# Managerial Economics

Second Edition

## Edwin Mansfield

Director, Center for Economics and Technology
University of Pennsylvania

**W.W. NORTON & COMPANY**

*New York   London*

To Katherine . . .
and her parents too

The text of this book is composed in Trump Medieval
with the display set in Trump Medieval Bold Italic
Composition by New England Typographic Service, Inc.
Manufacturing by Courier, Westford.

Library of Congress Cataloging-in-Publication Data

Mansfield, Edwin.
    Managerial economics / Edwin Mansfield. — 2nd ed.
        p.   cm.
    Includes index.
    1. Managerial economics.   I. Title
HD30.22.M354   1993          92–5317
338.5′024658—dc20

ISBN 0–393–96284–9

W.W. Norton & Company, Inc., 500 Fifth Avenue,
New York, N.Y. 10110
W.W. Norton & Company Ltd., 10 Coptic Street,
London WC1A 1PU

# About the Author

Edwin Mansfield is Professor of Economics and Director of the Center for Economics and Technology at the University of Pennsylvania. A graduate of Dartmouth College, he received his M.A. and Ph.D degrees from Duke University, as well as the Certificate and Diploma of the Royal Statistical Society. Before joining the University of Pennsylvania faculty, he taught at Carnegie-Mellon, Yale, Harvard, and the California Institute of Technology. He has been a consultant to many industrial firms and government agencies, and has been a member of the Advisory Committee of the U.S. Bureau of the Census, and the AAAS's Committee on Science, Engineering, and Public Policy. He has been chairman of the Visiting Committee at Rensselaer Polytechnic Institute. He has received the Certificate of Appreciation from the U.S. Secretary of Commerce, and in 1984 was appointed to the National Technology Medal Committee.

Professor Mansfield has been elected a fellow of the American Academy of Arts and Sciences, of the Econometric Society, of the Center for Advanced Study in the Behavioral Sciences, and he has held Fulbright and Ford Foundation fellowships. He has been a member of the board of directors of the American Productivity and Quality Center. He has served as U.S. chairman of the U.S.-U.S.S.R. Working Party on the Economics of Science and Technology, and was the first U.S. economist to be invited to visit and lecture in the People's Republic of China under the 1979 Sino-American agreements.

He is the author of 190 articles and 25 books. His textbooks on economics, microeconomics, managerial economics, and statistics have been adopted at over 1,000 colleges and universities, and have been translated for use abroad. He has been on the editorial board of eight journals, including the *Journal of the American Statistical Association*, and has been general editor of a series of books on technological change published by the University of Wisconsin Press. He has received the Publication Award of the Patent Law Association and the Honor Award of the National Technological University for research, teaching, and public service. He was included on the *Journal of Economic Perspectives'* list of 20 most cited economists in the United States.

# Contents

**Part One
Introduction**

**Part Two
Demand and Forecasting**

## Chapter 3
## Demand Theory

## Chapter 4
## Estimating Demand Functions

---

**Part Three**
**Production and Cost**

---

**Chapter 6**
**Production Theory**                                                    **203**

## Part Four
## Market Structure, Strategic Behavior, and Pricing

## Chapter 11
## Oligopoly and Strategic Behavior       418

## Part Five
## Risk Analysis and Capital Budgeting

## Part Six
## Government-Business Relations and the Global Economy

# *Preface*

The success of the first edition of this book was very gratifying, but, like any new textbook, extensive use in the classroom has produced lots of good ideas for improvements. Many of the hundreds of teachers who adopted the book have provided valuable comments and suggestions, which I appreciate very much. While the book's general structure and approach remain the same in this edition as in the previous one, there are many noteworthy improvements, described below.

*New Chapter on Managerial Economics in an International Setting.* Without question, the most important feature of this new edition is a chapter on managerial economics in the world economy. Competition in international markets is much rougher than in the past, and managers must be aware of the relevant principles of international economics and how they apply to real-world situations. Despite this fact, which has been trumpeted by many leading managers and teachers, no managerial economics textbook (that I know of) includes an extended discussion of this topic. One important aim of this new edition is to fill that void.

*New Introductory Material on Supply and Demand and on Principal-Agent Problems.* In Chapter 1, there is now a brief discussion of demand and supply curves and of price determination in competitive markets. This material will provide a useful orientation and review. Also, there is a treatment of principal-agent problems. Given the importance of these topics, it seems appropriate to introduce them at the outset.

*More Complete Discussion of Indifference Curves, Pricing Techniques, Externalities, and Public Goods.* Based on the reactions of users of the first edition, many teachers would like to have a fuller treatment of indifference curves, which is now included in a new appendix to Chapter 3. Also, a more extensive discussion of the long-run adjustment process and resource allocation under perfect competition is provided in Chapter 10, and new sections on two-part tariffs and bundling have been added. Further, in Chapter 15, there are more complete treatments of externalities and public goods.

*Revised Treatments of Game Theory and of Regression Techniques.* In Chapter 11, the material on game theory has been reorganized and beefed up; in particular, the discussions of Nash equilibrium and of reaction curves have been extended. In Chapter 4, the material on multiple regression techniques has been simplified. Also, much more emphasis has been put on the use of computer software and the interpretation of computer printouts, rather than on statistical formulas. In Chapter 13, there is a new discussion of the winner's curse.

*New Case Studies and Applications.* I have found from my own teaching experience, at the University of Pennsylvania (both in the Wharton School and in the College of Arts and Sciences) and at Carnegie-Mellon's Graduate School of Industrial Administration, that existing textbooks do not go far enough in demonstrating how the techniques presented in a managerial economics course are actually used by firms and analysts. In this second edition, there are well over 100 case studies and real-world applications (about 25 percent more than in the previous edition), of which the following are new: (1) The Comeback of the Xerox Corporation, (2) Harley-Davidson versus the Japanese Goliaths, (3) Bantam's Big Bet on Schwartzkopf's Book, (4) How Banc One Deals with the Principal-Agent Problem, (5) The 1991 Collapse of Wool Prices, (6) Why the Drop in the Price of Radio Stations?, (7) How the Japanese Motorcycle Makers Used the Coefficient of Determination, (8) Poultry Production in the United States, (9) The Time-Cost Trade-Off Function for Airliners, (10) Should We Continue to Make Autos from Steel?, (11) Economies of Scope in Advertising Agencies, (12) How Linear Programming Improves Aircraft Operations, (13) Acrimony in the OPEC Oil Cartel, (14) Pricing Electricity by the Hour, (15) Using Simulation Techniques in the Computer Industry, (16) Buying and Selling Pollution Permits at the Chicago Board of Trade, (17) Why Bridgestone Paid $2.6 Billion for Firestone's Tire Plants, (18) Airbus versus Boeing: Strategic Trade Policy in Action, (19) Is Airbus Playing by the Rules?, (20) Why So Many U.S. Plants Are Located South of the Border, (21) Reorganizing a Firm's Global R and D Network, and (22) A Free Trade Agreement for North America?

*Continued Emphasis on a Variety of Types of Cases.* As in the previous edition, a variety of types of cases are presented. Some ("Concepts in Context") describe how various important techniques have been used. Others ("Analyzing Managerial Decisions") go further and ask the student to answer questions related to the techniques being described. (Answers to these questions are included.) In addition, each chapter contains a section ("Consultant's Corner") that provides a brief case, generally based on an actual situation, where the student is asked to provide practical advice to a manager. Answers are provided at the end of the book. Further, each part of the book contains a case ("Managerial Economics in Context") that tries to bridge the material in various chapters, thus helping the student to integrate the material. Answers to these cases too are provided at the end of the book. For all of these types of cases, I have updated the material to make it as timely as possible.

*Numerical Examples and Answers to Problems.* Because managerial economics centers on the application of quantitative techniques, it is important that the student be ushered through many numerical examples. For example, to understand how price should be set under various sets of circumstances, the student should be given numerical examples that help to lay bare the essence of each price-setting technique. I have included many sections that are devoted entirely to working out such numerical examples. Also, answers to the odd-numbered end-of-chapter problems are included at the end of the book. This provides the student with useful feedback: he or she can see how a problem can be solved and whether he or she really understood the principles involved. In contrast to the previous edition, the answers to the even-numbered problems are in the *Instructor's Manual*, not the study guide, so these problems can be used to test students. New problems have been added, and old ones have been updated if needed.

*Chapter on Industrial Innovation and Technological Change.* American firms—as well as those in other countries—are constantly faced with decisions concerning innovation and technological change. It is no exaggeration to say that these decisions are among the most important facing any firm, particularly now that the traditional U.S. technological lead over other major countries has evaporated in many industries. Other textbooks in managerial economics devote little or no space to this topic. This is the first —and to date, only—one to provide a full chapter on this score.

*Chapter on Oligopoly and Strategic Behavior.* Advances in the analysis of strategic behavior have had an impact on thinking in boardrooms as well as classrooms. The previous edition was the first managerial economics textbook to devote a full chapter to oligopoly and strategic behavior. The reaction of instructors was enthusiastic, and we continue this practice in this new edition.

*Software Packages.* Given the major role played by the computer in today's firms, it is important in any modern managerial economics text that the student be introduced to the software packages available to help solve managerial problems. This is particularly important in the case of regression techniques and linear programming, where few real calculations are carried out any longer by hand. In this book, Chapter 4 and the appendix to Chapter 9 describe leading software packages in detail. Although the material is optional, experience indicates that it will be useful in many classes.

*Organization, Coverage, and Level.* Although this book contains a number of innovations, its overall organization and coverage is reasonably standard. All the topics usually taken up in a book of this sort are included, and the order in which they appear is similar to that in other books. Those instructors who wish to ignore the material on international economics, industrial innovation, strategic behavior, or software packages will find it easy to do so, since this material—included in Chapter 16, Chapter 7, the latter part of Chapter 11, and segments of Chapters 4 and 9—is self-contained and can be omitted without loss of continuity. Alternatively, some teachers omit Chapters 4, 5, and 9; this too can readily be done. It is important to note as well that this book is designed to be used by students with a wide range of abilities and backgrounds, not just a highly select few.

*Mathematical Sophistication.* Only a very modest mathematical background is required for an understanding of *Managerial Economics.* The elements of differential calculus that are used are explained in Chapter 2. For many students, this material can be skipped, since they will already have taken calculus courses, or it can be used to review the mathematics they have learned before. The emphasis in this book is on providing students with solid and effective evidence concerning the power and applicability of modern managerial economics and on making sure that they can use these techniques correctly and imaginatively. To accomplish these objectives, it is neither necessary nor appropriate to deluge students with mathematics.

*Problems and Problem Sets.* While real cases and examples whet a student's interest and sharpen his or her competence and intuition, they ordinarily must be supplemented with a substantial number of problems and problem sets. Besides the numerical examples included in the body of the chapters, there are a substantial number of problems at the end of each chapter. (As pointed out above, the answers to the odd-numbered problems are given at the end of the book.)

*Study Guide.* Because of the importance of hands-on experience with the techniques of this course, I have written a study guide *(Study Guide and Casebook for Managerial Economics)* to supplement the text. This supplement contains hundreds of problem sets, problems, and review questions (as well as their answers), which should be helpful to students. These problems and questions have been tested for effectiveness in the classroom. A new feature of the second edition is the inclusion of the following eight full-length classroom-tested cases, which should be very helpful and illuminating to students: (1) Apple Computer, Inc., 1987 . . . The Second Decade (by Phyllis Feddeler, Thomas Wheelen, and David Croll), (2) K. M. Westelle and Associates, Inc. (by Rhonda Aull), (3) Production Functions and Cost Functions in Oil Pipelines (by Leslie Cookenboo), (4) A Managerial Application of Cost Functions by a Railroad (by Edwin Mansfield and Harold Wein), (5) Applied CAD Knowledge, Inc. (by John Seeger and Raymond Kinnunen), (6) Catco Electronics Corporation (by Patrick Schul, William Cunningham, and Lynn Gill), (7) The Carriage House Inn (by Michael Everett), and (8) Revving Up for Relief: Harley-Davidson at the ITC (by Dorothy Robyn with assistance from Don Lippincott).

*Instructor's Manual.* An *Instructor's Manual* by Craig J. McCann of the University of South Carolina will be available to accompany this text. It includes suggestions for lectures and classroom discussion, as well as a test bank of roughly 700 multiple-choice questions. It should be of great help to many instructors.

In writing this book, I have benefited from the comments and suggestions of many colleagues and students. Particular thanks go to the following teachers who have commented in detail on all or part of the manuscript: Richard S. Bower, The Tuck School; Robert Carbaugh, Central Washington University; Thomas M. Carroll, University of Nevada (Las Vegas); Michael Claudon, Middlebury College; Mark Correll, University of Colorado; Alan Daskin, Boston University; George C. Dery, University of Lowell; Constantine Glezakos, California State University (Long Beach); H. Peter Gray, Rensselaer Polytechnic Institute; Theodore Groves, University of California (San Diego); James Hamilton, Wayne State University; Robert Hansen, The Tuck School; Kevin Hassett, Columbia University; Charles Hegji, Auburn University; George Hoffer, Virginia Commonwealth University; Jack Hou, California State University (Long Beach); Todd Idson, University of Miami; Lowell Jacobsen, William Jewell College; Charles E. Krider, University of Kansas; Michael Magura, University of Toledo; J. Peter Mattila, Iowa State University; Craig J. McCann, University of South Carolina; Marshall Medoff, California State University (Long Beach); Martin Milkman, Murray State University; J. Wilson Mixon, Berry College; Stephen Sheppard, Virginia Polytechnic Institute and State University; Sheldon H. Stein, Cleveland State University; John Clair Thompson, University of Connecticut; Samuel Wagner, Franklin and Marshall College; James Wetzel, Virginia Commonwealth University; and Pamela Whalley, Western Washington University. Also, Anthony Romeo of Unilever and Lorne Switzer of Concordia University suggested useful material and made valuable comments.

I am grateful to the Biometrika Trustees for permission to reprint material in Appendix Tables 3 to 7 and to the literary executor of the late Sir Ronald A. Fisher, F.R.S., Dr. Frank Yates, F.R.S., and the Longman Group, Ltd., London, for permission to reprint part of Appendix Table 4 from their book *Statistical Tables for Biological, Agricultural, and Medical Research* (6th edition, 1974). I would also like to thank W. Drake McFeely of W. W. Norton for his efficient handling of the publishing end of the work, and Edward D. Mansfield for his contribution to Chapter 9 (which he coauthored). As always, my wife, Lucile, has contributed an enormous amount to the completion of this book.

Philadelphia, 1992                                              E.M.

# Part One
# Introduction

# Chapter 1
# Introduction to Managerial Economics

What do Xerox, Harley-Davidson, and H. J. Heinz have in common? All three, like countless other firms, have used the well-established principles of managerial economics to improve their profitability. Managerial economics draws on economic analysis for such concepts as cost, demand, profit, and competition. It attempts to bridge the gap between the purely analytical problems that intrigue many economic theorists and the day-to-day decisions that managers must face. It now offers powerful tools and approaches for managerial policymaking.

In this opening chapter, we begin our study by presenting several case studies illustrating the problems that managerial economics can help solve. Although they cover only a small sample of the situations where managerial economics is useful, these illustrative problems should provide a reasonable first impression of the nature of managerial economics and its relevance to real business decisions. Also, we will examine the relationship between managerial economics and such related disciplines as microeconomics and the decision sciences, including statistics.

Next, we will take up basic models of decision making, as well as the theory of the firm. Since managerial economics is concerned with the ways in which business executives and other policymakers should make decisions, it is important at the outset that the nature of the decision-making process be analyzed and that the motivation of firms be discussed. Since profits play so major a role in business decision making, we will proceed to define profit and recognize how the economist's definition of profit differs

*1*

from that of the accountant. Finally, we will present an overview of the basic principles of demand and supply, a central topic that will be examined much more completely in subsequent chapters.

## CASE STUDY #1: THE COMEBACK OF THE XEROX CORPORATION

To illustrate the sorts of problems that managerial economics can help you solve, consider the Xerox Corporation, the famous producer of copiers. According to Mohan Kharbanda, Xerox's manager of business strategy, "Xerox had such a strong hold on the copier market throughout the 1960s and early 1970s that little attention was paid . . . when the Japanese began to offer small, inexpensive copiers in the mid-1970s. . . . Xerox of the mid-1970s was a bureaucratic company in which one function battled another, and operating people constantly bickered with corporate staff. . . . The result was painfully slow product development, high manufacturing costs, copiers that were hard to service, and unhappy customers. Then, in the mid-1970s, the Japanese camera makers entered the low end of the light-lens copier market. They used aggressive pricing to gain a foothold and procceded to gain a sizable market share. . . . The Japanese strategy worked well. Through the late 1970s, Xerox saw its market share erode at an alarming rate."[1]

By 1980, it was obvious that Xerox had enormous problems, but not so obvious what it could or should do about them. One basic problem was that the Japanese were selling their copiers at a much lower price than comparable Xerox copiers. (The Savin 750 copier sold for about 40 percent of the price of Xerox's comparable model.) The question arose: should Xerox cut its prices to match those of the Japanese? Moreover, the Japanese seemed to be able to produce their copiers much more inexpensively than Xerox could. How could Xerox determine how large the Japanese cost advantage was? And more importantly, how could it reduce its costs to the Japanese level? Further, the Japanese seemed to be much quicker than Xerox to bring new products to market. How could Xerox improve its performance in this regard?

To cope with these problems, top executives at Xerox carried out a wide variety of fundamental reforms. They instituted a formal system of "benchmarking" to identify the successful practices of Xerox's most efficient rivals. By emulating these practices, Xerox cut its costs, which helped make possible reductions in its prices. It also changed its product development process to reduce the time taken to get a new product to market. All these improvements, discussed in detail in subsequent chapters, are appli-

---

[1] M. Kharbanda, "Xerox Corporation," in J. Blackburn, *Time-Based Competition* (Homewood, Ill.: Business One Irwin, 1991), p. 178.

cations of the principles of managerial economics. Based on these reforms, Xerox has made a notable comeback. For example, in 1989, Xerox was awarded the U.S. Commerce Department's prestigious Malcolm Baldrige Award for significant and innovative approaches to quality.

## CASE STUDY #2: HARLEY-DAVIDSON VERSUS THE JAPANESE GOLIATHS

In contrast to Xerox, Harley-Davidson, a Wisconsin manufacturer of motorcycles, is a relatively small firm, with only about 2,000 employees. But like Xerox, it was hit hard by Japanese competition in the late 1970s. Honda and other Japanese motorcycle makers had lower production costs than Harley-Davidson, and they cut prices aggressively. Harley's share of the heavyweight motorcycle market fell from 78 percent in 1973 to 31 percent in 1980. According to Vaughn Beale, Harley-Davidson's chief executive officer, "We discovered that the key reason for our lack of competitiveness was poor management—by worldwide, not U.S. standards. We were being wiped out by the Japanese because they were better *managers*. It wasn't robotics, or culture, or morning calisthenics and company songs—it was professional managers who understood their business and paid attention to detail."[2]

Like Xerox, Harley-Davidson made a successful comeback. Indeed, in 1992, the firm was reported to be expanding its sales efforts in Japan and taking the fight to its Japanese rivals in their own backyard. Using many of the techniques described in later chapters, Harley reduced its costs and staved off bankruptcy. Harley's executives believe that just-in-time production, a relatively new technique described in Chapter 6, played a central role in the firm's improved performance. But a variety of other techniques we will study were also judged to be important. For example, Harley carried out studies to improve its marketing, production, and financial activities, and implemented the results.

Also, to understand many of Harley's problems, as well as the devices it used to avoid disaster, you must have at least a rudimentary knowledge of government policies toward business and of international economics, the topics of Chapters 15 and 16. Thus, in the early 1980s, the dollar rose in value relative to the Japanese yen, with the result that Japanese goods could be sold at comparatively low prices in the United States. This helped to enable Honda and other Japanese firms to sell their motorcycles at prices that Harley found difficult to meet. Further, the U.S. government helped Harley-Davidson to survive. As we shall see in Chapter 4, the firm asked the government to impose a tariff on Japanese motorcycles, which was done in 1983.

---

[2] P. Reid, *Well Made in America* (New York: McGraw-Hill, 1990), p. 65.

## CASE STUDY #3: HOW SHOULD HEINZ DISTRIBUTE ITS KETCHUP?

Having presented two case studies involving U.S.–Japanese competition, it should be obvious that some U.S. firms—as well as some Canadian and British firms—are being challenged by foreign competitors in a way that would have been hard to believe 20 years ago. As will become evident in subsequent chapters, one reason why U.S. firms find it difficult to compete is that whereas their managers used to understand the principles and techniques of managerial economics better than their foreign rivals, this is no longer true. These principles are now as well known in Tokyo and Seoul as in New York or Toronto.

But it would be as much a mistake to overemphasize as to neglect the role of foreign competition. Many of the typical firm's problems are regional or national in scope. For example, consider the H. J. Heinz Company, the leading ketchup producer, which makes its product in a variety of factories scattered around the United States and distributes it to warehouses that also are scattered around the country. Each factory has a certain daily capacity. Each warehouse has a certain daily requirement.

To minimize shipping costs, how much ketchup should each factory ship to each warehouse? At first glance, this may seem to be a simple problem. You may feel that trial and error will provide an adequate answer. But if so, you are likely to be wrong. (If you have the time, try to determine the optimal shipment from each factory to each warehouse, based on the data in Table 1.1. Then compare your results with the answer on page 359.)[3] In Chapter 9, we will see how linear programming, an important mathematical technique, can enable us to solve this problem. In fact, the H. J. Heinz Company has applied this technique to minimize its transportation costs, and has reported substantial savings as a result.

Managerial economics provides a wide variety of practical techniques that you can use to reduce costs and eliminate waste. For example, Chapter 6 describes how poultry producers have used economic techniques to improve their efficiency, and Chapter 9 shows how the Brisbane International Airport reduced the costs of transporting sand by the use of linear programming. Some of these applications—such as the reduction of the cost of transporting sand—may seem mundane, but the profits can be very substantial. Thus, the Brisbane International Airport saved $400,000 in transporting sand, based on a relatively simple use of managerial economics.

---

[3] The figures in Table 1.1 are illustrative, but accurate enough for present purposes.

TABLE 1.1    Daily Capacities of Factories, Requirements of Warehouses, and Freight Rates

| Factory | I | II | III | IV | V | VI | VII | VIII | IX | X | XI | XII | Daily requirements |
|---|---|---|---|---|---|---|---|---|---|---|---|---|---|
| Warehouse | | | | | Freight rates (cents per cwt.) | | | | | | | | (cwt.) |
| A | 16 | 16 | 6 | 13 | 24 | 13 | 6 | 31 | 37 | 34 | 37 | 40 | 1,820 |
| B | 20 | 18 | 8 | 10 | 22 | 11 | 8 | 29 | 33 | 25 | 35 | 38 | 1,530 |
| C | 30 | 23 | 8 | 9 | 14 | 7 | 9 | 22 | 29 | 20 | 38 | 35 | 2,360 |
| D | 10 | 15 | 10 | 8 | 10 | 15 | 13 | 19 | 19 | 15 | 28 | 34 | 100 |
| E | 31 | 23 | 16 | 10 | 10 | 16 | 20 | 14 | 17 | 17 | 25 | 28 | 280 |
| F | 24 | 14 | 19 | 13 | 13 | 14 | 18 | 9 | 14 | 13 | 29 | 25 | 730 |
| G | 27 | 23 | 7 | 11 | 23 | 8 | 16 | 6 | 10 | 11 | 16 | 28 | 940 |
| H | 34 | 25 | 15 | 4 | 27 | 15 | 11 | 9 | 16 | 17 | 13 | 16 | 1,130 |
| J | 38 | 29 | 17 | 11 | 16 | 27 | 17 | 19 | 8 | 18 | 19 | 11 | 4,150 |
| K | 42 | 43 | 21 | 22 | 16 | 10 | 21 | 18 | 24 | 16 | 17 | 15 | 3,700 |
| L | 44 | 49 | 25 | 23 | 18 | 6 | 13 | 19 | 15 | 12 | 10 | 13 | 2,560 |
| M | 49 | 40 | 29 | 21 | 10 | 15 | 14 | 21 | 12 | 29 | 14 | 20 | 1,710 |
| N | 56 | 58 | 36 | 37 | 6 | 25 | 8 | 19 | 9 | 21 | 15 | 26 | 580 |
| P | 59 | 57 | 44 | 33 | 5 | 21 | 6 | 10 | 8 | 33 | 15 | 18 | 30 |
| Q | 68 | 54 | 40 | 38 | 8 | 24 | 7 | 19 | 10 | 23 | 23 | 23 | 2,840 |
| R | 66 | 71 | 47 | 43 | 16 | 33 | 12 | 26 | 19 | 20 | 25 | 31 | 1,510 |
| S | 72 | 58 | 50 | 51 | 20 | 42 | 22 | 16 | 15 | 13 | 20 | 21 | 970 |
| T | 74 | 54 | 57 | 55 | 26 | 53 | 26 | 19 | 14 | 7 | 15 | 6 | 5,110 |
| U | 71 | 75 | 57 | 60 | 30 | 44 | 30 | 30 | 41 | 8 | 23 | 37 | 3,540 |
| Y | 73 | 72 | 63 | 56 | 37 | 49 | 40 | 31 | 31 | 10 | 8 | 25 | 4,410 |
| Daily capacity (cwt.) | 10,000 | 9,000 | 3,000 | 2,700 | 500 | 1,200 | 700 | 300 | 500 | 1,200 | 2,000 | 8,900 | 40,000 |

# RELATIONSHIPS OF MANAGERIAL ECONOMICS TO OTHER DISCIPLINES

Having considered three case studies illustrating the sorts of problems that managerial economics can help to solve, we can begin to describe how managerial economics is related to other disciplines. As shown in Figure 1.1, managerial economics provides a link between economic theory and the decision sciences in the analysis of managerial decision making. Traditional economic theory—which consists of **microeconomics** (focusing on individual consumers, firms, and industries) and **macroeconomics** (focusing on aggregate output, income, and employment)—contains a considerable amount of material that bears on managerial decision making, the role of microeconomics being particularly important in this regard. Managerial economics draws heavily from microeconomics, as well as from other areas of economic theory.

But managerial economics is quite different from microeconomics.

Whereas microeconomics is largely descriptive (that is, it attempts to describe how the economy works without indicating how it should operate), managerial economics is largely prescriptive (that is, it attempts to establish rules and techniques to fulfill specified goals). For example, microeconomics is concerned with the way in which computer manufacturers like IBM price their products, while managerial economics is concerned with how they *should* price their products. Of course, this is a difference of emphasis and degree, not of kind, but it nonetheless is important.

As shown in Figure 1.1, managerial economics draws heavily on the decision sciences, as well as traditional economics. The decision sciences provide ways to analyze the impact of alternative courses of action. Managerial economics uses optimization techniques, such as differential calculus and mathematical programming, to determine optimal courses of action for decision makers. To implement these techniques, statistical methods must be employed to estimate the relationships between relevant variables and to forecast their values. Thus, managerial economics has arisen from a complex mixture of various parts of economics and the decision sciences, including statistics.

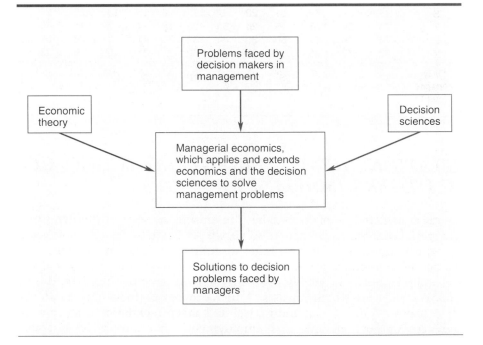

**FIGURE 1.1    Relationship between Managerial Economics and Related Disciplines**    Managerial economics provides a link between economic theory and the decision sciences in the analysis of managerial decision making.

Managerial economics plays two important roles in the study of business administration. First, the course in managerial economics, like the ones in accounting, quantitative methods, and management information systems, provides fundamental analytical *tools* that can and should be used in other courses, such as marketing, finance, and production. Second, courses in managerial economics, like those concerned with business policy, can serve an *integrating* role, showing how other areas such as marketing, finance, and production must be viewed as a whole in order to fulfill the goals of the firm.

Although managerial economics is at the heart of the study of business administration, it plays no less a part in the management of nonbusiness organizations like government agencies, hospitals, and schools. Regardless of whether one manages Dow Chemical, the Massachusetts General Hospital, or the University of New Mexico, one must pay attention to the efficient allocation of resources. Waste is waste, wherever it occurs. The principles of managerial economics are as important in reducing waste in nonbusiness organizations as they are in firms.

## THE BASIC PROCESS OF DECISION MAKING[4]

Both for firms and for nonbusiness organizations, the process of decision making can be divided into five basic steps, as indicated in Figure 1.2. These steps are as follows:

*Step 1: Establish or Identify the Objectives.* In making any decision, you, as decision maker, should determine what are the organization's (or individual's) objectives. Unless you know what it is that you are trying to achieve, there is no sensible way to make the decision. For example, consider the managers of Black and Decker, the power tool manufacturer, who had to decide in the 1970s whether the firm's consumer power tools should be redesigned. Their objectives were to bolster the company's profits, to attain a 15 percent annual growth rate, to remain independent, and to service world markets.[5]

*Step 2: Define the Problem.* One of the most difficult parts of decision making is to determine exactly what the problem is. Frequently executives confront a situation that is judged to be unsatisfactory. For example, Black and Decker's management felt that they had to change their operations drastically if they were to continue to be a domestic manufacturer doing business internationally. To meet this challenge, they had to determine exactly what the problem was, since otherwise they had little chance of

---

[4] For further discussion, see H. Simon, "The Decision-Making Process," in E. Mansfield, ed., *Managerial Economics and Operations Research*, 5th ed. (New York: Norton, 1987).

[5] A. Lehnerd, "Revitalizing the Manufacture and Design of Mature Global Products," in B. Guile and H. Brooks, eds., *Technology and Global Industry* (Washington, D.C.: National Academy Press, 1987).

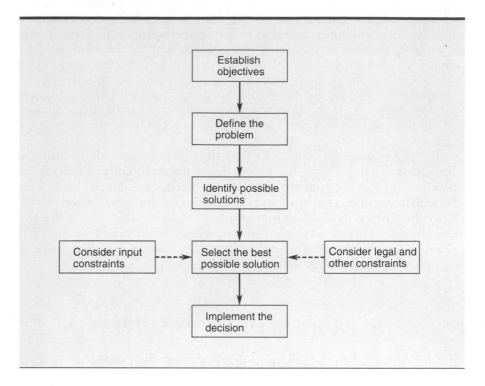

**FIGURE 1.2    Basic Process of Decision Making**    This process can be divided into the five basic steps shown above.

solving it. After considerable study, they concluded that the problem was the likelihood of increased foreign competition and the possibility that double insulation of power tools would be legally required. ("Double insulation" means that an additional insulation barrier is placed in an electrical device to protect the user from electrical shock if the main insulation system fails.)

***Step 3: Identify Possible Solutions.*** Once the problem is defined, you should try to construct and identify possible solutions. For example, Black and Decker considered a variety of options, including more effective production and marketing of its products based on existing designs, as well as redesigning its entire product line.

***Step 4: Select the Best Possible Solution.*** Having identified the set of alternative possible solutions, you must evaluate each one and determine which is best, given the objectives of the organization. In the case of Black and Decker, studies indicated that the best solution was to redesign the firm's consumer power tools. Black and Decker's managers "decided that a window of opportunity existed to improve their product lines and manufacturing capability. Moreover, they decided that if they did not take time to do it right the first time, they would never have the time or resources to do it over."[6]

*Step 5: Implement the Decision.* Having chosen a particular solution, this decision must be implemented in order to be effective. Even organizations as disciplined as armies find it difficult to carry out orders effectively. Since even the best decisions come to naught if they are not carried out, this phase of the decision-making process is of crucial importance. In the case of Black and Decker, the organization of the firm was changed, and a new job —vice president of operations—was created so that manufacturing, product development, and advanced manufacturing engineering were all under one manager. The firm's top management made sure the decision was implemented properly.

# THE THEORY OF THE FIRM

Although managerial economics is not concerned solely with the management of business firms, this is its principal field of application. To apply managerial economics to business management, we need a **theory of the firm,** a theory indicating how firms behave and what their goals are. Firms are complex organizations that vary enormously. Any theory or model (which means the same as theory) must be a simplification. The trick is to construct a model in such a way that irrelevant and unimportant considerations and variables are neglected, but the important factors—those that have an important effect on the phenomena the model is designed to illuminate—are included.

The basic model of the business enterprise stems from what economists designate as the theory of the firm. In its most stripped-down version, this theory assumes that the firm tries to maximize its profits. But this version is too stark to be useful in many circumstances, particularly where a problem facing the firm has important dynamic elements and where risk is involved. A richer version of this theory assumes that the firm tries to maximize its wealth or value. At present, this version is the dominant theory used by managerial economists.

To understand this theory, we must spell out what managerial economists mean by the **value** of the firm. Since a firm's value can be defined in a variety of ways,[7] it will prevent confusion if we provide a detailed definition at this point. Put briefly, *a firm's value will be defined here as the present value of its expected future cash flows.* In later chapters, we will learn more about what is meant by cash flow. For present purposes, we can regard a firm's cash flow as being the same as its profit. (For those who are

[6] Ibid., p. 50.

[7] For example, one could define a firm's value as its book value or liquidating value, among others.

unfamiliar with the concept of a "present value," or who want to review this concept, a detailed discussion is provided in Appendix A.)

Thus, expressed as an equation, the value of the firm equals

$$\text{Present value of expected future profits} = \frac{\pi_1}{1 + i} + \frac{\pi_2}{(1 + i)^2} + \cdots + \frac{\pi_n}{(1 + i)^n}$$

$$= \sum_{t=1}^{n} \frac{\pi_t}{(1 + i)^t} \tag{1.1}$$

where $\pi_t$ is the expected profit in year $t$, $i$ is the interest rate, and $t$ goes from 1 (next year) to $n$ (the last year in the planning horizon). Because profit equals total revenue (*TR*) minus total cost (*TC*), this equation can also be expressed as

$$\text{Present value of expected future profits} = \sum_{t=1}^{n} \frac{TR_t - TC_t}{(1 + i)^t}, \tag{1.2}$$

where $TR_t$ is the firm's total revenue in year $t$, and $TC_t$ is its total cost in year $t$.

A careful inspection of equation (1.2) suggests how a firm's managers and workers can influence its value. Consider, for example, the General Electric Company. Its marketing managers and sales representatives work hard to increase its total revenues, while its production managers and manufacturing engineers strive to reduce its total costs. At the same time, its financial managers play a major role in obtaining capital, and hence influence equation (1.2), while its research and development personnel invent new products and processes that both increase the firm's total revenues and reduce its total costs. All of these diverse groups affect General Electric's value, defined here as the present value of its expected profits.

## THE ROLE OF CONSTRAINTS

To repeat, managerial economists generally assume that firms want to maximize their value, as defined in equations (1.1) and (1.2). However, this does not mean that a firm has complete control over its value, and that it can set it at any level it chooses. On the contrary, firms must cope with the fact that there are many constraints on what they can achieve in this regard.

The constraints that limit the extent to which a firm's value can be increased are of various kinds. For one thing, the amount of certain types of inputs may be limited. In the relevant period of time, the firm may be unable to obtain more than a particular amount of specialized equipment, skilled labor, essential materials, or other inputs. Particularly if the period of time is relatively short, these input constraints may be quite severe. For example, because it takes many months to expand the capacity of a steel plant, many short-run problems facing a steel firm must be solved based on the recognition that plant capacity is essentially fixed. However, in dealing

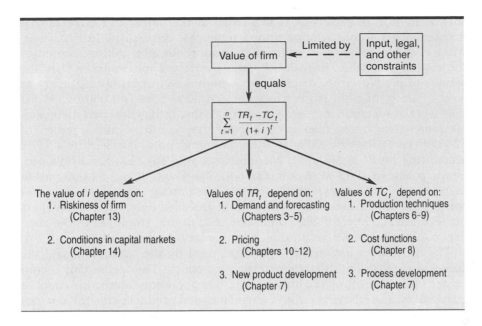

**FIGURE 1.3  *Determinants of the Value of a Firm***  A firm's value depends on factors influencing $TR_t$, $TC_t$, and $i$, as well as the constraints it faces.

with longer-run problems, the firm has more flexibility and can alter (within limits) its capacity.

Another important type of constraint that limits what firms can do is legal or contractual in nature. For example, a firm may be bound to pay wages exceeding a certain level because the minimum wage laws stipulate that it must do so. Also, it must pay taxes in accord with federal, state, and local laws. Further, it must act in accord with its contracts with customers and suppliers—or take the legal consequences. A wide variety of laws (ranging from environmental laws to antitrust laws to tax laws) limit what firms can do, and the contracts and other legal agreements made by firms further constrain their actions. As indicated in Figure 1.3, these constraints limit how much profit a firm can make, as well as the value of the firm itself.

Because there are constraints on a firm's actions and behavior, the relevant techniques used to analyze many of a firm's problems are **constrained optimization techniques,** such as linear programming (described in Chapter 9).

## WHAT ARE PROFITS?

Throughout previous sections, we have repeatedly encountered the term "profits." Practically all published profit figures are based on the accountants' definition of profits. It is important at the outset to recognize that managerial economists define profits somewhat differently. In particular, when economists speak of **profit**, they mean profit after taking account of the capital and labor provided by the owners. Thus, suppose that the owners of the Newark Grocery Store, who receive profits but no salary or wages, put in long hours for which they could receive $40,000 in 1993 if they worked for someone else. Also suppose that if they invested their capital somewhere other than in this firm, they could obtain a return of $24,000 on it in 1993. Under these circumstances, if the store's 1993 accounting profit is $60,000, economists would say that the firm's economic profits in 1993 were $60,000–$40,000–$24,000, or –$4,000, rather than the $60,000 shown in the store's accounting statements. In other words, the economists' concept of profit includes only what the owners make above and beyond what their labor and capital employed in the business could earn elsewhere. In this case, that amount is negative.

The differences between the concepts used by the accountant and the economist reflect the difference in their functions. The accountant is concerned with controlling the firm's day-to-day operations, detecting fraud or embezzlement, satisfying tax and other laws, and producing records for various interested groups. The economist is concerned primarily with decision making and rational choice among prospective alternatives. While the figures published on profits almost always conform to the accountant's, not the economist's, concept, the economist's is the more relevant one for many kinds of decisions. (And this, of course, is recognized by sophisticated accountants.) For example, suppose the owners of the Newark Grocery Store are trying to decide whether they should continue in business. If they are interested in making as much money as possible, the answer depends on the firm's profits as measured by the economist, not the accountant. If the firm's economic profits are greater than (or equal to) zero, the firm should continue in existence; otherwise, it should not. Hence, if 1993 is a good indicator of its prospective profitability, the Newark Grocery Store should not stay in existence.

# REASONS FOR THE EXISTENCE OF PROFIT

Why do economic profits exist? Three important reasons are innovation, risk, and monopoly power. Suppose that an economy is composed of competitive industries, that entry into these industries is completely free, and that no changes in technology—no new processes, no new products or other innovations—are permitted. Moreover, suppose that everyone can predict the future with perfect accuracy. Under these conditions, there will be no profits, because people will enter industries where profits exist, thus reducing these profits eventually to zero, and leave industries where losses exist, thus reducing these negative profits eventually to zero.

But in reality innovations of various kinds are made. For example, Genentech, the California biotechnology firm, introduces a new product like TPA (which dissolves blood clots that cause many heart attacks), or Varian Associates, the Palo Alto instruments firm, introduces the NMR spectrometer. The people who carry out these bold schemes are the **innovators,** those with vision and the daring to back it up. The innovators are not necessarily the inventors of new techniques or products, although in some cases the innovator and the inventor are the same. Often the innovator takes another's invention, adapts it, and introduces it to the market. Profits are a reward earned by successful innovators.

Risk also exists in the real world. Indeed one of the hazards in attempting to be an innovator is the **risk** involved. Profit is a reward for risk bearing. Assuming that people would like to avoid risk, they will prefer relatively stable, sure earnings to relatively unstable, uncertain earnings—*if the average level of earnings is the same.* Consequently, to induce people to take the risks involved in owning businesses in various industries, a profit —a premium for risk—must be paid to them.

Another reason for the existence of profits is the fact that markets are not perfectly competitive. Under perfect competition, there will be a tendency in the long run for economic profits to disappear. But this will not be the case if an industry is a monopoly or oligopoly. Instead, profits may well exist in the long run in such imperfectly competitive industries. Monopoly profits are fundamentally the result of "contrived scarcities." The monopolist takes account of the fact that the more it produces, the smaller the price it will receive. In other words, the monopolist realizes that it will spoil the market if it produces too much. Consequently, it pays the monopolist to limit its output, and this contrived scarcity is responsible for the existence of its profits.

# ORGANIZATIONAL FACTORS AND "SATISFICING"

Although managerial economists generally assume that firms want to maximize profit [and hence their value, as defined in equation (1.1)], other assumptions can be made. To see why it sometimes is sensible to make other assumptions, you must recognize that in many firms, particularly big ones, it is hard to know exactly where, how, and by whom decisions are made. Some firms, rather than being run by a single owner-manager, have large numbers of people in middle management, as well as the top brass occupying key management positions, all of whom participate in varying degrees in the formulation of company policy. Various groups within the firm develop their own party lines, and intrafirm politics is an important part of the process determining company policy. For example, if a firm is composed of two divisions (each making a different product), each division may fight to maintain and expand its share of the firm's budget, and each

## BANTAM'S BIG BET ON SCHWARZKOPF'S BOOK

In 1991, Bantam Books agreed to pay General Norman Schwarzkopf $6 million for the world rights to his not-yet-written memoirs. It was the highest bidder for the book. Macmillan bid $1.2 million; Viking Penguin, $3.2 million; and Random House, $5 million. According to estimates by one leading publisher, the following table shows Bantam's revenues, costs, and profits from this book under two sets of circumstances: (1) the hardcover version of this book sells 625,000 copies and the paperback version of this book sells 1.5 million copies; (2) the hardcover version sells 375,000 copies and the paperback version sells 1.2 million copies.

| | Sales of 625,000 hardcovers and 1.5 million paperbacks | Sales of 375,000 hardcovers and 1.2 million paperbacks |
|---|---|---|
| Revenues (price × number sold) | 15,132,062 | 10,642,587 |
| Costs | | |
|   Advance to Schwarzkopf | 6,000,000 | 6,000,000 |
|   Paper, printing, binding | 3,332,226 | 2,611,726 |
|   Print plates | 10,508 | 10,508 |
|   Marketing | 750,000 | 750,000 |
|   Other costs | 3,789,619 | 2,592,776 |
| Profit | 1,249,709 | −1,322,423 |

(a) According to publishing executives, it is very hard to sell more than 500,000 copies of a nonfiction hardcover, and very exceptional to sell 1 million copies. Is Bantam taking a substantial risk in publishing this book? (b) Simon and Schuster paid Ronald Reagan $7 million in 1989 for his memoirs, and is reported to have lost over $1 million on the book. Does this indicate that it is relatively easy to predict a book's sales? (c) According to Stuart Applebaum, a Bantam vice president, the fact that Schwarzkopf is now a Bantam author will help to boost the sale of all the company's books. If so, are the above profit figures accurate? (d) If Bantam makes a profit on this book, will this profit be, at least in part, a reward for risk-bearing?

*Jack Hoyt, President and CEO of Bantam Doubleday Dell Publishing Group, Inc.*

SOLUTION   (a) Based on the above table, it appears that, unless Bantam sells well above 375,000 hardcovers and 1.2 million paperbacks, it will lose money. Since, according to publishing executives, it is not easy to sell this many copies of a book, this investment seems to be risky. (b) No. It is by no means easy to predict a book's sales. (c) No. The above profit figures ignore whatever increase there may be in other books' profits due to Schwarzkopf's being a Bantam author. (d) Yes.*

* For further discussion, see *New York Times*, July 15, 1991.

may try to put the other in a subordinate position. Political struggles within the firm may play an important role in determining its objectives.

Under such circumstances, a firm may "satisfice" rather than attempt to maximize profit. In other words, it may aim at a satisfactory rate of profit rather than the maximum figure. A firm's aspiration level is the boundary between unsatisfactory and satisfactory outcomes. For example, the aspiration level might be a particular goal, such as "Our profit for this year should be $5 million." The firm may abandon the attempt to maximize profits because intrafirm politics rule out such a goal—and because the calculations required are too complicated and the available data are too poor. Instead the firm may attempt to attain certain minimal levels of performance.[8]

If the environment facing the firm is relatively constant, the aspiration level may tend to be slightly higher than the firm's performance. If performance is improving, the aspiration level may tend to lag behind actual performance. And if performance is decreasing, the aspiration level may tend to be above actual performance. Of course, if the aspiration level is close to the maximum profit, the findings obtained assuming satisficing are likely to be similar to those obtained by assuming profit maximization.

## MANAGERIAL INTERESTS AND THE PRINCIPAL-AGENT PROBLEM

Satisficing is not the only alternative to the assumption of profit maximization. When differences arise between profit maximization and the interests of the management group, executives are likely to follow policies favoring their own interests.[9] Important in this regard is the separation of owner-

[8] For example, see H. Simon, "Theories of Decision-Making in Economic and Behavioral Science," reprinted in E. Mansfield, ed., *Microeconomics: Selected Readings*, 5th ed. (New York: Norton, 1985).

[9] See R. Marris, *The Economic Theory of "Managerial" Capitalism* (New York: Free Press, 1964). For a study of intrafirm organization, see O. Williamson, *Markets and Hierarchies: Analysis and Antitrust Implications* (New York: Free Press, 1975).

ship from control in the large corporation in the United States. The owners of the firm—the stockholders—usually have little detailed knowledge of the firm's operations. Even if the board of directors is made up largely of people other than top management, top management usually has a great deal of freedom as long as it seems to be performing adequately. Consequently, the behavior of the firm may be dictated in part by the interests of the management group, the result being higher pay and more perquisites (and a larger staff) for managers than otherwise would be true.

Economists designate this as a *principal-agent problem*. A firm's managers are *agents* who work for the firm's owners, who are the *principals*. The principal-agent problem is that the managers may pursue their own objectives, even though this decreases the profits of the owners. Consider Joseph Wagner, a manager of a local textile firm. Because the cost of the benefits (large staff, company-paid travel, and so on) that he receives from the firm is borne entirely by the owners, he has an incentive to increase these benefits substantially. Since the owners of the firm find it difficult to distinguish between those benefits that bolster profits and those that do not do so, the manager has some leeway.

To deal with this problem, firms often establish contracts with their managers that give the latter an incentive to pursue objectives that are reasonably close to profit maximization. Thus, the firm's owners might give the managers a financial stake in the success of the firm. Many corporations have adopted stock option plans, whereby managers can purchase shares of common stock at less than market price. These plans give managers an incentive to promote the firm's profits and to act in accord with the owners' interests. There is some evidence that these plans do have an effect. For example, according to one recent study, if managers own between 5 and 20 percent of a firm, the firm is likely to perform better (in terms of profitability) than if they own less than 5 percent.

# DEMAND AND SUPPLY: A FIRST LOOK

Having described the nature of managerial economics, we turn now to an overview of the basic principles of demand and supply. Any manager, whether in Tokyo, Seoul, New York, or Toronto, must understand these basic principles, which are taken up in more detail in subsequent chapters. Our purpose here is to take a preliminary look at this topic, our first task being to define what we mean by a market.

For present purposes, a *market* can be defined as a group of firms and individuals that are in touch with each other in order to buy or sell some good. Of course, not every person in a market has to be in contact with every other person in the market. A person or firm is part of a market even if it is in contact with only a subset of the other persons or firms in the market.

Markets vary in the extent to which they are dominated by a few large

## HOW BANC ONE DEALS WITH THE PRINCIPAL-AGENT PROBLEM

Banc One is a superregional bank. During a period when the huge money-center banks like Citibank, Chase Manhattan, and others have been reported to be in deep trouble due to problems with commercial real estate loans and loans to third-world countries, Banc One has earned very substantial profits, over $400 million in 1990. In recent years, it has moved beyond its Ohio base and has established branch networks in Indiana, Wisconsin, Texas, Michigan, Kentucky, and Illinois by buying up smaller banks.

John B. McCoy, Banc One's chief executive officer, is constantly searching for new banks to buy. When a bank is acquired, its officers are put in the "key manager incentive compensation program," which is a strong part of the management culture at Banc One. According to this program, the president of a relatively small bank with $300 million in assets might get a salary of about $100,000. However, if he or she exceeds the profit targets for this bank for the year, he or she might get an additional bonus of $75,000. On the other hand, if this bank's profit is less than 1.1 percent of its assets, the president gets no bonus at all.

(a) Is this "key manager incentive compensation program" a way to deal with the principal-agent problem? (b) Under this program, does the president of each acquired bank have an incentive to cut unnecessary expenditure and to work hard to increase profit? (c) According to Keefe, Bruyette, and Woods, a bank research firm, only 5 of the 50 largest banks in the United States had profits exceeding 1.1 percent of assets in 1990. Does it appear that Banc One is setting stringent goals for presidents of acquired banks?

*SOLUTION* (a) Yes. If the president of an acquired bank is able to exceed the profit targets for his or her bank, he or she will receive a $75,000 bonus. Thus, the agent (the president) has a substantial incentive to work in the interests of the principal (Banc One's owners) and increase the bank's profits. (b) Yes. By cutting expenses and raising profits, the president can increase his or her salary from $100,000 to $175,000 per year. (c) Yes. To get the $75,000 bonus, the presidents have to achieve a level of performance exceeding that of about 90 percent of the 50 largest banks.*

*John B. McCoy, Chair and CEO of Banc One Corporation*

* For further discussion, see *New York Times*, July 7, 1991.

buyers or sellers. For example, in the United States, there was for many years only one producer of aluminum. This firm, the Aluminum Company of America, had great power in the market for aluminum. In contrast, the number of buyers and sellers in some other markets is so large that no single buyer or seller has any power over the price of the product. This is true in various agricultural markets, for example. When a market for a product contains so many buyers and sellers that none of them can influence the price, economists call the market *perfectly competitive.* In this introductory chapter, we make the simplifying assumption that markets are perfectly competitive. We will relax that assumption later.

## THE DEMAND SIDE OF A MARKET

Every market has a demand side and a supply side. The *demand* side can be represented by a *market demand curve,* which shows the amount of the commodity buyers would like to purchase at various prices. Consider Figure 1.4, which shows the demand curve for copper in the world market in

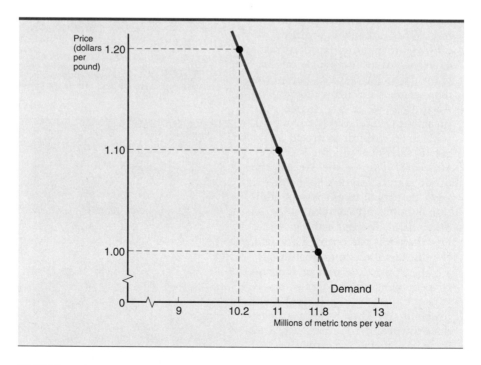

FIGURE 1.4   *The Market Demand Curve for Copper, World Market, 1991*
The market demand curve for copper shows the amount of copper that buyers would like to purchase at various prices.

1991.[10] The figure shows that about 11.8 million metric tons of copper will be demanded annually if the price is $1.00 per pound, about 11 million metric tons will be demanded annually if the price is $1.10 per pound, and about 10.2 million metric tons will be demanded annually if the price is $1.20 per pound. An important reason why copper is demanded in such substantial amounts is that it is very useful in constructing equipment to generate and transmit electricity.

The demand curve in Figure 1.4 shows the total demand—worldwide—at each price. Any demand curve pertains to a particular period of time, and the shape and position of the demand curve depend on the length of the period. The demand curve for copper slopes downward to the right. In other words, the quantity of copper demanded increases as the price falls. This is true of the demand curve for most commodities: they almost always slope downward to the right. This makes sense; one would expect increases in a good's price to result in a smaller quantity demanded.

Any demand curve is based on the assumption that the tastes, incomes, and number of consumers as well as the prices of other commodities, are held constant. Changes in any of these factors are likely to shift the position of a commodity's demand curve. Thus, if consumers' tastes shift toward goods that use considerable copper or if consumers' incomes increase (and they therefore buy more goods using copper), the demand curve for copper will shift to the right. In other words, holding the price of copper constant, more copper will be demanded than before. Much more will be said on this score in later sections (and in Chapter 3).

## THE SUPPLY SIDE OF A MARKET

The *supply* side of a market can be represented by a *market supply curve* that shows the amount of the commodity sellers would offer at various prices. Let's continue with the case of copper. Figure 1.5 shows the supply curve for copper in the world market in 1991, based on estimates made informally by industry experts.[11] According to the figure, about 9.4 million metric tons of copper would be supplied if the price of copper were $1.00 per pound, about 11 million tons if the price were $1.10 per pound, and about 12.6 million tons if the price were $1.20 per pound.

Any supply curve pertains to a particular period of time (1991 in Figure 1.5). Note that the supply curve for copper slopes upward to the right. In other words, the quantity of copper supplied increases as the price

[10] I am indebted to officials of the U.S. Bureau of Mines for providing me with relevant information. Of course, these estimates, based on a variety of studies of the copper industry, are only rough approximations, but they are good enough for present purposes.

[11] Officials of the U.S. Bureau of Mines provided me with relevant information. This supply curve is based on a variety of studies and assumptions. While it is only a rough approximation, it is good enough for present purposes.

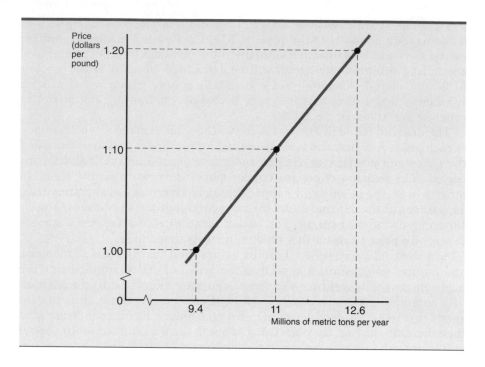

**FIGURE 1.5   The Market Supply Curve for Copper, World Market, 1991**
The market supply curve for copper shows the amount of copper that sellers would offer at various prices.

increases. This seems plausible, since increases in price give a greater incentive for firms to produce copper and offer it for sale. Also, there is more incentive to extract the copper from scrap metal. Empirical studies indicate that the supply curves for a great many commodities share this characteristic of sloping upward to the right.

Any supply curve is based on the assumption that technology, which we define as society's pool of knowledge regarding the industrial arts, is held constant. As technology progresses, it becomes possible to produce commodities more cheaply, so that firms often are willing to supply a given amount at a lower price than formerly. Thus, technological change often causes the supply curve to shift to the right. This certainly has occurred in the case of copper. There have been many important technological innovations in copper production, ranging from very large flotation cells to in-pit crushers of ore and conveyor belts to transport ore to the mill.

The supply curve for a product is also affected by the prices of the resources (labor, capital, and land) used to produce it. Decreases in the price of these inputs make it possible to produce commodities more cheaply, so that firms may be willing to supply a given amount at a lower price than they formerly would. Thus, decreases in the price of inputs may cause the supply curve to shift to the right. On the other hand, increases in the price of inputs may cause it to shift to the left. For example, if the wage rates of workers in the copper industry increase, the supply curve for copper may shift to the left. Much more will be said on this score in Chapter 10.

## EQUILIBRIUM PRICE

The two sides of a market, demand and supply, interact to determine the price of a commodity. To illustrate, consider the copper market. Let's put both the demand curve for copper (in Figure 1.4) and the supply curve for copper (in Figure 1.5) together in the same diagram. The result, shown in Figure 1.6, will help us determine the equilibrium price of copper. *An equilibrium price is a price that can be maintained. Any price that is not an equilibrium price cannot be maintained for long, since there are fundamental factors at work to cause a change in price.*

Let's see what would happen if various prices were established in the

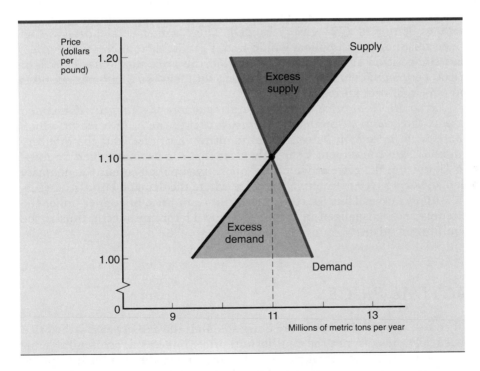

*FIGURE 1.6   Equilibrium Price of Copper, World Market, 1991*   The equilibrium price is $1.10 per pound, since the quantity demanded equals the quantity supplied at this price.

market. For example, if the price were $1.20 per pound, the demand curve indicates that 10.2 million metric tons of copper would be demanded, while the supply curve indicates that 12.6 million metric tons would be supplied. Thus, if the price were $1.20 per pound, there would be a mismatch between the quantity supplied and the quantity demanded per year, since the rate at which copper is supplied would be greater than the rate at which it is demanded. Specifically, as shown in Figure 1.6, there would be an *excess supply* of 2.4 million metric tons. Under these circumstances, some of the copper supplied by producers could not be sold, and, as inventories of copper built up, suppliers would tend to cut their prices in order to get rid of unwanted inventories. Thus, a price of $1.20 per pound would not be maintained for long—and for this reason, $1.20 per pound is not an equilibrium price.

If the price were $1.00 per pound, on the other hand, the demand curve indicates that 11.8 million metric tons would be demanded, while the supply curve indicates that 9.4 million metric tons would be supplied. Again we find a mismatch between the quantity supplied and the quantity demanded per year, since the rate at which copper is supplied would be less than the rate at which it is demanded. Specifically, as shown in Figure 1.6, there would be an *excess demand* of 2.4 million metric tons. Under these circumstances, some of the consumers who want copper at this price would have to be turned away empty-handed. There would be a shortage. And given this shortage, suppliers would find it profitable to increase the price, and competition among buyers would bid the price up. Thus, a price of $1.00 per pound could not be maintained for long—so $1.00 per pound is not an equilibrium price.

*The equilibrium price must be the price where the quantity demanded equals the quantity supplied. Obviously, this is the only price at which there is no mismatch between the quantity demanded and the quantity supplied; and consequently the only price that can be maintained for long.* In Figure 1.6, the price at which the quantity supplied equals the quantity demanded is $1.10 per pound, the price where the demand curve intersects the supply curve. Thus $1.10 is the equilibrium price of copper under the circumstances visualized in Figure 1.6, and 11 million metric tons is the equilibrium quantity.

## ACTUAL PRICE

Of course, the price we really are interested in is the *actual price*—the price that really prevails, not the equilibrium price. In general, economists simply assume that the actual price will approximate the equilibrium price, which seems reasonable enough, since the basic forces at work tend to push the actual price toward the equilibrium price. Thus, if conditions remain fairly stable for a time, the actual price should move toward the equilibrium price.

To see that this is true, consider the market for copper, as described in Figure 1.6. What if the price somehow is set at $1.20 per pound? As we saw in the previous section, there is downward pressure on the price of copper under these conditions. Suppose the price, responding to this pressure, falls to $1.15 per pound. Comparing the quantity demanded with the quantity supplied at $1.15 per pound, we find that there is still downward pressure on price, since the quantity supplied exceeds the quantity demanded at $1.15 per pound. The price, responding to this pressure, may fall to $1.12 per pound, but comparing the quantity demanded with the quantity supplied at this price, we find that there is still a downward pressure on price, since the quantity supplied exceeds the quantity demanded at $1.12 per pound.

So long as the actual price is greater than the equilibrium price, there will be a downward pressure on price. Similarly, so long as the actual price is less than the equilibrium price, there will be an upward pressure on price. Thus there is always a tendency for the actual price to move toward the equilibrium price. But this movement may not be fast. Sometimes it takes a long time for the actual price to get close to the equilibrium price because by the time it gets close, the equilibrium price changes (because of shifts in either the demand curve or the supply curve or both). All that safely can be said is that the actual price will move toward the equilibrium price. But of course this information is of great value, since all that a manager frequently needs to know is the direction in which a price will change.

## WHAT IF THE DEMAND CURVE SHIFTS?

Any supply-and-demand diagram like Figure 1.6 is essentially a snapshot of the situation during a particular period of time. The results in Figure 1.6 are limited to a particular period because the demand and supply curves in the figure, like any demand and supply curves, pertain only to a certain period. What happens to the equilibrium price of a product when its demand curve changes? This is an important question because managers must try to anticipate and forecast the changes that will occur in the prices of their products (as well as the prices of their inputs).

To illustrate the effects of a shift to the left of the demand curve, consider the situation in the copper industry during the 1980s. Because of the recession during the early 1980s, and reductions in the growth rate of electric power output, there was a decrease in the demand for copper. Also, due in part to the substitution of fiber optics and other materials for copper, there was a further decrease in copper demand. What this meant, of course, was that the demand curve for copper shifted *to the left*, as shown in the left-hand panel of Figure 1.7. According to this panel, one would expect that this leftward shift of the demand curve would have resulted in a decrease in the price of copper, from $P$ to $P_1$.

In fact, there was a very severe drop in the price of copper during this

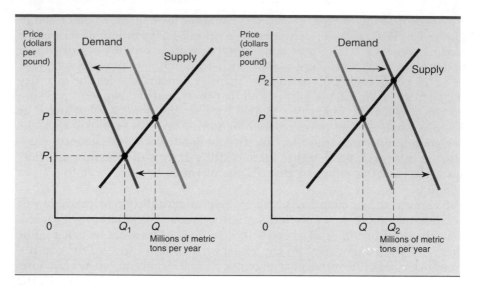

**FIGURE 1.7** *Effects of Leftward and Rightward Shifts of Demand Curve on Equilibrium Price of Copper* A leftward shift of the demand curve results in a decrease in the equilibrium price; a rightward shift results in an increase in the equilibrium price.

period. In 1980, the price was about $1 per pound; in 1986, it was about 60 cents per pound. Thus, our theory predicts exactly what occurred. It is important to recognize how momentous this price drop was—and how important it was for managers to understand why it occurred. Kennecott Copper, the nation's largest copper producer, cut operations at its Utah Copper Division by two-thirds and experienced heavy losses in the mid-1980s. Kennecott's president, G. Frank Joklik, was all too aware of the fact that this drastic price cut was due in part to a leftward shift in the demand curve for copper.[12]

On the other hand, suppose that the market demand curve for copper shifts *to the right,* as in the late 1980s. During this period, there was considerable economic growth in the United States and the demand for copper increased. As indicated in the right-hand panel of Figure 1.7, we would expect that such a rightward shift of the demand curve would result in an increase in the price of copper, from $P$ to $P_2$. In fact, the price of copper did increase during the late 1980s, from about 60 cents per pound in 1986 to about $1.30 per pound in 1989. Thus, in both the early and late 1980s, the

[12] J. Wheelen and J. D. Hunger, *Cases in Strategic Management and Business Policy* (Reading, Mass.: Addison-Wesley, 1987).

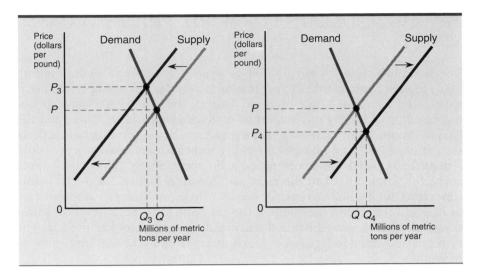

*FIGURE 1.8   Effects of Leftward and Rightward Shifts of Supply Curve on Equilibrium Price of Copper*   A leftward shift in the supply curve results in an increase in the equilibrium price; a rightward shift results in a decrease in the equilibrium price.

price of copper behaved in accord with our simple demand-and-supply analysis.

## WHAT IF THE SUPPLY CURVE SHIFTS?

What happens to the equilibrium price of a product when its supply curve changes? For example, suppose that, because of technological advances in copper production, firms like Kennecott Copper are willing and able to supply more copper at a given price than they used to, with the result that the supply curve shifts *to the right*, as shown in the right-hand panel of Figure 1.8. What will be the effect on the equilibrium price? Clearly, it will fall from $P$ (where the original supply curve intersects the demand curve) to $P_4$ (where the new supply curve intersects the demand curve).

On the other hand, suppose that there is a marked increase in the wage rates of copper workers, with the result that the supply curve shifts *to the left*, as shown in the left-hand panel of Figure 1.8. What will be the effect? The equilibrium price will increase from $P$ (where the original supply curve intersects the demand curve) to $P_3$ (where the new supply curve intersects the demand curve).

## THE 1991 COLLAPSE OF WOOL PRICES: A CASE STUDY

The basic principles of supply and demand are useful in understanding many markets, not just the copper market. Consider, for example, the fascinating and important case of wool. During the late 1980s, wool prices increased considerably due in part to increased demand by China and the Soviet Union. From 1987 to 1988, the price of wool for worsted clothing rose from $3.67 to $5.81 per pound. Expecting that wool prices would remain high, wool producers raised a lot more sheep. Thus, the supply curve for wool shifted to the right, as shown in Figure 1.9. At the same time, the Chinese and Soviets cut back on their purchases of wool because of lack of foreign currency (and in the case of China, because of organizational problems), thus shifting the demand curve for wool to the left. The result, as indicated in Figure 1.9, was a severe drop in the equilibrium price of wool.

Australia is the world's largest producer of wool, and for a time the Australian Wool Corporation propped up the price of wool by buying up any unsold Australian wool. But this did not work because wool production had

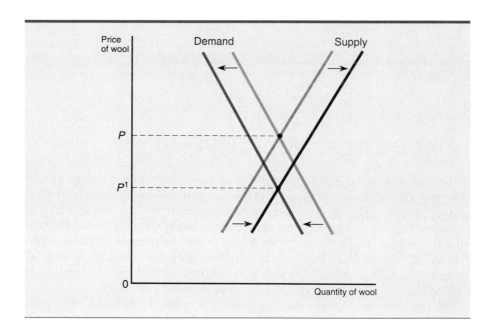

**FIGURE 1.9**   *Effect of Shifts in Demand Curve and Supply Curve in the late 1980s and early 1990s on the Equilibrium Price of Wool*   Because of the leftward shift in the demand curve and the rightward shift in the supply curve, the equilibrium price of wool dropped from $P$ to $P^1$.

## WHY THE DROP IN THE PRICE OF RADIO STATIONS?

From the mid-1980s to the early 1990s, the Federal Communications Commission (FCC), which regulates the nation's airwaves, approved over a thousand new radio stations. There is a market for radio stations, just as there is a market for wheat, corn, or lamb chops. Individuals and firms buy and sell radio stations. In effect, what the FCC did was to shift the supply curve for radio stations to the right, as shown below. That is, holding the price of a radio station constant, the quantity of radio stations increased substantially.

According to the demand-and-supply diagram below, one would expect the price of a radio station to fall considerably—from $P_1$ to $P_2$—as a consequence of the FCC's actions. In fact, this was exactly what occurred. According to Paul Kagan Associates, a market research firm in Carmel, California, the average price of a combined AM/FM radio station fell from about $6.2 million in 1987 to about $1.8 million in 1990.

*Alfred C. Sikes, Chairman, FCC*

Clearly, such a drop in the price of a station was of great concern to station owners.

Of course, the graph below is highly simplified. For one thing,

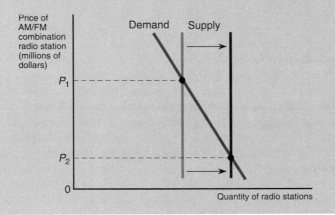

radio stations are by no means homogeneous, although we are treating them as if they were. For another thing, the demand curve for radio stations, as well as the supply curve for radio stations, may have shifted between 1987 and 1990. (In the diagram on page 27, we assume that the demand curve is fixed.) But the' important point is that this diagram, highly simplified though it is, provides a correct prediction of the central effect of the FCC's actions. By approving a lot of new stations, the FCC shifted the supply curve to the right, which would be expected to reduce the price of a station. This is the essential message of this diagram—and this message proved to be both correct and useful.*

* For further discussion, see *New York Times*, June 30, 1991.

grown so greatly and demand had fallen so sharply that the Australian Wool Corporation had to buy up so much wool that it exhausted its cash reserves and its credit. The firm turned for help to the Australian government, but its Parliament refused to guarantee further loans to buy up even more surplus wool. Eventually, in March 1991, the actual price of wool fell to about $2.50 per pound.

While this collapse of wool prices meant losses for wool producers, it helped clothing makers to reduce upward pressures on their own prices. In 1991, Giorgio Armani and Ralph Lauren, among others, cut their prices. Clearly, managers of both clothing makers and wool producers have an intense interest in the ups and downs of the wool market—and to understand these ups and downs, they must know the basic principles of demand and supply we have discussed. Managers in other industries must know these principles too. Much more will be said on this score in subsequent chapters.[13]

## SUMMARY

1. Managerial economics draws heavily on economics (particularly microeconomics) and the decision sciences. In contrast to microeconomics, which is largely descriptive, managerial economics is prescriptive. Courses in managerial economics provide fundamental analytical tools, as well as play a major integrating role. Managerial economics is at the core of the management of nonbusiness organizations like government agencies, as well as the management of firms.
2. Both for nonbusiness organizations and firms, the process of decision making can be divided into the following five steps. (1) Establish or

[13] I am grateful to officials of the Wool Bureau, who provided me with relevant data. Also, see *Philadelphia Inquirer*, October 27, 1991.

identify the organization's objectives. (2) Define the problem. (3) Identify possible solutions. (4) Select the best possible solution. (5) Implement the decision.

3. To apply managerial economics to business management, we need a theory of the firm. According to the theory accepted by most managerial economists, the firm tries to maximize its value, defined as the present value of its expected future cash flows (which for now are equated with profits). However, this maximization occurs subject to constraints, since the firm has limited inputs, particularly in the very short run, and must act in accord with a variety of laws and contracts.

4. Managerial economists define profits somewhat differently from the way accountants do. When economists speak of profit, they mean profit over and above what the owners' labor and capital employed in the business could earn elsewhere. To a considerable extent, the differences between the concepts of profit used by the accountant and the economist reflect the difference in their functions.

5. Three important reasons for the existence of profits are innovation, risk, and monopoly power. Profits and losses are the mainsprings of a free-enterprise economy. They are signals that indicate where resources are needed and where they are too abundant. They are important incentives for innovation and risk taking. They are society's reward for efficiency.

6. Although managerial economists generally assume that firms want to maximize profit (and hence their value), it is recognized that a principal-agent problem arises if managers pursue their own interests, even though this decreases the profits of the owners. To deal with this problem, the owners often give the managers a financial stake in the success of the firm.

7. Every market has a demand side and a supply side. The market demand curve shows the amount of a product that buyers would like to purchase at various prices. The market supply curve shows the amount of a product that sellers would offer at various prices. The equilibrium price is the price where the quantity demanded equals the quantity supplied.

8. Both demand curves and supply curves shift over time, thus resulting in changes in a product's price. Rightward shifts in the demand curve (and leftward shifts in the supply curve) tend to increase price. Leftward shifts in the demand curve (and rightward shifts in the supply curve) tend to decrease price.

## QUESTIONS AND PROBLEMS

1. "No self-respecting [top] executive joining a company from the outside these days does so without a front-end, or signing, bonus. And in many cases, the bonus is in the seven figures. At the same time, the entering executive may be given a bonus guarantee; hence, he does not have to

worry that if the company's fortunes sag right after he joins, he will lose some or all of his normal bonus. Typically, the bonus guarantee lasts for two or three years, although [sometimes] . . . the guarantee turns out to be for life."[14] Do long-term bonus guarantees help to solve the principal-agent problem, or do they tend to exacerbate it? Why?

2. Paul Fireman, chief executive officer of Reebok, signed an employment contract establishing his salary at $65,000 per year plus an annual bonus equal to 10 percent of the firm's pretax earnings in excess of $100,000. Was this contract an effective means of solving the principal-agent problem? Why, or why not?

3. What roles does managerial economics play in the study of business administration? What is its relationship to economic theory and the decision sciences?

4. What are the five basic steps in decision making? After the stock market crash on October 19, 1987, when the Dow-Jones average plummeted about 500 points, Louis Eckhardt, a New York broker, had to decide whether to buy IBM's stock. In his particular decision-making process, describe each of these five steps.

5. If the interest rate is 10 percent, what is the present value of the Monroe Corporation's profits in the next 10 years?

| Number of years in the future | Profit (millions of dollars) |
|---|---|
| 1 | 8 |
| 2 | 10 |
| 3 | 12 |
| 4 | 14 |
| 5 | 15 |
| 6 | 16 |
| 7 | 17 |
| 8 | 15 |
| 9 | 13 |
| 10 | 10 |

6. Describe in detail how the IBM Corporation's research laboratories can affect the value of the firm. When IBM scientists like Nobel Prize winner Alex Müller produced fundamental new findings concerning superconductors, did this have any impact on the value of the IBM Corporation?

7. What are the basic differences between the accounting and economic definitions of profits?

8. Smith-Kline Beecham, a major pharmaceutical firm, has made large profits from its anti-ulcers drug, Tagamet. In this case, have these profits been (a) the rewards for innovation, (b) compensation for risk bearing, (c) due to imperfect competition?

[14] G. Crystal, *In Search of Excess* (New York: Norton, 1991).

9. How does "satisficing" differ from the traditional economic theory of the firm?

10. List a dozen constraints that limit the extent to which the Exxon Corporation can increase its value. Are there political constraints? Technological constraints? Legal constraints? Social constraints? Time constraints?

11. In Figure 1.3, the value of $i$, the interest rate used in calculating the present value of the firm's expected future cash flows, is said to depend on the riskiness of the firm. Why is this the case?

12. The profits of Du Pont de Nemours and Company in 1991 were $1.4 billion. Does this mean that Du Pont's economic profit equaled $1.4 billion? Why or why not?

13. William Howe must decide whether or not to start a business renting beach umbrellas at an ocean resort during June, July, and August of next summer. He believes that he can rent each umbrella to vacationers at $5 a day, and he intends to lease 50 umbrellas for the 3-month period for $3,000. To operate this business, he does not have to hire anyone (but himself), and he has no expenses other than the leasing costs and a fee of $3,000 per month to rent the location of the business. Howe is a college student, and if he did not operate this business, he could earn $4,000 for the 3-month period doing construction work.
    (a) If there are 80 days during the summer when beach umbrellas are demanded, and if Howe rents all 50 of his umbrellas on each of these days, what will be his accounting profit for the summer?
    (b) What will be his economic profit for the summer?

14. Based on rough estimates by U.S. government economists, the demand curve for wheat in the United States in 1991 was
$$P = 12.4 - 4Q_D,$$
where $P$ is the farm price of wheat (in dollars per bushel) and $Q_D$ is the quantity of wheat demanded (in billions of bushels), and the supply curve for wheat in the United States in 1991 was
$$P = -2.6 + 2Q_S,$$
where $Q_S$ is the quantity of wheat supplied (in billions of bushels).
    (a) What was the equilibrium price of wheat in 1991?
    (b) What was the equilibrium quantity of wheat sold in 1991?
    (c) Must the actual price equal the equilibrium price? Why, or why not?

15. In July 1975, a frost destroyed most of Brazil's coffee crop. The price of coffee rose from about $.70 per pound to about $2.70 per pound.
    (a) Use a demand-and-supply diagram to indicate why this spectacular price increase occurred.
    (b) Do you think that the price remained for long at about $2.70 per pound? Why, or why not?

# Chapter 2
# Optimization Techniques

## INTRODUCTION

In 1987, John Welch, chairman of General Electric, sold the firm's Consumer Electronics Group to France's Thomson-Brandt. Why? Because he and his colleagues felt that it would enhance the performance of his firm. (The Consumer Electronics Group had been having difficulties competing with its Japanese and Korean rivals.) As we learned in the previous chapter, managerial economics is concerned with the ways in which managers should make decisions in order to maximize the effectiveness or performance of the organizations they manage. To understand how this can be done, you must understand the basic optimization techniques taken up in this chapter.

To begin with, we describe the nature of marginal analysis. While simple in concept, marginal analysis is a powerful tool that illuminates many central aspects of decision making regarding resource allocation. Next, we will examine the basic elements of differential calculus, including rules of differentiation and the use of derivatives to maximize or minimize a function. Finally, we will take up constrained optimization, and include an optional section on Lagrangian multipliers. Since Lagrangian multipliers require more mathematical sophistication than the rest of the chapter, the section dealing with them has been written so that it can be skipped without loss of continuity.

# FUNCTIONAL RELATIONSHIPS

To understand the optimization techniques described in this chapter, you must know how economic relationships are expressed. Frequently, the relationship between two or more economic variables can be represented by a *table* or *graph.* For example, Table 2.1 shows the relationship between the price charged by the Cherry Corporation and the number of units of output the company sells per day. Figure 2.1 represents the same relationship using a graph.

**TABLE 2.1   Relationship between Price and Quantity Sold, Cherry Corporation**

| Price per unit | Number of units sold per day |
|----------------|------------------------------|
| $10            | 150                          |
| 20             | 100                          |
| 30             | 50                           |
| 40             | 0                            |

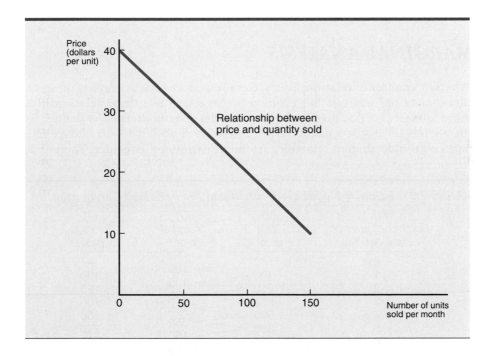

**FIGURE 2.1   Relationship between Price and Quantity Sold, Cherry Corporation**   This graph presents the data in Table 2.1.

While tables and graphs are extremely helpful, and will be used often in this book, another way of expressing economic relationships is through the use of *equations*. How can the relationship between the number of units sold and the price in Table 2.1 (and Figure 2.1) be expressed in the form of an equation? One way is to use the following functional notation:

$$Q = f(P), \tag{2.1}$$

where $Q$ is the number of units sold, and $P$ is price. This equation should be read as: "The number of units sold is a function of price," which means that the number of units sold *depends* on price. In other words, the number of units sold is the *dependent* variable, and price is the *independent* variable.

While equation (2.1) is useful, it does not tell us *how* the number of units sold depends on price. A more specific representation of this relationship is

$$Q = 200 - 5P. \tag{2.2}$$

Comparing this equation with the data in Table 2.1 (and Figure 2.1), you can verify that these data conform to this equation. For example, if the price equals $10, the number of units sold should be $200 - 5(10) = 150$, according to the equation. This is exactly what Table 2.1 (and Figure 2.1) shows. Regardless of what price you choose, the number of units sold is the same, no matter whether you consult Table 2.1, Figure 2.1, or equation (2.2).

## MARGINAL ANALYSIS

Whether economic relationships are expressed as tables, graphs, or equations, marginal analysis has enabled managers to use these relationships more effectively. The **marginal value** of a dependent variable is defined as the *change* in this dependent variable associated with a 1-unit *change* in a particular independent variable. As an illustration, consider Table 2.2,

TABLE 2.2   *Relationship between Output and Profit, Roland Corporation*

| (1)<br>Number of units of<br>output per day | (2)<br>Total<br>profit | (3)<br>Marginal<br>profit | (4)<br>Average<br>profit |
|---|---|---|---|
| 0 | 0 | | — |
| 1 | 100 | 100 | 100 |
| 2 | 250 | 150 | 125 |
| 3 | 600 | 350 | 200 |
| 4 | 1,000 | 400 | 250 |
| 5 | 1,350 | 350 | 270 |
| 6 | 1,500 | 150 | 250 |
| 7 | 1,550 | 50 | 221 |
| 8 | 1,500 | −50 | 188 |
| 9 | 1,400 | −100 | 156 |
| 10 | 1,200 | −200 | 120 |

which indicates in columns 1 and 2 the total profit of the Roland Corporation if the number of units produced equals various amounts. In this case, total profit is the dependent variable and output is the independent variable. Thus, the marginal value of profit (called **marginal profit**) is the *change* in total profit associated with a 1-unit *change* in output.

Column 3 of Table 2.2 shows the value of marginal profit. If output increases from 0 to 1 unit, column 2 shows that total profit increases by $100 (from 0 to $100). Thus, marginal profit in column 3 equals $100 if output is between 0 and 1 unit. If output increases from 1 to 2 units, total profit increases by $150 (from $100 to $250). Thus, marginal profit in column 3 equals $150 if output is between 1 and 2 units.

*The central point to bear in mind about a marginal relationship of this sort is that the dependent variable—in this case, total profit—is maximized when its marginal value shifts from positive to negative.* To see this, consider Table 2.2. So long as marginal profit is positive, the Roland Corporation can raise its total profit by increasing output. For example, if output is between 5 and 6 units, marginal profit is positive ($150); thus, the firm's total profit will go up (by $150) if output is increased from 5 to 6 units. But when marginal profit shifts from positive to negative, total profit will fall, not go up, with any further increase in output. In Table 2.2, this point is reached when the firm produces 7 units of output. If output is increased beyond this point (to 8 units), marginal profit shifts from positive to negative—and total profit goes down (by $50). Thus, as stated above, the dependent variable—in this case, total profit—is maximized when its marginal value shifts from positive to negative.

Since managers are interested in determining how to maximize profit (or other performance measures), this is a very useful result. It emphasizes the importance of looking at marginal values, and the hazards that may arise if average values are used instead. In Table 2.2, **average profit**—that is, total profit divided by output—is shown in column 4. It may seem eminently reasonable to choose the output whose average profit is highest. Countless managers have done so. But this is not the correct decision if one wants to maximize profit. Instead, as stressed in the previous paragraph, one should choose the output where marginal profit shifts from positive to negative.

To prove this, one need only find the output in Table 2.2 where average profit is highest. Based on a comparison of the figures in column 4, this output is 5 units; and according to column 2, total profit at this output equals $1,350. In the paragraph before last, we found that the output where marginal profit shifts from positive to negative is 7 units; and according to column 2, total profit at this point equals $1,550. Clearly, total profit is $200 higher if output is 7 rather than 5 units. Thus, if the managers of this firm were to choose the output where average profit is highest, they would sacrifice $200 per day in profits.

It is important to understand the relationship between average and marginal values: because the marginal value represents the change in the total, the average value must *increase* if the marginal value is *greater* than the average value; by the same token, the average value must *decrease* if the marginal value is *less* than the average value. Table 2.2 illustrates these propositions. For the first to fifth units of output, marginal profit is greater than average profit. Since the extra profit from each additional unit is greater than the average, the average is pulled up as more is produced. For the sixth to tenth units of output, marginal profit is less than average profit. Since the extra profit from each additional unit is less than the average, the average is pulled down as more is produced.

## RELATIONSHIP BETWEEN TOTAL, MARGINAL, AND AVERAGE VALUES

To explore further the relationships between total, marginal, and average values, consider Figure 2.2, which shows the relationship between total, average, and marginal profit, on the one hand, and output, on the other hand, for the Roland Corporation. The relationship between output and profit is exactly the same as in Table 2.2, but rather than using particular numbers to designate output or profit, we use symbols such as $Q_0$ and $Q_1$ for output levels and $\pi_0$ for a profit level. The results are of general validity, not true for only a particular set of numerical values.

At the outset, note that Figure 2.2 contains two panels. The upper panel (panel A) shows the relationship between total profit and output, while the lower panel (panel B) shows the relationship between average profit and marginal profit, on the one hand, and output, on the other. The horizontal scale of panel A is the same as that of panel B, the result being that a given output like $Q_0$ is the same distance from the origin (along the horizontal axis) in panel A as in panel B.

In practice, one seldom is presented with data concerning both (1) the relationship between total profit and output and (2) the relationship between average profit and output, because it is relatively simple to derive the latter relationship from the former. How can this be done? Take any output—say $Q_0$. *At this output, average profit equals the slope of the straight line from the origin to point E, the point on the total profit curve corresponding to output $Q_0$.* To see that this is the case, note that average profit at this output level equals $\pi_0/Q_0$, where $\pi_0$ is the level of total profit if output is $Q_0$. Because the slope of any straight line equals the vertical distance between two points on the line divided by the horizontal distance between them, the slope of the line from the origin to point $E$ equals $\pi_0/Q_0$.[1] Thus the slope of line $OE$ equals average profit at this output. (In other words, $K_0$ in panel B of Figure 2.2 is equal to the slope of line $OE$.) To determine the relationship between average profit and output from the relationship between total profit and output, we repeat this procedure for each level of output, not $Q_0$ alone. The resulting average profit curve is shown in panel B.

---

[1] The vertical distance between the origin and point $E$ equals $\pi_0$, and the horizontal distance between these two points equals $Q_0$. Thus, the vertical distance divided by the horizontal distance equals $\pi_0/Q_0$.

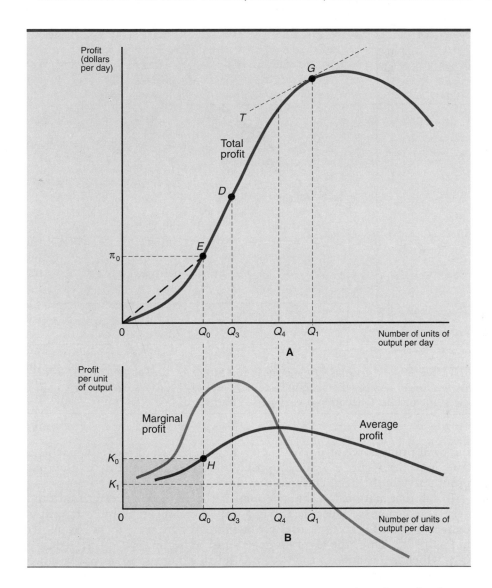

*FIGURE 2.2   Total Profit, Average Profit, and Marginal Profit, Roland Corporation*   The average and marginal profit curves in panel B can be derived geometrically from the total profit curve in panel A.

Turning to the relationship between marginal profit and output (in panel B), it is relatively simple to derive this relationship too from the relationship between total profit and output (in panel A). Take any output—say $Q_1$. *At this output, marginal profit equals the slope of the tangent to the total profit curve (in panel A) at the point where output is $Q_1$.* In other words, marginal profit equals the slope of line $T$ in Figure 2.2, which is tangent to

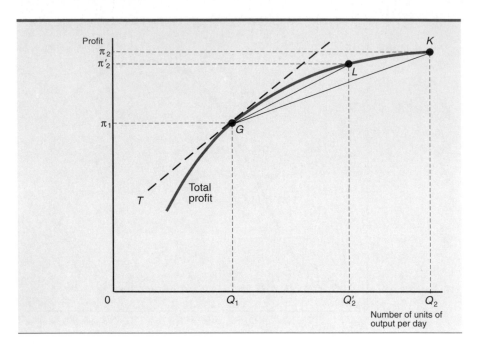

**FIGURE 2.3** *Marginal Profit Equals the Slope of the Tangent to the Total Profit Curve* As the distance between $Q_1$ and $Q_2$ becomes extremely small, the slope of line $T$ becomes a very good estimate of $(\pi_2 - \pi_1)/(Q_2 - Q_1)$.

the total profit curve at point $G$. As a first step toward seeing why this is true, consider Figure 2.3, which provides a magnified picture of the total profit curve in the neighborhood of point $G$.

Recall that marginal profit is defined as the extra profit resulting from a very small increase (specifically, a 1-unit increase) in output. If output increases from $Q_1$ to $Q_2$, total profit increases from $\pi_1$ to $\pi_2$, as shown in Figure 2.3. Thus, the extra profit per unit of output is $(\pi_2 - \pi_1) \div (Q_2 - Q_1)$, which is the slope of the $GK$ line. But this increase in output is rather large. Suppose that we decrease $Q_2$ so that it is closer to $Q_1$. In particular, let the new value of $Q_2$ be $Q'_2$. If output increases from $Q_1$ to $Q'_2$, the extra profit per unit of output equals $(\pi'_2 - \pi_1) \div (Q'_2 - Q_1)$, which is the slope of the $GL$ line. If we further decrease $Q_2$ until the distance between $Q_1$ and $Q_2$ is extremely small, the slope of the tangent (line $T$) at point $G$ becomes a very good estimate of $(\pi_2 - \pi_1) \div (Q_2 - Q_1)$. In the limit, for changes in output in a very small neighborhood around $Q_1$, the slope of the tangent *is* marginal profit. (This slope equals $K_1$ in panel B of Figure 2.2.) To determine the relationship between marginal profit and output from the relationship between total profit and output, we repeat this procedure for each level of output, not $Q_1$ alone. The resulting marginal profit curve is shown in panel B of Figure 2.2.

Sometimes one is given an average profit curve like that in panel B, but not the total profit curve. To derive the latter curve from the former, note that total profit equals average profit times output. Thus, if output equals $Q_0$, total profit equals $K_0$ times $Q_0$, which is the area of the shaded rectangle $OK_0HQ_0$ in panel B. In other words, $\pi_0$ in panel A equals the area of rectangle $OK_0HQ_0$ in panel B. To derive the relationship between total profit and output from the relationship between average profit and output, we repeat this procedure for each level of output. That is, we find the area of the appropriate rectangle of this sort corresponding to each output, not $Q_0$ alone. The resulting total profit curve is shown in panel A.

Finally, two further points should be made concerning the total, average, and marginal profit curves in Figure 2.2. First, you should be able to tell at a glance at panel A that marginal profit increases as output rises from zero to $Q_3$, and that it decreases as output rises further. Why is this so obvious from panel A? Because the slope of the total profit curve increases as one moves from the origin to point $D$. In other words, lines drawn tangent to the total profit curve become steeper as one moves from the origin to point $D$. Thus, since marginal profit equals the slope of this tangent, it must increase as output rises from zero to $Q_3$. To the right of point $D$, the slope of the total profit curve is decreasing as output increases. That is, lines drawn tangent to the total profit curve become less steep as one moves to the right of point $D$. Consequently, since marginal profit equals the slope of this tangent, it too must decrease when output rises beyond $Q_3$.

Second, panel B of Figure 2.2 confirms the proposition put forth on page 35: *The average profit curve must be rising if it is below the marginal profit curve, and it must be falling if it is above the marginal profit curve.* At output levels below $Q_4$, the average profit curve is below the marginal profit curve; thus, the average profit curve is rising because the higher marginal profits are pulling up the average profits. At output levels above $Q_4$, the average profit curve is above the marginal profit curve; thus, the average profit curve is falling because the lower marginal profits are pulling down the average profits.

## THE CONCEPT OF A DERIVATIVE

In the case of the Roland Corporation, we used Table 2.2—which shows the relationship between the firm's output and profit—to find the profit-maximizing output level. Frequently, a table of this sort is too cumbersome or inaccurate to be useful for this purpose. Instead, an equation is used to represent the relationship between the variable we are trying to maximize (in this case profit) and the variable or variables under the control of the decision maker (in this case, output). Given an equation of this sort, the powerful concepts and techniques of differential calculus can be employed to find optimal solutions to the decision maker's problem.

In previous sections, we defined the marginal value as the change in the

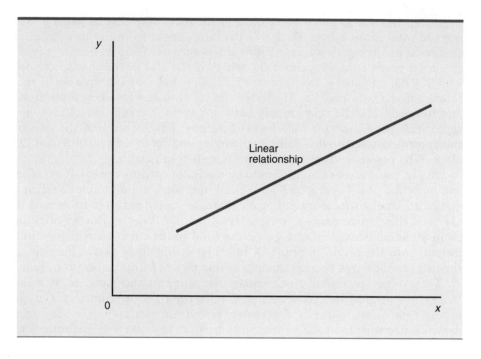

**FIGURE 2.4** *Linear Relationship between* **Y** *and* **X**   The relationship between $Y$ and $X$ can be represented as a straight line.

dependent variable resulting from a 1-unit change in an independent variable. If $Y$ is the dependent variable and $X$ is the independent variable,

$$Y = f(X), \tag{2.3}$$

according to the notation in equation (2.1). Using $\Delta$ (called delta) to denote change, a change in the independent variable can be expressed as $\Delta X$, and a change in the dependent variable can be expressed as $\Delta Y$. Thus, the marginal value of $Y$ can be estimated by

$$\frac{\text{Change in } Y}{\text{Change in } X} = \frac{\Delta Y}{\Delta X}. \tag{2.4}$$

For example, if a 2-unit increase in $X$ results in a 1-unit increase in $Y$, $\Delta X = 2$ and $\Delta Y = 1$, which means that the marginal value of $Y$ is about $\frac{1}{2}$. That is, the dependent variable $Y$ increases by about $\frac{1}{2}$ if the independent variable $X$ increases by 1.[2]

Unless the relationship between $Y$ and $X$ can be represented as a straight line (as in Figure 2.4), the value of $\Delta Y/\Delta X$ is not constant. For example, consider the relationship between $Y$ and $X$ in Figure 2.5. If a movement occurs

---

[2] Why do we say that $Y$ increases by about $\frac{1}{2}$, rather than by exactly $\frac{1}{2}$? Because $Y$ may not be linearly related to $X$. More is said on this score in the next paragraph of the text.

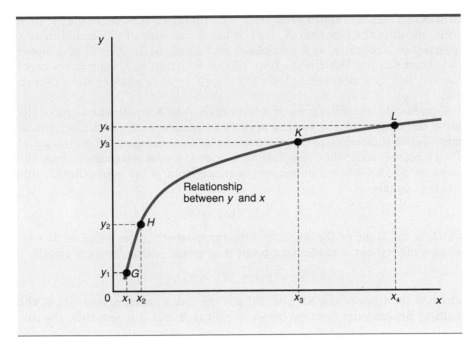

**FIGURE 2.5**    *How the Value of $\Delta Y / \Delta X$ Varies Depending on the Steepness or Flatness of the Relationship between* Y *and* X    Between points *G* and *H*, since the curve is steep, $\Delta Y / \Delta X$ is large. Between points *K* and *L*, since the curve is flat, $\Delta Y / \Delta X$ is small.

from point *G* to point *H*, a relatively small change in *X* (from $X_1$ to $X_2$) is associated with a big change in *Y* (from $Y_1$ to $Y_2$). Thus, between points *G* and *H*, the value of $\Delta Y / \Delta X$, which equals $(Y_2 - Y_1)/(X_2 - X_1)$, is relatively large. On the other hand, if a movement occurs from point *K* to point *L*, a relatively large change in *X* (from $X_3$ to $X_4$) is associated with a small change in *Y* (from $Y_3$ to $Y_4$). Consequently, between points *K* and *L*, the value of $\Delta Y / \Delta X$, which equals $(Y_4 - Y_3)/(X_4 - X_3)$, is relatively small.

The value of $\Delta Y / \Delta X$ is related to the steepness or flatness of the curve in Figure 2.5. Between points *G* and *H*, the curve is relatively *steep*, which means that a *small* change in *X* results in a *large* change in *Y*. Consequently, $\Delta Y / \Delta X$ is relatively large. Between points *K* and *L*, the curve is relatively *flat*, which means that a *large* change in *X* results in a *small* change in *Y*. Consequently $\Delta Y / \Delta X$ is relatively small.

*The derivative of* Y *with respect to* X *is defined as the limit of* $\Delta Y / \Delta X$ *as* $\Delta X$ *approaches zero.* Since the derivative of *Y* with respect to *X* is denoted by $dY/dX$, this definition can be restated as follows:

$$\frac{dY}{dX} = \frac{\text{limit}}{\Delta X \to 0} \frac{\Delta Y}{\Delta X} \qquad (2.5)$$

which is read: "The derivative of *Y* with respect to *X* equals the limit of the ratio $\Delta Y/\Delta X$ as $\Delta X$ approaches zero." To understand what is meant by a limit, consider the function $(X - 2)$. What is the limit of this function as $X$ approaches 2? Clearly, as $X$ gets closer and closer to 2, $(X - 2)$ gets closer and closer to zero. What is the limit of this function as $X$ approaches zero? Clearly, as $X$ gets closer and closer to zero, $(X - 2)$ gets closer and closer to $-2$.

Graphically, the derivative of $Y$ with respect to $X$ equals the *slope* of the curve showing $Y$ (on the vertical axis) as a function of $X$ (on the horizontal axis). To see this, suppose that we want to find the value of the derivative of $Y$ with respect to $X$ when $X$ equals $X_5$ in Figure 2.6. A rough measure is the value of $\Delta Y/\Delta X$ when a movement is made from point $A$ to point $C$; this measure equals

$$(Y_7 - Y_5) \div (X_7 - X_5),$$

which is the slope of the $AC$ line. A better measure is the value of $\Delta Y/\Delta X$ when a movement is made from point $A$ to point $B$; this measure equals

$$(Y_6 - Y_5) \div (X_6 - X_5),$$

which is the slope of the $AB$ line. Why is the latter measure better than the former? Because the distance between points $A$ and $B$ is less than the dis-

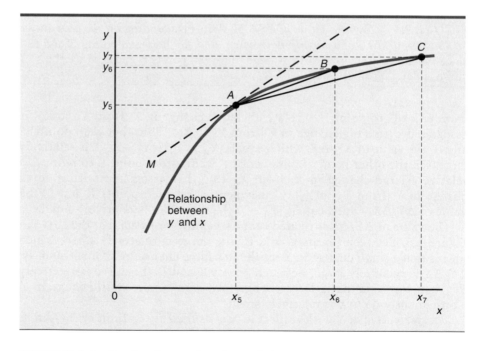

**FIGURE 2.6   Derivative as the Slope of the Curve**   When $X$ equals $X_5$, the derivative of $Y$ with respect to $X$ equals the slope of line $M$, the tangent to the curve at point $A$.

tance between points *A* and *C*. What we want is the value of $\Delta Y/\Delta X$ when $\Delta X$ is as small as possible. Clearly, *in the limit, as $\Delta X$ approaches zero, the ratio $\Delta Y/\Delta X$ is equal to the slope of the line M, which is drawn tangent to the curve at point A.*

## HOW TO FIND A DERIVATIVE

Managers like John Welch would like to know how to optimize the performance of their organizations. If *Y* is some measure of organizational performance and *X* is a variable under a particular manager's control, he or she would like to know the value of *X* that will maximize *Y*. To find out, it is very useful, as we shall see in the next section, to know the derivative of *Y* with respect to *X*. In this section, we learn how to find this derivative.

*Derivatives of Constants.* If the dependent variable *Y* is a constant, its derivative with respect to *X* is always zero. That is, if $Y = a$ (where *a* is a constant),

$$\frac{dY}{dX} = 0. \tag{2.6}$$

*Example:* Suppose that $Y = 6$, as shown in Figure 2.7. Since the value

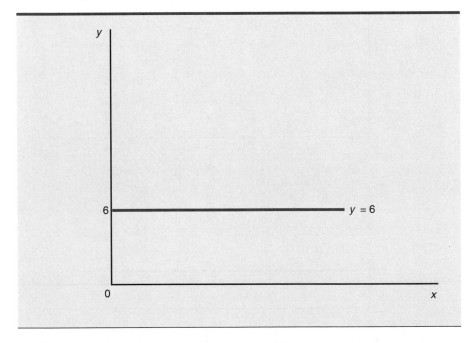

FIGURE 2.7   *Case Where* Y $= 6$   In this case, $dY/dX$ equals zero, since the slope of this horizontal line equals zero.

of $Y$ does not change as $X$ varies, $dY/dX$ must be equal to zero. To see how this can also be shown geometrically, recall from the previous section that $dY/dX$ equals the slope of the curve showing $Y$ as a function of $X$. As is evident from Figure 2.7, this slope equals zero, which means that $dY/dX$ must equal zero.

*Derivatives of Power Functions.* A power function can be expressed as

$$Y = aX^b,$$

where $a$ and $b$ are constants. If the relationship between $X$ and $Y$ is of this kind, the derivative of $Y$ with respect to $X$ equals $b$ times $a$ multiplied by $X$

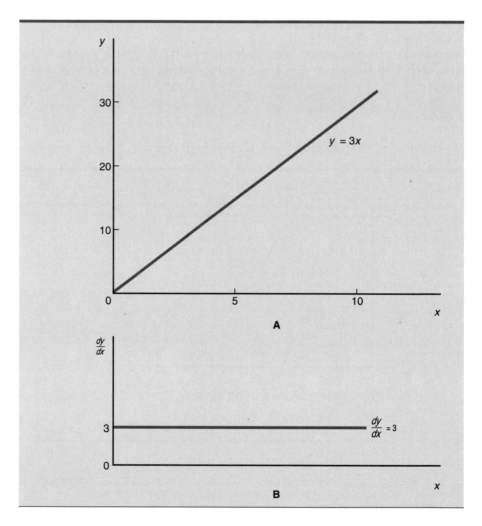

*FIGURE 2.8  Case Where* $Y = 3X$   In this case, $dY/dX$ equals 3, since the slope of the line in panel A equals 3.

raised to the $b - 1$ power:

$$\frac{dY}{dX} = b \cdot a \cdot X^{b-1}. \tag{2.7}$$

*Example:* Suppose that

$$Y = 3X,$$

which is graphed in panel A of Figure 2.8. Applying equation (2.7), we find that

$$\frac{dY}{dX} = 1 \cdot 3 \cdot X^{\circ}$$

$$= 3,$$

since $a = 3$ and $b = 1$. Thus, the value of $dY/dX$, which is graphed in panel B of Figure 2.8, is 3, regardless of the value of $X$. This makes sense, since the slope of the line in panel A is 3, regardless of the value of $X$. Recall once again from the previous section that $dY/dX$ equals the slope of the curve showing $Y$ as a function of $X$. In this case (as in Figure 2.7), this "curve" is a straight line.

*Example:* Suppose that

$$Y = 2X^2,$$

which is graphed in panel A of Figure 2.9. Applying equation (2.7), we find that

$$\frac{dY}{dX} = 2 \cdot 2 \cdot X^1$$

$$= 4X,$$

since $a = 2$ and $b = 2$. Thus, the value of $dY/dX$, which is graphed in panel B of Figure 2.9, is proportional to $X$. As would be expected, $dY/dX$ is negative when the slope of the curve in panel A is negative, and positive when this slope is positive. Why? Because as we have stressed repeatedly, $dY/dX$ equals this slope.

*Derivatives of Sums and Differences.* Suppose that $U$ and $W$ are two variables, each of which depends on $X$. That is,

$$U = g(X) \qquad W = h(X).$$

The functional relationship between $U$ and $X$ is denoted by $g$, and that between $W$ and $X$ is denoted by $h$. Suppose further that

$$Y = U + W.$$

In other words, $Y$ is the sum of $U$ and $W$. If so, the derivative of $Y$ with respect to $X$ is equal to the *sum* of the derivatives of the individual terms:

$$\frac{dY}{dX} = \frac{dU}{dX} + \frac{dW}{dX}. \tag{2.8}$$

On the other hand, if

$$Y = U - W,$$

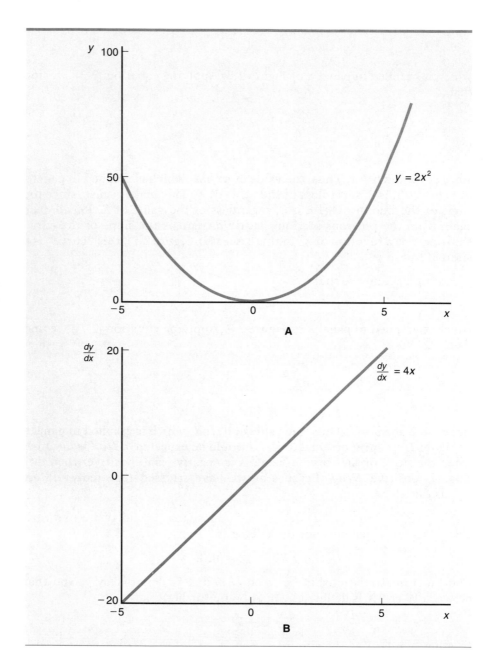

**A**

**B**

FIGURE 2.9   *Case Where* $Y = 2X^2$    In this case, $dY/dX = 4X$, since the slope of the curve in panel A equals $4X$.

the derivative of Y with respect to X is equal to the *difference* between the derivatives of the individual terms:

$$\frac{dY}{dX} = \frac{dU}{dX} - \frac{dW}{dX}.$$ (2.9)

*Example:* Consider the case where $U = g(X) = 3X^3$ and $W = h(X) = 4X^2$. If $Y = U + W = 3X^3 + 4X^2$,

$$\frac{dY}{dX} = 9X^2 + 8X.$$ (2.10)

To see why, recall from equation (2.8) that

$$\frac{dY}{dX} = \frac{dU}{dX} + \frac{dW}{dX}.$$ (2.11)

Applying equation (2.7),

$$\frac{dU}{dX} = 9X^2; \qquad \frac{dW}{dX} = 8X.$$

Substituting these values of the derivatives into equation (2.11), equation (2.10) follows.

*Example:* Suppose that $Y = U - W$, where $U = 8X^2$ and $W = 9X$. Then

$$\frac{dY}{dX} = 16X - 9,$$

since, according to equation (2.9),

$$\frac{dY}{dX} = \frac{dU}{dX} - \frac{dW}{dX}$$

and, applying equation (2.7),

$$\frac{dU}{dX} = 16X; \qquad \frac{dW}{dX} = 9.$$

*Derivatives of Products.* The derivative of the product of two terms is equal to the sum of the first term multiplied by the derivative of the second, plus the second term times the derivative of the first. Consequently, if $Y = U \cdot W$,

$$\frac{dY}{dX} = U \cdot \frac{dW}{dX} + W \cdot \frac{dU}{dX}.$$ (2.12)

*Example:* If $Y = 6X(3 - X^2)$, we can let $U = 6X$ and $W = 3 - X^2$, and

$$\frac{dY}{dX} = 6X \left( \frac{dW}{dX} \right) + (3 - X^2) \left( \frac{dU}{dX} \right)$$

$$= 6X (-2X) + (3 - X^2)(6)$$

$$= -12X^2 + 18 - 6X^2$$

$$= 18 - 18X^2.$$

## CONCEPTS IN CONTEXT

### THE ALLOCATION OF THE TANG BRAND ADVERTISING BUDGET

Managers and analysts use differential calculus to help solve all sorts of problems. Consider the work that Young and Rubicam, the prominent advertising agency, did for one of its General Foods accounts, TANG beverages. TANG is the trademark for an instant breakfast drink with an orange flavor. Young and Rubicam did a study to estimate the effects of advertising expenditures on the sales of TANG and found that the relationships between advertising expenditures and sales in two districts were of the following form:*

$$S_1 = 10 + 5A_1 - 1.5A_1{}^2$$

$$S_2 = 12 + 4A_2 - 0.5A_2{}^2$$

where $S_1$ is the sales of TANG (in millions of dollars per year) in the first district, $S_2$ is its sales in the second district, $A_1$ is the advertising expenditure on TANG (in millions of dollars per year) in the first district, and $A_2$ is the advertising expenditure in the second district.

Young and Rubicam wanted to determine the amount of additional sales that an extra dollar of advertising would generate in each district. To answer this question, the derivative of sales with respect to advertising expenditure was calculated for each district, the result being as follows:

$$\frac{dS_1}{dA_1} = 5 - 3A_1$$

$$\frac{dS_2}{dA_2} = 4 - A_2.$$

Thus, in each district, the effect on sales of an extra dollar of advertising depended on the amount spent on advertising. Supposing that $0.5 million was being spent on advertising in the first district and that $1 million was being spent on advertising in the second district,

$$\frac{dS_1}{dA_1} = 5 - 3(0.5) = 3.5$$

$$\frac{dS_2}{dA_2} = 4 - 1 = 3.$$

Consequently, an extra dollar of advertising generated an extra $3.50 of sales in the first district and an extra $3.00 of sales in the second district.

Based on these findings, Young and Rubicam made a number of recommendations to General Foods concerning the regional allocation of the TANG brand advertising budget. In particular, they recommended that, if General Foods wanted to boost the total sales of TANG, more should be spent on advertising in the first district, and less should be spent on it in the second district. This would not mean an increase in General Foods' total advertising budget, since the extra advertising expenditure in the first district would be offset by the reduced advertising expenditure in the second district.

How did Young and Rubicam come to this conclusion? The fact that an extra dollar of advertising would result in a greater addition to sales in the first district than in the second indicated that a reallocation of the advertising budget was called for. To see this, consider what would happen if a dollar extra was spent on advertising in the first district and a dollar less spent in the second. The result, as indicated above, would be an extra $3.50 of sales in the first district and a $3.00 reduction in sales in the second. The overall effect would be a $3.50 − $3.00 = $0.50 increase in total sales. Thus, if General Foods wanted to increase the sales of TANG beverages, a reallocation of the advertising budget in favor of the first district was to be recommended.[†]

*Although these equations are of the form derived by Young and Rubicam, the numerical coefficients are hypothetical. For present purposes, this is of no consequence. Our purpose here is to describe the general features of this case, and how differential calculus played a role, not the specific numbers. The methods that can be used to estimate such coefficients are described in Chapter 4. Also, note that sales in each district are assumed to depend on the level of advertising in this district only.

[†]F. DeBruicker, J. Quelch, and S. Ward, *Cases in Consumer Behavior*, 2d ed. (Englewood Cliffs, N.J.: Prentice-Hall, 1986). This case has been simplified in various respects for pedagogical reasons.

The first term, $6X$, is multiplied by the derivative of the second term, $-2X$; and the result is added to the second term, $3 - X^2$, times the derivative of the first, 6. As indicated above, the result is $18 - 18X^2$.

*Derivatives of Quotients.* If $Y = U/W$, the derivative of $Y$ with respect to $X$ equals

$$\frac{dY}{dX} = \frac{W \cdot \dfrac{dU}{dX} - U \cdot \dfrac{dW}{dX}}{W^2}. \tag{2.13}$$

In other words, the derivative of the quotient of two terms equals the denominator times the derivative of the numerator *minus* the numerator times the derivative of the denominator—all divided by the square of the denominator.

*Example:* Consider the problem of finding the derivative of the expression

$$Y = \frac{5X^3}{3 - 4X}.$$

If we let $U = 5X^3$ and $W = 3 - 4X$,

$$\frac{dU}{dX} = 15X^2; \quad \frac{dW}{dX} = -4.$$

Consequently, applying equation (2.13),

$$\frac{dY}{dX} = \frac{(3 - 4X)(15X^2) - 5X^3(-4)}{(3 - 4X)^2}$$

$$= \frac{45X^2 - 60X^3 + 20X^3}{(3 - 4X)^2}$$

$$= \frac{45X^2 - 40X^3}{(3 - 4X)^2}.$$

*Derivatives of a Function of a Function (Chain Rule).*[3] Sometimes a variable depends on another variable, which in turn depends on a third variable. For example, suppose that $Y = f(W)$ and $W = g(X)$. Under these circumstances, the derivative of $Y$ with respect to $X$ equals

$$\frac{dY}{dX} = \frac{dY}{dW} \cdot \frac{dW}{dX}. \tag{2.14}$$

In other words, to find this derivative, we find the derivative of $Y$ with respect to $W$, and multiply it by the derivative of $W$ with respect to $X$.

*Example:* Suppose that $Y = 4W + W^3$, and $W = 3X^2$. To find $dY/dX$, we begin by finding $dY/dW$ and $dW/dX$:

$$\frac{dY}{dW} = 4 + 3W^2$$

$$= 4 + 3(3X^2)^2$$

$$= 4 + 27X^4.$$

$$\frac{dW}{dX} = 6X.$$

Then to find $dY/dX$, we multiply $dY/dW$ and $dW/dX$:

$$\frac{dY}{dX} = (4 + 27X^4)(6X)$$

$$= 24X + 162X^5.$$

---

[3] This section can be skipped without loss of continuity.

# USING DERIVATIVES TO SOLVE MAXIMIZATION AND MINIMIZATION PROBLEMS

Having determined how you can find the derivative of $Y$ with respect to $X$, we now take up the way in which you can determine the value of $X$ that maximizes or minimizes $Y$. *The central point to recognize is that a maximum or minimum point can occur only if the slope of the curve showing $Y$ on the vertical axis and $X$ on the horizontal axis equals zero.* To see this, suppose that $Y$ equals the profit of the Monroe Company and $X$ is its output level. If the relationship between $Y$ and $X$ is as shown by the curve in panel A of Figure 2.10, the maximum value of $Y$ occurs when $X = 10$, and at this value of $X$ the slope of the curve equals zero.

Since the derivative of $Y$ with respect to $X$ equals the slope of this curve, it follows that $Y$ can be a maximum or minimum only if this derivative equals zero. To see that $Y$ really is maximized when this derivative equals zero, note that the relationship between $Y$ and $X$ in Figure 2.10 is

$$Y = -50 + 100X - 5X^2, \tag{2.15}$$

which means that

$$\frac{dY}{dX} = 100 - 10X. \tag{2.16}$$

Thus, if this derivative equals zero,

$$100 - 10X = 0$$

$$X = 10.$$

This is the value of $X$ where $Y$ is maximized, as we saw in the previous paragraph. The key point here is that *to find the value of $X$ that maximizes or minimizes $Y$, we must find the value of $X$ where this derivative equals zero.* Panel B of Figure 2.10 shows graphically that this derivative equals zero when $Y$ is maximized.

However, based only on the fact that this derivative is zero, one cannot distinguish between a point on the curve where $Y$ is maximized and a point where $Y$ is minimized. For example, in Figure 2.11, this derivative is zero both when $X = 5$ and when $X = 15$. In the one case (when $X = 15$), $Y$ is a maximum; in the other case (when $X = 5$), $Y$ is a minimum. To distinguish between a maximum and a minimum, one must find the *second derivative of $Y$ with respect to $X$, which is denoted by $d^2Y/dX^2$, and which is the derivative of* $dY/dX$. For example, in Figure 2.10, the second derivative of $Y$ with respect to $X$ is the derivative of the function in equation (2.16); thus, it equals $-10$.

The second derivative measures the slope of the curve showing the relationship between $dY/dX$ (the first derivative) and $X$. Just as the first derivative (that is, $dY/dX$) measures the slope of the $Y$ curve in panel A of Figure

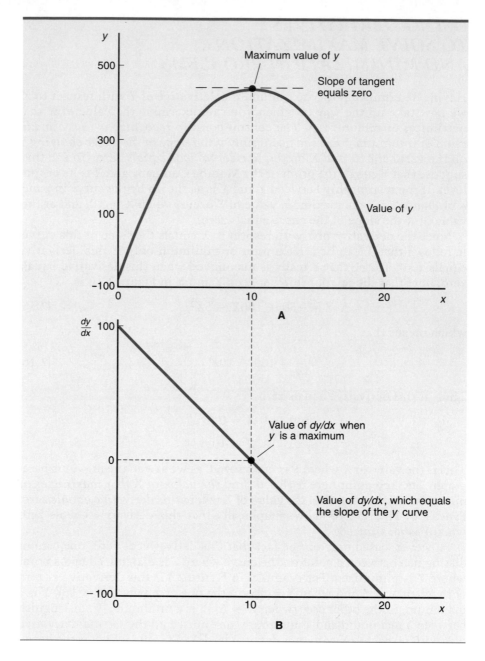

*FIGURE 2.10   Value of the Derivative When Y Is a Maximum*   When Y is a maximum (at $X = 10$), $dY/dX$ equals zero.

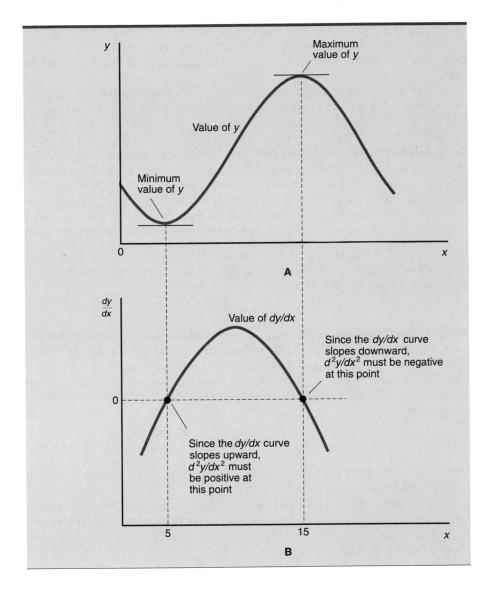

*FIGURE 2.11 Using the Second Derivative to Distinguish Maxima from Minima* At maxima (such as $X = 15$), $d^2Y/dX^2$ is negative; at minima (such as $X = 5$), $d^2Y/dX^2$ is positive.

2.11, so the second derivative (that is, $d^2Y/dX^2$) measures the slope of the $dY/dX$ curve in panel B of Figure 2.11. In other words, just as the first derivative measures the slope of the total profit curve, the second derivative measures the slope of the marginal profit curve. The reason why the second derivative is so important is that it is always *negative* at a point of *maximi-*

zation and always *positive* at a point of *minimization.* Thus, *to distinguish between maximization and minimization points, all that we have to do is determine whether the second derivative at each point is positive or negative.*

To understand why the second derivative is always negative at a maximization point and always positive at a minimization point, consider Figure 2.11. When the second derivative is *negative,* this means that the slope of the $dY/dX$ curve in panel B is *negative.* Because $dY/dX$ equals the slope of the Y curve in panel A, this in turn means that the slope of the Y curve decreases as X increases. At a maximum point, such as when $X = 15$, this must be the case. On the other hand, when the second derivative is *positive,* this means that the slope of the $dY/dX$ curve in panel B is *positive,* which is another way of saying that the slope of the Y curve in panel A increases as X increases. At a minimum point, such as when $X = 5$, this must be the case.

*Example:* To illustrate how one can use derivatives to solve maximization and minimization problems, suppose that the relationship between profit and output at the Kantor Corporation is

$$Y = -1 + 9X - 6X^2 + X^3,$$

where Y equals annual profit (in millions of dollars), and X equals annual output (in millions of units). This equation is valid only for values of X that equal 3 or less; capacity limitations prevent the firm from producing more than 3 million units per year. To find the values of output that maximize or minimize profit, we find the derivative of Y with respect to X and set it equal to zero.

$$\frac{dY}{dX} = 9 - 12X + 3X^2 = 0. \qquad (2.17)$$

Solving this equation for X, we find that two values of X—1 and 3—result in this derivative's being zero.[4]

To determine whether each of these two output levels maximizes or minimizes profit, we find the value of the second derivative at these two values of X. Taking the derivative of $dY/dX$, which is shown in equation (2.17) to equal $9 - 12X + 3X^2$, we find that

$$\frac{d^2Y}{dX^2} = -12 + 6X.$$

---

[4] If an equation is of the general quadratic form, $Y = aX^2 + bX + c$, the values of X where Y is 0 are

$$X = \frac{-b \pm \sqrt{b^2 - 4ac}}{2a}.$$

In the equation in the text, $a = 3$, $b = -12$, and $c = 9$. Thus,

$$X = \frac{12 \pm \sqrt{144 - 108}}{6} = 2 \pm 1.$$

Therefore, $Y = 0$ when X equals 1 or 3.

## ANALYZING MANAGERIAL DECISIONS

### THE OPTIMAL SIZE OF A HOSPITAL

As pointed out in Chapter 1, managerial economics is of use to non-profit organizations and government agencies as well as business firms. Take, for example, the case of hospitals. One very important question facing hospitals is: How big must a hospital be (in terms of patient days of care) to minimize the cost per patient day? According to one well-known study by Harold Cohen, the total cost (in dollars) of operating a hospital can be approximated by

$$C = 4,700,000 + .00013X^2,$$

where $X$ is the number of patient days.

(a) Derive a formula for the relationship between cost per patient day and the number of patient days. (b) Based on the results of this study, how big must a hospital be (in terms of patient days) to minimize the cost per patient day? (c) Show that your result minimizes, rather than maximizes, the cost per patient day. (d) Is the number of patient days a good measure of a hospital's output? Why or why not?

*Solution* (a) Let $Y$ be the cost per patient day. Since $Y = C/X$, the desired relationship is

$$Y = \frac{4,700,000}{X} + .00013X.$$

(b) To find the value of $X$ that minimizes $Y$, we set the derivative of $Y$ with respect to $X$ equal to zero:

$$\frac{dY}{dX} = \frac{-4,700,000}{X^2} + .00013 = 0.$$

Thus, $X = \sqrt{4,700,000 \div .00013}$, or approximately 190,000 patient days. (c) Since

$$\frac{d^2Y}{dX^2} = \frac{2(4,700,000)}{X^3},$$

$d^2Y/dX^2$ must be positive (since $X$ is positive). Thus, $Y$ must be a minimum, not a maximum, at the point where $dY/dX = 0$. (d) It is a very crude measure, since some patients have far more serious illnesses that require more intensive care than others.

If $X = 1$,

$$\frac{d^2Y}{dX^2} = -12 + 6(1) = -6.$$

Thus, since the second derivative is negative, profit is a maximum when output equals 1 million units. If $X = 3$,

$$\frac{d^2Y}{dX^2} = -12 + 6(3) = 6.$$

Thus, since the second derivative is positive, profit is a minimum when output equals 3 million units.

# THE MARGINAL-COST-EQUALS-MARGINAL-REVENUE RULE AND THE CALCULUS OF OPTIMIZATION

Once you know how elementary calculus can be used to solve optimization problems, it is easy to see that the fundamental rule for profit maximization—set marginal cost equal to marginal revenue—has its basis in the calculus of optimization. Figure 2.12 shows a firm's total cost and total revenue functions. Since total profit equals total revenue minus total cost, it is equal to the vertical distance between the total revenue and total cost curves at any level of output. This distance is maximized at output $Q_1$, where the slopes of the total revenue and total cost curves are equal. Since the slope of the total revenue curve is marginal revenue and the slope of the total cost curve is marginal cost, this means that profit is maximized when marginal cost equals marginal revenue.

Inspection of Figure 2.12 shows that $Q_1$ must be the profit-maximizing output. Outputs below $Q_0$ result in losses (since total cost exceeds total rev-

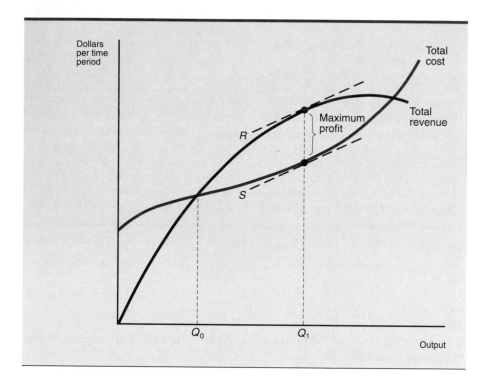

**FIGURE 2.12** *Marginal-Revenue-Equals-Marginal-Cost Rule for Profit Maximization* At the profit-maximizing output of $Q_1$, marginal revenue (equal to the slope of line $R$) equals marginal cost (the slope of line $S$).

## CONCEPTS IN CONTEXT

## AN ALLEGED BLUNDER IN THE STEALTH BOMBER'S DESIGN

Managerial economics is of great use in the aerospace industry, but this does not mean that errors sometimes will not occur. The B-2 "Stealth" bomber has cost billions of dollars to develop. According to Joseph Foa, an emeritus professor of engineering at George Washington University, its design is fundamentally flawed because two aerodynamicists made a mistake: they mistook a minimum point for a maximum point.

The B-2 is basically a jet-powered "flying wing" aircraft. In a secret study for the Air Force, the two aerodynamicists, William Sears and Irving Ashkenas (then at the Northrop Corporation), used mathematical formulas to determine how an aircraft's volume should be proportioned between wing and fuselage in order to maximize its range. Taking the derivative of range with respect to volume, they found that this derivative equaled zero when the total volume was almost all in the wing. Hence, they concluded that a "flying wing" design would maximize range.

But in a subsequent analysis, Foa showed that the second derivative was positive, not negative, under these circumstances. Thus, the "flying wing" design *minimized* range; it didn't maximize it. In Foa's words, "The flying wing was the aerodynamically worst possible choice of configuration."

This is a very interesting example of how important it is to look at the second derivative to make sure that you do not confuse a maximization point with a minimization point. While the backers of the B-2 bomber claim that it is a good plane despite this error, no one denies that the error is an embarrassment.*

*This discussion is based on W. Biddle, "Skeleton Alleged in the Stealth Bomber's Closet," *Science* (May 12, 1989).

enue), and obviously do not maximize profit. As output increases beyond $Q_0$, total revenue rises more rapidly than total cost, so profit must be going up. So long as the slope of the total revenue curve (which equals marginal revenue) exceeds the slope of the total cost curve (which equals marginal cost), profit will continue to rise as output increases. But when these slopes become equal (which means that marginal revenue equals marginal cost), profit will no longer rise—but will be at a maximum. Since these slopes become equal at an output of $Q_1$, this must be the profit-maximizing output.

Using the calculus, one can readily understand why firms maximize profit by setting marginal cost equal to marginal revenue. The first thing to note is that

$$\pi = TR - TC,$$

where $\pi$ equals total profit, $TR$ equals total revenue, and $TC$ equals total cost. Taking the derivative of $\pi$ with respect to $Q$ (output), we find that

$$\frac{d\pi}{dQ} = \frac{dTR}{dQ} - \frac{dTC}{dQ}.$$

For $\pi$ to be a maximum, this derivative must be zero, so it must be true that

$$\frac{dTR}{dQ} = \frac{dTC}{dQ}. \tag{2.18}$$

And since marginal revenue is defined as $dTR/dQ$ and marginal cost is defined as $dTC/dQ$, marginal revenue must equal marginal cost.[5]

## PARTIAL DIFFERENTIATION AND THE MAXIMIZATION OF MULTIVARIABLE FUNCTIONS

Up to this point, we have been concerned solely with situations where a variable depends on only one other variable. Although such situations exist, there are many cases where a variable depends on a number (often a large number) of other variables, not just one. For example, the Merrimack Company produces two goods, and its profit depends on the amount that it produces of each good. That is,

$$\pi = f(Q_1, Q_2), \tag{2.19}$$

where $\pi$ is the firm's profit, $Q_1$ is its output of the first good, and $Q_2$ is its output of the second good.

---

[5] Two points should be noted. (1) For profit to be maximized, $d^2\pi/dQ^2$ must be negative. (2) The analysis in this section (as well as earlier sections) results in the determination of a *local* maximum. Sometimes a local maximum is not a global maximum. For example, under some circumstances, the profit-maximizing (or loss-minimizing) output is zero, as we shall see in Chapter 10.

To find the value of each of the independent variables ($Q_1$ and $Q_2$ in this case) that maximizes the dependent variable ($\pi$ in this case), we need to know the marginal effect of each independent variable on the dependent variable, *holding constant the effect of all other independent variables.* For example, in this case, we need to know the marginal effect of $Q_1$ on $\pi$, when $Q_2$ is held constant, and we need to know the marginal effect of $Q_2$ on $\pi$, when $Q_1$ is held constant. To get this information, we obtain the partial derivative of $\pi$ with respect to $Q_1$ and the partial derivative of $\pi$ with respect to $Q_2$.

To obtain the *partial derivative of $\pi$ with respect to* $Q_1$, denoted by $\partial\pi/\partial Q_1$, one applies the rules for finding a derivative (on pp. 43 to 50) to equation (2.19), but treats $Q_2$ as a constant. Similarly, to obtain the *partial derivative of $\pi$ with respect to* $Q_2$, denoted by $\partial\pi/\partial Q_2$, one applies these rules to equation (2.19), but treats $Q_1$ as a constant.

*Example:* Suppose that the relationship between the Merrimack Company's profit (in thousands of dollars) and its output of each good is

$$\pi = -20 + 100Q_1 + 80Q_2 - 10Q_1{}^2 - 10Q_2{}^2 - 5Q_1Q_2. \qquad (2.20)$$

To find the partial derivative of $\pi$ with respect to $Q_1$, we treat $Q_2$ as a constant, and find that

$$\frac{\partial\pi}{\partial Q_1} = 100 - 20Q_1 - 5Q_2.$$

To find the partial derivative of $\pi$ with respect to $Q_2$, we treat $Q_1$ as a constant, and find that

$$\frac{\partial\pi}{\partial Q_2} = 80 - 20Q_2 - 5Q_1.$$

Once you have derived the partial derivatives, it is relatively simple to determine the values of the independent variables that maximize the dependent variable. All that you have to do is *set all of the partial derivatives equal to zero.* Thus, in the case of the Merrimack Company,

$$\frac{\partial\pi}{\partial Q_1} = 100 - 20Q_1 - 5Q_2 = 0 \qquad (2.21)$$

$$\frac{\partial\pi}{\partial Q_2} = 80 - 20Q_2 - 5Q_1 = 0. \qquad (2.22)$$

Equations (2.21) and (2.22) are two equations in two unknowns. Solving them simultaneously, we find that profit is maximized when $Q_1 = 4.267$ and $Q_2 = 2.933$. In other words, to maximize profit, the firm should produce 4.267 units of the first good and 2.933 units of the second good per period of time. If it does this, its profit will equal \$311 thousand per period of time.[6]

---

[6] Inserting 4.267 for $Q_1$ and 2.933 for $Q_2$ in equation (2.20), we find that

$$\pi = -20 + 100(4.267) + 80(2.933) - 10(4.267)^2 - 10(2.933)^2 - 5(4.267)(2.933)$$
$$= 311.$$

## THE EFFECTS OF ADVERTISING ON THE SALES OF TANG

On page 48, we encountered Young and Rubicam's study to estimate the effects of advertising expenditures on the sales of TANG, an instant breakfast drink marketed by General Foods. Specifically, the agency found that the relationship between advertising expenditures and sales in two districts were of the following form:

$$S_1 = 10 + 5A_1 - 1.5A_1{}^2$$

$$S_2 = 12 + 4A_2 - 0.5A_2{}^2$$

where $S_1$ is TANG's sales (in millions of dollars per year) in the first district, $S_2$ is its sales in the second district, $A_1$ is the advertising expenditure (in millions of dollars per year) on TANG in the first district, and $A_2$ is the advertising expenditure in the second district.

(a) If General Foods wants to maximize TANG's sales in the first district, how much should it spend on advertising? (b) If General Foods wants to maximize TANG's sales in the second district, how much should it spend on advertising? (c) Show that your answers to parts (a) and (b) maximize, rather than minimize, sales. (d) Would you recommend that General Foods attempt to maximize TANG's sales? Why or why not?

*Solution* (a) To find the value of $A_1$ that maximizes $S_1$, we set the derivative of $S_1$ with respect to $A_1$ equal to zero:

$$\frac{dS_1}{dA_1} = 5 - 3A_1 = 0.$$

Thus, $A_1 = \frac{5}{3}$ millions of dollars. (b) To find the value of $A_2$ that maximizes $S_2$, we set the derivative of $S_2$ with respect to $A_2$ equal to zero:

$$\frac{dS_2}{dA_2} = 4 - A_2 = 0.$$

Thus, $A_2 = 4$ millions of dollars. (c) Since $d^2S_1/dA_1{}^2 = -3$, $S_1$ must be a maximum at the point where $dS_1/dA_1 = 0$. Since $d^2S_2/dA_2{}^2 = -1$, $S_2$ must be a maximum at the point where $dS_2/dA_2 = 0$. If $S_1$ and $S_2$ were minimized, not maximized, the second derivatives would be positive, not negative. (d) No. As stressed in Chapter 1, firms generally are assumed to be interested in maximizing profit, not sales. In general, a firm is unlikely to increase its sales if it means a decrease in its profits. But in some cases, a firm may do this because, although profits may fall in the short run, they may increase in the long run. For example, a firm may make some sales at a loss in order to gain customers that eventually will enhance the firm's profits.*

*See F. DeBruicker, J. Quelch, and S. Ward, *Cases in Consumer Behavior*, as well as page 49 above.

To see why all of the partial derivatives should be set equal to zero, consider Figure 2.13, which shows the relationship in equation (2.20) between $\pi$, $Q_1$, and $Q_2$, in the range where $\pi$ is close to its maximum value. As you can see, this relationship is represented by a three-dimensional surface. The

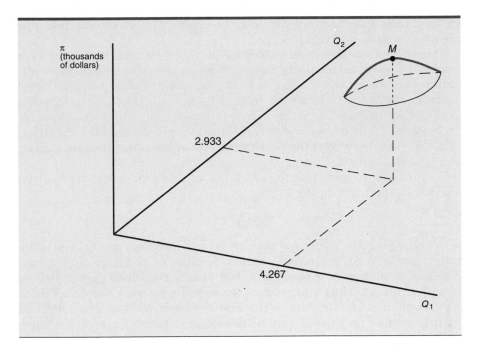

*FIGURE 2.13 Relationship between π, Q₁, and Q₂* At *M*, the point where π is a maximum, the surface representing this relationship is flat; its slope with regard to either $Q_1$ or $Q_2$ is zero.

---

maximum value of π is at point *M*, where this surface is level. A plane that is tangent to this surface at point *M* will be parallel to the $Q_1Q_2$ plane; in other words, its slopes with respect to either $Q_1$ or $Q_2$ must be zero. Thus, since the partial derivatives in equations (2.21) and (2.22) equal these slopes, they too must equal zero at the maximum point, *M*.[7]

## CONSTRAINED OPTIMIZATION

As we learned in Chapter 1, managers of firms and other organizations generally face constraints that limit the options available to them. A production manager may want to minimize his firm's costs, but he may not be permitted to produce less than is required to meet the firm's contracts with its customers. The top managers of a firm may want to maximize its

[7] The second-order conditions for distinguishing maxima from minima can be found in any calculus book. For present purposes, a discussion of these conditions is not essential. Also, note that the techniques presented in this section result in a local maximum, not necessarily a global maximum. (Recall note 5.)

profits, but in the short run they may be unable to change its product or augment its plant and equipment.

Constrained optimization problems of this sort can be solved in a number of ways. In relatively simple cases where there is only one constraint, one can use this constraint to express one of the decision variables —that is, one of the variables the decision maker can choose—as a function of the other decision variables. Then one can apply the techniques for unconstrained optimization described in the previous sections. In effect, what one does is convert the problem to one of unconstrained maximization or minimization.

To illustrate, suppose that the Kloster Company produces two products, and that its total cost equals

$$TC = 4Q_1^2 + 5Q_2^2 - Q_1Q_2, \tag{2.23}$$

where $Q_1$ equals its output per hour of the first product, and $Q_2$ equals its output per hour of the second product. Because of commitments to customers, the amount produced of both products combined cannot be less than 30 per hour. Kloster's president wants to know what output levels of the two products will minimize the firm's costs, given that the output of the first product plus the output of the second product equals 30 per hour.

This constrained optimization problem can be expressed as follows:

$$\text{Minimize } TC = 4Q_1^2 + 5Q_2^2 - Q_1Q_2$$

$$\text{subject to } Q_1 + Q_2 = 30.$$

Of course, the constraint is that $(Q_1 + Q_2)$ must equal 30. Solving this constraint for $Q_1$, we have

$$Q_1 = 30 - Q_2.$$

Substituting $(30 - Q_2)$ for $Q_1$ in equation (2.23), it follows that

$$TC = 4(30 - Q_2)^2 + 5Q_2^2 - (30 - Q_2)Q_2$$

$$= 4(900 - 60Q_2 + Q_2^2) + 5Q_2^2 - 30Q_2 + Q_2^2$$

$$= 3600 - 270Q_2 + 10Q_2^2. \tag{2.24}$$

The methods of unconstrained optimization described above can be used to find the value of $Q_2$ that minimizes TC. As indicated in earlier sections, we must obtain the derivative of $TC$ with respect to $Q_2$, and set it equal to zero.

$$\frac{dTC}{dQ_2} = -270 + 20Q_2 = 0$$

$$20Q_2 = 270$$

$$Q_2 = 13.5.$$

To make sure that this is a minimum, not a maximum, we obtain the second derivative, which is

$$\frac{d^2TC}{dQ_2{}^2} = 20.$$

Since this is positive, we have found a minimum.

To find the value of $Q_1$ that minimizes total cost, recall that the constraint requires that

$$Q_1 + Q_2 = 30,$$

which means that

$$Q_1 = 30 - Q_2.$$

Since we know that the optimal value of $Q_2$ is 13.5, it follows that the optimal value of $Q_1$ must be

$$Q_1 = 30 - 13.5 = 16.5.$$

Summing up, if the Kloster Company wants to minimize total cost subject to the constraint that the sum of the output levels of its two products be 30, it should produce 16.5 units of the first product and 13.5 units of the second product per hour.[8] (In other words, it should produce 33 units of the first product and 27 units of the second product every 2 hours.)


## LAGRANGIAN MULTIPLIERS[9]

If the technique described in the previous section is not feasible because the constraints are too numerous or complex, the method of Lagrangian multipliers can be used. This method of solving constrained optimization problems involves the construction of an equation—the so-called **Lagrangian function**—that combines the function to be minimized or maximized and the constraints. This equation is constructed so that two things are true: (1) When this equation is maximized (or minimized), the original function we want to maximize (or minimize) is in fact maximized (or minimized). (2) All the constraints are satisfied.

To illustrate how one creates a Lagrangian function, consider once again the problem faced by the Kloster Company. As indicated in the previous section, this firm wants to minimize $TC = 4Q_1{}^2 + 5Q_2{}^2 - Q_1Q_2$, subject

---

[8] Substituting 16.5 for $Q_1$ and 13.5 for $Q_2$ in equation (2.23), the firm's total cost will equal

$$TC = 4(16.5)^2 + 5(13.5)^2 - (16.5)(13.5)$$
$$= 4(272.25) + 5(182.25) - 222.75$$
$$= 1089 + 911.25 - 222.75$$
$$= 1777.5,$$

or $1,777.50.

[9] This section can be skipped without loss of continuity.

to the constraint that $Q_1 + Q_2 = 30$. The first step in constructing the Lagrangian function for this firm's problem is to restate the constraint so that an expression is formed that is equal to zero:

$$30 - Q_1 - Q_2 = 0. \tag{2.25}$$

Then if we multiply this form of the constraint by an unknown factor designated $\lambda$ (lambda), and add the result to the function we want to minimize (in equation [2.23]), we get the Lagrangian function, which is

$$L_{tc} = 4Q_1{}^2 + 5Q_2{}^2 - Q_1Q_2 + \lambda(30 - Q_1 - Q_2). \tag{2.26}$$

For reasons specified in the next paragraph, we can be sure that if we find the unconstrained maximum (or minimum) of the Lagrangian function, the solution will be exactly the same as the solution of the original constrained maximization (or minimization) problem. In other words, to solve the constrained optimization problem, all that we have to do is optimize the Lagrangian function. For example, in the case of the Kloster Company, we must find the values of $Q_1$, $Q_2$, and $\lambda$ that minimize $L_{tc}$ in equation (2.26). To do this, we must find the partial derivative of $L_{tc}$ with respect to each of these three variables—$Q_1$, $Q_2$, and $\lambda$:

$$\frac{\partial L_{tc}}{\partial Q_1} = 8Q_1 - Q_2 - \lambda$$

$$\frac{\partial L_{tc}}{\partial Q_2} = -Q_1 + 10Q_2 - \lambda$$

$$\frac{\partial L_{tc}}{\partial \lambda} = -Q_1 - Q_2 + 30.$$

As indicated in the section before last, we must set all three of these partial derivatives equal to zero in order to minimize $L_{tc}$. Thus,

$$8Q_1 - Q_2 - \lambda = 0 \tag{2.27}$$

$$-Q_1 + 10Q_2 - \lambda = 0 \tag{2.28}$$

$$-Q_1 - Q_2 + 30 = 0. \tag{2.29}$$

It is important to note that the partial derivative of the Lagrangian function with regard to $\lambda$ (that is, $\partial L_{tc}/\partial \lambda$), when it is set equal to zero [in equation (2.29)], is the constraint in our original optimization problem. [Recall equation (2.25).] This, of course, will always be true because of the way the Lagrangian function is constructed. Thus, if this derivative is zero, we can be sure that this original constraint is satisfied. And, if this constraint is satisfied, the last term on the right of the Lagrangian function is zero, so the Lagrangian function boils down to the original function that we wanted to maximize (or minimize). Consequently, by maximizing (or minimizing) the Lagrangian function, we solve the original constrained optimization problem.

Returning to the Kloster Company, equations (2.27), (2.28), and (2.29) are three simultaneous equations with three unknowns—$Q_1$, $Q_2$, and $\lambda$. If we solve this system of equations for $Q_1$ and $Q_2$, we get the optimal values of $Q_1$ and $Q_2$. Subtracting equation (2.28) from equation (2.27), we find that

$$9Q_1 - 11Q_2 = 0. \qquad (2.30)$$

Multiplying equation (2.29) by 9 and adding the result to equation (2.30), we can solve for $Q_2$:

$$
\begin{array}{rl}
-9Q_1 - 9Q_2 + 270 &= 0 \\
9Q_1 - 11Q_2 \phantom{+ 270} &= 0 \\
\hline
- 20Q_2 + 270 &= 0 \\
Q_2 &= 270/20 \\
&= 13.5.
\end{array}
$$

Thus, the optimal value of $Q_2$ is 13.5. Substituting 13.5 for $Q_2$ in equation (2.29), we find that the optimal value of $Q_1$ is 16.5.

The answer we get is precisely the same as in the previous section: the optimal value of $Q_1$ is 16.5, and the optimal value of $Q_2$ is 13.5. In other words, the Kloster Company should produce 16.5 units of the first product and 13.5 units of the second product per hour. But the method of Lagrangian multipliers described in this section is more powerful than that described in the previous section for at least two reasons. (1) It can handle more than a single constraint. (2) The value of $\lambda$ provides interesting and useful information to the decision maker.

Specifically, $\lambda$ (the so-called **Lagrangian multiplier**) measures the change in the variable to be maximized or minimized ($TC$ in this case) if the constraint is relaxed by one unit.[10] For example, if the Kloster Company wants to minimize total cost subject to the constraint that the total output of both products is 31 rather than 30, the value of $\lambda$ indicates by how much the minimum value of $TC$ will increase. What is the value of $\lambda$? According to equation (2.27),

$$8Q_1 - Q_2 - \lambda = 0.$$

Thus, since $Q_1 = 16.5$ and $Q_2 = 13.5$,

$$\lambda = 8(16.5) - 13.5 = 118.5.$$

Consequently, if the constraint is relaxed so that total output is 31 rather than 30, total cost will go up by $118.50.

For many managerial decisions, information of this sort is of great value. Suppose that a customer offers the Kloster Company $115 for one of its products, but to make this product, Kloster would have to stretch its total output to 31 per hour. Based on the findings of the previous paragraph,

---

[10] The values of $\lambda$ are analogous to the dual variables of linear programming, which will be discussed in Chapter 9.

---

CONSULTANT'S CORNER

## PLANNING TO MEET PEAK ENGINEERING REQUIREMENTS*

A leading computer manufacturer, after analyzing the history of its product development projects, found that there were regular patterns of manpower buildup and phaseout in its projects. Specifically, the number of engineers required to carry out such a project $t$ months after the start of the project could be approximated reasonably well by the following equation:

$$Y = at - bt^2, \quad \left(\text{for } 0 \leqslant t \leqslant \frac{a}{b}\right),$$

where $Y$ is the number of engineers required $t$ months after the start of the project, and $a$ and $b$ are numbers that vary from project to project (and that depend on the kind of product being developed).

The computer manufacturer wanted to use these results to estimate when the number of engi-neers required to carry out a particular product development project would hit its peak, and how great this peak requirement would be. Estimates of this sort would help the firm's managers in planning the allocation and utilization of the firm's engineering staff, and alert them to situations where its staff might have to be expanded or supplemented. The project for which the firm's managers wanted these estimates was to begin immediately. Based on previous experience with projects of this type, the firm's managers estimated that $a$ would be about 18 and $b$ would be about 1 for this project.

If you were a consultant to this firm, how would you make the estimates wanted by the firm's managers?

*This section is based on an actual case, although the equations and the situation have been simplified somewhat for pedagogical purposes.

---

Kloster would be foolish to accept this offer, since this extra product would raise its costs by $118.50, which is $3.50 more than the amount the customer offers to pay for it.

## COMPARING INCREMENTAL COSTS WITH INCREMENTAL REVENUES

Before concluding this chapter, we must point out that many business decisions can and should be made by comparing *incremental* costs with *incremental* revenues. Typically, a manager must choose between two (or more) courses of action, and what is relevant is the difference in costs between the two courses of action, as well as the difference in revenues between them. For example, if the managers of a machinery company are considering whether or not to add a new product line, they should compare the incremental cost of adding the new product line—that is, the extra cost resulting from its addition—with the incremental revenue, that is, the extra revenue resulting from its addition. If the incremental revenue exceeds the incremental cost, the new product line will add to the firm's profits.

Note that *incremental* cost is not the same as *marginal* cost. Whereas marginal cost is the extra cost from a very small (1-unit) increase in output, **incremental cost** is the extra cost from an output increase that may be very substantial. Similarly, **incremental revenue**, unlike marginal revenue, is the extra revenue from an output increase that may be very substantial. For example, suppose that you want to see whether a firm's profits will increase if it doubles its output. If the incremental cost of such an output increase is $5 million and the incremental revenue is $6 million, the firm will increase its profits by $1 million if it doubles its output. Marginal cost and marginal revenue cannot tell you this, because they refer only to a very small increase in output, not to a doubling of it.

While it may seem very easy to compare incremental costs with incremental revenues, there in fact are many pitfalls. One of the most common errors is to fail to recognize the irrelevance of *sunk* costs. Costs incurred in the past often are irrelevant in making today's decisions. Suppose you are going to make a trip and you want to determine whether it will be cheaper to drive your car or to go by plane. What costs should be included if you drive your car? Since the only *incremental* costs that will be incurred will be the gas and oil (and a certain amount of wear and tear on tires, engine, etc.), they are the only costs that should be included. Costs incurred in the past, such as the original price of the car, and costs that will be the same regardless of whether you make the trip by car or plane, such as your auto insurance, should not be included. On the other hand, if you are thinking about buying a car to make this and many other trips, these costs should be included. [11]

To illustrate the proper reasoning, consider the actual case of an airline which has deliberately run extra flights that do no more than return a little more than their out-of-pocket costs. Assume that this airline is faced with the decision of whether or not to run an extra flight between city A and city B. Assume that the fully allocated costs—the out-of-pocket costs plus a certain percent of overhead, depreciation, insurance, and other such costs—are $5,500 for the flight. Assume that the out-of-pocket costs—the actual sum that this airline has to disburse to run the flight—are $3,000, and the expected revenue from the flight is $4,100. In such a case, this airline will run the flight, which is the correct decision, since the flight will add $1,100 to profit. The incremental revenue from the flight is $4,100, and the incremental cost is $3,000. Overhead, depreciation, and insurance would be the same whether the flight is run or not. Thus, fully allocated costs are misleading here; the relevant concept of cost is out-of-pocket, not fully allocated costs.

Errors of other kinds can also mar firms' estimates of incremental costs.

---

[11] This example is worked out in more detail in the paper by E. Grant and W. Ireson in E. Mansfield, ed., *Managerial Economics and Operations Research*, 5th ed. (New York: Norton, 1987).

For example, a firm may refuse to produce and sell some items because it is already working near capacity, and the incremental cost of producing them is judged to be very high. In fact, however, the incremental cost may not be so high because the firm may be able to produce these items during the slack season (when there is plenty of excess capacity), since the potential customers may be willing to accept delivery then.

Also, incremental revenue frequently is misjudged. Take the case of a firm that is considering the introduction of a new product. The firm's managers may estimate the incremental revenue from the new product without taking proper account of the effects of the new product's sales on the sales of the firm's existing products. Whereas they may think that the new product will not cut into the sales of existing products, it may in fact do so, with the result that their estimate of incremental revenue may be too high.

## SUMMARY

1. Functional relationships can be represented by tables, graphs, or equations. The marginal value of a dependent variable is defined as the change in this variable associated with a 1-unit change in a particular independent variable. The dependent variable achieves a maximum when its marginal value shifts from positive to negative.
2. The derivative of $Y$ with respect to $X$, denoted by $dY/dX$, is the limit of the ratio $\Delta Y/\Delta X$ as $\Delta X$ approaches zero. Geometrically, it is the slope of the curve showing $Y$ (on the vertical axis) as a function of $X$ (on the horizontal axis). We have provided rules that enable us to find the value of this derivative.
3. To find the value of $X$ that maximizes or minimizes $Y$, we determine the value of $X$ where $dY/dX$ equals zero. To tell whether this is a maximum or a minimum, we find the second derivative of $Y$ with respect to $X$, denoted by $d^2Y/dX^2$, which is the derivative of $dY/dX$. If this second derivative is negative, we have found a maximum; if it is positive, we have found a minimum.
4. A dependent variable often depends on a number of independent variables, not just one. To find the value of each of the independent variables that maximizes the dependent variable, we determine the partial derivative of $Y$ with respect to each of the independent variables, denoted by $\partial Y/\partial X$, and set it equal to zero. To obtain the partial derivative of $Y$ with respect to $X$, we apply the ordinary rules for finding a derivative; however, all independent variables other than $X$ are treated as constants.
5. Managers of firms and other organizations generally face constraints that limit the options available to them. In relatively simple cases where there is only one constraint, we can use this constraint to express one of the decision variables as a function of the other decision variables, and we can apply the techniques for unconstrained optimization.

6. In more complex cases, constrained optimization problems can be solved by the method of Lagrangian multipliers. The Lagrangian function combines the function to be maximized or minimized and the constraints. To solve the constrained optimization problem, we optimize the Lagrangian function.

7. Many business decisions can and should be made by comparing incremental costs with incremental revenues. Typically, a manager must choose between two (or more) courses of action, and what is relevant is the difference in costs between the two courses of action, as well as the difference in revenues.

## PROBLEMS

1. For the Martin Corporation, the relationship between profit and output is the following:

| Output (number of units per day) | Profit (thousands of dollars per day) |
|---|---|
| 0 | −10 |
| 1 | − 8 |
| 2 | − 5 |
| 3 | 0 |
| 4 | 2 |
| 5 | 7 |
| 6 | 12 |
| 7 | 21 |
| 8 | 22 |
| 9 | 23 |
| 10 | 20 |

(a) What is the marginal profit when output is between 5 and 6 units per day? When output is between 9 and 10 units per day?

(b) At what output is average profit a maximum?

(c) Should the Martin Corporation produce the output where average profit is a maximum? Why or why not?

2. Determine the first derivative of the following functions:

(a) $Y = 3 + 10X + 5X^2$

(b) $Y = 2X(4 + X^3)$

(c) $Y = 3X \div (4 + X^3)$

(d) $Y = 4X \div (X - 3)$

3. The total cost function at the Duemer Company is $TC = 100 + 4Q + 8Q^2$, where $TC$ is total costs, and $Q$ is output.

(a) What is marginal cost when output is 10?

(b) What is marginal cost when output is 12?

(c) What is marginal cost when output is 20?

4. The Bartholomew Company's profit is related in the following way to its output: $\pi = -40 + 20Q - 3Q^2$, where $\pi$ is total profit and $Q$ is output.

(a) If the firm's output equals 8, what is its marginal profit?

(b) Derive an equation relating the firm's marginal profit to its output.

(c) What output will maximize the firm's profit?

5. Determine the second derivative of the following functions:

(a) $Y = 4 + 9X + 3X^2$

(b) $Y = 4X (3 + X^2)$

(c) $Y = 4X(2 + X^3)$

(d) $Y = 4/X + 3$

6. The Mineola Corporation hires a consultant to estimate the relationship between its profit and its output. The consultant reports that the relationship is

$$\pi = -10 - 6Q + 5.5Q^2 - 2Q^3 + .25Q^4.$$

(a) The consultant says that the firm should set $Q$ equal to 1 to maximize profit. Is it true that $d\pi/dQ = 0$ when $Q = 1$? Is $\pi$ a maximum when $Q = 1$?

(b) Mineola's executive vice president says that the firm's profit is a maximum when $Q = 2$. Is this true?

(c) If you were the chief executive officer of the Mineola Corporation, would you accept the consultant's estimate of the relationship between profit and output as being correct?

7. Find the partial derivative of $Y$ with respect to $X$ in each of the following cases:

(a) $Y = 10 + 3Z + 2X$

(b) $Y = 18Z^2 + 4X^3$

(c) $Y = 2Z^{.2}X^{.8}$

(d) $Y = 3Z \div (4 + X)$

8. The Stock Corporation makes two products, paper and cardboard. The relationship between $\pi$, the firm's annual profit (in thousands of dollars), and its output of each good is

$$\pi = -50 + 40Q_1 + 30Q_2 - 5Q_1^2 - 4Q_2^2 - 3Q_1Q_2,$$

where $Q_1$ is the firm's annual output of paper (in tons), and $Q_2$ is the firm's annual output of cardboard (in tons).

(a) Find the output of each good that the Stock Corporation should produce if it wants to maximize profit.

(b) If the community in which the firm is located imposes a tax of $5,000 per year on the firm, will this alter the answer to part (a)? If so, how will the answer change?

9. The Miller Company uses skilled and unskilled labor to do a particular construction project. The cost of doing the project depends on the number of hours of skilled labor and the number of hours of unskilled

labor that are used, the relationship being

$$C = 4 - 3X_1 - 4X_2 + 2X_1{}^2 + 3X_2{}^2 + X_1X_2,$$

where $C$ is cost (in thousands of dollars), $X_1$ is the number of hours (in thousands) of skilled labor, and $X_2$ is the number of hours (in thousands) of unskilled labor.

(a) Find the number of hours of skilled labor and the number of hours of unskilled labor that will minimize the cost of doing the project.

(b) If the Miller Company has to purchase a license costing $2,000 to do this project (and if the cost of this license is not included in $C$), will this alter the answer to part (a)? If so, how will the answer change?

10. Ilona Stafford manages a small firm that produces wool rugs and cotton rugs. Her total cost per day (in dollars) equals

$$C = 7X_1{}^2 + 9X_2{}^2 - 1.5X_1X_2,$$

where $X_1$ equals the number of cotton rugs produced per day, and $X_2$ equals the number of wool rugs produced per day. Because of commitments to retail stores that sell her rugs to consumers, she must produce 10 rugs per day, but any mix of wool and cotton rugs is acceptable.

(a) If she wants to minimize her costs (without violating her commitment to the retail stores), how many cotton rugs and wool rugs should she produce per day? (Do not use the method of Lagrangian multipliers.)

(b) Does it seem reasonable that she would want to minimize cost in a situation of this sort? Why or why not?

(c) Can she produce fractional numbers of rugs per day?

11. The Trumbull Company has developed a new product. Trumbull's chairman estimates that the new product will increase the firm's revenues by $5 million per year, and that it will result in extra out-of-pocket costs of $4 million per year, the fully allocated costs (including a percentage of overhead, depreciation, and insurance) being $5.5 million.

(a) Trumbull's chairman feels that it would not be profitable to introduce this new product. Is he right? Why or why not?

(b) Trumbull's vice president for research argues that since the development of this product has already cost about $10 million, the firm has little choice but to introduce it. Is he right? Why or why not?

12. (a) Use the method of Lagrangian multipliers to solve problem 10 above.

(b) Do you get the same answer as you do without using this method?

(c) What does $\lambda$ equal? What does this mean?

# Part Two

# Demand and Forecasting

# Chapter 3
# Demand Theory

## INTRODUCTION

Business firms spend enormous amounts of time, energy, and money analyzing the demand for their products—and with good reason. In 1983 and 1984, over 60 new types of business personal computers were introduced to the U.S. market, and most firms expected rapid growth. Whereas many industry forecasters claimed that about 27 or 28 million computers would be installed by 1987 or 1988, only 15 million had been shipped by 1986. By then, many firms had withdrawn from the production of personal computers—and some had gone out of business. Clearly, they had not understood the demand for their product. In this chapter, we focus attention on the theory of demand. In the following chapter, we will look much more closely at some of the techniques used to estimate the demand for a product.

## THE MARKET DEMAND CURVE

The **market demand schedule** for a good is a table that shows the total quantity of the good that would be purchased at each price. For example, suppose that the market demand schedule for personal computers is as shown

TABLE 3.1   *Market Demand Schedule for Personal Computers, 1993*

| Price per computer (dollars) | Quantity demanded per year (thousands) |
|---|---|
| 3,000 | 800 |
| 2,750 | 975 |
| 2,500 | 1,150 |
| 2,250 | 1,325 |
| 2,000 | 1,500 |

in Table 3.1.[1] According to this table, 1.5 million personal computers will be demanded per year if the price is $2,000 per computer, 800,000 will be demanded if the price is $3,000, and so on. Another way of presenting the data in Table 3.1 is by a **market demand curve,** which is a plot of the market demand schedule on a graph. The vertical axis of the graph measures the price per unit of the good, and the horizontal axis measures the quantity of the good demanded per unit of time. Figure 3.1 shows the market demand curve for personal computers, based on the figures in Table 3.1.

In Chapter 1, we provided an introductory look at the market demand curve. Now we must study this topic in more detail. Three things should be noted concerning Figure 3.1. First, the market demand curve shows the *total* quantity of personal computers demanded at each price, not the quantity demanded from a *particular* firm. We will discuss the demand for a particular firm's product in the next section of this chapter. Second, the market demand curve for personal computers slopes downward to the right. In other words, the quantity of personal computers demanded increases as the price falls. As we pointed out in Chapter 1, this is true of the demand curve for most goods; they almost always slope downward to the right. Third, the market demand curve in Figure 3.1 pertains to a particular period of time: 1993. As you will recall from Chapter 1, any demand curve pertains to some period of time, and its shape and position depend on the length and other characteristics of this period. For example, if we were to estimate the market demand curve for personal computers for the first week in 1993, it would be a different curve from the one in Figure 3.1, which pertains to the whole year. The difference arises partly because consumers can adapt their purchases more fully to changes in the price of personal computers in a year than in a week.

Besides the length of time period, what other factors determine the position and shape of the market demand curve for a good? As indicated in Chapter 1, one important factor is the **tastes of consumers.** If consumers show an increasing preference for a product, the demand curve will shift to the right; that is, at each price, consumers will desire to buy more than they

---

[1] These numbers are hypothetical, but adequate for present purposes. In subsequent chapters, we shall provide data describing the actual relationship between the price and quantity demanded of various goods. At this point, the emphasis is on the concept of a market demand schedule, not on the detailed accuracy of these numbers. In the appendix to this chapter, we show in more detail how the market demand schedule for a product is based on, and linked to, the tastes and characteristics of the consumers in the market for this product.

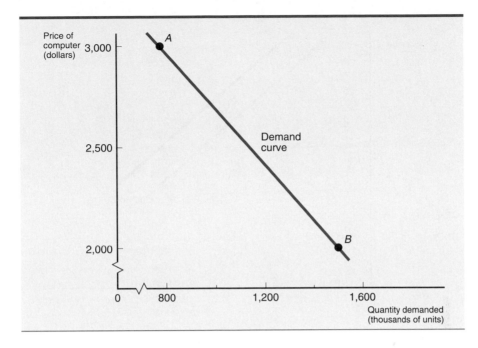

*FIGURE 3.1   Demand Curve for Personal Computers*   This demand curve is a graphical representation of the figures in Table 3.1.

did previously. On the other hand, if consumers show a decreasing preference for a product, the demand curve will shift to the left, since, at each price, consumers will desire to buy less than previously. For example, if people find that personal computers are more helpful than they thought, and if they begin to use them more and give them in larger numbers to their children and others, the demand curve for personal computers may shift to the right, as shown in Figure 3.2. The greater the shift in preferences, the farther the demand curve will shift.

Another factor that influences the position and shape of a good's market demand curve is the **level of consumer incomes.** For some types of products, the demand curve shifts to the right if per capita income increases; whereas for other types of commodities, the demand curve shifts to the left if per capita income rises. In the case of personal computers, one would expect that an increase in per capita income would shift the demand curve to the right, as shown in Figure 3.3. Still another factor that influences the position and shape of a good's market demand curve is the **level of other prices.** For example, one would expect that the quantity of personal computers demanded would increase if the price of software for such computers fell drastically.

Finally, the position and shape of a good's market demand curve is also affected by the size of the population in the relevant market. Thus, if the population increases, one would expect that, if all other factors were held equal, the quantity of personal computers demanded would go up. Of

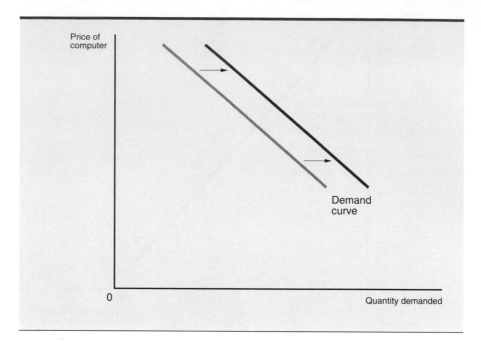

**FIGURE 3.2   *Effect of Increased Preference for Personal Computers on Market Demand Curve***   The demand curve for personal computers shifts to the right.

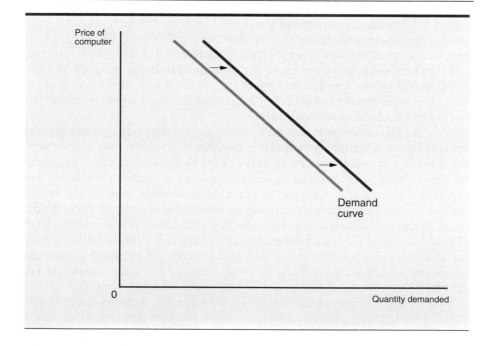

**FIGURE 3.3   *Effect of Increase in Per Capita Income on Market Demand Curve for Personal Computers***   The demand curve shifts to the right.

course, the population generally changes slowly, so this factor often has little effect in the very short run.

## INDUSTRY AND FIRM DEMAND FUNCTIONS

Building on the results of the previous section, we can define the **market demand function** for a product, which is the relationship between the quantity demanded of the product and the various factors that influence this quantity. Put generally, this market demand function can be written as

Quantity demanded
of good $X$       $= Q = f($price of $X$, incomes of consumers, tastes of consumers, prices of other goods, population, advertising expenditures, and so forth$)$.

To be useful for analytical and forecasting purposes, this equation must be made more specific. For example, if good $X$ is personal computers, the market demand function might be as follows:

$$Q = b_1P + b_2I + b_3S + b_4A, \tag{3.1}$$

where $Q$ equals the number of personal computers demanded in a particular year, $P$ is the average price of personal computers in that year, $I$ is per capita disposable income during that year, $S$ is the average price of software during that year, and $A$ is the amount spent on advertising by producers of personal computers in that year. The assumption in equation (3.1) is, of course, that the relationship is linear. (Also, we assume for simplicity that the population in the relevant market is essentially constant.)

Going a step further, it generally is necessary for managers and analysts to obtain numerical estimates of the $b$'s in equation (3.1). Employing the statistical techniques described in the following chapter, one usually can estimate these so-called **parameters** of the demand function. To illustrate the sorts of results that might be obtained, we might find that

$$Q = -700P + 200I - 500S + 0.01A. \tag{3.2}$$

According to equation (3.2), a \$1 increase in the price of a personal computer results in a decrease in the quantity demanded of 700 units per year; a \$1 increase in per capita disposable income results in a 200-unit increase in the quantity demanded; a \$1 increase in the price of software reduces the quantity demanded by 500 units per year; and a \$1 increase in advertising raises the quantity demanded by 0.01 units per year.

It is important to understand the relationship between the market demand function and the demand curve. The market demand curve shows the relationship between $Q$ and $P$ when all other relevant variables are held

## WALT DISNEY PRODUCTIONS AND ATTENDANCE AT THEME PARKS

Not even the land of Disney is immune to the harsh reality of demand curves. Disneyland in California and Walt Disney World in Florida are two major theme parks operated by Walt Disney Productions. A theme park, unlike an ordinary amusement park, offers rides, exhibits, shows, and restaurants in the context of an overall theme. Thus, Disneyland, the oldest theme park in the United States, is centered around cartoon and movie characters. When Disneyland opened in 1955, there were 17 attractions, which have been expanded over the years to 57. The seven major areas of the park are Adventureland, Bear Country, Fantasyland, Frontierland, Main Street, New Orleans Square, and Tomorrowland.

In the 1980s, Walt Disney Productions had revenues of over $1 billion, most of which came from its theme parks, which account for about a third of all theme park attendance in the United States. In 1980, Disneyland attracted 11.5 million people, but in 1984, it attracted only 9.9 million people. This decrease in attendance was painful to Disney's management, and they devoted considerable attention to trying to determine its causes.

To some extent, the decline in attendance may have been due to a movement (from point *A* to point *B* in the figure on p. 79) along the demand curve for attendance at the parks. During 1983, Disneyland's admission prices increased

by 6 percent. Also, higher gasoline prices tended to increase the cost of driving to Disneyland. For people who drive to theme parks, the driving cost can be regarded as part of the price of attending the parks. Thus, the higher total price of attendance may have been responsible for part of the drop in attendance.

But part of the drop seems to have been due to a leftward shift (shown in the figure on p. 79) in the demand curve for attendance at Disneyland. A harsh winter was blamed for the drop in attendance in 1983. The Olympics, which were held in neighboring Los Angeles, were blamed for the drop in 1984. Also, demographic

changes were cited. As the average age of the population increases and as the average family size decreases, fewer people may be interested in the child-centered themes featured in many parks. To Disney's management, this shift in the demand curve was of central importance. They had to try to determine whether they could push the demand curve to the right (by altering the parks, by advertising, and by other means) and whether it was worthwhile to try to do so.*

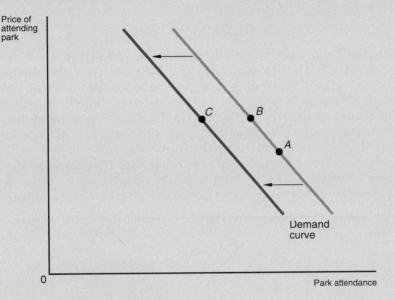

* H. Bartlett, *Cases in Strategic Management for Business* (New York: Dryden Press, 1988); and T. Wheelen and J. D. Hunger, *Cases in Strategic Management and Business Policy* (Reading, Mass.: Addison-Wesley, 1987).

constant. For example, suppose that we want to know what the relationship between quantity demanded and price would be if per capita disposable income is $13,000, if the average price of software is $400, and if advertising expenditure is $50 million. Since $I = 13,000$, $S = 400$, and $A = 50,000,000$, equation (3.2) becomes

$$Q = -700P + 200(13,000) - 500(400) + .01(50,000,000), \tag{3.3}$$

or

$$Q = 2,900,000 - 700P. \tag{3.4}$$

Solving this equation for $P$, we obtain

$$P = 4,143 - .001429Q,$$

which is graphed in Figure 3.1. This is the demand curve for personal computers, given that $I$, $S$, and $A$ are held constant at the stipulated levels.

Given the market demand function, managers and analysts can readily quantify the shifts in the demand curve that will result from changes in the variables other than the product's price. For example, how much of a shift will occur in the demand curve if the price of software falls from $400 to $200? Inserting 200 (rather than 400) for $S$ in equation (3.3), we find that

$$Q = 3,000,000 - 700P. \tag{3.5}$$

Solving this equation for $P$, we obtain

$$P = 4,286 - .001429Q, \tag{3.6}$$

which is graphed (together with the demand curve based on $S = 400$) in Figure 3.4. Clearly, the demand curve has shifted to the right, the quantity demanded being 100,000 more than when $S = 400$ (if $P$ is held constant).

Market demand functions can be formulated for individual firms as well as for entire industries. That is, one can formulate an equation like equation (3.2) to predict the sales of an individual producer of personal computers. In such an equation, the quantity demanded of the firm's good would be inversely related to its price but directly related to the prices charged by its competitors; and it would be directly related to its advertising expenditures but inversely related to the advertising expenditures of its

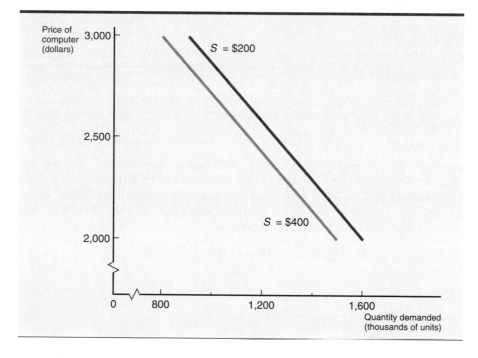

FIGURE 3.4  *Demand Curve for Personal Computers*  If the price of software falls from $400 to $200, the demand curve shifts to the right by 100,000 units.

competitors. It is important to distinguish between industry and firm demand functions, since they are quite different. Both are important to managers, because firms often are interested in the effects of variables like disposable income and advertising on industry sales, as well as on the sales of their own firm—which obviously is of primary significance.

## THE PRICE ELASTICITY OF DEMAND

Market demand curves vary with regard to the sensitivity of quantity demanded to price. For some goods, a small change in price results in a big change in quantity demanded; for other goods, a big change in price results in a small change in quantity demanded. To indicate how sensitive quantity demanded is to changes in price, economists use a measure called the **price elasticity of demand.** The price elasticity of demand is defined to be *the percentage change in quantity demanded resulting from a 1 percent change in price.* More precisely, it equals

$$\eta = -\frac{\partial Q}{\partial P} \cdot \frac{P}{Q}. \tag{3.7}$$

Suppose that a 1 percent reduction in the price of cotton shirts results in a 1.3 percent increase in the quantity demanded in the United States. If so, the price elasticity of demand for cotton shirts is 1.3. Convention dictates that we give the elasticity a positive sign despite the fact that the change in price is negative and the change in quantity demanded is positive. The price elasticity of demand generally will vary from one point to another on a demand curve. For instance, the price elasticity of demand may be higher when the price of cotton shirts is high than when it is low. Similarly, the price elasticity of demand will vary from market to market. For example, India may have a different price elasticity of demand for cotton shirts from that of the United States.

The price elasticity of demand for a product must lie between zero and infinity. If the price elasticity is zero, the demand curve is a vertical line; that is, the quantity demanded is unaffected by price. If the price elasticity is infinite, the demand curve is a horizontal line; that is, an unlimited amount can be sold at a particular price ($15 in Figure 3.5), but nothing can be sold if the price is raised even slightly. Figure 3.5 shows these two limiting cases.

## POINT AND ARC ELASTICITIES

If we have a market demand schedule showing the quantity of a commodity demanded in the market at various prices, how can we estimate the price elasticity of market demand? Let $\Delta P$ be a change in the price of the good and $\Delta Q$ be the resulting change in its quantity demanded. If $\Delta P$ is very small, we

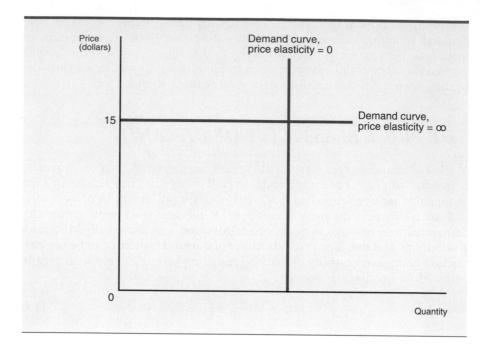

**FIGURE 3.5** *Demand Curves with Zero and Infinite Price Elasticities of Demand* The demand curve is a vertical line if the price elasticity is zero and a horizontal line if it is infinite.

**TABLE 3.2** *Quantity Demanded at Various Prices (Small Increments in Price)*

| Price (cents per unit of commodity) | Quantity demanded per unit of time (units of commodity) |
|---|---|
| 99.95 | 20,002 |
| 100.00 | 20,000 |
| 100.05 | 19,998 |

can compute the **point elasticity of demand:**

$$\eta = -\frac{\Delta Q}{Q} \div \frac{\Delta P}{P}. \tag{3.8}$$

For instance, consider Table 3.2, where data are given for very small increments in the price of a commodity. If we want to estimate the price elasticity of demand when the price is between 99.95 cents and $1, we obtain the following result:

$$\eta = -\frac{20,002 - 20,000}{20,000} \div \frac{99.95 - 100}{100} = .2.$$

Note that we used $1 as $P$ and 20,000 as $Q$. We could have used 99.95 cents

TABLE 3.3  *Quantity Demanded at Various Prices (Large Increments in Price)*

| Price (dollars per unit of commodity) | Quantity demanded per unit of time (units of commodity) |
|:---:|:---:|
| 3 | 50 |
| 4 | 40 |
| 5 | 3 |

as $P$ and 20,002 as $Q$, but it would have made no real difference to the answer.

But if we have data concerning only large changes in price (that is, if $\Delta P$ and $\Delta Q$ are large), the answer may vary considerably depending on which value of $P$ and $Q$ is used in equation (3.8). Consider the example in Table 3.3. Suppose that we want to estimate the price elasticity of demand in the price range between $4 and $5. Then, depending on which value of $P$ and $Q$ is used, the answer will be

$$\eta = -\frac{40-3}{3} \div \frac{4-5}{5} = 61.67$$

$$\eta = -\frac{3-40}{40} \div \frac{5-4}{4} = 3.70.$$

The difference between these two results is very large. To avoid this difficulty, it is advisable to compute the **arc elasticity of demand,** which uses the average value of $P$ and $Q$:

$$\eta = -\frac{\Delta Q}{(Q_1 + Q_2)/2} \div \frac{\Delta P}{(P_1 + P_2)/2}$$

$$= -\frac{\Delta Q(P_1 + P_2)}{\Delta P(Q_1 + Q_2)}, \tag{3.9}$$

where $P_1$ and $Q_1$ are the first values of price and quantity demanded, and $P_2$ and $Q_2$ are the second set. Thus, in Table 3.3,

$$\eta = -\frac{40-3}{(40+3)/2} \div \frac{4-5}{(4+5)/2} = 7.74.$$

## USING THE DEMAND FUNCTION TO CALCULATE THE PRICE ELASTICITY OF DEMAND

As we saw in a previous section, estimates frequently are made of the demand function for particular products. In equation (3.2), we provided the following hypothetical demand function for personal computers:

$$Q = -700P + 200I - 500S + 0.01A.$$

Given such a demand function, how can you calculate the price elasticity of demand?

The first step is to specify the point on the demand curve at which this price elasticity is to be measured. Assuming that per capita disposable income $(I)$ is $13,000, the average price of software $(S)$ is $400, and advertising expenditure $(A)$ is $50 million, we know from equation (3.4) that the relationship between quantity demanded and price is

$$Q = 2,900,000 - 700P. \tag{3.10}$$

Suppose that we want to measure the price elasticity of demand when price equals $3,000. At this point on the demand curve (point $A$ in Figure 3.1),

$$Q = 2,900,000 - 700(3,000)$$

$$= 800,000.$$

Next, we must evaluate the partial derivative of $Q$ with respect to $P$. Applying Chapter 2's rules for finding a derivative to equation (3.10), we find that the desired derivative equals

$$\frac{\partial Q}{\partial P} = -700.$$

According to equation (3.7), to obtain the price elasticity of demand, we must multiply $\partial Q/\partial P$ by $-P/Q$. Performing this multiplication, we get

$$-700\left(\frac{-3,000}{800,000}\right) = 2.62,$$

which means that the price elasticity of demand equals 2.62.

As a further illustration, let's calculate the price elasticity of demand when price equals $2,000 rather than $3,000. At this point on the demand curve (point $B$ in Figure 3.1),

$$Q = 2,900,000 - 700(2,000)$$

$$= 1,500,000.$$

Since $\partial Q/\partial P = -700$,

$$\eta = -\frac{\partial Q}{\partial P} \cdot \frac{P}{Q} = -(-700)\left(\frac{2,000}{1,500,000}\right) = 0.93.$$

Thus, the price elasticity of demand equals 0.93.

An important thing to note is that the price elasticity of demand can vary greatly from point to point on a particular demand curve. As we have just seen, on the demand curve in Figure 3.1, the price elasticity of demand is 2.62 at point $A$, but only 0.93 at point $B$. For any linear demand curve, the price elasticity of demand will vary from zero to infinity, as shown in Figure 3.6. If

$$P = c - dQ,$$

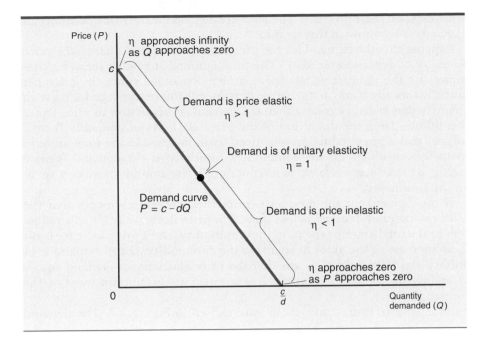

*FIGURE 3.6    Values of the Price Elasticity of Demand at Various Points along a Linear Demand Curve*    The price elasticity increases as price rises, approaching infinity as quantity approaches zero.

where $c$ is the intercept of the demand curve on the price axis, and $d$ is the slope (in absolute terms) of the demand curve, it follows that

$$Q = \frac{c}{d} - \frac{1}{d}P.$$

Thus, the price elasticity of demand is

$$-\frac{\partial Q}{\partial P} \cdot \frac{P}{Q} = \frac{1}{d} \cdot \frac{c - dQ}{Q}.$$

Clearly, if the demand curve is linear, the price elasticity approaches zero as $P(= C - dQ)$ gets very small, and approaches infinity as $Q$ gets very small.

# PRICE ELASTICITY AND TOTAL MONEY EXPENDITURE

Managers are interested in questions like: Will an increase in price result in an increase in the total amount spent by consumers on their product? Or will an increase in price result in a decrease in the total amount spent by consumers on their product? The answers depend on the price elasticity of demand, as we show in this section.

Suppose that the demand for the product is **price elastic,** that is, the price elasticity of demand exceeds 1. The total amount of money spent by consumers on the product equals the quantity demanded times the price per unit. In this situation, if the price is reduced, the percentage increase in quantity demanded is greater than the percentage reduction in price (since this follows from the definition of the price elasticity of demand). It then follows that a price reduction must lead to an increase in the total amount spent by consumers on the commodity. Similarly, if the demand is price elastic, a price increase leads to a reduction in the amount of money spent on the commodity.

If the demand for the product is **price inelastic** (which means that the price elasticity of demand is less than 1), a price decrease leads to a reduction in the total amount spent on the commodity, and a price increase leads to an increase in the amount spent on the commodity. If the demand is of **unitary elasticity** (which means that the price elasticity of demand equals 1), an increase or decrease in price has no effect on the amount spent on the commodity.

As an illustration, consider the case shown in Figure 3.7. The demand

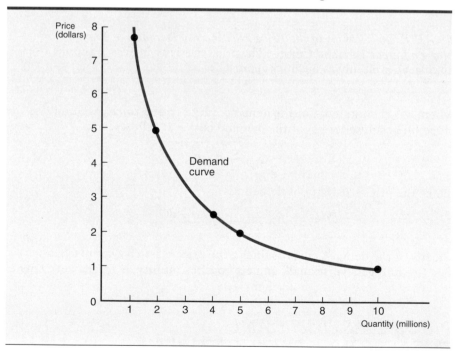

**FIGURE 3.7** *Demand Curve with Unitary Elasticity at All Points* The demand curve is a rectangular hyperbola if the price elasticity of demand is always 1.

## THE DEMAND FOR NEWSPRINT

Newsprint is an important commodity in both Canada and the United States. Suppose that the demand for newsprint can be represented as follows:

$$Q_1 = 17.3 - .0092P + 0.0067I,$$

where $Q_1$ equals the quantity demanded (in kilograms per capita), $P$ is the price of newsprint (in dollars per metric ton), and $I$ is income per capita (in dollars). (a) If there are 1 million people in the market, and if per capita income equals $10,000, what is the demand curve for newsprint? (b) Under these circumstances, what is the price elasticity of demand if the price of newsprint equals $400 per metric ton? (c) According to a 1984 study,* the demand curve for newsprint in the northeastern United States is

$$Q_2 = 2672 - 0.51P,$$

where $Q_2$ is the number of metric tons of newsprint demanded (in thousands). What is the price elasticity of demand for newsprint in the northeastern United States if price equals $500 per metric ton? (d) If the price of newsprint falls, will this result in an increase or decrease in the amount spent on newsprint in the northeastern United States? Why?

*Solution* (a) Since there are 1 million people in the market, and since $Q_1$ equals *per capita* quantity demanded, the quantity demanded equals 1 million times $Q_1$. Letting $Q'_1$ be the quantity demanded (in *millions* of kilograms),

$$Q'_1 = 17.3 - .0092P$$
$$+ .0067(10,000)$$
$$= 84.3 - .0092P.$$

(b) Since $dQ'_1/dP = -.0092$, the price elasticity of demand equals .0092 $P/Q_1$. Because $P = 400$ and $I = 10,000$, $Q'$ must equal $17.3 - .0092(400) + .0067(10,000) = 80.62$ million kilograms. Thus, the price elasticity of demand equals $.0092(400/80.62) = .05$. (c) Since $dQ_2/dP = -0.51$, and since $P = 500$, the price elasticity of demand equals $0.51(500) \div [2,672 - .51(500)] = .11$. (d) It will result in a decrease in the amount spent on newsprint because the demand for newsprint is price inelastic.

* F. Guder and J. Buongiorno, "An Interregional Analysis of the North American Newsprint Industry," *Interfaces* (September–October 1984), pp. 85–95.

curve shown there is a rectangular hyperbola, which means that

$$Q = \frac{m}{P},$$ (3.11)

where Q is the quantity demanded of the good, P is its price, and m is some constant. This kind of demand curve is of unitary elasticity at all points. Thus, changes in price have no effect on the total amount spent on the product. It is evident from equation (3.11) that, regardless of the price, the total amount spent on the product will be m ($10 million in Figure 3.7).

## TOTAL REVENUE, MARGINAL REVENUE, AND PRICE ELASTICITY

To its producers, the total amount of money spent on a product equals their total revenue. Thus, to the Ford Motor Company, the total amount spent on its cars (and other products) is its total revenue. Suppose that the demand curve for a firm's product is linear; that is,

$$P = a - bQ,$$ (3.12)

where a is the intercept on the price axis, and b is the slope (in absolute terms), as shown in panel A of Figure 3.8. Thus, the firm's total revenue equals

$$TR = P \cdot Q$$

$$= (a - bQ)Q$$

$$= aQ - bQ^2.$$ (3.13)

An important concept is **marginal revenue,** which, as we know from Chapter 2, is defined as $dTR/dQ$. In subsequent chapters, we will use this concept repeatedly. In the present case,

$$MR = \frac{dTR}{dQ}$$

$$= \frac{d(aQ - bQ^2)}{dQ}$$

$$= a - 2bQ,$$ (3.14)

which is also shown in panel A of Figure 3.8. Comparing the marginal revenue curve with the demand curve, we see that both have the same intercept on the vertical axis (this intercept being a), but that the marginal revenue curve has a slope that (in absolute terms) is twice that of the demand curve.

According to the definition in equation (3.7), the price elasticity of demand, $\eta$, equals $-(\partial Q/\partial P) \cdot (P/Q)$. Thus, since $\partial Q/\partial P = -1/b$ and

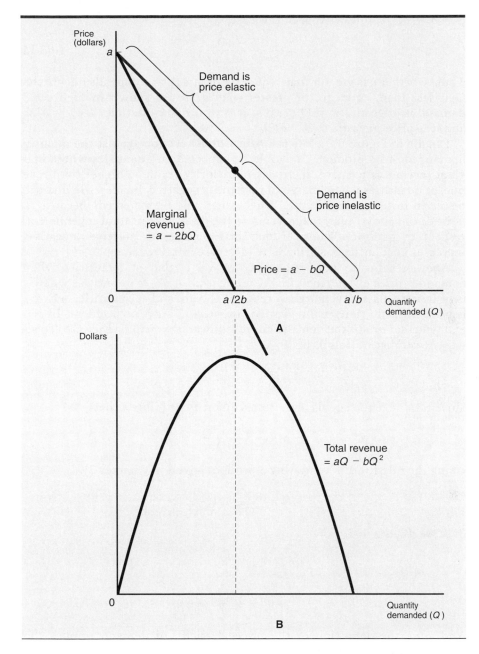

**FIGURE 3.8   *Relationship between Price Elasticity, Marginal Revenue, and Total Revenue***   If demand is price elastic, marginal revenue is positive, and increases in quantity result in higher total revenue. If demand is price inelastic, marginal revenue is negative, and increases in quantity result in lower total revenue.

$P = a - bQ$, it follows that in this case,

$$\eta = \frac{1}{b} \cdot \frac{a - bQ}{Q}. \tag{3.15}$$

Thus, whether $\eta$ is greater than, equal to, or less than 1 depends on whether $Q$ is less than, equal to, or greater than $a/2b$. As shown in Figure 3.8, demand is price elastic if $Q < a/2b$; it is of unitary elasticity if $Q = a/2b$; and it is price inelastic if $Q > a/2b$.

Panel B in Figure 3.8 plots the firm's total revenue against the quantity demanded of its product. As would be expected, at quantities where marginal revenue is positive, increases in quantity result in higher total revenue; at quantities where marginal revenue is negative, increases in quantity result in lower total revenue. Why would this be expected? Because, as pointed out above, marginal revenue is the derivative of total revenue with respect to quantity. Thus, if marginal revenue is positive (negative), increases in quantity must increase (decrease) total revenue.

Another thing to note about Figure 3.8 is that at quantities where demand is price elastic, marginal revenue is positive; at quantities where it is of unitary elasticity, marginal revenue is zero; and at quantities where it is price inelastic, marginal revenue is negative. This is no accident. In general, whether or not the demand curve is linear, this will be the case. To see why, recall that by definition,

$$MR = \frac{dTR}{dQ}.$$

Since total revenue equals price times quantity, it follows that

$$MR = \frac{d(P \cdot Q)}{dQ}.$$

Using the rule for differentiating a product (given in Chapter 2),

$$MR = P\frac{dQ}{dQ} + Q\frac{dP}{dQ}.$$

Because $dQ/dQ = 1$,

$$MR = P + Q\frac{dP}{dQ}$$

$$= P\left(1 + \frac{Q}{P} \cdot \frac{dP}{dQ}\right).$$

And since the definition of the price elasticity of demand implies that $Q/P \cdot dP/dQ = -1/\eta$,

$$MR = P\left(1 - \frac{1}{\eta}\right). \tag{3.16}$$

Equation (3.16) is a famous result, which shows that if $\eta > 1$, marginal revenue must be positive, if $\eta < 1$, marginal revenue must be negative, and if $\eta = 1$, marginal revenue must be zero. (This is what we set out to prove.) In later chapters, we will use equation (3.16) repeatedly. You should study it carefully, and understand it. To illustrate its meaning, what is the value of marginal revenue if price is $10 and the price elasticity of demand is 2? Based on equation (3.16), it equals $10(1 - \frac{1}{2}) = \$5$.

# DETERMINANTS OF THE PRICE ELASTICITY OF DEMAND

Table 3.4 shows the price elasticity of demand for selected products in the United States. What determines whether the demand for a product is price elastic or price inelastic? Why does the price elasticity of demand for restaurant meals equal 1.63 and the price elasticity of demand for gasoline and oil equal 0.14?

TABLE 3.4   *Price Elasticity of Demand, Selected Products, United States*

| Commodity | Price elasticity of demand |
|---|---|
| Tomatoes (fresh) | 4.60 |
| Restaurant meals | 1.63 |
| Glassware | 1.34 |
| Taxi service | 1.24 |
| Radios, TV service | 1.19 |
| Furniture | 1.01 |
| Housing | 1.00 |
| Alcohol | 0.92 |
| Movies | 0.87 |
| Air travel (foreign) | 0.77 |
| Shoes | 0.70 |
| Legal services | 0.61 |
| Auto repair | 0.36 |
| Medical insurance | 0.31 |
| Gasoline and oil | 0.14 |

*Source:* H. Houthakker and L. Taylor, *Consumer Demand in the United States*, 2d ed. (Cambridge, Mass.: Harvard University Press, 1970).

1. The price elasticity of demand for a product depends heavily on the number and closeness of the substitutes that are available. If a product has lots of close substitutes, its demand is likely to be price elastic. If the product's price is increased, a large proportion of its buyers will turn to the close substitutes that are available; if its price is reduced, a great many buyers of substitutes will switch to this product. The extent to which a product has close substitutes depends on how narrowly it is defined. As the definition of the product becomes narrower and more specific, the product would be expected to have more close substitutes, and its demand would be expected to become more price elastic. Hence, the demand for a particular brand of

gasoline is likely to be more price elastic than the overall demand for gasoline, and the demand for gasoline is likely to be more price elastic than the demand for all fuels taken as a whole.

2. The price elasticity of demand for a product may depend on the importance of the product in consumers' budgets. It is sometimes claimed that the demand for products like thimbles, rubber bands, and salt may be quite inelastic, since the typical consumer spends only a very small fraction of his or her income on such goods. In contrast, for products that bulk larger in the typical consumer's budget, like major appliances, the elasticity of demand may tend to be higher, since consumers may be more conscious of, and influenced by, price changes in the case of goods that require larger outlays. However, although a tendency of this sort is sometimes hypothesized, there is no guarantee that you can count on its being true.

3. The price elasticity of demand for a product is likely to depend on the length of the period to which the demand curve pertains. (As pointed out above, every market demand curve pertains to a certain time interval.) Demand is likely to be more elastic, or less inelastic, over a long period of time than over a short period of time because the longer the period of time, the easier it is for consumers and firms to substitute one good for another. If, for instance, the price of oil should decline relative to other fuels, the consumption of oil in the day after the price decline would probably increase very little. But over a period of several years, people would have an opportunity to take account of the price decline in choosing the type of fuel to be used in new houses and renovated old houses. In the longer period of several years, the price decline would have a greater effect on the consumption of oil than in the shorter period of one day.[2]

## USES OF THE PRICE ELASTICITY OF DEMAND

Managers display an avid interest, and for good reason, in the price elasticity of demand for their products. Consider Table 3.5, which provides estimates of the price elasticity of demand for first-class, regular economy, and excursion air tickets between the United States and Europe. The price elasticity of demand for first-class air tickets is much lower than for regular economy or excursion tickets, owing in part to the fact that the people who go first class—often business travelers and relatively wealthy people—are unlikely to change their travel plans if moderate increases or decreases occur in the price of an air ticket. Airline executives have studied these data carefully, with an eye toward the pricing of various kinds of tickets. Because the price elasticity of demand for first-class air tickets is relatively low, they have nudged up the prices for such tickets.

---

[2] However, for durable goods like automobiles, the price elasticity of demand may be greater in the short run than in the long run. If the price of automobiles goes up, the quantity demanded is likely to fall sharply because many consumers will put off buying a new car. But as time goes on and old cars wear out, the quantity of automobiles demanded will tend to increase.

TABLE 3.5   Elasticities of Demand for Air Tickets between United States and Europe

| Type of ticket | Price elasticity | Income elasticity |
|---|---|---|
| First class | 0.45 | 1.50 |
| Regular economy | 1.30 | 1.38 |
| Excursion | 1.83 | 2.37 |

Source: J. Cigliano, "Price and Income Elasticities for Airline Travel: The North Atlantic Market," Business Economics (September 1980).

It is important to recognize that no manager interested in maximizing profit will set price at a point where the demand for his or her product is price inelastic. To see why this is a mistake, recall from equation (3.16) that marginal revenue must be negative if demand is price inelastic (that is, if $\eta$ < 1). If marginal revenue is negative, a firm can increase its profit by raising its price and lowering its output. Why? Because its total revenue will increase if it sells less. (This, after all, is what it means to say that marginal revenue is negative.) Since the firm's total cost will not rise if less is sold, its profits will go up if it sells less.

Market researchers are continually engaged in studies to estimate the price elasticity of demand for particular products. The results enable firms to answer questions like: How much of an increase in sales can we expect if we reduce our price by 5 percent? To increase the amount we sell by 10 percent, how much must we reduce price? These are fundamental questions of the sort that firms confront repeatedly.

For example, take the soft drink industry. The price elasticity of demand for Royal Crown Cola has been estimated to be about 2.4, which means that the amount sold is very sensitive to price. A 1 percent reduction in the price of Royal Crown Cola (holding the prices of its competitors constant) results in a 2.4 percent increase in the quantity sold. Coke is even more price elastic, the price elasticity being about 5.5. Thus, a 1 percent reduction in the price of Coke (holding the prices of its competitors constant) results in a 5.5 percent increase in the quantity sold.[3] Clearly, the managers of Royal Crown and Coke need this information to function effectively—and they and their opposite numbers in firms across the country spend plenty to obtain such information.

## PRICE ELASTICITY AND PRICING POLICY

To see more specifically how managers use information concerning the price elasticity of demand for their products, let's consider in more detail

[3] J. Nevin, "Laboratory Experiments for Estimating Consumer Demand," Journal of Marketing Research (August 1974).

the important topic of pricing. According to equation (3.16),

$$MR = P\left(1 - \frac{1}{\eta}\right).$$

From Chapter 2, we know that marginal revenue equals marginal cost if a firm is maximizing profit, which means that

$$MC = P\left(1 - \frac{1}{\eta}\right), \tag{3.17}$$

where $MC$ equals marginal cost. [To obtain equation (3.17), we substitute $MC$ for $MR$ on the left-hand side of equation (3.16).] Solving equation (3.17) for $P$, we obtain

$$P = MC\left(\frac{1}{1 - 1/\eta}\right). \tag{3.18}$$

While equation (3.18) looks rather innocuous, it is in fact a very powerful and useful result. What it says is that the optimal price of a product depends on its marginal cost and its price elasticity of demand. Suppose that the marginal cost of a particular type of shirt is $10 and that its price elasticity of demand equals 2. According to equation (3.18), its optimal price is

$$P = 10\left(\frac{1}{1 - \frac{1}{2}}\right)$$

$$= 20 \text{ dollars.}$$

For present purposes, the central point to note is that the optimal price depends heavily on the price elasticity of demand. Holding constant the value of marginal cost, a product's optimal price is inversely related to its price elasticity of demand. Thus, if the shirt's price elasticity of demand were 5 rather than 2, its optimal price would be

$$P = 10\left(\frac{1}{1 - \frac{1}{5}}\right)$$

$$= 12\frac{1}{2} \text{ dollars.}$$

Given the importance of the price elasticity of demand in determining the optimal price of a product, it is not hard to see why managers are so intent on obtaining at least rough estimates of its value. (In Chapters 10 to 12, we will say much more about optimal pricing policies.)

## THE INCOME ELASTICITY OF DEMAND

As stressed in previous sections, price is not the only factor that influences the quantity demanded of a product. Another important factor is the level of money income among the consumers in the market. If shoppers have plenty of money to spend, the quantity demanded of men's suits is likely to be greater than it would be if they were poverty-stricken. Or if incomes in a particular city are high, the quantity demanded of cognac is likely to be greater than it would be if incomes were low.

The **income elasticity of demand** for a particular good is defined to be *the percentage change in quantity demanded resulting from a 1 percent change in consumers' income.* More precisely, it equals

$$\eta_I = \frac{\partial Q}{\partial I} \cdot \frac{I}{Q} \qquad (3.19)$$

where $Q$ is quantity demanded, and $I$ is consumers' income. For some products, the income elasticity of demand is positive, indicating that increases in consumers' money income result in increases in the amount of the good consumed. For example, one would generally expect luxury items like gourmet foods to have positive income elasticities. Other goods have negative income elasticities, indicating that increases in money income result in decreases in the amount of the good consumed. For example, inferior grades of vegetables and clothing might have negative income elasticities. In calculating the income elasticity of demand, it is assumed that the prices of all commodities are held constant.

Whether the income elasticity of demand for a firm's product is high or low can have a great impact on the firm's opportunities and problems. Firms making products with high income elasticities are likely to grow relatively rapidly as incomes rise in an expanding economy, whereas firms making products with low income elasticities are likely to experience more modest expansion. On the other hand, if the economy is jolted by a serious depression and incomes fall sharply, firms making products with low income elasticities are likely to experience less of a decrease in output than those making products with high income elasticities.

In forecasting the long-term growth of the quantity demanded for many major products, the income elasticity of demand is of key importance. According to studies by Princeton's Gregory Chow and Michigan State's Daniel Suits, among others, the income elasticity of demand for automobiles has been about 3, which means that a 1 percent increase in disposable income is associated with about a 3 percent increase in the quantity demanded of automobiles. Table 3.5 indicates that the income elasticity of demand for first-class air tickets between the United States and Europe is 1.50, which means that a 1 percent increase in disposable income is associated with about a 1.50 percent increase in the quantity demanded of such tickets. Table 3.6 shows the income elasticity of demand for other commodities. In measuring income elasticities, income can be defined as the aggregate income of consumers (as in Table 3.6) or as per capita income (as in the next section), depending on the circumstances.

---

TABLE 3.6    *Income Elasticity of Demand, Selected Commodities, United States*

| Commodity | Income elasticity of demand |
|---|---|
| Alcohol | 1.54 |
| Housing, owner-occupied | 1.49 |
| Furniture | 1.48 |
| Dental services | 1.42 |
| Restaurant meals | 1.40 |
| Shoes | 1.10 |
| Medical insurance | 0.92 |
| Gasoline and oil | 0.48 |
| Butter | 0.42 |
| Coffee | 0 |
| Margarine | −0.20 |
| Flour | −0.36 |

*Source:* H. Houthakker and L. Taylor, *Consumer Demand in the United States.*

## USING THE DEMAND FUNCTION TO CALCULATE THE INCOME ELASTICITY OF DEMAND

In a previous section, we learned how to calculate the price elasticity of demand, based on a product's demand function. Here we see how the income elasticity of demand can be calculated. Suppose that the demand function for good $X$ is

$$Q = 1,000 - 0.2P_x + 0.5P_y + .04I,$$

where $Q$ is the quantity demanded of good $X$, $P_x$ is the price of good $X$, $P_y$ is the price of good $Y$, and $I$ is per capita disposable income. The income elasticity of demand is

$$\eta_I = \frac{\partial Q}{\partial I} \cdot \frac{I}{Q}$$

$$= .04\frac{I}{Q}.$$

If $I = 10,000$ and $Q = 1,700$,

$$\eta_I = .04\left(\frac{10,000}{1,700}\right) = .24.$$

Thus, the income elasticity of demand equals .24, which means that a 1 percent increase in per capita disposable income is associated with a .24 percent increase in the quantity demanded of good $X$.

## ESTIMATING THE QUANTITY DEMANDED OF FRESH PREMIUM SALMON*

A leading producer of consumer goods, interested in entering the business of supplying salmon, carried out a study in 1988 to estimate the quantity that would be demanded of fresh premium salmon (Atlantic and Pacific) in 1990. The consumption of fresh premium salmon in 1986 was estimated to be as follows:

| Country | Thousands of tons consumed per year |
| --- | --- |
| United States | 90 |
| Canada | 14 |
| Japan | 110 |
| France | 35 |
| United Kingdom | 16 |
| Germany | 8 |
| Other European countries | 22 |
| Total | 295 |

Using a statistical analysis, the firm's analysts and managers estimated the income elasticity of demand for salmon to be about 4 (except in Japan, where it was estimated to be about 2). Income was expected to rise by about 10 percent in all countries between 1986 and 1990. The firm's managers wanted to estimate the total consumption of fresh premium salmon in these countries in 1990, assuming that price and other nonincome variables remained the same as in 1986.

How would you make such an estimate?

*This section is based on an actual case, although the numbers and situation have been simplified somewhat.

## CROSS ELASTICITIES OF DEMAND

Besides price and income, still another factor influencing the quantity demanded of a product is the price of other commodities. Holding constant the product's own price (as well as the level of money incomes) and allowing the price of another product to vary may result in important effects on the quantity demanded of the product in question. By observing these effects, we can classify pairs of commodities as **substitutes** or **complements,** and we can measure how close the relationship (either substitute or complementary) is. Consider two commodities, good $X$ and good $Y$. If good $Y$'s price goes up, what is the effect on $Q_x$, the quantity of good $X$ that is demanded? The **cross elasticity of demand** is defined as *the percentage change in the quantity demanded of good* X *resulting from a 1 percent change in the price of good* Y. Expressed in terms of derivatives,

$$\eta_{XY} = \frac{\partial Q_X}{\partial P_Y} \cdot \frac{P_Y}{Q_X}. \tag{3.20}$$

Goods $X$ and $Y$ are classified as substitutes if the cross elasticity of demand is positive. For instance, an increase in the price of wheat, when the price of corn remains constant, will tend to increase the quantity of corn demanded; thus, $\eta_{xy}$ is positive, and wheat and corn are classified as substitutes. On the other hand, if the cross elasticity of demand is negative, goods $X$ and $Y$ are classified as complements. Thus, an increase in the price of software may tend to decrease the purchase of personal computers, when the price of personal computers remains constant; thus, $\eta_{xy}$ is negative, and software and personal computers are classified as complements.

To illustrate the calculation of cross elasticities, suppose once again that the demand function for good $X$ is

$$Q_x = 1{,}000 - 0.2P_x + 0.5P_y + .04I,$$

where $Q_x$ is the quantity demanded of good $X$, $P_X$ is the price of good $X$, $P_Y$ is the price of good $Y$, and $I$ is per capita disposable income. The cross elasticity of demand between goods $X$ and $Y$ is

$$\eta_{xy} = \frac{\partial Q_X}{\partial P_Y} \cdot \frac{P_Y}{Q_X}$$

$$= 0.5\frac{P_Y}{Q_X}.$$

Although the value of the cross elasticity will depend on the values of $P_Y$ and $Q_X$, the goods will always be substitutes, since $\eta_{XY}$ must be positive, regardless of the values of $P_Y$ and $Q_X$. If $P_Y = 500$ and $Q_X = 1{,}500$,

$$\eta_{XY} = 0.5\left(\frac{500}{1500}\right) = .17.$$

The cross elasticity of demand is of fundamental importance to firms because they continually must do their best to anticipate what will happen

TABLE 3.7    *Cross Elasticity of Demand, Selected Pairs of Commodities, United States*

| Good X | Good Y | Cross elasticity of demand |
|--------|--------|----------------------------|
| Electricity | Natural gas | + 0.20 |
| California oranges | Florida interior oranges | + 0.14 |
| Butter | Margarine | + 0.67 |
| Pork | Beef | + 0.14 |

Source: R. Halvorsen, "Energy Substitution in U.S. Manufacturing," *Review of Economics and Statistics* (November 1977); and others.

to their own sales if their rivals change *their* prices. To do so, they need information concerning the cross elasticities of demand. Table 3.7 shows the cross elasticities of demand for selected pairs of commodities. In the following chapter, we will take up some of the statistical techniques used to estimate them.

## THE ADVERTISING ELASTICITY OF DEMAND

Although the price elasticity, income elasticity, and cross elasticities of demand are the most frequently used elasticity measures, they are not the only ones. For example, firms sometimes find it useful to calculate the **advertising elasticity of demand.** Suppose that the demand function for a particular firm's product is

$$Q = 500 - 0.5P + 0.01I + .82A,$$

where $Q$ is the quantity demanded of the product, $P$ is its price, $I$ is per capita disposable income, and $A$ is the firm's advertising expenditure. The advertising elasticity is defined as *the percentage change in the quantity demanded of the product resulting from a 1 percent change in advertising expenditure.* More precisely, it equals

$$\eta_A = \frac{\partial Q}{\partial A} \cdot \frac{A}{Q}. \tag{3.21}$$

Thus, in this case, since $\partial Q / \partial A = .82$,

$$\eta_A = .82 \frac{A}{Q}.$$

If $A/Q$—the amount of advertising per unit of the product demanded—is $2,

$$\eta_A = .82 \ (2) = 1.64.$$

## USING PIMS DATA TO ESTIMATE ELASTICITIES OF DEMAND

The PIMS (Profit Impact of Market Strategies) survey of major American firms has obtained annual expenditure and performance data for approximately 1,500 strategic business units. Using these data, Michael Hagerty, James Carman, and Gary Russell estimated for these firms the price elasticity of demand, as well as the elasticity of demand with respect to advertising, promotion, and sales force.* The elasticity of demand with respect to advertising is the percentage increase in quantity sold resulting from a 1 percent increase in spending on media advertising. The elasticity of demand with respect to promotion is the percentage increase in quantity sold resulting from a 1 percent increase in promotional expenditures (including premiums, catalogs, price promotions, and trade shows). The elasticity of demand with respect to sales force is the percentage increase in quantity sold resulting from a 1 percent increase in sales force expenditures (including sales force compensation, payments to brokers or agents, and sales force administrative expense). The average estimated values of these elasticities were as follows:

| Elasticity | Value |
|---|---|
| Price | .985 |
| Advertising | .003 |
| Promotion | .008 |
| Sales force | .304 |

(a) Do these results indicate that firms spend too much on advertising? (b) Do they indicate that an extra dollar spent on promotion will have a bigger effect on sales than an extra dollar spent on advertising? (c) Of what use are such elasticities to managers? (d) Do you think that these average values can be applied to any particular firm? Why or why not?

*Solution* (a) No. The fact that the elasticity of demand with respect to advertising is relatively low (.003) does not necessarily mean that an additional dollar spent on advertising would not be profitable, or that the last dollar spent was not profitable. (b) No. They indicate that a 1 percent increase in promotion would have a bigger effect on sales than a 1 percent increase in advertising. (c) They provide valuable information concerning the effects on sales of changes in price, advertising, promotion, or sales force. (d) No. These elasticities vary greatly from firm to firm, depending on the industry and other factors.

* M. Hagerty, J. Carman, and G. Russell, "Estimating Elasticities with PIMS Data: Methodological Issues and Substantive Implications," *Journal of Marketing Research* (February 1988), pp. 1–9. More will be said in Chapter 11 about the results of the PIMS surveys.

This elasticity is useful because it tells the firm's managers that a 1 percent increase in advertising expenditure results in a 1.64 percent increase in the quantity demanded. In later chapters, we shall see how information of this sort can be used to help guide major managerial decisions.

# THE CONSTANT-ELASTICITY DEMAND FUNCTION

In previous sections of this chapter, we generally have assumed that the demand function is linear. That is, the quantity demanded of a product has been assumed to be a linear function of its price, the prices of other goods, consumer income, and other variables. Another mathematical form that is frequently used is the **constant-elasticity demand function**. If the quantity demanded ($Q$) depends only on the product's price ($P$) and consumer income ($I$), this mathematical form is

$$Q = aP^{-b_1}I^{b_2}. \tag{3.22}$$

Thus, if $a = 200$, $b_1 = .3$, and $b_2 = 2$,

$$Q = 200P^{-.3}I^2.$$

An important property of this demand function is that the price elasticity of demand equals $b_1$, regardless of the value of $P$ or $I$. (This accounts for its being called the constant-elasticity demand function.) To see this, let's differentiate $Q$ with respect to price, the result being

$$\frac{\partial Q}{\partial P} = -b_1 aP^{-b_1-1}I^{b_2}$$

$$= \frac{-b_1}{P}(aP^{-b_1}I^{b_2})$$

$$= \frac{-b_1}{P}Q.$$

Thus,

$$-\frac{\partial Q}{\partial P} \cdot \frac{P}{Q} = b_1. \tag{3.23}$$

Since the left-hand side of equation (3.23) is defined to be the price elasticity of demand, it follows that the price elasticity of demand equals $b_1$, a constant whose value does not depend on $P$ or $I$.

Similarly, the income elasticity of demand equals $b_2$, regardless of the value of $P$ or $I$. To prove this, let's differentiate $Q$ with respect to income, the result being

$$\frac{\partial Q}{\partial I} = b_2 aP^{-b_1}I^{b_2-1}$$

$$= \frac{b_2}{I} \left( aP^{-b_1}I^{b_2} \right)$$

$$= \frac{b_2}{I} Q.$$

Thus,

$$\frac{\partial Q}{\partial I} \cdot \frac{I}{Q} = b_2. \tag{3.24}$$

Since the left-hand side of equation (3.24) is defined to be the income elasticity of demand, it follows that the income elasticity of demand equals $b_2$, another constant whose value does not depend on $P$ or $I$.

The constant-elasticity demand function is often used by managers and managerial economists, for several reasons. First, in contrast to the linear demand function, this mathematical form recognizes that the effect of price on quantity depends on the level of income, and that the effect of income on quantity depends on the level of price. The multiplicative relationship in equation (3.22) is often more realistic than the additive relationship in equation (3.1). Second, like the linear demand function, the constant-elasticity demand function is relatively easy to estimate. If we take logarithms of both sides of equation (3.22),

$$\log Q = \log a - b_1 \log P + b_2 \log I. \tag{3.25}$$

Since this equation is linear in the logarithms, the parameters—$a$, $b_1$, and $b_2$—can readily be estimated by regression analysis. In the following chapter, we will learn how such estimates can be made.

## SUMMARY

1. The market demand curve for a product shows how much of the product will be demanded at each price. The market demand curve shifts in response to changes in tastes, incomes, the prices of other products, and the size of the population.

2. The market demand function for a product is an equation showing how the quantity demanded depends on the product's price, the incomes of consumers, the prices of other products, advertising expenditure, and additional factors. Holding all factors other than the product's price constant, one can derive the market demand curve for the product from the market demand function. Market demand functions can be formulated for individual firms as well as for entire industries.

3. The price elasticity of demand is the percentage change in quantity demanded resulting from a 1 percent change in price; more precisely, it equals $-(\partial Q/\partial P)(P/Q)$. Whether a price increase (or decrease) results in an increase in the total amount spent by consumers on a product depends on the price elasticity of demand.

4. Marginal revenue is the change in total revenue resulting from a 1-unit

increase in quantity; that is, it equals the derivative of total revenue with respect to quantity. Marginal revenue equals $P(1 - 1/\eta)$, where $P$ is price and $\eta$ is the price elasticity of demand.

5. The price elasticity of demand for a product tends to be high if it has a large number of close substitutes. Also, it often tends to be higher in the long run than in the short run. It is sometimes asserted that the demand for a product is relatively price inelastic if the product accounts for a very small percentage of the typical consumer's budget, but this need not be the case.

6. The optimal price for a product depends on its price elasticity of demand, as well as on its marginal cost. To maximize profit, a firm should set its price equal to $MC[1 \div (1 - 1/\eta)]$, where $MC$ is marginal cost, and $\eta$ is the price elasticity of demand.

7. The income elasticity of demand is the percentage change in quantity demanded resulting from a 1 percent increase in consumer income; that is, it equals $(\partial Q/\partial I) \cdot (I/Q)$, where $I$ is the income of consumers. The income elasticity of demand may be positive or negative. Like the price elasticity of demand, it is of major importance in forecasting the long-term growth of the quantity demanded for many major products.

8. The cross elasticity of demand is the percentage change in the quantity demanded of product $X$ resulting from a 1 percent increase in the price of product $Y$; in other words, it equals $(\partial Q_X/\partial P_Y)(P_Y/Q_X)$. If $X$ and $Y$ are substitutes, it is positive; if they are complements, it is negative. This elasticity is important to managers because they must try to understand and forecast the effects of changes in other firms' prices on their own firm's sales.

9. If a demand curve is linear, the price elasticity of demand varies from point to point on the demand curve. As price approaches zero, the price elasticity of demand also approaches zero. As quantity demanded approaches zero, the price elasticity approaches infinity. In contrast, for a constant-elasticity demand function, the price elasticity of demand is the same, regardless of the product's price. Both linear demand functions and constant-elasticity demand functions are used frequently by managers and managerial economists.

## PROBLEMS

1. The Dolan Corporation, a maker of aircraft engines, determines that in 1993 the demand curve for its product is as follows:

$$P = 2,000 - 50Q,$$

where $P$ is the price (in dollars) of an engine, and $Q$ is the number of engines sold per month.

(a) To sell 20 engines per month, what price would Dolan have to charge?

(b) If it sets a price of $500, how many engines will Dolan sell per month?

(c) What is the price elasticity of demand if price equals $500?

(d) At what price, if any, will the demand for Dolan's engines be of unitary elasticity?

2. The Johnson Robot Company's marketing officials report to the company's chief executive officer that the demand curve for the company's robots in 1993 is

$$P = 3{,}000 - 40Q,$$

where $P$ is the price of a robot, and $Q$ is the number sold per month.

(a) Derive the marginal revenue curve for the firm.

(b) At what prices is the demand for the firm's product price elastic?

(c) If the firm wants to maximize its dollar sales volume, what price should it charge?

3. After a careful statistical analysis, the Chidester Company concludes that the demand function for its product is

$$Q = 500 - 3P + 2P_r + .1I,$$

where $Q$ is the quantity demanded of its product, $P$ is the price of its product, $P_r$ is the price of its rival's product, and $I$ is per capita disposable income (in dollars). At present, $P = \$10$, $P_r = \$20$, and $I = \$6{,}000$.

(a) What is the price elasticity of demand for the firm's product?

(b) What is the income elasticity of demand for the firm's product?

(c) What is the cross elasticity of demand between its product and its rival's product?

(d) What is the implicit assumption regarding the population in the market?

4. The Haas Corporation's executive vice president circulates a memo to the firm's top management in which he argues for a reduction in the price of the firm's product. He says that such a price cut will increase the firm's sales and profits.

(a) The firm's marketing manager responds with a memo pointing out that the price elasticity of demand for the firm's product is about 0.5. Why is this fact relevant?

(b) The firm's president concurs with the opinion of the executive vice president. Is he correct?

5. According to J. Fred Bucy, former president of Texas Instruments, his firm continually has made detailed studies of the price elasticity of demand for each of its major products in order to determine how much its sales will increase if it changes its price by a particular amount.[4] For example, Texas Instruments had to estimate the effect of a 10 percent reduction in the price of the TI-55, a hand calculator that the company

---

[4] See his paper in J. Backman and J. Czepiel, eds., *Changing Marketing Strategies in a New Economy* (Indianapolis: Bobbs-Merrill, 1977).

produces, and whether such a price reduction would increase sales by a large enough amount to be profitable.

(a) Prices for many electronics products have tended to drop dramatically. During the 1970s, simple four-function hand calculators fell in price from about $150 to less than $10. Other products that experienced similar price reductions were transistor radios and digital watches. Do the costs of producing such items tend to fall as larger and larger quantities of them are produced?

(b) In 1982, Texas Instruments reduced the price of its 99/4A home computer from $299 to $199, and its rivals followed suit. If the price elasticity of demand exceeded 1, did the price cut increase the amount spent on such computers?

6. The Hanover Manufacturing Company believes that the demand curve for its product is

$$P = 5 - Q,$$

where $P$ is the price of its product (in dollars) and $Q$ is the number of millions of units of its product sold per day. It is currently charging a price of $1 per unit for its product.

(a) Evaluate the wisdom of the firm's pricing policy.

(b) A marketing specialist says that the price elasticity of demand for the firm's product is 1.0. Is this correct?

7. Based on historical data, Richard Tennant has concluded: "The consumption of cigarettes is . . . [relatively] insensitive to changes in price. . . . In contrast, the demand for individual brands is highly elastic in its response to price. . . . In 1918, for example, Lucky Strike was sold for a short time at a higher retail price than Camel or Chesterfield and rapidly lost half its business."

(a) Explain why the demand for a particular brand is more elastic than the demand for all cigarettes. If Lucky Strike raised its price by 1 percent in 1918, was the price elasticity of demand for its product greater than 2?

(b) Do you think that the demand curve for cigarettes is the same now as it was in 1918? If not, describe in detail the factors that have shifted the demand curve, and whether each has shifted it to the left or right.

8. According to S. Sackrin of the U.S. Department of Agriculture, the price elasticity of demand for cigarettes is between 0.3 and 0.4, and the income elasticity of demand is about 0.5.

(a) Suppose the federal government, influenced by findings that link cigarettes and cancer, were to impose a tax on cigarettes that increased their price by 15 percent. What effect would this have on cigarette consumption?

(b) Suppose a brokerage house advised you to buy cigarette stocks because if incomes rose by 50 percent in the next decade, cigarette sales would be bound to spurt enormously. What would be your reaction to this advice?

9. The McCauley Company hires a marketing consultant to estimate the demand function for its product. The consultant concludes that this demand function is

$$Q = 100P^{-3.1}I^{2.3}A^{0.1},$$

where $Q$ is the quantity demanded per capita per month, $P$ is the product's price (in dollars), $I$ is per capita disposable income (in dollars), and $A$ is the firm's advertising expenditures (in thousands of dollars).
   (a) What is the price elasticity of demand?
   (b) Will increases in price result in increases or decreases in the amount spent on McCauley's product?
   (c) What is the income elasticity of demand?
   (d) What is the advertising elasticity of demand?
   (e) If the population in the market increases by 10 percent, what is the effect on the quantity demanded if $P$, $I$, and $A$ are held constant?
10. The Schmidt Corporation estimates that its demand function is as follows:

$$Q = 400 - 3P + 4I + .6A,$$

where $Q$ is the quantity demanded per month, $P$ is the product's price (in dollars), $I$ is per capita disposable income (in thousands of dollars), and $A$ is the firm's advertising expenditures (in thousands of dollars per month). Population is assumed to be constant.
   (a) During the next decade, per capita disposable income is expected to increase by $5,000. What effect will this have on the firm's sales?
   (b) If Schmidt wants to raise its price enough to offset the effect of the increase in per capita disposable income, by how much must it raise its price?
   (c) If Schmidt raises its price by this amount, will it increase or decrease the price elasticity of demand? Explain.
11. The marketing manager of the Summers Company must formulate a recommendation concerning the price to be charged for a new product. According to the best available estimates, the marginal cost of the new product will be $18, and the price elasticity of demand for this product will be 3.0.
   (a) What recommendation should she make, if Summers wants to maximize profit?
   (b) If her recommendation is accepted, what will be the new product's marginal revenue?
12. Market researchers at the Lawrence Corporation estimate that the demand function for the firm's product is

$$Q = 50P^{-1.5}I^{0.5},$$

where $Q$ is the quantity demanded, $P$ is the product's price, and $I$ is per capita disposable income. The marginal cost of the firm's product is estimated to be $10. Population is assumed to be constant.
   (a) Lawrence's price for its product is $20. Is this the optimal price? Why or why not?

(b) If it is not the optimal price, write a brief memorandum indicating what price might be better, and why.

# APPENDIX: FROM CONSUMER BEHAVIOR TO MARKET DEMAND

In this appendix, we show in more detail how the market demand curve for a consumer good is linked to, and based on, the tastes and characteristics of the consumers in the market for this good. Economists have devoted considerable effort to studies of consumer behavior. Our purpose here is to provide a brief sketch of the economist's theory of consumer behavior and to indicate how this theory can be used to derive the demand curve for a particular commodity—food. To make things as simple as possible, we assume that there are only two goods—food and clothing. This assumption can easily be relaxed.

*Indifference Curves*     Let's begin by defining an indifference curve. *An indifference curve contains points representing market baskets among which the consumer is indifferent.* To illustrate, consider Joan Ewing, a consumer in Houston, Texas. Certain market baskets—that is, certain combinations of food and clothing (the only commodities)—will be equally desirable for her. For example, she may be indifferent between a market basket containing 50 pounds of food and 5 pieces of clothing and a market basket containing 100 pounds of food and 2 pieces of clothing. These two market baskets can be represented by two points, $K$ and $L$ in Figure 3.9. In addition, other market baskets—each of which can be represented by a point in Figure 3.9—are just as desirable to Ms. Ewing as those represented by points $K$ and $L$. If we connect all these points, we get a curve that represents market baskets that are equally desirable to the consumer. In our case, Ms. Ewing is indifferent among all the market baskets represented by points on curve $I_1$ in Figure 3.9. Curve $I_1$ is therefore called an indifference curve.

Three important things should be noted about any consumer's indifference curves:

1. *A consumer has many indifference curves, not just one.* If Ms. Ewing is indifferent among all the market baskets represented by points on $I_2$ in Figure 3.9, $I_2$ is another of her indifference curves. Moreover, one thing is certain. She prefers any market basket on $I_2$ to any market basket on $I_1$, since $I_2$ includes market baskets with as much clothing and more food (or as much food and more clothing) than the market baskets on $I_1$. (Of course, consumers sometimes become so satiated with a commodity that they prefer less of it to more, but we assume for simplicity that this is not the case here.) Consequently, it must be true that market baskets on higher indifference curves like $I_2$ must be preferred to market baskets on lower indifference curves like $I_1$.

2. *Every indifference curve must slope downward and to the right,* so long as the consumer prefers more of each commodity to less. If one market basket has more of one commodity than a second market basket, it must have less of the other commodity than the second market basket—assuming that the two market baskets are to yield equal satisfaction to the consumer. This must be true so long as more of each commodity is preferred over less by the consumer.

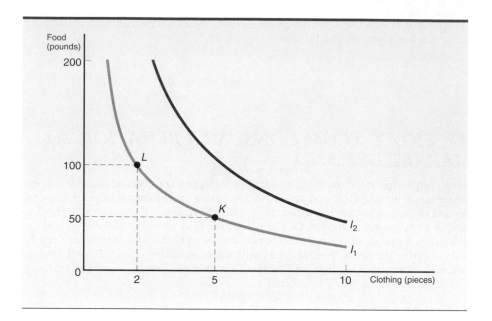

FIGURE 3.9    *Two of Ms. Ewing's Indifference Curves*   $I_1$ and $I_2$ are two of Ms. Ewing's indifference curves. Each shows market baskets that are equally desirable to Ms. Ewing.

3. *Indifference curves cannot intersect.* If they did, this would contradict the assumption that more of a commodity is preferred to less. For example, suppose that $I_1$ and $I_2$ in Figure 3.10 are two indifference curves and that they intersect. If this is the case, the market basket represented by point $D$ is equivalent in the eyes of the consumer to the one represented by point $C$, since both are on indifference curve $I_1$. Moreover, the market basket represented by point $E$ is equivalent in the eyes of the consumer to the one represented by point $C$, since both are on indifference curve $I_2$. And this means that the market basket represented by point $E$ must be equivalent in the eyes of the consumer to the one represented by point $D$. But this is impossible because market basket $E$ contains the same amount of food and two more pieces of clothing than does market basket $D$. Since more of a commodity is preferred to less, market basket $E$ must be preferred to market basket $D$.

*The Marginal Rate of Substitution*    Some consumers value an extra unit of a particular good highly; they would be willing to give their eye teeth to get an extra unit of it. Other consumers do not value an extra unit of this good at all highly; they wouldn't give up much of anything to get an extra unit of it. Obviously, in studying consumer behavior, it is useful to have a measure of the relative importance attached by the consumer to the acquisition of another unit of a particular good. The measure that economists use is called the marginal rate of substitution.

*The marginal rate of substitution of good* X *for good* Y *is defined as the number of units of good* Y *that must be given up if the consumer, after receiving an extra unit of good* X, *is to maintain a constant level of satisfaction.* Obviously, the larger

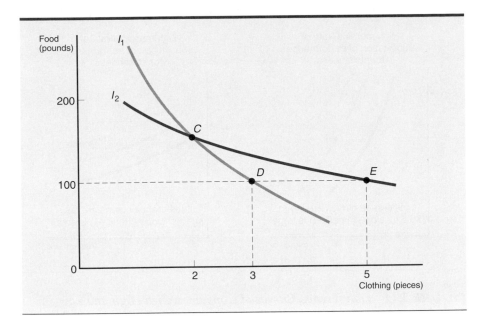

*FIGURE 3.10   Intersecting Indifference Curves: A Contradiction*
Indifference curves cannot intersect. If they did, the consumer would be
indifferent between $D$ and $C$, since both are on indifference curve $I_1$, and
between $E$ and $C$, since both are on indifference curve $I_2$. But this implies that
he or she must be indifferent between $D$ and $E$, which is impossible since $E$
contains the same amount of food and two more pieces of clothing than $D$.

the number of units of good $Y$ that the consumer is willing to give up to get an extra
unit of good $X$, the more important good $X$ is (relative to good $Y$) to the consumer.
To measure the marginal rate of substitution, we can obtain the slope of the consumer's indifference curve and multiply this slope by $-1$. This will give us the
number of units of good $Y$ that the consumer is willing to give up for an extra unit of
good $X$.

To illustrate, consider consumer preferences with regard to the characteristics of
automobiles. Two of the key characteristics of an automobile are stylishness and
performance (for example, speed, gasoline mileage, and handling). Some consumers
are willing to trade off a lot of stylishness for a little extra performance. For these
consumers, the indifference curves in Figure 3.11 are relatively steep, as in the left-
hand panel of Figure 3.11. The marginal rate of substitution of performance for stylishness is relatively high, since the slope of the indifference curves (times $-1$) is
relatively large. On the other hand, other consumers are willing to trade off a lot of
performance for a little extra stylishness. For these consumers, the indifference
curves in Figure 3.11 are relatively flat, as in the right-hand panel of Figure 3.11. The
marginal rate of substitution of performance for stylishness is relatively low, since
the slope of the indifference curves (time $-1$) is relatively small.

*The Concept of Utility*   As we have seen in previous paragraphs, the consumer's

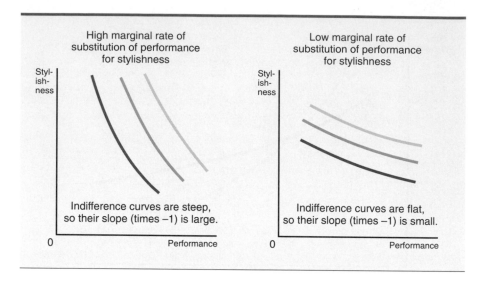

FIGURE 3.11    *Indifference Curves of Consumer with High and Low Marginal Rates of Substitution of Performance for Stylishness*    The left-hand panel shows the indifference curves of consumers who are willing to trade off a lot of stylishness for a little extra performance. The right-hand panel shows the indifference curves of consumers who are willing to trade off a lot of performance for a little extra stylishness.

indifference curves are a representation of his or her tastes. Given all of the indifference curves of a particular consumer, we attach a number, a *utility,* to each of the market baskets that might confront this consumer. *This utility indicates the level of enjoyment or preference attached by this consumer to this market basket.* Since all market baskets on a given indifference curve yield the same amount of satisfaction, they would have the same utility. Market baskets on higher indifference curves would have higher utilities than market baskets on lower indifference curves.

The reason why we attach these utilities to market baskets is that, once this is done, we can tell at a glance which market baskets the consumer would prefer over other market baskets. If the utility attached to one market basket is higher than that attached to another market basket, he or she will prefer the first over the second. If the utility attached to the first market basket is lower than the second, he or she will prefer the second over the first. If the utility attached to the first market basket equals the second, he or she will be indifferent between the two market baskets.

How should we pick these utilities? Any way will do as long as market baskets on the same indifference curve receive the same utility and market baskets on higher indifference curves receive higher utilities than market baskets on lower indifference curves. For example, if the consumer prefers market basket *R* to market basket *S*, and market basket *S* to market basket *T*, the utility of market basket *R* must be higher than the utility of market basket *S*, and the utility of market basket *S* must be higher than the utility of market basket *T*. But any set of numbers conforming to these requirements is an adequate measure of utility. Thus, the utility of market baskets R, S, and T may be 30, 20, and 10, or 6, 5, 4, respectively. Both are adequate utility measures, since all that counts is that the utility of market basket R be higher than that of market basket S, which in turn should be higher than that of market basket. T.

*The Budget Line*    *The consumer would like to maximize his or her utility, which means that he or she wants to achieve the highest possible indifference curve.* But whether or not a particular indifference curve is attainable depends on the consumer's money income and on commodity prices. Exactly what constraints are imposed on the consumer by the size of his or her money income and the nature of commodity prices? To make things concrete, let's return to Joan Ewing. Suppose that her total income is $600 per week and that she can spend this amount only on two commodities, food and clothing. Needless to say, it is unrealistic to assume that there are only two commodities in existence, but, to repeat what was said earlier, this makes it easier to present the model, and the results can easily be generalized to cases where more than two commodities exist.

Under these circumstances, the answer to how much of each commodity Ms. Ewing can buy depends on the price of a pound of food and the price of a piece of clothing. Suppose the price of a pound of food is $3 and the price of a piece of clothing is $60. Then if she spent all of her income on food, she could buy 200 pounds of food per week. On the other hand, if she spent all of her income on clothing, she could buy 10 pieces of clothing per week. Or she could, if she wished, buy some food and some clothing. There are a large number of combinations of amounts of food and clothing that she could buy, and each such combination can be represented by a point on the line in Figure 3.12. This line is called her budget line. *A consumer's budget line shows the market baskets that he or she can purchase, given the consumer's income and prevailing market prices.*

A shift will occur in the consumer's budget line if changes occur in the consumer's money income or in commodity prices. In particular, an increase in money income means that the budget line rises, and a decrease in money income means that the budget line falls. This is illustrated in Figure 3.13, which shows Ms. Ewing's budget line at money incomes of $300, $600, and $900 per week. As you can see, her budget line moves upward as her income rises.

Also, commodity prices affect the budget line. A decrease in a commodity's price causes the budget line to cut this commodity's axis at a point farther from the origin. Figure 3.14 shows Ms. Ewing's budget line when the price of a pound of food is $3 and when it is $6. You can see that the budget line cuts the vertical, or food, axis farther from the origin when the price of food is $3 per pound.

*The Equilibrium Market Basket*    Given the consumer's indifference curves and budget line, we are in a position to determine the consumer's equilibrium market basket—the market basket that, among all those that the consumer can purchase, yields the maximum utility. The first step is to combine the indifference curves with the budget line on the same graph. Figure 3.15 brings together Ms. Ewing's indifference curves (from Figure 3.9) and her budget line (from Figure 3.12). Based on the information assembled in Figure 3.15, it is a simple matter to determine her equilibrium market basket. *Her indifference curves show what she wants:* specifically, she wants to attain the highest possible indifference curve. Thus, she would rather be on indifference curve $I_2$ than on indifference curve $I_1$, and on indifference curve $I_3$ than on indifference curve $I_2$. But, as we have emphasized, she cannot choose any market

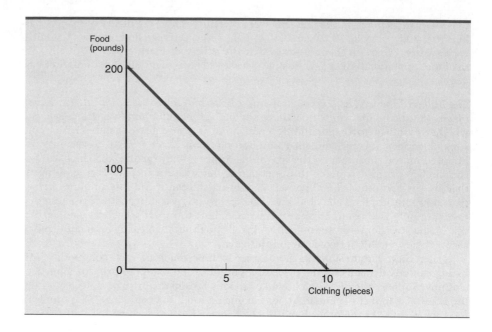

*FIGURE 3.12    Ms. Ewing's Budget Line*    The consumer's budget line shows the market baskets that can be purchased, given the consumer's income and prevailing commodity prices. This budget line assumes that Ms. Ewing's income is $600 per week, that the price of a pound of food is $3, and that the price of a piece of clothing is $60.

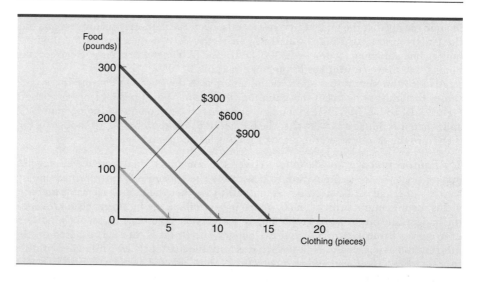

*FIGURE 3.13    Ms. Ewing's Budget Line at Money Incomes of $300, $600, and $900 per Week*    The higher the consumer's money income, the higher the budget line. Holding commodity prices constant, the budget line's slope remains constant.

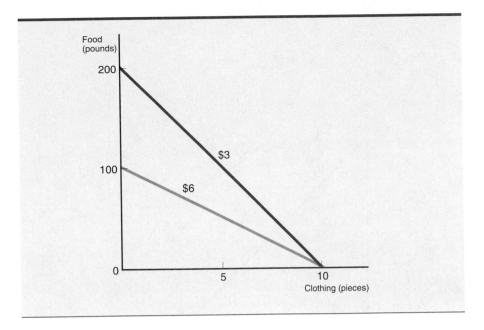

*FIGURE 3.14 Ms. Ewing's Budget Line at Food Prices of $3 and $6 per Pound* Holding constant Ms. Ewing's money income at $600 per week and the price of a piece of clothing at $60, the budget line cuts the vertical axis farther from the origin when the price of food is $3 than when it is $6.

basket she likes. *The budget line shows which market baskets her income and commodity prices permit her to buy.* Consequently, she must choose some market basket on her budget line.

Clearly, *the consumer's choice boils down to choosing that market basket on the budget line that is on the highest indifference curve. That is the equilibrium market basket.* For example, Ms. Ewing's equilibrium market basket is at point *H* in Figure 3.15; it consists of 100 pounds of food and 5 pieces of clothing per week. This is her equilibrium market basket because any other market basket on the budget line is on a lower indifference curve than point *H* is. But will a consumer like Ms. Ewing choose this market basket? Admittedly, it may take some time for the consumer to find out that this is the best market basket for him or her under the circumstances, but eventually one would expect a consumer to come very close to acting in the predicted manner.

*Deriving the Individual Demand Curve* A consumer's individual demand curve shows how much the consumer will purchase of the good in question at various prices of this good. Now we show how indifference curves can be used to derive the consumer's demand curve. In particular, let's return to the case of Ms. Ewing and show how her demand curve for food can be derived.

Assuming that food and clothing are the only goods, that Ms. Ewing's weekly

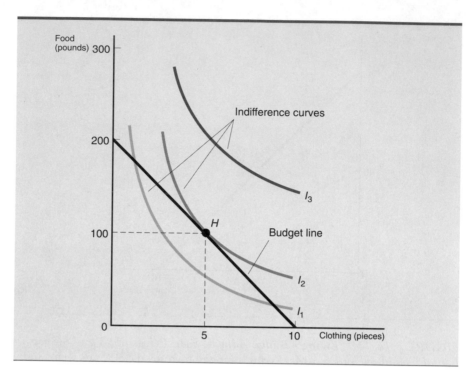

*FIGURE 3.15 Equilibrium Market Basket* Ms. Ewing's equilibrium market basket is at point *H*, containing 100 pounds of food and 5 pieces of clothing. This is the point on her budget line that is on the highest indifference curve $I_2$ she can attain.

income is $600, and that the price of clothing is $60 per piece of clothing, Ms. Ewing's budget line is budget line 1 in Figure 3.16, when the price of food is $3 per pound. Thus, as we saw in Figure 3.15, Ms. Ewing will buy 100 pounds of food per week under these circumstances.

But if the price of food increases to $6 per pound, and her income and the price of clothing remain constant, her budget line will be budget line 2 in Figure 3.16, and she will attain her highest indifference curve $I_1$ by choosing the market basket corresponding to point *K*, a market basket containing 50 pounds of food per week. Thus, if the price of food is $6 per pound, she will buy 50 pounds of food per week.

We have derived two points on Ms. Ewing's individual demand curve for food— those corresponding to food prices of $3 and $6 per pound. Figure 3.17 shows these two points, *U* and *V*. To obtain more points on her individual demand curve for food, all we have to do is assume a particular price of food, construct the budget line corresponding to this price (holding her income and the price of clothing constant), and find the market basket on this budget line that is on her highest indifference curve. Plotting the amount of food in this market basket against the assumed price of food, we obtain a new point on her individual demand curve for food. Connecting up all these points, we get her complete individual demand curve for food, shown in Figure 3.17.

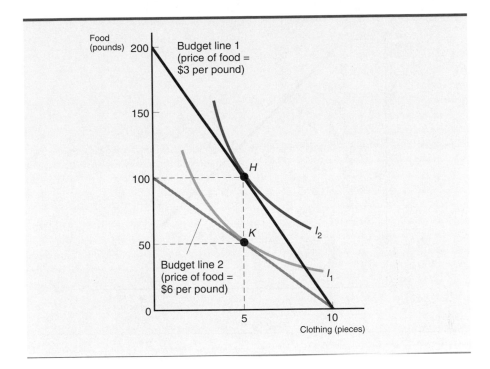

*FIGURE 3.16    Effect of Change in Price of Food on Ms. Ewing's Equilibrium Market Basket*    If the price of a pound of food is $3, Ms. Ewing's budget line is such that her equilibrium market basket is at point H, where she buys 100 pounds of food per week. If the price of a pound of food is $6, Ms. Ewing's budget line is such that her equilibrium market basket is at point K, where she buys 50 pounds of food per week.

*Deriving the Market Demand Curve*    We have just described how each consumer's individual demand curve for a commodity can be derived, given the consumer's tastes and income, as well as the prices of other commodities. Suppose that we have obtained the individual demand curve for each of the consumers in the market. How can these individual demand curves be used to derive the market demand curve?

The answer is easy. *To derive the market demand curve, we obtain the horizontal sum of all the individual demand curves.* In other words, to find the total quantity demanded in the market at a certain price, we add up the quantities demanded by the individual consumers at that price.

Table 3.8 shows the individual demand curves for food of four families: the Millers, Sarafians, Chases, and Grubers. For simplicity, suppose that these four families constitute the entire market for food. (This assumption can easily be relaxed; it just makes things simple.) Then the market demand curve for food is shown in the last column of Table 3.8. Figure 3.18 shows the families' individual demand curves for food, as well as the resulting market demand curve. To illustrate how the market demand curve is derived from the individual demand curves, suppose that the price

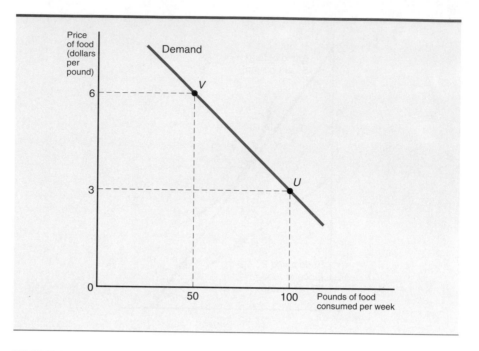

**FIGURE 3.17  Ms. Ewing's Individual Demand Curve for Food**  Ms. Ewing's individual demand curve for food shows the amount of food she will buy at various prices.

**TABLE 3.8  Individual Demand Curves and Market Demand Curve for Food**

| Price of food (dollars per pound) | Miller | Sarafian | Chase | Gruber | Market demand |
|---|---|---|---|---|---|
| | | Individual demand (hundreds of pounds per month) | | | |
| 3.00 | 51.0 | 45.0 | 5.0 | 2.0 | 103 |
| 3.20 | 43.0 | 44.0 | 4.2 | 1.8 | 93 |
| 3.40 | 36.0 | 43.0 | 3.4 | 1.6 | 84 |
| 3.60 | 30.0 | 42.0 | 2.6 | 1.4 | 76 |
| 3.80 | 26.0 | 41.4 | 2.4 | 1.2 | 71 |
| 4.00 | 21.0 | 41.0 | 2.0 | 1.0 | 65 |

of food is $3 per pound. Then the total quantity demanded in the market is 103 hundreds of pounds per month, since this is the sum of the quantities demanded at this price by the four families. (As shown in Table 3.8, this sum equals 51.0 + 45.0 + 5.0 + 2.0, or 103 hundreds of pounds.)

To conclude, this appendix has presented the theory of consumer behavior, which is built around indifference curves and budget lines, and has used this theory to show how the market demand curve for a commodity (in this case, food) can be derived from the indifference curves of individual consumers as well as their budget lines.

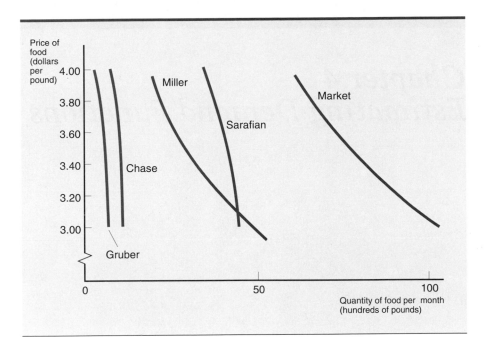

**FIGURE 3.18  Individual Demand Curves and Market Demand Curve for Food**  The market demand curve is the horizontal sum of all the individual demand curves.

# Chapter 4
# *Estimating Demand Functions*

## INTRODUCTION

C. Michael Armstrong, chairman of Hughes Aircraft, was at one time head of the IBM Corporation's marketing services. Many other top executives have had extensive knowledge of marketing and market research. This is not surprising. As stressed repeatedly in the previous chapter, an effective manager must have a good working knowledge of the demand function for his or her firm's products.

The previous chapter was concerned with the theory of demand; now we learn how you can estimate a product's demand function. Consumer surveys and market experiments can be useful in providing such information, but the technique most frequently used to estimate demand functions is regression analysis. Since regression analysis will be used repeatedly in subsequent chapters to estimate production functions and cost functions and for forecasting, we must devote considerable attention to this basic statistical technique.

## THE IDENTIFICATION PROBLEM

While it is very important that managers have reasonably accurate estimates of the demand functions for their own (and other) products, this does

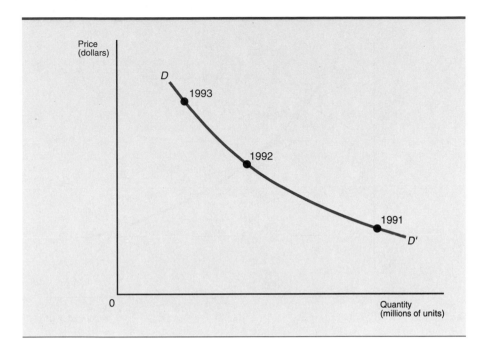

FIGURE 4.1  *Price Plotted against Quantity, 1991–93*  *DD'* is unlikely to be a good estimate of the demand curve.

not mean that it is always easy to obtain such estimates. One problem that may arise in estimating demand curves should be recognized at the outset. Given the task of estimating the demand curve for a particular product, you might be inclined to plot the quantity demanded of the product in 1993 versus its 1993 price, the quantity demanded in 1992 versus its 1992 price, and so forth. If the resulting plot of points for 1991 to 1993 were as shown in Figure 4.1, you might be tempted to conclude that the demand curve is *DD'*.

Unfortunately, things are not so simple. Price, as we saw in Chapter 1, is determined by both the demand and supply curves for this product if the market is competitive. Specifically, the equilibrium value of price is at the level where the demand and supply curves intersect. The important point to note is that the demand and supply curves for this product may have been different each year. Thus, as shown in Figure 4.2, the supply curve may have shifted (from $S_{91}$ in 1991 to $S_{92}$ in 1992 to $S_{93}$ in 1993), and the demand curve may have shifted (from $D_{91}$ in 1991 to $D_{92}$ in 1992 to $D_{93}$ in 1993). As indicated in Figure 4.2, *DD'* is not even close to being a good approximation to the demand curve for this product in any of these three years.

In the situation in Figure 4.2, if you were to conclude that *DD'* was the

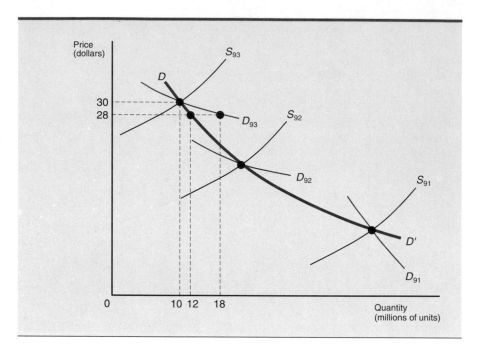

**FIGURE 4.2** *Estimated Demand Curve Contrasted with Actual Demand Curves* DD' is not at all similar to the actual demand curves.

demand curve, you would underestimate the price elasticity of demand for this product. In 1993, you would think that if price were lowered from $30 to $28, the quantity demanded would increase from 10 to 12 million units per year. In fact, as shown in Figure 4.2, such a price reduction would result in an increase of the quantity demanded to 18, not 12, million units per year. This is a mammoth error in anyone's book.

The point is that because we are not holding constant a variety of nonprice variables like consumer tastes, incomes, the prices of other goods, and advertising, we cannot be sure that the demand curve was fixed during the period when the measurements were made. If the demand curve was fixed, and if only the supply curve changed during the period, we could be confident that the plot of points in Figure 4.1 represented the demand curve. As shown in Figure 4.3, the shifts in the supply curve would trace out various points on the demand curve we want to measure.

How can we estimate a demand curve if it has not remained fixed in the past? There are many ways, some simple, some very complex. Econometric techniques recognize that price and quantity are related by both the supply curve and the demand curve, and that both of these curves shift in response to nonprice variables. Some basic econometric techniques, such as regression analysis, are presented later in this chapter; others are too complex to

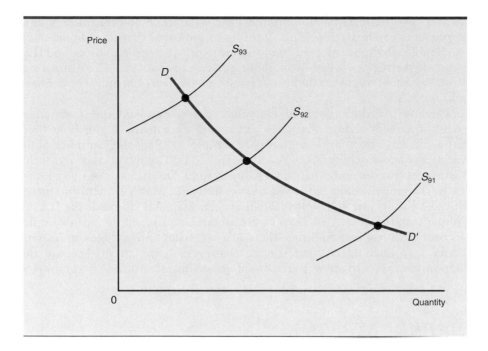

*FIGURE 4.3  Fixed Demand Curve and Shifting Supply Curve*   In this special case, *DD'* does represent the actual demand curve.

be taken up here.[1] Consumer interviews and market experiments are also widely used, as indicated in the next three sections.

## CONSUMER INTERVIEWS

To obtain information concerning the demand function for a particular product, firms frequently interview consumers and administer questionnaires concerning their buying habits, motives, and intentions. For example, a firm might ask a random sample of consumers how much more gasoline they would purchase if its price were reduced by 5 percent. Or a market researcher might ask a sample of consumers whether they liked a new type of perfume better than a leading existing brand, and if so, how much more they would be willing to pay for it (than for the existing brand).

Unfortunately, consumer surveys of this sort have many well-known limitations. The direct approach of simply asking people how much they would buy of a particular commodity at particular prices often does not seem to work very well. Frequently, the answers provided by consumers to

[1] See J. Johnston, *Econometric Methods*, 3d ed. (New York: McGraw-Hill, 1984); J. Kmenta, *Elements of Econometrics*, 2d ed. (New York: Macmillan, 1986); or E. Berndt, *The Practice of Econometrics* (Reading, Mass.: Addison-Wesley, 1991).

such a hypothetical question are not very accurate. However, more subtle approaches can be useful. Thus, interviews indicated that most buyers of a particular baby food selected it on their doctor's recommendation, and that most of them knew very little about prices of substitutes. This information, together with other data, suggested that the price elasticity of demand was quite low.[2]

Despite the limitations of consumer interviews and questionnaires, many managers believe that they can reveal a great deal about how their firms can serve the market better. For example, in 1986, the Campbell Soup Company's researchers contacted close to 110,000 people to talk about the taste, preparation, and nutritional value of food. On the basis of these interviews, Campbell changed the seasonings in five Le Menu dinners and introduced a line of low-salt soups (called Special Request). Some of the factors influencing the quality of survey results can be quite subtle. For example, according to research findings, there are sometimes advantages in respondents' keypunching answers, rather than verbalizing them, because the respondents tend to answer emotional questions more honestly this way.[3]

## MARKET EXPERIMENTS

Another method of estimating the demand curve for a particular commodity is to carry out direct market experiments. The idea is to vary the price of the product while attempting to keep other market conditions fairly stable (or to take changes in other market conditions into account). For example, a manufacturer of ink conducted an experiment some years ago to determine the price elasticity of demand for its product. They raised the price from 15 cents to 25 cents in four cities and found that demand was quite inelastic. Attempts were made to estimate the cross elasticity of demand with other brands as well.

Controlled laboratory experiments can sometimes be carried out. Consumers are given money and told to shop in a simulated store. The experimenter can vary the prices, packaging, and location of particular products, and see the effects on the consumers' purchasing decisions. While this technique is useful, it suffers from the fact that consumers participating in such an experiment know that their actions are being monitored. For that reason, the behavior may depart from what it normally would be.

Before carrying out a market experiment, you should weigh the costs against the benefits. Direct experimentation can be expensive or risky because customers may be lost and profits cut by the experiment. For example, if the price of a product is raised as part of an experiment, potential

---

[2] J. Dean, "Estimating the Price Elasticity of Demand," in E. Mansfield, ed., *Managerial Economics and Operations Research*, 4th ed. (New York: Norton, 1980).

[3] *New York Times*, November 8, 1987, p. 4F. Also, see W. Baumol, "The Empirical Determination of Demand Relationships," in E. Mansfield, ed., *Managerial Economics and Operations Research*, 5th ed. (New York: Norton, 1987).

buyers may be driven away. Also, since they are seldom really controlled experiments and since they are often of relatively brief duration and the number of observations is small, experiments often cannot produce all of the information that is needed. Nonetheless, market experiments can be of considerable value, as illustrated by the following actual case.

## L'EGGS: A MARKET EXPERIMENT

L'eggs Products, a subsidiary of the Hanes Corporation, markets L'eggs Pantyhose, the first major nationally branded and advertised hosiery product distributed through food and drug outlets. According to some estimates, it has been the largest-selling single brand in the hosiery industry. In 1973, Jack Ward, group product manager of the firm, was interested in determining the effect on sales of four temporary promotion alternatives: (1) a 40-cent price reduction for a package containing two pairs, (2) a 25-cent price reduction for a package containing two pairs, (3) a 20-cent price reduction per pair, and (4) a coupon mailed to homes worth 25 cents off if a pair was purchased.[4]

To test these four promotion alternatives, Jerry Clawson, director of marketing research, decided that each would be implemented in a carefully chosen test market, and the results would be compared with another market where no unusual promotion was carried out. Specifically, there was a 40-cent reduction (for two pairs) in Syracuse, New York, a 25-cent reduction (for two pairs) in Columbus, Ohio, a 20-cent reduction (for one pair) in Denver, and a 25-cent coupon in Cincinnati. The results in these markets were compared with those in Boise, Idaho, where no special promotion occurred.

According to the firm's sales research group, the results were as follows: "The 2 for 40¢-off promotion (Syracuse) was the most effective with a net short-term cumulative increase in sales of 53% felt over 6 weeks. The 20¢ price-off promotion (Denver) was the second most effective, with a net cumulative short-term increase of 20% felt over 8 weeks . . . . The 25¢ coupon promotion (Cincinnati) was the least effective promotion with a 3% short-term increase in sales felt over 8 weeks."[5]

This is an example of how firms go about obtaining information concerning their market demand functions. In this case, the firm's managers were interested in the effects of both the form and size of the price cut, and they were concerned only with a temporary price cut. In other cases, firms are interested in the effects of more long-term price changes or of changes in product characteristics or in advertising. But regardless of these differences, marketing research of this sort can play an important role in providing data for the estimation of demand functions.

[4] The material in this section is based on F. DeBruicker, J. Quelch, and S. Ward, *Cases in Consumer Behavior*, 2d ed. (Englewood Cliffs, N.J.: Prentice-Hall, 1986).

[5] Ibid., p. 335. For a discussion of the validity of these results, see ibid.

## REGRESSION ANALYSIS

Although consumer interviews and direct market experiments are important sources of information concerning demand functions, they are not used as often as regression analysis. Suppose that a firm's demand function has the following form:

$$Y = A + B_1X + B_2P + B_3I + B_4P_r, \qquad (4.1)$$

where $Y$ is the quantity demanded of the firm's product, $X$ is the selling expense (such as advertising) of the firm, $P$ is the price of its product, $I$ is the disposable income of consumers, and $P_r$ is the price of the competing product sold by its rival. What we want are estimates of the values of $A$, $B_1$, $B_2$, $B_3$, and $B_4$. Regression analysis enables us to obtain them, based on historical data concerning $Y$, $X$, $P$, $I$, and $P_r$.

In the rest of this chapter, we describe the nature and application of regression analysis, a statistical technique that can be used to estimate many types of economic relationships, not just demand functions. We begin with the simple case where the only factor influencing the quantity demanded is the firm's selling expense, and then turn to the more complicated (and realistic) case where the quantity demanded is affected by more than one factor, as it is in equation (4.1).

Regression analysis describes the way in which one variable is related to another. (As we will see later on in this chapter, regression techniques can handle more than two variables, but only two are considered at present.) Regression analysis derives an equation that can be used to estimate the unknown value of one variable on the basis of the known value of the other variable. For example, suppose that the Miller Pharmaceutical Company is scheduled to spend $4 million next year on selling expense (for promotion, advertising, and related marketing activities), and that it wants to estimate how much its next year's sales will be, based on the data in Table 4.1 regarding its sales and selling expense in the previous nine years. In this case, although the firm's selling expense next year is known, its next year's sales

TABLE 4.1 *Selling Expense and Sales, Miller Pharmaceutical Company, Sample of 9 Years*

| Selling expense (millions of dollars) | Sales (millions of units) |
|---|---|
| 1 | 4 |
| 2 | 6 |
| 4 | 8 |
| 8 | 14 |
| 6 | 12 |
| 5 | 10 |
| 8 | 16 |
| 9 | 16 |
| 7 | 12 |

are unknown. Regression analysis describes the way in which the firm's sales are related to its selling expense.

## SIMPLE REGRESSION MODEL

As you will recall from Chapter 1, a **model** is a simplified or idealized representation of the real world. In this section, we describe the model—that is, the set of simplifying assumptions—on which regression analysis is based. Let's begin by visualizing a population of all relevant pairs of observations of the independent and dependent variables. For instance, in the case of the Miller Pharmaceutical Company, we visualize a population of pairs of observations concerning sales and selling expense. This population would include all the levels of sales corresponding to all the levels of selling expense in the history of the firm.

The mean of a variable equals the sum of its values divided by their number. Thus, the mean of a variable that assumes four values, 3, 2, 1, 0, is $(3 + 2 + 1 + 0) \div 4$, or 1.5. Regression analysis assumes that *the mean value of Y, given the value of X, is a linear function of X*. In other words, the mean value of the dependent variable is assumed to be a linear function of the independent variable, the equation of this line being $A + BX$, as shown in Figure 4.4. This straight line is called the **population regression line** or the **true regression line.**

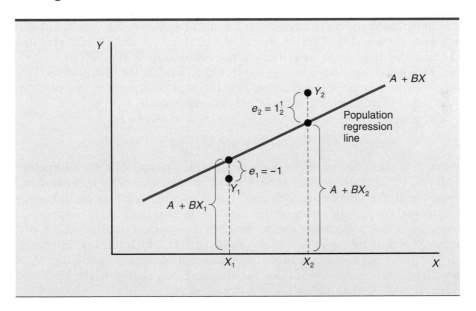

**FIGURE 4.4** *Regression Model*  The mean value of Y, given the value of X, falls on the population regression line.

Put differently, regression analysis assumes that

$$Y_i = A + BX_i + e_i,  \tag{4.2}$$

where $Y_i$ is the $i$th observed value of the dependent variable, and $X_i$ is the $i$th observed value of the independent variable. Essentially, $e_i$ is an **error term**, that is, a random amount that is added to $A + BX_i$ (or subtracted from it if $e_i$ is negative). Because of the presence of this error term, the observed values of $Y_i$ fall around the population regression line, not on it. Thus, as shown in Figure 4.4, if $e_1$ (the value of the error term for the first observation) is $-1$, $Y_1$ will lie 1 below the population regression line. And if $e_2$ (the value of the error term for the second observation) is $+1.50$, $Y_2$ will lie 1.50 above the population regression line. Regression analysis assumes that the values of $e_i$ are independent and that their mean value equals zero.[6]

Although the assumptions underlying regression analysis are unlikely to be met completely, they are close enough to the truth in a sufficiently large number of cases so that regression analysis is a powerful technique. Nonetheless, it is important to recognize at the start that if these assumptions are not at least approximately valid, the results of a regression analysis can be misleading.

## SAMPLE REGRESSION LINE

The purpose of a regression analysis is to obtain the mathematical equation for a line that describes the average relationship between the dependent and independent variable. This line is calculated from the sample observations and is called the **sample** or **estimated regression line**. It should not be confused with the population regression line discussed in the previous section. Whereas the population regression line is based on the entire population, the sample regression line is based only on the sample.

The general expression for the sample regression line is

$$\hat{Y} = a + bX,$$

where $\hat{Y}$ is the value of the dependent variable predicted by the regression line, and $a$ and $b$ are estimators of $A$ and $B$, respectively. (An estimator is a function of the sample observations that is used to estimate an unknown parameter. For example, the sample mean is an estimator that is often used to estimate the population mean.) Since this equation implies that $\hat{Y} = a$ when $X = 0$, it follows that $a$ is the value of $\hat{Y}$ at which the line intersects the $Y$ axis. Thus, $a$ is often called the $Y$ **intercept** of the regression line. And $b$, which clearly is the **slope** of the line, measures the change in the predicted value of $Y$ associated with a 1-unit increase in $X$.

---

[6] The values of $e_1$ and $e_2$ are independent if the probability distribution of $e_1$ does not depend on the value of $e_2$ and if the probability distribution of $e_2$ does not depend on the value of $e_1$. Regression analysis also assumes that the variability of the values of $e_i$ is the same, regardless of the value of $X$. Many of the tests described below assume too that the values of $e_i$ are normally distributed. For a description of the normal distribution, see Appendix B.

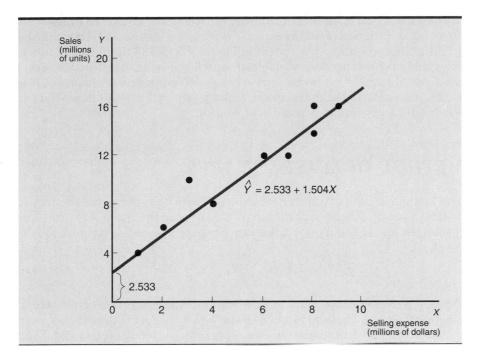

**FIGURE 4.5** **Sample Regression Line** This line is an estimate of the population regression line.

Figure 4.5 shows the estimated regression line for the data concerning sales and selling expense of the Miller Pharmaceutical Company. The equation for this regression line is

$$\hat{Y} = 2.533 + 1.504X,$$

where $\hat{Y}$ is sales in millions of units, and $X$ is selling expense in millions of dollars. What is 2.533? It is the value of $a$, the estimator of $A$. What is 1.504? It is the value of $b$, the estimator of $B$. For the moment, we are not interested in how this equation was determined; what we want to consider is how it should be interpreted.

At the outset, note the difference between $Y$ and $\hat{Y}$. Whereas $Y$ denotes an *observed* value of sales, $\hat{Y}$ denotes the *computed* or *estimated* value of sales, based on the regression line. For example, the first row of Table 4.1 shows that in the first year, the actual value of sales was 4 million units when selling expense was $1 million. Thus, $Y = 4.0$ millions of units when $X = 1$. In contrast, the regression line indicates that $\hat{Y} = 2.533 + 1.504(1)$, or 4.037 millions of units when $X = 1$. In other words, while the regression line predicts that sales will equal 4.037 millions of units when selling expense is $1 million, the actual sales under these circumstances (in the first year) was 4 million units.

It is essential to be able to identify and interpret the $Y$ intercept and slope of a regression line. What is the $Y$ intercept of the regression line in the case of the Miller Pharmaceutical Company? It is 2.533 millions of units. This means that if the firm's selling expense is zero, the estimated sales would be 2.533 millions of units. (As shown in Figure 4.5, 2.533 millions of units is the value of the dependent variable at which the regression line intersects the vertical axis.) What is the slope of the regression line in this case? It is 1.504. This means that the estimated sales go up by 1.504 millions of units when selling expense increases by $1 million.

## METHOD OF LEAST SQUARES

The method used to determine the values of $a$ and $b$ is the so-called method of least squares. Since the deviation of the $i$th observed value of Y from the regression line equals $Y_i - \hat{Y}_i$, the sum of these squared deviations equals

$$\sum_{i=1}^{n} (Y_i - \hat{Y}_i)^2 = \sum_{i=1}^{n} (Y_i - a - bX_i)^2, \qquad (4.3)$$

where $n$ is the sample size.[7] Using the minimization technique presented in Chapter 2, we can find the values of $a$ and $b$ that minimize the expression in equation (4.3) by differentiating this expression with respect to $a$ and $b$ and by setting these partial derivatives equal to zero:

$$\frac{\partial \sum_{i=1}^{n} (Y_i - \hat{Y}_i)^2}{\partial a} = -2 \sum_{i=1}^{n} (Y_i - a - bX_i) = 0 \qquad (4.4)$$

$$\frac{\partial \sum_{i=1}^{n} (Y_i - \hat{Y}_i)^2}{\partial b} = -2 \sum_{i=1}^{n} X_i (Y_i - a - bX_i) = 0. \qquad (4.5)$$

Solving equations (4.4) and (4.5) simultaneously, and letting $\overline{X}$ equal the mean value of $X$ in the sample and $\overline{Y}$ equal the mean value of Y, we find that

$$b = \frac{\sum_{i=1}^{n} (X_i - \overline{X})(Y_i - \overline{Y})}{\sum_{i=1}^{n} (X_i - \overline{X})^2}, \qquad (4.6)$$

$$a = \overline{Y} - b\overline{X}. \qquad (4.7)$$

---

[7] As pointed out in Chapter 1, $\Sigma$ is the mathematical summation sign. What does $\Sigma X_i$ mean? It means that the numbers to the right of the summation sign (that is, the values of $X_i$) should be summed from the lower limit on $i$ (which is given below the $\Sigma$ sign) to the upper limit on $i$ (which is given above the $\Sigma$ sign). Thus,

$$\sum_{i=1}^{n} X_i$$

means the same thing as $X_1 + X_2 + \cdots + X_n$.

The value of $b$ in equation (4.6) is often called the **estimated regression coefficient**.

From a computational point of view, it frequently is easier to use a somewhat different formula for $b$ than the one given in equation (4.6). This alternate formula, which yields the same answer as equation (4.6), is

$$b = \frac{n \sum_{i=1}^{n} X_i Y_i - \left( \sum_{i=1}^{n} X_i \right) \left( \sum_{i=1}^{n} Y_i \right)}{n \sum_{i=1}^{n} X_i^2 - \left( \sum_{i=1}^{n} X_i \right)^2}.$$

In the case of the Miller Pharmaceutical Company, Table 4.2 shows the calculation of $\Sigma X_i Y_i$, $\Sigma X_i^2$, $\Sigma X_i$, and $\Sigma Y_i$. Based on these calculations,

$$b = \frac{9(638) - (50)(98)}{9(340) - 50^2} = 1.504.$$

Thus, the value of $b$, the least-squares estimator of $B$, is 1.504, which is the result given in the previous section. In other words, an increase in selling expense of \$1 million results in an increase in estimated sales of about 1.504 millions of units.

Having calculated $b$, we can readily determine the value of $a$, the least-squares estimator of $A$. According to equation (4.7),

$$a = \overline{Y} - b\overline{X},$$

where $\overline{Y}$ is the mean of the values of $Y$, and $\overline{X}$ is the mean of the values of $X$. Since, as shown in Table 4.2, $\overline{Y} = 10.889$ and $\overline{X} = 5.556$, it follows that

$$a = 10.889 - 1.504(5.556)$$
$$= 2.533.$$

---

TABLE 4.2  *Computation of $\Sigma X_i$, $\Sigma Y_i$, $\Sigma X_i^2$, $\Sigma Y_i^2$, and $\Sigma X_i Y_i$*

| | $X_i$ | $Y_i$ | $X_i^2$ | $Y_i^2$ | $X_i Y_i$ |
|---|---|---|---|---|---|
| | 1 | 4 | 1 | 16 | 4 |
| | 2 | 6 | 4 | 36 | 12 |
| | 4 | 8 | 16 | 64 | 32 |
| | 8 | 14 | 64 | 196 | 112 |
| | 6 | 12 | 36 | 144 | 72 |
| | 5 | 10 | 25 | 100 | 50 |
| | 8 | 16 | 64 | 256 | 128 |
| | 9 | 16 | 81 | 256 | 144 |
| | 7 | 12 | 49 | 144 | 84 |
| Total | 50 | 98 | 340 | 1,212 | 638 |

$$\overline{X} = \frac{50}{9} = 5.556$$

$$\overline{Y} = \frac{98}{9} = 10.889$$

Thus, the least-squares estimate of $A$ is 2.533 millions of units, which is the result given in the previous section.

Having obtained $a$ and $b$, it is a simple matter to specify the average relationship in the sample between sales and selling expense for the Miller Pharmaceutical Company. This relationship is

$$\hat{Y} = 2.533 + 1.504X, \tag{4.8}$$

where $\hat{Y}$ is measured in millions of units, and $X$ is measured in millions of dollars. As we know, this line is often called the sample regression line, or the regression of $Y$ on $X$. It is the line that we presented in the previous section and that we plotted in Figure 4.5. Now we have seen how this line is derived. (However, a computer usually does the calculations.)

To illustrate how a regression line of this sort can be used, suppose that the managers of the firm want to predict the firm's sales if they decide to devote \$4 million to selling expense. Using equation (4.8), they would predict that its sales would be

$$2.533 + 1.504(4) = 8.549. \tag{4.9}$$

Since sales are measured in millions of units, this means that sales would be expected to be 8.549 millions of units.

## COEFFICIENT OF DETERMINATION

Once the regression line has been calculated, one wants to know how well this line fits the data. There can be huge differences in how well a regression line fits a set of data, as shown in Figure 4.6. Clearly, the regression line in panel F of Figure 4.6 provides a much better fit than the regression line in panel B of the same figure. How can we measure how well a regression line fits the data?

The most commonly used measure of the goodness of fit of a regression line is the coefficient of determination. For present purposes, it is not necessary to know the formula for the coefficient of determination because it is seldom calculated by hand. It is a particular item—often designated by $R^2$ or $R$-sq—on a computer printout, as we shall see in the section after next.

The value of the coefficient of determination varies between 0 and 1. *The closer it is to 1, the better the fit; the closer it is to 0, the poorer the fit.* In the case of the Miller Pharmaceutical Company, the coefficient of determination between sales and selling expense is .97, which indicates a very good fit. To get a feel for what a particular value of the coefficient of determination means, look at the six panels of Figure 4.6. Panel A shows that, if the coefficient of determination is 0, there is no relationship at all between the independent and dependent variables. Panel B shows that, if the coefficient of determination is .2, the regression line fits the data rather poorly. Panel C shows that, if it is .4, the regression line fits better, but not very well. Panel D shows that, if it is .6, the fit is reasonably good. Panel E shows

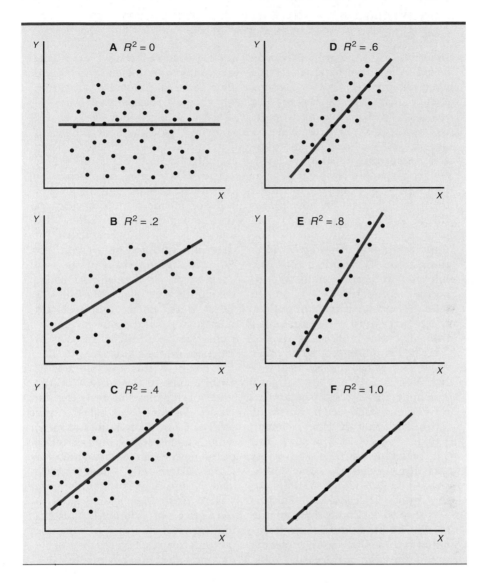

*FIGURE 4.6 Six Regression Lines: Coefficient of Determination\* Equals 0, 0.2, 0.4, 0.6, 0.8, and 1.0*

---

\* When there is only one independent variable, the coefficient of determination is often designated by $r^2$, rather than $R^2$, but computer printouts generally use $R^2$, regardless of the number of independent variables. We use $R^2$ here, even though there is only one independent variable. See note 8.

## HOW THE JAPANESE MOTORCYCLE MAKERS USED THE COEFFICIENT OF DETERMINATION

In late 1982, Harley-Davidson asked the International Trade Commission (ITC), a federal agency that investigates possible injuries to U.S. firms and workers by imports, for relief from Japanese imports of heavyweight motorcycles. According to Harley-Davidson, the Japanese were selling their motorcycles at prices too low for it to meet. Based on Section 201 of the 1974 Trade Act, the ITC can impose tariffs or quotas on imported goods to provide "additional time to permit a seriously injured domestic industry to become competitive. . . ." But to receive such tariff or quota relief, the industry must demonstrate that the injuries it suffers are due to increased imports, not some other cause such as bad management or a recession.

Harley-Davidson's petition to the ITC was contested by the major Japanese motorcycle makers: Honda, Kawasaki, Suzuki, and Yamaha. One of their arguments was that general economic conditions, not Japanese imports, were the principal cause of Harley-Davidson's declining share of the market. In other words, they attributed Harley-Davidson's problems to the recession of the early 1980s. They pointed out that heavyweight motorcycles, which cost about $7,000, were a "big-ticket luxury consumer product" and that their sales would be expected to fall in a recession.

To back up this argument, John Reilly of ICF, Inc., the Japanese firms' chief economic consultant, calculated a regression where Harley-Davidson's sales were the dependent variable and the level of blue-collar employment (a measure of general economic conditions) was the independent variable. He showed that the coefficient of determination was about .73. Then he calculated a regression where Harley-Davidson's sales were the dependent variable and the level of sales of Japanese motorcycles was the independent variable. He showed that the coefficient of determination was only about .22. From this comparison of the two coefficients of determination, he concluded that Harley-Davidson's sales were much more closely related to general economic conditions than to the level of sales of Japanese motorcycles.

Of course, this analysis tells us nothing about the effects of the price of Japanese motorcycles on Harley-Davidson's sales and profits. From many points of view, what was needed was an estimate of the market demand function for Harley-Davidson's motorcycles. Such an analysis would have related Harley-Davidson's sales to the price of Harley-Davidson's motorcycles, the price of Japanese motorcycles, the level of disposable income, and other variables discussed in Chapter 3. In any event, despite the evidence cited, the Japanese motorcycle manufacturers did not prevail. On the contrary, the ITC supported Harley-Davidson's petition, and on April 1, 1983 President Ronald Reagan imposed a substantial tariff (almost 50 percent) on imported (large) motorcycles.*

---

* See "Revving Up for Relief: Harley-Davidson at the ITC," a case in the study guide accompanying this textbook. For further discussion, see J. Gomez-Ibanez and J. Kalt, *Cases in Microeconomics* (Englewood Cliffs, N.J.: Prentice-Hall, 1990); and P. Reid, *Well Made in America* (New York: McGraw-Hill, 1990).

CONSULTANT'S CORNER

## PRICE AND MARKET SHARE FOR A NEW ELECTRICAL DRIVE*

A leading manufacturer of electrical products developed a new type of electrical drive. When the design engineering for this machine was finished, the firm's managers began to make long-range plans concerning the marketing of this product. By means of field surveys and through the analysis of published information, the firm's market research personnel estimated that about 10,000 electrical drives of this general sort would be sold per year. The share of the total market that this firm's new product would capture depended on its price. According to the market research department, the relationship between price and market share was as follows:

| Price | Market share |
|-------|--------------|
| $ 800 | 11.0 |
| 900 | 10.2 |
| 1,000 | 9.2 |
| 1,100 | 8.4 |
| 1,200 | 7.5 |
| 1,300 | 6.6 |
| 1,400 | 5.6 |

The firm's managers wanted advice in setting the price for their new drive, and, to help determine the optimal price, they wanted a simple equation expressing the annual quantity demanded of the new product as a function of its price. They also wanted whatever information could readily be provided concerning the reliability of this equation. In particular, they were interested in whether they could safely use this equation to estimate the quantity demanded if price were set at $1,500 or $1,600.

Prepare a brief report supplying the information requested. (Note that the figures on market share in the table are expressed in percentage points. Thus, if the price of this firm's new product is set at $800, it will capture 11.0 percent of the market for electrical drives of this general sort, according to the market research department.)

* This section is based on an actual case, although the numbers and situation are disguised somewhat.

that, if it is .8, the fit is good. Finally, panel F shows that, if it is 1.0, the fit is perfect.[8] (A fuller discussion of the coefficient of determination is provided in the appendix to this chapter.)

[8] If one is doing the calculations by hand, a convenient formula for the coefficient of determination is

$$r^2 = \frac{\left[ n \sum_{i=1}^{n} X_i Y_i - \left( \sum_{i=1}^{n} X_i \right) \left( \sum_{i=1}^{n} Y_i \right) \right]^2}{\left[ n \sum_{i=1}^{n} X_i^2 - \left( \sum_{i=1}^{n} X_i \right)^2 \right] \left[ n \sum_{i=1}^{n} Y_i^2 - \left( \sum_{i=1}^{n} Y_i \right)^2 \right]}.$$

Table 4.2 contains the quantities to be inserted in this formula.

Note too that the square root of $r^2$, called the **correlation coefficient,** is also used to measure how well a simple regression equation fits the data. (The sign of the square root is the same as that of $b$.)

As pointed out in note * of Figure 4.6, computer printouts generally refer to the coefficient of determination as $R^2$, although statisticians often call it $r^2$ when there is only one independent variable.

CONCEPTS IN CONTEXT

## COLOR BALANCE AND SHELF-LIFE PERFORMANCE OF POLAROID FILM

Regression analysis is important in many aspects of managerial economics, not just in estimating demand functions. For example, this technique helps the Polaroid Corporation, a leading manufacturer of cameras and film, to supply film at the peak of its usefulness. An extremely important consideration to Polaroid is how well films maintain their sensitivity, and whether they provide satisfactory photographic results and for how long. Information of this sort, together with data concerning average elapsed time between the purchase and utilization of film, enables Polaroid to make manufacturing adjustments to help consumers get good performance from Polaroid film.

One important characteristic of film is color balance—its ability to produce color. To see the effects of film age on color balance, Polaroid took 14 separate samples at monthly intervals, up to 13 months after manufacture. For each sample, the change in blue balance was measured. As shown in the graph below, the color balance becomes bluer (that is, "cooler," not as "warm") as the film ages.

Using the techniques described in this chapter, Polaroid estimated the regression line:

$$\hat{Y} = 8.194 + 6.756X,$$

where $Y$ is the change in blue balance, and $X$ is the age (in months) of the film. The coefficient of determination was 0.966, which indicates a close fit to the data.

According to Polaroid officials,

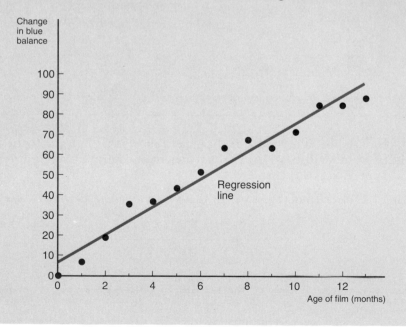

this application of regression analysis has been important. Together with data regarding consumer purchase and use patterns, it enabled "Polaroid to manufacture film that will have shifted those characteristics which determine picture quality to their optimum setting by the time the film is being used. In essence, Polaroid has the information to compensate in its manufacturing process for crucial alterations in film performance that happen as a result of the aging process."[*]

[*] D. Anderson, D. Sweeney, and T. Williams, *Statistics for Business and Economics*, 3d ed. (St. Paul, Minn.: West, 1987), p. 523.

# MULTIPLE REGRESSION

In previous sections of this chapter, we discussed regression techniques in the case where there is only one independent variable. In practical applications of regression techniques, it frequently is necessary and desirable to include two or more independent variables. Now we will extend our treatment of regression to the case in which there is more than one independent variable.

Whereas a **simple regression** includes only one independent variable, a **multiple regression** includes two or more independent variables. Multiple regressions ordinarily are carried out on computers with the aid of statistical software packages like Minitab, SAS, or SPSS. Thus, there is no reason for you to learn how to do them by hand. The first step in multiple regression analysis is to identify the independent variables, and to specify the mathematical form of the equation relating the mean value of the dependent variable to these independent variables.

In the case of the Miller Pharmaceutical Company, suppose that the firm's executives feel that its sales depend on its price, as well on its selling expense. More specifically, they assume that

$$Y_i = A + B_1 X_i + B_2 P_i + e_i, \qquad (4.10)$$

where $X_i$ is the selling expense (in millions of dollars) of the firm during the $i$th year, and $P_i$ is the price (in dollars) of the firm's product during the $i$th year (measured as a deviation from \$10, the current price). Of course, $B_2$ is assumed to be negative. This is a different model from that in equation (4.2). Here it is assumed that $Y_i$—the firm's sales in the $i$th year—depends on two independent variables, not one. Of course, there is no reason why more independent variables cannot be added, so long as data are available concerning their values, and so long as there is good reason to expect them to affect $Y_i$. But to keep matters simple, we assume that the firm's executives believe that only selling expense and price should be included as independent variables.[9]

The object of multiple regression analysis is to estimate the unknown constants $A$, $B_1$, and $B_2$ in equation (4.10). Just as in the case of simple regression, these constants are estimated by finding the value of each that minimizes the sum of the squared deviations of the observed values of the dependent variable from the values of the dependent variable predicted by the regression equation. Suppose that $a$ is an estimator of $A$, $b_1$ is an estimator of $B_1$, and $b_2$ is an estimator of $B_2$. Then the value of the dependent variable $\hat{Y}_i$ predicted by the estimated regression equation is

$$\hat{Y}_i = a + b_1 X_i + b_2 P_i,$$

and the deviation of this predicted value from the actual value of the dependent variable is

$$Y_i - \hat{Y}_i = Y_i - a - b_1 X_i - b_2 P_i.$$

Thus, if these deviations are squared and summed up, the result is

$$\sum_{i=1}^{n} (Y_i - \hat{Y}_i)^2 = \sum_{i=1}^{n} (Y_i - a - b_1 X_i - b_2 P_i)^2, \qquad (4.11)$$

where $n$ is the number of observations in the sample. As pointed out above, we choose the values of $a$, $b_1$, and $b_2$ that minimize the expression in equation (4.11). These estimates are called least-squares estimates, as in the case of simple regression.

Computer programs, described in the following section, are available to calculate these least-squares estimates. Based on the data in Table 4.3, the computer output shows that $b_1 = 1.76$, $b_2 = -0.35$, and $a = 2.53$. Consequently, the estimated regression equation is

$$Y_i = 2.53 + 1.76X_i - 0.35P_i. \qquad (4.12)$$

TABLE 4.3   Sales, Selling Expense, and Price, Miller Pharmaceutical Company, Sample of Nine Years

| Selling expense (millions of dollars) | Sales (millions of units) | Price (less $10) |
|---|---|---|
| 2 | 6 | 0 |
| 1 | 4 | 1 |
| 8 | 16 | 2 |
| 5 | 10 | 3 |
| 6 | 12 | 4 |
| 4 | 8 | 5 |
| 7 | 12 | 6 |
| 9 | 16 | 7 |
| 8 | 14 | 8 |

[9] As in the case of simple regression, it is assumed that the mean value of $e_i$ is zero, and that the values of $e_i$ are statistically independent. (Recall note 6.)

The estimated value of $B_1$ is 1.76, as contrasted with our earlier estimate of $B$, which was 1.50. In other words, a \$1 million increase in selling expense results in an increase in estimated sales of 1.76 millions of units, as contrasted with 1.50 millions of units in the simple regression in equation (4.8). The reason these estimates differ is that the present estimate of the effect of selling expense on sales holds constant the price, whereas the earlier estimate did not hold this factor constant. Since this factor affects sales, the earlier estimate is likely to be a biased estimate of the effect of selling expense on sales.[10]

## SOFTWARE PACKAGES AND COMPUTER PRINTOUTS

With few exceptions, regression analyses are carried out on computers, not by hand. Thus it is important that you know how to interpret computer printouts showing the results of regression calculations. Because there is a wide variety of "canned" programs for calculating regressions, there is no single format or list of items that are printed out. However, the various kinds of printouts are sufficiently similar so that it is worthwhile looking at two illustrations—Minitab and SAS—in some detail.

Figure 4.7 shows the Minitab printout from the multiple regression of the Miller Pharmaceutical Company's sales (designated as C1) on its selling expense (C2) and price (C3). According to this printout, the regression equation is

$$C1 = 2.529 + 1.758C2 - 0.352C3,$$

which differs slightly from Equation (4.12) due to rounding errors. The column headed "Coef" shows the estimated regression coefficient of each independent variable (called a "Predictor" on the printout). The intercept of the regression is the top figure in this vertical column (the figure in the horizontal row where the "Predictor" is "Constant"). The coefficient of determination (called R-sq) is shown in the middle of the printout. For a multiple regression, the coefficient of determination is often called the *multiple coefficient of determination.*[11]

Figure 4.8 shows the SAS printout for the same regression. To find the

---

[10] Of course, this regression is only supposed to be appropriate when $X_i$ and $P_i$ vary in a certain limited range. If $P_i$ is large and $X_i$ is small, the regression would predict a negative value of sales, which obviously is inadmissible. But as long as the regression is not used to make predictions for values of $X_i$ and $P_i$ outside the range of the data given in Table 4.3, this is no problem. For simplicity, we assume in equation (4.10) that the effect of price on the mean value of sales (holding selling expense constant) can be regarded as linear in the relevant range. Alternatively, we could have assumed that it was quadratic, or the constant-elasticity demand function discussed in Chapter 3 might have been used.

[11] The positive square root of the multiple coefficient of determination is called the multiple correlation coefficient and is denoted by $R$. It too is sometimes used to measure how well a multiple regression equation fits the data.

The *unadjusted* multiple coefficient of determination—R-sq in Figure 4.7—can never decrease as another independent variable is added; a related measure without this property is the *adjusted* multiple coefficient of determination—R-sq(adj.) in Figure 4.7. The latter is often denoted by $\overline{R}^2$.

```
MTB > regress c1 on 2 predictors in c2 and c3

The regression equation is
C1 = 2.53 + 1.76 C2 - 0.352 C3

Predictor          Coef      Stdev      t-ratio         P
Constant         2.5294     0.2884         8.77     0.000
C2               1.75805    0.06937       25.34     0.000
C3              -0.35187    0.07064       -4.98     0.002

s = 0.3702      R-sq = 99.4%      R-sq (adj) = 99.2%

Analysis of Variance

SOURCE           DF          SS          MS          F        P
Regression        2     144.067      72.033     525.72    0.000
Error             6       0.822       0.137
Total             8     144.889

SOURCE           DF      SEQ SS
C2                1     140.667
C3                1       3.399
```

**FIGURE 4.7** *Minitab Printout of Results of Multiple Regression*

```
Dependent Variable: C1

Analysis of Variance

                     Sum of      Mean
Source       DF      Squares     Square    F Value    Prob > F

Model         2    144.06678   72.03339    525.718      0.0001
Error         6      0.82211    0.13702
C Total       8    144.88889

   Root MSE     0.37016    R-Square   0.9943
   Dep Mean    10.88889    Adj R-sq   0.9924
   C.V.         3.39944

Parameter Estimates

              Parameter     Standard      T for H0:
Variable DF   Estimate         Error    Parameter = 0   Prob > |T

INTERCEP  1    2.529431    0.28842968         8.770      0.000
C2        1    1.758049    0.06937127        25.343      0.000
C3        1   -0.351870    0.07064425        -4.981      0.002
```

**FIGURE 4.8** *SAS Printout of Results of Multiple Regression*

## HOW GOOD ARE *WARD'S* PROJECTIONS OF AUTO OUTPUT?

The automobile industry and its suppliers, as well as other industries and government agencies, try in a variety of ways to forecast auto output in the United States. Each month, *Ward's Automotive Reports* asks eight U.S. automakers to state their domestic production plans for the next three to eight months. The figure below shows actual domestic auto production and *Ward's* projections made at the beginning of each quarter. The average error is about a half million cars per year, or about 6 percent.

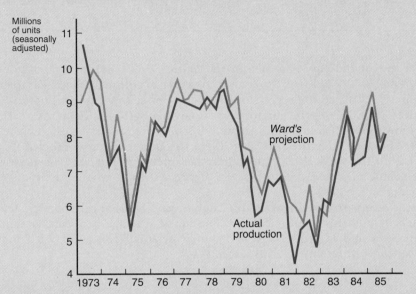

*Source:* **Various issues of *Ward's Automotive Reports* (1973–85); and unpublished data from the Bureau of Economic Analysis.**

To obtain a more precise estimate of the relationship between *Ward's* projections and actual output, Ethan Harris regressed actual output *(Y)* on *Ward's* projection *(X)* and the error in *Ward's* projection during the previous quarter *(E)*, the result being

$$Y = 0.275 + 0.909X + .277E.$$

The multiple coefficient of determination equals 0.838.

(a) If *Ward's* projection is 1 million cars higher in one quarter than in another, would you expect actual output to be 1 million cars higher? Why or why not? (b) If *Ward's* projection was 100,000 cars too high in the previous quarter, is it likely that actual output will be higher than it would if the projection had been 100,000 cars too low in the previous quarter? (c) Does the regression provide a good or poor fit to the data?

*Solution* (a) No. According to the equation, if $X$ increases by 1 million, $Y$ would be expected to increase by .909 times 1 million, or 909,000 (if $E$ remains the same). (b) Under these circumstances, it is likely that actual output will be higher than it would if the projection had been 100,000 cars too low in the previous quarter. To see this, note that the regression coefficient of $E$ in the regression equation is positive. Thus, increases in $E$ tend to be associated with increases in $Y$. (c) The fact that the multiple coefficient of determination is about .8 indicates that the fit is good (about like that in panel E of Figure 4.6).*

* For further discussion, see E. Harris, "Forecasting Automobile Output," *Federal Reserve Bank of New York Quarterly Review* (Winter 1985–86), reprinted in E. Mansfield, ed., *Managerial Economics and Operations Research*, 5th ed. (New York: Norton, 1987).

intercept of the equation, obtain the figure (2.529431) in the horizontal row labeled "INTERCEP" that is in the vertical column called "Parameter Estimate." To find the regression coefficient of selling expense, obtain the figure (1.758049) in the horizontal row labeled "C2" that is in the vertical column called "Parameter Estimate." To find the regression coefficient of price, obtain the figure (−0.351870) in the horizontal row labeled "C3" that is in the vertical column called "Parameter Estimate." The multiple coefficient of determination is the figure (0.9943) to the right of "R-square."

It is also worth noting that, although most advanced econometric work generally requires a statistical or econometric package, you can do simple regression and multiple regression on a personal computer with many spreadsheet programs, such as Lotus 1-2-3.

## INTERPRETING THE COMPUTER PRINTOUT

The following additional statistics are also of considerable importance: (1) the standard error of estimate, (2) the $F$-statistic, and (3) the $t$-statistics. Each is discussed briefly below. For more detailed discussions of each, see any business statistics textbook.[12]

*The Standard Error of Estimate.* A measure that is often used to indicate the accuracy of a regression model is the standard error of estimate, which is *a measure of the amount of scatter of individual observations about the regression line.* The standard error of estimate is denoted by s in the Minitab printout in Figure 4.7 and by ROOT MSE in the SAS printout in Figure 4.8. A comparison of these printouts shows that in the Miller Pharmaceuti-

[12] For example, E. Mansfield, *Statistics for Business and Economics*, 4th ed. (New York: Norton, 1991).

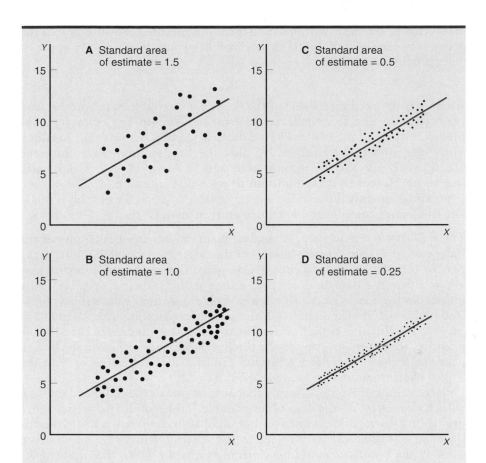

*FIGURE 4.9   Four Regression Lines: Standard Error of Estimate Equals 1.5, 1.0, 0.5, and 0.25*

cal multiple regression, the standard error is about 0.37 million units of sales. Of course, the answer will always be the same, no matter which package we use.

To illustrate what the standard error of estimate measures, consider Figure 4.9. In panel A, the standard error of estimate is 1.5, which is much higher than in panel D, where it is 0.25. This is reflected in the fact that there is a much greater amount of scatter of the points around the regression line in panel A than in panel D. As pointed out above, what the standard error of estimate measures is the amount of such scatter. Clearly, the amount of scatter decreases as we move from panel A to panel B to panel C to panel D. Similarly, the standard error of estimate decreases as we move from panel A to panel B to panel C to panel D.

The standard error of estimate is useful in constructing prediction intervals—that is, intervals within which there is a specified probability that the dependent variable will lie. If this probability is set at .95, a very approximate prediction interval is

$$\hat{Y} \pm 2s_e, \tag{4.13}$$

where $\hat{Y}$ is the predicted value of the dependent variable based on the sample regression, and $s_e$ is the standard error of estimate. For example, if the predicted value of the Miller Pharmaceutical Company's sales is 11 million units, the probability is about .95 that the firm's sales will be between 10.26 ($= 11 - 2 \times 0.37$) million units and 11.74 ($= 11 + 2 \times 0.37$) million units. However, it is important to note that equation (4.13) is a good approximation only if the independent variable is close to its mean; if this is not true, more complicated formulas must be used instead.[13]

*The F-Statistic.* Frequently the analyst wants to know whether any of the independent variables really influences the dependent variable. Thus, in the case of the Miller Pharmaceutical Company, the marketing director may ask whether the data indicate that either selling expense or price really influences the firm's sales. To answer such a question, one utilizes the *F*-statistic, which is also included in the computer printout. The value of *F* is provided in the fifth-from-bottom horizontal row of figures in the Minitab printout (see Figure 4.7) and in the top horizontal row of figures in the SAS printout (Figure 4.8). Both printouts indicate that the value of *F* in the Miller Pharmaceutical case equals about 525.72.

Large values of *F* tend to imply that at least one of the independent variables has an effect on the dependent variable. Tables of the *F* distribution, a probability distribution named (or initialed) after the famous British statistician R. A. Fisher, are used to determine *the probability that an observed value of the F-statistic could have arisen by chance, given that none of the independent variables has any effect on the dependent variable.* (See Appendix B.) This probability too is shown in the computer printout. It is denoted by "p" (immediately to the right of F) in the Minitab printout, and by "Prob > F" (immediately to the right of F VALUE) in the SAS printout. The value of this probability is .0001 (SAS) or .000 (Minitab); the difference is due to rounding.

[13] The formula for the standard error of estimate is

$$s_e = \sqrt{\sum_{i=1}^{n} (Y_i - \hat{Y}_i)^2 \div (n - k - 1)}$$

where $k$ is the number of independent variables.

If the error term is normally distributed (see Appendix B for a description of the normal distribution), the exact prediction interval (with .95 probability) is

$$\hat{Y} \pm t_{.025}\, s_e \sqrt{\frac{n+1}{n} + \frac{(X^* - \overline{X})^2}{\sum_{i=1}^{n} X_i^2 - \left(\sum_{i=1}^{n} X_i\right)^2 / n}}$$

where $t_{.025}$ is the value of a variable with the *t*-distribution with $(n-2)$ degrees of freedom that is exceeded with probability of .025, $X^*$ is the value of the independent variable, and $n$ is the sample size. (The *t*-distribution is taken up in Appendix B.) This assumes that there is only one independent variable. For further discussion, see ibid.

Having this probability in hand, it is easy to answer the marketing director's question. Clearly, the probability is extremely small—only about 1 in 10,000—that one could have obtained such a strong relationship between the dependent and independent variables sheerly by chance. Thus, the evidence certainly suggests that selling expense or price (or both) really influences the firm's sales.

*The* t-*statistic.* Managers and analysts often are interested in whether or not a particular independent variable influences the dependent variable. For example, the president of the Miller Pharmaceutical Company may want to determine whether the amount allocated to selling expense really affects the firm's sales. As we know from equation (4.12), the least-squares estimate of $B_1$ is 1.76, which suggests that selling expense has an effect on sales. But this least-squares estimate will vary from one sample to another, and by chance it may be positive even if the true value of $B_1$ is zero.

To test whether the true value of $B_1$ is zero, we must look at the t-statistic of $B_1$, which is presented in the printout. For Minitab, recall that $B_1$ is the regression coefficient of C2, since selling expense is denoted by C2. Thus, to find the t-statistic for $B_1$, we must locate the horizontal row of figures in the printout where the "Predictor" is C2, and obtain the figure in the vertical column called "t-ratio." If SAS is used, find the horizontal row of figures where the "Variable" is C2, and obtain the figure in the vertical column called "T for H0: Parameter = 0." If the error terms in the regression (that is, $e_i$) are normally distributed, the t-statistic has a well-known probability distribution—the t-distribution (see Appendix B).

All other things equal, the bigger the value of the t-statistic (in absolute terms), the smaller the probability that the true value of the regression coefficient in question really is zero. Based on the t-distribution, it is possible to calculate *the probability, if the true value of the regression coefficient is zero, that the* t-*statistic will be as large (in absolute terms) as we observe.* This probability too is presented in the computer printout. For both Minitab and SAS, this probability is immediately to the right of the t-statistic. For Minitab, it is in the vertical column labeled "p"; for SAS, it is in the vertical column labeled "Prob > |T|." Regardless of whether Minitab or SAS is used, this probability is shown to be about .0001. (See Figures 4.7 and 4.8.)

Given this probability, we can readily answer the question put forth by the president of the Miller Pharmaceutical Company. Recall that the president wanted to know whether the amount allocated to selling expense really affects the firm's sales. Given the results obtained in the previous paragraph, it seems extremely likely that the amount allocated to selling expense really does affect sales. After all, according to the previous paragraph, the probability is only about 1 in 10,000 that chance alone would have resulted in as large a t-statistic (in absolute terms) as we found, based on the firm's previous experience.[14]

[14] Note that this is a *two-tailed test* of the hypothesis that selling expense has no effect on sales. That is, it is a test of this hypothesis against the alternative hypothesis that the true regression coefficient of selling expense is either positive or negative. In many cases, a *one-tailed test*—for example, where the alternative hypothesis states that the true regression coefficient is positive only—may be more appropriate.

## MULTICOLLINEARITY

One important problem that can arise in multiple regression studies is **multicollinearity,** which is a situation in which two or more independent variables are very highly correlated. In the case of the Miller Pharmaceutical Company, suppose that there had been a perfect linear relationship in the past between the firm's selling expense and its price. In a case of this sort, it is impossible to estimate the regression coefficients of both independent variables ($X$ and $P$) because the data provide no information concerning the effect of one independent variable, holding the other independent variable constant. All that can be observed is the effect of both independent variables together, given that they both move together in the way they have in previous years.

Regression analysis estimates the effect of each independent variable by seeing how much effect this one independent variable has on the dependent variable when other independent variables are held constant. If two independent variables move together in a rigid, lockstep fashion, there is no way to tell how much effect each has separately; all that we can observe is the effect of both combined. If there is good reason to believe that the independent variables will continue to move in lockstep in the future as they have in the past, multicollinearity does not prevent us from using regression analysis to predict the dependent variable. Since the two independent variables are perfectly correlated, one of them in effect stands for both; and we therefore need use only one in the regression analysis. However, if the independent variables cannot be counted on to continue to move in lockstep, this procedure is dangerous, since it ignores the effect of the excluded independent variable.

In reality, you seldom encounter cases where independent variables are perfectly correlated, but you often encounter cases where independent variables are so highly correlated that, although it is possible to estimate the regression coefficient of each variable, these regression coefficients cannot be estimated at all accurately. To cope with such situations, it sometimes is

---

Frequently, a manager would like to obtain an interval estimate for the true value of a regression coefficient. In other words, he or she wants an interval that has a particular probability of including the true value of this regression coefficient. To find an interval that has a probability equal to $(1 - \alpha)$ of including this true value, you can calculate the following:

$$b_1 \pm t_{\alpha/2}s_{b1}, \tag{4.14}$$

where $s_{b1}$ is the standard error of $b_1$ (in the horizontal row labeled C2 and the vertical column labeled "Stdev" in the Minitab printout, or in the horizontal row labeled C2 and the vertical column labeled "Standard Error" in the SAS printout) and where $t_{\alpha/2}$ is the $\alpha/2$ point on the $t$-distribution with $(n - k - 1)$ degrees of freedom. (See Appendix B.) If $\alpha$ is set equal to .05, you obtain an interval that has a 95 percent probability of including $B_1$. Thus, in the case of the Miller Pharmaceutical Company, since $B_1 = 1.758$, $s_{b1} = 0.069$, and $t_{.025} = 2.447$, it follows that a 95 percent confidence interval for $B_1$ is

$$1.758 \pm 2.447(0.069),$$

or 1.589 to 1.927. For further discussion, see any business statistics textbook.

possible to alter the independent variables in such a way as to reduce multi-collinearity. Suppose that a managerial economist wants to estimate a regression equation where the quantity demanded per year of a certain good is the dependent variable, and the average price of this good and disposable income of American consumers are the independent variables. If disposable income is measured in money terms (that is, without adjustment for changes in the price level), there may be a high correlation between the independent variables. But if disposable income is measured in real terms (that is, with adjustment for changes in the price level), this correlation may be reduced considerably. Thus, the managerial economist may decide to measure disposable income in real rather than money terms in order to reduce multicollinearity.

If techniques of this sort cannot reduce multicollinearity, there may be no alternative but to acquire new data that do not contain the high correlation among the independent variables. Whether you (or your board of directors) like it or not, there may be no way to estimate accurately the regression coefficient of a particular independent variable that is very highly correlated with some other independent variable.

## *SERIAL CORRELATION*

Besides multicollinearity, another important problem that can occur in regression analysis is that the error terms (the values of $e_i$) are not independent; instead, they are serially correlated. For example, Figure 4.10 shows a case where if the error term in one period is positive, the error term in the next period is almost always positive. Similarly, if the error term in one period is negative, the error term in the next period almost always is negative. In such a situation, we say that the errors are serially correlated (or autocorrelated, which is another term for the same thing).[15] Because this violates the assumptions underlying regression analysis, it is important that we be able to detect its occurrence. (Recall that regression analysis assumes that the values of $e_i$ are independent.)

To see whether serial correlation is present in the error terms in a regression, we can use the Durbin-Watson test. Let $\hat{e}_i$ be the difference between $Y_i$ and $\hat{Y}_i$, the value of $Y_i$ predicted by the sample regression. To apply the Durbin-Watson test, we (or in most cases, the computer) must calculate

$$d = \frac{\sum\limits_{i=2}^{n} (\hat{e}_i - \hat{e}_{i-1})^2}{\sum\limits_{i=1}^{n} \hat{e}_i^2}. \tag{4.15}$$

---

[15] This is a case of positive serial correlation. (It is the sort of situation frequently encountered in managerial economics.) If the error term in one period tends to be positive (negative) if the error term in the previous period is negative (positive), this is a case of negative serial correlation. More is said about this below.

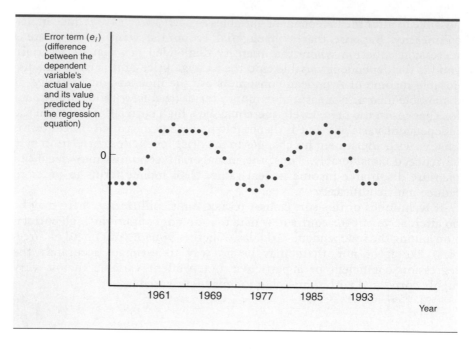

**FIGURE 4.10** *Serial Correlation of Error Terms* If the error term in one year is positive, the error term in the next year is almost always positive. If the error term in one year is negative, the error term in the next year is almost always negative.

Durbin and Watson have provided tables that show whether $d$ is so high or so low that the hypothesis that there is no serial correlation should be rejected. (Note that $d$ is often called the Durbin-Watson statistic.)

Suppose we want to test this hypothesis against the alternative hypothesis that there is **positive** serial correlation. (Positive serial correlation would mean that $e_i$ is directly related to $e_{i-1}$, as in Figure 4.10.) If so, we should reject the hypothesis of no serial correlation if $d < d_L$ and accept this hypothesis if $d > d_u$. If $d_L \leq d \leq d_u$, the test is inconclusive. The values of $d_L$ and $d_u$ are shown in Appendix Table 7. (Note that these values depend on the sample size $n$ and on $k$, the number of independent variables in the regression.) On the other hand, suppose that the alternative hypothesis is that there is **negative** serial correlation. (Negative serial correlation would mean that $e_i$ is inversely related to $e_{i-1}$.) If so, we should reject the hypothesis of no serial correlation if $d > 4 - d_L$ and accept this hypothesis if $d < 4 - d_u$. If $4 - d_u < d \leq 4 - d_L$, the test is inconclusive.[16]

---

[16] For a two-tailed test of both positive and negative serial correlation, reject the hypothesis of no serial correlation if $d < d_L$ or if $d > 4 - d_L$, and accept this hypothesis if $d_u < d < 4 - d_u$. Otherwise, the test is inconclusive. For a two-tailed test, the significance level is double the significance level shown in Appendix Table 7.

## HOW FED ECONOMISTS FORECAST AUTO OUTPUT

Since purchases by the auto industry account for more than half of the rubber and lead consumed in this country, as well as a major portion of the steel, aluminum, and a variety of other materials, it is obvious that many firms and government agencies, as well as the auto firms themselves, are interested in forecasting auto output. In 1985, the Federal Reserve Bank of New York published an article describing how the regression techniques described in this chapter have been used for this purpose. According to the author, Ethan Harris, the quantity of autos produced quarterly depends on five variables: (1) real disposable income, (2) the ratio of retail auto inventories to sales, (3) the average price of new cars (relative to the overall consumer price index), (4) the price level for nonauto durable goods, and (5) the prime rate (the interest rate banks charge their best customers).

The regression results, based on data from the first quarter of 1973 to the third quarter of 1985, are shown on page 148. The probability that the *t*-statistic for each of the regression coefficients will be as large (in absolute terms) as it is here, if the true value of the regression coefficient is zero, is less than .01, except for the case of the nonauto price.

The value of the adjusted multiple coefficient of determination is .862, the standard error of estimate is 532, and the Durbin-Watson statistic (*d*) is 2.26. According to Ethan Harris, this regression equation has predicted auto output with a mean (absolute) error of about 6.9 percent.

(a) Would you expect the regression coefficient of the inventory-sales ratio to be negative? If so, why? (b) Can we be reasonably sure that the true value of the regression coefficient of the inventory-sales ratio is nonzero? Why or why not? (c) Is there evidence of positive serial correlation of the error terms?

| Variable | Regression coefficient | t-statistic |
|---|---|---|
| Constant | −22,302 | −4.5 |
| Disposable income | 12.9 | 6.6 |
| Prime rate | −97.8 | −3.2 |
| Inventory-sales ratio | −19.9 | −6.1 |
| Auto price | 230 | 5.0 |
| Nonauto price | 6.0 | 2.1 |

(d) Can we use this regression as an estimate of the demand curve for autos? Why or why not?

*Solution* (a) Yes. If inventories are large relative to sales, one would expect auto firms to produce less than they would if inventories were small. (b) Yes. According to the discussion above, the probability that the $t$-statistic for the regression coefficient of the inventory-sales ratio would be as great as 6.1 (in absolute terms) would be less than .01, if the true regression coefficient were zero. Thus, if this true regression coefficient were zero, it is exceedingly unlikely that the $t$-statistic (in absolute terms) would equal its observed value or more. (c) No. Since the value of $n$ is approximately 50 and $k = 5$, Appendix Table 7 shows that $d_L = 1.26$ and $d_u = 1.69$ if the significance level equals .025. The observed value of the Durbin-Watson statistic (2.26) is greater than $d_u$ (1.69), which means that we should accept the hypothesis that there is no positive serial correlation. (d) No. One important indication that this is true is the fact that the regression coefficient of the auto price is positive. Clearly, this regression equation cannot be used as an estimate of the demand curve for autos.

One way to deal with the problem of serial correlation, if it exists, is to take first differences of all of the independent and dependent variables in the regression. For example, in the case of the Miller Pharmaceutical Company, we might use the change in sales relative to the previous year (rather than the level of sales) as the dependent variable. And the change in selling expense relative to the previous year (rather than the level of selling expense) and the change in price relative to the previous year (rather than the level of price) might be used as the independent variables in the regression.[17]

---

[17] The use of first differences, while useful in some cases, is not always appropriate. For further discussion, see J. Johnston, *Econometric Methods.*

It is also important to avoid specification errors, which result when one or more significant explanatory variables are not included in the regression. If specification errors arise, the estimated regression coefficients may be biased, and the regression equation may not predict very well. Also, problems can arise if the independent variables in a regression contain substantial measurement errors, since the regression coefficients of these variables often tend to be biased toward zero.

## FURTHER ANALYSIS OF THE RESIDUALS

In the previous section, we used $\hat{e}_i$—the difference between the actual value of $Y_i$ and its value predicted by the sample regression—to test for serial correlation. Since it is a measure of the extent to which $Y_i$ *cannot* be explained by the regression, $\hat{e}_i$ is often called the **residual** for the $i$th observation. Now we describe additional ways in which the residuals—that is, the values of $\hat{e}_i$—can be used to test whether the assumptions underlying regression analysis are met. We begin by plotting the value of each residual against the value of the independent variable. (For simplicity, we suppose that there is only one independent variable.) That is, we plot $\hat{e}_i$ against $X_i$, which is the independent variable.

Suppose that the plot is as shown in Figure 4.11. As you can see, the values of the residuals are much more variable when $X_i$ is large than when it is small. In other words, the variation in $\hat{e}_i$ increases as $X_i$ increases. Since regression analysis assumes that *the variation in the error terms is the same, regardless of the value of the independent variable,* the plot in Figure 4.11 indicates that this assumption is violated. Two ways to remedy this situation are to use a weighted least-squares regression or to change the

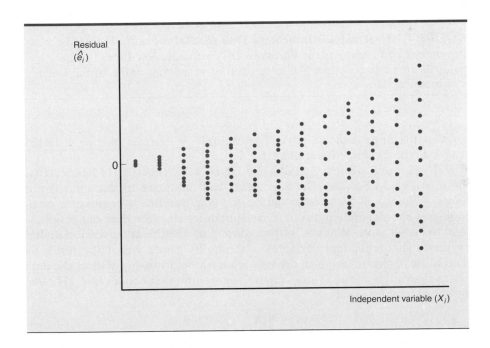

**FIGURE 4.11** *Residuals Indicating That the Variation in the Error Terms Is Not Constant* As you can see, the residuals vary less when $X$ is small than when it is large.

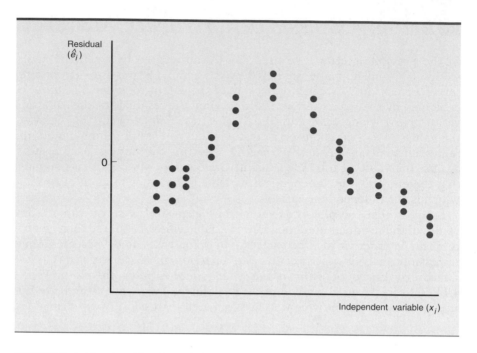

**FIGURE 4.12** *Residuals Indicating That the Relationship between the Dependent and Independent Variables Is Nonlinear, Not Linear* The residuals are negative when X is very small or very large, and positive when X is of medium size.

form of the dependent variable. For example, we might use log $Y$ rather than $Y$ as the dependent variable.[18]

If the plot of $\hat{e}_i$ against $X_i$ looks like Figure 4.12, this is an indication that the relationship between the dependent and independent variables is not linear. When $X$ is very low and very high, the linear regression **over-estimates** the dependent variable, as shown by the fact that the residuals tend to be negative. When $X$ is of medium size, the linear regression **under-estimates** the dependent variable, as shown by the fact that the residuals tend to be positive. It appears that a quadratic relationship will fit the data better than a linear one. Thus, rather than assume that equation (4.2) holds, we should assume that

$$Y_i = A + B_1 X_i - B_2 X_i^2 + e_i.$$

Using the multiple regression techniques described above, the values of $A$, $B_1$, and $B_2$ can be estimated.

[18] For further details, see ibid.

# THE DEMAND FUNCTION FOR CIGARETTES: A CASE STUDY

Having discussed regression techniques in some detail, let's take up an actual case where they were used to estimate a product's demand function. Many groups in the United States, including tobacco firms like Phillip Morris and RJR Nabisco and government agencies like the Federal Trade Commission, have a great interest in the demand function for cigarettes. Using annual data for 1947 to 1982, an estimate was made in 1984 of the demand function for cigarettes in the United States. The constant-elasticity demand function (discussed in Chapter 3) was regarded as a more appropriate mathematical form than a linear equation. Thus, the logarithm of the quantity demanded was the dependent variable, and the logarithms of price, income, advertising, and the price of a substitute product (cigars) were (some of) the independent variables.[19]

Specifically, the resulting regression equation was[20]

$$\log Q = -2.55 - 0.29 \log P + 0.08 \log A - 0.09 \log I$$
$$\phantom{\log Q = -2.55} (-2.07) \qquad (4.48) \qquad (-1.00)$$

$$+ 0.14 \log P_c - 0.10C - 0.06\,D, \qquad\qquad (4.16)$$
$$\phantom{+} (0.92) \qquad (-5.19)\ (-3.60)$$

where $Q$ is annual cigarette consumption, $P$ is the average price of cigarettes, $A$ is total cigarette advertising, $I$ is per capita income, $P_c$ is the average price of cigars, $C$ is a variable that equals 1 if the year under consideration is after the issuance of the 1953 American Cancer Society report linking cigarette smoking with cancer and 0 otherwise, and $D$ is a variable that equals 1 if the year under consideration is during the period (1968 to 1970) when the Federal Communications Commission required that one antismoking commercial be aired for every four prosmoking advertisements and 0 otherwise.

The number in parentheses under each regression coefficient is its $t$-statistic. The value of $\overline{R}^2$—the adjusted multiple coefficient of determination —for this regression is .91, which indicates a good fit. The Durbin-Watson statistic is 1.54, which provides no evidence of serial correlation. According to the computer printout, the probability is less than .05 that the $t$-statistic for the regression coefficient of $\log P$ would be as large (in absolute terms) as it is if its true value was zero. The same is true for the $t$-statistics of $\log A$, $C$, and $D$. Thus, we can be reasonably confident that these variables ($\log P$, $\log A$, $C$, and $D$) really have an effect on cigarette consumption.

---

[19] Recall from equation (3.25) on page 102 that if we take logarithms of the dependent and independent variables, the demand function is linear, if the constant-elasticity demand function is used.

[20] Actually, equation (4.16) has been simplified in various ways. Some independent variables have been omitted to make the results more tractable for pedagogical purposes. Note too that the logarithms are natural logarithms. For the full results, see R. Porter, "The Impact of Government Policy on the U.S. Cigarette Industry," in P. Ippolito and D. Scheffman, eds., *Empirical Approaches to Consumer Protection Economics* (Washington, D.C.: Federal Trade Commission, 1984).

To interpret this estimated demand function for cigarettes, the first thing to note is that the regression coefficients are all estimated elasticities. To see this, turn back to page 102 and look at equation (3.25). This equation shows that for a constant-elasticity demand function, the coefficient of log $P$ is the price elasticity of demand (denoted there by $b_1$) and the coefficient of log $I$ is the income elasticity of demand (denoted there by $b_2$). Thus, based on equation (4.16), the estimated price elasticity of demand for cigarettes is 0.29, and the estimated income elasticity of demand for cigarettes is $-0.09$. By the same token, the cross elasticity of demand between cigarettes and cigars is 0.14, and the advertising elasticity of demand for cigarettes is 0.08.

This estimated demand function is of great importance to tobacco executives. As emphasized in the previous chapter, managers must be vitally interested in the price elasticity, income elasticity, cross elasticity, and advertising elasticity of their product. Between 1980 and 1990, the cigarette industry raised its prices over 50 percent. "Like clockwork, the industry raises prices twice a year, in the November–December period and in May–June,"[21] according to Patrick Jackman of the Bureau of Labor Statistics. Given the fact that the price elasticity of demand is only about 0.29, this is understandable. After all, increases in price do not discourage cigarette consumption very much.

The results also provide an interesting estimate of the effect on cigarette consumption of the evidence that cigarettes may cause cancer. The fact that the regression coefficient of $C$ is negative indicates that, holding the other independent variables constant, cigarette consumption was significantly lower after the American Cancer Society report on this topic than before its publication.

The negative regression coefficient of $D$ is also interesting. What it means is that, when other independent variables are held constant, cigarette consumption was significantly lower during the period when the Federal Communications Commission required antismoking commercials than during other periods. To tobacco executives, this result is very useful because it indicates how vulnerable their sales are to such antismoking ads.

Finally, as we have stressed repeatedly in this chapter, one of the principal uses of estimated demand functions is for forecasting. Suppose you have a pretty good idea of next year's values of $P$, $A$, $I$, $P_c$, $C$, and $D$. To forecast cigarette consumption next year, all you have to do is plug these values into the above regression equation.[22] Of course, this does not mean that forecasting is a simple business, or that this is the only way to make such forecasts. On the contrary, forecasting is a very difficult and exacting activity, and there are a number of forecasting techniques, all of which are in common use. In the next chapter, we will take them up in detail.

---

[21] *New York Times*, July 30, 1991.

[22] As pointed out in note 20, equation (4.16) is abridged for pedagogical reasons. What should be used for forecasting is, of course, the full equation of the sort reported in *ibid.*

# SUMMARY

1. An identification problem may occur if price in various periods is plotted against quantity demanded, and the resulting relationship is used to estimate the demand curve. Because nonprice variables are not held constant, the demand curve may have shifted over time. Nonetheless, sophisticated econometric methods may be used to estimate the demand function. Also, market experiments and consumer interviews may be of value. For example, firms sometimes vary price from one city or region to another, and see what the effects are on quantity demanded. An actual illustration of this sort was the evaluation of the four promotion alternatives by L'eggs Products.

2. Regression analysis is useful in estimating demand functions and other economic relationships. The regression line shows the average relationship between the dependent variable and the independent variable. The method of least squares is the standard technique used to fit a regression line to a set of data. If the regression line is $\hat{Y} = a + bX$, and if $a$ and $b$ are calculated by least squares,

$$b = \frac{\sum_{i=1}^{n} (X_i - \overline{X})(Y_i - \overline{Y})}{\sum_{i=1}^{n} (X_i - \overline{X})^2}$$

$$a = \overline{Y} - b\overline{X}.$$

This value of $b$ is often called the estimated regression coefficient.

3. Whereas a simple regression includes only one independent variable, a multiple regression includes more than one independent variable. An advantage of multiple regression over a simple regression is that you frequently can predict the dependent variable more accurately if more than one independent variable is used. Also, if the dependent variable is influenced by more than one independent variable, a simple regression of the dependent variable on a single independent variable may result in a biased estimate of the effect of this independent variable on the dependent variable.

4. The first step in multiple regression analysis is to identify the independent variables, and then to specify the mathematical form of the equation relating the mean value of the dependent variable to the independent variables. For example, if $Y$ is the dependent variable and $X$ and $P$ are identified as the independent variables, one might specify that

$$Y_i = A + B_1 X_i + B_2 P_i + e_i,$$

where $e_i$ is an error term. To estimate $B_1$ and $B_2$ (called the true regression coefficients of $X$ and $P$) as well as $A$ (the intercept of this true regression equation), we use the values that minimize the sum of squared deviations of $Y_i$ from $\hat{Y}_i$, the value of the dependent variable predicted by the estimated regression equation.

5. In a simple regression, the coefficient of determination is used to measure the closeness of fit of the regression line. In a multiple regression, the multiple coefficient of determination, $R^2$, plays the same role. The closer $R^2$ is to zero, the poorer the fit; the closer it is to 1, the better the fit.

6. The $F$-statistic can be used to test whether any of the independent variables has an effect on the dependent variable. The standard error of estimate can help to indicate how well a regression model can predict the dependent variable. The $t$-statistic for the regression coefficient of each independent variable can be used to test whether this independent variable has any effect on the dependent variable. Computer printouts show the probability that the $t$-statistic would be as big (in absolute terms) as we have observed, given that this independent variable has no effect on the dependent variable.

7. A difficult problem that can occur in multiple regression is multicollinearity, a situation where two or more of the independent variables are highly correlated. If multicollinearity exists, it may be impossible to estimate accurately the effect of particular independent variables on the dependent variable. Another frequently encountered problem arises when the error terms in a regression are serially correlated. The Durbin-Watson test can be carried out to determine whether this problem exists. Plots of the residuals can help to detect cases where the variation of the error terms is not constant or where the relationship is nonlinear, not linear.

8. Despite the difficulties cited above, regression analysis is useful in estimating demand functions. As an illustration, an actual estimate of the demand function for cigarettes was described in some detail.

## PROBLEMS

1. The Klein Corporation's marketing department, using regression analysis, estimates the firm's demand function, the result being

$$Q = -104 - 2.1P + 3.2I + 1.5A + 1.6Z,$$

$$R^2 = .89 \qquad \text{Standard error of estimate} = 108,$$

where $Q$ is the quantity demanded of the firm's product (in tons), $P$ is the price of the firm's product (in dollars per ton), $I$ is per capita income (in dollars), $A$ is the firm's advertising expenditure (in thousands of dollars), and $Z$ is the price (in dollars) of a competing product. The regression is based on 200 observations.

(a) According to the computer printout, the probability is .005 that the $t$-statistic for the regression coefficient of $A$ would be as large (in absolute terms) as it is in this case, if in fact $A$ had no effect on $Q$. Interpret this result.

(b) If $I = 5,000$, $A = 20$, and $Z = 1,000$, what is the Klein Corporation's demand curve?

(c) If $P = 500$ (and the conditions in part [b] hold), estimate the quantity demanded of the Klein Corporation's product.

(d) How well does this regression equation fit the data?

2. Since the Hawkins Company's costs (other than advertising) are essentially all fixed costs, it wants to maximize its total revenue (net of advertising expenses). According to a regression analysis (based on 124 observations) carried out by a consultant hired by the Hawkins Company,

$$Q = -23 - 4.1P + 4.2I + 3.1A,$$

where $Q$ is the quantity demanded of the firm's product (in dozens), $P$ is the price of the firm's product (in dollars per dozen), $I$ is per capita income (in dollars), and $A$ is advertising expenditure (in dollars).

(a) If the price of the product is $10 per dozen, should the firm increase its advertising?

(b) If the advertising budget is fixed at $10,000, and per capita income equals $8,000, what is the firm's marginal revenue curve?

(c) If the advertising budget is fixed at $10,000, and per capita income equals $8,000, what price should the Hawkins Company charge?

3. The 1980 sales and profits of seven steel companies were as follows:

| Firm | (Billions of dollars) Sales | Profit |
|------|------|------|
| Armco | 5.7 | 0.27 |
| Bethlehem | 6.7 | 0.12 |
| Bundy | 0.2 | 0.00 |
| Carpenter | 0.6 | 0.04 |
| Republic | 3.8 | 0.05 |
| U.S. Steel (now USX) | 12.5 | 0.46 |
| Westran | 0.5 | 0.00 |

(a) Calculate the sample regression line, where profit is the dependent variable and sales is the independent variable.

(b) Estimate the 1980 average profit of a steel firm with sales of $2 billion then.

(c) Can this regression line be used to predict a steel firm's profit in 1998? Explain.

4. The Cherry Manufacturing Company's chief engineer examines a random sample of 10 spot welds of steel. In each case, the shear strength of the weld and the diameter of the weld are determined, the results being as follows:

| Shear strength (pounds) | Weld diameter (thousandths of an inch) |
|---|---|
| 680 | 190 |
| 800 | 200 |
| 780 | 209 |
| 885 | 215 |
| 975 | 215 |
| 1,025 | 215 |
| 1,100 | 230 |
| 1,030 | 250 |
| 1,175 | 265 |
| 1,300 | 250 |

(a) Does the relationship between these two variables seem to be direct or inverse? Does this accord with common sense? Why or why not? Does the relationship seem to be linear?

(b) Calculate the least-squares regression of shear strength on weld diameter.

(c) Plot the regression line. Use this regression line to predict the average shear strength of a weld 1/5 inch in diameter. Use the regression line to predict the average shear strength of a weld 1/4 inch in diameter.

5. The Kramer Corporation's marketing manager calculates a regression where the quantity demanded of the firm's product (designated as C1) is the dependent variable and the price of the product (designated as C2) and consumers' disposable income (designated as C3) are independent variables. The Minitab printout for this regression is shown below:

```
MTB > regress c1 on 2 predictors in c2 and c3
The regression equation is
C1 = 40.8 − 1.02 C2 + 0.00667 C3
```

| Predictor | Coef | Stdev | t-ratio | p |
|---|---|---|---|---|
| Constant | 40.833 | 1.112 | 36.74 | 0.000 |
| C2 | −1.02500 | 0.06807 | −15.06 | 0.000 |
| C3 | 0.006667 | 0.005558 | 1.20 | 0.244 |

$s = 1.361$    R-sq $= 91.6\%$    R-sq (adj) $= 90.8\%$

Analysis of Variance

| SOURCE | DF | SS | MS | F | p |
|---|---|---|---|---|---|
| Regression | 2 | 422.92 | 211.46 | 114.11 | 0.000 |
| Error | 21 | 38.92 | 1.85 | | |
| Total | 23 | 461.83 | | | |

| SOURCE | DF | SEQ SS |
|---|---|---|
| C2 | 1 | 420.25 |
| C3 | 1 | 2.67 |

(a) What is the intercept of the regression?

(b) What is the estimated regression coefficient of the product's price?

(c) What is the estimated regression coefficient of disposable income?

(d) What is the multiple coefficient of determination?

(e) What is the standard error of estimate?

(f) What is the probability that the observed value of the $F$-statistic could have arisen by chance, given that neither of the independent variables has any effect on the dependent variable?

(g) What is the probability, if the true value of the regression coefficient of price is zero, that the $t$-statistic will be as large (in absolute terms) as we observe?

(h) What is the probability, if the true value of the regression coefficient of disposable income is zero, that the $t$-statistic will be as large (in absolute terms) as we observe?

(i) Describe briefly what this regression means.

6. Railroad executives must understand how the costs incurred in a freight yard are related to the output of the yard. The two most important services performed by a yard are switching and delivery, and it seems reasonable to use the number of cuts switched and the number of cars delivered during a particular period as a measure of output. (A **cut** is a group of cars that rolls as a unit onto the same classification track; it is often used as a unit of switching output.) A study[23] of one of the nation's largest railroads assumed that

$$C_i = A + B_1 S_i + B_2 D_i + e_i,$$

where $C_i$ is the cost incurred in this freight yard on the $i$th day, $S_i$ is the number of cuts switched in this yard on the $i$th day, $D_i$ is the number of cars delivered in this yard on the $i$th day, and $e_i$ is an error term. Data were obtained regarding $C_i$, $S_i$, and $D_i$ for 61 days. Based on the procedures described in this chapter, these data were used to obtain estimates of $A$, $B_1$, and $B_2$. The resulting regression equation was

$$\hat{C}_i = 4,914 + 0.42 S_i + 2.44 D_i,$$

where $\hat{C}_1$ is the cost (in dollars) predicted by the regression equation for the $i$th day.

(a) If you were asked to evaluate this study, what steps would you take to determine whether the principal assumptions underlying regression analysis were met?

(b) If you were satisfied that the underlying assumptions were met, of what use might the above regression equation be to the railroad? Be specific.

(c) Before using the above regression equation, what additional statistics would you like to have? Why?

---

[23] For a much more detailed account of this study, see E. Mansfield and H. Wein, "A Managerial Application of a Cost Function by a Railroad," a case in the study guide accompanying this textbook.

(d) If the Durbin-Watson statistic equals 2.11, is there evidence of serial correlation in the residuals?

7. Mary Palmquist, a Wall Street securities analyst, wants to determine the relationship between the nation's gross national product (GNP) and the profits (after taxes) of the General Electric Company. She obtains the following data concerning each variable:

| Year | Gross national product (billions of dollars) | General Electric's profits (millions of dollars) |
|------|-------------------|----------------------|
| 1965 | 688 | 355 |
| 1966 | 753 | 339 |
| 1967 | 796 | 361 |
| 1968 | 868 | 357 |
| 1969 | 936 | 278 |
| 1970 | 982 | 363 |
| 1971 | 1,063 | 510 |
| 1972 | 1,171 | 573 |
| 1973 | 1,306 | 661 |
| 1974 | 1,407 | 705 |
| 1975 | 1,529 | 688 |
| 1976 | 1,706 | 931 |

(a) What are the least-squares estimates of the intercept and slope of the true regression line, where GE's profits are the dependent variable and GNP is the independent variable?

(b) On the average, what effect does a $1 increase in gross national product seem to have on the profits of GE?

(c) If Ms. Palmquist feels that next year's GNP will be $2 trillion, what forecast of GE's profits will she make on the basis of the regression?

(d) What is the coefficient of determination between the nation's gross national product and GE's profits?

(e) Do the results obtained in previous parts of this problem prove that changes in GE's profits are caused by changes in the gross national product? Can we be sure that GE's profit is a linear function of the GNP? What other kinds of functions might be as good or better?

(f) If you were the financial analyst, would you feel that this regression line was an adequate model to forecast GE's profits? Why or why not?

8. In the manufacture of cloth, the weft packages should not disintegrate unduly during weaving. A direct measure of the tendency to disintegrate exists, but it is very laborious and uneconomical to carry out. In addition, there are indirect measures based on laboratory tests. The Brockway Textile Company would like to determine the extent to which one of these indirect measures is correlated with the direct measure. If the correlation is high enough, the firm believes that it may be able to use the indirect measure instead of the direct measure.

An experiment was carried out in which both the direct and indirect measures of the tendency to disintegrate were calculated for 18 lots of packages. The results were as shown below:

| Lot | Measure | |
| --- | Direct | Indirect |
| 1 | 31 | 6.2 |
| 2 | 31 | 6.2 |
| 3 | 21 | 10.1 |
| 4 | 21 | 8.4 |
| 5 | 57 | 2.9 |
| 6 | 80 | 2.9 |
| 7 | 35 | 7.4 |
| 8 | 10 | 7.3 |
| 9 | 0 | 11.1 |
| 10 | 0 | 10.7 |
| 11 | 35 | 4.1 |
| 12 | 63 | 3.5 |
| 13 | 10 | 5.0 |
| 14 | 51 | 4.5 |
| 15 | 24 | 9.5 |
| 16 | 15 | 8.5 |
| 17 | 80 | 2.6 |
| 18 | 90 | 2.9 |

(a) What is the coefficient of determination between the two measures?

(b) What is the linear regression line you would use to predict the value of the direct measure on the basis of knowledge of the indirect measure?

(c) Based on your findings, write a brief report indicating the factors to be weighed in deciding whether to substitute the indirect measure for the direct measure.

9. The Kingston Company hires a consultant to estimate the demand function for its product. Using regression analysis, the consultant estimates the demand function to be

$$\log Q = 2.01 - 0.148 \log P + 0.258 \log Z,$$

where $Q$ is the quantity demanded (in tons) of Kingston's product, $P$ is the price (in dollars per ton) of Kingston's product, and $Z$ is the price (in dollars per ton) of a rival product.

(a) Calculate the price elasticity of demand for Kingston's product.

(b) Calculate the cross elasticity of demand between Kingston's product and the rival product.

(c) According to the consultant, $\overline{R}^2 = .98$ and the standard error of estimate is .001. If the number of observations is 94, comment on the goodness of fit of the regression.

10. During the 1960s, the Boston and Maine Railroad conducted an experiment in which it reduced fares by about 28 percent for approximately a year in order to estimate the price elasticity of demand. This large fare reduction resulted in essentially no change in the railroad's revenues.
    (a) What problems exist in carrying out an experiment of this sort?
    (b) Taken at face value, what seemed to be the price elasticity of demand?

11. Because of a shift in consumer tastes, the market demand curve for high-quality red wine has shifted steadily to the right. If the market supply curve has remained fixed (and is upward sloping to the right), there has been an increase over time in both the price of such wine and in the quantity sold.
    (a) If one were to plot price against quantity sold, would the resulting relationship approximate the market demand curve?
    (b) If not, what would this relationship approximate?

12. The Brennan Company uses regression analysis to obtain the following estimate of the demand function for its product:

$$\log Q = 2 - 1.2 \log P + 1.5 \log I,$$

where $Q$ is quantity demanded, $P$ is price, and $I$ is consumers' disposable income.
    (a) Brennan's president is considering a 5 percent price reduction. He argues that these results indicate that it will result in a 6 percent increase in the number of units sold by the firm. Do you agree? Why or why not?
    (b) The firm's treasurer points out that, according to the computer printout, the probability that the $t$-statistic of $\log P$ would be as large (in absolute value) as it is, given that $\log P$ has no real effect on $\log Q$, is about .5. He says that the estimate of the price elasticity is unreliable. Do you agree? Why or why not?
    (c) How can the firm obtain a more accurate estimate of the price elasticity of demand?

# APPENDIX: THE COEFFICIENT OF DETERMINATION AND THE CONCEPT OF EXPLAINED VARIATION

In this appendix, we provide a fuller explanation of what the coefficient of determination is and how it can be interpreted. To begin with, we must discuss the concept of **variation,** which refers to a sum of squared deviations. The total variation in the dependent variable $Y$ equals

$$\sum_{i=1}^{n} (Y_i - \overline{Y})^2. \tag{4.17}$$

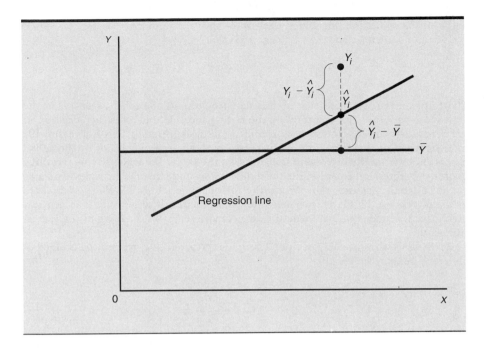

**FIGURE 4.13** *Division of* $(Y_i - \overline{Y})$ *into Two Parts:* $(Y_i - \hat{Y}_i)$ *and* $(\hat{Y}_i - \overline{Y})$
This division is carried out to measure how well the regression line fits
the data.

In other words, the total variation equals the sum of the squared deviations of $Y$
from its mean.

To measure how well a regression line fits the data, we divide the total variation
in the dependent variable into two parts: (1) the variation that *can* be explained by
the regression line; and (2) the variation that *cannot* be explained by the regression
line. To divide the total variation in this way, we must note that for the $i$th observation,

$$(Y_i - \overline{Y}) = (Y_i - \hat{Y}_i) + (\hat{Y}_i - \overline{Y}), \qquad (4.18)$$

where $\hat{Y}_i$ is the value of $Y_i$ that would be predicted on the basis of the regression line.
In other words, as shown in Figure 4.13, the discrepancy between $Y_i$ and the mean
value of $Y$ can be split into two parts: the discrepancy between $Y_i$ and the point on
the regression line directly below (or above) $Y_i$ and the discrepancy between the

[24] To derive this result, we square both sides of equation (4.18) and sum the result over all values of $i$.
We find that

$$\sum_{i=1}^{n}(Y_i - \overline{Y})^2 = \sum_{i=1}^{n}[(Y_i - \hat{Y}_i) + (\hat{Y}_i - \overline{Y})]^2$$

$$= \sum_{i=1}^{n}(Y_i - \hat{Y}_i)^2 + \sum_{i=1}^{n}(\hat{Y}_i - \overline{Y})^2 + 2\sum_{i=1}^{n}(Y_i - \hat{Y}_i)(\hat{Y}_i - \overline{Y}).$$

The last term on the right-hand side equals zero, so the equation at the top of p. 162 follows.

point on the regression line directly below (or above) $Y_i$ and $\overline{Y}$.

It can be shown (see note 24 on page 161) that

$$\sum_{i=1}^{n} (Y_i - \overline{Y})^2 = \sum_{i=1}^{n} (Y_i - \hat{Y}_i)^2 + \sum_{i=1}^{n} (\hat{Y}_i - \overline{Y})^2.$$

The term on the left-hand side of this equation shows the *total variation* in the dependent variable. The first term on the right-hand side measures the *variation in the dependent variable that is not explained by the regression*. This is a reasonable interpretation of this term, since it is the sum of squared deviations of the actual observations from the regression line. Clearly, the larger the value of this term, the poorer the regression equation fits the data. The second term on the right-hand side of the equation measures the *variation in the dependent variable that is explained by the regression*. This is a reasonable interpretation of this term, since it shows how much the dependent variable would be expected to vary on the basis of the regression alone.

To measure the closeness of fit of a simple regression line, we use the **coefficient of determination**, which equals

$$1 - \frac{\sum_{i=1}^{n} (Y_i - \hat{Y}_i)^2}{\sum_{i=1}^{n} (Y_i - \overline{Y})^2}. \tag{4.19}$$

In other words, the coefficient of determination equals

$$1 - \frac{\text{variation not explained by regression}}{\text{total variation}}$$

$$= \frac{\text{variation explained by regression}}{\text{total variation}}. \tag{4.20}$$

Clearly, the coefficient of determination is a reasonable measure of the closeness of fit of the regression line, since it equals the proportion of the total variation in the dependent variable that is explained by the regression line. The closer it is to 1, the better the fit; the closer it is to zero, the poorer the fit.

When a multiple regression is calculated, the multiple coefficient of determination is used to measure the goodness of fit of the regression. The multiple coefficient of determination is defined as

$$R^2 = 1 - \frac{\sum_{i=1}^{n} (Y_i - \hat{Y}_i)^2}{\sum_{i=1}^{n} (Y_i - \overline{Y})^2}, \tag{4.21}$$

where $\hat{Y}_i$ is the value of the dependent variable that is predicted from the regression equation. Thus, as in the case of the simple coefficient of determination covered earlier,

$$R^2 = \frac{\text{variation explained by regression}}{\text{total variation}}, \tag{4.22}$$

which means that $R^2$ *measures the proportion of the total variation in the dependent variable that is explained by the regression equation.*

# Chapter 5
# Business and Economic Forecasting

In 1992, Chrysler was scheduled to begin delivering its new two-seater car, the Viper, to customers. Its top executives forecasted that about 3,000 Vipers would be sold annually (at a price of about $50,000) during the mid-1990s. This forecast was important in determining whether Chrysler decided to develop and market this new car.

Practically all problems in managerial economics involve forecasting. No matter whether you are a sales representative, an engineer, an accountant, or chairman of the board, you must constantly be involved in forecasting. In this chapter, we take up the techniques used by many business and economic forecasters. At the outset, it should be recognized that these techniques are far from precise. Nonetheless, they generally are more trustworthy than unaided intuition or hunch. As we shall see, regression—which we studied in the previous chapter—plays a major role in many of these techniques, including the econometric models that have become increasingly important in recent decades.

It is very important that you be able to understand and evaluate various forecasting techniques, since you can cost your firm a lot of money by betting heavily on what turns out to be a bad forecast. Take the case of videotex, a computer-based service that allows consumers to shop and bank electronically. A market research firm forecasted in 1983 that there would be 1.9 million users, then in 1984 revised its estimate to 95,000 users—a huge downward revision. Many major firms put too much stock in such overly optimistic forecasts. In March 1986, Knight-Ridder Newspapers and the Times-Mirror Company left the business after losing $80 million.

## SURVEY TECHNIQUES

One of the simplest forecasting devices is to survey firms or individuals and to determine what they believe will occur. For example, Table 5.1 shows the results of a survey carried out by the Steel Service Center Institute, a trade association composed of steel service centers. Each month, the institute asks a representative sample of member companies what the trend of general economic activity is expected to be for the next three months. These firms account for approximately 30 percent of the total industry shipments of industrial steel products. This sample was chosen to show all sizes of firms, regions of the country, and types of products. If the percent of these firms expecting a downward trend goes up, as in June 1988, this is an interesting fact. While it does not necessarily mean that an economic slowdown will occur, it tells us something about the expectations and state of mind of relevant business executives.

---

TABLE 5.1 *Percentage of Steel Service Centers Expecting the Trend of General Economic Activity for the Next Three Months to Be Up, the Same, or Down, 1988.*

| Month | Up | Same | Down | Total |
|---|---|---|---|---|
| January | 26 | 66 | 7 | 100 |
| February | 30 | 63 | 7 | 100 |
| March | 31 | 61 | 8 | 100 |
| April | 26 | 71 | 3 | 100 |
| May | 20 | 74 | 6 | 100 |
| June | 12 | 63 | 25 | 100 |

*Source: Business Conditions* (Cleveland: Steel Service Service Center Institute, June 6, 1988). Because of rounding errors, figures may not sum to total.

---

Other surveys are carried out to forecast firms' expenditures. For example, the U.S. Department of Commerce and the Securities and Exchange Commission conduct surveys of business intentions to buy plant and equipment. Still other surveys are aimed at measuring consumer intentions. The Survey Research Center at the University of Michigan and other such groups provide information on planned purchases of automobiles, appliances, and housing. Also, they indicate the extent of consumer confidence in the economy, which is an important factor influencing consumers' spending decisions. Surveys of this type are of value in forecasting the sales of many products. They provide a wealth of information to the forecaster.

At least two types of information can be obtained from surveys. First, they can provide us with the respondent's forecast of some variable over which he or she has no control. For example, the University of Michigan obtains data from consumers concerning their forecasts of the rate of inflation. Second, surveys can provide us with information concerning what people or firms believe they will do. For example, the National Federation of Independent Business surveys firms to determine whether, and to what extent, they plan to increase their prices.[1]

Suppose a survey is used to forecast some variable, such as the sales of a particular firm. How can we determine how reliable this forecasting technique seems to be? One commonly used measure of the size of the forecast error is the **root-mean-squared forecast error,** which is defined as

$$E = \sqrt{\sum_{i=1}^{n} (Y_i - F_i)^2 / n},$$

where $F_i$ is the $i$th forecast, $Y_i$ is the corresponding actual value, and $n$ is the number of forecasts for which we have data concerning the size of the forecast errors. Thus, if the forecasts for 1992, 1993, and 1994 are $110 million, $120 million, and $130 million, and if the actual values are $105 million, $122 million, and $127 million, respectively, the root-mean-squared forecast error equals

$$\sqrt{\frac{(105 - 110)^2 + (122 - 120)^2 + (127 - 130)^2}{3}} = 3.56,$$

or $3.56 millions of dollars. This measure of forecast error is used to evaluate forecasts, no matter whether they are based on surveys or other techniques. Clearly, the lower the root-mean-squared forecast error, the better the forecasting technique.

## TAKING APART A TIME SERIES

Although surveys are of considerable use, most major firms seem to base their forecasts in large part on the quantitative analysis of economic time series. The classical approach to economic forecasting, devised primarily by economic statisticians, was essentially descriptive. It assumed that an economic time series could be decomposed into four components: trend, seasonal variation, cyclical variation, and irregular movements. More specifically, it assumed that the value of an economic variable at a certain time could be represented as the product of each of these four components. For example, the value of a company's sales in January 1993 was viewed as equal to

$$Y = T \times S \times C \times I, \tag{5.1}$$

[1] See W. Dunkelberg, "The Use of Survey Data in Forecasting," in E. Mansfield, ed., *Managerial Economics and Operations Research*, 5th ed. (New York: Norton, 1987).

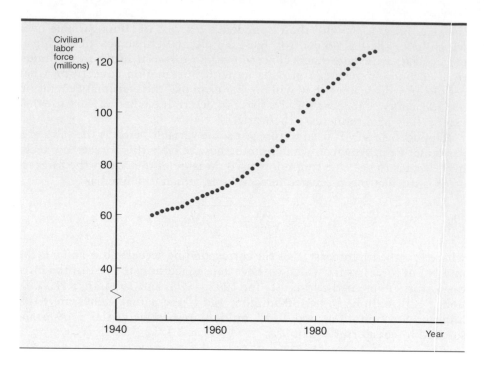

**FIGURE 5.1** *Civilian Labor Force of the United States, 1947–91* This series exhibits a strong upward trend.

where $T$ is the trend value of the firm's sales during that month, $S$ is the seasonal variation attributable to January, $C$ is the cyclical variation occurring that month, and $I$ is the irregular variation that occurred then.[2] Each of these components is defined below.

**Trend:** *A trend is a relatively smooth long-term movement of a time series.* For instance, the civilian labor force of the United States increased rather steadily between 1947 and 1991, as shown in Figure 5.1. Thus, there has been an upward trend in the U.S. civilian labor force. Of course, not all trends are upward. The trend in farm employment in the United States has generally been downward, as shown in Figure 5.2.[3] Whether upward or downward, the trend of a time series is represented by a smooth curve. In

---

[2] In some versions of this model, the components are added rather than multiplied. That is, it is assumed that

$$Y = T + S + C + I,$$

where $Y$ is the value of the time series.

[3] In still other cases, the trend is horizontal; that is, there is no upward tendency or downward tendency in the time series. In these cases, it is often said that there is no trend.

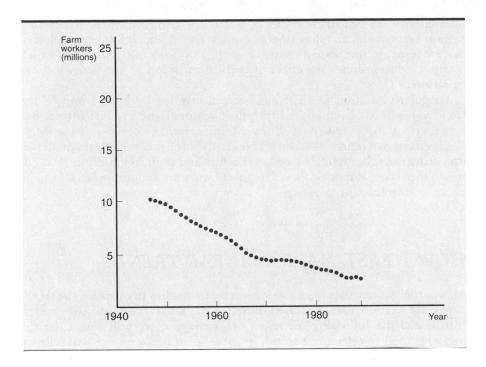

*FIGURE 5.2 Farm Employment in the United States, 1947–90* This series exhibits a strong downward trend.

equation (5.1), $T$ is the value of the firm's sales that would be predicted for January 1993, based on such a curve.

**Seasonal variation:** *In a particular month, the value of an economic variable is likely to differ from what would be expected on the basis of its trend, because of seasonal factors.* For example, consider the sales of a firm that produces Christmas trees. Since the demand for Christmas trees is much higher in the winter than in the summer, one would expect that the monthly time series of the firm's sales would show a pronounced and predictable seasonal pattern. Specifically, sales each year would tend to be higher in December than during the rest of the year. As we shall see, it is possible to calculate *seasonal indexes* that estimate how much each month departs from what would be expected on the basis of its trend. In equation (5.1), we must multiply the trend value $T$ by the seasonal index $S$ to allow for the effect of this seasonal variation.

**Cyclical variation:** *Another reason why an economic variable may differ from its trend value is that it may be influenced by the so-called business cycle.* The general tempo of economic activity in our society has exhibited a cyclical nature, with booms being followed by recessions, and recessions being followed by expansions. These cycles have not been regular or consistent (which is one reason why many economists prefer the term "business fluctuations" to "business cycles"); but unquestionably there has been a certain cyclical ebb and flow of economic activity, which has been reflected in a great many time series. For this reason, $T \times S$ is multiplied by $C$, which is supposed to indicate the effect of cyclical variation on the firm's sales in equation (5.1).

**Irregular variation:** Once it has been multiplied by both $S$ and $C$, the trend value $T$ has been altered to reflect seasonal and cyclical forces. But besides these forces, *a variety of short-term, erratic forces are also at work.* Their effects are represented by $I$. Essentially, $I$ reflects the effects of all factors other than the trend, seasonal variation, and cyclical variation. According to the classical model, these irregular forces are too unpredictable to be useful for forecasting purposes.

## HOW TO ESTIMATE A LINEAR TREND

Managerial economists have carried out many studies to estimate the trend, seasonal variation, and cyclical variation in particular economic time series. In this and the following sections of this chapter, we will encounter the methods used to estimate a trend; in subsequent sections, we will take up seasonal and cyclical variation. First, we consider the case where the long-term overall movement of the time series seems to be fairly close to linear. For example, this seems true for the sales of the IBM Corporation during the period 1974 to 1989. (These sales are plotted in Figure 5.3.) In a case where the trend seems to be linear, analysts frequently use the method of least squares to calculate the trend. In other words, they assume that if the long-term forces underlying the trend were the only ones at work, the time series would be approximately linear. Specifically, they assume that

$$Y_t = A + Bt, \tag{5.2}$$

where $Y_t$ is the trend value of the variable at time $t$. (Note that $t$ assumes values like 1993 or 1994 if time is measured in years.) The **trend value** is the value of the variable that would result if only the trend were at work. The deviation of $Y$, the actual value of the variable, from the trend value is the **deviation from trend**.

To illustrate the calculation of a linear trend, let's examine IBM's annual sales from 1974 to 1989. Since sales in year $t$ is the dependent variable and $t$ is the independent variable, it follows from our discussion in Chapter 4 that

$$b = \frac{\sum_{t=t_0}^{t_0+n-1} (S_t - \bar{S})(t - \bar{t})}{\sum_{t=t_0}^{t_0+n-1} (t - \bar{t})^2}, \tag{5.3}$$

$$a = \bar{S} - b\bar{t}, \tag{5.4}$$

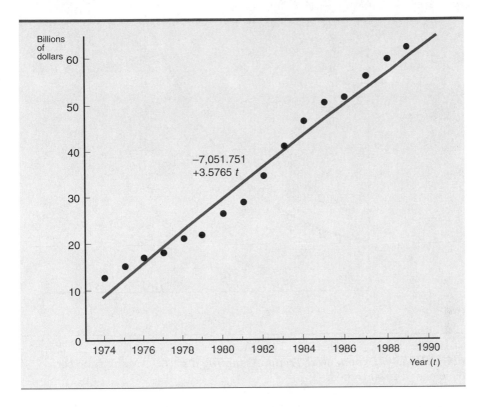

*FIGURE 5.3   Linear Trend in Sales, IBM Corporation, 1974–89*   IBM's sales have risen rather steadily throughout the period.

where $S_t$ is sales (in billions of dollars) in year $t$, $t_0$ is the earliest year in the time series (that is, 1974), and $t_0 + n - 1$ is the latest year in the time series (that is, 1989).

Inserting the data underlying Figure 5.3 into equations (5.3) and (5.4), we find that the trend line is

$$S_t = -7,051.751 + 3.5765t. \tag{5.5}$$

This trend line is plotted in Figure 5.3.

## HOW TO ESTIMATE A NONLINEAR TREND

Many time series do not exhibit linear trends. In some such cases, a quadratic function of time provides an adequate trend. Such a trend can be represented as

$$Y_t = A + B_1t + B_2t^2.$$

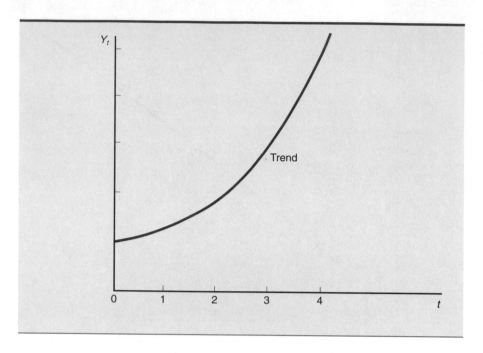

**FIGURE 5.4   *Exponential Trend, Assuming β = 1.5*   Many time series have exponential trends.**

To estimate $A$, $B_1$, and $B_2$, we can use the multiple regression techniques described in Chapter 4. As indicated there, standard computer programs are available to make these computations. The regression contains two independent variables: $t$ and $t^2$. Whether or not a quadratic trend is more appropriate than a linear trend can be determined by seeing whether it fits the data significantly better than a linear trend.

For many variables, an exponential curve provides a better-fitting trend than a quadratic curve. The equation for such a trend (shown in Figure 5.4) is

$$Y_t = \alpha \beta^t, \tag{5.6}$$

where $Y_t$ is the trend value of the time series at time $t$. A trend of this sort seems to fit many business and economic time series. It represents a situation where the variable grows at a constant percentage rate per year. Thus, if a firm's sales grow at about 5 percent per year, they are likely to exhibit an exponential trend.

If there is an exponential trend, we can take logarithms of both sides of equation (5.6), the result being

$$\log Y_t = A + Bt, \tag{5.7}$$

**TABLE 5.2** *Exponential Trend for Consumption as a Percentage of Gross National Product, United States, 1940–80*

| Year | Y | log Y | t' | log Y(t') | (t')² |
|------|------|--------|------|----------|--------|
| 1940 | 71.0 | 1.8513 | −20 | −37.026 | 400 |
| 1950 | 67.0 | 1.8261 | −10 | −18.261 | 100 |
| 1960 | 64.1 | 1.8069 | 0 | 0 | 0 |
| 1970 | 62.6 | 1.7966 | 10 | 17.966 | 100 |
| 1980 | 63.4 | 1.8021 | 20 | 36.042 | 400 |
| Total | | 9.0830 | 0 | −1.279 | 1,000 |

*Source: Economic Report of the President* (Washington, D.C.: Government Printing Office, 1985).

where $A = \log \alpha$, and $B = \log \beta$. Since equation (5.7) is linear, we can estimate $A$ and $B$ by the method of least squares. Then we can take antilogs of $A$ and $B$ to estimate $\alpha$ and $\beta$, the unknown coefficients in equation (5.6). (The average rate of increase of $Y_t$ equals $\beta - 1$.)[4] In this way, we can estimate the nonlinear trend shown in equation (5.6).

To illustrate, consider a managerial economist who in 1981 wanted to estimate the trend in the ratio of U.S. consumption expenditures to gross national product. Table 5.2 shows this ratio (expressed as a percentage and given at 10-year intervals) from 1940 to 1980. To calculate an exponential trend for this ratio, our analyst took logarithms of the ratios and obtained the figures in the third column of the table. The least-squares estimator of $B$ is

$$b = \frac{\Sigma \log Y(t')}{\Sigma t'^2} \tag{5.8}$$

and the least-squares estimator of $A$ is

$$a = \frac{\Sigma \log Y}{n} \tag{5.9}$$

if time is coded as shown in Table 5.2. [That is, time (t') equals −20, −10, 0, 10, and 20, which means that 1960 is the new origin. Thus, the mean of $t'$ equals zero, which explains why equations (5.8) and (5.9) are correct.][5]

---

[4] If $Y$ grows at a constant rate of $100r$ percent per year,

$$Y_t = Y_0 (1 + r)^t$$

where $Y_0$ is the value of $Y$ in some base year (say 1980), and $Y_t$ is its value $t$ years after the base year. Taking logarithms of both sides of this equation,

$$\log Y_t = \log Y_0 + [\log (1 + r)] \, t.$$

Thus, $\log (1 + r)$ equals $B$, and the antilog of $B$—which is $\beta$—equals $(1 + r)$. Consequently, $r = \beta - 1$. In other words, as stated in the text, the average rate of increase of $Y_t$—which is $r$—equals $\beta - 1$.

[5] Since $\log Y$ is the dependent variable and $t'$ is the independent variable, we know from Chapter 4 that, if $\overline{\log Y}$ is the mean of $\log Y$, the least-squares estimate of $B$ equals

$$\frac{\Sigma(\log Y - \overline{\log Y})\,(t' - \bar{t}')}{\Sigma(t' - \bar{t}')^2}.$$

Inserting the figures from Table 5.2 into equations (5.8) and (5.9), our analyst found that

$$b = \frac{-1.279}{1000} = -.001279$$

$$a = \frac{9.083}{5} = 1.8166.$$

Since the antilog of $b$ is .9971 and the antilog of $a$ is 65.6, the regression line in equation (5.6) was estimated to be

$$Y_t = 65.6(0.9971)^{t'},$$

where $t'$ is measured in years from 1960. This is the formula for the exponential trend in this case. (Note that $Y_t$ decreases by about $1 - .9971 = .0029$, or .29 percent per year.)

It is important to recognize that trends, whether linear or nonlinear, do not always continue. For example, based on this analysis, our analyst would seem justified in forecasting that the ratio of consumption expenditures to gross national product would be lower in 1990 than in 1980, the last year the analyst could include in the analysis. In fact, however, this ratio was higher in 1990 than in 1980. The moral is simple: Don't assume blindly that past trends cannot be reversed.

## SEASONAL VARIATION

Many time series consist of monthly or quarterly rather than annual data. For such time series, managerial economists and decision makers must recognize that seasonal variation is likely to be present in the series. Seasonal variation in many economic time series is due to the weather. For example, sales of soft drinks are higher in the summer than in the winter. In other cases, such as the sales of Christmas trees, seasonal variation is due to the location of a specific holiday (Christmas) on the calendar. Still other reasons for seasonal variation are the fact that some industries tend to grant vacations at a particular time of year, or that taxes have to be paid at certain times of the year, or that schools tend to open at particular times of the year.

Managerial economists have devised methods for estimating the pattern

---

Since $\bar{t}' = 0$, this expression equals the right-hand side of equation (5.8). [Note that $\Sigma \overline{\log Y} (t' - \bar{t}') = 0$.] We also know from Chapter 4 that the least-squares estimate of $A$ equals
$$\overline{\log Y} - b\bar{t}'.$$

Since $\bar{t}' = 0$, this expression equals the right-hand side of equation (5.9). [Note that $\overline{\log Y} = (\Sigma \log Y)/n$.]

of seasonal variation in a particular time series. In other words, they can determine the extent to which a particular month or quarter is likely to differ from what would be expected on the basis of the trend and cyclical variation in the same series. [In terms of the traditional model in equation (5.1), they can determine the value of $S$ for each month or quarter.] For example, the marketing vice president for a manufacturer of soft drinks may tell the company's board of directors that U.S. production of soft drinks tends in June to be 5.9 percent higher than what the trend and cyclical variation in soft drink production would indicate. Or she may tell them that U.S. production of soft drinks in December tends to be 7.0 percent lower than the trend and cyclical variation would indicate.

*The seasonal variation in a particular time series is described by a figure for each month, the **seasonal index**, which shows the way in which that month tends to depart from what would be expected on the basis of the trend and cyclical variation in the time series.* For example, Table 5.3 shows the seasonal variation in U.S. production of soft drinks. January's production tends to be about 93.4 percent of the amount expected on the basis of trend and cyclical variation; February's production tends to be about 89.3 percent of this amount; March's production tends to be about 90.7 percent of this amount; and so on. Figures of this sort can be used in a number of ways. *One important application is to forecast what the time series will be in the future.* For example, suppose that based on the trend and cyclical variation, it appears likely that about 30 million gallons of soft drinks will be produced next January. If this is the case, a reasonable forecast of actual January production is .934 (30 million) = 28.02 million gallons, since January's production tends to be 93.4 percent of the amount expected on the basis of trend and cyclical variation.

---

**TABLE 5.3**   *Seasonal Variation in Production of Soft Drinks in the United States*

| Month | Seasonal index |
|---|---|
| January | 93.4 |
| February | 89.3 |
| March | 90.7 |
| April | 94.9 |
| May | 99.0 |
| June | 105.9 |
| July | 112.4 |
| August | 113.4 |
| September | 108.3 |
| October | 103.9 |
| November | 95.8 |
| December | 93.0 |

## CALCULATION OF SEASONAL VARIATION

One way of calculating the seasonal variation in a time series is to use the regression techniques described in Chapter 4. Suppose, for example, that a business analyst has a time series composed of quarterly values; that is, each observation pertains to the first, second, third, or fourth quarter of a year. If the analyst believes that the time series has a linear trend, he or she may assume that the value of the observation at time $t$ equals

$$Y = A + B_1 t + B_2 Q_1 + B_3 Q_2 + B_4 Q_3 + e_t, \qquad (5.10)$$

where $Q_1$ equals 1 if time $t$ is the first quarter and zero otherwise, $Q_2$ equals 1 if time $t$ is the second quarter and zero otherwise, $Q_3$ equals 1 if time $t$ is the third quarter and zero otherwise, and $e_t$ is an error term.

It is important to understand the meaning of $B_1$, $B_2$, $B_3$, and $B_4$ in equation (5.10). Clearly, $B_1$ is the slope of the linear trend, but what are $B_2$, $B_3$, and $B_4$? The answer is that $B_2$ is *the difference between the expected value of an observation in the first quarter and the expected value of an observation in the fourth quarter, when the effects of the trend are removed.* (The **expected value** of an observation is its long-term mean value. To find its expected value, one multiplies each possible value of the observation by the probability of this value, and sums up the results.) To see that this is true, note that if an observation pertains to time $t$, the first quarter of a particular year, its expected value equals

$$A + B_1 t + B_2,$$

according to equation (5.10). Similarly, if an observation pertains to time $t + 3$, the fourth quarter of the same year, its expected value equals

$$A + B_1 (t + 3),$$

according to equation (5.10). Thus, the difference between the expected value of an observation in the first quarter and the expected value of an observation in the fourth quarter equals

$$(A + B_1 t + B_2) - [A + B_1 (t + 3)] = B_2 - 3B_1 .$$

And if we remove the effects of the trend (which is responsible for the last term on the right, $-3B_1$), this difference equals $B_2$, which is what we set out to prove. When the effects of the trend are removed, one can show in the same way that $B_3$ is *the difference between the expected value of an observation in the second quarter and the expected value of an observation in the fourth quarter;* and $B_4$ is *the difference between the expected value of an observation in the third quarter and the expected value of an observation in the fourth quarter.*

Consequently, if equation (5.10) is valid, the analyst can represent the seasonal variation in the time series by the three numbers $B_2$, $B_3$, and $B_4$. To estimate each of these numbers, ordinary multiple regression techniques can be used. The dependent variable is $Y$, and the independent variables are

## FORECASTING THE DEMAND FOR BLOOD TESTS AT NORTH CAROLINA MEMORIAL HOSPITAL

At North Carolina Memorial Hospital, which is interested in forecasting the number of blood tests it will perform, a simple model has been constructed that assumes that the number of tests per month increases according to a linear trend, and that the seasonal variation can be represented in the way described in equation (5.11). In other words, it is assumed that

$$Q = A + B_1 t + B_2 M_1 + B_3 M_2 + \cdots + B_{12} M_{11} + e_t,$$

where $Q$ is the number of blood tests performed at the hospital in month $t$, $M_1$ equals 1 if month $t$ is January and zero otherwise, $\ldots$, $M_{11}$ equals 1 if month $t$ is November and zero otherwise, and $e_t$ equals an error term. Thus, $B_2$ is the difference between January and December in the expected number of tests, $B_3$ is the difference between February and December in the expected number of tests, and so on (when the effects of the trend are removed).

(a) Indicate how one can estimate the values of $A$, $B_1$, $B_2$, $\ldots$, $B_{12}$. (b) Potential patients are reluctant to seek medical care during the Christmas holidays. Would you expect $B_2$ to be positive or negative? Why? (c) According to the hospital, the model forecasts "are being used to plan vacation schedules for . . . employees and to order supplies for the tests."* Why would forecasts of this sort be useful for these purposes? (d) Forecasts based on this simple model have been reported to be "excellent."

Forecasting errors have averaged only about 4.4 percent. On the other hand, forecasts based on exponential smoothing (a technique described in the Appendix) did not perform so well. Do you think that a model of this sort will always outperform exponential smoothing?

*Solution* (a) The values of these parameters can be estimated by calculating a multiple regression where $Q$ is the dependent variable and $t$, $M_1$, $M_2$, $\ldots$, $M_{11}$ are the independent variables. (b) Positive, because $B_2$ is the difference between January and December in the expected number of tests, when the effects of the trend are removed. Because patients tend not to want such tests during the holidays, December would be expected to be below January in this regard. (c) If one can forecast the demand for blood tests, it is possible to estimate the number of employees and the quantity of supplies needed at various times. Clearly, this information is useful in scheduling vacations and purchases, among other things. (d) No. In some cases, one forecasting technique works well; in others, it works less well. No technique is universally better than the others discussed in this chapter.

* E. Gardner, "Box-Jenkins vs. Multiple Regression: Some Adventures in Forecasting the Demand for Blood Tests," *Interfaces* (August 1979), pp. 49–54.

$t$, $Q_1$, $Q_2$, and $Q_3$. The latter three independent variables—$Q_1$, $Q_2$, and $Q_3$—are dummy variables. (A **dummy variable** is defined as a variable that can assume only two values: zero or 1.) Using the regression methods described in Chapter 4, the constants in equation (5.10)—$A$, $B_1$, $B_2$, $B_3$, and $B_4$—can be estimated by the ordinary least-squares technique.

When using this procedure, the analyst assumes that seasonal effects are *added* to the trend value, as shown in equation (5.10). This differs from the traditional model in equation (5.1), where it is assumed that seasonal effects *multiply* the trend value. (See note 2.) The former assumption is appropriate in some cases, while the latter assumption is appropriate in others. Techniques based on both assumptions are useful.[6]

To illustrate how this regression procedure can be used to estimate the seasonal variation in monthly data, suppose you have monthly data concerning the sales of a particular firm. If there is a linear trend, you can assume that

$$Y = A + B_1 t + B_2 M_1 + B_3 M_2 + \cdots + B_{12} M_{11} + e_t, \qquad (5.11)$$

where $Y$ is the firm's sales in month $t$, $M_1$ equals 1 if month $t$ is January and zero otherwise, $M_2$ equals 1 if month $t$ is February and zero otherwise, . . . , $M_{11}$ equals 1 if month $t$ is November and zero otherwise, and $e_t$ equals an error term. Using ordinary multiple regression techniques, you can estimate $A$, $B_1$, $B_2$, . . . , $B_{12}$. The estimates of $B_2$, $B_3$, . . . , $B_{11}$, and $B_{12}$ indicate the seasonal variation in the firm's sales. In particular, $B_2$ is the difference between January and December in the expected value of sales, $B_3$ is the difference between February and December in the expected value of sales, and so on, until $B_{12}$ is the difference between November and December in the expected value of sales (when the effects of the trend are removed).

## CYCLICAL VARIATION

Time series in business and economics frequently exhibit cyclical variation, such variation often being termed the **business cycle**. To illustrate what we

[6] To calculate the seasonal variation based on the latter assumption, a 4-quarter—or 12-month, if the data are monthly—moving average can be used. For the details, see any business statistics book.

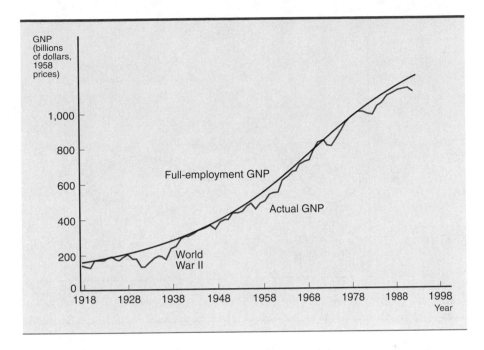

FIGURE 5.5   *Gross National Product (1958 Dollars), United States, 1919–91 (Excluding World War II)*   National output has fluctuated considerably.

mean by the business cycle or **business fluctuations,** let's look at how national output has grown in the United States since World War I. Figure 5.5 shows the behavior of gross national product (GNP) in constant dollars in the United States since 1919. Clearly, output has grown considerably during this period; indeed, GNP is more than five times what it was fifty years ago. But this growth has not been steady. While the long-term trend has been upward, there have been periods—1919–21, 1929–33, 1937–38, 1944–46, 1948–49, 1953–54, 1957–58, 1969–70, 1973–75, 1980, 1981–82, and 1990–91—when national output has declined.

The **full-employment level** of GNP is defined as the total amount of goods and services that could have been produced if there had been full employment. Figure 5.5 shows that national output tends to rise and approach (and perhaps exceed)[7] its full-employment level for a while, then falters and falls below this level, then rises to approach it once more, then falls below it again, and so on. For example, output remained close to the full-employment level in the prosperous mid-1920s, fell far below this level in the depressed 1930s, and rose again to this level once we entered World

---

[7] During a period of inflationary pressure, national output may exceed its full-employment level.

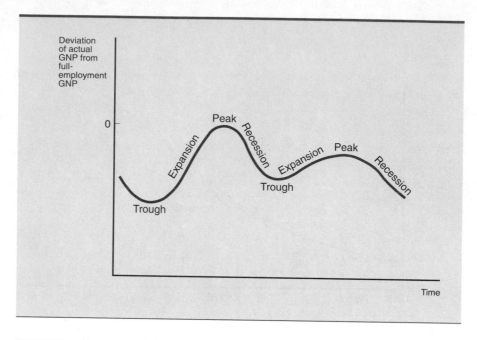

**FIGURE 5.6** *Four Phases of Business Fluctuations* The peak occurs when national output is highest relative to its full-employment value; the trough occurs when national output is lowest relative to its full-employment value.

War II. This movement of national output is sometimes called the business cycle, but it must be recognized that these "cycles" are far from regular or consistent.

Each cycle can be divided by definition into four phases, as shown in Figure 5.6. *The **trough** is the point where national output is lowest relative to its full-employment level. **Expansion** is the subsequent phase during which national output rises. The **peak** occurs when national output is highest relative to its full-employment level. Finally, **recession** is the subsequent phase during which national output falls.*[8]

*Many business and economic time series go up and down with the business cycle.* For example, industrial output tends to be above its trend line at the peak of the business cycle and tends to fall below its trend line at the trough. Similarly, such diverse series as the money supply, industrial employment, and stock prices reflect the business cycle. However, not all series go up and down at exactly the same time. Some turn upward before others at a trough, and some turn downward before others at a peak. As we shall see below, the fact that some time series tend to precede others in

[8] The peak and trough may also be defined in terms of deviations from the long-term trend of GNP rather than in terms of deviations from the full-employment level of GNP.

cyclical variation sometimes is used to forecast the pace of economic activity.

# ELEMENTARY FORECASTING TECHNIQUES

In general, all forecasting techniques are extremely fallible, and all forecasts should be treated with caution. Nonetheless, businesses and government agencies have no choice but to make forecasts, however crude. Since firms, governments, and private individuals must continually make decisions that hinge on what they expect will happen, they must make implicit forecasts even if they do not make explicit ones. Thus, the central question is how best to forecast, not whether to forecast. In this section, we present some elementary forecasting techniques that are commonly applied. Even among small firms, recent evidence indicates that about three-quarters of the firms use techniques of this sort.[9] However, these techniques should be viewed as crude first approximations rather than as highly sophisticated methods. More sophisticated techniques are taken up subsequently.

The simplest type of forecasting method is a straightforward extrapolation of a trend. For example, let's return to the IBM Corporation. At the end of 1989, suppose that IBM wanted to forecast its 1990 sales. During the period 1974–89, we know from our earlier discussion that the firm's sales could be represented (approximately) by the following trend line:

$$S_t = -7,051.751 + 3.5765t,$$

where $t$ equals the year in question. To forecast its 1990 sales, IBM could simply insert 1990 for $t$ in the above equation. Thus, the forecast for 1990 is

$$-7,051.751 + 3.5765(1990) = 65.484,$$

or 65.484 billions of dollars. As shown in Figure 5.7, this forecast is a simple extension, or extrapolation, of the trend line into the future.

How accurate would this forecast have been? IBM's sales for 1990 were $69.0 billion, so this forecast was in error by about 6 or 7 percent. Whether this is good or bad performance depends on the purpose of the forecast. For some purposes, you need very accurate forecasts; for others, you don't.

Decision makers often need forecasts of monthly rather than annual amounts. In such cases, it is necessary to recognize that seasonal variation, as well as trend, is likely to affect the value for a particular month. To see how a forecast can be made under such circumstances, consider a clothing manufacturer that wants to forecast its sales during each month of 1996. On the basis of data for each month during the period 1970 to 1993, the

[9] R. Coccari, "How Quantitative Business Techniques are Being Used," *Business Horizons* (July 1989).

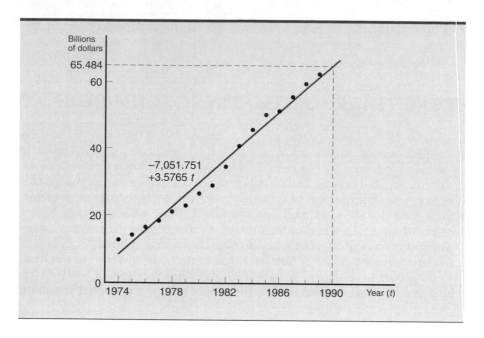

**FIGURE 5.7   Simple Trend Extrapolation to Forecast 1990 Sales of IBM Corporation**   The forecast was 65.484 billions of dollars.

firm determines that its sales seem to conform to the following trend:

$$S_t = 12,030 + 41t,$$

where $S_t$ is the trend value of the firm's monthly sales (in thousands of dollars), and $t$ is time measured in months from January 1995. Thus, if this trend continues, the expected sales for each month in 1996 would be as shown in the second column of Table 5.4. But this ignores whatever seasonal variation exists in the firm's sales. In order to include seasonal variation, suppose that the clothing manufacturer's marketing manager analyzes past sales data and finds that the monthly seasonal index for sales is as shown in the third column of Table 5.4. (Seasonal effects here are multiplicative, not additive.) Thus, if this seasonal pattern continues in 1996 as in the past, we would expect that actual sales each month would equal the trend value (in the second column) times the seasonal index (in the third column) divided by 100. The result, which is shown in the fourth column of Table 5.4, is a forecast that includes both the trend and the seasonal variation.

Needless to say, this entire procedure is simply a mechanical extrapolation of the firm's sales data into the future. The assumption is made that the past trend and the past seasonal variation will continue. Moreover, it is assumed that the trend and seasonal variation are the predominantly

**TABLE 5.4**  *Forecast of Sales of Clothing Manufacturer, 1996*

| Month | Forecasted trend value of sales* | Seasonal index | Forecasted sales (reflecting both trend and seasonal variables)* |
|---|---|---|---|
| January | 12,522 | 90 | 11,270 |
| February | 12,563 | 80 | 10,050 |
| March | 12,604 | 80 | 10,083 |
| April | 12,645 | 90 | 11,380 |
| May | 12,686 | 110 | 13,955 |
| June | 12,727 | 120 | 15,272 |
| July | 12,768 | 80 | 10,214 |
| August | 12,809 | 110 | 14,090 |
| September | 12,850 | 120 | 15,420 |
| October | 12,891 | 100 | 12,891 |
| November | 12,932 | 100 | 12,932 |
| December | 12,973 | 120 | 15,568 |

* Expressed in units of $1,000.

important factors that will determine sales in the coming months. The validity of this assumption depends on many considerations, including the extent to which the time series in question (in this case, sales) is affected by cyclical factors and the extent to which the economy is likely to change its cyclical position. In the next section, we will turn our attention to a particular method of forecasting business fluctuations.

# HOW LEADING INDICATORS ARE USED

Managers and analysts want to modify their forecasts in order to reflect prospective overall changes in economic activity. For example, if the president of the clothing firm in Table 5.4 is convinced that a serious depression will occur in 1996, he is likely to modify the forecasts in Table 5.4 accordingly. But how does the president of the clothing firm—or anyone else—predict whether there is going to be a depression? There are a variety of ways of doing this, all of which are very imperfect. In this section, we discuss an essentially empirical approach, reserving a discussion of more sophisticated techniques for a later section.

One of the simplest ways to forecast business fluctuations is to use **leading indicators,** which are certain economic series that typically go down or up before gross national product does. The National Bureau of Economic Research has carried out detailed and painstaking examinations of the behavior of various economic variables over a long period of time, and has attempted to find out whether each variable turns downward before, at, or after the peak of the business cycle, and whether it turns upward before, at, or after the trough. Variables that go down before the peak and up before

## DECIDING WHETHER TO FINANCE THE PURCHASE OF AN OIL FIELD*

In 1985, a leading bank was deciding whether or not to approve a loan application from an oil and gas company. This loan was to finance the purchase of an oil and gas field. The bank projected the oil and gas company's most likely production levels and profits, and estimated how much money the company would have available to meet its debt. To make these estimates, it was necessary to forecast the price of crude oil. In the bank's view, the oil industry had very good prospects for returning to the prosperity of the 1970s.

The thirteen-year forecast of the oil price that was provided by the bank's head office for the purpose of evaluating this loan was as follows:

| Year | Price (per barrel) | Year | Price (per barrel) |
|------|--------------------|------|--------------------|
| 1986 | $25 | 1993 | $39 |
| 1987 | 27 | 1994 | 41 |
| 1988 | 29 | 1995 | 43 |
| 1989 | 31 | 1996 | 45 |
| 1990 | 33 | 1997 | 47 |
| 1991 | 35 | 1998 | 49 |
| 1992 | 37 | | |

You've now got the benefit of hindsight, but even in 1985 you should have been suspicious of the bank's forecast. If the bank hired you to evaluate its forecasting procedure in this case, what comments would you make?

* This section is based on an actual case, although the numbers and situation are simplified somewhat.

the trough are called **leading series.** Variables that go down at the peak and up at the trough are called **coincident series.** Variables that go down after the peak and up after the trough are called **lagging series.**

According to the bureau, some important leading series are new orders for durable goods, the average work week, building contracts, stock prices, certain wholesale prices, and claims for unemployment insurance. These are the variables that tend to turn downward before the peak and upward before the trough.[10] Coincident series include employment, industrial production, corporate profits, and gross national product, among many others. Some typical lagging series are retail sales, manufacturers' inventories, and personal income.

These leading series—or leading indicators, as they often are called—are used frequently as forecasting devices. There are sound economic reasons why these series turn downward before a peak or upward before a trough: in some cases, leading series indicate changes in spending in strategic areas of the economy, while in others, they indicate changes in managers' and investors' expectations. In order to guide business executives in their planning, it is important to try to spot turning points—peaks and troughs—in advance. This, of course, is the toughest part of economic forecasting. Economists sometimes use leading indicators as evidence that a turning point is about to occur. If a large number of leading indicators turn down, this is viewed as a sign of a coming peak. The upturn of a large number of leading indicators is thought to signal an impending trough.

Experience with leading indicators has been only partially successful. The economy has seldom turned downward in recent years without a warning from these indicators, but unfortunately these indicators have turned down on a number of occasions—in 1952 and 1962, for example—when the economy did *not* turn down subsequently. Thus, leading indicators sometimes provide false signals. Also, in periods of expansion, they sometimes turn downward too far ahead of the real peak. And in periods of recession, they sometimes turn upward only a very short while before the trough, so that we've turned the corners before anything can be done. Nonetheless, leading indicators are not worthless; they are watched closely and used to supplement other, more sophisticated forecasting techniques.[11]

# HOW ECONOMETRIC MODELS ARE USED

Managers and analysts have tended in recent years to base their forecasts more and more on multiple regression techniques and multi-equation models. Increased emphasis has been put on the construction and estima-

[10] Of course, claims for unemployment insurance turn upward before the peak and downward before the trough.

[11] See R. Ratti, "A Descriptive Analysis of Economic Indicators," in E. Mansfield, ed., *Managerial Economics and Operations Research*, 5th ed.

tion of an equation or system of equations to show the effects of various independent variables on the variable or variables one wants to forecast. For example, we may want to estimate the quantity of automobiles produced by American auto firms next quarter. According to a study published by the Federal Reserve Bank of New York (which was described on page 139), the following regression equation is useful for this purpose:[12]

$$A = -22,302 + 12.9D - 97.8I - 19.9R + 230P + 6.0N,$$

where $A$ is the quantity of autos produced quarterly, $D$ is real disposable income, $I$ is the prime interest rate, $R$ is the inventory-sales ratio, $P$ is the auto price, and $N$ is the nonauto price level. To forecast the quantity of autos produced quarterly, one estimates the values of the independent variables and inserts them into this equation.

Multi-equation models, like the Wharton Econometric Model, are used to forecast many variables, such as gross national product. The Wharton model contains hundreds of equations variously intended to explain the level of expenditures by households, the level of business investment, aggregate output and employment, and wages, prices, and interest rates. The forecasts produced by the Wharton model (and other large models like it) are followed closely by major business firms and government agencies. Indeed, some firms (like General Electric) have constructed their own multi-equation models. Of course, this does not mean that these large models have an unblemished forecasting record; on the contrary, they, like all other forecasting techniques, are quite fallible. However, these models continue to be widely used in business and government.

Both the single-equation model used to forecast the quantity of autos produced and the Wharton model, with its hundreds of equations, are examples of econometric models. An **econometric model** is a system of equations (or a single equation) estimated from past data that is used to forecast economic and business variables. The essence of any econometric model is that it blends economic theory with modern statistical methods.

## THE WHARTON ECONOMETRIC MODEL

Let's look in more detail at the Wharton model, one of the most widely used econometric models. Composed of hundreds of equations, this model has been in operation for over twenty years. In addition to being used to forecast gross national product, it attempts to forecast the composition of gross national product, the price level, unemployment, and other major variables pertaining to the national economy. With the help of computers,

[12] E. Harris, "Forecasting Automobile Output," *Federal Reserve Bank of New York Quarterly Review* (Winter 1985–86), reprinted in E. Mansfield, ed., *Managerial Economics and Operations Research*, 5th ed.

## FORECASTING SHIPMENTS OF CEMENT BY CEMCO

CEMCO is a small cement producer that has used an econometric model to forecast its sales and profits. According to this model, national cement shipments depend on the amount of residential construction and business fixed investment. Assuming its price is unchanged, CEMCO's shipments of cement are assumed to depend on national cement shipments. Holding national cement shipments constant, CEMCO can increase its shipments by reducing its price. However, its rivals are likely to meet such a price cut, whereas they are less likely to match a price increase.

In 1984, CEMCO shipped 453,000 tons of cement. Based on this model, and alternative assumptions concerning the firm's future price, the forecasted shipments for 1985 to 1987 were as follows (in thousands of tons):

| Assumed future change in CEMCO's price | 1985 | 1986 | 1987 |
|---|---|---|---|
| No price change | 468 | 457 | 504 |
| 10 percent price increase | 306 | 296 | 329 |
| 10 percent price decrease | 473 | 459 | 509 |

(a) As stated above, the firm's model assumes that (1) national cement shipments depend on the amount of residential construction and business fixed investment, and (2) its shipments depend on national cement shipments (if its price does not change). Does it appear that the company expected both residential construction and

business fixed investment to be higher in 1986 than in 1985? Why or why not? (b) With regard to increases in price, does the demand for the firm's cement seem to be price elastic or price inelastic? Explain. (c) Does the price elasticity of demand seem to be lower for price decreases than for price increases? Is this reasonable? Why or why not?

*Solution* (a) No. If the company had expected both residential construction and business fixed investment to be higher in 1986 than in 1985, it would have forecasted an increase in national cement shipments, which in turn would have implied an increase in CEMCO's cement shipments (assuming no price change). In fact, as shown in the above table, it forecasted that its cement shipments would be lower in 1986 than in 1985. (b) Price elastic. A 10 percent increase in price seems to reduce shipments by about one-third. (c) Yes. It seems reasonable if, as stated above, the firm's rivals are likely to meet a price reduction, but unlikely to meet a price increase.*

* F. G. Adams, *The Business Forecasting Revolution* (New York: Oxford University Press, 1986), pp. 219–36. A couple of numbers have been changed for pedagogical reasons.

the coefficients of the many equations in this model can be estimated and revised from time to time.

Every three months the Wharton model is used to produce forecasts for the next two years. During the 1960s, its forecasting performance was particularly impressive; the average error of its forecasts of gross national product during the period 1959 to 1967 was only about $3 billion (less than $\frac{1}{2}$ of 1 percent). During the mid-1970s, its forecasting performance was less impressive, owing in part to political events such as the huge price increases imposed by the OPEC oil producers. (Obviously, such events are difficult to predict and incorporate into such a model.)

Because of the model's large size, it is not feasible to list all its equations. But it is possible to describe the nature of some of the more important equations, thus providing some feel for the structure of the model. To begin with, there are equations to explain the level of personal consumption expenditures, one equation pertaining to autos, one to nonautomotive durables, one to nondurables, and one to services. In each of these equations, the level of expenditure is dependent on disposable income and prices, among other things. This, of course, is in keeping with basic economic theory.

Next, there are equations that are used to explain the level of investment, one equation pertaining to business purchases of plant and equipment, one pertaining to construction of houses and apartments, and one pertaining to changes in inventories. In the case of expenditures on plant and equipment, the relevant equation makes these expenditures dependent on changes in output or the extent of capacity utilization as well as on the cost of capital. In the case of residential investment, the tightness of monetary markets is an important explanatory variable in the relevant equation.

Further, there are equations to explain output and employment. These variables are determined in the model primarily by the level of aggregate demand, which depends on consumption expenditure, investment, imports and exports, and government expenditures. Equations are included to explain imports and exports, these variables being functions of things like the prices of imported goods relative to domestic goods and the competitiveness of U.S. export prices relative to world prices. To estimate employment, production functions are estimated.[13] Given the estimates of output, these production functions can be used to forecast employment. Unemployment can also be forecasted, based on information concerning the size of the labor force.

Finally, there are equations to explain wages, prices, and interest rates. The wage equations make the rate of increase of wages depend on the rate of unemployment and the rate of increase of prices. The price level is determined by the extent of capacity utilization, among other things. A number of equations relate to the monetary sector of the economy. These equations attempt to explain interest rates, the money supply, and other financial variables.[14]

# THE PURVERE CORPORATION: A NUMERICAL EXAMPLE

To illustrate the nature of multi-equation econometric models, consider the Purvere Corporation, a seller of automotive equipment. Purvere's total revenues come from three sources: (1) the sale of the equipment, (2) the servicing of the equipment, and (3) the sale of accessories to customers who buy equipment or have it serviced. Based on regression analysis, Purvere's managers have found that its revenues from each of these sources can be represented by the following three equations:

$$E_t = 100 - 4P_t + .02\, G_t, \tag{5.12}$$

$$S_t = 10 + .05\, E_{t-1}, \tag{5.13}$$

$$A_t = 25 + .1Y_t, \tag{5.14}$$

where $E_t$ is the company's revenue from equipment sales in year $t$, $P_t$ is the price of its equipment, $G_t$ is gross national product (in billions of dollars), $S_t$

---

[13] A production function is the relationship between input and output for a firm, industry, or the economy as a whole. See Chapter 6.

[14] See Wharton Econometric Forecasting Associates, "The Wharton Econometric Model," and S. NcNees, "How Accurate Are Economic Forecasts?," both in E. Mansfield, ed., *Managerial Economics and Operations Research*, 5th ed. Because the Wharton model is constantly being updated and revised, its structure changes continually over time.

is its revenue from servicing its equipment, $A_t$ is its revenue from accessory sales, and $Y_t$ is its total sales (which equal $E_t + S_t + A_t$). $E_t$, $S_t$, $A_t$, and $P_t$ are expressed in thousands of dollars.

According to equation (5.12), Purvere's equipment sales are inversely related to its price and directly related to gross national product. According to equation (5.13), its service revenues are directly related to its equipment sales during the previous year (because the equipment is serviced about a year after it is bought). According to equation (5.14), its revenue from accessory sales is directly related to its total sales.

Purvere's president wants to use this model to forecast next year's total sales, which equal (in year $t$)

$$Y_t = E_t + S_t + A_t = (100 + 10 + 25) - 4P_t + .02G_t + .05E_{t-1} + .1Y_t.$$

Thus,

$$(1 - .1)Y_t = 135 - 4P_t + .02G_t + .05E_{t-1},$$

or

$$Y_t = \frac{1}{0.9}(135 - 4P_t + .02G_t + .05E_{t-1}). \tag{5.15}$$

This equation can be used to forecast next year's value of $Y$ if we know the price of Purvere's equipment next year, the value of GNP next year, and the firm's revenues from equipment sales this year. Suppose that price will be 10 and that this year's equipment sales will be 100. Then

$$Y_t = \frac{1}{0.9}(135 - 4 \times 10 + .05 \times 100 + .02G_t)$$

$$= \frac{1}{0.9}(100 + .02G_t).$$

To forecast $Y_t$, we must know $G_t$, the value of gross national product next year. Obviously, the best we can do is to utilize the best available forecast of next year's GNP. Suppose that Purvere's president decides to rely on the Wharton model's forecast, which is that GNP next year will be about $6,100 billion. If so, his sales forecast for next year will be

$$Y_t = \frac{1}{0.9}(100 + .02 \times 6,100) = \frac{1}{0.9}(222) = 247,$$

or $247,000.

Note that Purvere's president is linking his company model in equations (5.12) to (5.14) to the Wharton model, which is providing the forecasted value of $G_t$. This is frequently the way firms use the forecasts of macroeconomic models like the Wharton model. For example, Cummins Engine Company bases its sales forecasts in part on macroeconomic forecasts obtained from the Wharton model. (See page 189.)

Before leaving this example, it is important to recognize that it is highly

## HOW THE CUMMINS ENGINE COMPANY FORECASTS SALES

The Cummins Engine Company makes and sells diesel engines. This firm's sales forecasting for the truck market (the market considered here) is the responsibility of four executives: the manager of economic forecasting, the vice president for automotive sales, the director of automotive market planning, and the manager of marketing services. The forecasting process begins with a macroeconomic forecast obtained from the Wharton model. Wharton's quarterly model is used for Cummins' short-term forecasts, covering the next eight quarters. Wharton's annual model is used for the firm's long-term forecasts, which add eight years to the short-term forecasts.

*Henry B. Schacht, Chairman and CEO of Cummins Engine Company, Inc.*

In particular, it is assumed that the demand for new trucks depends on (1) truckers' output, which in turn depends on production and consumption in the economy as a whole, (2) the size and age of the existing stock of trucks in the country, and (3) the expected freight rate level, as well as a number of variables that indicate the nature of the financial environ-

*FIGURE I*   *Quarterly Sales*

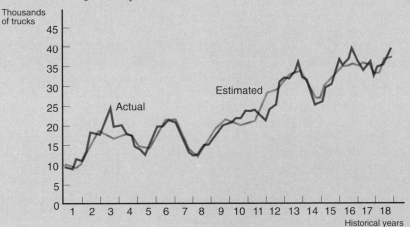

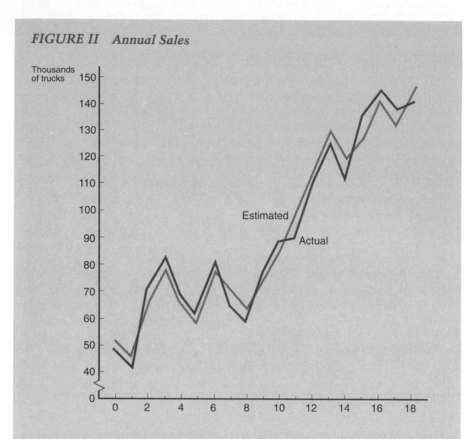

*FIGURE II   Annual Sales*

ment. An econometric model based on these assumptions has been quite accurate. Figure I shows that the short-term forecasts have been close to the mark, $R^2$ being about .93. Figure II shows the goodness of fit of the long-term model, the value of $R^2$ being .98. According to Cummins officials, the absolute average percentage forecasting error has been below 4.5 percent for one to five quarters out.

To forecast Cummins' sales to the diesel truck industry, two approaches are used. According to the first approach, the forecasted number of new trucks is multiplied by a percentage representing Cummins' expected and intended market share. According to the second approach, each manufacturer of trucks is studied, and a detailed forecast is made by the market research and sales departments of the number of engines that Cummins can expect to sell to this manufacturer. When these two forecasts are reconciled, the result is an official engine sales forecast for the next six months.*

simplified. Firms frequently use multi-equation models containing many variables, not just the handful contained in equations (5.12) to (5.14). Some of these additional variables utilized to forecast company sales were identified and discussed in Chapter 3. General Electric, for example, has used an iterative process "in which the initial values are obtained from individual economic relationships but the final results are strongly influenced by the experience, 'feel,' and intuition of business economists. This procedure has the advantage of 'taking everything into account' along with the disadvantage of being time consuming. The GE group, like the large model forecasters, forecasts more than a hundred economic variables, including items of special interest to the company such as total appliance sales and electric power generation."[15]

## *"STUDY YOUR RESIDUALS"*

Before concluding this chapter, it is important to consider Nobel laureate Paul A. Samuelson's well-known statement: "To the scientific forecaster I say, 'Always study your residuals.' " What Samuelson meant was that in evaluating any forecasting technique, it is useful to calculate the difference between each observation and what the technique predicts this observation will be. These differences—or residuals (defined in Chapter 4)—are very useful in indicating whether your forecasting technique excludes some important explanatory variables and whether its assumptions are valid.

To illustrate, suppose you are using an econometric model to forecast your firm's sales, and the difference between each year's sales and what this model predicts these sales to be is as shown in Figure 5.8. To improve this technique, you should think hard about why the model made the errors that it did. Based on Figure 5.8, it might occur to you, for example, that many of the years when the residuals were large and positive were years when your firm had an unusually large sales force, and that many of the years when the residuals were large and negative were years when your firm had an unusually small sales force. If the size of your firm's sales force is not included as an independent variable in your model, there may be good reason to include it.

By continually studying your forecasting errors, and improving your forecasting techniques, significant progress can be made. Although it generally is unrealistic to expect business and economic forecasts to be very precise, they are likely to be considerably more trustworthy than forecasts that are not based on the principles of managerial economics.

---

[15] S. McNees, "The Recent Record of Thirteen Forecasters," *New England Economic Review* (September 1981), p. 291.

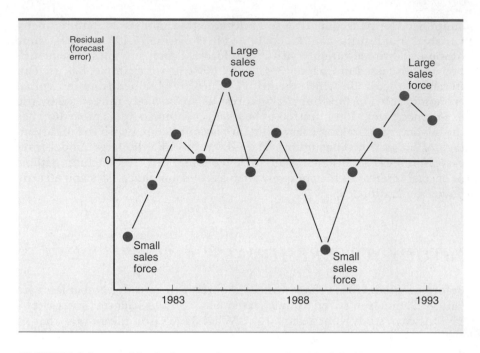

**FIGURE 5.8** *Residuals from Sales Forecasting Model* The years (1981 and 1989) when the residuals are large and negative are ones when the sales force was small; the years (1985 and 1992) when they are large and positive are ones when the sales force was large.

## SUMMARY

1. Although surveys are of considerable use, most major firms seem to base their forecasts in large part on the quantitative analysis of economic time series. The classical approach to business forecasting assumes that an economic time series can be decomposed into four components: trend, seasonal variation, cyclical variation, and irregular movements.

2. If the trend in a time series is linear, simple regression may be used to estimate an equation representing the trend. If it seems to be nonlinear, a quadratic equation may be estimated by multiple regression, or an exponential trend may be fitted. An exponential trend is appropriate when the variable increases at a relatively constant percentage rate per year. To fit such a trend, we use the logarithm of the variable, not the variable itself, as the dependent variable in the regression.

3. The seasonal variation in a particular time series is described by a figure for each month (the seasonal index) that shows the extent to which that month's value typically departs from what would be expected on the

basis of trend and cyclical variation. Such seasonal indexes, together with the trend, can be useful for forecasting. Regression analysis, including dummy variables, can be employed to estimate seasonal indexes.

4. Cyclical variation, as well as trend and seasonal variation, is reflected in many time series. Variables that go down before the peak and up before the trough are called leading indicators. If a large number of leading indicators turn downward, this is viewed as a sign of a coming peak. If a large number turn upward, this is thought to signal an impending trough. Although these indicators are not very reliable, they are watched closely and are used to supplement other, more sophisticated forecasting techniques.

5. The simplest kind of forecasting method is a straightforward extrapolation of a trend. To allow for seasonal variation, either multiplicative or additive seasonal effects can be included. This entire procedure is simply a mechanical extrapolation of the time series into the future.

6. In recent years, managerial economists have tended to base their forecasts less on simple extrapolations and more on equations (or systems of equations) showing the effects of various independent variables on the variable (or variables) one wants to forecast. These equations (or systems of equations), which are estimated using the techniques described in Chapter 4, are called econometric models. Examples are the Wharton model and the models used by CEMCO and Cummins Engine Company.

## PROBLEMS

1. The following seasonal index was calculated for the room occupancy of a motel located on a major interstate highway in the Southeast. The motel's customers are largely tourists and commercial truckers who regularly travel this highway. This index is based on actual data for 1987 to 1991.[16]

| | | | |
|---|---|---|---|
| January | 74.8 | July | 116.8 |
| February | 79.8 | August | 117.4 |
| March | 92.9 | September | 105.4 |
| April | 108.8 | October | 103.7 |
| May | 107.5 | November | 100.3 |
| June | 112.0 | December | 80.6 |

(a) Is there pronounced seasonal variation in this motel's business? All other things equal, by what percentage, on the average, does room occupancy in the peak month exceed that in the lowest month?

(b) What factors would you expect to be responsible for the observed

---

[16] B. Bettegowda, "Calculation of Seasonal Index for Motel Room Occupancy," National Technological University, 1991.

seasonal variation? In calculating the seasonal index, it was assumed that the index for a particular month like January was the same from 1987 to 1991. Some observers have questioned whether this assumption is correct, given that a recession occurred in 1990 and 1991. Why might the recession have changed the pattern of seasonal variation?

(c) If you were the motel's manager, how might a seasonal index of this sort be of use? Be specific.

2. The Union Carbide Corporation's sales during the period 1960 to 1975 are given below:

| Year | Sales (billions of dollars) | Year | Sales (billions of dollars) |
|------|------|------|------|
| 1960 | 1.5 | 1968 | 2.7 |
| 1961 | 1.6 | 1969 | 2.9 |
| 1962 | 1.6 | 1970 | 3.0 |
| 1963 | 1.7 | 1971 | 3.0 |
| 1964 | 1.9 | 1972 | 3.3 |
| 1965 | 2.1 | 1973 | 3.9 |
| 1966 | 2.2 | 1974 | 5.3 |
| 1967 | 2.5 | 1975 | 5.7 |

(a) Fit a linear trend to these data.

(b) Fit an exponential trend line to these data.

(c) In 1980, Union Carbide's sales were $9.994 billion. Suppose that in 1976, both the linear trend line and the exponential trend line had been used to forecast the firm's 1980 sales. Which forecast would have been more accurate?

(d) In 1984, Union Carbide's sales were $9.508 billion. Suppose that in 1976, both the linear trend line and the exponential trend line had been used to forecast the firm's 1984 sales. Which forecast would have been more accurate?

3. The Milton Company's statistician calculates a seasonal index for the firm's sales; the results are shown in the second column below. The firm's monthly 1993 sales are shown in the third column.

| Month | Seasonal index | 1993 sales (millions of dollars) |
|------|------|------|
| January | 97 | 2.5 |
| February | 96 | 2.4 |
| March | 97 | 2.7 |
| April | 98 | 2.9 |
| May | 99 | 3.0 |
| June | 100 | 3.1 |
| July | 101 | 3.2 |
| August | 103 | 3.1 |
| September | 103 | 3.2 |
| October | 103 | 3.1 |
| November | 102 | 3.0 |
| December | 101 | 2.9 |

(a) If one divides each month's sales figure by its seasonal index (divided by 100), it is said to be "deseasonalized." That is, the seasonal element is removed from the data. Why is this true?
(b) Calculate deseasonalized sales figures for 1993.
(c) Why would the managers of the Milton Company want deseasonalized sales figures?

4. The equation describing the sales trend of the Secane Chemical Company is

$$S_t = 21.3 + 1.3t,$$

where $S_t$ is the sales (in millions of dollars per month) of the firm, and $t$ is time measured in months from January 1989. The firm's seasonal index of sales is

| | | | | | |
|---|---|---|---|---|---|
| January | 103 | May | 101 | September | 121 |
| February | 80 | June | 104 | October | 101 |
| March | 75 | July | 120 | November | 75 |
| April | 103 | August | 139 | December | 78 |

(a) Construct a monthly sales forecast for the firm for 1995.
(b) Why would the managers of the Secane Chemical Company want monthly sales forecasts of this kind?

5. On October 1, 1985, the U.S. Department of Commerce announced that the index of leading indicators rose seven-tenths of 1 percent in August 1985, the fourth consecutive monthly gain.
(a) During August, the average work week rose. Is the average work week among the leading indicators? If so, did its increase help to raise the index?
(b) During August, stock prices fell. Is the level of stock prices among the leading indicators? If so, did its fall help to raise the index?

6. The Allen Company's monthly sales have the following trend:

$$C_t = 4.12 + 0.32t,$$

where $C_t$ is the sales (in millions of dollars per month) of the firm, and $t$ is time measured in months from July 1988. The firm's seasonal index of sales is

| | | | | | |
|---|---|---|---|---|---|
| January | 81 | May | 137 | September | 79 |
| February | 98 | June | 122 | October | 101 |
| March | 102 | July | 104 | November | 74 |
| April | 76 | August | 101 | December | 125 |

(a) Construct a monthly sales forecast for the firm in 1994.
(b) The firm's president feels strongly that a recession will occur in late 1994. Would this influence your answer to part (a)? If so, how?

7. According to a small econometric model devised by Irwin Friend and Paul Taubman,

$$\Delta C = 2.18 + .37\Delta Y + .10\Delta C_{-1},$$

$$\Delta I = 1.50 + .13(\Delta Y - \Delta Y_{-1}),$$

$$\Delta Y = \Delta C + \Delta I + \Delta G,$$

where $\Delta Y$ is the change in GNP between this period and last, $\Delta I$ is the change in investment expenditure, $\Delta C$ is the change in consumption expenditure, $\Delta G$ is the change in government expenditure plus net exports, $\Delta C_{-1}$ is the change between last period and the period before it in consumption expenditure, and $\Delta Y_{-1}$ is the change between last period and the period before it in GNP.
   (a) Express $\Delta Y$ as a function of $\Delta C_{-1}$, $\Delta Y_{-1}$, and $\Delta G$.
   (b) Can the equation you derived in part (a) be used to forecast the change in GNP? If so, how?

8. In the Wharton Econometric Model, housing starts (divided by the number of households) is specified to be a function of (1) the mortgage rate, (2) a consumer sentiment index, (3) capacity utilization, (4) the occupancy rate, and (5) deposit inflows into savings intermediaries.
   (a) Indicate why each of these five variables might be expected to influence the number of housing starts.
   (b) What factors influence these five variables? What sort of multi-equation system might be constructed for forecasting purposes?

9. The General Electric Corporation's sales from 1950 to 1976 were as follows:

| Year | Sales (billions of dollars) | Year | Sales (billions of dollars) |
|---|---|---|---|
| 1950 | 2.2 | 1964 | 4.9 |
| 1951 | 2.6 | 1965 | 6.2 |
| 1952 | 3.0 | 1966 | 7.2 |
| 1953 | 3.5 | 1967 | 7.7 |
| 1954 | 3.3 | 1968 | 8.4 |
| 1955 | 3.5 | 1969 | 8.4 |
| 1956 | 4.1 | 1970 | 8.8 |
| 1957 | 4.3 | 1971 | 9.6 |
| 1958 | 4.2 | 1972 | 10.5 |
| 1959 | 4.5 | 1973 | 11.9 |
| 1960 | 4.2 | 1974 | 13.9 |
| 1961 | 4.5 | 1975 | 14.1 |
| 1962 | 4.8 | 1976 | 15.7 |
| 1963 | 4.9 | | |

   (a) Using the method of least squares, derive a linear trend.
   (b) Plot General Electric's sales against time. Also, plot the trend line derived in (a) against time. (Time here is the year to which the sales figure pertains.)

(c) Does a visual inspection of how well the linear trend fits suggest that an exponential trend would do better? That a quadratic trend would do better?

(d) Using this linear trend, what would have been the sales forecast for General Electric in 1991? How accurate would it have been?

10. The SAS printout of the regression of the IBM Corporation's annual sales (designated as Y) on the year to which the sales figure pertains (designated as YEAR) is shown below. This regression is based on data for 1974 to 1986.

(a) If you had used this regression as a linear trend in 1986, what would have been your forecast of IBM's 1987 sales, based on this trend?

(b) IBM's actual sales in 1987 were $54.2 billion. How accurate would your forecast have been?

DEP VARIABLE: Y
ANALYSIS OF VARIANCE

| SOURCE | DF | SUM OF SQUARES | MEAN SQUARE | F VALUE | PROB>F |
|--------|-----|----------------|-------------|---------|--------|
| MODEL | 1 | 2164.18549 | 2164.18549 | 288.750 | 0.0001 |
| ERROR | 11 | 82.44527481 | 7.49502498 | | |
| C TOTAL | 12 | 2246.63077 | | | |

| | | | | | |
|--------|-----|----------------|-------------|---------|--------|
| ROOT MSE | | 2.737704 | R-SQUARE | 0.09633 | |
| DEP MEAN | | 29.43846 | ADJ R-SQ | 0.9600 | |
| C.V. | | 9.299753 | | | |

PARAMETER ESTIMATES

| VARIABLE | DF | PARAMETER ESTIMATE | STANDARD ERROR | T FOR H0: PARAMETER=0 | PROB>\|T\| |
|----------|-----|--------------------|-----------------|-----------------------|-----------|
| INTERCEP | 1 | −6798.29780 | 401.80637 | −16.919 | 0.0001 |
| YEAR | 1 | 3.44835165 | 0.20293215 | 16.993 | 0.0001 |

## HOW TO FORECAST THE SALES OF PAPER, ACCORDING TO McKINSEY*

Bill Barnett of McKinsey and Company, a leading management consulting firm, has described how a management team constructed a forecast of the sales of uncoated white paper in the United States. The first step was to divide the total demand into more homogeneous components. (See the table below.)

Then in each of these end-use categories, the analysts tried to identify, understand, and forecast the factors influencing demand.

To illustrate, take the case of reprographics paper. The management team, using existing data, divided reprographics paper into two types: plain-paper copy paper

| End-use category | Percent of total 1985 sales |
|---|---|
| Business forms | 25 |
| Commercial printing | 25 |
| Reprographics | 20 |
| Envelopes | 10 |
| Other converting | 5 |
| Stationery and tablet | 5 |
| Books | 5 |
| Other | 5 |
| Total | 100 |

and nonimpact page printer paper. With regard to plain-paper copy paper, there was evidence that sales tended to be directly related to the level of business activity (as measured by macroeconomic variables like gross national product). Holding the level of business activity constant, it appeared that the quantity of plain-paper copy paper demanded was related to the average cost (including labor time, equipment, and paper) of making a copy. As indicated in the graph on the right, the analysts found an inverse relationship between the average cost per copy and the quantity demanded.

Because further declines in cost per copy seemed unlikely, the management team forecasted a slowing in the growth of sales of plain-

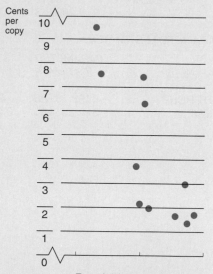

Tons of plain-paper copy paper per billion dollars of real GNP

paper copy paper. Since 1983, there seemed to be a decrease in the rate of growth of sales of this product; the team forecasted that this decrease would continue. (In addition, the analysts looked carefully at how sensitive their conclusions were to alternative assumptions regarding the rate of growth of gross national product and the rate of reduction of cost per copy.) According to Barnett, this sort of approach to sales forecasting is frequently very effective.

(a) Can regression techniques be used to estimate the relationship between cost per copy and the quantity demanded of plain-paper copy paper? If so, how?

(b) What statistic would you use to measure how strong this relationship is?

(c) Can one calculate the elasticity of demand for plain-paper copy paper with respect to cost per copy? Of what use might it be?

(d) During 1978 to 1986, the quantity demanded of plain-paper copy paper grew at an average annual rate of 7 percent. Does this mean that an exponential curve provides the best representation of the trend in quantity demanded?

(e) Does the procedure described above to forecast demand result in a seasonal index for sales of plain-paper copy paper? If not, how might such a seasonal index be calculated? Of what use might it be?

(f) How might this forecasting procedure utilize the results of macroeconomic econometric models such as the Wharton model?

* The material on which this case is based comes from F. W. Barnett, "Four Steps to Forecast Total Market Demand," *Harvard Business Review* (July–August 1988).

# APPENDIX: EXPONENTIAL SMOOTHING AND FORECASTING

One frequently used method of calculating a trend is to use **exponential smoothing.** According to this method, *the trend value at time* t *is a weighted average of all available previous values, where the weights decline geometrically as one goes backward in time.* As an illustration, suppose that a firm has been in existence for five years and that its sales have been $2 million, $6 million, $6 million, $4 million, and $8 million. (See Figure 5.9.) Then, the trend value in the fifth year would be a weighted average of $2 million, $6 million, $6 million, $4 million, and $8 million, where the weights decline geometrically as we go backward in time. Specifically, the weight attached to the observation at time $t$ equals $\theta$, the weight attached to the observation at time $t - 1$ equals $(1 - \theta)\theta$, the weight attached to the observation at time $t - 2$ equals $(1 - \theta)^2\theta$, the weight attached to the observation at time $t - 3$ equals $(1 - \theta)^3\theta, \ldots$, and the weight attached to the observation at the earliest relevant time (time 0) equals $(1 - \theta)^t$. Clearly, the weights decline geometrically as one goes backward in time; that is, the weight attached to the observation at time $t - 1$ is $(1 - \theta)$ times the weight attached to the observation at time $t$; the weight attached to the observation at time $t - 2$ is $(1 - \theta)$ times the weight attached to the observation at time $t - 1$; and so on.

To calculate an exponentially smoothed time series, you must choose a value of $\theta$, which is designated the **smoothing constant.** If we choose a value of 0.5 for $\theta$, the exponentially smoothed value of the firm's sales in each of the five years is as follows:

$$S_0 = 2$$

$$S_1 = (.5)(6) + (1 - .5)(2) = 4$$

$$S_2 = (.5)(6) + (1 - .5)(.5)(6) + (1 - .5)^2(2) = 5$$

$$S_3 = (.5)(4) + (1 - .5)(.5)(6) + (1 - .5)^2(.5)(6)$$
$$+ (1 - .5)^3(2) = 4.5$$

$$S_4 = (.5)(8) + (1 - .5)(.5)(4) + (1 - .5)^2(.5)(6)$$
$$+ (1 - .5)^3(.5)(6) + (1 - .5)^4(2) = 6.25,$$

where $S_0$ is the exponentially smoothed value of the firm's sales in the first year of its existence, $S_1$ is this value in the second year, $S_2$ the value in the third year, and so on. Figure 5.9 shows both the original time series and the exponentially smoothed time series.

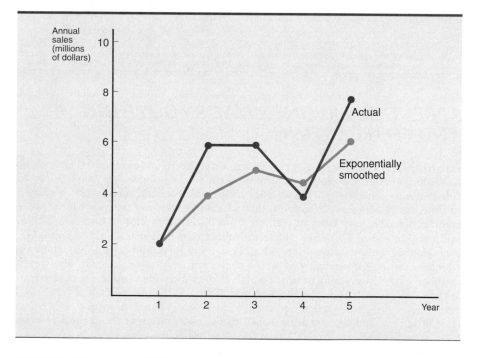

FIGURE 5.9  *Sales of Firm, Actual and Exponentially Smoothed*  Year 1 is the firm's first year in existence, year 2 is its second year, and so on.

To compute the value of such a smoothed time series at time $t$, all you really need is the value of the smoothed time series at time $t - 1$ and the actual value of the time series at time $t$. This is because the smoothed value of the time series at time $t$ is a simple weighted average of the smoothed value at time $t - 1$ and the actual value at time $t$. If $S_t$ is the smoothed value at time $t$,

$$S_t = \theta Y(t) + (1 - \theta)S_{t-1}, \qquad (5.16)$$

where $Y(t)$ is the value of the time series at time $t$.[17] Thus, to calculate an exponentially smoothed time series, you do not need to keep all the previous values of the actual time series; *all you need to keep is the value of the exponentially smoothed series in the previous period.* From this information alone (together with the current value of the series and the smoothing constant), you can calculate the smoothed value of the series in the current period. For instance, consider the firm in the previous paragraph. If the firm's sales in its sixth year of existence are $10 million, the smoothed value of sales for the sixth year is

$$(0.5)(10) + (1 - 0.5)(6.25) = 8.125,$$

or $8.125 million.

In choosing the value of the smoothing constant $\theta$, you must pick a number between zero and 1. (In other words, $0 \leq \theta \leq 1$.) If $\theta$ is close to 1, past values of the time series are given relatively little weight (compared with recent values) in calculating smoothed values. If $\theta$ is close to zero, past values of the time series are given considerable weight (as compared with recent values) in calculating smoothed values. If the time series contains a great deal of random variation, it is often advisable to choose a relatively small value of $\theta$, since this results in relatively little weight being put on $Y(t)$, which is more influenced than $S_{t-1}$ by this variation. On the other hand, if one wants the smoothed time series to reflect relatively quickly whatever changes occur in the average level of the time series, the value of $\theta$ should be set at a high level.

*Forecasting Based on Exponential Smoothing*   Exponential smoothing is also used for forecasting purposes. When used in this way, the basic equation for exponential smoothing is

$$F_t = \theta A(t - 1) + (1 - \theta)F_{t-1}, \qquad (5.17)$$

where $A(t - 1)$ is the actual value of the time series at time $(t - 1)$, and $F_t$ is the forecast for time $t$. Because the forecast is being made at time $(t - 1)$, the actual value of the time series at this time is known. The forecast for time $t$ is simply a weighted average of the actual value at time $(t - 1)$ and the *forecasted* value for time $(t - 1)$, where the actual value is weighted by $\theta$ and the forecasted value is weighted

---

[17] Let's prove that equation (5.16) is true. If $Y(t)$ is the actual value of the time series at time $t$, then equation (5.16) implies that

$$
\begin{aligned}
S_t &= \theta Y(t) + (1 - \theta)S_{t-1} \\
&= \theta Y(t) + (1 - \theta)[\theta Y(t - 1) + (1 - \theta)S_{t-2}] \\
&= \theta Y(t) + (1 - \theta)\theta Y(t - 1) + (1 - \theta)^2[\theta Y(t - 2) + (1 - \theta)S_{t-3}] \\
&= \theta Y(t) + (1 - \theta)\theta Y(t - 1) + (1 - \theta)^2\theta Y(t - 2) + \cdots + (1 - \theta)^t Y(0).
\end{aligned}
$$

Since the last expression on the right-hand side is equivalent to the definition of an exponentially smoothed time series in the first paragraph of this appendix, it follows that equation (5.16) is true.

by $(1 - \theta)$. It can readily be demonstrated that the forecast for time $t$ is the weighted sum of the actual values prior to time $t$, where the weight attached to each value declines geometrically with the age of the observation.

To see how exponential smoothing can be used for forecasting purposes, let's return to the firm in Figure 5.9, which had been in existence for five years. Sales during the first year were $2 million, and we assume that the firm's sales forecast for the first year was also $2 million. What will be its sales forecast for the second year? To make such a forecast, the firm begins by choosing a value for the smoothing constant $\theta$. (Values of .3 or less are often used.) Suppose that a value of .2 is chosen. Then the forecast for the second year is .2(2) + .8(2) = 2, or $2 million. Since the firm's actual sales in the second year turn out to be $6 million, its sales forecast for the third year will be .2(6) + .8(2) = 2.8, or $2.8 million. Since the firm's actual sales in the third year turn out to be $6 million, its sales forecast for the fourth year will be .2(6) + .8(2.8) = 3.44, or $3.44 million. And so on. Exponential smoothing is often used in this way to make forecasts, particularly where there is a need for a cheap, fast, and rather mechanical method to make forecasts for a large number of items. For example, to implement various kinds of inventory control models, demand forecasts for hundreds or thousands of items may be required.

**Problem** The Dickson Corporation wants to calculate an exponentially smoothed time series from the following data:

| 1983 | 2 | 1988 | 28 |
|------|-----|------|----|
| 1984 | 4 | 1989 | 38 |
| 1985 | 8 | 1990 | 50 |
| 1986 | 12 | 1991 | 70 |
| 1987 | 20 | 1992 | 90 |

(a) Calculate an exponentially smoothed time series, letting the smoothing constant equal 1/4.

(b) Calculate an exponentially smoothed time series, letting the smoothing constant equal 1/2.

(c) Calculate an exponentially weighted time series, letting the smoothing constant equal 3/4.

# Part Three

# Production and Cost

# Chapter 6
# Production Theory

## INTRODUCTION

When Chrysler manufactured the Viper, the two-seater car it introduced in 1992, it decided to use some novel production methods. In particular, this car was the first Chrysler with an all-plastic body. Decisions of this sort are of fundamental importance, whatever business a firm is engaged in. Any firm's managers and engineers must decide how to produce the firm's product. To maximize profit, they must strive to produce the product efficiently and at minimal cost. This means that they must constantly keep abreast of new methods and compare their productive performance with those of their rivals. While the secrets of efficient production are not as complex (or secret) as you might think, the price of efficiency, like that of liberty, is eternal vigilance. In this chapter, we present the essential aspects of production theory and indicate how business analysts, executives, and economists use them.

## THE PRODUCTION FUNCTION
## WITH ONE VARIABLE INPUT

For any product, the **production function** is a table, a graph, or an equation showing the maximum output rate of the product that can be achieved from any specified set of usage rates of inputs. The production function summarizes the characteristics of existing technology at a given time; it shows the technological constraints that the firm must reckon with. In this chapter, we assume that the firm takes the production function as given; in the next chapter, when we analyze the process of technological change, we study the firm's attempts to change the production function.

Consider the simplest case—when there is one input whose quantity is fixed and one input whose quantity is variable. Suppose that the fixed input is the service of five machine tools, the variable input is labor, and the product is a metal part. Suppose that John Thomas, owner of the Thomas Machine Company, a very small machine shop, decides to find out what the effect on annual output will be if he applies various numbers of units of labor during the year to the five machine tools (and if he maximizes output). He discovers that one full-time laborer can make 12 hundred parts per year on the machines. But he can make more parts per year by hiring more workers, as we see in Table 6.1. The results in Table 6.1 can be regarded as the production function in this situation, if the Thomas Machine Company is maximizing the output of the labor and machines it uses. Alternatively,

TABLE 6.1   *Output of Metal Parts When Various Amounts of Labor Are Applied to Five Machine Tools, Thomas Machine Company*

| Amount of labor (annual number of units) | Output of parts (hundreds per year) |
|:---:|:---:|
| 1 | 12 |
| 2 | 27 |
| 3 | 42 |
| 4 | 56 |
| 5 | 68 |
| 6 | 76 |
| 7 | 76 |
| 8 | 74 |

the curve in Figure 6.1, which presents exactly the same results, can be regarded as the production function.

The production function provides basic information concerning the nature of a firm's production technology; it shows us the maximum *total output* that can be realized by using each combination of quantities of inputs. Two other important concepts are the average product and the marginal product of an input. The **average product** of an input is total product (that is, total output) divided by the amount of the input used to produce this amount of output. The **marginal product** of an input is the addition to

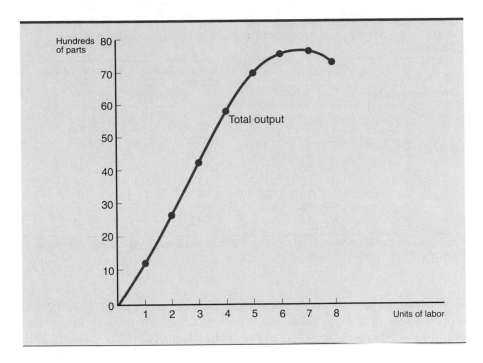

**FIGURE 6.1** *Relationship between Total Output and Amount of Labor Used on Five Machine Tools, Thomas Machine Company* The production function shows the relationship between output (in this case, number of parts produced) and input (in this case, units of labor).

total output resulting from the addition of the last unit of the input, when the amounts of other inputs used are held constant.[1]

Returning to the Thomas Machine Company, we can calculate the average product and the marginal product of labor, based on the production function in Table 6.1. Both the average product and the marginal product of labor will vary, of course, depending on how much labor is used. If $Q(L)$ is the total output rate when $L$ units of labor are used per year, the average product of labor when $L$ units of labor are used per year is $Q(L)/L$. And the marginal product of labor when between $L$ and $(L - 1)$ units of labor are used per year is $Q(L) - Q(L - 1)$. Hence, the average product of labor is 12 hundred parts per unit of labor when 1 unit of labor is used, and the marginal product of labor is 15 hundred parts per unit of labor when between 1 and 2 units of labor are used. The results for other amounts of labor are shown in Table 6.2.

---

[1] More precisely, the marginal product of an input is the derivative of output with regard to the quantity of the input. That is, if Q is output and x is the quantity of the input, the marginal product of the input equals $dQ/dx$, if the quantity of all other inputs is fixed.

**TABLE 6.2**  *Average and Marginal Products of Labor, Thomas Machine Company*

| Amount of labor | Total output | Average product of labor | Marginal product of labor* |
|---|---|---|---|
| | | (hundreds of parts) | |
| 0 | 0 | — | — |
| 1 | 12 | 12.0 | 12 |
| 2 | 27 | 13.5 | 15 |
| 3 | 42 | 14.0 | 15 |
| 4 | 56 | 14.0 | 14 |
| 5 | 68 | 13.6 | 12 |
| 6 | 76 | 12.7 | 8 |
| 7 | 76 | 10.9 | 0 |
| 8 | 74 | 9.2 | -2 |

\* These figures pertain to the interval between the indicated amount of labor and one unit less than the indicated amount of labor.

The average product curve for labor is shown in panel A of Figure 6.2; the numbers are taken from Table 6.2. As is often (but not always) the case for production processes, the average product of labor (which is the only variable input in this case) rises, reaches a maximum, and then falls. Panel B of Figure 6.2 shows the marginal product curve for labor. (These numbers also

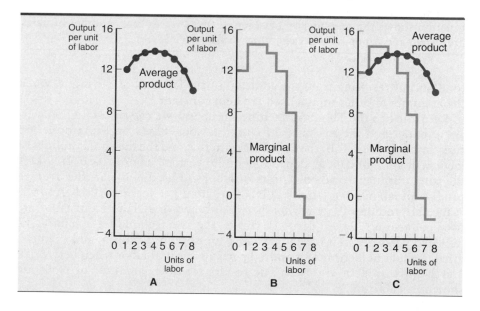

**FIGURE 6.2**  *Average and Marginal Product Curves for Labor*  Marginal product exceeds average product when the latter is increasing, and is less than average product when the latter is decreasing.

are taken from Table 6.2.) The marginal product of labor also rises, reaches a maximum, and then falls. This too is typical of many (but not all) production processes. Finally, panel c of Figure 6.2 shows both the average product curve and the marginal product curve for labor. As is always the case, marginal product equals average product when the latter reaches a maximum.

To see why this is true, let's apply the calculus techniques presented in Chapter 2. If x is the amount of the variable input that is used, and Q is the output rate, then the average product of the variable input is $Q \div x$, and the marginal product of the variable input is $dQ/dx$. (See note 1.) From Chapter 2, page 49, we know that

$$\frac{d(Q/x)}{dx} = \frac{x \cdot \frac{dQ}{dx} - Q\frac{dx}{dx}}{x^2}$$

$$= \frac{1}{x}\left(\frac{dQ}{dx} - \frac{Q}{x}\right).$$

When average product is a maximum, $d(Q/x)/dx$ equals zero. Thus,

$$\frac{d(Q/x)}{dx} = \frac{1}{x}\left(\frac{dQ}{dx} - \frac{Q}{x}\right) = 0,$$

which means that $dQ/dx$ must equal $Q/x$ when the average product is a maximum. But since $dQ/dx$ is the marginal product and $Q/x$ is the average product, this proves the proposition in the previous paragraph: When the average product is a maximum, the average product equals the marginal product.

## THE LAW OF DIMINISHING MARGINAL RETURNS

Having defined the production function and the average and marginal products of an input, we are ready to present one of the most famous laws of managerial economics—the law of **diminishing marginal returns**. This law states that *if equal increments of an input are added, and the quantities of other inputs are held constant, the resulting increments of product will decrease beyond some point; that is, the marginal product of the input will diminish*. This law is illustrated by Table 6.2; beyond 3 units of labor, the marginal product of labor decreases.

Three things should be noted concerning the law of diminishing marginal returns. First, this law is an empirical generalization, not a deduction from physical or biological laws. Second, it is assumed that technology remains fixed. The law of diminishing marginal returns cannot predict the effect of an additional unit of input when technology is allowed to change. Third, it is assumed that there is at least one input whose quantity is being held constant. The law of diminishing marginal returns does not apply to cases where there are increases in all inputs.

It is not hard to see why the law of diminishing marginal returns holds true. Take, for example, the case of the Thomas Machine Company, which has a fixed number of machine tools. If this firm hires more and more workers, the marginal product of a worker will eventually begin to decrease, because workers will have to wait in line to use the machine tools, and because the extra workers will have to be assigned to less and less important tasks.

## THE OPTIMAL LEVEL OF UTILIZATION OF AN INPUT

If a firm has one fixed input and one variable input, how much of the variable input should it utilize? This is a very important question for the managers of business firms, large or small. To answer it, we must define the marginal revenue product of the variable input and the marginal expenditure on the variable input. These two concepts must be understood if we are to answer the question.

The **marginal revenue product** is the amount that an additional unit of the variable input adds to the firm's total revenue. That is, letting $MRP_Y$ be the marginal revenue product of input $Y$,

$$MRP_Y = \frac{\Delta TR}{\Delta Y},$$ (6.1)

where $\Delta TR$ is the change in total revenue resulting from a change of $\Delta Y$ in the amount of input $Y$ used by the firm.[2] It can easily be proved that the marginal revenue product of input $Y$ equals input $Y$'s marginal product times the firm's marginal revenue. To see this, note that marginal revenue $(MR)$ equals $\Delta TR/\Delta Q$, where $\Delta Q$ is the change in the firm's output, and that

$$MRP_Y = \frac{\Delta TR}{\Delta Y} = \frac{\Delta TR}{\Delta Q} \cdot \frac{\Delta Q}{\Delta Y}.$$

Thus, since $\Delta Q/\Delta Y$ equals input $Y$'s marginal product $(MP_Y)$, it follows that

$$MRP_Y = MR \cdot MP_Y,$$ (6.2)

which is what we set out to prove.

The **marginal expenditure** is the amount that an additional unit of the variable input adds to the firm's total costs. That is, letting $ME_Y$ be the marginal expenditure on input $Y$,

$$ME_Y = \frac{\Delta TC}{\Delta Y},$$ (6.3)

[2] More precisely, $MRP_y = dTR/dY$.

where $\Delta TC$ is the change in total cost resulting from a change of $\Delta Y$ in the amount of input Y used by the firm.[3] If the firm can buy all it wants of input Y at a price of $10 a unit, $ME_Y$ will equal $10. In some cases, however, the firm must raise the price of input Y in order to get more of it; in such cases, $ME_Y$ will exceed the price of input Y.

To maximize its profits, the firm should utilize the amount of input Y where the marginal revenue product equals the marginal expenditure. In other words, the firm should set

$$MRP_Y = ME_Y. \qquad (6.4)$$

This follows from our discussion of marginal analysis in Chapter 2. To maximize profit, a firm should expand any activity as long as the marginal benefits exceed the marginal costs. It should stop expanding it when the marginal benefit (in this case, $MRP_Y$) equals the marginal cost (in this case, $ME_Y$).

# THE RONDO CORPORATION: A NUMERICAL EXAMPLE

To illustrate, consider the case of the Rondo Corporation, a producer of pocket calculators that has a fixed amount of plant and equipment, but that can vary the number of workers it hires per day. The relationship between the number of calculators produced per day $(Q)$ and the number of workers hired per day $(L)$ is

$$Q = 98L - 3L^2. \qquad (6.5)$$

The Rondo Corporation can sell all the calculators it can produce (with its current plant and equipment) for $20 per calculator, so its marginal revenue equals $20. It can also hire as many workers as it likes for $40 per day. How many workers should it hire per day?

To apply the results of the previous section, we must determine the marginal revenue product of labor $(MRP_L)$ and the marginal expenditure on labor $(ME_L)$ in this firm. Using equation (6.2),

$$MRP_L = 20MP_L,$$

since the firm's marginal revenue equals $20. Since $MP_L = dQ/dL$,

$$MRP_L = 20\frac{d(98L - 3L^2)}{dL} = 20(98 - 6L).$$

Thus, if $MRP_L$ is to equal $ME_L$, the number of workers hired must be such that

$$20(98 - 6L) = 40,$$

---

[3] More precisely, $ME_y = dTC/dY$.

ANALYZING MANAGERIAL DECISIONS

## HOW TO DETERMINE THE OPTIMAL HORSEPOWER FOR AN OIL PIPELINE

Crude oil is carried by pipelines from oil fields and storage areas over hundreds of miles to urban and industrial centers. The output of such a pipeline is the amount of oil carried per day, and the two principal inputs are the diameter of the pipeline and the horsepower applied to the oil carried. Leslie Cookenboo of the Exxon Corporation estimated the production function for a pipeline with a 10-inch diameter to be as follows:

$$Q = 286H^{.37},$$

where $Q$ is the amount of crude oil carried per day, and $H$ is horsepower.

(a) Derive a formula for the marginal product of horsepower. (b) Do increases in horsepower result in diminishing marginal returns? (c) Derive a formula for the average product of horsepower. (d) If the marginal revenue from an extra unit of crude oil carried per day is $2, what is the marginal revenue product of horsepower? (e) If an oil-pipeline firm can add all of the horsepower it wants at a price of $30 per unit of horsepower, what is the marginal expenditure on horsepower? (f) Under the circumstances described above, what is the amount of horsepower that an oil-pipeline firm should use?

*Solution* (a) The marginal product of horsepower equals $dQ/dH = .37(286)H^{-.63} = 105.82H^{-.63}$. (b) Yes. The marginal product of horsepower decreases as horsepower increases, as shown by the formula in the answer to part (a). (c) The average product of horsepower equals $Q \div H = 286H^{-.63}$. (d) Using equation (6.2), the marginal revenue product of horsepower equals $2 times $(105.82H^{-.63}) = $211.64H^{-.63}$. (e) $30. (f) Using equation (6.4), the firm should set the marginal revenue product of horsepower equal to marginal expenditure. Thus,

$$211.64H^{-.63} = 30$$

$$H^{-.63} = .14175$$

$$H = 22.22.$$

The optimal amount of horsepower is 22.22 units.*

* For further discussion, see L. Cookenboo, "Production Functions and Cost Functions in Oil Pipelines," in the study guide accompanying this textbook.

since the firm's marginal expenditure on labor equals $40. Solving this equation, we find that $L$ must equal 16. So, if the Rondo Corporation wants to maximize profit, it should hire 16 workers per day.

## THE PRODUCTION FUNCTION WITH TWO VARIABLE INPUTS

Up to this point, we have been concerned with the case where there is only one variable input. Now we take up the more general case where there are two variable inputs. These variable inputs can be thought of as working with one or more fixed inputs, or they may be thought of as the only two inputs (in which case the situation is the long run, since all inputs are variable). In either case, it is easy to extend the results to as many inputs as one likes.

When we increase the number of variable inputs from one to two, the production function becomes slightly more complicated, but it is still the relationship between various combinations of inputs and the maximum amount of output that can be obtained from them. Really, the only change is that output is a function of two variables rather than one. To illustrate, suppose that the Monroe Machine Company, which produces a metal part (different from that produced by the Thomas Machine Company), can vary the quantities of both machine tools and labor. Its production function is given in Table 6.3. The average product of either machine tools or labor can be computed simply by dividing the total output by the amount of either machine tools or labor that is used. The marginal product of each input can be obtained by holding the other input constant. For example, the marginal product of a machine tool when 4 units of labor are used and when between 3 and 4 machine tools are used is 51 hundred parts per machine tool; the marginal product of labor when 4 machine tools are used and when between 3 and 4 units of labor are used is 21 hundred parts per unit. If $X_1$ is the amount of the first input and $X_2$ is the amount of the second input, the

TABLE 6.3 *Production Function, Two Variable Inputs, Monroe Machine Company*

| Amount of labor (units) | Number of machine tools | | | |
|---|---|---|---|---|
| | 3 | 4 | 5 | 6 |
| | (hundreds of parts produced per year) | | | |
| 1 | 5 | 11 | 18 | 24 |
| 2 | 14 | 30 | 50 | 72 |
| 3 | 22 | 60 | 80 | 99 |
| 4 | 30 | 81 | 115 | 125 |
| 5 | 35 | 84 | 140 | 144 |

production function is

$$Q = f(X_1, X_2), \tag{6.6}$$

where $Q$ is the firm's output rate. The marginal product of the first input is $\partial Q/\partial X_1$; the marginal product of the second input is $\partial Q/\partial X_2$.

One can also represent the production function by a surface, like that in Figure 6.3. The production surface is $OAQB$.[4] The height of a point on this surface denotes the quantity of output. Dropping a perpendicular down from a point on the production surface to the "floor" and seeing how far the resulting point is from the labor and machine tool axes indicates how much of each input is required to produce this much output. For example, to produce $G'G$ units of output requires $OB_1$ $(= A_1 G')$ units of labor and $OA_1$ $(= B_1 G')$ machine tools. Conversely, one can take any amounts of machine tools and labor, say $OA_2$ machine tools and $OB_2$ units of labor, and find out how much output they will produce by measuring the height of the

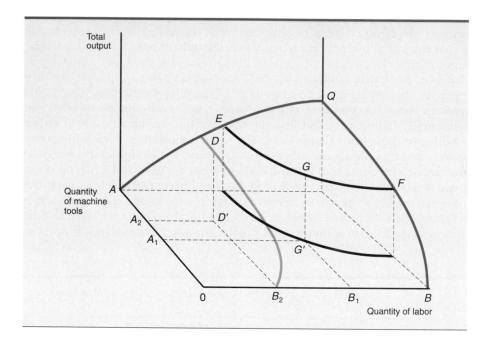

FIGURE 6.3 *Production Function, Two Variable Inputs* The production surface, **OAQB**, shows the amount of total output that can be obtained from various combinations of quantities of machine tools and labor.

---

[4] This surface is not meant to represent the numerical values in Table 6.3, but is a general representation of how a production surface of this sort is likely to appear.

## HOW NUCOR STAYS ON THE PRODUCTION FUNCTION

Nucor, the sixth-largest steel firm in the United States, has not had a quarterly loss in well over 20 years. In 1988, while the average integrated steel company in the United States produced 400 tons of steel per employee, Nucor produced about 980 tons per employee. Part of the reason for this difference is that Nucor is a "mini-mill," not an integrated steel firm. The mini-mills have a different production function from that of the integrated mills. They use electric arc furnaces to make a narrow product line from scrap steel. In contrast to the integrated steel producers, American mini-mills have prospered in recent years.

Another reason for Nucor's relatively high output per employee is that the firm's managers work hard to keep the firm *on* the production function. As pointed out on page 214, the production function includes only *efficient* input combinations. For example, if a unit of output can be produced with 3 units of labor and 3 units of capital, an input combination containing 4 units of labor and 3 units of capital will not be included because it is inefficient. Firms that are inefficient are *off* the production function. They produce less output than is possible, given the amount of inputs they use.

Kenneth Iverson, Nucor's president, has described some of the ways he and his colleagues promote efficiency:

> *You can tell a lot about a company by looking at its organization charts. . . . If you*
> *see a lot of staff, you can bet it is not a very efficient organization. . . . Secondly, don't have assistants. We do not have that title and prohibit it in our company. . . . In this organization . . . the division managers report directly to me. . . . And one of the most important things is to restrict as much as possible the number of management layers.*
>
> *Each division is a profit center and the division manager has control over the day-to-day decisions that make that particular division profitable or not profitable. We expect the division to provide division contribution, which is earnings before corporate expenses. We do not allocate our corporate expenses,*

*F. Kenneth Iverson, Chairman and CEO of Nucor Corporation*

*because we do not think there is any way to do this reasonably and fairly. We do focus on earnings. And we expect a division to earn 25% return on total assets employed, before corporate expenses, taxes, interest or profit sharing. And we have a saying in the company—if a manager doesn't provide that for a number of years, we are either going to get rid of the division or get rid of the division manager, and it's generally the division manager.*

It is essential to recognize that a firm's managers have the job of keeping their firm on the production function. This is not a job for engineers and technicians alone. To illustrate, consider the words of one Nucor manager:

*When I came to this plant four years ago, we had too*

*many people, too much overhead. We had 410 people at the plant and I could see, because I knew how many people we had in the Nebraska plant, we had many more than we needed. That was my yardstick and we set about to reduce those numbers by attrition. . . . We have made a few equipment changes that made it easier for the men, giving them an opportunity to make better bonuses. Of course the changes were very subtle in any given case but overall in four years we have probably helped the men tremendously. With 55 fewer men, perhaps 40–45 fewer in the production area, we are still capable of producing the same number of tons as four years ago.\**

\* H. Bartlett, *Cases in Strategic Management for Business* (New York: Dryden Press, 1988); *American Productivity and Quality Center Letter* 8, no. 7 (January 1989); and *Business Week* (November 19, 1990).

production surface at $D'$, the point where labor input is $OB_2$ and machine tool input is $OA_2$. According to Figure 6.3, the answer equals $D'D$.

The production function does not include many of the different ways in which a given output can be produced because it includes only *efficient* combinations of inputs. For example, if 2 units of labor and 3 units of capital can produce 1 unit of output, this combination of inputs and output will not be included in the production function if it is also possible to produce 1 unit of output with 2 units of labor and 2 units of capital. The former input-output combination is clearly inefficient, since it is possible to obtain the result with the same amount of labor and less capital.

## ISOQUANTS

An **isoquant** is a curve showing all possible (efficient) combinations of inputs that are capable of producing a certain quantity of output. If we know the production function, we can readily derive the isoquant pertaining to any level of output. In Figure 6.3, suppose we want to find the isoquant corresponding to an output of $G'G$. All we need to do is to cut the production surface at the height of $G'G$ parallel to the base plane, the result being $EGF$, and to drop perpendiculars from $EGF$ to the base. Clearly, this results in a curve that includes all efficient combinations of machine tools and labor that can produce $G'G$ metal parts. Using the notation in equation (6.6), an isoquant shows all combinations of $X_1$ and $X_2$ such that $f(X_1, X_2)$ equals a certain output rate.

Several isoquants, each pertaining to a different output rate, are shown in Figure 6.4. The two axes measure the quantities of inputs that are used. In contrast to the previous diagrams, we assume that labor and capital—not labor and machine tools (a particular form of capital)—are the relevant inputs in this case. The curves show the various combinations of inputs that can produce 100, 200, and 300 units of output. For example, consider the isoquant pertaining to 100 units of output per period of time. According to this isoquant, it is possible to attain this output rate if $L_0$ units of labor and $K_0$ units of capital are used per period of time. Alternatively, this output rate can be attained if $L_1$ units of labor and $K_1$ units of capital—or $L_2$ units of labor and $K_2$ units of capital—are used per period of time.

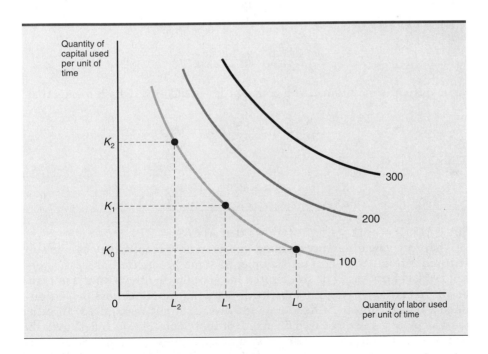

**FIGURE 6.4  *Isoquants***  These three isoquants show the various combinations of capital and labor that can produce 100, 200, and 300 units of output.

## THE MARGINAL RATE OF TECHNICAL SUBSTITUTION

As we have just seen, there ordinarily are a number of efficient ways that a particular output can be produced. The **marginal rate of technical substitution** shows the rate at which one input can be substituted for another input, if output remains constant. If, as in equation (6.6), the quantity of output produced by a firm is a function of the amounts of two inputs used,

$$Q = f(X_1, X_2),$$

the marginal rate of technical substitution is

$$MRTS = -\frac{dX_2}{dX_1}, \tag{6.7}$$

given that $Q$ is held constant.

Geometrically, the marginal rate of technical substitution is $-1$ times the slope of the isoquant. This makes sense, since $dX_2/dX_1$ is the slope of the isoquant. Note that the marginal rate of technical substitution equals $MP_1/MP_2$, where $MP_1$ is the marginal product of input 1, and $MP_2$ is the marginal product of input 2. It can be shown that

$$dQ = \frac{\partial Q}{\partial X_1} dX_1 + \frac{\partial Q}{\partial X_2} dX_2.$$

Since output is maintained at a constant level, $dQ = 0$, which means that

$$\frac{\partial Q}{\partial X_1} dX_1 + \frac{\partial Q}{\partial X_2} dX_2 = 0.$$

Thus,

$$\frac{dX_2}{dX_1} = -\frac{\partial Q}{\partial X_1} \div \frac{\partial Q}{\partial X_2} = -\frac{MP_1}{MP_2}. \tag{6.8}$$

Since $MRTS = -dX_2/dX_1$, it follows that $MRTS = MP_1/MP_2$.

There are vast differences among inputs in how readily they can be substituted for one another. For example, in some production processes, one kind of labor can easily be substituted for another; in others, this is not true at all. In extreme cases, no substitution among inputs is possible; to produce a unit of output, a fixed amount of each input is required. In other words, inputs must be used in fixed proportions. Figure 6.5 shows the firm's isoquants in such a case; as you can see, they are right angles. Very few production processes allow no substitution among inputs at all, but in some cases the amount of substitution is very limited.

Isoquants may also have positively sloped segments, or bend back upon

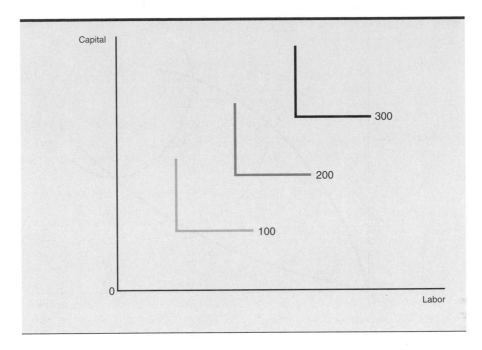

**FIGURE 6.5** *Isoquants in the Case of Fixed Proportions*   If inputs must be used in fixed proportions, the isoquants are right angles.

themselves, as shown in Figure 6.6. Above *OU* and below *OV*, the slope of the isoquants is positive, which implies that increases in both capital and labor are required to maintain a certain output rate. If this is the case, the marginal product of one or the other input must be negative. Above *OU*, the marginal product of capital is negative; thus, output will increase if less capital is used, while the amount of labor is held constant. Below *OV*, the marginal product of labor is negative; thus, output will increase if less labor is used, while the amount of capital is held constant. The lines *OU* and *OV* are called **ridge lines.**

No profit-maximizing firm will operate at a point outside the ridge lines, since it can produce the same output with less of both inputs, which must be cheaper. Consider point *H* in Figure 6.6. Because this is a point where the isoquant is positively sloped—and thus outside the ridge lines—it requires a greater amount of both labor and capital than some other point (for example, point *E*) on the same isoquant. Since both capital and labor have positive prices, it must be cheaper to operate at point *E* than at point *H*. The moral is: Don't operate at a point outside the ridge lines, if you want to maximize profit.

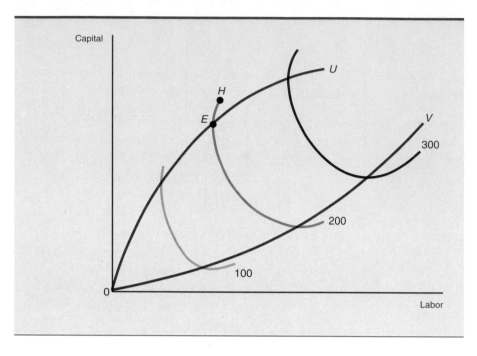

**FIGURE 6.6**  *Economic Region of Production*  No profit-maximizing firm
will operate at a point outside the ridge lines, *OU* and *OV*.

## THE OPTIMAL COMBINATION OF INPUTS

If a firm wants to maximize profit, it will try to minimize the cost of producing a given output or maximize the output derived from a given level of
cost.[5] Suppose the firm takes input prices as given, and that there are two
inputs, capital and labor, that are variable in the relevant time period. What
combination of capital and labor should the firm choose if it wants to maximize the quantity of output derived from the given level of cost?

To begin to answer this question, let's determine the various combinations of inputs that the firm can obtain for a given expenditure. For example, if capital and labor are the inputs and the price of labor is $P_L$ per unit
and the price of capital is $P_K$ per unit, the input combinations that can be
obtained for a total outlay of $M$ are such that

$$P_L L + P_K K = M, \tag{6.9}$$

---

[5] The conditions for minimizing the cost of producing a given output are the same as those for maximizing the output from a given cost. This is shown in the present section. Thus, we can view the firm's
problem in either way.

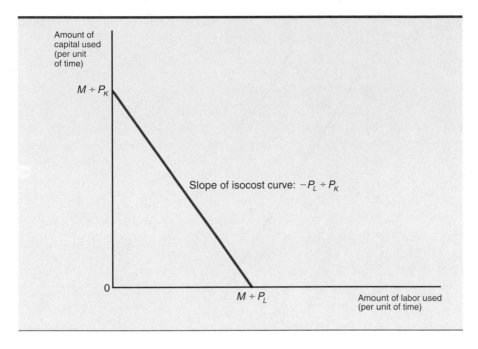

**FIGURE 6.7** *Isocost Curve* The isocost curve shows the combinations of inputs that can be obtained for a total outlay of $M$.

where $L$ is the amount of the labor input, and $K$ is the amount of the capital input. Given $M$, $P_L$, and $P_K$, it follows that

$$K = \frac{M}{P_K} - \frac{P_L L}{P_K}. \tag{6.10}$$

Thus, the various combinations of capital and labor that can be purchased, given $P_L$, $P_K$, and $M$, can be represented by a straight line like that shown in Figure 6.7. (Capital is plotted on the vertical axis, labor is plotted on the horizontal.) This line, which has an intercept on the vertical axis equal to $M/P_K$ and a slope of $-P_L/P_K$, is called an **isocost curve**.

If we superimpose the relevant isocost curve on the firm's isoquant map, we can determine graphically which combination of inputs will maximize the output for the given expenditure. The firm should pick the point on the isocost curve that is on the highest isoquant, for example, $R$ in Figure 6.8. This is a point where the isocost curve is tangent to the isoquant. Thus, since the slope of the isocost curve is the negative of $P_L/P_K$ and the slope of the isoquant is the negative of $MP_L/MP_K$ (as we pointed out in the previous section), it follows that the optimal combination of inputs is one where $MP_L/MP_K = P_L/P_K$. Or put differently, the firm should choose an input combination where $MP_L/P_L = MP_K/P_K$.

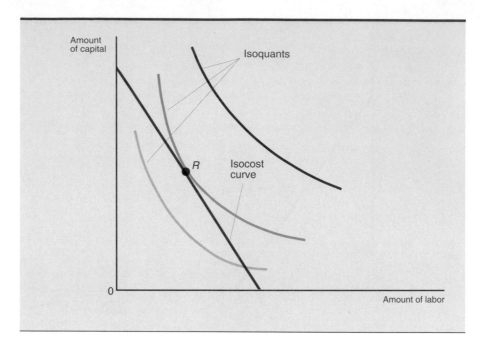

**FIGURE 6.8   Maximization of Output for Given Cost**   To maximize output for a given cost, the firm should choose the input combination at point *R*.

If there are more than two inputs, the firm will maximize output by distributing its expenditures among various inputs in such a way that the marginal product of a dollar's worth of any one input is equal to the marginal product of a dollar's worth of any other input used. Thus, the firm will choose an input combination such that

$$\frac{MP_a}{P_a} = \frac{MP_b}{P_b} = \cdots = \frac{MP_n}{P_n}, \tag{6.11}$$

where $MP_a, MP_b, \ldots, MP_n$ are the marginal products of inputs $a, b, \ldots, n$, and $P_a, P_b, \ldots, P_n$ are the prices of inputs $a, b, \ldots, n$. (For further proof of the decision rule in equation (6.11), see the chapter appendix.)

To determine the input combination that will minimize the cost of producing a given output, we use a graph similar to Figure 6.8. Moving along the isoquant corresponding to the stipulated output level, we must find the point on the isoquant that lies on the lowest isocost curve, for example, $S$ in Figure 6.9. Input combinations on isocost curves like $C_0$ that lie below $S$ are cheaper than $S$, but they cannot produce the desired output. Input combinations on isocost curves like $C_2$ that lie above $S$ will produce the desired output but at a higher cost than $S$. It is obvious that the optimal point, $S$, is a

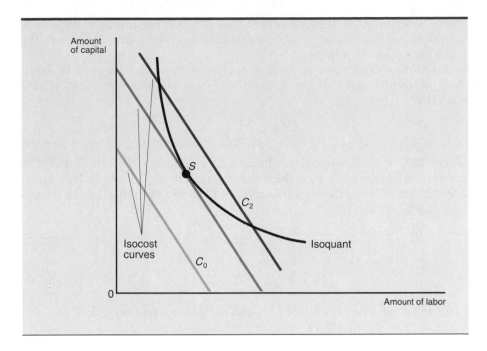

**FIGURE 6.9** *Minimization of Cost for Given Output* To minimize the cost of producing the amount of output corresponding to this isoquant, the firm should choose the input combination at point $S$.

point where the isocost curve is tangent to the isoquant. Thus, to minimize the cost of producing a given output or to maximize the output from a given cost outlay, the firm must equate $MP_L/MP_K$ and $P_L/P_K$—which means that $MP_L/P_L = MP_K/P_K$. And if more than two inputs are needed, the firm must satisfy equation (6.11).

## THE BEISWANGER COMPANY: A NUMERICAL EXAMPLE

To illustrate how the technique presented in the previous section can be used, consider the Beiswanger Company, a small firm engaged in engineering analysis. Beiswanger's president has determined that the firm's output per month $(Q)$ is related in the following way to the number of engineers used $(E)$ and the number of technicians used $(T)$:

$$Q = 20E - E^2 + 12T - 0.5T^2. \tag{6.12}$$

The monthly wage of an engineer is \$4,000, and the monthly wage of a technician is $2,000. If Beiswanger allots $28,000 per month for the total combined wages of engineers and technicians, how many engineers and technicians should it hire?

Based on the previous section, if the Beiswanger Company is to maximize output, it must choose a combination of engineers and technicians such that

$$\frac{MP_E}{P_E} = \frac{MP_T}{P_T}, \tag{6.13}$$

where $MP_E$ is the marginal product of an engineer, $MP_T$ is the marginal product of a technician, $P_E$ is the wage of an engineer, and $P_T$ is the wage of a technician. Taking partial derivatives of $Q$ in equation (6.12) with respect to $E$ and $T$, we find that

$$MP_E = \frac{\partial Q}{\partial E} = 20 - 2E, \tag{6.14a}$$

$$MP_T = \frac{\partial Q}{\partial T} = 12 - T. \tag{6.14b}$$

Inserting these expressions for $MP_E$ and $MP_T$ into equation (6.13), and noting that $P_E = 4,000$ and $P_T = 2,000$, it follows from equation (6.13) that

$$\frac{20 - 2E}{4,000} = \frac{12 - T}{2,000},$$

$$\frac{2,000(20 - 2E)}{4,000} = 12 - T,$$

$$10 - E = 12 - T,$$

which implies that $T = E + 2$.

Since Beiswanger will spend $28,000 per month on the total combined wages of engineers and technicians,

$$4,000E + 2,000T = 28,000.$$

Substituting $(E + 2)$ for $T$,

$$4,000E + 2,000(E + 2) = 28,000,$$

which means that $E = 4$ (and $T = 6$). Thus, to maximize the output from the $28,000 outlay on wages, Beiswanger should hire 4 engineers and 6 technicians.

## THE MILLER COMPANY: ANOTHER NUMERICAL EXAMPLE

To show how the analysis in the section before last can be used to determine the input combination that will minimize the cost of producing a given output, consider the Miller Company, where the relationship between output per hour ($Q$) and the number of workers ($L$) and the number of machines ($K$) used per hour is as follows:

$$Q = 10\sqrt{LK}.$$

The wage of a worker is \$8 per hour, and the price of a machine is \$2 per hour. If the Miller Company produces 80 units of output per hour, how many workers and machines should it use?

According to equation (6.11), the Miller Company should choose an input combination such that

$$\frac{MP_L}{P_L} = \frac{MP_K}{P_K},$$

where $MP_L$ is the marginal product of a worker, $MP_K$ is the marginal product of a machine, $P_L$ is the wage of a worker, and $P_K$ is the price of using a machine. Since $Q = 10\sqrt{LK}$,

$$MP_L = \frac{\partial Q}{\partial L} = 5\sqrt{K/L},$$

$$MP_K = \frac{\partial Q}{\partial K} = 5\sqrt{L/K}.$$

Thus, if $MP_L/P_L = MP_K/P_K$,

$$\frac{5\sqrt{K/L}}{8} = \frac{5\sqrt{L/K}}{2}.$$

Multiplying both sides of this equation by $\sqrt{K/L}$, we get

$$\frac{5K}{8L} = \frac{5}{2},$$

which means that $K = 4L$. And since $Q = 80$,

$$10\sqrt{LK} = 80$$

$$10\sqrt{L(4L)} = 80$$

$$L = 4.$$

Thus, to minimize cost, the Miller Company should hire 4 workers and use 16 machines.

## OPTIMAL LOT SIZE

In previous sections, we have described how a firm's managers can find the input combination that minimizes the cost of producing a particular quantity of output. In this section, we extend our analysis to include more than one time period, and recognize that many firms produce goods in lots or batches, which are produced intermittently. A central question for such firms is: What is the optimal lot size? Managerial economists have devoted considerable attention to this question. By using the optimization techniques described in earlier chapters, this question can readily be answered, thus extending our analysis in previous sections.

Suppose that the Monarch Company, a manufacturer of trucks, has to produce 100,000 parts of a particular type, since each of its trucks requires such a part. Each time that the firm begins to produce this type of part, it incurs a setup cost of $20,000 because it has to devote considerable labor time to setting up the equipment that produces this part. The advantage of producing large lots is that this cuts the total setup costs incurred during the year. If the firm were to produce its annual requirement of 100,000 parts in one huge lot, it would only have to set up the equipment once, the result being that its total setup costs for the year would be $20,000. If it produced its annual requirement of 100,000 parts in two lots (each of 50,000), it would have to set up the equipment twice, the result being that the total setup costs for the year would be $40,000. The relationship between the size of a lot and the annual total setup costs is shown in Figure 6.10.

The reason why firms often do not produce large lots is that they result in large inventories that are expensive to maintain and finance. If, for example, the firm produces all 100,000 of the parts in one huge lot at the

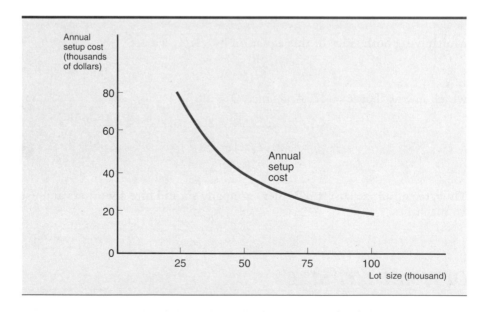

FIGURE 6.10 *Relationship between the Size of Lot and the Annual Setup Costs* The larger the lot size, the lower the annual setup costs.

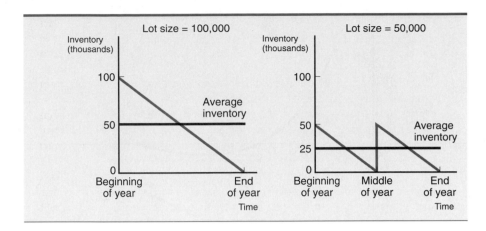

**FIGURE 6.11** *Size of Inventory during the Year* Average inventory is 50,000 parts if the lot size equals 100,000 and 25,000 parts if the lot size equals 50,000.

beginning of the year, its inventory equals 100,000 parts at the beginning of the year and zero parts at the end of the year. Its average inventory is 50,000 parts, as shown in the left-hand panel of Figure 6.11. On the other hand, if the firm produces the annual requirement of 100,000 parts in two lots (each of 50,000 units), its inventory equals 50,000 parts at the beginning of the year and zero parts at the end of six months; then after the second lot is produced, its inventory jumps back up to 50,000 parts, after which it declines once again to zero parts at the end of the year. Thus, its average inventory is 25,000 parts, as shown in the right-hand panel of Figure 6.11.

If the annual cost of holding inventory is proportional to the average inventory, the relationship between the size of a lot and the annual cost of holding inventory is shown in Figure 6.12. Adding the annual setup costs for each lot size (taken from Figure 6.10 and reproduced in Figure 6.12) to the inventory costs, we obtain the total annual cost for each lot size. Under the conditions shown in Figure 6.12, the optimal lot size is 70,711, where the total annual costs are a minimum.

In general, how can we determine the optimal lot size? Total annual setup costs equal $20,000Q/L$ dollars, where $Q$ is the total annual requirement of the relevant part, and $L$ is the number of identical parts of this sort produced in a lot. If 80 cents is the annual cost of holding each identical part of this sort in inventory for a year, the annual cost of holding inventory equals $0.8L/2$ dollars. Adding the annual setup costs and the annual costs of holding inventory, we obtain the following expression for the total annual costs:

$$C = 0.8L/2 + 20{,}000Q/L.$$

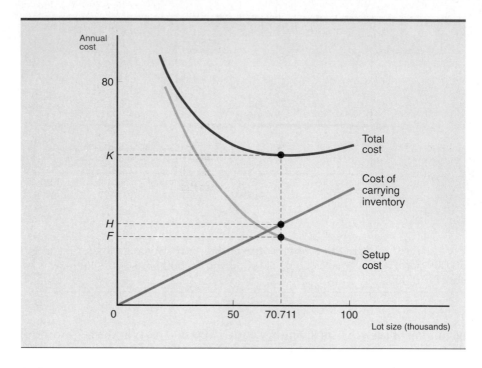

**FIGURE 6.12** *Relationship between Size of Lot and Total Annual Costs* Total cost is the sum of the cost of carrying inventory and the setup cost. Thus, the "Total cost" curve is the vertical sum of the "Cost of carrying inventory" curve and the "Setup cost" curve. For example, if the lot size is 70,711, annual setup cost equals *OF*, annual inventory cost equals *OH*, and annual total cost equals *OF* + *OH* = *OK*.

To minimize total annual costs, we set

$$\frac{dC}{dL} = 0.4 - \frac{20,000Q}{L^2} = 0.$$

Solving for *L*, we find that to minimize total annual costs, *L* should equal

$$\sqrt{\frac{20,000Q}{0.4}}. \tag{6.15}$$

More generally, the optimal lot size equals $\sqrt{2SQ/b}$, where *S* is the cost per setup and *b* is the annual cost of carrying each good of this sort in inventory.

In the case of the Monarch Company described above, *Q* equals 100,000. Thus, to minimize total annual costs, *L* should equal $\sqrt{20,000(100,000)/0.4}$ = $\sqrt{5 \text{ billion}}$ = 70,711. In other words, the optimal lot size is 70,711, which means that 70,711 identical parts of this sort should be produced in each lot. (Of course, there is no reason for the number of setups per year to be an integer number. For example, one could have 5 setups during each two-year period, or $2\frac{1}{2}$ setups per year.)[6]

# WHAT TOYOTA TAUGHT THE WORLD

The Japanese have forged ahead of the rest of the world in some areas of production. For one thing, they have succeeded in lowering the cost per setup, thus reducing the optimal lot size. For example, in the late 1970s, Toyota Motor Company's workers took about 10 minutes to set up the 800-ton presses used in forming auto hoods and fenders, whereas this took about 6 hours in the United States. (See Table 6.4 for other cases.) To see that such a reduction in the cost per setup will reduce the optimal lot size, consider the Monarch Company, discussed in the previous section. If this firm can reduce the cost per setup from $20,000 to $5,000, the optimal lot size will be $\sqrt{5,000Q/0.4}$, not $\sqrt{20,000Q/0.4}$, which means that the optimal lot size will be cut in half (holding Q constant).

TABLE 6.4 *Reductions in Time Required to Set Up Selected Machines, Japanese Firms*

| Firm | Machine | Initial setup time | New setup time |
|------|---------|--------------------|----------------|
| Toyota | Bolt maker | 8 hours | 1 minute |
| Mazda | Ring gear cutter | 6.5 hours | 15 minutes |
| Mazda | Die casting machine | 1.5 hours | 4 minutes |
| Mitsubishi | 8-arbor boring machine | 24 hours | 3 minutes |

Source: J. Blackburn, *Time-Based Competition.*

A big advantage of reducing lot sizes is that less inventory has to be held. At least one senior Japanese manager has stated that "inventory is the root of all evil." Toyota's famous just-in-time production system (page 229) calls for every part's arrival just when it is needed, or just when a machine is available. This can result in a great increase in efficiency. Less work-in-process inventory cuts the cost of holding inventory, as well as speeds up the production cycle time, and makes it simpler to monitor the progress of work through the factory.[7]

According to some estimates, 35,000 American firms are experimenting with just-in-time production systems, and at least 500 are trying to use them throughout their organizations. The results have sometimes been

---

[6] See J. Magee, "Guides to Inventory Policy: Functions and Lot Sizes," in E. Mansfield, ed. *Managerial Economics and Operations Research*, 5th ed.

[7] R. Hayes and S. Wheelwright, *Restoring Our Competitive Edge* (New York: Wiley, 1984). Also, see National Research Council, "The Japanese Cost and Quality Advantages in the Auto Industry," in E. Mansfield, ed., *Managerial Economics and Operations Research*, 5th ed.

stunning. For example, consider Northern Telecom's plant in Santa Clara, California, which makes printed circuit boards. Managers report that output increased by 25 percent, without additional workers, and that inventories were reduced by over 80 percent.

Another technique adopted by the Japanese is focused manufacturing. For example, Toyota, in making forklift trucks, restricted its production to a comparatively narrow line of 6 families of trucks in its factory in Nagoya. In this way, it reduced the complexity of its production operations, which in turn decreased the number of parts, the level of inventories, the required amount of supervision, and the number of errors and defects. Table 6.5 compares the average cost of producing a forklift truck at Toyota with that at a West European factory that produced 20 families of trucks in its factory. As you can see, Toyota's cost was about 20 percent lower than the West European firm.[8]

TABLE 6.5 *Cost of Producing a Forklift Truck (European Cost = 100)*

| | Factory | |
| --- | --- | --- |
| | West European | Toyota |
| Number of product families | 20 | 6 |
| Cost per truck | | |
|     Materials | 75 | 65 |
|     Direct labor | 4 | 2 |
|     Overhead | 21 | 14 |
|     Total cost | 100 | 81 |

*Source:* J. Abegglen and G. Stalk, *Kaisha.*

American, European, and other firms have responded by adopting similar techniques. For example, the West European manufacturer of forklift trucks in Table 6.5 reduced the number of product families made in its plant from 20 to 6. The result was about the same as in Japan: cost per truck fell by 19 percent.[9] One important point that this illustrates is that Japanese firms have no monopoly on production knowledge and expertise. Indeed, many of the ideas that the Japanese have utilized with great success—for example, quality control techniques—originated in the United States. Where American firms have sometimes gone wrong is that they have been slow to put these ideas into practice. Consequently, they sometimes have used more inputs than were required, and have operated off, not on, the industry production function. (The industry production function is the production function of the most efficient firms in the industry.)

---

[8] J. Abegglen, and G. Stalk, *Kaisha: The Japanese Corporation* (New York: Basic Books, 1985). Of course, from a marketing point of view, there can be disadvantages in reducing the variety of products produced. They must be balanced against the cost reductions.
[9] Ibid.

## ADVANTAGES OF JUST-IN-TIME PRODUCTION

During the 1950s and 1960s, the Toyota Motor Company originated and developed the just-in-time system of production, which has had an enormous effect in Japan and elsewhere. According to this system, materials, parts, and components are produced and delivered just before they are needed. One advantage is that inventories of parts and of work in process are reduced considerably, but this is only part of the story. In addition, the time and cost required to change from the production of one part or model to another are reduced, thus cutting setup costs and enabling the firm to produce small lots economically.

A careful comparison of an automobile plant using the just-in-time system with an automobile plant not using it resulted in the following data:*

|  | Plant using just-in-time system | Plant not using just-in-time system |
| --- | --- | --- |
| Cars produced per day | 1,000 | 860 |
| Total factory workers | 1,000 | 2,150 |
| Workers per car per day |  |  |
| Direct labor | 0.79 | 1.25 |
| Overhead personnel | 0.21 | 1.25 |
| Total | 1.00 | 2.50 |

(a) Based on this comparison, does it appear that the average product of labor is higher with the just-in-time system than without it? (b) Does such a system increase the average product of overhead personnel to a greater extent than it does the average product of direct labor? (c) If changeovers from one part or model to another require a great deal of time, the required planning and management effort is greater than it would be if such changeovers could be accomplished quickly. Does this help to explain why the average product of overhead personnel increases so much? (d) According to James Abegglen and George Stalk, "Many Japanese companies by adopting the just-in-time system doubled the productivity of their factory labor forces and almost doubled the productivity of the assets they employed." Did this result in a shift in these firm's isoquants, or a movement along fixed isoquants?

*Solution* (a) Yes. The number of cars produced per day divided by the number of workers is 1.0 in the plant using the just-in-time system, but only 0.4 in the plant not using the just-in-time system. (b) Based on the above figures, this seems to be the case. The average product of labor—the number of cars produced per day divided by the number of workers—is the reciprocal of the number of workers per car per day. Thus, the average product of *overhead* workers is $1/0.21 = 4.76$ using the just-in-time system, but $1/1.25 = 0.8$ without it. On the other hand, the average product of workers *engaged in direct labor* is $1/0.79 = 1.27$ using the just-in-time system, but $1/1.25 = 0.8$ without it. Clearly, the percentage increase in average product is greater for overhead workers than for direct labor. (c)

Yes. One reason why the just-in-time system decreases overhead labor considerably is that the time required for planning and management is reduced because change-overs are faster. (d) The firms' isoquants shifted inward toward the origin.

* J. Abegglen and G. Stalk, *Kaisha*.

## RETURNS TO SCALE

In previous sections, we have learned how technology in a particular industry can be represented by a production function and have described the characteristics of production functions (and of related concepts like the marginal and average product) that seem to hold in general for production processes. However, one important characteristic of production functions has not been described: how output responds in the long run to changes in the *scale* of the firm. In other words, suppose we consider a long-run situation in which all inputs are variable, and suppose the firm increases the amount of all inputs by the same proportion. What will happen to output?

Clearly, there are three possibilities: First, output may increase by a larger proportion than each of the inputs. For example, a doubling of all inputs may lead to more than a doubling of output. This is the case of **increasing returns to scale.** Second, output may increase by a smaller proportion than each of the inputs. For example, a doubling of all inputs may lead to less than a doubling of output. This is the case of **decreasing returns to scale.** Third, output may increase by exactly the same proportion as the inputs. For example, a doubling of all inputs may lead to a doubling of output. This is the case of **constant returns to scale.**

It may seem that production functions must necessarily exhibit constant returns to scale. If two factories are built with the same plant and the same types of workers, it may appear obvious that twice as much output will result. But things are not so simple. If a firm doubles its scale, it may be able to use techniques that could not be used at the smaller scale. Some inputs are not available in small units; for example, we cannot install half a robot. Because of indivisibilities of this sort, increasing returns to scale may occur. Thus, although one could double a firm's size by simply building two small factories, this may be inefficient. One large factory may be more efficient than two smaller factories of the same total capacity because it is large enough to use certain techniques and inputs that the smaller factories cannot employ.

Increasing returns to scale also arise because of certain geometrical relations. Since the volume of a box that is $2 \times 2 \times 2$ feet is 8 times as great as the volume of a box that is $1 \times 1 \times 1$ foot, the former box can carry 8 times as much as the latter box. But since the area of the six sides of the $2 \times 2 \times 2$-foot box is 24 square feet and the area of the six sides of the $1 \times 1 \times 1$-foot box is 6 square feet, the former box only requires 4 times as much wood as the latter. Greater specialization also can result in increasing returns to scale: as more men and machines are used, it is possible to subdivide tasks and allow various inputs to specialize. Also, economies of scale may arise because of probabilistic considerations: for example, because the aggregate behavior of a bigger number of customers tends to be more stable, a firm's inventory may not have to increase in proportion to its sales.

Why do decreasing returns to scale occur? The most frequently cited reason is the difficulty of coordinating a large enterprise. It can be difficult even in a small firm to obtain the information required to make important decisions; in a large firm, the difficulties tend to be greater. It can be difficult even in a small firm to be certain that management's wishes are being carried out; in a larger firm, these difficulties too tend to be greater. Although the advantages of a large organization are obvious, there are often very great disadvantages. For example, in certain kinds of research and development, there is evidence that large engineering teams tend to be less effective than smaller ones and that large firms tend to be less effective than small ones.

Whether or not there are constant, increasing, or decreasing returns to scale in a particular situation is an empirical question that must be settled case by case. There is no simple, all-encompassing answer. In some industries, the available evidence may indicate that increasing returns are present over a certain range of output. In other industries, decreasing or constant returns may be present. Moreover, it is important to note that the answer is likely to depend on the level of output that is considered. There may be increasing returns to scale at small output levels and constant or decreasing returns to scale at larger output levels.

## THE OUTPUT ELASTICITY

To measure whether there are increasing, decreasing, or constant returns to scale, the **output elasticity** can be computed. *The output elasticity is defined as the percentage change in output resulting from 1 percent increase in all inputs.* If the output elasticity exceeds 1, there are increasing returns to scale; if it equals 1, there are constant returns to scale; and if it is less than 1, there are decreasing returns to scale.

As an illustration, consider the Lone Star Company, a maker of aircraft parts, which has the following production function:

$$Q = .8L^{.3}K^{.8},$$

## CHOOSING THE SIZE OF AN OIL TANKER*

Leading oil companies, as well as independent shipowners like Aristotle Onassis, Stavos Niarchos, and Y. K. Pao, have invested billions of dollars in oil tankers. An oil tanker can be regarded as a large cylinder. The surface area of a cylinder is not proportional to its volume; instead, as a cylinder's volume increases, its surface area goes up less than proportionately. Thus, a tanker that can carry 200,000 deadweight tons is only about twice as broad, long, and deep as a tanker that can carry 20,000 deadweight tons.

Up to the late 1970s, there was a trend toward larger tankers, as indicated below:

| Year | Average tanker size (thousands of deadweight tons) |
|------|----------------------------------------------------|
| 1956 | 16.2 |
| 1964 | 23.5 |
| 1967 | 35.0 |
| 1973 | 64.0 |
| 1978 | 103.0 |

In the fall of 1977, there was a substantial surplus of tanker capacity. According to one major oil company's estimates of the supply and demand for tanker capacity, the quantity supplied exceeded the quantity demanded by almost 30 percent in 1976.

If there were no oversupply of tankers, and if you were a consultant to an oil company that was interested in building a new tanker, would you advise the company to build a tanker that can carry about 20,000 deadweight tons?

* For further discussion, see Michael Porter, *Cases in Competitive Strategy* (New York: Free Press, 1983).

where $Q$ is the number of parts produced per year, $L$ is the number of workers hired, and $K$ is the amount of capital used. This is a Cobb-Douglas production function (named after Charles Cobb and Paul Douglas, who pioneered in its application), which will be discussed in more detail in the section after next. ($Q$ is measured in millions of parts.)

To calculate the output elasticity at the Lone Star Company, let's see what happens to $Q$ if we multiply both inputs ($L$ and $K$) by 1.01. Clearly, the new value of $Q$, that is, $Q'$, equals

$$Q' = .8(1.01L)^{.3}(1.01K)^{.8}$$
$$= .8(1.01)^{1.1}L^{.3}K^{.8}$$
$$= (1.01)^{1.1}(.8L^{.3}K^{.8})$$
$$= (1.01)^{1.1}Q$$
$$= 1.011Q.$$

Thus, if the quantity of both inputs increases by 1 percent, output increases by 1.1 percent, which means that the output elasticity equals 1.1.

## HOW FIRMS OBTAIN INFORMATION CONCERNING THE PRODUCTION FUNCTION: COMPETITIVE BENCHMARKING AT XEROX[10]

Having discussed at length the key role of the production function in managerial decision making, we must look carefully at how managers obtain information concerning the production function. How does Hewlett-Packard or Merck or Exxon find out how to get the most out of a particular combination of inputs, and what the maximum output obtainable from this input combination is? One way that firms try to solve this problem is by sending out teams of engineers and technicians to visit other firms to obtain information concerning best-practice methods and procedures. In this way, they try to determine whether they are operating on the industry production function—or whether they are inefficient relative to other firms. This practice, known as **competitive benchmarking,** has produced valuable results for many companies, such as the Xerox Corporation.

In 1979, Xerox, confronted with a falling share of the market and reduced profitability of its basic copier business, began a searching examination of its methods. (Recall Chapter 1.) Starting with an engineering study of rival products, including an examination of Fuji Xerox, its partly owned subsidiary in Japan, Xerox's executives found strong evidence that it was not as efficient as its major Japanese rivals.

---

[10] This section is based largely on R. Hayes, S. Wheelwright, and K. Clark, *Dynamic Manufacturing* (New York: Free Press, 1988).

Interestingly, Xerox found that it could learn a great deal from firms in seemingly unrelated fields. For example, Xerox executives, intent on improving their warehousing operations, searched for a firm to study in this regard. After looking in trade journals and discussing warehousing systems with consultants, they decided to visit L.L. Bean, the Maine apparel and footwear seller, which had acquired a strong reputation for customer service and which had distribution problems similar to Xerox's.

---

TABLE 6.6    *Comparison of Warehouse Operations in 1982*

| Measure of output per worker per day | L.L. Bean | Xerox |
|---|---|---|
| Orders per worker per day | 550 | 117 |
| Lines* per worker per day | 1,440 | 497 |

\* A line is a standard measure of travel distance for one trip to a storage bin.
*Source:* R. Hayes, S. Wheelwright, and K. Clark, *Dynamic Manufacturing.*

---

Xerox's managers found that although L.L. Bean's warehouse operations were largely manual, it had achieved a high degree of output per worker. Table 6.6 compares output per worker in L.L. Bean's warehouse operation in 1982 with a proposed operation at Xerox. In large part, Bean's superiority could be attributed to differences in methods; it arranged materials so that big-selling items were closer to stock pickers, and it chose storage locations to minimize forklift travel distance.

In this way, Xerox learned what the production function was for this type of warehousing operation. Based on these findings, it modernized its own warehousing operations. Competitive benchmarking is a very important technique and is applicable in a wide variety of areas. Xerox's top managers felt that it was responsible for much of the improvement in the firm's performance during the 1980s. Many other firms swear by the effectiveness and significance of this technique.

## MEASUREMENT OF PRODUCTION FUNCTIONS

Although techniques like competitive benchmarking are valuable, they generally can provide only part of the information managers need concerning production functions. Thus, managerial economists have devised other methods, based largely on the regression techniques described in Chapter 4, to measure production functions. As we will see in subsequent sections of this chapter, the results often have proved very useful. One of the first steps in estimating a production function is to choose the mathematical form of the production function. If labor and capital are the only inputs used, one possible mathematical form is the following cubic equation:

$$Q = aLK + bL^2K + cLK^2 - dL^3K - eLK^3, \qquad (6.16)$$

where $Q$ is output, $L$ is the quantity of labor input, and $K$ is the quantity of capital output. This mathematical form exhibits first increasing and then decreasing returns to scale. Also, the marginal product of each input first increases and then decreases as more and more of the input is used. To see that this is true, consider the marginal product of labor, which equals

$$\frac{\partial Q}{\partial L} = (aK + cK^2 - eK^3) + 2bKL - 3dKL^2.$$

Clearly, the marginal product of labor is a quadratic function of the amount of labor used; it increases at first and then decreases as more and more labor is employed.

Another mathematical form that is more commonly used is the Cobb-Douglas form, which we encountered in the section before last. With only two inputs, this form is

$$Q = aL^bK^c. \tag{6.17}$$

One advantage of this form is that the marginal productivity of each input depends on the level of all inputs employed, which is often realistic. Consider the marginal product of labor, which equals

$$\frac{\partial Q}{\partial L} = baL^{b-1}K^c.$$

Obviously, the marginal product of labor depends on the values of both $L$ and $K$. Another advantage is that if logarithms are taken of both sides of equation (6.17),

$$\log Q = \log a + b \log L + c \log K. \tag{6.18}$$

Thus, the regression techniques in Chapter 4 can be used to estimate $b$ and $c$ (as well as $\log a$). If we regress $\log Q$ on $\log L$ and $\log K$, the regression coefficients are these estimates.

Note that if the Cobb-Douglas production function is used, we can easily estimate the returns to scale. If the sum of the exponents (that is, $b + c$) exceeds 1, increasing returns to scale are indicated; if the sum of the exponents equals 1, constant returns to scale prevail; and if the sum of the exponents is less than 1, decreasing returns to scale are indicated. This is because, if the Cobb-Douglas production functions prevails, the output elasticity equals the sum of the exponents. For example, in the section before last, the output elasticity of the Lone Star Company was 1.1, which equaled the sum of the exponents (.3 and .8).

There is no cut-and-dried way to determine which mathematical form is best, since the answer depends on the particular situation. Frequently, a good procedure is to try more than one mathematical form and see which one fits the data best. The important thing is that the chosen form provide a faithful representation of the actual situation. To determine whether this is the case, it often is useful to see how well a particular estimated production function can forecast the quantity of output resulting from the combination of inputs actually used.

# THREE TYPES OF STATISTICAL ANALYSIS

Having chosen a mathematical form for the production function, there remains the question of which of three types of data to use. One possibility is to use time-series data concerning the amount of various inputs used in various periods in the past and the amount of output produced in each period. For example, you might obtain data concerning the amount of labor, the amount of capital, and the amount of various raw materials used in the steel industry during each year from 1958 to 1993. On the basis of such data and information concerning the annual output of steel during 1958 to 1993, you might estimate the relationship between the amounts of the inputs and the resulting output, using regression techniques like those discussed in Chapter 4.

The second possibility is to use cross-section data concerning the amount of various inputs used and output produced in various firms or sectors of the industry at a given time. For example, you might obtain data concerning the amount of labor, the amount of capital, and the amount of various raw materials used in various firms in the steel industry in 1993. On the basis of such data and information concerning the 1993 output of each firm, you might use regression techniques to estimate the relationship between the amounts of the inputs and the resulting output.

The third possibility is to use technical information supplied by the engineer or the agricultural scientist. This information is collected by experiment or from experience with the day-to-day workings of the technical process. There are advantages to be gained from approaching the measurement of the production function from this angle because the range of applicability of the data is known, and, unlike time-series and cross-section studies, we are not restricted to the narrow range of actual observations.[11]

Regardless of which approach you use, it is important to recognize that the data may not always represent technically efficient combinations of inputs and output. For example, because of errors or constraints, the amount of inputs used by the steel industry in 1993 may not have been the minimum required to produce the 1993 output of the steel industry. Since the production function theoretically includes only efficient input combinations, a case of this sort should be excluded, if our measurements are to be pristine pure. In practice, however, such cases are not always excluded (or recognized), and the resulting estimate of the production function contains errors on this account.

Another important difficulty is the measurement of capital input. The principal problem stems from the fact that the stock of capital is composed of various types and ages of machines, buildings, and inventories. Combining them into a single measure—or a few measures—is not easy. In addi-

---

[11] For an illustration of this approach, see L. Cookenboo, "Production Functions and Cost Functions in Oil Pipelines" in the study guide accompanying this textbook.

tion, errors can arise because various data points, which are assumed to be on the same production function, are in fact on different ones. Moreover, biases can occur because of identification problems somewhat similar to those discussed on pages 118 to 121.

With regard to the engineering approach, it is difficult to combine the results for the processes for which engineers have data into an overall plant or firm production function. Since engineering data generally pertain to only a part of the firm's activities, this is often a very hard job. For example, engineering data tell us little or nothing about the firm's marketing or financial activities.

## THE TELEPHONE INDUSTRY IN CANADA: A CASE STUDY

Despite these difficulties, estimates of production functions have proved of considerable interest and value. To illustrate the empirical results that have been obtained, A. Dobell, L. Taylor, L. Waverman, T. Liu, and M. Copeland[12] found that the production function in the telephone industry in Canada was

$$Q = AL^{.70}K^{.41}, \tag{6.19}$$

where $A$ is the level of output when both $L$ and $K$ equal 1. Based on this equation, it appears that a 1 percent increase in labor (holding the amount of capital constant) will result in a 0.70 percent increase in output. To prove that this is true, note that

$$\frac{\partial Q}{\partial L} = .70AL^{-.30}K^{.41}$$

$$= .70\frac{Q}{L}.$$

Thus,

$$\frac{\partial Q}{\partial L} \cdot \frac{L}{Q} = .70. \tag{6.20}$$

Since $(\partial Q/\partial L)\,(L/Q)$ is (approximately) equal to the percentage increase in output resulting from a 1 percent increase in labor, a 1 percent increase in labor will result in a 0.70 percent increase in output.

Based on the estimated production function in equation (6.19), one can also determine the effect on output of a 1 percent increase in capital.

---

[12] A. Dobell, L. Taylor, L. Waverman, T. Liu, and M. Copeland, "Communications in Canada," *Bell Journal of Economics and Management Science* (1972).

Because

$$\frac{\partial Q}{\partial K} = .41AL^{.70}K^{-.59}$$

$$= .41\frac{Q}{K},$$

it follows that a 1 percent increase in capital will raise the output of the telephone industry by .41 percent. Why? Because $(\partial Q/\partial K)(K/Q) = 0.41$.

In addition, equation (6.19) provides valuable information concerning returns to scale in the Canadian telephone industry. Because the production function is of the Cobb-Douglas form, the output elasticity equals the sum of the exponents; that is, it equals $0.70 + 0.41 = 1.11$. (Recall our discussion on page 235.) Since the output elasticity is the percentage change in output resulting from a 1 percent increase in all inputs, this means that a 1 percent increase in all inputs would result in a 1.11 percent increase in output. Clearly these results indicate increasing returns to scale.

Estimated production functions of this sort are of enormous value to managers and analysts, since they enable the manager or analyst to estimate the marginal product of each input, and to determine whether there are increasing, decreasing, or constant returns to scale. As we have stressed in this chapter, information of this kind is of fundamental importance in deciding how to minimize a firm's costs. In a world where competition is intense and costs matter greatly, it is no wonder that firms find estimated production functions valuable.

## POULTRY PRODUCTION IN THE UNITED STATES: ANOTHER CASE STUDY

As a further illustration, consider the production of broiler chickens, which is a big industry in the United States (1990 production value: $8.4 billion). To estimate the production function, an experiment was carried out in which broilers were fed various amounts of corn and soybean oilmeal, and the gain in weight of each broiler was carefully measured.[13] Based on regression analysis of the sort described in Chapter 4, it was found that

$$G = .03 + .48C + .64S - .02C^2 - .05S^2 - .02CS, \qquad (6.21)$$

where $G$ is the gain in weight (in pounds per broiler), $C$ is pounds of corn per broiler, and $S$ is pounds of soybean oilmeal per broiler. The multiple coefficient of determination ($R^2$) is very high, about .998.

---

[13] Organization for Economic Cooperation and Development, *Interdisciplinary Research in Input/Output Relationships and Production Functions to Improve Decisions and Efficiency for Poultry Production,* Paris, 1966.

Based on equation (6.21), we can obtain isoquants for poultry production. Suppose that we want to obtain the isoquant pertaining to a weight gain of 1 pound. In other words, we want to find the various combinations of amounts of corn per broiler and soybean oilmeal per broiler that will result in a weight gain per broiler of 1 pound. To find these combinations, we set $G = 1$, the result being

$$1 = .03 + .48C + .64S - .02C^2 - .05S^2 - .02CS. \qquad (6.22)$$

Then we set $C$ equal to various values and see what each resulting value of $S$ is. For example, suppose that $C = 1$. Then

$$1 = .03 + .48(1) + .64S - .02(1^2) - .05S^2 - .02(1)S,$$

or

$$1 = .03 + .48 - .02 + (.64 - .02)S - .05S^2,$$

or

$$0 = -.51 + .62S - .05S^2.$$

Thus, $S = -.62 + \sqrt{.62^2 - 4(-.05)(-.51)}/2(-.05) = 0.9$. Consequently, if a broiler is to gain 1 pound of weight, it must be fed 0.9 pound of soybean oilmeal, as well as 1 pound of corn.[14]

If we let $C = 1.1$, we can find the corresponding value of $S$ by substituting 1.1 for $C$ in equation (6.22) and solving for $S$. If we let $C = 1.2$, we can find the corresponding value of $S$ by substituting 1.2 for $C$ in equation (6.22) and solving for $S$. Proceeding in this way, we can find more and more points on the isoquant corresponding to a weight gain of 1 pound. The resulting isoquant is shown in Figure 6.13. Isoquants of this sort are of great importance to managers. Coupled with data regarding input prices, they can be used to determine how much of each input should be used to minimize costs. (Recall Figure 6.9.)

In fact, poultry producers have used the isoquant in Figure 6.13 to determine how much corn and soybean oilmeal to feed a broiler, if they want a 1-pound weight gain. To see how they have done this, suppose that the price of a pound of corn is two-thirds of the price of a pound of soybean oilmeal. Then the slope of each isocost curve in Figure 6.13 equals $-2/3$, since, as pointed out in Figure 6.7, the slope equals $-1$ times the price of the input on the horizontal axis (corn) divided by the price of the input on the vertical axis (soybean oilmeal). For the cost of the weight gain to be a minimum, the isocost curve should be tangent to the isoquant, which means that the slope of the isoquant should also equal $-2/3$. As shown in Figure 6.13, this occurs when 1.2 pounds of corn and 0.6 pounds of soybean oilmeal are used. Thus,

---

[14] To obtain this expression for $S$, we use the formula in note 4, Chapter 2. (See page 54.) There is another possible value of $S$, which corresponds to the use of the minus sign (rather than the plus sign) before $\sqrt{b^2 - 4ac}$ in this formula, but this other value is not relevant here.

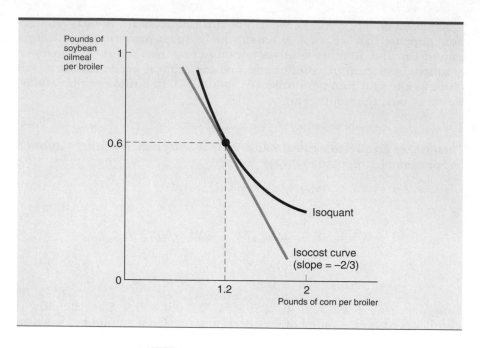

**FIGURE 6.13** *Isoquant for 1-Pound Weight Gain for a Broiler and Isocost Curve if Corn Price is 2/3 of Soybean Oilmeal Price* The optimal input combination is 1.2 pounds of corn and 0.6 pound of soybean oilmeal.

*Source:* Organization for Economic Cooperation and Development, *Interdisciplinary Research.*

this is the optimal input combination if the price of a pound of corn is two-thirds the price of a pound of soybean oilmeal.

## SUMMARY

1. The production function is the relationship between the quantities of various inputs used per period of time and the maximum quantity of the good that can be produced per period of time. Given the production function for a particular firm, one can calculate the average product of an input and the marginal product of an input.

2. To determine how much of a particular input to utilize, a firm should compare the marginal revenue product of the input with the marginal expenditure on the input. To maximize profit, the firm should utilize the amount of the input that results in the marginal revenue product being equal to the marginal expenditure.

3. An isoquant is a curve showing all possible (efficient) combinations of inputs that are capable of producing a particular quantity of output. The marginal rate of technical substitution shows the rate at which one input can be substituted for another input, if output remains constant. No profit-maximizing firm will operate at a point where the isoquant is positively sloped.

4. To minimize the cost of producing a particular output, a firm should allocate its expenditures among various inputs in such a way that the ratio of the marginal product to the input price is the same for all inputs used. Graphically, this amounts to choosing the input combination where the relevant isoquant is tangent to an isocost curve.

5. Many firms produce goods in lots. The optimal lot size equals $\sqrt{2SQ/b}$, where $S$ is the cost per setup, $Q$ is the total annual requirement of the relevant good, and $b$ is the annual cost of holding each good of this sort in inventory. It is important that firms produce lots of approximately optimal size; otherwise, their costs will be higher than is necessary or desirable.

6. If the firm increases all inputs by the same proportion and output increases by more (less) than this proportion, there are increasing (decreasing) returns to scale. Increasing returns to scale may occur because of indivisibility of inputs, various geometrical relations, or specialization. Decreasing returns to scale can also occur; the most frequently cited reason is the difficulty of managing a huge enterprise. Whether or not there are constant, increasing, or decreasing returns to scale is an empirical question that must be settled case by case.

7. Competitive benchmarking is frequently used to obtain information concerning the production function. Also, using techniques of the sort described in Chapter 4, business analysts, engineers, and others have estimated production functions in many firms and industries. Statistical analysis of time series and cross-section data, as well as engineering data, have been carried out. For example, many studies have fit the Cobb-Douglas production function to the data. The results have proved of considerable value to managers, here and abroad.

## PROBLEMS

1. In the Elwyn Company, the relationship between output $(Q)$ and the number of hours of skilled labor $(S)$ and unskilled labor $(U)$ is as follows:

$$Q = 300S + 200U - 0.2S^2 - 0.3U^2.$$

The hourly wage of skilled labor is \$10, and the hourly wage of unskilled labor is \$5. The firm can hire as much labor as it wants at these wage rates.

(a) Elwyn's chief engineer recommends that the firm hire 400 hours of skilled labor and 100 hours of unskilled labor. Evaluate this recommendation.

(b) If the Elwyn Company decides to spend a total of $5,000 on skilled and unskilled labor, how many hours of each type of labor should it hire?

(c) If the price of a unit of output is $10 (and does not vary with output), how many hours of unskilled labor should the company hire?

2. Based on a regression analysis like those in Chapter 4, the Washington Company finds that its production function is as follows:

$$\log Q = 1.50 + .76 \log L + .24 \log K,$$

where $Q$ is its daily output, $L$ is the number of workers employed per day, and $K$ is the number of machines used per day. The Washington Company's product is sold in a competitive market, the price per unit being $10. The firm cannot influence the wage of workers or the price of machines.

(a) If the wage of a worker is $30 per day, how many workers per unit of output should the firm hire?

(b) What percentage of the firm's revenues will be spent on labor? Why?

(c) Will this percentage vary, depending on the daily wage of a worker? Why or why not?

3. A consulting firm specializing in agriculture determines that the following combinations of hay and grain consumption per lamb will result in a 25-pound gain on a lamb:

| Pounds of hay | Pounds of grain |
|---|---|
| 40 | 130.9 |
| 50 | 125.1 |
| 60 | 120.1 |
| 70 | 115.7 |
| 80 | 111.8 |
| 90 | 108.3 |
| 110 | 102.3 |
| 130 | 97.4 |
| 150 | 93.8 |

(a) The firm's president wants to estimate the marginal product of a pound of grain in producing lamb. Can he do so on the basis of these data?

(b) The firm's president is convinced that constant returns to scale prevail in lamb production. If this is true, and if hay and grain consumption per lamb are the only inputs, how much gain will accrue if the hay consumption per lamb is 100 pounds and the grain consumption per lamb is 250.2 pounds?

(c) What is the marginal rate of technical substitution of hay for grain when between 40 and 50 pounds of hay (and between 130.9 and 125.1 pounds of grain) are consumed per lamb?

(d) A major advance in technology occurs that allows farmers to produce a 25-pound gain on a lamb with less hay and grain than the above table indicates. If the marginal rate of technical substitution (at each rate of consumption of each input) is the same after the technological advance as before, can you draw the new isoquant corresponding to a 25-pound gain on a lamb?

4. The Ascot Corporation, which produces stationery, hires a consultant to estimate its production function. The consultant concludes that

$$Q = .9P + .06L,$$

where $Q$ is the number of pounds of stationery produced by Ascot per year, $L$ is the number of hours of labor per year, and $P$ is the number of pounds of paper used per year.

(a) Does this production function seem to include all of the relevant inputs? Explain.

(b) Does this production function seem reasonable, if it is applied to all possible values of $L$? Explain.

(c) Does this production function exhibit diminishing marginal returns?

5. A Cobb Douglas production function was estimated for six types of farms, there being 5 inputs in the production function: (1) land, (2) labor, (3) equipment, (4) livestock and feed, and (5) other resource services. The exponent of each input was as shown below:

| | | | | Exponent | |
| | | | | Livestock | Other resource |
| Farm type | Land | Labor | Equipment | and feed | services |
| --- | --- | --- | --- | --- | --- |
| Crop farms | 0.24 | 0.07 | 0.08 | 0.53 | 0.02 |
| Hog farms | 0.07 | 0.02 | 0.10 | 0.74 | 0.03 |
| Dairy farms | 0.10 | 0.01 | 0.06 | 0.63 | 0.02 |
| General farms | 0.17 | 0.12 | 0.16 | 0.46 | 0.03 |
| Large farms | 0.28 | 0.01 | 0.11 | 0.53 | 0.03 |
| Small farms | 0.21 | 0.05 | 0.08 | 0.43 | 0.03 |

(a) Do there appear to be increasing returns to scale in any of these six types of farms?

(b) In what type of farm does a 1 percent increase in labor have the largest percentage effect on output?

(c) Based on these results, would you expect that output would increase if many of the farms included in this sample were merged?

6. According to the chief engineer at the Zodiac Company, $Q = AL^\alpha K^\beta$, where $Q$ is the output rate, $L$ is the rate of labor input, and $K$ is the rate of capital input. Statistical analysis indicates that $\alpha = 0.8$ and $\beta = 0.3$. The owner of the firm claims that there are increasing returns to scale in the plant.

(a) Is the owner correct?

(b) If $\beta$ were 0.2 rather than 0.3, would she be correct?

(c) Does output per unit of labor depend only on $\alpha$ and $\beta$? Why or why not?

7. Based on data obtained by the U.S. Department of Agriculture, the relationship between a cow's total output of milk and the amount of grain it is fed is as follows:

| Amount of grain (pounds) | Amount of milk (pounds) |
| --- | --- |
| 1,200 | 5,917 |
| 1,800 | 7,250 |
| 2,400 | 8,379 |
| 3,000 | 9,371 |

(This relationship assumes that forage input is fixed at 6,500 pounds of hay.)

(a) Calculate the average product of grain when each amount is used.

(b) Estimate the marginal product of grain when between 1,200 and 1,800 pounds are fed, when between 1,800 and 2,400 pounds are fed, and when between 2,400 and 3,000 pounds are fed.

(c) Does this production function exhibit diminishing marginal returns?

8. The owner of the Hughes Car Wash believes that the relationship between the number of cars washed and labor input is

$$Q = -0.8 + 4.5L - 0.3L^2,$$

where $Q$ is the number of cars washed per hour, and $L$ is the number of people employed per hour. The firm receives $5 for each car washed, and the hourly wage rate for each person employed is $4.50. The cost of other inputs like water is trivial, and hence they are ignored.

(a) How many people should be employed to maximize profit?

(b) What will be the firm's hourly profit?

(c) Is the above relationship between output and labor input valid for all values of $L$? Why or why not?

9. An electronics plant's production function is $Q = 5LK$, where $Q$ is its output rate, $L$ is the amount of labor it uses per period of time, and $K$ is the amount of capital it uses per period of time. The price of labor is $1 per unit of labor, and the price of capital is $2 per unit of capital. The firm's vice president for manufacturing hires you to determine what combination of inputs the plant should use to produce 20 units of output per period.

(a) What advice would you give him?

(b) Suppose that the price of labor increases to $2 per unit. What effect will this have on output per unit of labor?

(c) Is this plant subject to decreasing returns to scale? Why or why not?

10. In its Erie, Pennsylvania, plant, General Electric has installed a flexible manufacturing system to produce locomotives. Flexible manufacturing systems, which are very sophisticated forms of factory automation, operate with a minimum of manual intervention. They are integrated systems of machines under full programmable control. According to General Electric, the new system compares as follows with the old one:

|  | Old system | New system |
|---|---|---|
| Number of machines | 29 | 9 |
| Number of workers | 86 | 16 |
| Annual output | 4,100 | 5,600 |

(a) Does the new system increase the average product of labor?

(b) Does it increase the average product of machines?

(c) According to a study by Harvard's Ramchandran Jaikumar, American firms generally do not exploit flexible manufacturing systems as well as they might. For one thing, the percentage of time that such systems are actually functioning, rather than awaiting adjustments or repair, seems to be relatively low. He believes that American firms should invest more in skilled engineering personnel. Can steps of this sort result in shifts of the production function?

(d) How can a firm determine whether such steps are worthwhile?[15]

11. The Arbor Company produces metal fasteners. The cost per setup is $8,000, and the annual cost of holding each fastener in inventory for a year is $40. What is the optimal lot size if the Arbor Company produces each of the following annual outputs?

(a) 1,000

(b) 10,000

(c) 100,000

12. A.B. Volvo, the Swedish auto firm, opened a new car-assembly plant at Udevalla in 1988. The idea was to have a small team of highly skilled workers build an entire car. According to the proponents, it would reduce the tedium associated with the conventional assembly line and cut absenteeism and turnover among workers. In 1991, there were reports that it takes 50 hours of labor to assemble a car at Udevalla, in contrast to 25 hours at Volvo's conventional assembly plant at Ghent, Belgium. If you were Volvo's chief executive officer, what questions would you ask Udevalla's managers, and what steps would you take?

---

[15] For further discussion, see S. Miller, *Impacts of Industrial Robotics* (Madison: University of Wisconsin Press, 1988); R. Jaikumar, "Postindustrial Manufacturing," *Harvard Business Review* (November–December 1986); and E. Mansfield, "Flexible Manufacturing Systems: Economic Effects in Japan, United States, and Western Europe," *Japan and the World Economy*, 1992.

# APPENDIX: LAGRANGIAN MULTIPLIERS AND OPTIMAL INPUT COMBINATIONS

In this chapter, we stated that equation (6.11) must be satisfied if a firm is to maximize output for a given expenditure level, or if it is to minimize the cost of producing a specified amount of output. In this appendix, we show how the decision rule in equation (6.11) can be derived using the method of Lagrangian multipliers (discussed in Chapter 2). To simplify matters, the firm is assumed to employ only two inputs.

*Maximizing Output from a Specified Expenditure Level*     Suppose that a firm's production function is

$$Q = f(X_1, X_2),$$

where $Q$ is output, $X_1$ is the amount used of the first input, and $X_2$ is the amount used of the second input. The firm's total expenditure on both inputs is specified to equal $E^*$. Thus,

$$X_1 P_1 + X_2 P_2 = E^*,$$

where $P_1$ is the price of the first input, and $P_2$ is the price of the second input. The firm wants to maximize the quantity of output from this specified level of expenditure. Thus, the firm wants to maximize $Q$, where

$$Q = f(X_1, X_2), \tag{6.23}$$

subject to the constraint that

$$E^* - X_1 P_1 - X_2 P_2 = 0. \tag{6.24}$$

Following the procedure described in Chapter 2, we can use the method of Lagrangian multipliers to solve this problem. The first step is to construct the Lagrangian function, which is the right-hand side of equation (6.23) plus $\lambda$ times the left-hand side of equation (6.24):

$$L_1 = f(X_1, X_2) + \lambda (E^* - X_1 P_1 - X_2 P_2),$$

where $\lambda$ is the Lagrangian multiplier. Taking the partial derivatives of $L_1$ with respect to $X_1$, $X_2$, and $\lambda$, and setting them all equal to zero, we obtain

$$\frac{\partial L_1}{\partial X_1} = \frac{\partial f(X_1, X_2)}{\partial X_1} - \lambda P_1 = 0 \tag{6.25}$$

$$\frac{\partial L_1}{\partial X_2} = \frac{\partial f(X_1, X_2)}{\partial X_2} - \lambda P_2 = 0 \tag{6.26}$$

$$\frac{\partial L_1}{\partial \lambda} = E^* - X_1 P_1 - X_2 P_2 = 0. \tag{6.27}$$

These are the conditions for output maximization subject to the expenditure constraint.

Letting $MP_1$ be the marginal product of the first input and $MP_2$ be the marginal product of the second input, the following is true (by definition):

$$\frac{\partial f(X_1, X_2)}{\partial X_1} = \frac{\partial Q}{\partial X_1} = MP_1$$

$$\frac{\partial f(X_1, X_2)}{\partial X_2} = \frac{\partial Q}{\partial X_2} = MP_2.$$

Thus, equations (6.25) and (6.26) can be restated as follows:

$$MP_1 - \lambda P_1 = 0$$

$$MP_2 - \lambda P_2 = 0,$$

which implies that

$$MP_1 = \lambda P_1 \qquad\qquad (6.28)$$

$$MP_2 = \lambda P_2. \qquad\qquad (6.29)$$

Dividing each side of equation (6.28) by the corresponding side of equation (6.29), we find that

$$\frac{MP_1}{MP_2} = \frac{P_1}{P_2},$$

or

$$\frac{MP_1}{P_1} = \frac{MP_2}{P_2}, \qquad\qquad (6.30)$$

which is the decision rule in equation (6.11) when there are only two inputs. Thus, we have proved what we set out to prove—that this decision rule can be derived using the method of Lagrangian multipliers when the object is to maximize output subject to an expenditure constraint.

*Minimizing the Cost of a Specified Amount of Output*     Suppose this firm is committed to produce a specified quantity of output, $Q^*$, which means that

$$f(X_1, X_2) = Q^*.$$

The firm's problem is to minimize its costs, which equal

$$C = X_1 P_1 + X_2 P_2, \qquad\qquad (6.31)$$

subject to the constraint that

$$Q^* - f(X_1, X_2) = 0. \qquad\qquad (6.32)$$

Following the procedure described in Chapter 2, we can use the method of Lagrangian multipliers to solve this problem. The first step is to construct the Lagrangian function, which is the right-hand side of equation (6.31) plus $\lambda$ times the left-hand side of equation (6.32):

$$L_2 = X_1 P_1 + X_2 P_2 + \lambda [Q^* - f(X_1, X_2)],$$

where $\lambda$ is the Lagrangian multiplier. Taking the partial derivatives of $L_2$ with respect to $X_1$, $X_2$, and $\lambda$, and setting them all equal to zero, we obtain

$$\frac{\partial L_2}{\partial X_1} = P_1 - \lambda \frac{\partial f(X_1, X_2)}{\partial X_1} = 0 \tag{6.33}$$

$$\frac{\partial L_2}{\partial X_2} = P_2 - \lambda \frac{\partial f(X_1, X_2)}{\partial X_2} = 0 \tag{6.34}$$

$$\frac{\partial L_2}{\partial \lambda} = Q^* - f(X_1, X_2) = 0. \tag{6.35}$$

These are the conditions for cost minimization subject to the output constraint.

Substituting $MP_1$ for $\partial f(X_1, X_2)/\partial X_1$ and $MP_2$ for $\partial f(X_1, X_2)/\partial X_2$ in equations (6.33) and (6.34), we get the following:

$$P_1 - \lambda MP_1 = 0$$

$$P_2 - \lambda MP_2 = 0,$$

which implies that

$$P_1 = \lambda MP_1 \tag{6.36}$$

$$P_2 = \lambda MP_2. \tag{6.37}$$

Dividing each side of equation (6.36) by the corresponding side of equation (6.37), we find that

$$\frac{P_1}{P_2} = \frac{MP_1}{MP_2},$$

or

$$\frac{MP_1}{P_1} = \frac{MP_2}{P_2},$$

which is the decision rule in equation (6.11) when there are only two inputs. Thus, we have proved what we set out to prove—that this decision rule can be derived using the method of Lagrangian multipliers when the object is to minimize cost subject to an output constraint.

# Chapter 7
# Technological Change and Industrial Innovation

American companies traditionally have tended to be at the forefront of new technology. Their long-term profitability and success in the marketplace have often resulted from new products and processes, and these products and processes have come largely, but not exclusively, from an active commitment to research and development. Recent decades, however, have seen much soul-searching among managers about the apparent decline of innovation in some American industries. Given the present threat, particularly from Japan, to American technological leadership, the ability to manage innovation—once virtually taken for granted—is now high on many corporate agendas. In this chapter, we discuss various models and techniques that have proved useful in this regard.

## TECHNOLOGICAL CHANGE

**Technological change**—the advance of technology—often takes the form of new methods of producing existing products and new techniques of organization, marketing, and management. Technological change results in a change in the production function. If the production function were readily observable, a comparison of the production function at two different times would provide the manager with a simple measure of the effect of

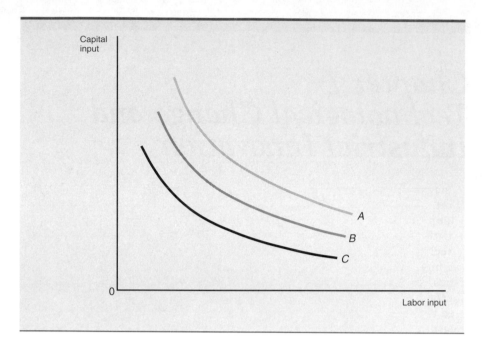

**FIGURE 7.1** *Change over a Period of Time in the Position of an Isoquant* If the isoquant shifted from position A to position B, technological change had less impact than it would have had if it had shifted to position C.

technological change during the intervening period. If there were only two inputs, labor and capital, and if there were constant returns to scale, the characteristics of the production function at a given date could be captured fully by a single isoquant.[1] One could simply look at the changing position of this isoquant to see the effects of technological change. If this isoquant shifted from position A to position B in Figure 7.1 during a certain period of time, technological change had less impact during this period than it would have had if the curve had shifted to position C.

Technological change may also result in the availability of new products. Video cassette recorders, for example, did not exist several decades ago, much less were they found in so many households. Nylon was first brought to markets in the 1930s; today it is hard to imagine what life would be like without it. In many cases, the availability of new products can be regarded as a change in the production function, since they are merely more efficient ways of meeting old wants if these wants are defined with proper breadth.

---

[1] Recall from Chapter 6 that if there are constant returns to scale, an x-percent increase in all inputs results in an x-percent increase in output. Thus, if there are constant returns to scale, there is at a given time a unique relationship between capital input per unit of output and labor input per unit of output. This relationship holds for any output and completely summarizes the efficient input combinations.

This is particularly true in the case of new goods used by firms, which may result in little or no change in the final product shipped to consumers. In other cases, however, the availability of new products cannot realistically be viewed as a change in the production function, since the new products represent an important difference in kind.

## LABOR PRODUCTIVITY

Managers have long been interested in productivity—the ratio of output to input. The oldest and most commonly studied productivity measure is **labor productivity,** output per hour of labor. One determinant of the rate of growth of labor productivity is the rate of technological change, a high rate of technological change being likely to result, all other things being equal, in a high rate of growth of labor productivity. However, the rate of technological change is not the sole determinant of the rate of growth of labor productivity, the consequence being that although labor productivity is often used to measure the rate of technological change, it is in fact an incomplete measure.

Figure 7.2 shows how changes in labor productivity can produce false signals concerning the rate of technological change. Suppose that the relevant isoquant is II′ and the input prices at the beginning of the period are such that the isocost curves are $A$, $B$, $C$ and so on. The least-cost combination of inputs is $L_1$ of labor and $C_1$ of capital. Now suppose that input prices change, and labor becomes more expensive relative to capital, the result being that the isoquant curves shift to $A'$, $B'$, $C'$, and so on. Under these new circumstances, the least-cost combination of inputs to produce the same output is $L_2$ of labor and $C_2$ of capital. Since output remains constant and labor input decreases, labor productivity increases as a result of the change in input prices. But this productivity increase is not an indication of technological change, there being no change at all in the production function.

## TOTAL FACTOR PRODUCTIVITY

A better measure of the rate of technological change is **total factor productivity,** which relates changes in output to changes in both labor and capital inputs, not changes in labor inputs alone. Assume that the production function is of the simple form

$$Q = \alpha(bL + cK), \tag{7.1}$$

where $Q$ is the quantity of output, $L$ is the quantity of labor, $K$ is the quantity of capital, and $b$ and $c$ are constants. Dividing both sides of equation

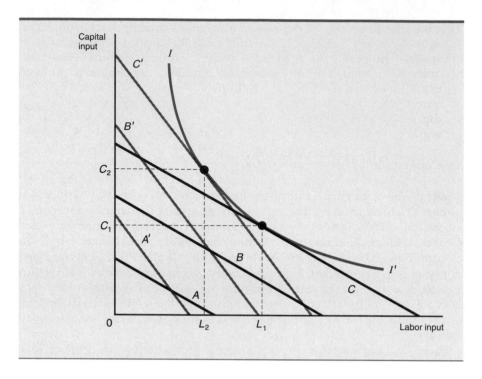

*FIGURE 7.2  Productivity Increase without Technological Change*
Because labor becomes more expensive relative to capital, labor productivity increases.

(7.1) by $(bL + cK)$, we have

$$\frac{Q}{bL + cK} = \alpha, \tag{7.2}$$

which is total factor productivity. In this simple case, changes in total factor productivity measure changes in efficiency.

If a firm uses more than two inputs, total factor productivity equals

$$\frac{Q}{a_1 I_1 + a_2 I_2 + \cdots + a_n I_n}, \tag{7.3}$$

where $I_1$ is the amount of the first input used, $I_2$ is the amount of the second input used, . . . , and $I_n$ is the amount of the $n$th input used. In calculating total factor productivity, firms often let $a_1$ equal the price of the first input, $a_2$ equal the price of the second input, . . . , and $a_n$ equal the price of the $n$th input in some base period, as we shall see below. The principal advantage of total factor productivity over labor productivity is its inclusion of more types of inputs, not labor alone. It otherwise shares many of the limitations of labor productivity.

Firms calculate total factor productivity in order to measure changes over time in the efficiency of their operations. It is important for a firm's managers to be aware of the extent to which productivity has increased in response to new techniques and other factors. For example, consider flexible manufacturing systems, a major innovation in industries like machinery. (Recall page 245.) According to Messerschmidt, a leading West German firm, the flexible manufacturing system that it installed at its Augsburg facility reduced the labor requirements to produce a given output by over 50 percent and reduced the capital investment required by 10 percent.[2]

To calculate the changes in total factor productivity for a firm or plant over a period of time, managers must obtain data concerning the quantity of output and the quantities of inputs utilized in each period. For example, suppose that the Landau Company uses three inputs—labor, energy, and raw materials. In 1993, it uses 10,000 hours of labor, 100,000 kilowatt-hours of energy, and 5,000 pounds of materials to produce 400,000 pounds of output. In 1995, it uses 12,000 hours of labor, 150,000 kilowatt-hours of energy, and 6,000 pounds of materials to produce 700,000 pounds of output. What is total factor productivity in each year?

As a first step toward answering this question, we must get data concerning the price of each input in some base period, say 1993. Suppose that the price of labor is $8 per hour, the price of a kilowatt-hour of energy is 2 cents, and the price of a pound of materials is $3. Then, inserting these figures into the expression in (7.3), we find that total factor productivity in 1993 is

$$\frac{400,000}{8(10,000) + 0.02(100,000) + 3(5,000)} = 4.12,$$

and total factor productivity in 1995 is

$$\frac{700,000}{8(12,000) + 0.02(150,000) + 3(6,000)} = 5.98.$$

Thus, from 1993 to 1995, total factor productivity increases by 45 percent —from 4.12 to 5.98.

Note that the base-year input prices are used for all years, not just the base year. For example, the 1993 input prices would be used for all years, not just 1993, in the case of the Landau Company. In this way, we hold constant input prices and do not let changes in them over time affect our results.[3]

---

[2] National Research Council, *Toward a New Era in Manufacturing* (Washington, D.C.: National Academy Press, 1986), p. 118.

[3] Of course, this does not mean that the value of total factor productivity is not affected by the base-year prices. For example, if the price of labor in the base period were $10 (rather than $8) per hour, our results would be different. But changes *over time* in input prices are not allowed to influence our results.

## USING TOTAL FACTOR PRODUCTIVITY
## TO TRACK FACTORY PERFORMANCE

To illustrate how changes in total factor productivity can be used to track factory performance, consider a manufacturing plant studied by Harvard's Robert Hayes, Steven Wheelwright, and Kim Clark.[4] Figure 7.3 shows the behavior of total factor productivity in this plant during a 10-year period. As you can see, total factor productivity increased at a healthy pace up to 1976. This was the period during which the plant was started up. Because it takes time for a factory to operate properly, one would expect that total factor productivity would increase substantially in this start-up phase.

From 1977 to 1983, there was no evidence of any strong, persistent increase in total factor productivity. Instead, there was an increase in 1977–79, a fall in 1979–80, and an increase in 1981–82. In 1982, total factory productivity was only somewhat higher than in 1976. The data in Figure

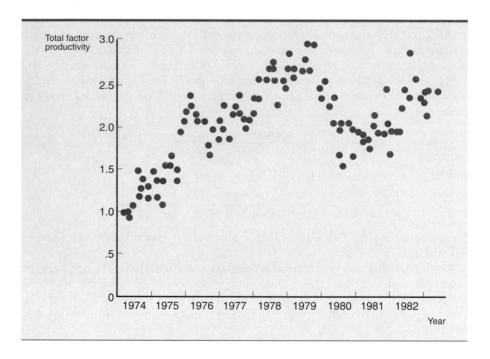

*FIGURE 7.3   Total Factor Productivity, Actual Manufacturing Plant*
Total factor productivity increased up to 1976, but in 1982 was only slightly higher than in 1976.

*Source:* R. Hayes, S. Wheelwright, and K. Clark, ***Dynamic Manufacturing.***

[4] R. Hayes, S. Wheelwright, and K. Clark, *Dynamic Manufacturing* (New York: Free Press, 1988).

---

CONSULTANT'S CORNER

### EVALUATING A LARGE-SCALE PROGRAM OF PRODUCT AND PROCESS IMPROVEMENT*

General Electric, a leading manufacturer of dishwashers, decided to invest about $40 million to make major changes in its product and manufacturing process. The new dishwasher was to be redesigned around a one-piece plastic tub and one-piece plastic door. To make sure the product would meet the desired quality standards, tight specifications were set both for the firm and its suppliers. In revamping the manufacturing process, automation was stressed, the object being to improve quality as well as to cut costs. Also, an attempt was made to coordinate product and process development, which was not the traditional procedure.

Because of the resulting changes in product and process technology, the following changes occurred between 1980 and 1984:

|  | 1980 | 1984 |
|---|---|---|
| Average cost of dishwasher (1980 = 100) | 100 | 88 |
| Output per employee (1980 = 100) | 100 | 142 |
| Number of calls by customers for service (1980 = 100) | 100 | 55 |
| Percent of dishwashers rejected (based on mechanical/electrical test) | 10% | 2.5% |

If you were a consultant to this firm, and if you were asked to evaluate this investment program, what would be your conclusions? What additional data would you request from the firm?

* For further discussion, see R. Hayes and S. Wheelwright, *Restoring Our Competitive Edge* (New York: Wiley, 1984).

---

7.3 indicate that this factory experienced little in the way of technological change from 1977 to 1983. Hayes, Wheelwright, and Clark report that these data triggered an investigation of the causes for this poor performance, and that this investigation indicated that it was due in considerable part to the way the factory managed equipment introductions.[5] Obviously, this information was of use to the firm's top managers.

In passing, note that the fact that total factor productivity fell during 1979–80 does not mean that there was *negative* technological change then. If the factory's sales decreased during this period, perhaps because of cyclical factors (recall Chapter 5), this could cause such a decline in total factor productivity. Also, it sometimes takes time for new equipment to reach its full efficiency. When it is first used, productivity may fall temporarily because of "teething" problems.

[5] Ibid.

# RESEARCH AND DEVELOPMENT:
# A LEARNING PROCESS

Particularly in science-based industries like electronics and chemicals, a firm's success depends on the extent and nature of the research and development that it carries out. Research and development encompasses work of many kinds. Basic research is aimed purely at the creation of new knowledge, applied research is expected to have a practical payoff, and development is aimed at the reduction of research findings to practice. Inventions can occur in either the research phase or the development phase of organized research and development activity.

Chance plays a crucial role in research and development, and a long string of failures frequently occurs before any kind of success is achieved. A research or development project can be regarded as a process of uncertainty reduction, or learning. Suppose, for example, that a firm that is trying to fabricate a part can use one of two alloys and that it is impossible to use standard sources to determine their characteristics. Suppose that strength is of paramount importance and that the firm's estimates of the strengths of the alloys, alloy X and alloy Y, are represented by the probability distributions in part A of Table 7.1. If the firm were forced to make a choice immediately, it would probably choose alloy Y, since it believes that there is better than a 50–50 chance that alloy Y will turn out to be stronger than alloy X.

TABLE 7.1 *Subjective Probability Distribution of Strength of Alloys X and Y*

| Extent of strength | A. Before test Alloy X | Alloy Y | B. After test Alloy X | Alloy Y |
|---|---|---|---|---|
|  | Probabilities | | | |
| Exceptionally high | .20 | .30 | .10 | .10 |
| Very high | .40 | .50 | .20 | .80 |
| High | .20 | .10 | .60 | .10 |
| Medium | .10 | .05 | .10 | .00 |
| Low | .10 | .05 | .00 | .00 |
| Total | 1.00 | 1.00 | 1.00 | 1.00 |

However, there is a good chance that this decision might turn out to be wrong, the consequence being that the part would be weaker than if alloy X had been used. Thus, the firm may decide to perform a test prior to making the selection. On the basis of the test results, the firm will formulate new estimates, represented by the probability distributions in part B of Table 7.1. These probability distributions show less dispersion than the ones in part A; in other words, the firm believes it is able to pinpoint more closely the strength of each alloy in part B than in part A. Because of the tests, the firm feels more certainty concerning which alloy will prove stronger.

# PARALLEL DEVELOPMENT EFFORTS

Research and development is more risky than most other economic activities. Many development projects use parallel efforts to help cope with uncertainty. For example, in the development of the atomic bomb, there were several methods of making fissionable materials, and no consensus existed among scientists as to which of these alternatives was most promising. To make sure that the best one was not discarded, all methods were pursued in parallel. The wisdom of this decision was borne out by the fact that the method that was first to produce appreciable quantities of fissionable material was one that had been considered relatively unpromising early in the development program's history.

How can a firm's managers tell whether it is optimal to run parallel research and development efforts? What factors determine the optimal number of parallel efforts? Suppose that a firm can select x approaches, spend $C$ dollars on each one over a period of $n$ months, choose the one that looks most promising at the end of the period, and carry it to completion, dropping the others. Suppose that the only relevant criterion is the extent of the development costs, the usefulness of the result and the development time being assumed to be the same regardless of which parallel effort is pursued. For further simplification, suppose that all approaches look equally promising. Under these circumstances, the optimal value of x—the number of parallel research and development efforts—is inversely related to $C$ and directly related to the amount learned in the next $n$ months. As the cost of running each effort increases, the optimal number of parallel efforts decreases. As the prospective amount of learning increases, the optimal number of parallel efforts goes up.

To illustrate why it is sometimes cheaper to run parallel development efforts, consider a case in which each approach has a 50–50 chance of costing $5 million and a 50-50 chance of costing $8 million. Since we assume that all approaches are equally promising, these probabilities are the same for all approaches. The expected total cost of development is the sum of the total costs of development if each possible outcome occurs times the probability of the occurrence of this outcome. If a single approach is used, the expected total costs of development are

$$.5(\$5 \text{ million}) + .5(\$8 \text{ million}) = \$6.5 \text{ million}, \qquad (7.4)$$

since there is a .5 probability that total costs with any single approach will be $5 million and a .5 probability that they will be $8 million.

If two approaches are run in parallel and if the true cost of development using each approach can be determined after $C$ dollars are spent on each approach, the expected total costs of development are

$$.25(\$8 \text{ million}) + .75(\$5 \text{ million}) + C = \$5.75 \text{ million} + C, \qquad (7.5)$$

if each approach is carried to the point at which $C$ dollars have been spent on it, and if the cheaper approach is chosen at that point (and the other approach is dropped). Why? Because there is a .25 probability that total

CONCEPTS IN CONTEXT

## PARALLEL DEVELOPMENT EFFORTS AT IBM

The IBM Corporation, which spent about $5 billion on research and development in 1990, is one of the world's leading high-technology companies. Nonetheless, IBM, like other firms, must face the fact that R and D is a risky activity, and that it is not able to predict with confidence whether a particular R and D project will be successful or not. Recognizing this fact, parallel development efforts have played a major role in IBM's history, as indicated by the following quotation from one IBM manager:

*John F. Akers, Chairman of IBM*

> *Parallel projects are crucial—no doubt of it. When I look back over the last dozen products we've introduced, I find in well over half the instances the big development project that we "bet on" via the system came a cropper somewhere along the way. In every instance—and we've gone back and taken a look and I do mean every— there were two or three (about five once) other small projects, you know, four-to-six person groups, two people in one instance, who had been working on parallel technology or parallel development efforts. It had been with scrounged time and bodies. But that's a time-honored thing. We wink at it. It pays off. Looking at the projects where the initial bets failed, the subsequently developed project came in ahead of the original schedule in three instances. It's just amazing what a handful of dedicated people can do when they are really turned on. Of course they had an advantage. Since they were so resource-constrained, they had to design a simple product in the first place.\**

\* H. Bartlett, *Cases in Strategic Management for Business* (New York: Dryden Press, 1988).

costs with the better of the two approaches will be $8 million and a .75 probability that they will be $5 million. In addition, there is the certainty that a cost of *C* will be incurred for the approach that is dropped. (The *C* dollars spent on the project that is not dropped are included in its total costs, given above.) The reason why there is a .25 chance that total costs with the better of the two approaches is $8 million is that this will occur only when the total cost of both approaches turns out to be $8 million—and the probability that this will occur is .5 times .5, or .25. Comparing equation (7.4) with equation (7.5), it is obvious that the expected total cost of development is lower with two parallel approaches than with a single approach if $C$ is less than $750,000.

More generally, if the probability is $P$ that the development cost will be $C_1$ and $(1 - P)$ that it will be $C_2$ (where $C_2 < C_1$), the expected cost if a single approach is used is

$$PC_1 + (1 - P)C_2.$$

If two approaches are run in parallel, the expected cost is

$$P^2C_1 + (1 - P^2)C_2 + C,$$

which is less than the cost of a single approach if

$$P^2C_1 + (1 - P^2)C_2 + C < PC_1 + (1 - P)C_2. \tag{7.6}$$

Thus, if the inequality in (7.6) holds, two parallel approaches will result in a lower expected cost than a single approach.[6]


## WHAT MAKES FOR SUCCESS?

Even companies in the same industry may differ markedly in their ability to make R and D pay off commercially. During a four-year period, for instance, three evenly matched chemical companies found the proportion of their R and D expenditures that earned a profit to be 69 percent, 54 percent, and 39 percent, respectively. These differences are too large to be attributed to errors of measurement or definition. What can explain them?[7]

An R and D project's likelihood of economic success is the product of three separate factors: (1) the probability of technical success, (2) the probability of commercialization (given technical success), and (3) the probability of economic success (given commercialization). One econometric study shows that all three of these probabilities are directly related to how quickly an R and D project is evaluated for its economic, as opposed to technical, potential. Also, in those companies whose R and D staff members do not work closely or responsively with marketing staff, the integra-

---

[6] See R. Nelson, "Uncertainty, Learning, and the Economics of Parallel Research and Development Efforts," *Review of Economics and Statistics* (1961), for an early paper on this topic. Also, see B. Dean and J. Goldhar, eds., *Management of Research and Innovation*, vol. 15 of *Studies in the Management Sciences* (Amsterdam: North-Holland, 1980).

[7] For references and sources of information for the data presented in this and the next three sections, see E. Mansfield, "How Economists See R and D," *Harvard Business Review* (November–December 1981). Also, see K. Clark and T. Fujimoto, *Product Development Performance* (Boston: Harvard Business School Press, 1991); and R. Stobaugh, *Innovation and Competition* (Boston: Harvard Business School Press, 1988).

tion of R and D activity with market realities is haphazard, belated, or both. Yet commercially successful innovation depends on just this sort of integration. Numerous case studies of successful and unsuccessful innovation come to the same conclusion: the closer the link between marketing and R and D, the greater the probability of commercialization (given technical completion).

Consider, by way of illustration, the experience of three chemical companies of roughly the same size and level of R and D expenditure that underwent reorganization at roughly the same time. In two of them, the reorganization produced a closer integration of R and D with marketing by improving the channels of communication between them as well as by noticeably increasing marketing's input to R and D decision making. In the third, however, integration decreased; R and D paid even less attention to marketing than it had before the reorganization.

Data on the probability of commercialization (given technical completion) of 330 R and D projects in these companies—projects carried out anywhere from three to seven years before reorganization to five to eight years after it—are highly suggestive. They show an increase of about 20 percentage points for the two companies that more closely linked R and D with marketing and a decrease of about 20 percentage points for the third.

More generally, a substantial portion of a company's R and D efforts may lie fallow because other parts of the company do not make proper use of them. One survey of executive opinion has noted the widely held belief that the economic success rate of R and D projects would increase by half if marketing and production people fully exploited them. If this figure is anywhere close to the truth, the faulty interface between R and D and the other functions has a very serious effect on the productivity of industrial R and D.

## PROJECT SELECTION

However well-founded the fears of excessively detailed control, some managerial oversight of R and D is essential. To make effective use of its R and D capacity, a company must first spell out its business objectives and then communicate them to its scientists and engineers. Research, after all, makes sense only when undertaken in areas relevant to economic goals.

Simply taking on a team of scientists and allowing them to do research in their favorite fields may produce novel results—but results that are unlikely to have much immediate commercial value. Most companies, therefore, have found it worthwhile to make economic evaluations of both project proposals and continuing projects. Without question, these evaluations have been useful, since they have forced managers to make their assumptions explicit. Research suggests that the sooner such evaluations are carried out, the greater a project's chances of ultimate commercial success.

The nature of these evaluations is different for a research as opposed to a development project. As a project moves from the laboratory toward the market, it receives more intensive scrutiny from both a technical and an economic angle. In the early research phase, the screening of proposals will probably be quick and informal, since costs at this stage are still low and predicting outcomes is very difficult. But as projects enter the development phase, where costs and predictability are higher, they require a far more detailed process of economic evaluation.

Managerial economists have developed a number of more or less sophisticated models to help solve these problems of evaluation. Some employ relatively straightforward adaptations of capital budgeting techniques. For example, the net present value or internal rate of return (both discussed in Chapter 14) of each project may be calculated and compared. Others, described in Chapter 9, use mathematical programming techniques. For the following reasons, the more complicated versions of these models have not found extensive use: (1) Many of the models fail to recognize that R and D is essentially a process of buying information, that unsuccessful projects can provide valuable information, and as a result that the real task is to facilitate sequential decision making under conditions of uncertainty. (2) Application of the more sophisticated models is not cheap. (3) Perhaps most important, the models often rest on overly optimistic estimates that are not very reliable—estimates that reflect both the uncertainty of the undertaking and the desire by researchers and others to "sell" projects to top management.

# INNOVATION

An invention, when applied for the first time, is called an **innovation**. The distinction between an invention and an innovation becomes somewhat blurred in cases like Du Pont's nylon, where the inventor and the innovator are the same firm. In these circumstances, the final stages of development may entail at least a partial commitment to a market test. However, in many cases, the firm that is the inventor is not in a position to—and does not want to—apply its invention, because its business is invention, not production; or because it is a supplier, not a user, of the equipment embodying the innovation; or for some other reason. In these cases, the distinction remains relatively clear-cut.

Regardless of whether the break between invention and innovation is clean, innovation is a key stage in the process leading to the full evaluation and utilization of an invention. The innovator—the firm that is first to apply the invention—must be willing to take the risks involved in introducing a new and untried process, good, or service. In many cases these risks are high. Although R and D can provide a great deal of information regarding the technical characteristics and cost of production of the invention—and market research can provide considerable information regarding the demand for it—there are many areas of uncertainty that can be resolved only by actual production and marketing of the invention. By obtaining needed information regarding the actual performance of the invention, the innovator plays a vital social role.

## DO AMERICAN FIRMS NEGLECT PROCESS INNOVATION?

Innovations are generally of two types—**product innovations** (new and improved products) and **process innovations** (new and improved processes). Some leading managers, engineers, and economists have warned that American firms tend to neglect process innovation. While this is not easy to prove or disprove, it is interesting to note that Japanese firms devote about two-thirds of their R and D budgets to work on processes, whereas comparable American firms devote only about one-third of their budgets to such work. American firms devote the bulk of their energy and resources to the development and introduction of new products, rather than new processes. A host of important new products, like the videotape recorder and the xerox copier, have come from American industrial laboratories. These new products have been of enormous significance to consumers and others, here and abroad, but in many cases, a substantial share of their profits has gone to foreign producers, who have devised ways of producing these new products better and more cheaply than we did.

Take the case of the industrial robot, which was invented largely by George C. Devol, an engineer who headed Devol Research Associates. The first commercial robots based on Devol's 1954 patent were sold in 1961, but American firms were not quick to make use of them. In 1966, our robotics technology began to be transferred to Japan, where robots spread more rapidly than in this country, improvements were made in some aspects of robot design, and the costs of robots were lowered. By 1983, the U.S. Department of Commerce acknowledged that in robots, "the Japanese enjoy undisputed superiority in terms of their producers' experience, capacity, financial strength, and market position."

As the President's Commission on Industrial Competitiveness, headed by Hewlett-Packard's John Young, pointed out in 1985, "It does us little good to design state-of-the-art products, if within a short time our foreign competitors can manufacture them more cheaply." But despite such warnings and criticisms, the available evidence suggests that American firms, although far more concerned about this problem than they were ten or fifteen years ago, had effected no perceptible increase between 1976 and 1985 in the proportion of their R and D expenditures devoted to new or improved processes.

According to some observers, this problem reflects the relatively low status of manufacturing—relative to finance, marketing, research, and other functions of the firm—in some American companies. The best engineering talent often has been drawn into research and design, not manufacturing. Jobs in manufacturing have tended to have lower pay and less prospect for promotion than those in other areas. Relatively few chief executive officers of major corporations have come from manufacturing. This is in contrast to countries like Japan and Germany, where manufacturing seems to be much more highly regarded.

The nature of process improvements also seems to fit less easily into the structure and operation of many of our firms than into those of their foreign competitors. Processes tend to be improved by many incremental changes, and the work force is very important in suggesting and accepting them. Relative to countries like Japan, our workers often have poor vocational and technical educations, and our firms often invest less in worker skills, partly because worker turnover tends to be high.

## TIME-COST TRADE-OFFS

For a particular innovator, there is likely to be a time-cost trade-off function, like that in Figure 7.4. If the firm cuts the total time taken to develop and introduce the innovation, it incurs higher costs. As the development

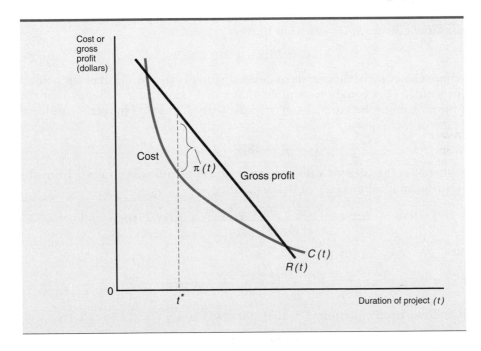

*FIGURE 7.4* *Time-Cost Trade-Off Function and Optimal Duration of Project* The optimal duration of the project is *t\** years.

schedule is shortened, more tasks must be carried out concurrently rather than sequentially, and since each task provides information that is useful in carrying out the others, there are more false starts and wasted designs. Also, diminishing returns set in as more and more technical workers are assigned simultaneously to the project.

Faced with this time-cost trade-off function, how quickly should the firm develop and introduce the innovation? Clearly, the answer depends on the relationship between the present value of profit (gross of innovation cost) from the innovation and how quickly the firm develops and introduces it. (For a detailed discussion of the concept of present value, see Appendix A.) If $R(t)$ is the present value of gross profit if the duration of the project is $t$ years, and if the time-cost trade-off function is $C(t)$, profit equals

$$\pi(t) = R(t) - C(t), \tag{7.7}$$

and the first-order condition for profit maximization is

$$\frac{dC}{dt} = \frac{dR}{dt}. \tag{7.8}$$

Thus, in Figure 7.4, the optimal duration of the project is $t^*$ years, since $\pi(t)$ —which is the vertical difference between $R(t)$ and $C(t)$—is greatest when this is the duration of the project.

To illustrate, consider the Hanover Company, which wants to develop a new plastic. Its vice president for research and development believes that the time-cost trade-off function for this project is

$$C = 520 - 100t + 5t^2,$$

where $C$ is cost (in thousands of dollars), and $t$ is the duration of the project (in years). This equation assumes that $t \geqslant 1$, since it is believed that the project cannot be carried out in less than a year. Hanover's president believes that

$$R = 480 - 20t,$$

where $R$ is the present value of profit (gross of innovation cost) from the innovation (in thousands of dollars). Since

$$\frac{dC}{dt} = \frac{d(520 - 100t + 5t^2)}{dt} = -100 + 10t,$$

and

$$\frac{dR}{dt} = \frac{d(480 - 20t)}{dt} = -20,$$

it follows from equation (7.8) that the firm should choose $t$ so that

$$-100 + 10t = -20$$

$$t = 8.$$

## THE TIME-COST TRADE-OFF FUNCTION FOR AIRLINERS

Keith Hartley of the University of York and W. Corcoran of the University of Newcastle (both English universities) have estimated the time-cost trade-off function for the development of airliners (like the Boeing 707 or McDonnell Douglas DC-10) in the United States and the United Kingdom. Their results are shown in the graph below.

(a) If an aircraft manufacturer in the United Kingdom decides to reduce the duration of a development project by 10 percent, by about how much will the cost of the project increase? (b) Holding the duration of a development project constant, does the cost of the project tend to be different in the United States from that in the

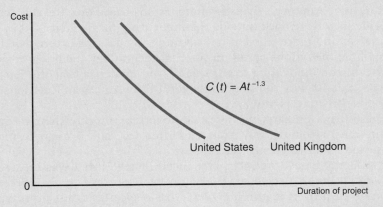

$$C(t) = At^{-1.3}$$

United States    United Kingdom

Cost

Duration of project

0

United Kingdom? (c) What factors may account for this difference between the United States and the United Kingdom in the time-cost trade-off function for airliners?

*Solution* (a) The cost will increase by about 15 percent. To see this, let $t' = 0.9t$. Then according to the formula in the above graph, $C(t') = A(t')^{-1.3} = A(0.9t)^{-1.3} = 0.9^{-1.3}At^{-1.3} = 0.9^{-1.3}C(t) = 1.15C(t)$, since $0.9^{-1.3} = 1.15$. Thus, $C$ increases by about 15 percent when $t$ is reduced by 10 percent (to $0.9t$). (b) Yes. The cost tends to be less in the United States than in the United Kingdom. (c) Hartley and Corcoran suggest that one factor may be that American aircraft manufacturers benefit from defense

contracts to a greater extent than their British counterparts do. Thus, the American manufacturers can develop a commercial airliner more cheaply (holding the duration of the development project constant) than can the British firms. (More will be said on this score in Chapter 16.)*

*For further discussion, see K. Hartley and W. Corcoran, *Journal of Industrial Economics* (March 1978).

In other words, the Hanover Company should carry out the project in about 8 years.

## INNOVATION TIME AND COST: JAPAN VERSUS THE UNITED STATES

Time-cost trade-off functions vary from firm to firm, because some firms are more adept than others in developing and introducing particular types of products. According to recent findings, Japanese firms in many high-technology industries tend to have time-cost trade-off functions that are to the left of their American rivals for innovations based on external technology (technology developed outside the innovating firm). That is, they tend to be quicker and more efficient in utilizing and adapting external technology. But for innovations based on internal technology (technology developed within the innovating firm), there is no evidence that the Japanese time-cost trade-off functions are to the left of the American functions. The situation is shown in Figure 7.5.

Japanese firms, in carrying out an innovation, allocate their resources quite differently from the way American firms do. Table 7.2 shows, for 100 Japanese and American firms, the proportion of the total cost of developing and introducing a new product (introduced in 1985) that was incurred in each of the following stages of the innovation process: applied research, preparation of project requirements and basic specifications, prototype or pilot plant, tooling and manufacturing equipment and facilities, manufacturing start-up, and marketing start-up. The percentage of total innovation cost devoted in Japan to tooling and manufacturing equipment and facilities is almost double that in the United States. This reflects Japan's emphasis on process engineering and efficient manufacturing facilities. On the other hand, the percentage of innovation cost devoted to marketing start-up costs—that is, the expenses of pre-introduction marketing activities—in the United States is almost double that in Japan.

TABLE 7.2   *Percentage Distribution of Innovation Cost, 100 Firms, Japan and the United States, 1985*

| Stage of innovation process | Japan | United States |
|---|---|---|
| Applied research | 14 | 18 |
| Preparation of product specifications | 7 | 8 |
| Prototype or pilot plant | 16 | 17 |
| Tooling and manufacturing equipment and facilities | 44 | 23 |
| Manufacturing start-up | 10 | 17 |
| Marketing start-up | 8 | 17 |
| Total | 100 | 100 |

*Source:* E. Mansfield, "Industrial Innovation in Japan and the United States," *Science* (September 30, 1988). Because of rounding errors, figures may not sum to total.

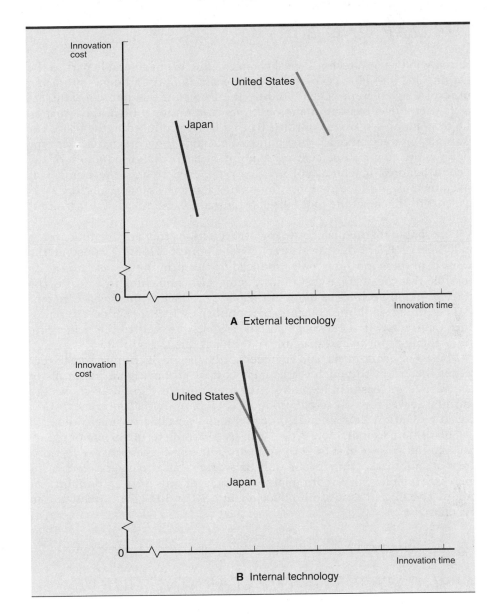

**FIGURE 7.5   *Illustrative Time-Cost Trade-Off Functions***   For an
innovation based on external technology, the Japanese time-cost trade-off
function seems to be to the left of the American function.

*Source:* E. Mansfield, "The Speed and Cost of Industrial Innovation in Japan and the
United States: External vs. Internal Technology," *Management Science* (October 1988).

## THE LEARNING CURVE

In many industries, technological change is due in considerable part to the learning and on-the-job experience that occurs as a firm produces more and more of a given item. Thus, holding the firm's output rate constant, its average cost declines with increases in its *cumulative* total output (that is, the total number of items of this sort that it has produced in the past). For example, production of the first hundred machine tools of a particular type may require about 50 percent more hours of labor than production of the second hundred machine tools of this type, even though the number of machine tools produced per month remains about the same. Thus, the average cost of this machine tool falls substantially as cumulative total output grows.

One should distinguish between cost reductions that are due to *learning* and those that are due to greater current output. Holding constant the number of these machine tools produced by this firm in the past, it is quite possible that the average cost of producing such a machine tool during the current period declines as more of them are produced. But this is different from learning. Holding constant the number of such machine tools produced currently, if the average cost is inversely related to the firm's previous total output of this machine tool, this is due to learning.

Managers, economists, and engineers often use the **learning curve** to represent the extent to which the average cost of producing an item falls in response to increases in its cumulative total output. Figure 7.6 shows the learning curves for two actual products: a piece of optical equipment (produced by Optical Equipment Company) and a portable turbine (produced by Solar International, Inc.). As you can see, learning results in major reductions in the average cost of both products. Of course, these cost reductions are not automatic: they occur only if workers and managers strive for increased efficiency. But for many products of this sort, a doubling of cumulative output tends to produce about a 20 or 30 percent reduction in average cost.

## APPLICATIONS OF THE LEARNING CURVE

Many firms have adopted pricing strategies based on the learning curve. Consider the case of Texas Instruments, a major producer of semiconductor chips and other electronic products. When the semiconductor industry was relatively young, Texas Instruments priced its product at less than its then-current average costs in order to increase its output rate and its cumulative total output. Believing that the learning curve was relatively steep, it hoped that this would reduce its average costs to such an extent that it would be profitable to produce and sell at this low price. This strategy was extremely successful. As Texas Instruments continued to cut price, its rivals began to

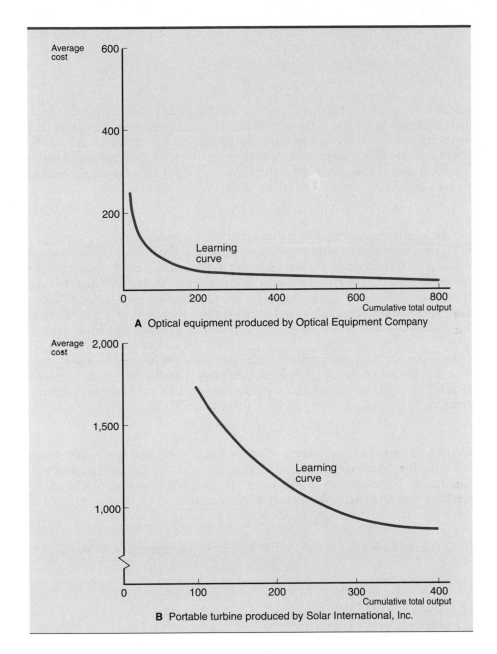

*FIGURE 7.6 Learning Curves* Average cost declines with increases in cumulative total output.

*Source:* R. Hayes and S. Wheelwright, *Restoring Our Competitive Edge.* The cost data are incomplete, but this makes no difference for present purposes.

withdraw from the market, its output continued to go up, its costs were reduced further, and its profits rose.[8]

The learning curve is expressed as follows:

$$C = aQ^b, \tag{7.9}$$

where $C$ is the input cost of the $Q^{th}$ unit of output produced. If this relationship holds exactly, $a$ is the cost of the first unit produced. The value of $b$ is negative, since increases in cumulative total output reduce cost. If the absolute value of $b$ is large, cost falls more rapidly with increases in cumulative total output than it would if the absolute value of $b$ were small. Taking logarithms of both sides of equation (7.9),

$$\log C = \log a + b \log Q. \tag{7.10}$$

In this logarithmic form, $b$ is the slope of the learning curve.

To estimate the learning curve from historical data concerning cost and cumulative output, one can use the regression techniques in Chapter 4. As shown in equation (7.10), $\log C$ is a linear function of $\log Q$. Thus, to estimate $a$ and $b$, we can regress $\log C$ on $\log Q$. (In other words, $\log C$ is the equivalent of $Y$ in Chapter 4, and $\log Q$ is the equivalent of $X$.) Of course, the values of $a$ and $b$ will vary from product to product and from firm to firm.

To illustrate how the learning curve can be used in specific cases, suppose that the controller of the Killian Company, a maker of a particular type of machine tool, finds that for her firm the learning curve (in logarithmic form) is

$$\log C = 4.0 - .30 \log Q,$$

where $C$ is expressed in dollars. (That is, $\log a = 4.0$ and $b = -.30$.) From this equation, she can estimate how much the cost per unit will go down in the future. For example, if she wants to estimate the cost of the $100^{th}$ machine tool of a particular type, the answer is

$$\log C = 4.0 - .30 \log 100 = 4.0 - .30(2) = 3.4.$$

Since the antilog of 3.4 is 2,512, the answer is that the cost will be $2,512.

## *HENRY FORD'S MODEL T AND DOUGLAS AIRCRAFT'S DC-9*

The learning curve is nothing new. Between 1908 and 1923, the price of Henry Ford's famous Model T automobile fell from over $3,000 to under $1,000, owing in considerable measure to cost reductions that were due to

---

[8] For a classic paper concerning learning curves, see K. Arrow, "The Economic Implications of Learning by Doing," *Review of Economic Studies* (June 1962). The Boston Consulting Group was a leading advocate of their application to corporate planning.

learning. Ford worked hard to push costs down in this way. Standardization was increased. His product line was less diverse than those of his competitors, and model improvements occurred less frequently. The production throughput time was reduced, and the division of labor was increased.

However, not all firms have been as successful as the Ford Motor Company in reducing costs in this way. In cases where labor turnover is high or where a firm cannot obtain workers with the necessary skills, expected cost reductions that are due to learning may not materialize. For example, when Douglas Aircraft planned the production of the DC-9 airframe, it anticipated little problem in getting qualified workers. But when the time came, the labor market was so tight in Los Angeles, that Douglas soon lost 12,000 of the 35,000 workers it hired. The result was that, contrary to the firm's expectations, costs did not fall as a result of learning, substantial losses were incurred, and the firm was forced into a merger (resulting in McDonnell Douglas).[9]

# TECHNOLOGICAL FORECASTING

Managers must try, as best they can, to forecast the rate and direction of technological change. If a rival introduces a major new product or process, it may have a devastating effect on a firm's profits. For example, in the first several years after its introduction, Glaxo's anti-ulcers drug, Zantac, took over half of the market away from Smith-Kline Beecham's anti-ulcers drug, Tagamet. Or consider the case of the early plastics, which were brittle and highly flammable, had low resistance to heat, and were subject to early discoloration. Because of competition from new products, virtually none is presently on the market.

It is widely agreed that technology is a relatively difficult variable to forecast, because there is so much uncertainty concerning what will be produced by R and D efforts, and what breakthroughs will occur, and when. How do the people engaged in technological forecasting go about making their forecasts? According to various surveys, simple intuitive projections seem to play a very important role in technological forecasting. For example, suppose a firm wants to forecast the maximum speed of commercial aircraft in the year 2000. One way of obtaining such a forecast is simply to ask an expert, or group of experts, to guess as best they can what the maximum speed will be at that time. Certainly, this approach is straightforward enough and relatively cheap. But it runs into a number of difficulties. First, technologists are no more in agreement about the future than managers are, the result being that the answer is likely to vary, depending on the choice of expert. Second, even when based on the opinion of distinguished experts, such forecasts can contain large errors.

---

[9] J. Macklin, "Douglas Aircraft's Stormy Flight Path," *Fortune* (December 1966).

To cope with some of the problems involved in simply asking a group of experts for a consensus guess, Olaf Helmer and T. Gordon, while at the RAND Corporation, developed a technique known as the Delphi method, which attempts to utilize expert opinion more effectively. For example, to forecast the maximum speed of commercial aircraft in the year 2000, users of the Delphi method would ask a number of experts to formulate separate and independent estimates. The median and interquartile range (the span encompassing the middle 50 percent) of the estimates would be communicated to each of the experts, and they would be asked to reconsider their previous answers and revise them if they wanted to. Then those people whose answers lay outside the interquartile range would be asked to state why they disagreed to this extent from the other members of the group. Their replies would be circulated among the group, and the members would be asked once again to make a forecast. This iterative process would continue until there was a reasonable convergence of the individual forecasts.

The Delphi method has been used in fields as diverse as defense, pharmaceuticals, political science, and educational technology. According to its developers, it is a useful tool for technological forecasting. However, it is important to recognize the obvious fact that the results of the Delphi method can be no better than the foresight of the individual experts. And as noted above, this foresight can be very imperfect. Moreover, by relying so heavily on a consensus, the Delphi method assumes that collective judgment is better than individual judgment. This is a dangerous assumption, as evidenced by the many important technological advances that have been made by individuals and groups that acted contrary to prevailing majority —and elite—opinion.

Another technique that plays an important role in technological forecasting is simple trend extrapolation. For example, to forecast the maximum speed of commercial aircraft in the year 2000, one could obtain a time series of the maximum speed of such aircraft at various points in history, and project the historical trend into the future. (Essentially, the procedure is like that used for IBM's sales on page 179.) In fact, this simple sort of extrapolation technique has been used in the U.S. Department of Defense, where much of the work on technological forecasting originated. It has also been used in commercial work of various kinds.

The problem with naive extrapolation techniques of this sort is that unless the fundamental factors determining the technological parameter in question operate much as they have in the past, previous trends will not necessarily be a good guide to the future. For example, a host of factors, including the allocation of R and D resources and the pressure of environmental concerns, may see to it that the maximum speed of commercial aircraft increases at quite a different rate than it has in the immediate past.

Besides trend extrapolation, technological forecasters sometimes use lead-lag relationships. For example, to forecast the maximum speed of commercial aircraft in the year 2000, one could plot the maximum speed of commercial aircraft against the maximum speed of military aircraft. Finding that commercial speeds have lagged military speeds, one might be able to use this relationship to make the desired forecast. Of course, here too the problem is that the historical relationship may not continue into the future.[10]

## INPUT-OUTPUT MODELS

The available evidence indicates that most technology forecasts, both in industry and in government, are based on the simple intuitive methods and extrapolation techniques described in the previous section. In addition, however, there has been some experimentation with more sophisticated types of forecasting techniques, including input-output models.

Input-output analysis assumes that inputs are used in fixed proportions in producing any product and that there are constant returns to scale. For example, in the production of steel, it assumes that for every ton of steel produced, a certain amount of iron ore, a certain amount of coke, a certain amount of fuel, and so on would be required. The amount of each input required per unit of output is assumed to be the same, regardless of the level of output. For example, if a certain amount of iron ore is required to produce 1 million tons of steel, it is assumed that 20 times that amount is required to produce 20 million tons of steel.

Suppose the economy consists of only three industries: coal, chemicals, and electric power. Each industry uses the products of the other industries in the proportions shown in Table 7.3. For instance, the second column of Table 7.3 states that every dollar's worth of coal requires 20 cents' worth of electric power, 10 cents' worth of coal, and 70 cents' worth of labor.[11]

According to the best available forecasts, consumers next year will consume $100 million of electric power, $30 million of coal, and $40 million

TABLE 7.3  *Amount of Each Input Used per Dollar of Output*

|  | Type of output | | |
|---|---|---|---|
|  | Electric power (dollars) | Coal (dollars) | Chemicals (dollars) |
| Electric power | 0.2 | 0.2 | 0.2 |
| Coal | 0.4 | 0.1 | 0.2 |
| Chemicals | 0.2 | 0.0 | 0.1 |
| Labor | 0.2 | 0.7 | 0.5 |
| Total | 1.0 | 1.0 | 1.0 |

[10] For further discussion, see E. Mansfield, "Technological Forecasting," in T. S. Khachaturov, ed., *Methods of Long-Term Planning and Forecasting* (London: Macmillan, 1976), from which some of this material is drawn.

[11] In some cases, outputs and inputs are measured in physical units rather than dollars. For example, coal output and coal input might be measured in tons per year, and labor input might be measured in labor-hours per year. Clearly, one can carry out the analysis in either way.

of chemicals. Input-output analysis is concerned with the question: How much will have to be produced by each industry in order to meet these levels of consumption? To begin to solve this problem, consider the case of coal. If electric power output is $E$, chemical output is $C$, and coal output is $L$ ($E$, $C$, and $L$ are measured in millions of dollars), it follows from Table 7.3 that

$$L = .4E + .1L + .2C + 30 \tag{7.11}$$

if the forecasted level of coal consumption is achieved. Why? Because an amount of coal equal in value to $.4E$ must be produced to meet the needs of the electric power industry, an amount of coal equal in value to $.1L$ must be produced to meet the needs of the coal industry, an amount of coal equal in value to $.2C$ must be produced to meet the needs of the chemical industry, and an amount of coal equal in value to 30 must be produced for consumption. Thus, the total output of coal must be equal to the sum of these four terms, as shown in equation (7.11).

If we construct similar equations for electric power output and chemical output, we find that

$$E = .2E + .2L + .2C + 100 \tag{7.12}$$

$$C = .2E + .1C + 40 \tag{7.13}$$

if the forecasted levels of consumption are to be met. For example, equation (7.13) must hold because chemical output must equal the amount needed by the electric power industry ($.2E$) plus the amount needed by the chemical industry itself ($.1C$) plus 40 for consumption.

Equations (7.11) to (7.13) are three simultaneous linear equations in three variables, $L$, $E$, and $C$. Using straightforward techniques, we can solve for these unknowns[12]; the solution is $L = 131$, $E = 178$, and $C = 84$. This provides the answer to our question: $131 million of coal, $178 million of electric power, and $84 million of chemicals must be produced if the forecasted consumption levels are to be met.

Technological forecasters try to forecast the changes in input-output coefficients (the numbers in Table 7.3), and see what the effects of these changes will be. One way they have tried to forecast input-output coefficients in a particular industry is to assume that new technologies have a weight proportional to investment in new capacity. By observing the changes in the industry's average input-output structure, and its expenditures on new plant and equipment, one can estimate what the input-output coefficients for the new "layer" of capital must have been. Then, to make short-term projections, one can assume that the coefficients for the new layer will remain constant, and increase the weight given to these coeffi-

---

[12] From equation (7.13), we know that $2E = .9C - 40$, which means that $E = 4.5C - 200$. If we substitute this expression for $E$ in equation (7.11), we find that
$$.9L = .4(4.5C - 200) + .2C + 30.$$
If we substitute the same expression for $E$ in equation (7.12), we find that
$$.2L = .8(4.5C - 200) - .2C - 100.$$
Solving these two equations simultaneously, we obtain $L$ and $C$; and using the fact that $E = 4.5C - 200$, it is easy to obtain $E$ as well.

cients (in proportion to expected investment). This method, used by the Harvard Economic Research Project, is rough. All that its users claim is that it gives "ballpark" estimates.[13]

# DIFFUSION MODELS

Another type of technological forecasting technique is based on the use of econometric diffusion models, which analyze the rate at which an innovation spreads. Although these models forecast the diffusion of new processes and products that are already in existence rather than the occurrence of future inventions, this limitation may be less important than it seems, since the inventions that have already occurred are sometimes all that really matter in the short and intermediate run. In part, this is because it frequently takes a long time for an invention to be commercially introduced. For example, it took about nine years before catalytic cracking, a major innovation in oil refining, was first used.

The diffusion process, like the earlier stages in the creation and assimilation of new processes and products, is essentially a learning process. However, rather than being confined to a research laboratory or to a few firms, the learning takes place among a considerable number of users and producers. When the innovation first appears, potential users are uncertain of its nature and effectiveness, and they tend to view its purchase as an experiment. Sometimes considerable additional research and development is required before the innovation is successful; sometimes, despite attempts at redesign and improvement, the innovation never is a success. Information regarding the existence, characteristics, and availability of the innovation is circulated by the producers through advertisements and salesmen; information regarding the reaction of users to the innovation tends to be circulated informally and through the trade press.

Figure 7.7 illustrates an important aspect of the process by which new techniques spread throughout an industry. The figure shows that the probability that a firm not using an innovation will adopt it in the next few months is influenced by the proportion of firms in the industry that already are using it. Specifically, as the number of firms adopting an innovation increases, the probability of its adoption by a nonuser increases. This is because the risks associated with its introduction grow smaller, competitive pressures mount, and bandwagon effects increase as experience and information regarding an innovation accumulate.

Other important aspects of the diffusion process are brought out by Figure 7.8. Panel A shows that the probability that a nonuser will adopt the innovation is higher for more profitable innovations than for less profitable innovations, holding constant the proportion of firms in the industry that

[13] A. Carter, "Technological Forecasting and Input-Output Analysis," *Technological Forecasting and Social Change* (1970), pp. 331–45.

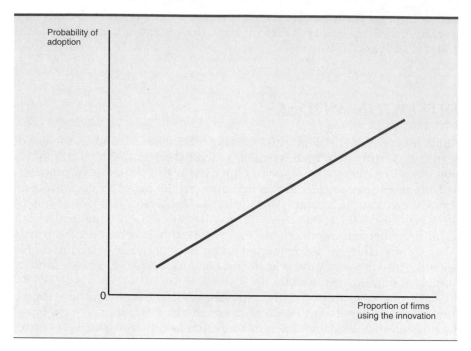

**FIGURE 7.7    Relation between Probability of a Nonuser's Adopting a Process Innovation and the Proportion of Firms Already Using the Innovation**    This relationship tends to be direct.

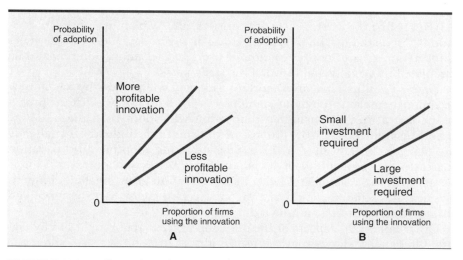

**FIGURE 7.8    Effect of Profitability of the Innovation and Size of Investment Required to Adopt the Innovation on Probability of Adoption** This probability tends to be directly related to profitability and inversely related to the size of the investment.

are already using it. The more profitable the investment in an innovation promises to be, the greater will be the probability that a firm's estimate of its potential profitability will compensate for the risks involved in its installation.

Panel B of Figure 7.8 shows that the probability that a nonuser will adopt the innovation is higher for innovations requiring fairly small investments, holding constant the proportion of firms in the industry that are already using it (and the profitability of the innovation). This is because firms will be more cautious before committing themselves to large, expensive projects, and they will have more difficulty in financing them.

If the relationship in Figure 7.7 holds, it can be shown that $P(t)$, the proportion of firms using the innovation, will increase in accord with the S-shaped growth curve shown in Figure 7.9. The formula for this growth curve (often called the logistic curve) is

$$P(t) = \frac{1}{1 + e^{-(A + Bt)}}, \tag{7.14}$$

where $A$ and $B$ are parameters that vary from innovation to innovation. Whether the diffusion process goes on slowly, as in curve $L$ in Figure 7.9, or quickly, as in curve $M$, depends on the profitability of the innovation and the size of the investment it requires. This model has much in common with the models used by epidemiologists to represent the spread of contagious diseases. Firms in a wide variety of industries have found that it has

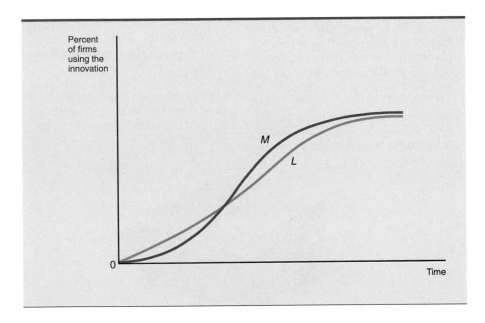

**FIGURE 7.9** *Growth over a Period of Time in Proportion of Firms Using the Innovation* Both growth curves $L$ and $M$ are S-shaped.

## THE DEVELOPMENT AND INTRODUCTION OF CANON'S PERSONAL COPIER

In 1980, Canon, the Japanese copier firm, began work on the development of a small model for the home or office that would be virtually service-free. The copy speed —6, 8, or 10 copies per minute —didn't matter much, but it was felt that its cost should be less than $1,000. About 140 top R and D personnel were recruited from various parts of the firm, and worked in great secrecy for 2½ years to achieve this result. The project cost Canon about $8 million. To field-test the resulting machines, Canon employees used them in their homes. Until a day before the announcement of the new copier, practically no one knew the characteristics of the new machine, the Canon PC-10.*

(a) This new machine cost Canon less than $300 to manufacture because it was so well designed for automatic assembly. Thus, it was sold to American dealers for $400 to $420. The cartridge unit could be assembled totally by robots without human hands touching it. Were both product and process innovations involved in this project? (b) Canon devoted $15 million to advertising this new copier in 1983. Jack Klugman, star of TV's "The Odd Couple" and "Quincy" series, appeared in television ads in the United States. What sorts of potential customers were these marketing efforts aimed at? (c) By the end of 1983, sales reached 10,000 per month; by 1985, they were more than 30,000 per month. To speed up delivery, Canon began shipping machines in cargo jets. What sorts of techniques might have been used to forecast the sales of this copier?

*Solution* (a) Yes. The new copier was a product innovation; the new methods used to produce it were process innovations. (b) Klugman seemed to represent small retailers, executives, and the several million Americans who have offices in their homes. These were some of the most important potential customers. (c) The diffusion models described in this chapter might have been useful in this regard.

* G. Jacobson and J. Hillkirk, *Xerox: American Samurai* (New York: Macmillan, 1987).

been able to explain reasonably well the available data concerning the diffusion process.[14]

# FORECASTING THE RATE OF DIFFUSION OF NUMERICALLY CONTROLLED MACHINE TOOLS

To illustrate the use of diffusion models for forecasting purposes, consider a study carried out for the Small Business Administration to forecast the percentage of firms in the tool and die industry that would be using numerically controlled machine tools two years after the time of the study.[15] When the study was carried out, about 20 percent of the firms in the National Tool, Die, and Precision Machining Association were using numerically controlled machine tools. To use the model described in the previous section, data were obtained, both from a mail survey and from an interview study, of the past growth over time in the percentage of tool and die firms using such machine tools. Based on these data, and using the regression techniques in Chapter 4, estimates of A and B in equation (7.14) were made. To see how these estimates were calculated, note that equation (7.14) implies that

$$\ln \{P(t)/[1 - P(t)]\} = A + Bt. \tag{7.15}$$

Thus, A and B can be estimated by regressing $\ln \{P(t)/[1 - P(t)]\}$ on $t$.[16] (The natural logarithm of any number—say X—is designated as $\ln X$.)

Given estimates of A and B, equation (7.14) can be used to forecast $P(t)$ for future values of $t$. Based on the interview data, the model forecasted that about 33 percent of the firms would be using numerically controlled machine tools. Based on the mail-survey data, the model forecasted that about 37 percent of the firms would be using them.

To see how these forecasts compared with those obtained on the basis of other methods, two alternative types of forecasts were made. First, the firms—both in interviews with a carefully selected sample of industry executives and in the mail survey of the industry—were asked whether they planned to begin using numerical control in the next two years. Since there was considerable lead time required in obtaining numerical control, it seemed reasonable to suppose that their replies would have some forecasting value. The results of the interviews indicated that about 16 percent of nonusers planned to use numerical control; the results of the mail survey indicated that this was the case for 28 percent of the nonusers. Thus, the forecast was 33 percent, based on the interview data, or 43 percent, based on the mail survey.

---

[14] See. E. Mansfield, *Industrial Research and Technological Innovation* (New York: Norton, 1968); E. Mansfield et al., *The Production and Application of New Industrial Technology* (New York: Norton, 1977); V. Mahajan and Y. Wind, eds., *Innovation Diffusion Models of New Product Acceptance* (Cambridge, Mass.: Ballinger, 1986); and E. Mansfield, "The Diffusion of Flexible Manufacturing Systems in Japan, Europe, and the United States," *Management Science*, in press.

[15] See E. Mansfield et al., *New Industrial Technology*.

[16] This is only a rough estimation technique, but it is adequate for present purposes.

## THE SPREAD OF INDUSTRIAL ROBOTS IN JAPAN AND THE UNITED STATES

The industrial robot is one of the most important manufacturing innovations of recent decades. Based on data obtained from 175 firms in Japan and the United States, the growth over time in the proportion of firms that have begun to use robots in each country can be approximated reasonably well by the logistic function in equation (7.14). Let $b_{ij}$ be the least-squares estimate of $B_{ij}$ (the value of $B$ in the $i$th industry in the $j$th country), let $\pi_{ij}$ be the average rate of return from robots (divided by the required rate of return) in the $i$th industry in the $j$th country, and let $D_{ij}$ be the number of years from the first introduction of robots in 1961 to their first use in the $i$th industry in the $j$th country. If we regress $b_{ij}$, which is a measure of the rate of diffusion of robots in the $i$th industry in the $j$th country, on $\pi_{ij}$ and $D_{ij}$, we find that

$$b_{ij} = \begin{bmatrix} -.341 \\ -.234 \end{bmatrix} + 0.25\,\pi_{ij} + 0.031\,D_{ij},$$

where the top figure in brackets pertains to Japan, and the bottom figure pertains to the United States.*

(a) Holding $\pi_{ij}$ and $D_{ij}$ constant, is there any tendency for the rate of diffusion to be higher in Japan than in the United States? (b) Does this mean we can be sure that the rate of diffusion was no greater in Japan than in the United States? (c) According to the President's Commission on International Competitiveness, Japan has been quicker than the United States to use robots

in large numbers. Do the above results contradict this conclusion? (d) The logistic function in equation (7.14) has been used to forecast the percentage of firms in each industry (in Japan and the United States) that will use robots by the year 2000. Of what use are such forecasts to producers of industrial robots?

*Solution* (a) No. Holding $\pi_{ij}$ and $D_{ij}$ constant in the two countries, the rate of diffusion tends to be higher in the United States than in Japan, since the top figure in brackets (which pertains to Japan) is less than the bottom figure in brackets (which pertains to the United States). (b) No. Because $D_{ij}$ tends to be greater in Japan than in the United States, one would expect that $b_{ij}$ would tend to be greater in Japan than in the United

States. (c) No. The above results pertain entirely to the interfirm rate of diffusion, not to the intrafirm rates of diffusion. (d) They help them make the proper deci- sions concerning plant capacity, among other things. Robot pro- ducers are intensely interested in how rapidly the market for their product will expand.

* E. Mansfield, "The Diffusion of Industrial Robots in Japan and the United States," *Research Policy* (1989).

Second, forecasts were obtained from the machine tool builders, the firms that presumably are closest to and best informed about the market for numerically controlled machine tools. About 25 of the 150 members of the National Machine Tool Builders Association provided forecasts. The results showed a considerable amount of variation, but the median forecast was about 30 percent.

How accurate were these forecasts? Which forecasting approach was most accurate? Table 7.4 shows that the model's forecast based on the data from the mail survey was almost precisely correct and that the model's fore- cast based on the interview data was off by only 4 percentage points. Regardless of whether we look at results based on the interview data or the mail survey, the model forecasts better than the other two techniques. Moreover, it forecasts better than simple extrapolation by "naive" models.[17] Certainly, this is encouraging. Based on these and other results, it appears that this simple model may be of use in forecasting the rate of diffusion. Of course, this does not mean that it is anything more than a crude device—or that it can be applied in situations where its basic assumptions do not hold. But it does mean that, used with caution, the model may perform at least as well as other commonly used forecasting devices.

TABLE 7.4   *Alternative 2-Year Forecasts of the Percentage of Firms in the U.S. Tool and Die Industry Using Numerical Control, and the Actual Percentage*

| Type of forecast | Based on interview data | Based on mail survey |
|---|---|---|
| | (percent) | |
| Model | 33 | 37 |
| Plans of tool and die firms | 33 | 43 |
| Median forecast by machine tool builders | 30 | 30 |
| Actual percentage | 37 | 37 |

[17] Specifically, the model forecasted better than naive models that assumed that the increase in the percentage of firms using numerical control would be the same amount, in absolute or relative terms, during the next two years as it had been during the previous two years.

# SUMMARY

1. Technological change is the advance of technology, such advance often resulting in a change in the production function for an existing product or in a new product. The rate of technological change is often measured by changes in productivity. Changes in total factor productivity are often used by firms to measure changes in efficiency.

2. Research and development can be regarded as a process of uncertainty reduction, or learning. Chance plays a large role in research and development, and many projects use parallel efforts to help cope with uncertainty. Techniques are presented in this chapter to indicate when parallel efforts should be used.

3. An R and D project's likelihood of economic success is the product of three separate factors: (a) the probability of technical success, (b) the probability of commercialization (given technical success), and (c) the probability of economic success (given commercialization). All three seem to be directly related to how quickly an R and D project is evaluated for its economic, as opposed to only technical, potential.

4. To promote successful R and D, there must be a strong linkage between R and D and marketing personnel, and project selection techniques must be effective. However, this does not mean that the more complicated quantitative selection techniques need be used.

5. For a particular innovation, there is likely to be a time-cost trade-off function. If the firm cuts the total time taken to develop and introduce the innovation, it incurs higher costs. Time-cost trade-off functions vary from firm to firm, because some firms are more adept and experienced than others in developing and introducing a particular innovation. The optimal duration of the project is the time interval where the discounted gross profits exceed the discounted cost by the maximum amount.

6. In many industries, there is a learning curve, which shows the extent to which the average cost of producing an item falls in response to increases in its tumulative total output. This learning curve plays an important role in pricing. For example, Texas Instruments successfully priced its product at less than its then-current average cost to move quickly down the learning curve. Regression techniques can be applied to estimate the learning curve for a particular product.

7. Technological forecasting techniques, such as the Delphi method and trend extrapolation, have often been used. Input-output models also have been adapted for this purpose.

8. As the number of firms adopting a new process increases, the probability of its adoption by a nonuser increases. Also, the probability that a nonuser will adopt the innovation is higher for more profitable innovations than for less profitable innovations, and for innovations requiring small investments than for those requiring large investments. A model based on these propositions can sometimes be of use in forecasting the rate of diffusion of an innovation.

# PROBLEMS

1. The Monroe Corporation uses three inputs: labor, energy, and materials. In 1994, it uses 20,000 hours of labor, 50,000 kilowatt-hours of energy, and 10,000 pounds of materials to produce 200,000 pounds of output. In 1995, it uses 30,000 hours of labor, 100,000 kilowatt-hours of energy, and 14,000 pounds of materials to produce 300,000 pounds of output. In 1994, the price of labor is $10 per hour, the price of a kilowatt-hour of energy is 2 cents, and the price of a pound of materials is $5.
   (a) What is total factor productivity in 1994?
   (b) What is total factor productivity in 1995?
   (c) What is the base year in the above calculations?
2. The chief scientist at the Roosevelt Laboratories estimates that the cost (in millions of dollars) of developing and introducing a new type of anti-ulcers drug equals

$$C = 100 - 19t + 0.5t^2, \quad \text{for } 1 \le t \le 6,$$

where $t$ is the number of years taken to develop and introduce the new drug. The discounted profit (gross of innovation cost) from a new drug of this type (in millions of dollars) is estimated to equal

$$R = 110 - 15t, \quad \text{for } 1 \le t \le 6.$$

   (a) The managers of the Roosevelt Laboratories are committed to develop and introduce this new drug within 6 years, and it is impossible to develop and introduce it in less than 1 year. What project duration would minimize cost?
   (b) Why does $R$ decline as $t$ increases?
   (c) What is the optimal project duration? Why?
3. The Flynn Company produces a particular type of commercial truck. Its chief engineer regresses the logarithm of the input cost of the $Q^{\text{th}}$ truck produced on the logarithm of $Q$, the result being

$$\log C = 5.1 - .25 \log Q,$$

where $C$ is input cost (in dollars).
   (a) What is the estimated input cost of the 100th truck produced?
   (b) What is the estimated input cost of the 200th truck produced?
   (c) By what percentage does unit input cost decline if output is doubled (from 100 to 200 trucks)?
4. The Martin Company's president wants to estimate the proportion of chemical firms that will be using a particular new process in 1998. One of her assistants regresses $\ln \{m(t)/[n - m(t)]\}$ on $t$, where $m(t)$ is the number of chemical firms using this process in year $t$, and $n$ is the total number of chemical firms that can use this process. Measuring $t$ in years from 1983, the regression is

$$\ln \left[ \frac{m(t)}{n - m(t)} \right] = -4.0 + .22t.$$

(a) Prove that if the proportion of chemical firms using the new process increases in accord with the logistic curve in equation (7.14), ln $\{m(t)/[n - m(t)]\}$ will be a linear function of t.

(b) Based on the above regression, can you estimate A and B [the parameters of the logistic curve in equation (7.14)]? If so, how?

(c) Forecast the percentage of chemical firms using the new process in 1998.

5. Suppose the following table shows the amount of each type of input used per dollar of output:

| Type of input | Output (dollars) | | |
|---|---|---|---|
| | Electric power | Coal | Chemicals |
| Electric power | $0.1 | $0.3 | $0.0 |
| Coal | 0.5 | 0.1 | 0.0 |
| Chemicals | 0.2 | 0.0 | 0.9 |
| Labor | 0.2 | 0.6 | 0.1 |
| Total | 1.0 | 1.0 | 1.0 |

Suppose that this economy expects to consume $100 million of electric power, $50 million of coal, and $50 million of chemicals. If so, how much labor must be used?

6. The Bureau of Labor Statistics has produced data showing that output per hour of labor in blast furnaces using the most up-to-date techniques has sometimes been about twice as large as the industry average.

(a) How can such large differences exist at a given time? Why don't all firms continually adopt the most up-to-date techniques?

(b) Should firms always adopt techniques that maximize output per hour of labor? Why or why not?

(c) Should firms adopt techniques that maximize output per dollar of capital? Why or why not?

7. The Russell Corporation is trying to develop an improved engine that will emit fewer pollutants. There are two possible approaches to this technical problem. If either one is adopted, there is a 50-50 chance that it will cost $2 million to develop the engine and a 50-50 chance that it will cost $1 million to do so.

(a) If the firm chooses one of the approaches and carries it to completion, what is the expected cost of developing the engine?

(b) If the two approaches are run in parallel and if the true cost of development using each approach can be determined after $150,000 has been spent on each approach, what is the expected cost of developing the engine? (Note that the total cost figure for each approach, if adopted, includes the $150,000.)

(c) Should parallel approaches be used?

8. To help decide whether particular research and development (R and D) projects should be carried out, some firms compare the estimated cost

of each project with the estimated profits it will earn. To carry out such an analysis, the firm's personnel must estimate how much the R and D project would cost if it were carried out. In one major drug firm, the frequency distribution of 49 projects by the ratio of actual to estimated cost is as shown below:

| Actual cost divided by estimated cost | Number of projects |
| --- | --- |
| Less than 1.01 | 6 |
| 1.01 and under 2.01 | 24 |
| 2.01 and under 3.01 | 16 |
| 3.01 and under 4.01 | 3 |

(a) If this firm were using this technique to help determine whether particular R and D projects should be carried out, what problems would be encountered?

(b) How might the firm try to cope with these problems?

9. The Monroe Corporation wants to develop a new process that will reduce its costs by 10 percent. There are two ways to go about developing such a process. If the first way is adopted, there is a .6 probability that it will cost $5 million to develop the process, and a .4 probability that it will cost $3 million to do so. If the second way is adopted, there is a .7 probability that it will cost $3 million, and a .3 probability that it will cost $5 million.

(a) If the first way is adopted, what is the expected cost of developing the new process?

(b) If the second way is adopted, what is the expected cost?

(c) If the two approaches can be run in parallel, and if the true cost of development using each approach can be determined after $500,000 has been spent on each approach, what is the expected cost? (Assume that the outcomes of the two approaches are independent. Also, note that the total cost figure for each approach, if adopted, includes the $500,000.)

10. Based on past growth of the percentage of firms in the machinery industry using robots, this percentage can be approximated by the following equation:

$$P(t) = \frac{1}{1 + e^{(6.1 - .41t)}}$$

where $P(t)$ is this percentage and $t$ is measured in years from 1970.

(a) During what year did about 25 percent of the firms in the machinery industry use robots?

(b) During what year did 50 percent of the firms in this industry use robots?

# Chapter 8
# *The Analysis of Costs*

## *INTRODUCTION*

According to a recent study, which will be described in this chapter, a small advertising agency's costs can be reduced significantly by carrying out a variety of types of advertising jointly, rather than separately. This result is of importance to the top executives of the many small advertising agencies on Madison Avenue and elsewhere, since firms, whether in advertising or in any other industry, must try to contain their costs.

To make wise decisions concerning how much to produce and what prices to charge, a firm's executives also must understand, and pay proper attention to, the relationship between their firm's output rate and its costs. In this chapter, we learn to analyze in detail the nature of this relationship, both in the short and long runs. Moreover, building on our previous discussion in Chapter 4, we examine the results of empirical studies of the relationship between output and cost in various firms, and describe the nature and usefulness of the break-even chart, which is commonly used by many firms to analyze the effects of variations in output on their profits.

## *OPPORTUNITY COSTS*

Managerial economists define the cost of producing a particular product as the value of the other products that the resources used in its production could have produced instead. For example, the cost of producing locomotives is the value of the goods and services that could be obtained from the manpower, equipment, and materials used currently in locomotive production. The costs of inputs to a firm are their values in their most valuable alternative uses. These costs, together with the firm's production function (which indicates how much of each input is required to produce various amounts of the product), determine the cost of producing the product. This is called the **opportunity cost doctrine.**

The opportunity cost of an input may not equal its **historical cost,** which is defined to be the amount the firm actually paid for it. For example, if a firm invests $1 million in a piece of equipment that is quickly outmoded and is too inefficient relative to new equipment to be worth operating, its value is clearly not $1 million. Although conventional accounting rules place great emphasis on historical costs, managerial economists emphasize that historical costs can be misleading.

There are two types of costs, both of which are generally important. The first type is **explicit costs,** which are the ordinary items that accountants include as the firm's expenses. They are the firm's payroll, payments for raw materials, and so on. The second type is **implicit costs,** which include the cost of resources owned and used by the firm's owner. Unfortunately, accountants and managers, in calculating the costs of the firm often omit the second type of costs.

Implicit costs arise because the opportunity cost doctrine must be applied to the inputs supplied by the owner of the firm. Consider John Harvey, the proprietor of a firm who invests his own labor and capital in the business. These inputs should be valued at the amount he would have received if he had used these inputs in another way. If he could have received a salary of $25,000 if he worked for someone else, and if he could have received dividends of $20,000 if he invested his money in someone else's firm, he should value his labor and his capital at these rates. To exclude these implicit costs can be a serious mistake.

## *SHORT-RUN COST FUNCTIONS*

Given the firm's cost of producing each level of output, we can define the firm's **cost functions,** which play a very important role in managerial economics. A firm's cost functions show various relationships between its costs and its output rate. The firm's production function and the prices it pays for inputs determine the firm's cost functions, which can pertain to the short run or the long run.

The **short run** is a time period so short that the firm cannot alter the quantity of some of its inputs. As the length of the time period increases, the amounts of more and more inputs become variable. Any time span between one where the quantity of no input is variable and one where the quantity of all inputs is variable could reasonably be called the short run. However, a more restrictive definition is generally employed: we say that

## HOW HARLEY-DAVIDSON HAS REDUCED COSTS

Harley-Davidson Motor Company, a producer of motorcycles, has experienced very tough competition, particularly from Japanese rivals. (Recall Chapter 1.) Faced with a decreasing share of the market and lower profits, it took a number of major steps to increase manufacturing efficiency and reduce costs. For one thing, it phased out many of its machining operations in 1981, and began to purchase its metal from steel service centers, which are companies that supply steel products and provide just-in-time delivery.

According to Harley-Davidson officials, this program, which became fully operational in 1985, has reduced its work-in-process inventory by nearly $24 million. This has meant a substantial cost reduction. Why? Because it costs money to house inventories, to tie up capital in inventories, and to hire people to move materials in and out of inventory. If a firm can reduce its inventories, it can cut these costs significantly.

Specifically, suppose that Harley-Davidson had borrowed the money to finance its work-in-process inventory and that the interest rate on its loan was 15 percent. By reducing the amount that it had to borrow by $24 million (the amount of the reduction in its work-in-process inventory), Harley-Davidson reduced its annual costs by $.15 \times 24 = \$3.6$ million.

To some extent, Harley-Davidson has adopted the sort of just-in-time system pioneered by Toyota and other Japanese firms. (Recall page 229.) As pointed out by one Harley-Davidson executive, "The plant doesn't have enough real estate to physically accommodate the larger mill orders. Timely service center deliveries have enabled us to make more productive use of our floor space."* This story also illustrates the importance of fostering and maintaining good working relationships between firms and their suppliers. Often economies can be realized if relationships of this sort are improved.

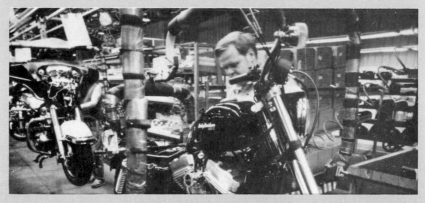

* A. Sharkey, "Making Industry More Competitive," *The Chicago Purchasor* (November–December 1986), pp. 11–12. Also, see "Revving Up for Relief: Harley-Davidson at the ITC," a case in the study guide accompanying this textbook.

TABLE 8.1  *Fixed, Variable, and Total Costs, Media Corporation*

| Units of output | Total fixed cost (dollars per day) | Total variable cost (dollars per day) | Total cost (dollars per day) |
|---|---|---|---|
| 0 | 2,000 | 0 | 2,000 |
| 1 | 2,000 | 100 | 2,100 |
| 2 | 2,000 | 180 | 2,180 |
| 3 | 2,000 | 280 | 2,280 |
| 4 | 2,000 | 392 | 2,392 |
| 5 | 2,000 | 510 | 2,510 |
| 6 | 2,000 | 650 | 2,650 |
| 7 | 2,000 | 800 | 2,800 |
| 8 | 2,000 | 960 | 2,960 |
| 9 | 2,000 | 1,140 | 3,140 |
| 10 | 2,000 | 1,340 | 3,340 |
| 11 | 2,000 | 1,560 | 3,560 |
| 12 | 2,000 | 2,160 | 4,160 |

the short run is the time interval so brief that the firm cannot alter the quantities of plant and equipment. These are the firm's **fixed inputs,** and they determine the firm's **scale of plant.** Inputs like labor, which the firm can vary in quantity in the short run, are the firm's **variable inputs.**

Three concepts of total cost in the short run must be considered: total fixed cost, total variable cost, and total cost. **Total fixed costs** are the total costs per period of time incurred by the firm for fixed inputs. Since the amount of the fixed inputs is fixed (by definition), the total fixed cost will be the same regardless of the firm's output rate. Examples of fixed costs may be depreciation of plant and equipment and property taxes. Table 8.1 shows the costs of the Media Corporation, a producer of sofas. According to Table 8.1, this firm's total fixed costs are $2,000 per day; the firm's total fixed cost function is shown graphically in Figure 8.1.

**Total variable costs** are the total costs incurred by the firm for variable inputs. They go up as the firm's output rate rises, since higher output rates require higher variable input rates, which mean bigger variable costs. For example, the larger the product of a woolen mill, the larger the quantity of wool that must be used, and the higher the total cost of the wool. The Media Corporation's total variable cost schedule is shown in Table 8.1. Figure 8.1 shows the corresponding total variable cost function. Up to a particular output rate (2 units of output), total variable costs are shown to rise at a decreasing rate; beyond that output level, total variable costs rise at an increasing rate. This latter characteristic of the total variable cost function follows from the law of diminishing marginal returns. At low levels of output, increases in the variable inputs may result in increases in their productivity, with the result that total variable costs increase with output, but at a decreasing rate. (More will be said on this score on page 292.)

Finally, **total costs** are the sum of total fixed costs and total variable costs. To derive the total cost column in Table 8.1, add total fixed cost and total variable cost at each output. The total cost function for the Media Corpora-

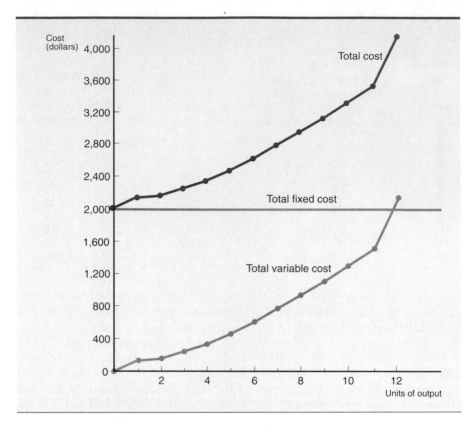

**FIGURE 8.1** *Fixed, Variable, and Total Costs, Media Corporation*
The total cost function and the total variable cost function have the same
shape, since they differ by only a constant amount, which is total fixed cost.

tion is shown in Figure 8.1. The total cost function and the total variable
cost function have the same shape, since they differ by only a constant
amount, which is total fixed cost.

# AVERAGE AND MARGINAL COSTS

While the total cost functions are of great importance, managers must be
interested as well in the average cost functions and the marginal cost function. There are three average cost functions, corresponding to the three
total cost functions. **Average fixed cost** is total fixed cost divided by output.
Average fixed cost declines with increases in output; mathematically, the
average fixed cost function is a rectangular hyperbola. Table 8.2 and Figure
8.2 show the average fixed cost function for the Media Corporation.

TABLE 8.2  *Average and Marginal Costs, Media Corporation*

| Units of output | Average fixed cost (dollars) | Average variable cost (dollars) | Average total cost (dollars) * | Marginal cost (dollars) |
|---|---|---|---|---|
| 1 | 2,000 | 100 | 2,100 | |
| | | | | 80 |
| 2 | 1,000 | 90 | 1,090 | |
| | | | | 100 |
| 3 | 667 | 94 | 760 | |
| | | | | 112 |
| 4 | 500 | 98 | 598 | |
| | | | | 118 |
| 5 | 400 | 102 | 502 | |
| | | | | 140 |
| 6 | 333 | 108 | 442 | |
| | | | | 150 |
| 7 | 286 | 114 | 400 | |
| | | | | 160 |
| 8 | 250 | 120 | 370 | |
| | | | | 180 |
| 9 | 222 | 127 | 349 | |
| | | | | 200 |
| 10 | 200 | 134 | 334 | |
| | | | | 220 |
| 11 | 182 | 142 | 324 | |
| | | | | 600 |
| 12 | 167 | 180 | 347 | |

* Because of rounding errors, average total cost may not equal average fixed cost plus average variable cost.

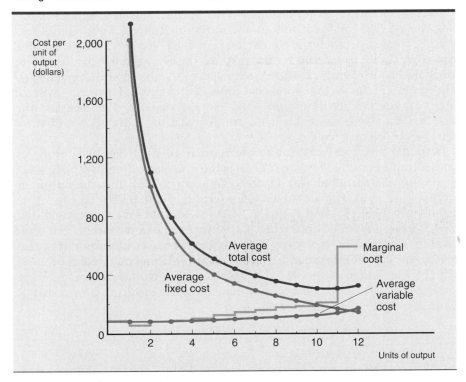

FIGURE 8.2  *Average and Marginal Cost Curves, Media Corporation*
Average total cost achieves its minimum at a higher output rate than average variable cost, because the increases in average variable cost are up to a point more than offset by decreases in average fixed cost.

**Average variable cost** is total variable cost divided by output. For the Media Corporation, the average variable cost function is shown in Table 8.2 and Figure 8.2. At first, output increases result in decreases in average variable cost, but beyond a point, they result in higher average variable cost. The theory of production in Chapter 6 leads us to expect this curvature of the average variable cost function. If $AVC$ is the average variable cost, $TVC$ is the total variable cost, $Q$ is the quantity of output, $U$ is the quantity of the variable input, and $W$ is the price of the variable input, it must be true that

$$AVC = \frac{TVC}{Q} = W\frac{U}{Q}.$$

Consequently, since $Q/U$ is the average product of the variable input ($AVP$),

$$AVC = W\frac{1}{AVP}. \tag{8.1}$$

Hence, since $AVP$ generally rises and then falls with increases in output and since $W$ is constant, $AVC$ must decrease and then go up with increases in output.

**Average total cost** is total cost divided by output. For the Media Corporation, the average total cost function is shown in Table 8.2 and Figure 8.2. Average total cost equals the sum of average fixed cost and average variable cost, which helps to account for the shape of the average total cost function. For those levels of output where both average fixed cost and average variable cost decrease, average total cost must decrease too. However, average total cost reaches its minimum after average variable cost, because the increases in average variable cost are for a time more than offset by decreases in average fixed cost.

**Marginal cost** is the addition to total cost resulting from the addition of the last unit of output. That is, if $C(Q)$ is the total cost of producing $Q$ units of output, the marginal cost between $Q$ and $(Q - 1)$ units of output is $C(Q) - C(Q - 1)$. For the Media Corporation, the marginal cost function is shown in Table 8.2 and Figure 8.2. At low output levels, marginal cost may decrease (as it does in Figure 8.2) with increases in output, but after reaching a minimum, it goes up with further increases in output. The reason for this behavior is found in the law of diminishing marginal returns. If $\Delta TVC$ is the change in total variable costs resulting from a change in output of $\Delta Q$ and if $\Delta TFC$ is the change in total fixed costs resulting from a change in output of $\Delta Q$, marginal cost equals

$$\frac{\Delta TVC + \Delta TFC}{\Delta Q}.$$

But $\Delta TFC$ is zero because fixed costs are fixed; thus marginal cost equals

$$\frac{\Delta TVC}{\Delta Q}.$$

Moreover, if the price of the variable input is taken as given by the firm, $\Delta TVC = W(\Delta U)$, where $\Delta U$ is the change in the quantity of the variable

## THE EFFECTS OF OUTPUT ON THE COST OF PRODUCING AIRCRAFT

In 1985, the National Research Council made a study of the American aircraft industry that stressed the importance to airplane manufacturers of serving the entire world market. As evidence, the council presented the following graph, based on data supplied by McDonnell Douglas.*

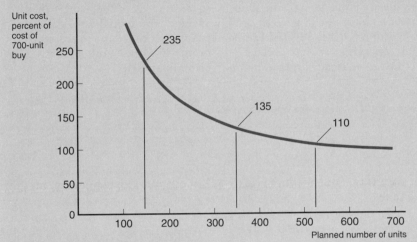

(a) As indicated in this graph, the cost per airplane of producing 525 aircraft of a particular type is about 10 percent higher than the cost per airplane of producing 700 aircraft of this type. Assuming that this graph pertains to the short run, by what percentage does average fixed cost increase if 525 rather than 700 aircraft are produced? (b) If average fixed cost is 30 percent of average total cost if 700 aircraft are produced and 36 percent of average total cost if 525 aircraft are produced, is it true that average total cost is about 10 percent higher if 525 rather than 700 aircraft are produced? (c) According to the council, "If a foreign government elected to incur a cost penalty in order to establish a domestic [aircraft] industry that serves 25 percent of the world market, the effect would be to dramatically change the pricing and thus the profit prospects for a privately funded U.S. manufacturer." What sorts of changes in pricing and profit prospects would occur? Why? (d) The council goes on to say: "With the opportunity for profit reduced or destroyed due to a split market, the U.S. firm might well choose not to enter, and the foreign competitor would then have the total market available." Why?

*Solution* (a) If the number of aircraft produced is 525 rather than 700, average fixed cost is *TFC* ÷ 525 rather than *TFC* ÷ 700, where *TFC* equals total fixed cost. Thus, average fixed cost increases by 33 percent. (b) For 700 aircraft, average total cost equals $X \div .30 = 3.33X$, where $X$ is average fixed cost when 700 aircraft are produced. For 525 aircraft, average total cost equals $1.33X \div .36 = 3.69X$, since average fixed cost equals $1.33X$ when 525 aircraft are produced. Thus, average total cost increases by about 11 percent (from $3.33X$ to $3.69X$) if 525 rather than 700 aircraft are produced. (c) Because American airplane manufacturers would be shut out of part of the market, they would be likely to sell fewer airplanes, the result being that their average total cost would be higher. Thus, their profits would be reduced, or their prices would have to go up, or both. (d) If the American airplane manufacturer felt that it was shut out of so large a part of the market that its average cost would be too high to enable it to make a reasonable profit, it would not build the airplane in question.

* National Research Council, *The Competitive Status of the U.S. Civil Aviation Manufacturing Industry*, (Washington, D.C.: National Academy Press, 1985).

input resulting from the increase of $\Delta Q$ in output. Consequently, marginal cost equals

$$MC = W\frac{\Delta U}{\Delta Q} = W\frac{1}{MP}, \tag{8.2}$$

where $MP$ is the marginal product of the variable input. Because $MP$ generally increases, attains a maximum, and declines with increases in output, marginal cost normally decreases, attains a minimum, and then increases.[1]

If the total cost function is continuous, marginal cost is defined as $dTC/dQ$, where $TC$ is total cost. (Recall Chapter 2.) Suppose, for example, that a firm's total cost function is

$$TC = 20 + 3Q + 0.2Q^2,$$

where $TC$ is expressed in thousands of dollars, and $Q$ is expressed in units of output. This firm's marginal cost function will be

$$MC = \frac{dTC}{dQ} = 3 + 0.4Q.$$

Note that marginal cost always equals average cost when the latter is a minimum. If $AC$ is this firm's average cost,

$$AC = \frac{TC}{Q} = \frac{20}{Q} + 3 + 0.2Q.$$

[1] However, this is not always true, as indicated in Figure 8.6 below, where short-run marginal cost always rises as output increases.

Taking the derivative of $AC$ with respect to $Q$, and setting it equal to zero, we find the value of $Q$ where $AC$ is a minimum:

$$\frac{dAC}{dQ} = -\frac{20}{Q^2} + 0.2 = 0$$

$$Q = 10.$$

When $Q$ equals 10, both marginal cost and average cost equal 7 thousands of dollars. (Substitute 10 for $Q$ in the above equations for $MC$ and $AC$, and see for yourself that this is true.) Thus, as pointed out above, marginal cost equals average cost when the latter is a minimum.

# LONG-RUN COST FUNCTIONS

In the **long run,** all inputs are variable, and a firm can build any scale or type of plant that it wants. There are no fixed cost functions (total or average) in the long run, since no inputs are fixed. A useful way to look at the long run is to consider it a **planning horizon.** While operating in the short run, the firm must continually be planning ahead and deciding its strategy in the long run. Its decisions concerning the long run determine the sort of short-run position the firm will occupy in the future. For example, before the IBM Corporation makes the decision to add a new type of product to its line, the firm is in a long-run situation, since it can choose among a wide variety of types and sizes of equipment to produce the new product. But once the investment is made, IBM is confronted with a short-run situation, since the type and size of equipment is, to a considerable extent, frozen.

Assume it is possible for a firm to construct only three alternative scales of plant; the short-run average cost function for each scale of plant is represented by $G_1G_1'$, $G_2G_2'$, and $G_3G_3'$ in Figure 8.3. In the long run, the firm can build (or convert to) any one of these possible scales of plant. Which scale is most profitable? Obviously, the answer depends on the long-run output rate to be produced, since the firm will want to produce this output at a minimum average cost. For example, if the anticipated output rate is $Q$, the firm should pick the smallest plant, since it will produce $Q$ units of output per period of time at a cost per unit, $C$, which is smaller than what the medium-sized plant (its cost per unit being $B$) or the large plant (its cost per unit being $A$) can do. However, if the anticipated output rate is $S$, the firm should pick the largest plant.

The **long-run average cost function** shows the minimum cost per unit of producing each output level when any desired scale of plant can be built. In Figure 8.3, the long-run average cost function is the solid portion of the short-run average cost functions, $G_1DEG_3'$. The broken-line segments of the short-run functions are not included since they are not the lowest average costs, as is obvious from the figure.

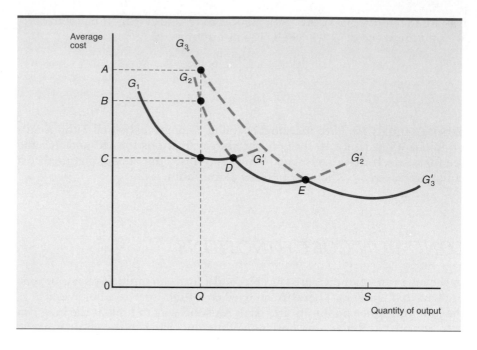

**FIGURE 8.3** *Short-Run Average Cost Functions for Various Scales of Plant* The long-run average cost function is the solid portion of the short-run average cost functions, $G_1DEG_3'$.

Now we must abandon the simplifying assumption that there are only three alternative scales of plant. In fact, there are many alternative scales, so the firm is confronted with a host of short-run average cost functions, as shown in Figure 8.4. The minimum cost per unit of producing each output level is given by the long-run average cost function, $LL'$. The long-run average cost function is tangent to each of the short-run average cost functions at the output where the plant corresponding to the short-run average cost function is optimal. (Mathematically, the long-run average cost function is the envelope of the short-run functions.)

If you have the long-run average cost of producing a given output, you can readily derive the long-run total cost of the output, since the latter is simply the product of long-run average cost and output. Figure 8.5 shows the relationship between long-run total cost and output; this relationship is called the **long-run total cost function.** Given the long-run total cost function, you can readily derive the **long-run marginal cost function,** which shows the relationship between output and the cost resulting from the production of the last unit of output, if the firm has time to make the optimal changes in the quantities of all inputs used. Of course, long-run marginal cost must be less than long-run average cost when the latter is decreasing,

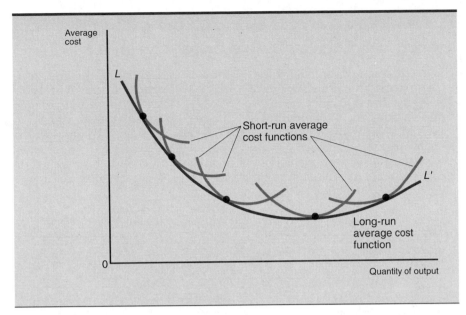

**FIGURE 8.4 *Long-Run Average Cost Function*** The long-run average cost function, which shows the minimum long-run cost per unit of producing each output level, is the envelope of the short-run functions.

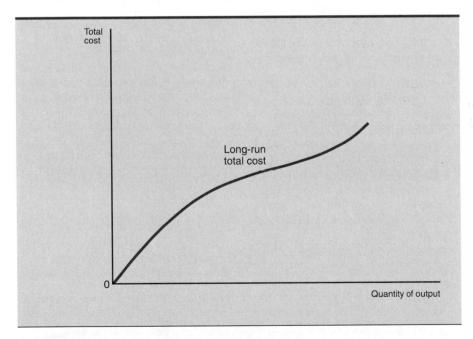

**FIGURE 8.5 *Long-Run Total Cost Function*** The long-run total cost of a given output equals the long-run average cost (given in Figure 8.4) times output.

## SHOULD WE CONTINUE TO MAKE AUTOS FROM STEEL?

In recent years, auto makers have begun to substitute synthetic materials for steel. Engineers at the Materials Systems Laboratory of the Massachusetts Institute of Technology have made careful studies of the costs of producing an automobile fender. Assuming that the annual production volume of the fender is 100,000, the average cost of a fender is as shown below if sheet steel or four alternative plastics fabrication technologies (injection moulding, compression moulding, reaction injection moulding, and thermoplastic sheet stamping) are used to make the fender:

| Cost | Sheet steel | Injection moulding | Compression moulding | Reaction injection moulding | Thermo-plastic sheet |
|------|------|------|------|------|------|
| Materials | $4.25 | $ 8.50 | $4.84 | $4.89 | $5.75 |
| Labor | .24 | .42 | .63 | .83 | 0.52 |
| Capital | .66 | 2.62 | 1.57 | 1.40 | 2.18 |
| Tooling | 2.57 | .86 | .71 | .57 | .71 |
| Total* | 7.71 | 12.39 | 7.75 | 7.70 | 9.17 |

If the annual production volume is 200,000, rather than 100,000, the cost per fender if sheet metal is used in its production is less than $7—and less than the cost if any of the plastics fabrication technologies are used at this production volume.

(a) If 100,000 fenders are made per year, does the cost per fender differ significantly if sheet steel is used from the cost if reaction injection moulding (or compression moulding) is used? (b) Compared with reaction injection moulding (or compression moulding), sheet steel uses less (or less costly) materials, labor, and capital. Why then doesn't it have lower average total costs? (c) If sheet steel is used, are there economies of scale in fender production? (d) Steel is commonly thought to be the most advantageous material for high-volume production of auto fenders. Does this seem to be true?

*Solution* (a) No. The cost is $7.71 for sheet steel versus $7.70 for reaction injection moulding (and $7.75 for compression moulding). (b) Sheet steel has much higher tooling costs per fender than does reaction injection moulding (or compression moulding). (c) Yes. Whereas the cost per fender is $7.71 when 100,000 fenders are produced per year, it is less than $7 when 200,000 are produced per year. (d) Yes. For a production volume of 200,000 per year, sheet steel, according to the figures quoted, has a lower average cost than any of the plastics fabrication techniques.[†]

* Figures do not sum to totals because of rounding errors.
† For further discussion, see G. Amendola, "The Diffusion of Synthetic Materials in the Automobile Industry," *Research Policy* (1990). Note that the production volume for Chrysler's Viper (cited on pages 163 and 203) was much smaller than considered here.

equal to long-run average cost when the latter is a minimum, and greater than long-run average cost when the latter is increasing. It can also be demonstrated that when the firm has built the optimal scale of plant for producing a given level of output, long-run marginal cost will be equal to short-run marginal cost at that output.[2]

# THE CROSBY CORPORATION: A NUMERICAL EXAMPLE

To illustrate the relationship between a firm's long-run and short-run cost functions, consider the Crosby Corporation, a hypothetical producer of flashlights. Crosby's engineers have determined that the firm's production function is

$$Q = 4\sqrt{K \cdot L}, \tag{8.3}$$

where $Q$ is output (in thousands of flashlights per month), $K$ is the amount of capital used per month (in thousands of units), and $L$ is the number of hours of labor employed per month (in thousands). Because Crosby must pay $8 per hour for labor and $2 per unit for capital, its total cost (in thousands of dollars per month) equals

$$TC = 8L + 2K$$

$$= \frac{Q^2}{2K} + 2K, \tag{8.4}$$

---

[2] Suppose that the long-run average cost of producing an output rate of $Q$ is $L(Q)$ and that the short-run average cost of producing this output with the $i$th scale of plant is $A_i(Q)$. Let $M(Q)$ be the long-run marginal cost and $R_i(Q)$ be the short-run marginal cost with the $i$th scale of plant. If the firm is maximizing profit, it is operating where short-run and long-run average costs are equal; in other words, $L(Q) = A_i(Q)$. Also, the long-run average cost function is tangent to the short-run average cost function, which means that

$$\frac{dL(Q)}{dQ} = \frac{dA_i(Q)}{dQ} \quad \text{and} \quad Q\frac{dL(Q)}{dQ} = Q\frac{dA_i(Q)}{dQ}.$$

From these conditions, it is easy to prove that the long-run marginal cost, $M(Q)$, equals the short-run marginal cost, $R_i(Q)$.

$$M(Q) = \frac{d[QL(Q)]}{dQ} = L(Q) + \frac{QdL(Q)}{dQ}.$$

$$R_i(Q) = \frac{d[QA_i(Q)]}{dQ} = A_i(Q) + \frac{QdA_i(Q)}{dQ}.$$

Since we know from the previous paragraph that $L(Q) = A_i(Q)$ and $Q\,dL(Q)/dQ = QdA_i(Q)/dQ$, it follows that $R_i(Q)$ must equal $M(Q)$.

since equation (8.3) implies that

$$L = \frac{Q^2}{16K}.$$

In the short run, which is a time period so brief that a firm cannot vary the quantity of its plant and equipment, $K$ is fixed. Because the Crosby Corporation has 10 thousand units of capital, $K = 10$. Substituting 10 for $K$ in equation (8.4), the short-run cost function is

$$TC_s = \frac{Q^2}{20} + 20, \tag{8.5}$$

where $TC_s$ is short-run total cost. Thus, the short-run average total cost function is

$$AC_s = \frac{TC_s}{Q} = \frac{Q}{20} + \frac{20}{Q},$$

and the short-run marginal cost function is

$$MC_s = \frac{dTC_s}{dQ} = \frac{Q}{10}.$$

In the long run, no input is fixed. To determine the optimal amount of capital input to be used to produce an output of $Q$ units per month, Crosby's managers should minimize total cost. Based on equation (8.4),

$$\frac{dTC}{dK} = -\frac{Q^2}{2K^2} + 2.$$

Setting this derivative equal to zero, we find that the cost-minimizing value of $K$ is

$$K = \frac{Q}{2}.$$

Substituting $Q/2$ for $K$ in equation (8.4), we see that the long-run cost function is

$$TC_L = 2Q, \tag{8.6}$$

where $TC_L$ is long-run total cost. Thus, since $TC_L/Q = 2$, long-run average cost equals \$2 per flashlight.

Figure 8.6 shows the relationship between the Crosby Corporation's short-run average and marginal costs and its long-run average costs. As is always the case (recall page 294), the short-run marginal cost function intersects the short-run average cost function at its minimum point—where $Q = 20$ and $AC_s = 2$, in this case. Because it is horizontal (owing to constant returns to scale), the long-run average cost function is tangent to the short-run average cost function at the latter's minimum point. Note that the fact that the long-run average cost function is horizontal is unusual. Instead, as illustrated in the following section, there are economies of scale (over at least some range of output) in a wide variety of industries.

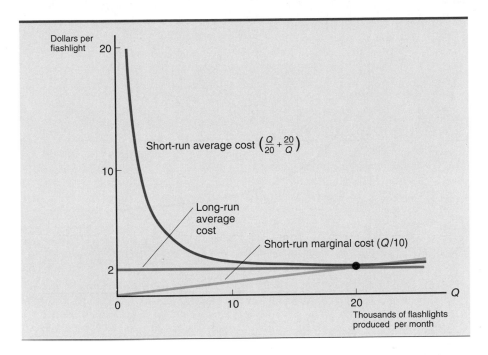

**FIGURE 8.6** *Short-Run Average and Marginal Cost and Long-Run Average Cost, Crosby Corporation* Because the long-run average cost function is horizontal, it is tangent to the short-run average cost function at the latter's minimum point.

## ECONOMIES OF SCALE IN PRODUCING METHANOL FROM COAL: A CASE STUDY

The long-run average cost curve is important for practical decision making by managers because it shows whether, and to what extent, larger plants have cost advantages over smaller ones. In cases where big plants have lower average costs than smaller ones, we often say that there are **economies of scale.** To illustrate, consider the production of methanol, an important chemical, from coal. Figure 8.7 shows the long-run average cost curve for a plant of this kind, based on data provided by Badger, Du Pont, and Exxon engineers.[3]

As you can see, there are marked economies of scale. If a plant produces only 0.5 million gallons of methanol per day, the cost per gallon is about 48 cents; if it produces 16 million gallons per day, the cost per gallon is about

[3] R. Kermode, A. Nicholson, and J. Jones, "Methanol from Coal: Cost Projections to 1990," *Modern Cost Engineering* (New York: McGraw-Hill, 1984). Figure 8.7 is based on a yield of 200 gallons per ton of coal.

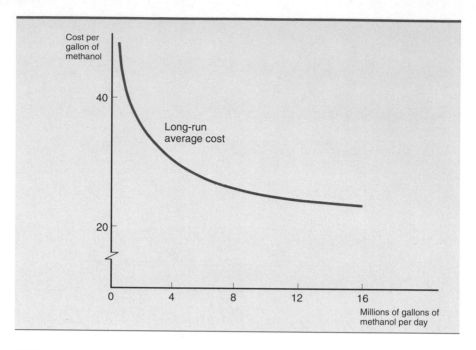

**FIGURE 8.7** *Long-Run Average Cost Function, Methanol Produced from Coal* This cost function, based on engineering data, indicates substantial economies of scale.

*Source:* R. Kermode, A. Nicholson, and J. Jones, "Methanol from Coal."

2.3 cents. Curves like Figure 8.7 are constructed by engineers for a huge variety of chemical (and other industrial) processes. Without such information, managers could not make rational decisions concerning the size of plant they should build.

## MEASUREMENT OF SHORT-RUN COST FUNCTIONS: THE CHOICE OF A MATHEMATICAL FORM

To analyze many important problems, managers must estimate cost functions—or **cost curves,** as they are often called—in particular firms and industries. One of the initial steps in estimating a cost function is to choose the mathematical form of the relationship between output and cost. As a first approximation, managers often assume that short-run total cost is a linear function of output, which means that marginal cost tends to be constant in the relevant output range. (See Figure 8.8.) In fact, as we shall see

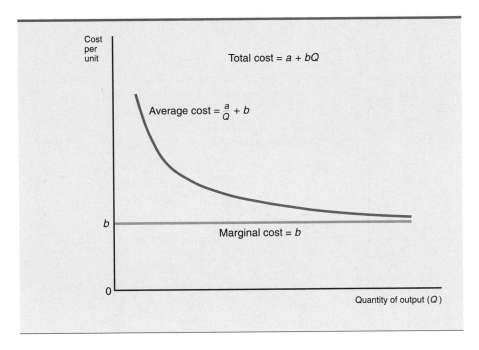

**FIGURE 8.8** *Average Cost and Marginal Cost, Linear Total Cost Function* Marginal cost is constant.

below, a linear function often fits the data for particular firms and plants quite well in the short run. To some extent, this may reflect the fact that some empirical studies are biased toward constant marginal cost by the nature of accounting data and the statistical methods used. Also, the data used in these studies often do not cover periods when the firm was operating close to the peak of its capacity, which is when marginal cost would be expected to increase substantially. Although marginal costs may well be relatively constant over a wide range, it is inconceivable that they do not eventually increase with increases in output. Thus, a linear function is likely to be appropriate for only a restricted range of output.

It is also possible to assume that total cost is a quadratic or cubic function of output. If the quadratic form is chosen, marginal cost increases with output, as shown in Figure 8.9. If the cubic form is chosen, marginal cost first decreases and then increases with output, as shown in Figure 8.10. Whether these forms are better than the linear form depends on whether they fit the data better. In many cases, they seem to do no better in this regard than the linear form. However, before deciding that the linear form is satisfactory, you should be careful to inspect the residuals from the estimated cost function to see whether there is evidence of departures from linearity. (Recall our discussion on pages 149 to 150 of the appropriate inspection procedure.)

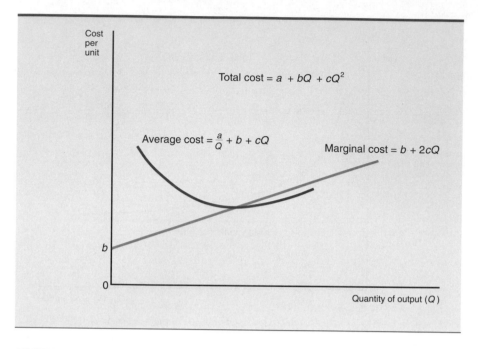

**FIGURE 8.9** *Average Cost and Marginal Cost, Quadratic Total Cost Function* Marginal cost increases as output rises.

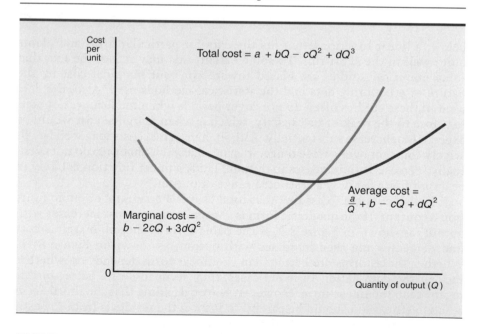

**FIGURE 8.10** *Average Cost and Marginal Cost, Cubic Total Cost Function* Marginal cost first falls and then rises as output increases.

# NATURE AND LIMITATIONS OF AVAILABLE DATA

Having chosen a mathematical form, one must decide upon the type of data to be used in estimating a cost function. One possibility is to use time-series data, and relate the total cost of a firm in each time period to its output level in that period. Regression analysis (described in Chapter 4) is frequently used to estimate this relationship. Another possibility is to use cross-section data, and relate the total costs of a variety of firms (during the same period of time) to their output levels. Figure 8.11 plots the 1993 output of eight firms in a given industry against their 1993 total costs. Here too regression analysis can be used to estimate the relationship. A third possibility is to use engineering data to construct cost functions.

Regardless of which of these types of data is used, there are a number of important difficulties in estimating cost functions. Accounting data, which are generally the only cost data available, suffer from a number of deficiencies, when used for this purpose. The time period used for accounting purposes generally is longer than the economist's short run. Accountants often use arbitrary allocations of overhead and joint costs. The depreciation of an asset over a period of time is determined largely by the tax laws rather than economic criteria. Many inputs are valued at historical, rather than opportunity, cost.

Engineering data also suffer from important limitations. Engineering

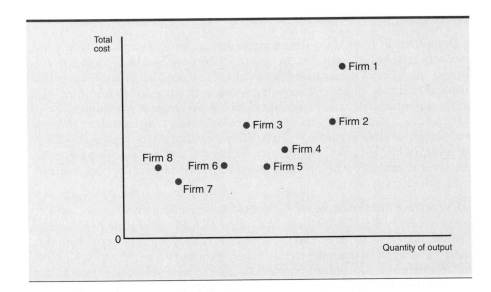

**FIGURE 8.11   *Relationship between Total Cost and Output, Cross Section*
Each firm's level of cost during 1993 is plotted against the firm's output level during that year. Such a relationship generally is only a very rough approximation to the relevant cost function.

data, like cost accounting data, relate to processes within the firm. There is an inevitable arbitrariness involved in allocating costs that are jointly attached to the production of more than one product in multiproduct firms. Also, a problem in using such data to estimate cost functions for an entire firm is that the costs of various processes may affect one another and may not be additive.

If you are considering the use of cross-section data, it is important to watch out for the so-called regression fallacy. Because the output produced and sold by a firm is only partly under its control, actual and expected output often differ. When firms are classified by actual output, firms with very high output levels may be producing at an unusually high level, and firms with very low output levels may be producing at an unusually low level. Since firms producing at an unusually high level of output may be producing at lower average costs than firms producing at an unusually low level of output, cross-section studies may be biased, the observed cost of producing various output levels being different from the minimum cost of producing these output levels.

# KEY STEPS IN THE ESTIMATION PROCESS

Having chosen a mathematical form and having decided upon the type of data to be used, the following six steps should be carried out before using the regression techniques described in Chapter 4 to estimate a short-run cost function.

*1. Definition of Cost.* As pointed out at the beginning of this chapter, the relevant concept of cost for managerial decision making ordinarily is opportunity cost, not cost based on accounting data. You must be careful to insure that the accounting data—or engineering data, for that matter—on which an estimated cost function is based are reasonably indicative of opportunity costs. If not, they should be adjusted. For example, suppose that historical data regarding a firm's depreciation costs are based on the tax laws, rather than on opportunity costs of the relevant equipment. To remedy this problem, the cost data should be revised to reflect opportunity costs, not tax conventions.

*2. Correction for Price Level Changes.* When using time-series data to estimate cost functions, it is important that changes over time in the prices of all inputs be recognized and measured. What we want is a cost function based on next year's input prices, if next year is the period to which the analysis pertains. Since our historical data are based on input prices at various times in the past, we need a price index that will allow us to adjust our historical cost data for changes in the prices of various inputs. Moreover, since various inputs may experience quite different rates of inflation, we frequently must obtain or construct a separate price index for each of a number of major types of inputs. Using these price indexes, we must convert the available historical cost data into cost data reflecting next year's input prices, not those in the past.

3. *Relating Cost to Output.* If an estimated cost function is to be reasonably accurate, it is important that our cost data distinguish properly between costs that vary with output and those that do not do so. For many types of equipment, as well as other assets, depreciation depends on both the passage of time and the extent to which they are used, the result being that it is very difficult, if not impossible, to determine solely from accounting data how much the depreciation cost varies with output alone. Also, some costs do not vary with output, so long as output does not exceed some critical level. But above this critical level, these costs may increase considerably. For example, up to some output level, a firm may be able to get along with one machine tool of a particular type, but beyond that output level, it may have to get an additional machine tool.

4. *Matching Time Periods.* Major errors sometimes occur because the cost data do not pertain to the same time periods as the output data. To see what mayhem this can cause, suppose that we were to plot a firm's 1993 cost against its 1992 output, its 1992 cost against its 1991 output, and so on. Would the resulting plot of points be a good estimate of the firm's cost function? Of course not. Instead, we should relate a firm's costs in a particular period to its level of output *in that same period.* However, this rule must be modified in cases where some of the costs of producing output in one period do not arise until subsequent periods. These delayed costs must be recognized, measured, and charged against the period when the output occurred. Thus, costs of maintenance and repairs, when they are delayed, should be treated in this way.

5. *Controlling Product, Technology, and Plant.* As stressed earlier in this chapter, when we estimate a firm's cost function, we do so based on a fixed definition of the firm's product, as well as on a fixed level of technology and (for short-run cost functions) a fixed scale of plant. This means that we must be careful to insure that the product mix of the firm does not change over time, if we are carrying out a time-series analysis. Also, the analysis cannot include observations from so long a period of time that some observations pertain to different levels of technology (or different scales of plant) from those of other observations.

6. *Length of Period and Sample Size.* Since there are important advantages in having a reasonably large number of observations extending over a period that is not so long that technology has changed greatly, many analyses are based on observations of monthly cost and output. Often there are about thirty or forty such observations. However, one problem with the use of monthly data is that one month's output may result in costs that occur in subsequent months. There is no simple rule that can be used to specify the best length of period. Like so many aspects of this subject, the answer depends in considerable part on the quality and level of detail of the firm's accounting records.

# A HOSIERY MILL'S SHORT-RUN COST FUNCTIONS

If a conscientious effort is made to carry out each of the steps described in previous sections, and if one is careful to avoid the pitfalls cited above, it generally is possible to estimate cost functions that are of considerable use in promoting better managerial decisions. To illustrate how cost functions have been estimated, let's consider a pioneering study by the late Joel Dean of Columbia University of the cost behavior of a hosiery knitting mill that was a part of a large silk hosiery manufacturing firm.[4] This mill began with the wound silk and carried the work up to the point where the stockings were ready to be sent to other plants for dyeing and finishing. Thus, this mill's operations were carried on by skilled labor and highly mechanized equipment.

Besides studying total cost, Dean obtained cost functions for productive labor cost, nonproductive labor cost, and overhead cost. As a first step, he plotted the monthly cost of each kind against monthly output. Then a simple regression equation of the form $TC = a + bQ$ was fitted to the observations for combined (that is, total) cost and its three components. The resulting regression equations are shown in Table 8.3. (Total cost is in dollars, and output is in dozens of pairs of stockings.)

---

TABLE 8.3    *Regressions of Combined Cost and Its Components on Output, Hosiery Mill*

| | (Monthly observations) | | | |
| --- | --- | --- | --- | --- |
| | Combined cost | Productive labor cost | Nonproductive labor cost | Overhead cost |
| Simple regression equation | $TC = 2935.59 + 1.998Q$ | $TC = -1695.16 + 1.780Q$ | $TC = 992.23 + 0.097Q$ | $TC = 3638.30 + 0.121Q$ |
| Standard error of estimate | 6109.83 | 5497.09 | 399.34 | 390.58 |
| Correlation coefficient ($r$) | 0.973 | 0.972 | 0.952 | 0.970 |

*Source:* J. Dean, "Statistical Cost Functions of a Hosiery Mill."

---

The regression equation for combined cost is illustrated graphically in Figure 8.12. As you can see, the linear form of the equation fits quite well. The regression line is $TC = 2,935.59 + 1.998Q$. The slope of the regression line equals 1.998, which indicates that marginal cost was $1.998. Aver-

---

[4] J. Dean, "Statistical Cost Functions of a Hosiery Mill," *Studies in Business Administration*, University of Chicago Press, 14, no. 3 (1941).

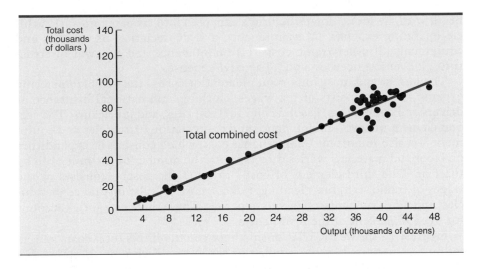

**FIGURE 8.12** *Regression of Total Cost on Output, Hosiery Mill* In the output range covered by these data, the total cost function seems to be approximately linear.

age cost (in dollars) was

$$AC = 1.998 + \frac{2,935.59}{Q}.$$

Using this equation, the firm's managers could estimate average costs for any output level in the range covered by the data. For example, if they planned to produce 20,000 dozen pairs of stockings next month, their estimate of the total cost per dozen pairs of stockings would be

$$1.998 + \frac{2,935.59}{20,000} = 2.145,$$

or about $2.15.

# A TRANSPORTATION FIRM'S SHORT-RUN COST FUNCTIONS

In the five decades since Joel Dean's pioneering study of the hosiery mill, a great many studies of this sort have been carried out, and statistical and economic techniques have advanced considerably. Nonetheless, the basic approach has not changed very much. To illustrate, consider one of the largest road passenger transport firms in the United Kingdom. Jack Johnston, a well-known econometrician, estimated this firm's cost functions.[5] To

[5] J. Johnston, *Statistical Cost Analysis* (New York: McGraw-Hill, 1960).

begin with, he broke down the firm's expenses into six categories: (1) vehicle operating expense, (2) maintenance and depreciation of vehicles and equipment, (3) other traffic costs, (4) maintenance and renewal of structures, (5) vehicle licenses, and (6) general expenses.

The largest and most important element of cost is the vehicle operating expense, which consists of the wages, clothing, and national insurance of drivers and conductors, gasoline and fuel oil, tires, and lubricants. The second element of cost—maintenance and depreciation of vehicles and equipment—is also important. Maintenance cost, which consists of expenditure on labor and materials, varies directly with the number of car-miles run by the firm. The third element of cost—other traffic costs—consists of the wages of traffic staff, bus cleaning, tickets, cost of tolls, insurance of vehicles, and other such miscellaneous expenses. These three categories account for over 90 percent of the firm's costs.

Figure 8.13 shows the relationship between the firm's total costs and its output, as measured by the number of car-miles. (Each point pertains to a four-week period.) Using more sophisticated statistical methods than were available to Dean, Johnston estimated the firm's total cost function; this

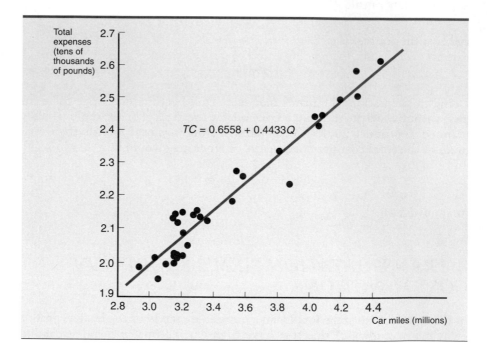

FIGURE 8.13 *Relationship between Total Costs and Car-Miles, Road Passenger Transportation Firm* As in Figure 8.12, the total cost function seems to be approximately linear.

*Source:* J. Johnston, *Statistical Cost Analysis.*

estimate is included in Figure 8.13. The equation for this cost function is

$$TC = 0.6558 + 0.4433Q,$$

where *TC* is total cost (in tens of thousands of British pounds), and *Q* is car-miles (in millions).

For values of car-miles ranging from 3.2 to 4.0 million, a 10 percent increase in the firm's output is associated with an increase of about 7 percent in its total cost. Thus, the short-run average cost function is downward sloping to the right, a 10 percent increase in output being associated, on the average, with about a 3 percent decrease in average cost per unit of output. Empirical results of this sort are of basic importance to a firm's managers. Any manager, to be effective, must have a good working knowledge of his or her firm's short-run cost structure.

# *LONG-RUN STATISTICAL COST ESTIMATION*

The same sorts of regression techniques used by Dean or Johnston to estimate short-run cost functions can also be used to estimate long-run cost functions. However, it is very difficult to find cases where the scale of a firm has changed, but technology and other relevant variables have remained constant. Thus, it is hard to use time-series data to estimate long-run cost functions. Generally, regression analyses based on cross-section data have been used instead. Specifically, a sample of firms (or plants) of various sizes is chosen, and a firm's (or plant's) total cost is regressed on its output, as well as other independent variables, such as regional differences in wage rates or other input prices.

Cross-section analysis of this sort, while useful, faces a number of difficulties, some of which have been noted above. (1) Firms may use different accounting methods, with the result that their cost data are not comparable. Thus, the true relationship between cost and output may be obscured. (2) Firms in different regions of the country may pay quite different wage rates (and other input prices may differ considerably among regions). Unless input prices are held constant (by including them as independent variables in the regression), the estimated relationship between cost and output may be biased. (3) Whereas the long-run cost function is based on the assumption that firms are minimizing cost, the actual data used in the statistical analysis may pertain to firms that are not operating efficiently. Thus, the estimated cost function may exaggerate how much it would cost an efficient firm to produce a particular output.

Despite these difficulties, a great many valuable studies of long-run cost functions have been carried out. In general, these studies have found that there are very significant economies of scale at low output levels, but that these economies of scale tend to diminish as output increases, and that the long-run average cost function eventually becomes close to horizontal at high output levels. In other words, long-run average cost functions tend to

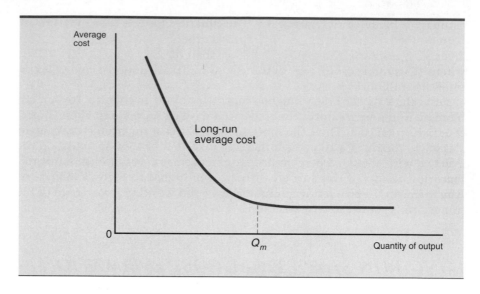

**FIGURE 8.14** *Typical Long-Run Average Cost Curve*   Its shape is L-shaped, not U-shaped (as in Figure 8.4). The minimum efficient scale is $Q_m$.

look like Figure 8.7, which pertains to methanol. In contrast to the U-shaped curve in Figure 8.4, which often is postulated in microeconomic theory, the long-run average cost curve tends to be L-shaped, as in Figure 8.14.

Given that this is the case, managers and others are particularly interested in estimating the **minimum efficient scale** of plant or firm in a particular industry. The minimum efficient scale of plant is defined as the smallest output at which long-run average cost is a minimum. If the long-run average cost curve is as shown in Figure 8.14, the minimum efficient scale of plant is $Q_m$. One reason why managers are so interested in the minimum efficient scale is that plants below this size are at a competitive disadvantage, since their costs are higher than their larger rivals. Table 8.4

**TABLE 8.4**   *Cost Disadvantage of Plants That Are 50 Percent of Minimum Efficient Scale*

| Industry | Cost disadvantage (percent) | Industry | Cost disadvantage (percent) |
|---|---|---|---|
| Flour mills | 3.0 | Synthetic rubber | 15.0 |
| Bread baking | 7.5 | Detergents | 2.5 |
| Paper printing | 9.0 | Bricks | 25.0 |
| Sulphuric acid | 1.0 | Machine tools | 5.0 |

*Source:* F. M. Scherer, *Industrial Market Structure and Economic Performance,* 2d ed. (Chicago: Rand McNally, 1980).

shows, for various industries, the cost disadvantage of plants that are 50 percent of minimum efficient scale. In synthetic rubber, such plants have average costs that are 15 percent higher than those of plants of minimum efficient scale.

The minimum efficient scale of plant or firm in a particular industry can be estimated from the long-run average cost function, which, as we have seen, can be approximated on the basis of the regression techniques described above. Another way to estimate the minimum efficient scale of plant or firm is through engineering analysis. Using their knowledge of the relevant production technology, engineers can determine the optimal input combination to produce each quantity of output. The long-run total cost function can then be estimated by multiplying the optimal quantity of each input by its price and summing to obtain the total cost. From the long-run total cost function, we can readily obtain the long-run average cost function, from which the minimum efficient scale can be determined. (The long-run average cost function for methanol in Figure 8.7 was derived in this way.)[6]

# THE LONG-RUN AVERAGE COST FUNCTION FOR ELECTRIC POWER: A CASE STUDY

To illustrate the estimation of long-run cost functions, consider the study made by Laurits Christenson and William Greene of the American electric power industry.[7] Based on cross-section data for all investor-owned utilities with more than $1 million in revenues, they used the regression techniques described in Chapter 4 to estimate the long-run average cost functions prevailing in 1955 and 1970, the results being shown in Figure 8.15. In accord with the previous section, the long-run cost curve in both years appears to have been L-shaped, not U-shaped.

The minimum efficient scale of firm seems to have been at an output of about 12 billion kilowatt-hours in 1970. Figure 8.15 shows that there was a substantial reduction in average costs between 1955 and 1970, as indicated by the fact that the 1970 average cost curve is well below the 1955 curve. In considerable part, this cost reduction was due to technological change of the sort we studied in Chapter 7.

---

[6] For a case study, see L. Cookenboo, "Production Functions and Cost Functions in Oil Pipelines," in the study guide accompanying this textbook.

[7] L. Christenson and W. Greene, "Economies of Scale in U.S. Electric Power Generation," *Journal of Political Economy* (1976). The mathematical form used in this study is the translog cost function, which is a more general (and more complex) relationship than those discussed above.

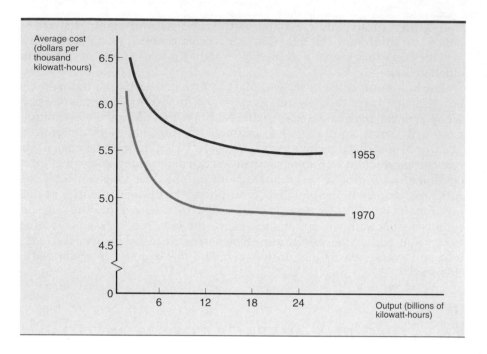

**FIGURE 8.15    Long-Run Average Cost Function, Electric Power**
Between 1955 and 1970, the average cost function fell considerably. The minimum efficient scale of firm seemed to have been at an output of about 12 billion kilowatt-hours in 1970.

## THE SURVIVOR TECHNIQUE

Still another way to estimate the minimum efficient scale is to use the **survivor technique** pioneered by the late Nobel laureate George Stigler. To use this technique, we classify the firms in an industry by size and compute the percentage of the industry output coming from each size class at various times. If the share of one size class diminishes over time, it is assumed to be relatively inefficient; whereas if its share increases, it is assumed to be relatively efficient. Thus, if firms or plants below a particular size tend to account for a smaller share of industry output, this may indicate that they are below the minimum efficient scale. However, because of the effects of regulation, barriers to entry, collusion, and a variety of other factors, average cost may not be as closely linked to survival as assumed by the survivor technique. Thus, this technique should be viewed with appropriate caution.

In Figure 8.16, we show Stigler's estimate of the long-run average cost function for ingot steel production. Apparently, firms with less than about $2\frac{1}{2}$ percent and greater than about 25 percent of the market had relatively

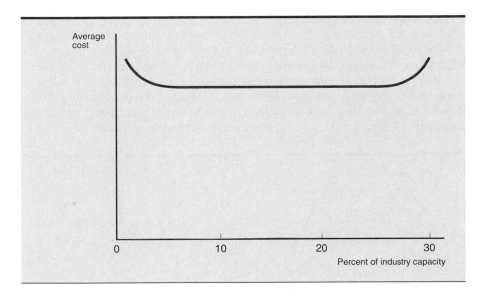

**FIGURE 8.16   Long-Run Average Cost Function, Steel Ingot Production**
Firms with less than about $2\frac{1}{2}$ and more than 25 percent of the market seem
to have had relatively high average costs.

high average costs. Firms in these size categories declined (as a percentage
of industry output) during the period he studied. As you can see, one of the
major limitations of the survivor technique is that it tells us nothing about
the *extent* of the cost differentials among firms of different sizes. This is
reflected in the fact that there is no scale on the vertical axis in Figure 8.16.

To illustrate the use of the survivor technique, consider the question of
whether or not efficiencies might arise from common ownership of multiple radio stations within a market. In 1988, economists at the Federal Trade
Commission carried out an analysis based on the survivor technique to see
whether AM-FM radio combinations have increased in number relative to
independently owned and operated stations. According to their results, this
has been the case. They interpret these findings as suggesting that common
ownership may result in significant economies.[8]

## THE IMPORTANCE OF FLEXIBILITY

Based on the measurement techniques described in previous sections, one
can derive for various types of plants the relationship between output and

[8] K. Anderson and J. Woodbury, "Do Government-Imposed Ownership Restrictions Inhibit Efficiency?" Bureau of Economics, Federal Trade Commission, December 1988.

average total cost. Suppose that the Marion Manufacturing Company is faced with the task of deciding which of two types of plant (type 1 or type 2) to build. The nature and quality of the output of one type of plant do not differ from the nature and quality of the output of the other type of plant. The average total cost function for each type of plant is shown in panel A of Figure 8.17. Suppose the executives of the Marion Manufacturing Company believe that they will want to produce about 10,000 units of output per month. Which of the two types of plant should they build?

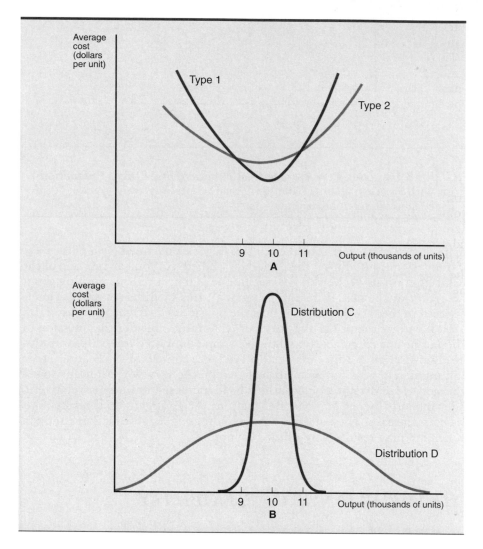

FIGURE 8.17 *Average Cost Function, Type 1 and Type 2 Plants, and Two Probability Distributions of Output (C and D)* If the probability distribution of output is *D*, a type 2 plant is likely to be preferable to a type 1 plant.

The answer depends on how certain they are of the output of the plant. Suppose that the probability distribution of the plant's output is distribution $C$ (in panel B of Figure 8.17). In this case, a type 1 plant probably is preferable because it is very likely that the plant will be called on to produce 9,000 to 11,000 units per month, and in that range the type 1 plant produces at lower average cost than does the type 2 plant. However, if the probability distribution of output is distribution $D$ (in panel B of Figure 8.17), the type 2 plant is likely to be preferable, because it is very likely that the plant will be called on to produce fewer than 9,000 or more than 11,000 units, and in those ranges the type 2 plant produces at lower average cost than does the type 1 plant.

This case illustrates the importance of flexibility. While the type 1 plant is more economical if output is close to 10,000 units, the type 2 plant is more flexible. If output is likely to depart greatly from 10,000 units, the type 2 plant is the better choice.

## ECONOMIES OF SCOPE

Firms commonly produce more than one product. Oil firms like Exxon and Mobil produce both petroleum and chemical products; drug firms like Merck and Smith-Kline Beecham produce both vaccines and tranquilizers; and publishers like Random House and Simon and Schuster produce both mysteries and biographies. In many cases, a firm obtains production or cost advantages when it produces a combination of products rather than just one. These advantages sometimes arise because certain production facilities used to make one product can also be used to make another product, or because by-products resulting from the making of one product are useful in making other products.

**Economies of scope** exist when the cost of producing two (or more) products jointly is less than the cost of producing each one alone. For example, suppose that the Martin Company produces 1,000 milling machines and 500 lathes per year at a cost of $15 million, whereas if a firm produced 1,000 milling machines only, the cost would be $12 million, and if it produced 500 lathes only, the cost would be $6 million. In this case, the cost of producing both the milling machines and the lathes is less than the total cost of producing each separately. Thus, there are economies of scope.

To gauge the extent of economies of scope, the following measure is sometimes calculated:

$$S = \frac{C(Q_1) + C(Q_2) - C(Q_1 + Q_2)}{C(Q_1 + Q_2)},\tag{8.7}$$

where $S$ is the degree of economies of scope, $C(Q_1)$ is the cost of producing $Q_1$ units of the first product alone, $C(Q_2)$ is the cost of producing $Q_2$ units of the second product alone, and $C(Q_1 + Q_2)$ is the cost of producing $Q_1$ units of the first product in combination with $Q_2$ units of the second product. If there are economies of scope, $S$ is greater than zero because the cost

## ECONOMIES OF SCOPE IN ADVERTISING AGENCIES

In recent years, there has been considerable controversy over the extent to which there are economies of scope in the advertising industry. An advertising agency can provide many products. According to Alvin Silk and Ernst Berndt of MIT, these products (that is, types of advertising) can be categorized into the following nine categories: (1) network television, (2) spot television, (3) general magazines, (4) special print media (such as business publications), (5) newspapers, (6) direct response advertising, (7) radio, (8) outdoor and media services, and (9) nonmedia services. To what extent are an advertising agency's costs reduced by producing a mix of these products rather than producing them separately?

On the basis of a recent statistical analysis, Silk and Berndt estimated that the percentage cost reduction from joint production for 401 advertising agencies was as follows:

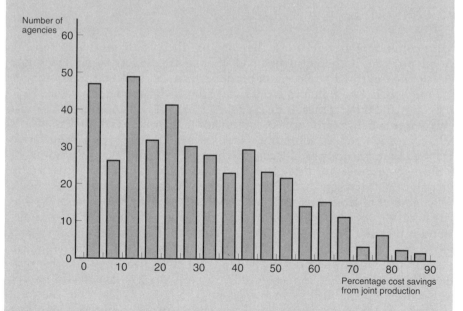

As you can see, the cost saving from joint production of these products ranged from essentially 0 to about 86 percent, depending on which advertising agency is considered. On the average, this cost saving was about 26 percent.

Clearly, there are very substantial economies of scope in advertising. However, it is important to recognize that these economies of scope are much more important for small advertising agencies than for large ones. For the handful of very large agencies with gross annual incomes of $100 million or more, economies of scope seem to be virtually nonexistent, according to the estimates provided by Silk and Berndt. But for small agencies with gross annual incomes of a few million dollars, economies of scope are very significant. Top advertising executives like Charlotte Beers, head of Ogilvy and Mather, must be concerned with findings of this sort.*

*Charlotte Beers, Chairman and CEO of Ogilvy and Mather Worldwide*

* For further discussion, see A. Silk and E. Berndt, "Scale and Scope Effects on Advertising Agency Costs," Working Paper No. 3463, National Bureau of Economic Research, October 1990.

of producing both products together—$C(Q_1 + Q_2)$—is less than the cost of producing each alone—$C(Q_1) + C(Q_2)$. Clearly, $S$ measures the percentage saving as a result of producing them jointly rather than individually. Thus, in the case of the Martin Company,

$$S = \frac{\$12 \text{ million} + \$6 \text{ million} - \$15 \text{ million}}{\$15 \text{ million}} = 0.20,$$

which means that there is a 20 percent saving of this sort. The larger the value of $S$, the bigger the economies of scope.

To managers, it is very important that economies of scope be recognized and exploited. For example, a small airline may find that its regularly scheduled passenger service can be profitably supplemented by providing cargo services, since the cost of flying both passengers and cargo is much less than that of specializing in either passenger or cargo services. Similarly, in the trucking industry, there are substantial economies, particularly for small firms, in combining short hauls, intermediate hauls, and long hauls. A firm's managers must constantly be alert to the potential profitability of extending its product line, or of adding new product lines. Thus, in 1977, when the Xerox Corporation introduced its 9700 electronic printer, it had to consider whether and to what extent this new product line complemented its existing copier business, and whether there were economies of scope.

## BREAK-EVEN ANALYSIS

An analytical tool frequently employed by managerial economists is the **break-even chart,** an important application of cost functions. Generally, a break-even chart assumes that the firm's average variable costs are constant in the relevant output range; hence, the firm's total cost function is assumed to be a straight line. Since average variable cost is constant, the extra cost of an extra unit—marginal cost—must be constant too, and equal to average variable cost. In Figure 8.18, we assume that the Carson Company's fixed costs are $600,000 per month and that its variable costs are $2 per unit of output per month.

To construct a break-even chart, you plot the firm's total revenue curve on the same chart with its total cost function. Typically, it is assumed that the price the firm receives for its product will not be affected by the amount it sells, with the result that total revenue is proportional to output. Consequently, the total revenue curve is a straight line through the origin. Figure 8.18 shows the Carson Company's total revenue curve, assuming that the

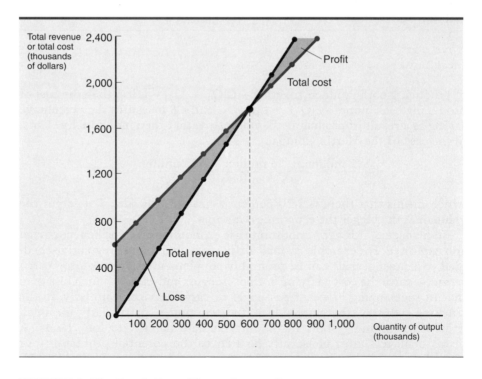

*FIGURE 8.18   Break-Even Chart, Carson Company*   The break-even point, the output level that must be reached if the firm is to avoid losses, is 600,000 units of output per month.

price of the product will be $3 per unit. The break-even chart, which combines the total cost function and the total revenue curve, shows the monthly profit or loss resulting from each sales level. For example, Figure 8.18 shows that if the Carson Company sells 300,000 units per month, it will make a loss of $300,000 per month. The chart also shows the **break-even point,** the output level that must be reached if the firm is to avoid losses; in Figure 8.18, the break-even point is 600,000 units of output per month.

Under the right conditions, break-even charts can produce useful projections of the effect of the output rate on costs, receipts, and profits. For example, a firm may use a break-even chart to determine the effect of a projected decline in sales on profits. Or it may use it to determine how many units of a particular product it must sell in order to break even. However, break-even charts must be used with caution, since the assumptions underlying them may be inappropriate. If the product price is highly variable or costs are difficult to predict, the estimated total cost function and the estimated total revenue curve may be subject to substantial errors.

Break-even charts are used extensively. It is worth noting that, while the total cost function generally is assumed to be a straight line in break-even charts, this assumption can easily be dropped, and a curvilinear total cost function can be used instead. But for fairly small changes in output, a linear approximation is probably good enough in many cases. Also, as pointed out above, empirical studies suggest that the total cost function is often close to linear, as long as the firm is not operating at or close to capacity.

## ALGEBRAIC BREAK-EVEN ANALYSIS

In the previous section, we showed how a break-even analysis can be carried out geometrically; now let's see how such an analysis can be carried out algebraically. Let $P$ be the price of the good, $Q$ be the quantity produced and sold, $AVC$ be the average variable cost, and $TFC$ be the firm's total fixed cost. The break-even point is the output, $Q_B$, at which total revenue equals total cost. Thus, since total revenue equals $P \cdot Q$ and total cost equals $TFC + AVC \cdot Q$, it follows that

$$P \cdot Q_B = TFC + AVC \cdot Q_B,$$

$$(P - AVC)Q_B = TFC$$

$$Q_B = \frac{TFC}{P - AVC}. \tag{8.8}$$

In the case of the Carson Company, $P = \$3$, $AVC = \$2$, and $TFC = \$600,000$. Consequently,

$$Q_B = \frac{600,000}{3 - 2} = 600,000,$$

which agrees with our finding based on Figure 8.18. Of course, this algebraic procedure will always produce the same results as the geometric procedure in the previous section.

# PROFIT CONTRIBUTION ANALYSIS

In making short-run decisions, firms often find it useful to carry out various types of profit contribution analysis. The profit contribution is the difference between total revenue and total variable cost; on a per-unit basis, it is equal to price minus average variable cost. Thus, in the case of the Carson Company, where price is $3 and average variable cost is $2, the per-unit profit contribution is $3 − $2, or $1. This profit contribution can be used to help pay the firm's fixed costs, and, once these costs are met, to build up the firm's profits.

## CONSULTANT'S CORNER

### AN INTRAFIRM DISPUTE OVER A BREAK-EVEN CHART*

An accountant at a small company that manufactures and sells three types of office chairs constructed a break-even chart for the company as a whole. He used as a measure of output the total number of chairs produced during each year. To obtain an estimate of the average variable cost of a chair, he took the mean of the average variable costs of the three types of chairs. To obtain an estimate of the price of a chair, he took the mean of the prices of the three types of chairs. Using these figures, he constructed a break-even chart (based on linear total cost and total revenue curves) that indicated that the company was operating at an output well above the break-even point and that profit would increase rapidly as output increased.

When the accountant presented these findings, the company's president said that they were misleading because the analysis lumped together the three types of chairs. For one type, the plant was operating at capacity, and marginal cost would increase substantially if output were increased. For another type of chair, it had become increasingly obvious that the price was too high, and was about to be reduced. For the third type of chair, only a few were produced, so it was incorrect to weight it as heavily as the other two types in the analysis. The firm's president also pointed out that as the firm's output increased, the first and second types accounted for bigger and bigger shares of total output.

If you were a consultant to this company, which of the points raised by the president would you regard as relevant, and why?

* This section is based on an actual case, although the numbers and situation have been disguised somewhat.

To illustrate how profit contribution analysis can be used, suppose that the Carson Company wants to determine how many units of output it will have to produce and sell to earn a profit of $1 million per month. The required sales equals

$$Q = \frac{\text{total fixed cost} + \text{profit target}}{\text{profit contribution (per unit)}}$$

$$= \frac{\$600,000 + \$1,000,000}{\$1}$$

$$= 1,600,000 \text{ units.}$$

As another example, suppose that the Carson Company is selling only 500,000 units per month, which means that it is losing $100,000 per month. The firm's marketing director hopes to land an order for 50,000 units of the firm's product. How much will this order reduce the firm's loss? To find out, one can multiply the order size (50,000 units) by the per-unit profit contribution ($1) to get the increase in profit (or reduction in loss, which is what is the case here); the result is $50,000.

## SUMMARY

1. Managerial economists define the cost of producing a particular product as the value of the other products that the resources used in its production could have produced instead. This is the product's opportunity cost, and it may differ from historical cost, which is generally the basis for accounting statements.
2. In the short run, it is important to distinguish between a firm's fixed and variable costs. The firm's total and average costs, total and average fixed costs, and total and average variable costs can all be plotted against output. So can the firm's marginal cost. The resulting cost functions, or cost curves (as they are often called), show how changes in output will affect the firm's costs, a major concern of any firm.
3. The long-run average cost function shows the minimum cost per unit of producing each output level when any desired scale of plant can be built. The long-run average cost function is tangent to each of the short-run average cost functions at the output where the plant corresponding to the short-run average cost function is optimal. The long-run average cost curve is important to managers because it shows the extent to which larger plants have cost advantages over smaller ones.
4. Many studies based on the statistical analysis of cross-section and time-series data, as well as engineering studies, have been carried out to estimate the cost functions of particular firms. The regression techniques described in Chapter 4 have played an important role here. Both short-run and long-run cost functions can be estimated, as illustrated by the

many examples we have considered. A detailed account of the relevant procedures and problems has been given.

5. In choosing among plants, a major consideration is flexibility if the output of the plant is highly uncertain. Some plants, while they have higher costs than others at the most likely output, have lower costs than the others over a wide range of output. If one cannot predict output reasonably well, flexible plants of this sort may be best.

6. Economies of scope occur when the cost of producing two (or more) products jointly is less than the cost of producing them separately. Such economies may arise because production facilities used to make one product can also be used to make another product, or because by-products resulting from the making of one product can be useful in making other products.

7. Break-even analysis compares total revenue and total cost, graphically or algebraically. A break-even chart combines the total cost function and the total revenue curve, both of which are generally assumed to be linear, and shows the profit or loss resulting from each sales level. The break-even point is the sales level that must be achieved if the firm is to avoid losses. Firms often find it useful to carry out various types of profit contribution analysis. The profit contribution is the difference between total revenue and total variable cost; on a per-unit basis, it is equal to price minus average variable cost.

## PROBLEMS

1. In 1985, the National Academy of Engineering, using data developed at the Massachusetts Institute of Technology, estimated the costs of producing steel with three different technologies: (1) coke, blast furnace, basic oxygen furnace, ingots, and finishing mills, (2) coke, blast furnace, basic oxygen furnace, continuous casting, and finishing mills, and (3) steel scrap, electric arc furnace, continuous casting, and finishing mills. Under reasonable assumptions concerning input prices, the estimated average costs per ton were as follows:

| Cost category | Coke, blast furnaces, basic oxygen furnace, ingots, finishing mills | Coke, blast furnaces, basic oxygen furnace, continuous casting, finishing mills | Steel scrap, electric arc furnace, continuous casting, finishing mills |
|---|---|---|---|
| Process materials | $148.34 | $136.19 | $122.78 |
| Energy | 21.15 | 15.98 | 41.58 |
| Direct labor | 83.43 | 75.09 | 67.43 |
| Capital | 102.06 | 99.93 | 54.08 |
| Other | 46.74 | 41.67 | 24.47 |
| Total | 401.73 | 368.86 | 310.34 |

(a) The academy's report concludes that "unless significant changes occur in other technologies, the electric-furnace continuous-casting route will dominate domestic production by 1995." Why?

(b) At the same time, the report notes that the price of scrap (which is used in this route) "could increase as electric furnace production expands because of the increased demand." Why is this relevant?

(c) The academy also concludes that, regardless of which of these technologies is used, cost per ton is about 25–30 percent higher if wages are $26 per hour rather than $2 per hour. What does this imply concerning the competitiveness of American steel producers relative to producers in Korea and elsewhere that pay wages far below American levels?

(d) If the above cost figures are long-run average costs, under what circumstances would they also equal long-run marginal costs?

2. The Haverford Company is considering three types of plants to make a particular electronic device. Plant A is much more highly automated than plant B, which in turn is more highly automated than plant C. For each type of plant, average variable cost is constant so long as output is less than capacity, which is the maximum output of the plant. The cost structure for each type of plant is as follows:

|  | Plant A | Plant B | Plant C |
| --- | --- | --- | --- |
| Average variable costs |  |  |  |
| Labor | $1.10 | $2.40 | $3.70 |
| Materials | .90 | 1.20 | 1.80 |
| Other | .50 | 2.40 | 2.00 |
| Total | $2.50 | $6.00 | $7.50 |
| Total fixed costs | $300,000 | $ 75,000 | $ 25,000 |
| Annual capacity | 200,000 | 100,000 | 50,000 |

(a) Derive the average cost of producing 100,000, 200,000, 300,000, and 400,000 devices per year with plant A. (For outputs exceeding the capacity of a single plant, assume that more than one plant of this type is built.)

(b) Derive the average cost of producing 100,000, 200,000, 300,000, and 400,000 devices per year with plant B.

(c) Derive the average cost of producing 100,000, 200,000, 300,000, and 400,000 devices per year with plant C.

(d) Using the results of parts (a)–(c), plot the points on the long-run average cost curve for the production of these electronic devices for outputs of 100,000, 200,000, and 400,000 devices per year.

3. The Abner Corporation, a retail seller of television sets, wants to determine how many television sets it must sell in order to earn a profit of $10,000 per month. The price of each television set is $300, and the average variable cost is $100.

(a) What is the required sales volume if the Abner Corporation's monthly fixed costs are $5,000 per month?

(b) If the firm were to sell each television set at a price of $350 rather than $300, what would be the required sales volume?

(c) If the price is $350, and if average variable cost is $85 rather than $100, what would be the required sales volume?

4. According to a statistical study, the following relationship exists between an electric light and power plant's fuel costs (C) and its 8-hour output as a percent of capacity (Q):

$$TC = 16.68 + 0.125Q + 0.00439Q^2.$$

(a) When Q increases from 50 to 51, what is the increase in the cost of fuel for this electric plant?

(b) Of what use might the result in part (a) be to the plant's managers?

(c) Derive the marginal (fuel) cost curve for this plant, and indicate how it might be used by the plant's managers.

5. The following table pertains to the Lincoln Company. Fill in the blanks below:

| Output | Total cost | Total fixed cost | Total variable cost | Average fixed cost | Average variable cost |
|---|---|---|---|---|---|
| 0 | 50 | ——— | ——— | ——— | ——— |
| 1 | 75 | ——— | ——— | ——— | ——— |
| 2 | 100 | ——— | ——— | ——— | ——— |
| 3 | 120 | ——— | ——— | ——— | ——— |
| 4 | 135 | ——— | ——— | ——— | ——— |
| 5 | 150 | ——— | ——— | ——— | ——— |
| 6 | 190 | ——— | ——— | ——— | ——— |
| 7 | 260 | ——— | ——— | ——— | ——— |

6. The Deering Manufacturing Company's short-run average cost function in 1993 is

$$AC = 3 + 4Q,$$

where AC is the firm's average cost (in dollars per pound of the product), and Q is its output rate.

(a) Obtain an equation for the firm's short-run total cost function.

(b) Does the firm have any fixed costs? Explain.

(c) If the price of the Deering Manufacturing Company's product (per pound) is $3, is the firm making profits or losses? Explain.

(d) Derive an equation for the firm's marginal cost function.

7. The president of the Tacke Corporation believes that statistical research by his staff shows that the firm's long-run total cost curve can be represented as follows:

$$TC = \alpha_0 Q^{\alpha_1} P_L^{\alpha_2} P_K^{\alpha_3},$$

where TC is the firm's total cost, Q is its output, $P_L$ is the price of labor, and $P_K$ is the price of capital.

(a) Tacke's president says that $\alpha_1$ measures the elasticity of cost with respect to output—that is, the percentage change in total cost resulting from a 1 percent change in output. Is he correct? Why or why not?

(b) He also says that if $\alpha_1 < 1$, economies of scale are indicated, whereas if $\alpha_1 > 1$, diseconomies of scale are indicated. Is he correct? Why or why not?

(c) According to Tacke's president, the $\alpha$'s can be estimated by regressing $\log (TC/P_K)$ on $\log Q$ and $\log (P_L/P_K)$. Is he correct? Why or why not?

8. Engineers sometimes rely on the "0.6 rule," which states that the increase in cost is given by the increase in capacity raised to the 0.6 power; that is,

$$C_2 = C_1 (X_2/X_1)^{0.6},$$

where $C_1$ and $C_2$ are the costs of two pieces of equipment, and $X_1$ and $X_2$ are their respective capacities.

(a) Does the 0.6 rule suggest economies of scale?

(b) Some experts have stated that in the chemical and metal industries, the 0.6 rule can be applied to entire plants rather than individual pieces of equipment. If so, will the long-run average cost curve in these industries tend to be negatively sloped?

(c) Can you think of a way to test whether this rule is correct?

9. The Dijon Company's total variable cost function is as follows:

$$TVC = 50Q - 10Q^2 + Q^3,$$

where $Q$ is the number of units of output produced.

(a) What is the output level where marginal cost is a minimum?

(b) What is the output level where average variable cost is a minimum?

(c) What is the value of average variable cost and marginal cost at the output specified in the answer to part (b)?

10. The Berwyn Company is considering the addition of a new product to its product line. The firm has plenty of excess manufacturing capacity to produce the new product, and its total fixed costs would be unaffected if the new product were added to its line. Nonetheless, the firm's accountants decide that a reasonable share of the firm's present fixed costs should be allocated to the new product. Specifically, they decide that a $300,000 fixed charge will be absorbed by the new product. The variable cost per unit of making and selling the new product is $14, which is composed of the following:

| Direct labor | 8.20 |
| Direct materials | 1.90 |
| Other | 3.90 |
| Total | 14.00 |

(a) Should the Berwyn Company add the new product to its line if it can sell about 10,000 units of this product at a price of $25?

(b) Should it add the new product if it can sell about 10,000 units at a price of $20?

(c) Should it add the new product if it can sell about 10,000 units at a price of $15?

(d) What is the minimum price (that the firm can get for the new product) that will make it worthwhile to add the new product to its line?

11. The Jolson Corporation produces 1,000 wood cabinets and 500 wood desks per year, the total cost being $30,000. If the firm produced 1,000 wood cabinets only, the cost would be $23,000. If the firm produced 500 wood desks only, the cost would be $11,000.

(a) Calculate the degree of economies of scope.

(b) Why do economies of scope exist?

12. The Smith Company made and sold 10,000 metal tables last year. When output was between 5,000 and 10,000 tables, its average variable cost was $24. In this output range, each table contributed 60 percent of its revenue to fixed costs and profits.

(a) What was the price per table?

(b) If the Smith Company increases its price by 10 percent, how many tables will it have to sell next year to obtain the same profit as last year?

(c) If the Smith Company increases its price by 10 percent, and if its average variable cost increases by 8 percent as a result of wage increases, how many tables will it have to sell next year to obtain the same profit as last year?

# APPENDIX: BREAK-EVEN ANALYSIS AND OPERATING LEVERAGE

Managers must continually make comparisons among alternative systems of production. Should one type of plant be replaced by another? How does your plant stack up against your competitor's? Break-even analysis can be extended to help make such comparisons more effective. In this appendix, we show how you can analyze how total costs and profits vary with output, depending on how automated or mechanized the plant may be. This is an important topic, since top-level managers often have to make such comparisons.

At the outset, it is essential to recognize that some plants, because they are much more mechanized than others, have relatively high fixed costs, but relatively low average variable costs. Consider firms I, II, and III in Figure 8.19. Firm I's plant has fixed costs of $100,000 per month, which are much higher than those of the plants operated by firms II or III; however, its average variable cost of $2 is much lower than that of firms II or III. Essentially, firm I has substituted capital for labor and materials. It has built a highly automated plant with high fixed costs, but low average variable cost.

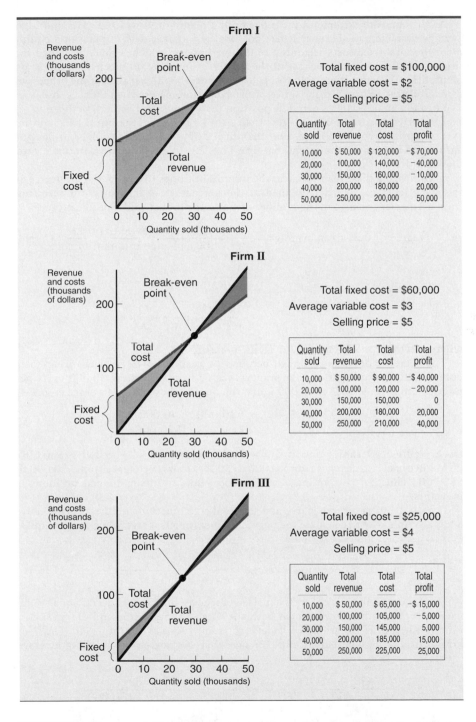

**FIGURE 8.19 Break-Even Analysis and Operating Leverage** Firm I has relatively high fixed costs and low variable costs, firm III has relatively low fixed costs and high variable costs, and firm II is in the middle.

At the opposite extreme, firm III has built a plant with low fixed costs, but high average variable cost. Because it has not invested a great deal in plant and equipment, its total fixed costs are only $25,000 per month, which is much less than for firms I and II. However, because of the relatively low level of mechanization at its plant, firm III's average variable cost is $4, considerably higher than at the other two firms. Relative to firm I, firm III uses more labor and materials and less capital.

Firm II's plant occupies a middle position (between firms I and III) in this regard. Its total fixed cost of $60,000 is less than firm I's but more than firm III's, and its average variable cost of $3 is greater than firm I's but less than firm III's. It has not automated its plant to the extent that firm I has, but it has done more in this regard than firm III.

In comparing these plants, one of the important things to consider is the **degree of operating leverage**, which is defined as the percentage change in profit resulting from a 1 percent change in the number of units of product sold. Specifically,

$$\text{Degree of operating leverage} = \frac{\text{percentage change in profit}}{\text{percentage change in quantity sold}}$$

$$= \frac{\Delta\pi/\pi}{\Delta Q/Q}$$

$$= \frac{\Delta\pi}{\Delta Q} \cdot \frac{Q}{\pi} \text{ or } \frac{d\pi}{dQ} \cdot \frac{Q}{\pi}, \quad (8.9)$$

where $\pi$ is the firm's profits, and $Q$ is the quantity sold.

The degree of operating leverage, because it measures how a given change in sales volume affects profits, is of great importance. If firm I is selling 40,000 units per month, and if we let $\Delta Q = 10,000$ units, the degree of operating leverage equals

$$\frac{\Delta\pi}{\Delta Q} \cdot \frac{Q}{\pi} = \frac{\$50,000 - \$20,000}{10,000} \cdot \frac{40,000}{\$20,000} = 6,$$

since Figure 8.19 shows that if $\Delta Q = 10,000$ units, $\Delta\pi = \$50,000 - \$20,000$. (Why? Because if $Q$ changes from 40,000 to 50,000 units, $\pi$ changes from $20,000 to $50,000.) Thus, a 1 percent increase in quantity sold results in a 6 percent increase in profits.

If both the total revenue curve and the total cost function are linear, as in Figure 8.19, a simple way to calculate the degree of operating leverage when output equals $Q$ is to use the following formula:

$$\text{Degree of operating leverage} = \frac{Q(P - AVC)}{Q(P - AVC) - TFC} \quad (8.10)$$

where $P$ equals selling price, $AVC$ equals average variable cost, and $TFC$ equals total fixed cost. It can be shown that if both the total revenue curve and the total cost function are linear, equation (8.10) yields the same result as equation (8.9). Thus, for firm I, if $Q = 40,000$, equation (8.10) says that the degree of operating leverage equals

$$\frac{Q(P - AVC)}{Q(P - AVC) - TFC} = \frac{40,000(\$5 - \$2)}{40,000(\$5 - \$2) - \$100,000}$$

$$= \frac{\$120,000}{\$120,000 - \$100,000} = 6,$$

since $P$ equals $5, $AVC$ equals $2, and $TFC$ equals $100,000. The result is the same as in the previous paragraph. (In both cases, it is 6.)

It is interesting and important to compare the degree of operating leverage of the three firms, since this comparison reveals a great deal about how these plants differ. If $Q = 40,000$, the degree of operating leverage for firm II equals

$$\frac{Q(P - AVC)}{Q(P - AVC) - TFC} = \frac{40,000(\$5 - \$3)}{40,000(\$5 - \$3) - \$60,000} = 4.$$

For firm III, it equals

$$\frac{Q(P - AVC)}{Q(P - AVC) - TFC} = \frac{40,000(\$5 - \$4).}{40,000(\$5 - \$4) - \$25,000} = 2.67.$$

Thus, a 1 percent increase in sales volume results in a 6 percent increase in profit at firm I, a 4 percent increase in profit at firm II, and a 2.67 percent increase in profit at firm III. Clearly, firm I's profits are much more sensitive to changes in sales volume than firm III's profits; firm II is in the middle in this regard.

# Chapter 9
# Linear Programming*

One of the most important and widely used techniques in managerial economics is linear programming, which can be used to help solve a wide variety of managerial problems related to production, marketing, and finance. In Chapter 1, we pointed out that H. J. Heinz has used linear programming to determine how much of its product should be shipped from each of its factories to each of its warehouses. This is only one of thousands of industrial applications of linear programming, ranging from increasing the efficiency of oil refineries to helping banks choose the composition of their assets. In this chapter, we describe what linear programming is and how it can be used.

## WHAT IS LINEAR PROGRAMMING?

**Linear programming** is a technique that allows decision makers to solve maximization and minimization problems where there are certain constraints that limit what can be done. Used initially in the aftermath of World War II to help schedule the procurement activities of the United States Air Force, linear programming has become a very powerful tool for the solution of managerial problems. Its remarkable growth has been facili-

* This chapter is coauthored by Edward D. Mansfield.

tated by the development of computers that can handle the many computations required to solve large linear programming problems.

While linear programming is an important tool of managerial economics, it is purely a mathematical technique which can only tell us the implications of the data that the decision maker or the analyst has gathered (or assumed). If these data (or assumptions) are wrong, the solution will in general be wrong too.

Linear programming is used in cases where there is some objective function to be maximized or minimized. This objective function is a linear function of the variables to be determined. The values of these variables must satisfy certain constraints, which are in the form of inequalities. (Note that this differs from the Lagrangian technique, where the constraints are in the form of equalities.) The best way to learn what we mean by an objective function or a constraint is to take up a variety of cases. Let's begin with the American Textile Company.

# PRODUCTION PLANNING: ONE OUTPUT

Suppose that one of the operations of the American Textile Company is the finishing of cotton cloth. The output rate of the finishing department is limited by the capacity of its finishing equipment and the amount of labor available to carry out the work. The firm's managers are considering which of three finishing processes to use: processes 1, 2, and 3. They know that the profit per batch of cotton cloth finished with process 1 is $1.00; similarly, it is $0.90 for process 2, and $1.10 for process 3. They also know that process 1 uses 3 machine-hours of finishing capacity per batch of cotton cloth processed, that process 2 uses 2.50 machine-hours, and that process 3 uses 5.25 machine-hours. Also, process 1 uses 0.4 hours of labor per batch of cotton cloth processed, process 2 uses 0.50 hours, and process 3 uses 0.35 hours. Finally, 6,000 machine-hours per week is the maximum finishing capacity, and 600 hours per week is the maximum amount of labor that the firm can use.

Letting $Q_1$ equal the number of batches of cotton cloth processed per week on process 1, $Q_2$ equal the number processed on process 2, and $Q_3$ equal the number processed on process 3, the American Textile Company's production problem can be regarded as the following linear programming problem: Maximize

$$\pi = 1.00Q_1 + 0.90Q_2 + 1.10Q_3 \tag{9.1}$$

subject to the constraints

$$3Q_1 + 2.50Q_2 + 5.25Q_3 \le 6,000 \tag{9.2}$$

$$0.40Q_1 + 0.50Q_2 + 0.35Q_3 \le 600 \tag{9.3}$$

$$Q_1 \ge 0; Q_2 \ge 0; Q_3 \ge 0. \tag{9.4}$$

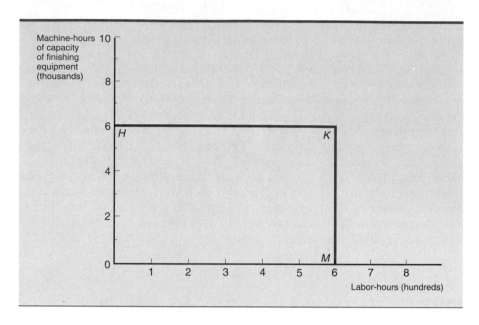

FIGURE 9.1   *Feasible Input Combinations*   Since a maximum of 600
labor-hours and 6,000 machine-hours are available, the feasible region is the
rectangle *OHKM.*

The **objective function,** sometimes called the criterion function, is the function to be maximized in a linear programming problem. In this case, it is the
expression for the firm's profits given in equation (9.1). The **constraints** are
given in inequalities (9.2) to (9.4). Inequality (9.2) states that the total
machine-hours per week of finishing capacity must be less than or equal to
6,000. Inequality (9.3) states that the total hours of labor per week must be
less than or equal to 600. Inequality (9.4) contains nonnegativity constraints, which may seem so obvious as to be unnecessary to state. But they
are not obvious to a computer, which might otherwise come up with a solution with a negative output. Finally, note that the objective function and
the constraints are all linear in $Q_1$, $Q_2$, and $Q_3$, the levels at which the processes are operated.

To solve this problem, we begin by graphing the feasible input combinations.[1] Figure 9.1, which has the total hours per week of labor time used by
all three processes along the horizontal axis and the total machine-hours per
week of finishing capacity used by all three processes along the vertical
axis, shows the combinations of total labor-hours and total machine-hours

[1] The ensuing discussion of this problem is similar in many respects (although the problem itself is
quite different) to that of W. Baumol, *Economic Theory and Operations Analysis,* 3d ed. (Englewood
Cliffs, N.J.: Prentice-Hall, 1972), pp. 296–310.

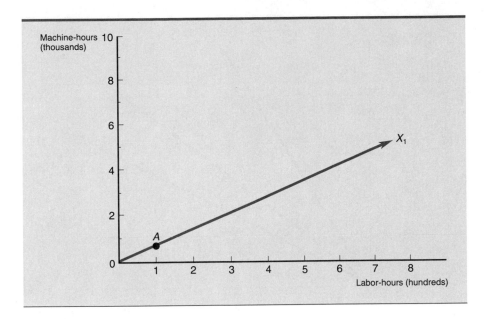

*FIGURE 9.2    Representation of Process 1 by a Ray*   The ray $OX_1$ includes all points at which finishing capacity is combined with labor in the ratio of 7.5:1.

that are feasible. The feasible region is the rectangle *OHKM*, since a maximum of 600 labor-hours and 6,000 machine-hours are available.

As pointed out above, each process is defined to have fixed input proportions. Since all points where input proportions are unchanged lie along a straight line through the origin, we can represent each process by such a line, or **ray.** In Figure 9.2, the ray $OX_1$ represents process 1. Process 1 uses 3 machine-hours of finishing capacity and 0.4 hours of labor per batch processed. That is, it uses 7.5 machine-hours of finishing capacity for every hour of labor. Thus, the ray $OX_1$ includes all points at which finishing capacity is combined with labor in the ratio of 7.5: 1. Each point on this ray implies a certain output level. For example, point *A*, where 100 hours of labor and 750 machine-hours of finishing capacity are used, implies an output of 250 batches per week, since process 1 uses 0.4 hours of labor and 3 machine-hours of finishing capacity per batch. Moreover, since all points at which labor and finishing capacity are combined in the ratio of 7.5: 1 are included in the ray $OX_1$, every possible output corresponds to some point on $OX_1$. It is possible to construct rays representing each of the three processes. Figure 9.3 shows all of them, with $OX_2$ representing process 2, and $OX_3$ representing process 3. Each ray is constructed in the same way as $OX_1$ was constructed for process 1.

Using these rays, we can draw isoquants—curves that include all input

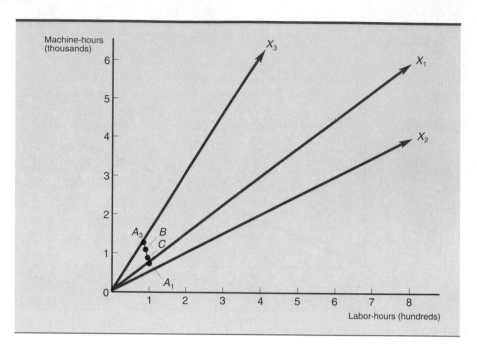

**FIGURE 9.3** *Rays for Processes 1, 2, and 3*   The isoquant corresponding to an output of 250 batches per week contains all points on the line segment that joins $A_1$ to $A_3$.

combinations that can produce a particular amount of output.[2] An isoquant means the same thing here as it did in Chapter 6; the only difference is that an isoquant here does not exhibit the smoothness of the isoquants in Chapter 6. To illustrate, let's draw the isoquant for an output of 250 batches per week. In Figure 9.3, point $A_1$ on $OX_1$ is the point corresponding to an output of 250 batches per week, and point $A_3$ on $OX_3$ is the point corresponding to an output of 250 batches per week. Thus, $A_1$ and $A_3$ are points on the isoquant corresponding to an output of 250 batches per week. Moreover, any point on the line segment that joins $A_1$ to $A_3$ is also on this isoquant, because the firm can simultaneously use both process 1 and process 3 to produce 250 batches per week. For example, point $B$ corresponds to the case in which process 1 is used to produce 25 batches and process 3 is used to produce 225 batches, and point $C$ corresponds to the case in which process 1 is used to produce 150 batches and process 3 is used to produce 100 batches. By varying the proportion of total output produced by each process, one can obtain all points on the line segment that joins $A_1$ to $A_3$.

---

[2] For simplicity, we treat each batch that is finished as an equal amount of output, regardless of which process is used. Obviously, this may not be true, but for present purposes, it makes no essential difference.

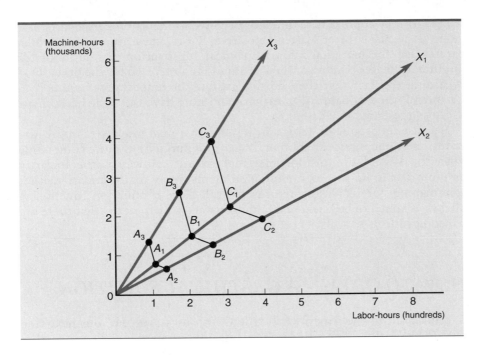

**FIGURE 9.4  Isoquants for Selected Levels of Output**  $A_3A_1A_2$ is the isoquant corresponding to an output of 250 batches per week; $B_3B_1B_2$ is the isoquant corresponding to an output of 500 batches per week; and $C_3C_1C_2$ is the isoquant corresponding to an output of 750 batches per week.

In Figure 9.4, to complete the isoquant corresponding to an output of 250 batches per week, we join $A_1$ to $A_2$, the point on $OX_2$ that represents an output of 250 batches per week. Thus, the entire isoquant is $A_3A_1A_2$. (At first glance, one might wonder why the line segment joining $A_3$ to $A_2$ is not part of the isoquant. After all, it does represent various combinations of labor and finishing capacity that can produce 250 batches a week. The reason for its exclusion is that all points on the line segment joining $A_3$ to $A_2$ are inefficient. They use as much of one input and more of the other input than some point on $A_3A_1A_2$. Thus, the points on $A_3A_2$ are clearly not on the isoquant—and they are not part of the solution to the firm's problem.) Other isoquants are also shown in Figure 9.4: $B_3B_1B_2$ is the isoquant corresponding to an output of 500 batches per week, and $C_3C_1C_2$ is the isoquant corresponding to an output of 750 batches per week.

Three points should be noted about the characteristic shape of isoquants in linear programming problems. First, they consist of a series of connected line segments, not the smooth curves of the conventional theory presented in Chapter 6. If the number of possible processes is very large, however, the isoquants may approximate the smooth conventional curves.[3] Second, their slope is negative, or at least nonpositive. Third, they are convex, which means that the marginal rate of technical substitution of one input for another decreases as more of the first input is substituted for the other. Disregarding the fact that they do not exhibit the smoothness assumed in Chapter 6, the isoquants of linear programming have the same basic shape as those presented in Chapter 6.

Because the isoquants show a decreasing marginal rate of technical substitution of one input for another, linear programming is quite compatible with the law of diminishing marginal returns. However, the linearity assumptions in linear programming problems imply that there are neither diminishing nor increasing returns to scale. The production function is always assumed to be linear and homogeneous, which means that there are constant returns to scale.

## HOW TO OBTAIN A GRAPHICAL SOLUTION

Getting back to the American Textile Company's problem, our next step toward a solution of this linear programming problem is the construction of isoprofit curves. After this is done, we can obtain a solution by graphical means. Just as each isoquant in Figure 9.4 represents the locus of input combinations that can produce a given output, each **isoprofit curve** is constructed to include all input combinations that can produce a given amount of profit.

To illustrate, let's construct the isoprofit curve corresponding to a profit of \$200. Because the profit per batch is \$1.00 for process 1, the point on $OX_1$ corresponding to an output of 200 batches per week is on this isoprofit curve. Because each batch produced with process 1 requires 3 machine-hours of finishing capacity and 0.4 hours of labor, the point on $OX_1$ corresponding to an output of 200 batches per week is $L$ in Figure 9.5. Similarly, because the profit per batch is \$0.90 for process 2, the point on $OX_2$ corresponding to an output of 222.2 batches per week is on this isoprofit curve. This is point $B$. Moreover, because the profit per batch is \$1.10 for process 3, the point on $OX_3$ corresponding to an output of 181.8 batches per week is also on this isoprofit curve. This is point $C$. Finally, for the same reason as in the case of the isoquants, we can also include all points on the lines that join these points. Thus, the isoprofit curve corresponding to a profit of \$200 per week is $CLB$ in Figure 9.5.

Using the same procedure, we can construct isoprofit curves corresponding to other levels of profit. As in the case of the isoquants in Figure 9.4, the isoprofit curves in Figure 9.5 are parallel to one another. For example, if we

---

[3] The basic reason why they are not smooth is that only a finite number of processes are assumed to be available to the firm. As the number of processes grows larger and larger, the isoquants become closer and closer to the smooth isoquants of conventional theory.

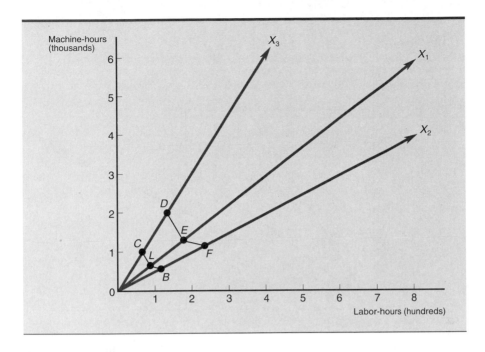

*FIGURE 9.5   Isoprofit Curves for Selected Profit Levels*   The isoprofit curve corresponding to a profit of $200 per week is *CLB*. The isoprofit curve corresponding to a profit of $400 per week is *DEF*.

compare *DEF*, the isoprofit curve corresponding to $400, with *CLB*, the isoprofit curve corresponding to $200, we find that they are parallel. That is, the slope of *CL* equals the slope of *DE*, and the slope of *LB* equals the slope of *EF*.

Having constructed the isoprofit curves, we can easily solve the firm's problem. All we need to do is add the isoprofit curves to the diagram (Figure 9.1) showing the feasible input combinations. This is done in Figure 9.6. Clearly, the problem is to find the point in the rectangle *OHKM* of feasible input combinations that lies on the highest isoprofit curve. It is obvious from Figure 9.6 that the optimal point is *K*. If we construct various isoprofit curves, like $U_3U_1U_2$, $V_3V_1V_2$, and so forth, the highest isoprofit curve we can construct that includes any points in *OHKM* is $V_3V_1V_2$. The only point in *OHKM* that lies on $V_3V_1V_2$ is *K*.

Granting that *K* is the optimum point, how can we tell what the optimum values of $Q_1$, $Q_2$, and $Q_3$ are? First, since *K* lies on the line segment $V_3V_1$, it means that it is optimal only to use processes 3 and 1. This illustrates the fact that the optimal solution of a linear programming problem of this sort will generally entail the use of no more processes than there are constraints: two, in this case (excluding the nonnegativity constraints). Sec-

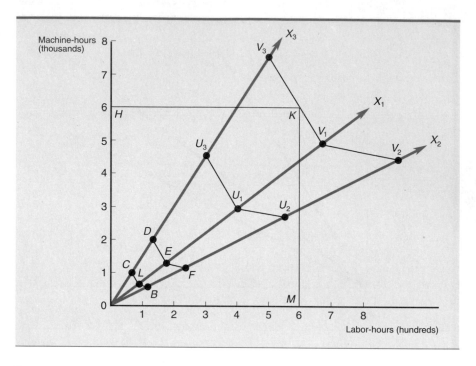

**FIGURE 9.6** *Isoprofit Curves and Feasible Input Combinations* The optimum point is $K$, where 6,000 machine-hours of finishing capacity and 600 hours of labor are used. It is optimal to use only processes 3 and 1.

ond, since $K$ is the point where a total of 6,000 machine-hours of finishing capacity and 600 hours of labor are used,

$$3Q_1 + 5.25Q_3 = 6{,}000 \tag{9.5}$$

$$0.40Q_1 + 0.35Q_3 = 600. \tag{9.6}$$

Solving equations (9.5) and (9.6) simultaneously, we find that the optimal values are $Q_3 = 571.4$ and $Q_1 = 1{,}000$. In other words, the American Textile Company will maximize its profit if it produces about 571 batches per week on process 3 and 1,000 batches per week on process 1.

## THE CASE OF UNLIMITED RESOURCES

To illustrate further the use of linear programming in solving production problems, suppose that the American Textile Company is no longer constrained by limits on the amount of labor and finishing capacity it can use.

Instead, it can hire all of the labor it wants at $12.00 an hour, and it can rent all of the finishing capacity it wants at $1.60 per machine-hour. Suppose it can use any of the three processes just described, and its problem is to choose that combination of processes that will produce 400 batches per week of finished cotton cloth at minimum cost. The price received per batch is the same for all processes. (Note that the figures given on page 333 concerning the profit per batch made by each process are no longer valid, since the price received per batch is now the same for all processes.)

Now the American Textile Company's production problem can be regarded as the following linear programming problem: Minimize

$$C = 9.60Q_1 + 10.00Q_2 + 12.60Q_3 \qquad (9.7)$$

subject to the constraints

$$Q_1 + Q_2 + Q_3 = 400 \qquad (9.8)$$

$$Q_1 \geq 0; Q_2 \geq 0; Q_3 \geq 0. \qquad (9.9)$$

The objective function in this case is cost, $C$, which is given in equation (9.7). To derive this equation, note that the cost of each batch produced by process 1 is $9.60, since process 1 requires 3 machine-hours of finishing capacity (at $1.60 a machine-hour) and 0.4 hours of labor (at $12.00 an hour). Thus, the total cost of the batches produced by process 1 is $9.60Q_1$. Similarly, the total cost of the batches produced by process 2 is $10.00Q_2$, and the total cost of the batches produced by process 3 is $12.60Q_3$. The only constraint, other than the nonnegativity constraints in inequality (9.9), is equation (9.8), which states that the total production from all processes must equal 400.

This problem is easy to solve. Using the methods described in the section before last, we can construct the isoquant corresponding to an output of 400 batches per week. This isoquant, labeled *ABC*, is shown in Figure 9.7. Next we can construct isocost curves, each of which shows the various combinations of quantities of labor and finishing capacity that can be obtained at a given level of cost. The isocost curves corresponding to costs of $4,000 and $3,600 are labeled $NN^1$ and $SS^1$ in Figure 9.7. Clearly, the problem is to find the point on the isoquant, *ABC*, that lies on the lowest isocost curve. It is evident that the optimal point is *B*, which means that all of the output should be produced with process 1.

A comparison of this problem with the one discussed on page 220 of Chapter 6 shows that they are one and the same. In both cases, we are determining the input combination and production technique that minimize the cost of producing a given output. Moreover, Figure 6.9 (page 221), which shows the solution according to conventional theory, is very similar to Figure 9.7, which shows the solution in this case. What is the difference between the two cases? In Chapter 6 we assumed we were somehow given a smooth production function, whereas here we assume we are given the technical characteristics of the relevant processes. The situation analyzed here is generally the more realistic one.

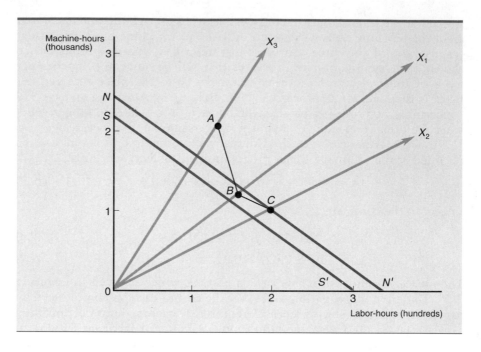

**FIGURE 9.7** *Optimal Solution: Cost Minimization Problem* Since the isoquant is *ABC* and the isocost curves are $NN^1$ and $SS^1$, the optimal point is *B*, which means that all of the output should be made with process 1.

# PRODUCTION PLANNING: MULTIPLE PRODUCTS

Turning now to a more complex case, suppose that the National Auto Company produces two kinds of output, automobiles and trucks.[4] It has four kinds of facilities, each of which is fixed in capacity: automobile assembly, truck assembly, engine assembly, and sheet metal stamping. The problem is: How many automobiles and how many trucks should the firm produce? The profit per automobile or the profit per truck depends on the price of an automobile or a truck, the variable costs of producing an automobile or a truck, and the firm's fixed costs. Assume that the price and average variable cost of each product are constant; that is, they do not vary with output in

---

[4] This is an adaptation of the well-known example found in R. Dorfman, "Mathematical or Linear Programming: A Nonmathematical Exposition," reprinted in E. Mansfield, ed., *Managerial Economics and Operations Research*, 5th ed. (New York: Norton, 1987). Different numbers have been used to simplify the result. For applications in the oil industry, see W. Garvin and others, "Applications of Linear Programming in the Oil Industry," in E. Mansfield, ed., *Managerial Economics and Operations Research*, 5th ed.

## HOW LINEAR PROGRAMMING IMPROVES AIRCRAFT OPERATIONS

Linear programming is used in a wide variety of industries and firms. Consider, for example, the case of Delta Airlines, which uses linear programming to reduce the costs of moving flight crews from place to place. Because of work rules limiting the number of hours per day that crew members can fly, as well as waiting time in airports and other factors, a substantial percentage of the time of pilots and flight attendants is essentially unproductive, from the point of view of the airline.

To try to cut down on this unproductive time, Delta faces a very difficult analytical problem. Specifically, in 1992, it had to schedule a very large work force (9,000 pilots and 17,000 flight attendants), and it had to take into account roughly 2,500 route segments daily to more than 220 cities worldwide, using more than 500 aircraft of nine types flown from a dozen different crew bases. Clearly, the problem is very complex.

In the early 1990s, Delta used a new technique based on linear programming to help solve this problem, the result being an estimated annual saving of about $14 million. Besides the monetary savings, there were improvements in working conditions since crew members, particularly flight attendants, now had schedules that took them away from their home bases for less time than before. Moreover, schedules could be formulated more rapidly than in the past. (A crew planner could do in a day what formerly took most of a week.)

Government agencies, like firms, use linear programming to help solve a variety of problems concerning aircraft operations. For example, the Air Force Military Aircraft Command has used linear programming to help perform aircraft operations more efficiently. In some problems involving the scheduling of military support aircraft, over 300,000 variables and almost 15,000 constraints were considered. While problems of this sort are far more complex than those considered in this chapter, the basic ideas are no different from those taken up here.[*]

*Ronald W. Allen, Chairman of the Board and CEO, Delta Air Lines*

[*]These examples were described in D. Werkheiser, "Karmarkar Algorithm," National Technological University, 1991.

the relevant range. Specifically, assume that the price of an automobile is $20,000, the price of a truck is $30,000, the average variable costs of an automobile are $19,700, and the average variable costs of a truck are $29,750.

The National Auto Company wants to maximize profits. Neglecting fixed costs (which will be the same regardless of what the firm does), the firm's profits (per hour) equal

$$\pi = 300Q_a + 250Q_t, \tag{9.10}$$

where $Q_a$ is the number of automobiles produced by the firm per hour, and $Q_t$ is the number of trucks produced by the firm per hour. Because the firm receives $300 (that is, $20,000 − $19,700) above the variable cost for each automobile it produces, and because the firm receives $250 (that is, $30,000 − $29,750) above the variable cost for each truck it produces, the firm's profits (before deducting fixed costs) must equal $300 times its output of automobiles plus $250 times its output of trucks.

What are the constraints on the decisions of the firm's managers? Its capacities for automobile assembly, truck assembly, engine assembly, and sheet metal stamping are fixed. Table 9.1 shows the proportion of each facility's total capacity required to produce one automobile or one truck. From this table, we can represent the constraints on the production of automobiles and trucks by the following inequalities:

$$.05Q_a \leq 1 \tag{9.11}$$

$$.04Q_t \leq 1 \tag{9.12}$$

$$.02Q_a + .033Q_t \leq 1 \tag{9.13}$$

$$.033Q_a + .025Q_t \leq 1 \tag{9.14}$$

$$Q_a \geq 0; \; Q_t \geq 0. \tag{9.15}$$

Inequalities (9.11) and (9.12) represent the constraints imposed by existing automobile and truck assembly capacity. Since each automobile that is produced per hour utilizes 5 percent of the automobile assembly capacity, it follows that .05 times the output per hour of automobiles must be less than or equal to 1. Figure 9.8 plots the firm's automobile production

---

TABLE 9.1  *Percentage of National Auto Company's Capacity Required to Make an Automobile or Truck (per Hour)*

| Capacity | Automobile | Truck |
|----------|------------|-------|
| Auto assembly | 5 | 0 |
| Engine assembly | 2 | $3\frac{1}{3}$ |
| Sheet metal | $3\frac{1}{3}$ | $2\frac{1}{2}$ |
| Truck assembly | 0 | 4 |

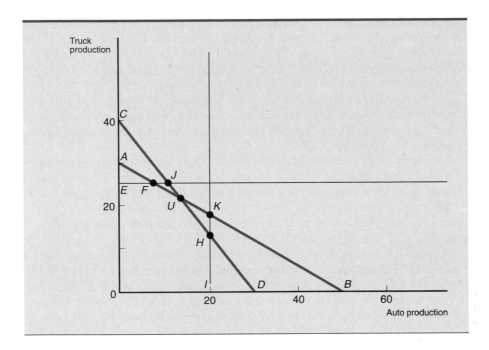

**FIGURE 9.8   Feasible Output Combinations, National Auto
Company**   The feasible combinations of output of automobiles and trucks all
lie within the area *OEFUHI*.

against its truck production. The vertical line at 20 automobiles per hour
shows the effects of this constraint, since 20 is the maximum automobile
output compatible with this constraint. Similarly, since each truck that is
produced per hour utilizes 4 percent of the truck assembly capacity, it follows that .04 times the output per hour of trucks must be less than or equal
to 1. The horizontal line in Figure 9.8 at 25 trucks per hour shows the
effects of this constraint, since 25 is the maximum truck output compatible
with this constraint.

Inequality (9.13) says that no more than the existing capacity for engine
assembly can be used. Since each automobile produced per hour utilizes 2
percent of the existing engine assembly capacity and since each truck produced per hour utilizes $3\frac{1}{3}$ percent of the existing engine assembly capacity,
it follows that .02 times the output per hour of automobiles plus .033 times
the output per hour of trucks must be less than or equal to 1. Thus, the line
*AB* in Figure 9.8 separates feasible combinations of automobile and truck
outputs from those that are beyond the existing engine assembly capacity.
To be feasible, the combination of outputs must be on, or within, the triangle *OAB*.

Inequality (9.14) says that no more than the existing sheet metal stamping capacity can be used. Since each automobile produced per hour takes up $3\frac{1}{3}$ percent of the available metal stamping capacity and since each truck produced per hour takes up $2\frac{1}{2}$ percent of the available metal stamping capacity, it follows that .033 times the output per hour of automobiles plus .025 times the output per hour of trucks must be less than or equal to 1. Thus, the line CD in Figure 9.8 separates feasible combinations of automobile and truck outputs from those that are beyond the existing sheet metal stamping capacity. To be feasible, the combination of outputs must be on, or within, the triangle OCD.

To satisfy all of these constraints, the combination of output of automobiles and trucks must lie within the area OEFUHI in Figure 9.8. Any point outside this area violates at least one of the constraints. For example, point C uses more engine assembly capacity and truck assembly capacity than is available, and point K uses more sheet metal stamping capacity than is available.

This is a linear programming problem. The objective function is given by equation (9.10), and the constraints are given in inequalities (9.11) to (9.15). There are two processes, automobile production and truck production, each of which uses the four types of capacities in fixed (but different) proportions. The optimal solution to this problem can be found graphically by adding a family of isoprofit lines to Figure 9.8. This is done in Figure 9.9. Each isoprofit line shows the various combinations of automobile production and truck production that will result in the same total profit (gross of fixed costs). If $\pi$ is this profit, the equation for an isoprofit line is

$$Q_t = \frac{\pi}{250} - \frac{300}{250} Q_a. \tag{9.16}$$

Clearly, you should find the point in the feasible area, OEFUHI, that lies on the highest isoprofit line.

Figure 9.9 shows that the optimal solution is at point U, where the National Auto Company produces 13.6 automobiles and 21.8 trucks per hour. With these output rates, the firm's profit (gross of fixed costs) is $9,547 per hour.[5]

## EXTREME POINTS AND THE SIMPLEX METHOD

As we pointed out at the beginning of this chapter, one important reason why the linear programming approach is used is that powerful computa-

[5] How can a firm produce 13.6 autos per hour? By producing 68 autos every 5 hours. In cases in which the solution must be composed of integers, an extension of linear programming called integer programming must be used. See W. Baumol, *Economic Theory*, Chapter 8. Note that it is easy to find the coordinates of U by making inequalities (9.13) and (9.14) into equations and solving them simultaneously for $Q_a$ and $Q_t$.

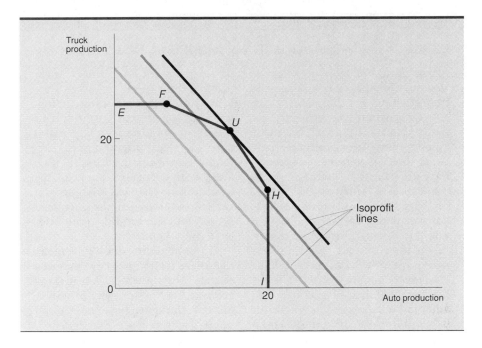

*FIGURE 9.9   Optimal Output Combination, National Auto Company*   The optimal output combination is at point *U*, where the firm produces 13.6 automobiles and 21.8 trucks per hour.

tional techniques have been developed to find the numerical solutions to linear programming problems. These computational techniques make use of the following fact: the optimal solution will lie at one of the *extreme points*—or corners—of the feasible area.[6] This rule is consistent with the cases discussed in the previous paragraphs. For example, in Figure 9.9, the optimal point, *U*, was an extreme point of the feasible area *OEFUHI*; and in Figure 9.6, the optimal point, *K*, was an extreme point of the feasible area *OHKM*. This fact reduces greatly the number of points that must be examined to find the optimal solution, since it demonstrates that all we need to bother with are the extreme points of the feasible area.

For example, consider Figure 9.9. There are six extreme points of the feasible area *OEFUHI*. To find the optimal solution, we need only compute the profit (gross of fixed costs) at each of these points. At the origin 0, profit obviously is zero. At $E(Q_a = 0$ and $Q_t = 25)$, profit is \$6,250. At $I(Q_a = 20$ and $Q_t = 0)$, profit is \$6,000. We must find the coordinates of the other

[6] Of course, it sometimes happens that other points are as good as (but not better than) any extreme point. See H. Wagner, *Principles of Operations Research*, 2d ed. (Englewood Cliffs, N.J.: Prentice-Hall, 1975). Also, see G. Dantzig, "Linear Programming: Examples and Concepts," in E. Mansfield, ed., *Managerial Economics and Operations Research*, 5th ed.

## USING LINEAR PROGRAMMING TO CHOOSE R AND D PROJECTS

Research and development, as we saw in Chapter 7, is enormously important to productivity. It can also be enormously expensive, and hard choices have to be made among competing projects. Many firms and government agencies have used linear programming techniques to help choose R and D projects. To illustrate their use, suppose that Du Pont has a list of $n$ possible R and D projects that it might carry out and that to undertake project $i$ would cost $C_i$ dollars. Moreover, suppose that project $i$ has a probability of success of $P_i$ and that, if successful, it will result in a profit (gross of R and D costs) of $\pi_i$. Then, if Du Pont can spend no more than $C$ dollars on R and D and if it wants to maximize the expected value of profit, its problem can be represented as follows:

$$\text{Maximize} \sum_{i=1}^{n} X_i(P_i\pi_i - C_i)$$

subject to the constraint that

$$\sum_{i=1}^{n} X_iC_i \leqslant C$$

and

$$X_i = 0, 1.$$

In other words, Du Pont's problem is to choose the $X_i$—where $X_i = 1$ if project $i$ is accepted and 0 if it is rejected—in such a way that it maximizes the expected value of profit, subject to the constraint that the total amount spent on R and D does not exceed $C$.

Because the $X_i$ can only be zero or 1, this is not an ordinary linear programming problem; it is a so-called integer programming problem. But for present purposes, this is not of importance. The major point is that programming techniques have been used in this way. Surveys indicate that many of the laboratories—particularly the bigger laboratories—in the chemical, drug, and electronics industries have used them.

However, this does not mean that these techniques have played a central role in the decision-making process. One reason why programming techniques have not found more extensive use is that data concerning $P_i$, $\pi_i$, and $C_i$ often are very rough. There frequently is consider-

*E. S. Woolard, Jr., Chairman and CEO of E. I. duPont de Nemours and Co.*

able disagreement over a project's value of $P_i$, some people feeling that the project is likely to succeed, others feeling that it is a loser. The value of $\pi_i$ is often difficult to estimate as well. Even $C_i$, the cost of the project, can be hard to forecast, because engineers and scientists often present overly optimistic estimates to help sell projects to top management. The moral is that while programming techniques are powerful and useful, they cannot be used effectively without reliable basic data. If the numbers in the objective function and constraints are subject to very large errors, one should view the results with appropriate caution.

---

ANALYZING MANAGERIAL DECISIONS

## MOVING SAND AT THE BRISBANE AIRPORT

When the Brisbane International Airport was redeveloped, about 2 million cubic meters of sand dredged from a nearby bay had to be moved by pipeline to various sites. Additional sand was brought to help compress the swampy grounds at the sites, and the excess sand was transported from these areas to other places around the airport by truck or scraper. The distance from each source to each destination, as well as the quantity of sand available from each source and the quantity required at each destination, are shown below. The use of linear programming in this case resulted in a saving in transport costs of about $400,000.*

| Source | Destination | | | | | | | | | Quantity available (cubic meters) |
|---|---|---|---|---|---|---|---|---|---|---|
| | Local-izer N | Exten-sion | Low areas | Roads | Car park | Local-izer S | Fire station | Oil industry | Perimiter Road | |
| | Distance (meters) from source to destination | | | | | | | | | |
| Apron | 22 | 26 | 12 | 10 | 18 | 18 | 11 | 8.5 | 20 | 960 |
| Terminal | 20 | 28 | 14 | 12 | 20 | 20 | 13 | 10 | 22 | 201 |
| Airline area | 16 | 20 | 26 | 20 | 1.5 | 28 | 6 | 22 | 18 | 71 |
| Mainte-nance | 20 | 22 | 26 | 22 | 6 | | 2 | 21 | 18 | 24 |
| Access road | 22 | 26 | 10 | 4 | 16 | | 24 | 14 | 21 | 99 |
| Quantity required (cubic meters) | 62 | 217 | 444 | 315 | 50 | 7 | 20 | 90 | 150 | 1355 |

* C. Perry and M. Iliff, "From the Shadows: Earthmoving on Construction Projects," *Interfaces* (February 1983), pp. 79–84.

(a) If the cost of hauling sand is proportional to the amount of sand times the distance hauled, what is an expression for the quantity that the airport executives should maximize or minimize? (b) What constraints must be satisfied? (c) In fact, the airport's managers used linear programming (the LINDO package described on page 369) to solve this problem. They found that all of the sand required in the low areas should come from the apron. Does this make sense? Why or why not? (d) Two figures in the above table are omitted. Can the problem be solved without them? How can one estimate them?

the distance hauled. It is proportional to the total cost of hauling the sand. The values of $D_{ij}$ are given. The problem is to find the values of $T_{ij}$ that minimize $\sum_i \sum_j T_{ij} \cdot D_{ij}$. (b) The amount of sand moved from the $i$th source must not exceed the amount available. The amount of sand moved to the $j$th destination must not be less than the amount required. For all $i$ and $j$, $T_{ij}$ must be nonnegative. (c) The low areas are quite close (12 meters) to the apron, which seems to suggest that this is reasonable, but in a complex problem of this sort, it is not easy to tell at a glance what the solution is. If it were easy, there would be no need for sophisticated analytical techniques like linear programming. (d) No. To estimate them, determine the distance between localizer $S$, on the one hand, and the maintenance area and the access road, on the other hand.

*Solution* (a) Minimize $\sum_i \sum_j T_{ij} \cdot D_{ij}$ where $T_{ij}$ is the number of cubic meters of sand to be moved from source $i$ to destination $j$, and $D_{ij}$ is the distance (in meters) from source $i$ to destination $j$. This is the sum of the amount of sand times

three extreme points before we can compute the level of profit at them. To find the coordinates of $F$, we must make inequalities (9.12) and (9.13) into equations and solve them simultaneously; to find the coordinates of $U$, we must make inequalities (9.13) and (9.14) into equations and solve them simultaneously; and to find the coordinates of $H$, we must make inequalities (9.11) and (9.14) into equations and solve them simultaneously. We find that point $F$ is $Q_a = 8\frac{1}{3}$ and $Q_t = 25$, the result being that profit is \$8,750. Point $U$ is $Q_a = 13.6$ and $Q_t = 21.8$, the result being that profit is \$9,547. Point $H$ is $Q_a = 20$ and $Q_t = 13\frac{1}{3}$, the result being that profit is \$9,333$\frac{1}{3}$. Consequently, on the basis of these few computations, we can tell that point $U$ must be the optimal solution.

If the number of processes and constraints are too large for the graphical analysis used in previous sections, this kind of comparison of extreme point or corner solutions may be employed to find the optimal solution. The **simplex method**, which may be used for this purpose, is a systematic procedure for comparing extreme point or corner solutions.[7] Combined with the speed and capacity of modern computers, it can solve extremely large problems rapidly.

## THE DUAL PROBLEM AND SHADOW PRICES

Using linear programming, you can do more than just find an optimal production program. You can also find values to be placed on particular resources or inputs. To illustrate, suppose that the National Auto Company wants to determine the value of adding an extra amount of sheet metal capacity. To find out, you could carry out the programming problem described above, assuming that the firm had a small amount of additional sheet metal capacity. Then you could compare the maximum profit obtainable with the extra amount of sheet metal capacity with the maximum profit obtainable without it. The increase, if there is an increase, in maximum profit is, of course, a measure of the value of the extra amount of sheet metal capacity.

While this method of finding the value of an extra unit of a particular input is perfectly correct, it is cumbersome. An important feature of linear programming problems is that you can obtain such values without going through this cumbersome procedure. Every linear programming problem has a corresponding problem called its **dual.** (The original problem is called the **primal** problem.) If the primal is a maximization problem, the dual is a minimization problem; if the primal is a minimization problem, the dual is a maximization problem. The solutions to the dual are **shadow prices,** the values you seek.

Thus, the shadow price of each type of capacity (in the problem concerning the National Auto Company) tells you what would happen to the firm's profits if the company were somehow able to increase this type of capacity. Clearly, these shadow prices are of great practical importance. They show which types of capacity are bottlenecks, or effective constraints on output, since capacity that is underutilized receives a zero shadow price. More important, they indicate how much it would be worth to management to expand each type of capacity. A comparison can then be made between the extra profit that is due to expansion and the extra costs that must be incurred. If the costs are lower than the extra profits, as indicated by the shadow price, the expansion seems desirable. For instance, if the National Auto Company can rent an additional 1 percent of sheet metal capacity at $300 an hour and if an extra 1 percent of such capacity would increase profits by $400, the firm's managers should rent the extra capacity.

---

[7] In 1984, N. Karmarkar of Bell Labs suggested another algorithm resulting in faster solutions of linear programming problems, but we need not be concerned here with that algorithm.

## RELATIONSHIP BETWEEN PRIMAL AND DUAL PROBLEMS

To illustrate the relationship between the primal and dual problems, suppose that the Ajax Chemical Company produces carbon black and ether, that the profit contribution per unit of carbon black produced is $50, and that the profit contribution per unit of ether produced is $80. Ajax wants to maximize the total profit contribution, which equals

$$\pi = 50Q_1 + 80Q_2, \tag{9.17}$$

where $Q_1$ is the number of units of carbon black produced, and $Q_2$ is the number of units of ether produced. To produce carbon black and ether, the firm uses labor and equipment. Each unit of carbon black produced requires 2 hours of labor and 3 machine-hours of equipment. Each unit of ether produced requires 3 hours of labor and 2 machine-hours of equipment. Since the firm has available only 4,000 hours of labor and 5,400 machine-hours of equipment (and cannot hire more),

$$2Q_1 + 3Q_2 \le 4{,}000 \tag{9.18}$$

$$3Q_1 + 2Q_2 \le 5{,}400. \tag{9.19}$$

Also, $Q_1 \ge 0$ and $Q_2 \ge 0$.

The primal problem is to find the values of $Q_1$ and $Q_2$ that maximize $\pi$ [in equation (9.17)] subject to the constraints in (9.18) and (9.19). What is the corresponding dual problem? As pointed out in the previous section, it involves minimization, rather than maximization. Specifically, the problem is to minimize the total value of resources (labor and equipment) available, given that $S_L$ and $S_E$ are the prices of labor and equipment. This total value equals

$$V = 4{,}000\,S_L + 5{,}400\,S_E. \tag{9.20}$$

These prices ($S_L$ and $S_E$) are the shadow prices discussed in the previous section. The constraints in the dual problem are

$$2S_L + 3S_E \ge 50 \tag{9.21}$$

$$3S_L + 2S_E \ge 80. \tag{9.22}$$

Also, $S_L \ge 0$ and $S_E \ge 0$. The constraint in (9.21) says that the total value of resources used in the production of a unit of carbon black must be at least equal to the profit from this unit, and the constraint in (9.22) says that the total value of resources used in the production of a unit of ether must be at least equal to the profit from this unit.

The dual problem is to find the values of $S_L$ and $S_E$ that minimize $V$ in equation (9.20) subject to the constraints in (9.21) and (9.22). These values of $S_L$ and $S_E$, which can be determined using the graphical techniques described above, are the shadow prices of labor and equipment. They are the prices that a manager should be willing to pay for these resources. Put differently, they are the opportunity cost of using these resources. If a resource is not fully utilized, its shadow price will be zero, since an extra unit of this resource would not increase profit. The firm already has more of this resource than it can use effectively. On the other hand, if a resource is fully utilized, its shadow price will be positive, since its opportunity cost will be positive.

## SLACK VARIABLES

To specify a linear programming problem algebraically, it is useful to use so-called slack variables to represent the amounts of various inputs that are *unused.* For example, consider the Ajax Chemical Company, discussed in the previous section. According to inequality (9.18), the amount of labor used must be less than or equal to 4,000 hours. If we let $U_L$ be a slack variable equaling the number of hours of labor that are unused, we can convert inequality (9.18) into the following equation:

$$2Q_1 + 3Q_2 + U_L = 4,000. \tag{9.23}$$

To see that this equation is correct, recall that the number of hours of labor used by the firm is $2Q_1 + 3Q_2$; thus, this amount plus the number of unused hours of labor, $U_L$, must equal 4,000 hours, the amount that is available.

Similarly, if we let $U_M$ be a slack variable equaling the number of machine-hours that are unused, we can convert inequality (9.19) into the following equation:

$$3Q_1 + 2Q_2 + U_M = 5,400. \tag{9.24}$$

To see that this is correct, recall that the number of machine-hours used by the firm is $3Q_1 + 2Q_2$; thus, this amount plus the number of unused machine-hours, $U_M$, must equal 5,400 hours, the amount that is available.

Besides allowing us to state the constraints in equality form, which simplifies the algebraic analysis, the introduction of these slack variables provides important information because their values are of significance. If the slack variable for an input turns out to be zero, this means that this input is fully utilized when the firm is maximizing profit. If it turns out to be positive, this means that some of this input is redundant.

## ALGEBRAIC SOLUTION OF LINEAR PROGRAMMING PROBLEMS

Having defined a slack variable, we can readily show how algebraic techniques, rather than the graphical methods described above, can be used to solve linear programming problems. Consider once again the Ajax Chemical Company, which, as we know from the previous sections, wants to maximize the total profit contribution

$$\pi = 50Q_1 + 80Q_2, \tag{9.25}$$

where $Q_1$ is the number of units of carbon black produced, and $Q_2$ is the number of units of ether produced. Since no more than 4,000 hours of labor can be used,

$$2Q_1 + 3Q_2 + U_L = 4,000. \tag{9.26}$$

And since no more than 5,400 machine-hours can be used,

$$3Q_1 + 2Q_2 + U_M = 5,400. \tag{9.27}$$

Recall from the previous section that $U_L$ is the number of unused labor hours, and $U_M$ is the number of unused machine-hours. Both are slack variables.

As emphasized on page 347, the optimal solution of any linear programming problem will always lie at one of the extreme points—or corners—of the feasible area. In Ajax's problem, the feasible area is the shaded area in Figure 9.10, since only points in this area satisfy the constraints. [See ine-

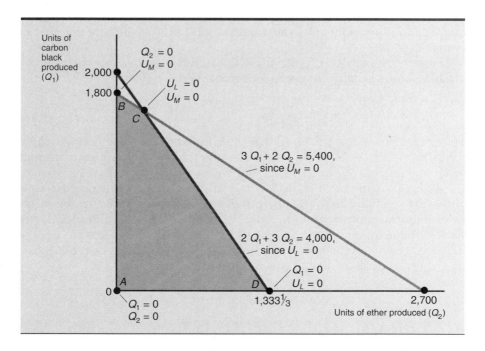

**FIGURE 9.10** *Identification of Which Variables Equal Zero at Each Corner (A, B, C, D) of the Feasible Area* Two of the four variables ($Q_1$, $Q_2$, $U_L$, $U_M$) equal zero at each corner.

qualities (9.18) and (9.19).] Thus, there are four corners: $A$, $B$, $C$, and $D$. To solve this problem algebraically, we determine the values of $Q_1$, $Q_2$, $U_L$, and $U_M$ at each of these corners. As shown in Figure 9.10, two of these four variables equal zero at each corner.[8] The corner where the total profit contribution is highest is the optimal solution.

*Point A.* Since point $A$ is at the origin, both $Q_1$ and $Q_2$ are zero. Substituting these values into equations (9.26) and (9.27), we find that $U_L = 4,000$ and $U_M = 5,400$. Moreover, if we substitute these values into equation (9.25), we see that $\pi = 0$. These results are contained in the first row of Table 9.2.

---

TABLE 9.2 *Algebraic Solution of Ajax Chemical Company's Linear Programming Problem*

| Corner | $Q_1$ | $Q_2$ | $U_L$ | $U_M$ | $\pi$ |
|--------|-------|-------|-------|-------|-------|
| A | 0 | 0 | 4,000 | 5,400 | 0 |
| B | 1,800 | 0 | 400 | 0 | 90,000 |
| C | 1,640 | 240 | 0 | 0 | 101,200 |
| D | 0 | $1,333\frac{1}{3}$ | 0 | $2,733\frac{1}{3}$ | $106,666\frac{2}{3}$ |

---

*Point B.* Since point $B$ is on the vertical axis, $Q_2$ is zero. Also, since point $B$ is on the line in Figure 9.10 where $U_M = 0$, it follows that $U_M$ is zero. Substituting these values into equations (9.26) and (9.27), we obtain

$$2Q_1 + 3(0) + U_L = 4,000$$

$$3Q_1 + 2(0) + 0 = 5,400,$$

which implies that

$$Q_1 = \frac{5,400}{3} = 1,800$$

and

$$U_L = 4,000 - 2(1,800),$$

$$= 400.$$

Since $Q_1 = 1,800$ and $Q_2 = 0$, equation (9.25) tells us that $\pi = 90,000$, which is entered in the second row of Table 9.2.

*Point C.* Since point $C$ is at the intersection of the line in Figure 9.10 where $U_L = 0$ and the line where $U_M = 0$, it follows that both $U_L$ and $U_M$ are zero. Substituting these values into equations (9.26) and (9.27), we obtain

$$2Q_1 + 3Q_2 + 0 = 4,000$$

$$3Q_1 + 2Q_2 + 0 = 5,400.$$

---

[8] In almost all linear programming problems, the number of non-zero-valued variables at each corner equals the number of constraints in the problem. (Recall page 339.) In this case, there are two constraints: inequalities (9.18) and (9.19).

Solving these two equations simultaneously, we find that $Q_1 = 1,640$ and $Q_2 = 240$. Thus, based on equation (9.25),

$$\pi = 50(1,640) + 80(240)$$

$$= 101,200,$$

as shown in the third row of Table 9.2.

*Point D.* Since point $D$ is on the horizontal axis, $Q_1$ is zero. Also, since point $D$ is on the line in Figure 9.10 where $U_L = 0$, it follows that $U_L$ is zero. Substituting these values into equations (9.26) and (9.27), we get

$$2(0) + 3Q_2 + 0 = 4,000$$

$$3(0) + 2Q_2 + U_M = 5,400,$$

which implies that

$$Q_2 = \frac{4,000}{3} = 1,333\tfrac{1}{3}$$

and

$$U_M = 5,400 - 2(1,333\tfrac{1}{3})$$

$$= 2,733\tfrac{1}{3}.$$

Since $Q_1 = 0$ and $Q_2 = 1,333\tfrac{1}{3}$, equation (9.25) tells us that $\pi = 106,666\tfrac{2}{3}$, which is entered in the fourth row of Table 9.2.

*Optimal Solution.* As pointed out above, the corner where the total profit contribution, $\pi$, is highest is the optimal solution. The last column of Table 9.2 shows the value of $\pi$ at each corner. Clearly, $\pi$ is highest at corner $D$, which is where $Q_1 = 0$ and $Q_2 = 1,333\tfrac{1}{3}$. Thus, Ajax's optimal solution is to produce $1,333\tfrac{1}{3}$ units of ether and no carbon black.

# MINIMIZATION OF SHIPPING COSTS AT THE ESSEX CORPORATION

Most linear programming problems faced by firms are much more complicated than that facing the Ajax Chemical Corporation. Consider the Essex Corporation, which has two production plants and three warehouses. The plants are in Florida and Texas; the warehouses are in California, Illinois, and New York. The cost of shipping a ton of Essex's product from each plant to each warehouse is provided in Table 9.3. Table 9.4 shows the number of tons of the product produced (per day) by each plant and the number of tons demanded (per day) by each warehouse. As you can see, the total amount produced by the two plants ($4,000 + 3,000 = 7,000$ tons) is exactly equal to the total amount demanded by the three warehouses ($2,500 + 2,000 + 2,500 = 7,000$ tons).

TABLE 9.3   Cost of Shipping a Ton of the Essex Corporation's Product from Each Plant to Each Warehouse

| Plant | California | Warehouse Illinois | New York |
|---|---|---|---|
| Florida | $15 | $10 | $7 |
| Texas | 6 | 8 | 11 |

TABLE 9.4   Daily Output of Plants and Daily Demands by Warehouses, Essex Corporation

| Plant | Output (tons) | Warehouse | Demand (tons) |
|---|---|---|---|
| Florida | 4,000 | California | 2,500 |
| Texas | 3,000 | Illinois | 2,000 |
|  | 7,000 | New York | 2,500 |
|  |  |  | 7,000 |

The problem that the Essex Corporation wants to solve is: How many tons of product should each plant ship to each warehouse? Because shipping costs are high in many industries, this can be a very significant problem. The Essex Corporation wants to minimize its total shipping cost, which equals

$$15A + 10B + 7C + 6D + 8E + 11F, \tag{9.28}$$

where $A$ is the number of tons shipped (per day) from the Florida plant to the California warehouse, $B$ is the number of tons shipped from the Florida plant to the Illinois warehouse, $C$ is the number of tons shipped from the Florida plant to the New York warehouse, $D$ is the number of tons shipped from the Texas plant to the California warehouse, $E$ is the number of tons shipped from the Texas plant to the Illinois warehouse, and $F$ is the number of tons shipped from the Texas plant to the New York warehouse.

There are three sets of constraints. First, total shipments to each warehouse must meet its demand, which means that the following inequalities must hold:

$$A + D \geq 2,500 \tag{9.29}$$

$$B + E \geq 2,000 \tag{9.30}$$

$$C + F \geq 2,500. \tag{9.31}$$

Second, total shipments from each plant cannot exceed its production rate, which means that the following inequalities must hold:

$$A + B + C \leq 4,000 \tag{9.32}$$

$$D + E + F \leq 3,000. \tag{9.33}$$

ANALYZING MANAGERIAL DECISIONS

## HOW H. J. HEINZ MINIMIZES ITS SHIPPING COSTS

The H. J. Heinz Company manufactures ketchup in a variety of factories scattered around the United States and distributes this ketchup to warehouses that are also scattered around the country. To determine how much ketchup each factory should send to each warehouse, Heinz has used linear programming techniques. The capacities of each factory, the requirements of each warehouse, and freight rates are given below:*

| | Factory | | | | | | | | | | | | Daily requirements (cwt.) |
| | I | II | III | IV | V | VI | VII | VIII | IX | X | XI | XII | |
| | Freight rates (cents per cwt.) | | | | | | | | | | | | |
|---|---|---|---|---|---|---|---|---|---|---|---|---|---|
| Warehouse | | | | | | | | | | | | | |
| A | 16 | 16 | 6 | 13 | 24 | 13 | 6 | 31 | 37 | 34 | 37 | 40 | 1,820 |
| B | 20 | 18 | 8 | 10 | 22 | 11 | 8 | 29 | 33 | 25 | 35 | 38 | 1,530 |
| C | 30 | 23 | 8 | 9 | 14 | 7 | 9 | 22 | 29 | 20 | 38 | 35 | 2,360 |
| D | 10 | 15 | 10 | 8 | 10 | 15 | 13 | 19 | 19 | 15 | 28 | 34 | 100 |
| E | 31 | 23 | 16 | 10 | 10 | 16 | 20 | 14 | 17 | 17 | 25 | 28 | 280 |
| F | 24 | 14 | 19 | 13 | 13 | 14 | 18 | 9 | 14 | 13 | 29 | 25 | 730 |
| G | 27 | 23 | 7 | 11 | 23 | 8 | 16 | 6 | 10 | 11 | 16 | 28 | 940 |
| H | 34 | 25 | 15 | 4 | 27 | 15 | 11 | 9 | 16 | 17 | 13 | 16 | 1,130 |
| J | 38 | 29 | 17 | 11 | 16 | 27 | 17 | 19 | 8 | 18 | 19 | 11 | 4,150 |
| K | 42 | 43 | 21 | 22 | 16 | 10 | 21 | 18 | 24 | 16 | 17 | 15 | 3,700 |
| L | 44 | 49 | 25 | 23 | 18 | 6 | 13 | 19 | 15 | 12 | 10 | 13 | 2,560 |
| M | 49 | 40 | 29 | 21 | 10 | 15 | 14 | 21 | 12 | 29 | 14 | 20 | 1,710 |
| N | 56 | 58 | 36 | 37 | 6 | 25 | 8 | 19 | 9 | 21 | 15 | 26 | 580 |
| P | 59 | 57 | 44 | 33 | 5 | 21 | 6 | 10 | 8 | 33 | 15 | 18 | 30 |
| Q | 68 | 54 | 40 | 38 | 8 | 24 | 7 | 19 | 10 | 23 | 23 | 23 | 2,840 |
| R | 66 | 71 | 47 | 43 | 16 | 33 | 12 | 26 | 19 | 20 | 25 | 31 | 1,510 |
| S | 72 | 58 | 50 | 51 | 20 | 42 | 22 | 16 | 15 | 13 | 20 | 21 | 970 |
| T | 74 | 54 | 57 | 55 | 26 | 53 | 26 | 19 | 14 | 7 | 15 | 6 | 5,110 |
| U | 71 | 75 | 57 | 60 | 30 | 44 | 30 | 30 | 41 | 8 | 23 | 37 | 3,540 |
| Y | 73 | 72 | 63 | 56 | 37 | 49 | 40 | 31 | 31 | 10 | 8 | 25 | 4,410 |
| Daily capacity (cwt.) | 10,000 | 9,000 | 3,000 | 2,700 | 500 | 1,200 | 700 | 300 | 500 | 1,200 | 2,000 | 8,900 | 40,000 |

The optimal daily shipment from each factory to each warehouse is shown in the table on page 359. For example, all of warehouse A's ketchup should come from factory I.

(a) According to officials of the H. J. Heinz Company, one of the most important advantages gained from the introduction of linear programming was that senior members of the distribution department no longer had to spend so much time preparing shipping programs.

* A. Henderson and R. Schlaifer, "Mathematical Programming," in E. Mansfield, ed., *Managerial Economics and Operations Research,* 5th ed. These data are approximate, but adequate for our purposes.

|  | Factory | | | | | | | | | | | | |
|  | I | II | III | IV | V | VI | VII | VIII | IX | X | XI | XII | Total |
|---|---|---|---|---|---|---|---|---|---|---|---|---|---|
| **Warehouse** | | | | | | | | | | | | | |
| A | 1,820 | | | | | | | | | | | | 1,820 |
| B | 1,530 | | | | | | | | | | | | 1,530 |
| C | | 2,360 | | | | | | | | | | | 2,360 |
| D | 100 | | | | | | | | | | | | 100 |
| E | | 280 | | | | | | | | | | | 280 |
| F | | 730 | | | | | | | | | | | 730 |
| G | 940 | | | | | | | | | | | | 940 |
| H | | | | 1,130 | | | | | | | | | 1,130 |
| J | | 4,150 | | | | | | | | | | | 4,150 |
| K | 700 | | 3,000 | | | | | | | | | | 3,700 |
| L | 1,360 | | | | | 1,200 | | | | | | | 2,560 |
| M | | 140 | | 1,570 | | | | | | | | | 1,710 |
| N | 580 | | | | | | | | | | | | 580 |
| P | | | | | | | | 30 | | | | | 30 |
| Q | | 1,340 | | | 500 | | | | 500 | | | 500 | 2,840 |
| R | 810 | | | | | | 700 | | | | | | 1,510 |
| S | | | | | | | | 90 | | | | 880 | 970 |
| T | | | | | | | | | | | | 5,110 | 5,110 |
| U | 2,160 | | | | | | | 180 | | 1,200 | | | 3,540 |
| Y | | | | | | | | | | | 2,000 | 2,410 | 4,410 |
| **Total** | 10,000 | 9,000 | 3,000 | 2,700 | 500 | 1,200 | 700 | 300 | 500 | 1,200 | 2,000 | 8,900 | 40,000 |

Who did it instead? (b) They also said that an important advantage of linear programming was the peace of mind resulting from being sure that the program is the lowest-cost program possible. Does this mean that if the data on freight rates are incorrect, the program will still be optimal? (c) What is the H. J. Heinz Company trying to minimize or maximize? (d) Explain in detail the nature of the constraints.

*Solution* (a) A computer, together with some lower-level people. (b) No. The model used here is essentially the same as that used to minimize shipping costs in the case of the Essex Corporation. If the data concerning freight rates, daily requirements, or daily capacities are wrong, the results obviously may be wrong as well. (c) Heinz is trying to minimize its total freight bill, which can be represented as $\sum_i \sum_j U_{ij} V_{ij}$, where $U_{ij}$ equals the freight rate from factory $i$ to warehouse $j$, and $V_{ij}$ equals the amount shipped per day from factory $i$ to warehouse $j$. (d) One set of constraints says that the total shipments from each factory cannot exceed its capacity. That is, $\sum_j V_{ij} \leq K_i$, where $K_i$ is the capacity of the $i$th factory. Another set of constraints says that the total shipments to each warehouse must meet its requirements. That is, $\sum_i V_{ij} \geq R_j$, where $R_j$ is the required total shipment to the $j$th warehouse. In addition, there are nonnegativity constraints saying that the shipment from each factory to each warehouse must be nonnegative. That is, $V_{ij} \geq 0$.

---

## EVALUATING THE ORGANIZATION OF A SHIPPING PROGRAM*

A leading manufacturer and distributor of a consumer good was organized around the principle of decentralized management. In accord with this principle, each of the firm's six regional warehouses was under the supervision of a regional sales manager, who decided how much of the firm's product to order from each of the firm's plants. Because the regional warehouse had to pay the freight costs, it was felt that each regional sales manager would formulate its orders so as to minimize both its own freight costs and those of the firm as a whole.

But one of the firm's plants was located far from all of the firm's warehouses, and none of the regional sales managers willingly ordered from it. Only when the other plants turned down orders, pleading lack of capacity to fulfill them, did the regional sales managers order from this distant plant. In general, the other plants accepted orders on a "first come, first served" basis, and turned down those that were received last.

If you were a consultant to this firm, what suggestions would you make concerning the organization of the firm's shipping program?

* For a much more detailed examination of a similar situation, see N. Harlan, C. Christenson, and R. Vancil, *Managerial Economics: Text and Cases* (Homewood, Ill.: Irwin, 1962).

---

Third, $A, B, \ldots, F$ must be nonnegative:

$$A \geq 0, B \geq 0, C \geq 0, D \geq 0, E \geq 0, F \geq 0. \qquad (9.34)$$

As explained in detail in the chapter appendix, computer programs are generally used in practice to solve linear programming problems. Figure 9.11 shows the computer printout for this problem. (For an explanation of such printouts, see the appendix.) Based on this printout, the Essex Corporation should ship 1,500 tons per day from the Florida plant to the Illinois warehouse, 2,500 tons per day from the Florida plant to the New York warehouse, 2,500 tons per day from the Texas plant to the California warehouse, and 500 tons per day from the Texas plant to the Illinois warehouse. The minimum shipping cost is $51,500 per day.

## WHAT THE FEDERAL RESERVE TOLD THE BANKS

Based on previous sections of this chapter, one might get the impression that linear programming is applicable only to manufacturing and logistic problems. This is by no means true. For example, the Federal Reserve Bank

```
$ LINDO
 LINDO (UC 2 MARCH 85)
 : MIN 15A + 10B + 7C + 6D + 8E + 11F
 ? SUBJECT TO
 ? A + D > 2500
 ? B + E > 2000
 ? C + F > 2500
 ? A + B + C < 4000
 ? D + E + F < 3000
 ? END

 : LOOK ALL

 MIN     15 A + 10 B + 7 C + 6 D + 8 E + 11 F
 SUBJECT TO
         2) A + D >= 2500
         3) B + E >= 2000
         4) C + F >= 2500
         5) A + B + C <= 4000
         6) D + E + F <= 3000
 END

 : GO
     LP OPTIMUM FOUND AT STEP 4

          OBJECTIVE FUNCTION VALUE

 1)       51500.0000

 VARIABLE            VALUE                REDUCED COST
        A              0.000000              7.000000
        B           1500.000000              0.000000
        C           2500.000000              0.000000
        D           2500.000000              0.000000
        E            500.000000              0.000000
        F              0.000000              6.000000

 ROW            SLACK OR SURPLUS           DUAL PRICES
        2)             0.000000             -8.000000
        3)             0.000000            -10.000000
        4)             0.000000             -7.000000
        5)             0.000000              0.000000
        6)             0.000000              2.000000

 NO. ITERATIONS=          4
```

FIGURE 9.11  *Solution of Essex Corporation's Problem*

of Richmond has instructed commercial banks in the use of linear programming.[9] Consider the illustrative case of the First National Bank, which has only two types of assets, loans and investments. Because the First National Bank has $400 million that must be allocated between these two types of assets,

$$I + L \le 400, \tag{9.35}$$

where $I$ is the amount of investments, and $L$ is the amount of loans made by the bank.

[9] A. Broaddus, "Linear Programming: A New Approach to Bank Portfolio Management," *Federal Reserve Bank of Richmond Monthly Review* (November 1972).

The First National Bank wants its loans to equal at least $150 million, so

$$L \geq 150. \tag{9.36}$$

Also, since investments can be turned more readily into cash than loans, the bank wants the amount of its investments to equal at least 20 percent of the total of its loans and investments. Thus,

$$I \geq .20 \, (L + I),$$

or

$$L \leq 4I. \tag{9.37}$$

The bank's managers want to maximize profit. If the bank earns a 16 percent return on its loans and a 10 percent return on its investments, its profit equals

$$\pi = .16L + .10I. \tag{9.38}$$

Thus, the bank managers' problem is to maximize $\pi$ subject to the constraints in (9.35), (9.36), and (9.37) and the constraints that $I > 0$ and $L > 0$. This is a linear programming problem. It can be solved graphically, as shown in Figure 9.12. If all the constraints are met, the bank must choose a point in the shaded area in Figure 9.12. To see this, note that the bank must choose a point on or above the line where $L = 150$ in order to meet the constraint in (9.36), it must choose a point on or below the line where $I + L = 400$ to meet the constraint in (9.35), and it must choose a point on or below the line where $L = 4I$ to meet the constraint in (9.37).

From equation (9.38), we can construct the isoprofit lines in Figure 9.12. To maximize profit, the bank's managers should choose the point in the shaded area on the highest isoprofit line. Clearly, this point is $A$, where the bank devotes $320 million to loans and $80 million to investments. This example, while extremely simple, is a useful illustration of linear programming's power in solving nonmanufacturing problems. Without question, this technique is just as relevant in finance or marketing as in production.

# SUMMARY

1. Linear programming is a technique that allows decision makers to solve maximization and minimization problems where there are certain constraints that limit what can be done. It is useful to look at production decisions from the programming point of view because, unlike the conventional theory in Chapter 6, programming does not take the production function as being given to the manager before he or she attacks the problem. Also, the programming analysis is easier to apply in many respects, and powerful computational techniques are available to obtain solutions.

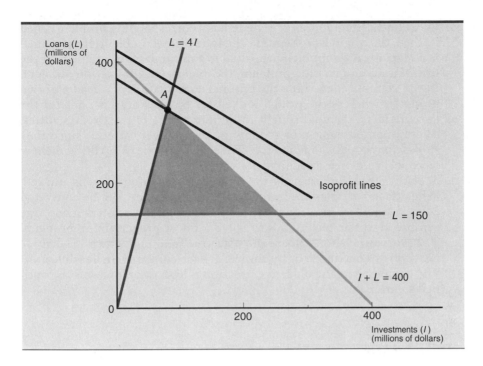

*FIGURE 9.12  Optimal Portfolio of Loans and Investments*  The optimal point is *A*, where the bank invests $320 million in loans and $80 million in investments.

2. A manager often has to choose which one (or which combination) of a number of alternative processes to use to produce a particular product, given that the firm has only a limited amount of certain inputs. We solved the problem by graphical techniques. Isoprofit curves were constructed and superimposed on a diagram showing the feasible input combinations, and the point was chosen that, among those that were feasible, was on the highest isoprofit curve. In addition, we considered a variant of this problem in which the firm is no longer constrained by limitations on inputs.

3. Frequently, a firm produces more than one product, and has various fixed facilities that set limits on the amount of each product that can be produced. The firm's managers must determine the optimal combination of outputs of the products. This problem was also solved by graphical means, with isoprofit lines superimposed on a diagram showing feasible output combinations. In addition, in the context of this example, we discussed the fact that the optimal solution of a linear programming problem will lie at one of the extreme points or corners of the feasible area.

4. Every linear programming problem has a corresponding problem called its dual; the original problem is called the primal problem. If the primal is a maximization problem, the dual is a minimization problem; if the primal is a minimization problem, the dual is a maximization problem. In the example concerning the optimal combination of outputs of two products, whereas the primal looked for optimal output rates for the two products, the dual sought to impute values to the fixed facilities. These imputed values, or shadow prices, are very useful, since they show what would happen to the firm's profits if the company somehow were able to increase each type of capacity.

5. A slack variable represents the amount of an input that is unused. When slack variables are introduced, the constraints can be converted from inequalities into equations. Once such a conversion is made, one can use algebraic techniques to solve a linear programming problem. The procedure is to evaluate the objective function, which is what we are trying to maximize or minimize, at each corner of the feasible area. The corner where the objective function is highest or lowest is the optimal solution.

## PROBLEMS

1. Martin Casey, the executive vice president of the Summit Company, must allocate the firm's workers and machine tools to the production of three types of metal file cabinets, with the following characteristics:

| Input requirements or profit | Product | | |
| --- | --- | --- | --- |
| | Large cabinets | Medium cabinets | Small cabinets |
| Hours of labor per cabinet | 25 | 15 | 10 |
| Hours of machine time per cabinet | 40 | 15 | 5 |
| Profit per cabinet | $50 | $25 | $12.50 |

The firm has a total of 3,500 hours of labor and 2,500 hours of machine time that it can use per day.
(a) What is the objective function?
(b) What are the constraints?
(c) How many hours of labor and machine time should Mr. Casey allocate to the production of each product?

2. Frank Chidester, the chief engineer of the Cartwright Company, must decide which of three processes to use to produce the firm's product, paper napkins. The characteristics of each process are given as follows:

| Input requirements | | Process | |
|---|---|---|---|
| (per ton of output) | A | B | C |
| Hours of skilled labor | 2 | 4 | 1 |
| Hours of unskilled labor | 1 | 1 | 1 |
| Hours of machine time | 3 | 1 | 5 |

The price of an hour of skilled labor is $11; the price of an hour of unskilled labor is $5; and the price of an hour of machine time is $15. The firm is committed to produce 100 tons of output per day, and it can hire as much of each input as it wants.

(a) What is the objective function?

(b) What are the constraints?

(c) Which process (or processes) should Mr. Chidester choose?

(d) Is this really a linear programming problem? Why or why not?

3. The Adams Company can use three processes, X, Y, and Z, to produce a particular good. To make one unit of the good, process X requires 2 hours of labor and 1 hour of machine time, process Y requires 1.5 hours of labor and 1.5 hours of machine time, and process Z requires 1.1 hours of labor and 2.2 hours of machine time.

(a) Using a graph where labor-hours are measured along the vertical axis and machine hours are measured along the horizontal axis, draw the rays corresponding to the three processes.

(b) Using the graph in part (a), draw the isoquant corresponding to an output of 100 units of the good.

4. Based on the use of linear programming, the vice president of the Summers Company finds that the shadow price of skilled labor is $15 per hour, and the shadow price of sewing machine time is zero.

(a) What are the implications of the shadow price of skilled labor?

(b) What are the implications of the shadow price of sewing machine time?

5. Consider Martin Casey's situation (described in problem 1) once again. Suppose that he wants to determine how much an extra hour of labor is worth and how much an extra hour of machine time is worth.

(a) What is the dual problem?

(b) What is the solution to the dual problem?

(c) How much is an extra hour of each input worth?

6. The Murray Company uses two inputs, machine-hours of finishing capacity and hours of labor.

(a) If there are at most 2,000 machine-hours and 200 labor-hours available per week, draw the set of feasible input combinations in a graph.

(b) Process X utilizes 1 machine-hour and 1 labor-hour to produce a unit of output. Graph the ray depicting this process.

(c) Process Y utilizes 1/2 machine-hour and 2 labor-hours to produce a unit of output, and process Z utilizes 2 machine-hours and 1/2 labor-hour to produce a unit of output. Graph the rays for these additional two processes.

(d) Graph the isoquant corresponding to 1,000 units of output (given the three processes described above).

(e) Suppose that the firm can rent all of the machine-hours it wants at $10 an hour and all of the labor-hours it wants at $10 an hour. Which process should it use to produce 1,000 units of output?

7. In its Mexican plant, the Brown Company can use three processes, A, B, and C, to produce a particular good. To make one unit of the good, process A requires 2 hours of labor and 1 hour of machine time, process B requires 1.5 hours of labor and 1.5 hours of machine time, and process C requires 1.1 hours of labor and 2.2 hours of machine time. The firm must pay $3 per hour for labor and $2 per hour for machine time, but it cannot use more than 120 hours of machine time per week, since this is all that is available in the short run.

(a) If it has committed itself to produce 100 units of the product per week, how many units should it produce with process A?

(b) How many units should it produce with process B?

(c) How many units should it produce with process C?

8. In problem 7, suppose the Brown Company can use more than 120 hours of machine-time per week. Under these circumstances, how many units should it produce with process A? process B? process C?

9. According to the computer printout in Figure 9.13 on page 370, the shadow price (dual price) of a minute of labor time is 2.5 cents, and the shadow price of a minute of machine time is 65 cents.

(a) If George Kramer (described in the Appendix) can hire additional labor at $5 an hour, should he hire any additional labor?

(b) If he can hire additional machines at $35 per hour, should he hire any additional machines?

10. The Dartmouth Company has plants in Kentucky and Oregon, and warehouses in Florida, Oklahoma, and Arizona. The cost of shipping a ton of its product from each plant to each warehouse is as follows:

| | Warehouse | | |
| --- | --- | --- | --- |
| Plant | Florida | Oklahoma | Arizona |
| Kentucky | $4 | $6 | $7 |
| Oregon | 11 | 7 | 6 |

The daily outputs of the plants cannot exceed 4,000 tons (Kentucky) and 5,000 tons (Oregon). The daily demands of the warehouses cannot fall below 2,500 tons (Florida), 3,500 tons (Oklahoma), and 3,000 tons (Arizona).

(a) What is the objective function?

(b) What are the constraints?

*(c) To minimize total shipping costs, how many tons of product should the Kentucky plant ship to each of the warehouses?

*(d) To minimize total shipping costs, how many tons of product should the Oregon plant ship to each of the warehouses?

MANAGERIAL ECONOMICS IN CONTEXT

## APPLE'S LISA-MACINTOSH DEVELOPMENT PROJECT†

In 1982, Steve Jobs, the chief executive officer of Apple Computer, started the development of a new family of products—the Lisa-Macintosh personal computers. This new family of products was aimed at the business market and the professional personal computer market, not the educational market, where Apple was particularly strong. The Lisa-Macintosh development effort was carried out by a small team reporting directly to Jobs. It was an ambitious project assigned to very competent people who had day-to-day contact with the firm's top management.

The Lisa, priced at $8,000 to $10,000 per unit, was viewed initially as the central member of the product family. The idea was to develop it first, have it show the power of the new technology it would embody, and use it to help launch a higher-volume product (that would be derived from it): the Macintosh. Both the Lisa and Macintosh were regarded as primarily engineering projects; marketing received secondary consideration. The features of the Lisa did not jibe at all well with the needs of corporate offices, which were particularly interested in field support, application software, and connectivity. The Macintosh seemed to be more appropriate for small businesses and universities than for large corporations.

Although highly innovative in design, Lisa's sales never lived up to expectations. Macintosh's design had to be changed a number of times before it was suitable for its market. Originally, the Mac's introduction was scheduled for March 1983, but it was postponed several times and did not occur until early 1984, when a television ad was aired during the Super Bowl that showed IBM as Big Brother and Macintosh as an alternative business computer. Regardless of the ads, the Mac did not make a big

*Steve Jobs*

---

\* These questions are for students who can use a computer package like LINDO. (See the appendix.)

hit in the business market at which it was aimed, one reason being the lack of software available.

At first, Apple planned to have a highly automated plant ready to produce the Macintosh when it was first marketed. But when the plant, which cost about $20 million, was finally started up in early 1984, it was only partially automated, and within eight months of its opening, about $7 million of its automation equipment was removed because of lack of effectiveness. One problem may have been that Apple's previous plants were not nearly so highly automated. Until 1981, its production experience had been limited largely to relatively labor-intensive assembly work.

Apple's earnings fell dramatically, owing in part to the shortcomings of the Lisa-Macintosh development project. (See Table 1.) On September 17, 1985, Steve Jobs resigned as chairman. His successor, John Sculley, feeling that Apple had excessive manufacturing capacity, closed the firm's Dallas plant, and over 20 percent of the firm's work force was let go. Apple was a quite different company from what it was at the start of the Lisa-Macintosh development project.

(a) If the average price Apple received for a Macintosh was $1,500, and if the average variable cost was $1,200, what was the break-even point, if the total fixed costs were $15 million per year?

(b) If the time-cost trade-off function for the Macintosh project was such that a 1-year reduction in the duration of the project would have cost $2 million, what factors would you consider in determining whether the extra $2 million should have been spent?

(c) Was Apple's input combination for the production of the Macintosh on or off the production function? That is, was it efficient or inefficient?

(d) What were the disadvantages in developing the Lisa and Macin-

TABLE 1   Income Statement, Apple Computer

|  | Three months ended: | |
|---|---|---|
|  | September 27, 1985 | September 28, 1984 |
| Net sales | $409,709 | $477,400 |
| Cost and expenses | 373,899 | 432,528 |
| Operating income before provision for consolidation | 35,810 | 44,872 |
| Provision for consolidation | 3,373 | — |
| Interest and other income, net | 4,654 | 3,861 |
| Income before income taxes | 43,837 | 48,733 |
| Provision for income taxes | 21,480 | 17,927 |
| Net income | 22,357 | 30,806 |
| Earnings per share | $.36 | $.50 |

*Source:* T. Wheelen and J. D. Hunger, *Cases in Strategic Management and Business Policy.* All items except per-share amounts are in thousands of dollars.

tosh without giving marketing more than secondary consideration?

(e) Is it generally best to use the most capital-intensive and most highly automated factory possi-

ble? Why or why not?

(f) Might linear programming have been useful in deciding which type of production facility to construct and how to operate it? If so, how?

---

† The material in this case came from R. Hayes, S. Wheelwright, and K. Clark, *Dynamic Manufacturing* (New York: Free Press, 1988); and T. Wheelen and J. D. Hunger, *Cases in Strategic Management and Business Policy* (Reading, Mass.: Addison-Wesley, 1987). Also, see P. Feddeler, T. Wheelen, and D. Croll, "Apple Computer, Inc., 1987 ... The Second Decade", a case in the study guide accompanying this textbook.

---

# APPENDIX: A SOFTWARE PACKAGE TO SOLVE LINEAR PROGRAMMING PROBLEMS

In practice, most linear programming problems are solved using computer programs, not graphical or algebraic techniques. One popular and easy-to-use software package for linear programming problems is called LINDO (Linear Interactive Discrete Optimizer). Whether or not you have this package, it is worthwhile to describe it briefly, to illustrate how easy it is to solve linear programming problems with computers.

Once LINDO is accessed on your computer, a colon will appear in the far left-hand side of the screen. LINDO must be instructed to minimize or maximize whatever objective function we are using. To do so, we enter "MIN" or "MAX" and the objective function after the colon. We next enter "SUBJECT TO," which indicates to LINDO that what follows will be the constraints. When all of the constraints have been entered,[10] "END" is entered, which indicates to LINDO that all of the information needed to solve the problem has been provided. Finally, "LOOK ALL" is entered, which asks LINDO to show us the objective function and constraints that were entered. This is a useful check to insure that no errors have been made. We are now ready to run the program and solve the linear programming problem. After instructing LINDO to "GO" after the colon, the solution to the problem is given.[11]

To illustrate, consider George Kramer, who owns a firm that produces scarves and neckties. He realizes a profit of 50 cents per scarf and $2 per necktie. A scarf requires only 30 seconds of labor to produce, whereas a necktie takes 15 minutes of labor. In all, Kramer has 12,000 minutes of labor per week that can be allocated to producing either scarves or neckties. The firm's machines can be used to make both scarves and neckties. A scarf requires 0.75 minutes of machine time; a necktie

---

[10] When entering the constraints, LINDO interprets > as greater than *or equal to* and < as less than *or equal to*. This is because there is no way on many keyboards to input "greater than or equal to" or "less than or equal to." Note that when we enter the "LOOK ALL" command, LINDO has read these inequalities in the above-mentioned fashion.

[11] For present purposes, you may ignore the number of iterations and the step at which the solution is found. This information will not be used here.

requires 2.5 minutes of machine time. In all, the firm has 5,000 minutes of machine time available to produce these goods each week.

Since George Kramer wishes to maximize profits, his objective function can be written as follows:

$$\text{Maximize } Z = .5X + 2Y, \tag{9.39}$$

where $Z$ is his total weekly profit, $X$ is the number of scarves produced per week, and $Y$ is the number of neckties produced per week. The labor constraint is

$$.5X + 15Y \le 12,000, \tag{9.40}$$

where the coefficients of $X$ and $Y$ are the minutes of labor needed to produce a scarf and necktie, respectively, and 12,000 is the total number of labor minutes at Kramer's disposal per week. The machinery constraint is

$$.75X + 2.5Y \le 5,000, \tag{9.41}$$

where the coefficients of $X$ and $Y$ are the numbers of minutes of machine time needed to produce a scarf and a necktie, respectively, and 5,000 is the total number of machine-minutes available each week.

Using LINDO, the first step is to enter the objective function and the constraints, as indicated in Figure 9.13, which shows the computer printout for the problem. After this information is entered, we can use the "LOOK ALL" command to check its accuracy. The "GO" command tells LINDO to solve the problem. LINDO pro-

```
$ LINDO
 LINDO (UC 2 MARCH 85)
: MAX .5X + 2Y
? SUBJECT TO
? .5X + 15Y < 12000
? .75X + 2.5Y < 5000
? END

: LOOK ALL

MAX      0.5 X + 2 Y
SUBJECT TO
        2) 0.5 X + 15 Y <= 12000
        3) 0.75 X + 2.5 Y <= 5,000
END

: GO
        LP OPTIMUM FOUND AT STEP  2

                    OBJECTIVE FUNCTION VALUE

1)                  3550.00000
VARIABLE            VALUE               REDUCED COST
        X           4500.000000             0.000000
        Y            650.000000             0.000000

    ROW             SLACK OR SURPLUS        DUAL PRICES
        2)           0.000000               0.025000
        3)           0.000000               0.650000

NO. ITERATIONS=      2
```

**FIGURE 9.13** *Solution of George Kramer's Problem*

vides the "objective function value," which is the maximum profit Mr. Kramer can obtain given the constraints he faces: $3,550 per week. It also provides the optimal mix of scarves $(X)$ and neckties $(Y)$ that the firm should produce. In order to maximize profits, given the constraints, Kramer should produce 4,500 scarves and 650 neckties weekly. The column labeled "Slack or Surplus" tells us that the slack variable for both inputs equals zero; that is, that each minute of labor and machine time is being utilized when this product mix is used. Further, the column labeled "Dual Prices" provides us with the shadow prices for labor and machine time. The shadow price (or dual price) for a minute of labor time is 2.5 cents, and the shadow price for a minute of machine time is 65 cents.

# Part Four

# Market Structure, Strategic Behavior, and Pricing

# Chapter 10
# Perfect Competition, Monopoly, and Monopolistic Competition

In 1992, Amgen was one of the leading lights of the high-tech biotechnology industry; it produced EPO, an antianemia agent. Two central decisions that Gordon Binder, chairman of the company, and his colleagues had to make were: What should be the firm's output rate? What price should it charge?

Regardless of whether a firm is high-tech or low-tech, young or old, its executives must address these same questions, and the answers depend on the structure of the market. In this chapter, we take up the results for three market structures: perfect competition, monopoly, and monopolistic competition. (In the next chapter, we will study the fourth market structure—oligopoly.) Besides considering how firms should price their products and set their output rates, we also take up the way in which they should determine their advertising expenditures. Although the model presented here is a simple one, it should provide some useful insights into this difficult and important problem.

## MARKET STRUCTURE

As pointed out in Chapter 1, a **market** consists of a group of firms and individuals who are in touch with each other in order to buy or sell some good or service. Economists have generally found it useful to classify markets into four broad types: **perfect competition, monopoly, monopolistic competition,** and **oligopoly.** In perfect competition and monopolistic competition, there are *many* sellers, each of which produces only a small part of the industry's output. In monopoly, on the other hand, the industry consists of only a *single* seller. Oligopoly is an intermediate case where there are a *few* sellers. Thus, Baltimore Gas and Electric, if it is the only supplier of electricity in a particular market, is a monopoly. And since there are only a small number of automobile manufacturers, the market for automobiles is an oligopoly.

Market structures vary substantially in the extent to which an individual firm controls its price. A firm under perfect competition has *no control* over price. For example, a farm producing corn (which for present purposes can be regarded as a perfectly competitive firm) has no control over the price of corn. On the other hand, a monopolist is likely to have *considerable control* over price. In the absence of public regulation, Baltimore Gas and Electric would have considerable control over the price of electricity in Baltimore. A firm under monopolistic competition or oligopoly is likely to have *less* control over price than a monopolist and *more* control over price than a perfectly competitive firm.

These market structures also vary in the extent to which the firms in an industry produce standardized (that is, identical) products. Firms in a perfectly competitive market all produce *identical* products. Thus, one farmer's wheat is essentially the same as another farmer's. In a monopolistically competitive industry like shirt manufacturing, firms produce *somewhat different* products. One firm's shirts differ in style and quality from another firm's shirts. In an oligopoly, firms *sometimes*, but not always, produce identical products. And in a monopoly, there can be *no difference* among firms in their products, since the industry contains only one firm.

How easily firms can enter the industry differs from one market structure to another. In perfect competition, **barriers to entry** are *low.* Thus, only a small investment is required to enter many parts of agriculture. Similarly, there are *low* barriers to entry in monopolistic competition. But in oligopolies such as autos and oil refining, there tend to be *very considerable* barriers to entry because it is so expensive to build an auto plant or an oil refinery (and for many other reasons too). In monopoly, entry is blocked; once entry occurs, the monopoly no longer exists.

Market structures also differ in the extent to which firms compete on the basis of advertising and differences in product characteristics, rather than price. In perfect competition, there is *no nonprice competition.* (If every farmer produces identical corn, and has to take the market price, why devote some of the proceeds to advertising?) In monopolistic competition, there is *considerable emphasis* on nonprice competition. Thus, shirt manufacturers compete by trying to develop better styles and by advertising to accentuate the advantages of their product lines. Oligopolies also tend to rely *heavily* on nonprice competition. For example, computer firms try to

**TABLE 10.1** *Characteristics of Perfect Competition, Monopolistic Competition, Oligopoly, and Monopoly*

| Market structure | Examples | Number of producers | Type of product | Power of firm over price | Barriers to entry | Nonprice competition |
|---|---|---|---|---|---|---|
| Perfect competition | Parts of agriculture are reasonably close | Many | Standardized | None | Low | None |
| Monopolistic competition | Retail trade | Many | Differentiated | Some | Low | Advertising and product differentiation |
| Oligopoly | Computers, oil, steel | Few | Standardized or differentiated | Some | High | Advertising and product differentiation |
| Monopoly | Public utilities | One | Unique product | Considerable | Very high | Advertising |

increase their sales by building better computers and by advertising. Monopolists also engage in advertising, although this advertising is directed not at capturing the sales of other firms in the industry, since no other firms exist, but rather at increasing total market demand.

Table 10.1 provides a summary of many of the key features of each market structure. Be sure to look this table over before proceeding further.

# MARKET PRICE UNDER PERFECT COMPETITION

In a perfectly competitive industry, market price, as we saw in Chapter 1, is determined by the market demand and supply curves. There is a market demand curve, which shows the total amount that individual buyers of the commodity will purchase, and a market supply curve, which shows the total amount that individual suppliers of the commodity will supply. Figure 10.1 shows the market demand and supply curves for a good produced in a perfectly competitive market. As is ordinarily the case, the market supply curve slopes upward to the right. That is, increases in price generally result in higher industry output because firms find it profitable to expand production. Also, in accord with Chapters 1 and 3, the market demand curve slopes downward to the right. That is, increases in price generally result in less of the product being demanded.

To determine the equilibrium price, which is the price that will eventu-

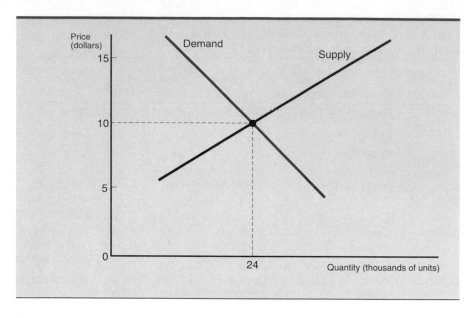

**FIGURE 10.1   Determination of Price in a Perfectly Competitive Market**   Equilibrium price is $10, and equilibrium quantity is 24 thousand units.

ally prevail in this market,[1] we must find the price where market supply equals market demand. The demand curve in Figure 10.1 is

$$P = 22 - 0.5Q_D, \qquad (10.1)$$

where $P$ is the price (in dollars) of this good, and $Q_D$ is the quantity demanded (in thousands of units). The supply curve in Figure 10.1 is

$$P = 4 + 0.25Q_S, \qquad (10.2)$$

where $Q_S$ is the quantity supplied. Since the equilibrium price is at the level where $Q_D$ (the quantity demanded) equals $Q_S$ (the quantity supplied),

$$22 - 0.5Q = 4 + 0.25Q$$

$$18 = 0.75Q$$

$$Q = 24.$$

Substituting 24 for $Q_D$ in equation (10.1), we find that $P = \$10$. [If we substitute 24 for $Q_S$ in equation (10.2), we get the same result.] Thus, as shown in Figure 10.1, price would be expected to equal $10, and output would be expected to equal 24 thousand units.

[1] Recall from Chapter 1 that an equilibrium price is a price that can be maintained. If conditions do not change, the actual price tends to equal the equilibrium price.

## FORECASTING THE PRICE OF SALMON*

A major producer of consumer goods (the same firm discussed on page 97) set out in 1987 to forecast the price of fresh salmon in 1990. Such a forecast was needed in deciding whether or not the firm should enter the business of supplying salmon. Its analysts estimated the quantity of fresh salmon that would be supplied in 1990. Because of substantial plans to expand the production of farmed Atlantic and Pacific salmon in Canada, Chile, Japan, and Ireland, this projected supply was considerably greater than the actual supply at the time the forecast was made. In addition, the firm's analysts estimated the quantity of fresh salmon that would be demanded in 1990, using the sorts of techniques described in previous chapters. Their results showed that if the price of salmon remained unchanged at its 1987 level, the quantity sup-

plied would exceed the quantity demanded by about 15 percent in 1990.

The firm's analysts also estimated the price elasticity of demand for fresh salmon to be about 1.5. This estimate too was based on the sorts of techniques described in previous chapters. Like the other estimates presented above, it was regarded as being rough, but useful.

If you had been a consultant to this firm in 1987, and if you had been asked to use these estimates to forecast the change in the salmon price from 1987 to 1990, what would have been your forecast? (The firm's analysts believed that the quantity supplied in 1990 would be approximately equal to their estimates, regardless of whatever changes occurred in price between 1987 and 1990.)

* This section is based on an actual case, although the numbers and situation have been disguised somewhat.

While Figure 10.1 shows that both total quantity demanded and total quantity supplied depend on price, this does not mean that an individual firm can affect price. According to the market demand curve in equation (10.1),

$$P = 22 - 0.5Q.$$

If there are 1,000 firms in this market, each produces, on the average, only 24 units of the product. Even if an individual firm doubles its output (from 24 to 48 units), the effect on price is minuscule. Specifically, an increase in output of 24 units results in a price reduction of only 1.2 cents—or about $\frac{1}{10}$ of 1 percent.[2] What this means is that the demand curve for the output of

[2] If output increases by 24 units, $Q$ increases by .024, since $Q$ is measured in thousands of units. If $Q$ increases by .024, $P$ falls by 0.5(.024) = .012, according to the demand curve in equation (10.1). Since $P$ is measured in dollars, this amounts to 1.2 cents.

an individual firm under perfect competition is essentially *horizontal*. Thus, whereas the demand curve for the output of the entire industry slopes downward to the right (as shown in Figure 10.1), the demand curve for the output of any single firm can be regarded as horizontal.

## SHIFTS IN SUPPLY AND DEMAND CURVES

Shifts in the market supply or demand curves result in changes in price. (Recall Chapter 1.) For example, if the supply curve in Figure 10.1 shifts to the left, the price would be expected to rise. Such shifts in market supply and demand curves are of the utmost significance to managers, who must try to anticipate their occurrence and their effects—and respond to them as best they can. Consider the case of the Coca-Cola Company, which takes about 10 percent of all sugar sold in the United States. Because of shifts in sugar's supply and demand curves (which resulted in worldwide shortages), the price of beet and cane sugar rose from 19 cents per pound in September 1978 to 26 cents per pound in January 1979. The effect on Coca-Cola was particularly severe, since a change of 1 cent per pound in sugar prices can cause a $20 million swing in the firm's operating profits. Its managers responded (in accord with the principles set forth in Chapter 6) by switching from sugar to high-fructose corn sweeteners, which are cheaper than sugar.

For present purposes, the point is that managers must understand the factors affecting the supply and demand curves of products they buy and sell. There is no need to dwell at length on the factors causing shifts in demand curves, since they have been discussed in Chapter 3. But it is worth recalling from Chapter 1 that two of the most important factors causing shifts in supply curves are improvements in technology (discussed in Chapter 7) and changes in input prices. Improvements in technology tend to shift a product's supply curve to the right, since they permit firms to reduce their costs. On the other hand, increases in input prices tend to shift a product's supply curve to the left, since they push up the firms' costs. For agricultural products, the supply curve also shifts in response to weather conditions. For example, in 1986, a drought in Brazil cut the coffee crop by about 60 percent, causing a significant shift to the left of the supply curve for coffee.

## THE OUTPUT DECISION OF A PERFECTLY COMPETITIVE FIRM

How much output should a perfectly competitive firm produce? As we saw in the section before last, a perfectly competitive firm cannot affect the

TABLE 10.2    Cost and Revenue, Perfectly Competitive Firm

| Output per period | Price (dollars) | Total revenue (dollars) | Total fixed cost (dollars) | Total vari- able cost (dollars) | Total cost (dollars) | Total profit (dollars) |
|---|---|---|---|---|---|---|
| 0 | 20 | 0 | 24 | 0 | 24 | −24 |
| 1 | 20 | 20 | 24 | 4 | 28 | −8 |
| 2 | 20 | 40 | 24 | 6 | 30 | 10 |
| 3 | 20 | 60 | 24 | 10 | 34 | 26 |
| 4 | 20 | 80 | 24 | 16 | 40 | 40 |
| 5 | 20 | 100 | 24 | 26 | 50 | 50 |
| 6 | 20 | 120 | 24 | 46 | 70 | 50 |
| 7 | 20 | 140 | 24 | 76 | 100 | 40 |
| 8 | 20 | 160 | 24 | 138 | 162 | −2 |

market price of its product, and it can sell any amount of its product that it wants (within its capabilities) at the market price. To illustrate the firm's situation, consider the example in Table 10.2. The market price is $20 a unit, and the firm can produce as much as it chooses. Hence, the firm's total revenue at various output rates is given in column 3 of Table 10.2. The firm's total fixed cost, total variable cost, and total cost are given in columns 4, 5, and 6 of Table 10.2. Finally, the last column shows the firm's total profit.

Figure 10.2 shows the relationship between total revenue and total cost, on the one hand, and output, on the other. The vertical distance between the total revenue curve and the total cost curve is the profit at the corresponding output rate. Below 2 units of output and above 7 units of output, this distance is negative. Since the firm can sell either large or small volumes of output at the same price per unit, the total revenue curve is a straight line through the origin. (Specifically, total revenue = price times quantity, so since price is constant, total revenue is proportional to quantity.) Since a perfectly competitive firm takes the price as given, this will always be true under perfect competition.

Both Table 10.2 and Figure 10.2 show that the output rate that will maximize the firm's profits is either 5 or 6 units per time period. These are the output rates where the profit figure in the last column of Table 10.2 is the highest and where the vertical distance between the total revenue and total cost curves in Figure 10.2 is the largest.[3]

It is worthwhile to present the marginal revenue and marginal cost curves, as well as the total revenue and total cost curves. Table 10.3 shows marginal revenue and marginal cost at each output rate. Figure 10.3 shows the resulting marginal revenue and marginal cost curves. Because the firm

---

[3] If the firm can produce a fractional number of units per time period and if the firm's total cost curve is linear between outputs of 5 and 6 units per time period, profits will be maximized if the firm produces 5 or 6 units per time period—or any output in between.

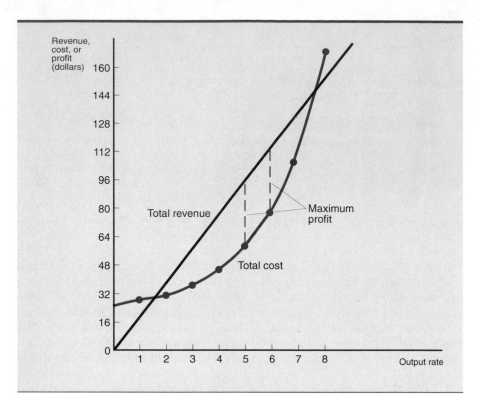

**FIGURE 10.2  Relationship between Total Cost and Total Revenue, Perfectly Competitive Firm**  The output rate that will maximize the firm's profits is either 5 or 6 units per time period. At either of these output rates, profit (total revenue minus total cost) equals $50.

**TABLE 10.3**  *Marginal Revenue and Marginal Cost, Perfectly Competitive Firm*

| Output per period | Marginal revenue (dollars) | Marginal cost* (dollars) |
|:---:|:---:|:---:|
| 1 | 20 | 4 |
| 2 | 20 | 2 |
| 3 | 20 | 4 |
| 4 | 20 | 6 |
| 5 | 20 | 10 |
| 6 | 20 | 20 |
| 7 | 20 | 30 |
| 8 | 20 | 62 |

* This is the marginal cost between the indicated output level and 1 unit less than this output level.

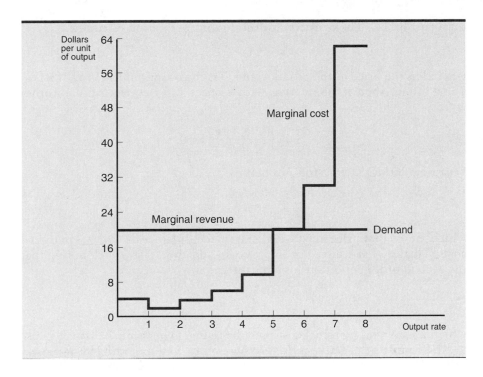

*FIGURE 10.3   Marginal Revenue and Marginal Cost, Perfectly Competitive Firm*   When output is at the profit-maximizing level of 5 or 6 units, price (= marginal revenue) equals marginal cost.

takes the price as a given, which is constant for all units that it may wish to sell, marginal revenue equals price, since the change in total revenue resulting from a 1-unit change in sales necessarily equals the price. (If the price of a bushel of wheat is $3, then the extra revenue from selling one more bushel is $3.) Thus the marginal revenue curve is the same as the firm's demand curve, which (for reasons discussed above) is horizontal.

The central point to note is that the maximum profit is achieved at the output rate where *price (= marginal revenue) equals marginal cost.* Both the figures in Table 10.3 and the curves in Figure 10.3 indicate that price equals marginal cost at an output rate of between 5 and 6 units, which we know from the earlier Table 10.2 or Figure 10.2 to be the profit-maximizing outputs.

## SETTING MARGINAL COST EQUAL TO PRICE

In general, the optimal output for a perfectly competitive firm will be the one where marginal cost equals price. To prove that this is the case, let the total cost be *TC*. The equation for total profit per period of time is

$$\pi = PQ - TC,$$

where *P* is the price of the product, and *Q* is the output of the firm. If $\pi$ is at a maximum, then its derivative with respect to *Q* equals zero. In other words,

$$\frac{d\pi}{dQ} = \frac{d(PQ - TC)}{dQ} = 0.$$

Because $dPQ/dQ = P$, it follows that

$$P - \frac{dTC}{dQ} = 0, \tag{10.3}$$

which means that price must equal marginal cost (since $dTC/dQ$ is marginal cost). This is what we set out to prove. In addition, it is worth noting that the second-order condition for a maximum is

$$\frac{d^2TC}{dQ^2} > 0,$$

which means that marginal cost must be rising. (This must be true because $d^2\pi/dQ^2$ must be negative if this is a maximum, and if $d^2\pi/dQ^2$ is negative, $d^2TC/dQ^2$ must be positive.)

Even if a firm is doing its best, it may not be able to earn a profit. If the price is $P_2$ in Figure 10.4, short-run average costs exceed the price at all possible outputs. Because the short run is too short (by definition) to permit the firm to alter the scale of its plant, it cannot liquidate its plant in the short run. All the firm can do is to produce at a loss or discontinue production. Its decision should depend on whether the price of the product will cover average variable costs. If there exists an output rate where price exceeds average variable costs, it will pay the firm to produce, despite the fact that price does not cover average total costs. If there does not exist an output rate where price exceeds average variable costs, the firm is better off to produce nothing at all. Hence, if the average variable cost curve is as shown in Figure 10.4, the firm will produce if the price is $P_2$, but not if it is $P_1$.

To see why this is so, it is essential to recognize that, if the firm produces nothing, it must still pay its fixed costs. Thus, if the loss resulting from production is less than the firm's fixed costs (the loss from shutting down), it is more profitable (in the sense that losses are smaller) to produce than not to produce. On a per-unit basis, this implies that it is better to produce than to discontinue production if the loss per unit of production is less than average fixed costs, that is, if $ATC - P < AFC$, were *ATC* is average total costs, *P* is price, and *AFC* is average fixed cost. But this will be so if $ATC < AFC + P$, since *P* has merely been added to both sides of the inequality. Subtracting *AFC* from both sides, this will be so if $ATC - AFC < P$. But $ATC - AFC$ is average variable costs, which means

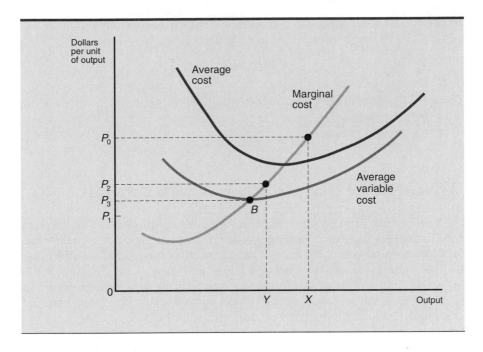

**FIGURE 10.4** *Short-Run Average and Marginal Cost Curves* If price is $P_0$, the firm will produce an output of $X$; if price is $P_2$, it will produce an output of $Y$; and if price is less than $P_3$, it will produce nothing.

that we have shown what we set out to show: that it is better to produce than to discontinue production if price exceeds average variable costs.

To summarize, if the firm maximizes profit or minimizes losses, it sets its output rate so that short-run marginal cost equals price. But this proposition, like most others, has an exception: if the market price is below the firm's average variable costs at any conceivable output rate, the firm will minimize losses by discontinuing production.

As an illustration, consider the Green Company, a perfectly competitive firm with the following total cost function:

$$TC = 800 + 6Q + 2Q^2,$$

where $TC$ is total cost (in dollars), and $Q$ is the firm's output per day. If the price of its product equals \$30, the firm should set its output so that

$$MC = \frac{dTC}{dQ} = 6 + 4Q = 30. \tag{10.4}$$

In other words, it should set marginal cost equal to price (\$30). Solving equation (10.4) for $Q$, we find that the firm should set output equal to 6 units per day. To make sure that price is no less than average variable cost at this output, we note that since the firm's total variable cost equals $6Q + 2Q^2$, its average variable cost equals

$$AVC = \frac{6Q + 2Q^2}{Q} = 6 + 2Q.$$

Thus, if $Q = 6$, average variable cost equals $6 + 2(6)$, or \$18, which is less than the price of \$30.

# LONG-RUN EQUILIBRIUM OF THE FIRM

In the long run, how much will a competitive firm produce? The long-run equilibrium position of the firm is at the point at which its long-run average total costs equal price. If price is in excess of average total costs for any firm, economic profits are being earned and new firms will enter the industry. This will increase supply, thereby driving down price and hence profits. If price is less than average total costs for any firm, that firm will eventually leave the industry. As firms exit, supply falls, causing price and profits to rise. Only when economic profits are zero (which means that long-run average cost equals price) will the firm be in long-run equilibrium.

Recall from Chapter 1 that economic profits are not the same as accounting profits. Economic profits are profits above and beyond what the owners of the firm could obtain elsewhere from the resources they invest in the firm. Thus, long-run equilibrium occurs when the owners receive no more (and no less) than they could obtain elsewhere from these resources.

More specifically, price must be equal to the *lowest value* of long-run average total costs. That is, firms must be producing at the minimum point on their long-run average cost curves. To see why, note that, if firms maximize their profits, they must operate where price equals long-run marginal cost. Also, we have just seen that they must operate where price equals long-run average cost. But if both of these conditions are satisfied, it follows that long-run marginal cost must equal long-run average cost. And we know from Chapter 8 that long-run marginal cost is equal to long-run average cost only at the point at which long-run average cost is a minimum. Consequently, this point must be the equilibrium position of the firm.

To illustrate this equilibrium position, consider Figure 10.5. When all adjustments are made, price equals $G$. Since price is constant, the demand curve is horizontal, and therefore the marginal revenue curve is the same as the demand curve, both being $GG'$. The equilibrium output of the firm is $V$, and its optimal-sized plant is described by the short-run average and marginal cost curves, $AA'$ and $MM'$. At this output and with this plant, we see that long-run marginal cost equals short-run marginal cost equals price. This insures that the firm is maximizing profit. Also, long-run average cost equals short-run average cost equals price: this insures that economic profits are zero. Because the long-run marginal cost and long-run average

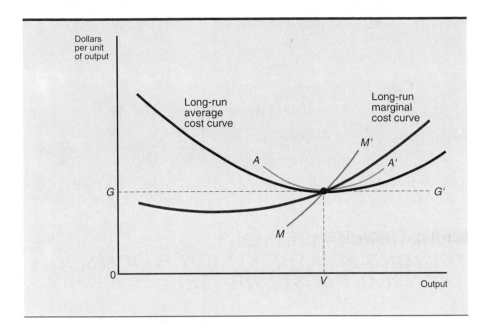

**FIGURE 10.5** *Long-Run Equilibrium, Perfectly Competitive Firm* In long-run equilibrium, the firm produces an output of $V$, and price = marginal cost (both long-run and short-run) = average cost (both long-run and short-run).

cost must be equal, the equilibrium point is at the bottom of the long-run average cost curve.

For example, suppose that the Milton Company's long-run average cost curve is

$$AC = 200 - 4Q + .05Q^2, \tag{10.5}$$

where $AC$ is long-run average cost (in dollars), and $Q$ is the firm's output per day. Since the Milton Company is a perfectly competitive firm, its output in the long run will equal the value of $Q$ that minimizes $AC$. To determine this value of $Q$, we obtain the derivative of $AC$ with respect to $Q$:

$$\frac{dAC}{dQ} = -4 + .10Q.$$

Setting $dAC/dQ$ equal to zero, we find that $Q = 40$. Thus, if the firm maximizes profit, its output in the long run will equal 40 units per day.

As indicated above, average cost will equal marginal cost at this output. To see this, note that since total cost equals $Q$ times $AC$,

$$TC = Q(200 - 4Q + .05Q^2)$$
$$= 200Q - 4Q^2 + .05Q^3,$$

where $TC$ is total cost. Taking the derivative of $TC$ with respect to $Q$,

$$MC = \frac{dTC}{dQ} = 200 - 8Q + .15Q^2,$$

where $MC$ equals marginal cost. Since $Q = 40$,

$$MC = 200 - 8(40) + .15(40)^2 = 120.$$

Also, inserting 40 for $Q$ in equation (10.5),

$$AC = 200 - 4(40) + .05(40)^2 = 120.$$

Thus, marginal cost equals average cost when $Q = 40$. (Both marginal cost and average cost equal \$120.)

# THE LONG-RUN ADJUSTMENT PROCESS: A CONSTANT-COST INDUSTRY

Having looked at the behavior of the perfectly competitive firm in the short and long run, we turn to the long-run adjustment process of a perfectly competitive industry. To begin with, we assume that the industry is a *constant-cost industry*, which means that expansion of the industry does not result in an increase in input prices. Figure 10.6 shows long-run equilibrium under conditions of constant cost. The left-hand panel shows the short- and long-run cost curves of a typical firm in the industry. The right-hand panel shows the demand and supply curves in the market as a whole, $D$ being the original demand curve and $S$ being the original short-run supply curve. It is assumed that the industry is in long-run equilibrium, with the result that the price (\$6 per unit) equals the minimum value of long-run (and short-run) average cost.

Suppose now that the demand curve shifts to $D_1$. In the short run, with the number of firms fixed, the price of the product will rise from \$6 to \$7 per unit; each firm will expand output from 5,000 to 6,000 units per day; and each firm will be making economic profits since the new price, \$7, exceeds the short-run average costs of the firm when output is 6,000 units per day. The result is that firms will enter the industry and shift the supply curve to the right. In the case of a constant-cost industry, the entrance of the new firms does not influence the costs of the existing firms. The inputs used by this industry are used by many other industries as well, and the appearance of the new firms in this industry does not bid up the price of inputs and hence raise the costs of existing firms. Neither does the entry of the new firms reduce existing firms' costs.

Thus, a constant-cost industry *has a horizontal long-run supply curve*. Since output can be increased by increasing the number of firms producing 5,000 units of output per day at an average cost of \$6 per unit, the long-run supply curve is horizontal at \$6 per unit. So long as the industry remains in

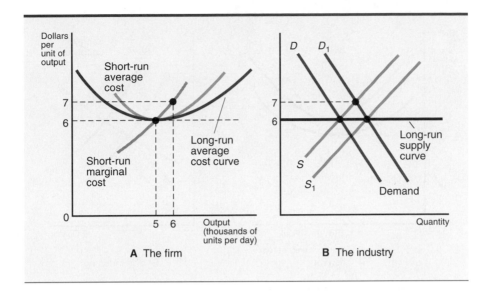

FIGURE 10.6   *Long-Run Equilibrium: Constant-Cost Industry*   A
constant-cost industry has a horizontal long-run supply curve, as shown in
panel B. If demand shifts upward from $D$ to $D_1$, the consequent increase in
price (to $7 per unit) results in the entry of firms, which shifts the supply
curve to the right (to $S_1$), thus pushing the price back to its original level
($6 per unit).

a state of constant costs, its output can be increased indefinitely. If price
exceeds $6 per unit, firms would enter the industry; if price were less than
$6 per unit, firms would leave the industry. Thus, long-run equilibrium can
only occur in this industry when price is $6 per unit. And industry output
can be raised or lowered, in accord with demand conditions, without changing this long-run equilibrium price.

## THE LONG-RUN ADJUSTMENT PROCESS: AN INCREASING-COST INDUSTRY

Not all industries are constant-cost industries. Next, let's consider the case
of an *increasing-cost industry*, which occurs when the expansion of the
industry results in an increase in input prices.[4] An increasing-cost industry

[4] Besides constant-cost and increasing-cost industries, there are also decreasing-cost industries, which
are the most unusual case, although quite young industries may fall into this category. External economies, which are cost reductions that occur when the industry expands, may be responsible for the existence of decreasing-cost industries. For example, the expansion of an industry may lead to an
improvement in transportation that reduces the costs of each firm in the industry. A decreasing-cost
industry has a negatively sloped long-run supply curve.

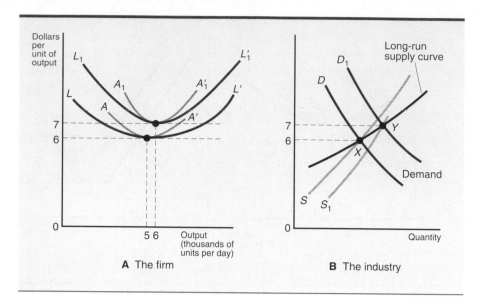

**A** The firm

**B** The industry

---

**FIGURE 10.7  Long-Run Equilibrium: Increasing-Cost Industry**  An increasing-cost industry has a positively sloped long-run supply curve, as shown in panel B. After long-run equilibrium is achieved, increases in output require increases in the price of the product.

---

is shown in Figure 10.7. The original conditions are the same as in Figure 10.6, $D$ being the original demand curve, $S$ being the original supply curve, $6 per unit being the equilibrium price, and the long- and short-run average cost curves of each firm being $LL'$ and $AA'$ in the left panel. As in Figure 10.6, the original position is one of long-run equilibrium, since the price equals the minimum value of long-run (and short-run) average cost.

Assume now that the demand curve shifts to $D_1$, with the result that the price of the product goes up and firms earn economic profits, thus attracting new entrants. More and more inputs are needed by the industry, and in an increasing-cost industry, the price of inputs goes up with the amount used by the industry. Thus, the cost of inputs increases for the established firms as well as the new entrants and the average cost curves are pushed up to $L_1L_1'$ and $A_1A_1'$.

If each firm's marginal cost curve is shifted to the left by the increase in input prices, the industry supply curve will tend to shift to the left. But this tendency is more than counterbalanced by the effects of the increase in the number of firms, which shifts the industry supply curve to the right. The latter effect must more than offset the former effect because otherwise there would be no expansion in total industry output. (No new resources would have been attracted to the industry.) The process of adjustment must go on until a new point of long-run equilibrium is reached. In Figure 10.7, this point is where the price of the product is $7 per unit and each firm produces 6,000 units per day;[5] the new short-run supply curve is $S_1$.

An increasing-cost industry *has a positively sloped long-run supply curve.* That is, after long-run equilibrium is achieved, increases in output require increases in the price of the product. For example, points $X$ and $Y$ in Figure 10.7 are both on the long-run supply curve for the industry. The difference between constant-cost and increasing-cost industries is as follows: *In constant-cost industries, new firms enter in response to an increase in demand until price returns to its original level, whereas in increasing-cost industries, new firms enter until the minimum point on the long-run average cost curve has increased to the point where it equals the new price.*[6]

Finally, some industries are neither constant-cost nor increasing-cost industries; they are decreasing-cost industries. Their long-run supply curve is negatively sloped. For further discussion of these industries, which are less frequently encountered than constant-cost or increasing-cost industries, see note 4.

# HOW A PERFECTLY COMPETITIVE ECONOMY ALLOCATES RESOURCES

It is very important for managers to understand how a competitive economy allocates resources. Without such an understanding, they cannot interpret or anticipate the fundamental changes that occur in many industries. To illustrate this allocation process, let's take a simple case: consumers become more favorably disposed toward corn and less favorably disposed toward rice than in the past. What will happen in the short run? The increase in the demand for corn increases the price of corn, and results in some increase in the output of corn. However, the output of corn cannot be increased very substantially because the capacity of the industry cannot be expanded in the short run. Similarly, the fall in the demand for rice reduces the price of rice, and results in some reduction in the output of rice. But the output of rice will not be curtailed greatly because firms will continue to produce as long as they can cover variable costs.

The alteration in the relative prices of corn and rice tells producers that a

---

[5] We cannot be sure that the firm's new output exceeds its old output as shown in Figure 10.7. It is possible for its new output to be less than or equal to its old output.

[6] This is not the only way in which equilibrium can be achieved in increasing-cost industries. It is also possible that the increase in input prices (due to the expansion of industry output) raises average cost more than the increase in demand raises average revenue. Thus firms may experience losses, some may leave the industry, and the remaining firms may produce at a bigger scale.

reallocation of resources is needed. Because of the increase in the price of corn and the decrease in the price of rice, corn producers are earning economic profits and rice producers are showing economic losses. This will trigger a redeployment of resources. If some variable inputs in the production of rice can be used as effectively in the production of corn, these variable inputs may be withdrawn from rice production and switched to corn production. Even if there are no variable inputs that are used in both corn and rice production, adjustment can occur in various interrelated markets, with the result that corn production gains resources and rice production loses resources.

When short-run equilibrium is achieved in both the corn and rice industries, the reallocation of resources is not yet complete since there has not been enough time for producers to build new capacity or liquidate old capacity. In particular, neither industry is operating at minimum average cost. The corn producers may be operating at greater than the output level where average cost is a minimum; and the rice producers may be operating at less than the output level where average cost is a minimum.

What will occur in the long run? The shift in consumer demand from rice to corn will result in greater adjustments in output and smaller adjustments in price than in the short run. In the long run, existing firms can leave rice production and new firms can enter corn production. Because of short-run economic losses in rice production, some rice land and related equipment will be allowed to run down, and some firms engaged in rice production will be liquidated. As firms leave rice production, the supply curve shifts to the left, causing the price to rise above its short-run level. The transfer of resources out of rice production will cease when the price has increased, and costs have decreased, to the point where losses no longer occur.

Whereas rice production is losing resources, corn production is gaining them. The short-run economic profits in corn production will stimulate the entry of new firms. The increased demand for inputs will raise input prices and cost curves in corn production, and the price of corn will be depressed by the movement to the right of the supply curve because of the entry of new firms. Entry stops when economic profits are no longer being earned. At that point, when long-run equilibrium is achieved, there will be more firms and more resources used in the corn industry than in the short run.

Eventually, long-run equilibrium is achieved in both industries, and the reallocation of resources is complete. It is important to note that this reallocation can affect industries other than corn and rice. If rice land and equipment can be easily adapted to the production of corn, which seems unlikely, rice producers can simply change to the production of corn. If not, the resources used in rice production are converted to some use other than corn, and the resources that enter corn production come from some use other than rice production.

# PRICE AND OUTPUT DECISIONS UNDER MONOPOLY

Let's turn now from perfect competition to monopoly. An unregulated monopolist, if it maximizes profit, will choose the price and output at which the difference between total revenue and total cost is largest. For example, if a monopolist's total revenue and total cost curves are as shown in Table 10.4, it will choose an output rate of either 5 or 6 units per time period and a price of $331 or $311. Figure 10.8 shows the situation graphically.[7]

**TABLE 10.4   Cost, Revenue, and Profit of Monopolist**

| Output | Price (dollars) | Total revenue (dollars) | Total cost (dollars) | Total profit (dollars) |
|---|---|---|---|---|
| 2 | 400 | 800 | 640 | 160 |
| 3 | 350 | 1,050 | 790 | 260 |
| 4 | $342\frac{1}{2}$ | 1,370 | 960 | 410 |
| 5 | 331 | 1,655 | 1,150 | 505 |
| 6 | 311 | 1,866 | 1,361 | 505 |
| 7 | 278 | 1,946 | 1,590 | 356 |
| 8 | 250 | 2,000 | 1,840 | 160 |

Under monopoly, the firm will maximize profit if it sets its output rate at the point at which marginal cost equals marginal revenue. Table 10.5 and Figure 10.9 show that this is true in this example. It is easy to prove that this is generally a necessary condition for profit maximization. If $TR$ is the monopolist's total revenue and $TC$ is its total cost, the monopolist's profit equals

$$\pi = TR - TC$$

and

$$\frac{d\pi}{dQ} = \frac{dTR}{dQ} - \frac{dTC}{dQ}.$$

Setting $d\pi/dQ = 0$ to obtain the conditions under which profit is a maximum, we find that

$$\frac{dTR}{dQ} = \frac{dTC}{dQ}. \tag{10.6}$$

[7] If the monopolist can produce a fractional number of units per time period and if the monopolist's total cost curve and total revenue curve are linear between 5 and 6 units per time period, profits will be maximized if the monopolist produces 5 or 6 units per time period—or any output in between.

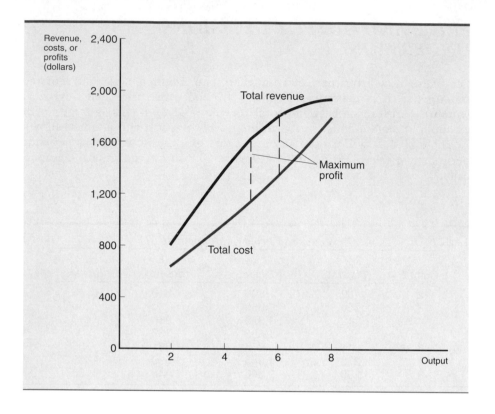

**FIGURE 10.8** *Total Revenue, Total Cost, and Total Profit of Monopolist*
To maximize profit, the monopolist will choose an output rate of 5 or 6 units per period of time.

**TABLE 10.5** *Marginal Cost and Marginal Revenue of Monopolist*

| Output | Marginal cost* (dollars) | Marginal revenue* (dollars) | Total profit (dollars) |
|---|---|---|---|
| 3 | 150 | 250 | 260 |
| 4 | 170 | 320 | 410 |
| 5 | 190 | 285 | 505 |
| 6 | 211 | 211 | 505 |
| 7 | 229 | 80 | 356 |
| 8 | 250 | 54 | 160 |

*These figures pertain to the interval between the indicated quantity of output and one unit less than the indicated quantity of output.

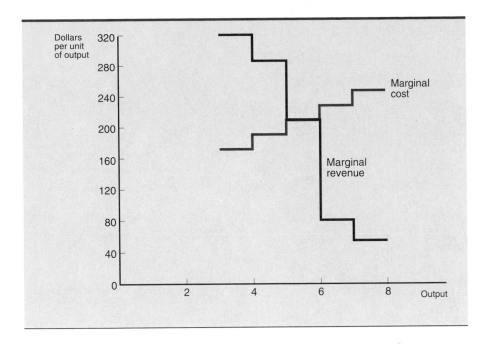

*FIGURE 10.9   Marginal Revenue and Marginal Cost of Monopolist*   At the monopolist's profit-maximizing output (5 or 6 units), marginal cost equals marginal revenue.

Thus, marginal revenue must equal marginal cost when profits are maximized, since the expression on the left-hand side is marginal revenue and the expression on the right-hand side is marginal cost.

It is easy to represent graphically the price and output decisions of the monopolist. Figure 10.10 shows the demand curve, the marginal revenue curve, the marginal cost curve, and the average total cost curve faced by the firm. To maximize profit, it should produce the output, $Q$, where the marginal cost curve intersects the marginal revenue curve. If the monopolist produces $Q$ units, the demand curve shows that it must set a price of $P$. It is important to recognize that, since the monopolist is the only member of the industry, the demand curve for the output of the monopolist is the industry demand curve. Thus, in contrast to perfect competition where the demand curve for the output of an individual firm is horizontal, the demand curve for the monopolist's output slopes downward to the right, as shown in Figure 10.10.

If an industry is monopolized, it generally will set a higher price and lower output than if it is perfectly competitive. The perfectly competitive firm operates at the point at which price equals marginal cost, whereas the monopolist operates at a point at which price exceeds marginal cost. To see

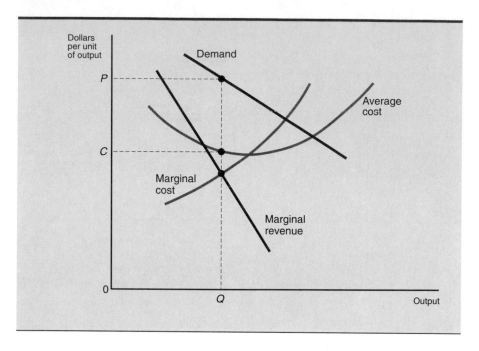

**FIGURE 10.10** *Output and Price Decisions of Monopolist* In equilibrium, the monopolist produces Q units of output and sets a price of P. (Note that, in contrast to perfect competition, the demand curve slopes downward to the right.)

that the monopolist's price exceeds marginal cost, recall from equation (3.16) that

$$MR = P\left(1 - \frac{1}{\eta}\right),$$

where *MR* is marginal revenue, *P* is price, and $\eta$ is the price elasticity of demand. Since the monopolist sets marginal revenue equal to marginal cost, *MC*, it follows that at the point where profit is maximized,

$$MC = P\left(1 - \frac{1}{\eta}\right),$$

so that

$$P = MC \div \left(1 - \frac{1}{\eta}\right).$$

Thus, since $\eta > 0$, it follows that $(1 - 1/\eta) < 1$, which means that *P* must exceed *MC*.

## NEWSPAPER MONOPOLY IN DETROIT

# The Detroit News
# Detroit Free Press

In 1991, there were only 63 communities in the United States with more than one daily newspaper—and only 12 of them had rival newspapers that were separately owned and commercially independent. Take the case of Detroit. In early 1989, the *Detroit Free Press* and the *Detroit News* obtained approval from the United States Court of Appeals to establish a newspaper monopoly in Detroit. Arguing that the *Free Press* was a failing newspaper, they took advantage of a special exemption from antitrust law, allowed under the Newspaper Preservation Act of 1970. (This exemption was created to keep alive competing editorial voices in major cities.) The two newspapers were allowed to continue to print newspapers under their own names, but all commercial operations would be merged.

Because the merged newspapers were legally permitted to fix prices and allocate markets as they pleased, they would constitute a monopoly, even though their newspapers were printed under two different names. The result would be a very substantial increase in profit. Before they combined, each lost more than $10 million a year; after they combined, experts estimated that they would make more than $150 million a year. This is eloquent testimony to the effect of monopoly on profit.

The reasons for this increase in profit were summarized as follows by the *New York Times:* "The formation of the monopoly enterprise would end an all-out war for control of advertising and circulation dollars, sending . . . rates skyrocketing for readers and advertisers."* This, of course, is entirely consistent with our discussion on page 393. A monopolist, free from the constraints imposed by direct competition, can set a higher price—and obtain a higher profit level—than it could if it had to compete with rival firms. The demand curve facing the monopolist in Figure 10.10 is the market demand curve—the demand curve for newspapers in Detroit in this case. This is quite different from the demand curve facing a perfectly competitive firm.

*New York Times, September 18, 1988.*

For the above reasons, monopoly newspapers command a higher market value than newspapers with competition. According to William McCluskey, the managing director of a media investment banking concern, a well-run monopoly would sell for about four times revenues, whereas a newspaper with competitors would sell for much less.

Detroit is not the only city with newspapers that have combined—or that are about to combine—their commercial arrangements: the *Pittsburgh Post-Gazette* and the *Pittsburgh Press* have combined, as have the *Miami Herald* and the *Miami News*, as well as the *San Francisco Chronicle* and the *San Francisco Examiner*. According to Stephen Barnett of the University of California law school, "Every industry would like to operate monopolistically. It's just that the newspaper industry has the political power to convince Congress to give it to them."†

†Ibid. Also, see *New York Times*, January 28, 1989 and September 22, 1991.

---

ANALYZING MANAGERIAL DECISIONS

## XEROX'S REACTION TO THE SAVIN 750 COPIER

As pointed out in Chapter 1, the Xerox Corporation's share of U.S. copier revenues was close to 100 percent in 1970. According to a McKinsey consultant who worked with Xerox,

*I can remember as late as 1975 looking at internal Xerox reports showing that market share was a word they had never heard of. They did not have any formal market share information. It had always been 100 percent. Right then, some people started to accumulate some information and the Japanese weren't even listed. . . . The whole company, in terms of competition, was focused on IBM at that time. Everybody was convinced that if they were going to have any competition, it was going to come from IBM. When IBM came out with its first product, a shudder went through Xerox. Later, it was Kodak. Xerox totally missed the fundamental strategy of the Japanese, which was going in at the low end of the market and working up, going for the soft underbelly.*

By 1980, Xerox's market share had fallen to 46 percent. One reason was the appearance of a number of low-priced copiers that were introduced in the late 1970s. Perhaps the most successful was the Savin 750, which was introduced in 1975. It had about a third of the parts and a third of the weight of conventional Xerox machines. It cost Ricoh, the Japanese firm that produced it, about $500 to $600 to build, and was sold to Savin for about $1,600. Savin in turn sold it to the customer for $4,995. Xerox's comparable copier, the model 3100, sold for about $12,000. The Savin 750 averaged 17,000 copies between failures and took less than 30 minutes to repair. Xerox machines averaged 6,000 to 10,000 copies between failures and took up to twice as long to repair.

(a) What effect do you think the appearance of the Savin 750 had on the demand curve for Xerox's model 3100? (b) In response to the Savin 750, Xerox slashed price. Was this the rational thing to do? (Use a diagram to illustrate your answer.) (c) If the two machines sold for the same price, was the Savin 750 likely to outsell the Xerox 3100? (d) Did the market structure of the copier industry change in the 1970s? If so, how?

*Solution* (a) The demand curve for Xerox's model 3100 was pushed downward and to the left by the appearance of the Savin 750. (b) Given the shift in the demand curve for the model 3100, the marginal revenue curve shifted as well. Let $Q_0$ be the output at which the new marginal revenue curve intersected the model 3100's marginal cost curve. If the price at which Xerox could sell an output of $Q_0$ (based on the new demand curve) was below the old price of $12,000, it was rational (in the sense that it increased profit) to reduce price, since only at a lower price would consumers purchase the new profit-maximizing output level. (c) Yes, because of the Savin 750's greater reliability and lower repair costs. According to some knowledgeable observers, the low service costs of the Savin 750 were very

The following graph illustrates the situation:

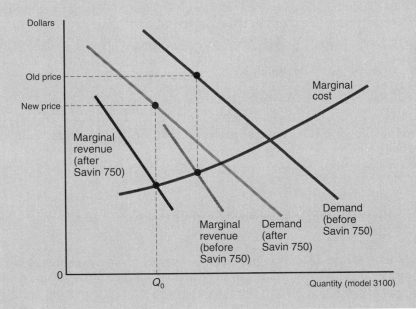

important factors in its success. far from being monopolized in
(d) Yes. Whereas it was close to a 1980. Concentration in the indus-
monopoly in 1970, this market was try decreased.*

* For further discussion, see T. Bresnahan, "Post-Entry Competition in the Plain Paper Copier Mar-
ket," *American Economic Review* (May 1985); G. Jacobson and J. Hillkirk, *Xerox: American Samurai*
(New York: Macmillan, 1987); and H. Bartlett, *Cases in Strategic Management for Business* (New York:
Dryden Press, 1988).

# THE RALEIGH COMPANY: A NUMERICAL EXAMPLE

To illustrate how price and output can be chosen to maximize profit, consider the Raleigh Company, a monopolist producing and selling a product
with the following demand curve:

$$P = 30 - 6Q, \tag{10.7}$$

where $P$ is price (in thousands of dollars), and $Q$ is the firm's output (in
thousands of units). The firm's total cost function is

$$TC = 14 + 3Q + 3Q^2, \tag{10.8}$$

where $TC$ is total cost (in millions of dollars).

From the demand curve in equation (10.7), we can determine the firm's
total revenue (in millions of dollars), which is

$$TR = P \cdot Q = (30 - 6Q)Q = 30Q - 6Q^2.$$

Thus, marginal revenue equals

$$\frac{dTR}{dQ} = \frac{d(30Q - 6Q^2)}{dQ} = 30 - 12Q.$$

From the total cost function in equation (10.8), we can determine marginal
cost, which is

$$MC = \frac{dTC}{dQ} = \frac{d(14 + 3Q + 3Q^2)}{dQ} = 3 + 6Q.$$

Setting marginal revenue equal to marginal cost,

$$30 - 12Q = 3 + 6Q,$$

which means that $Q = 1.5$. Inserting 1.5 for $Q$ in the demand curve in
equation (10.7), we find that $P = 30 - 6(1.5)$, or 21. Thus, to maximize
profit, the Raleigh Company should set a price of $21 thousand and pro-
duce and sell 1.5 thousand units. If it does so, its profit equals
$[30(1.5) - 6(1.5)^2] - [14 + 3(1.5) + 3(1.5)^2] = 6.25$ millions of dollars.

# TWO-PART TARIFFS

A monopolist sometimes requires the consumer to pay an initial fee for the right to buy its product as well as a usage fee for each unit of the product that he or she buys. This is known as a *two-part tariff*. There are many cases where this pricing technique is used. For example, telephone companies charge a basic monthly fee for telephone service plus an amount for message units.

If a monopolist uses this pricing technique, it must determine how high the initial fee must be, as well as the size of the usage fee. Clearly, the lower the initial fee, the greater the number of consumers that will purchase the right to buy the product. Thus lower initial fees are likely to result in greater profits from the sales of the product. But this may not be best for the firm, since it also receives profits from the initial fees it charges—and if it lowers the initial fee, these profits will fall. Consequently, the monopolist would be expected to choose the initial fee and usage fee so that its total profit—from both the sales of the product and from initial fees—is a maximum.

To illustrate the use of a two-part tariff, consider Disneyland, the California amusement park discussed in Chapter 3. Disneyland used to charge each person a price to enter the park and an extra amount for each ride he or she went on. In the early 1980s, Disneyland eliminated the fee for individual rides and raised the entrance fee. Presumably, Disneyland's managers felt that this would increase the park's profits.

# BUNDLING

Another pricing technique sometimes used by monopolists is *bundling*, in which a firm requires customers who buy one of its products to buy another of its products as well. This procedure can increase the firm's profits if customers have quite different tastes. To see why bundling can be profitable, consider a movie company that leases two movies, *Casablanca* and *The Godfather*. For simplicity, suppose that there are only two theaters, the Alvin and the Palace, and that the maximum amount that each theater is willing to pay to lease each movie is as shown in Table 10.6.

TABLE 10.6  *Maximum Price That Each Theater Would Pay for Two Movies, Leased Separately or as a Bundle (Case Where Bundling Is Profitable)*

|  | Theater | |
| --- | --- | --- |
| Movie | Alvin | Palace |
| Casablanca | $12,000 | $ 9,000 |
| The Godfather | 8,000 | 10,000 |
| Bundle (both movies combined) | $20,000 | $19,000 |

If the movies are leased separately, the most that can be charged for *Casablanca* is $9,000 and the most that can be charged for *The Godfather* is $8,000. Why? Because if the movie company is foolish enough to set prices above these levels, it will not be able to lease its films to both theaters. Thus, the most it can get for both films is $9,000 + $8,000 = $17,000. But what if the movie company insists that a theater must lease both movies? In this case, as shown in Table 10.6, the most that the Alvin is willing to pay for both is $20,000 and the most that the Palace is willing to pay for both is $19,000. Thus, the movie company can charge $19,000 for both movies combined, which is more than the amount ($17,000) that it could obtain if it leased them separately.

The managers of the movie company will find it more profitable to lease them as a bundle than to lease them separately so long as there is an inverse relationship between the amount that a theater is willing to pay for one movie and the amount that it is willing to pay for the other movie. (Panel A of Figure 10.11 shows that the relationship in Table 10.6 is in fact inverse.) But if this relationship is direct, there will be no advantage to the movie company in bundling them. For example, if the maximum prices the theaters would pay are shown in Table 10.7, the most that can be gotten for *Casablanca* (leased separately) is $9,000 and the most that can be gotten

TABLE 10.7  *Maximum Price That Each Theater Would Pay for Two Movies, Leased Separately or as a Bundle (Case Where Bundling Is Not Profitable)*

| | Theater | |
|---|---|---|
| Movie | Alvin | Palace |
| Casablanca | $12,000 | $ 9,000 |
| The Godfather | 8,000 | 7,000 |
| Bundle (both movies combined) | $20,000 | $16,000 |

for *The Godfather* (leased separately) is $7,000. Thus, if they are leased separately, the most that can be gotten from them both is $9,000 + $7,000 = $16,000, which is the same as the amount that can be gotten if they are bundled. (Panel B of Figure 10.11 shows that there is in fact a direct relationship in Table 10.7 between the amount that a theater would be willing to pay for one movie and the amount it would be willing to pay for the other.)

## MONOPOLISTIC COMPETITION

Having taken up perfect competition and monopoly, let's turn now to monopolistic competition. The central feature of monopolistic competition is *product differentiation.* Unlike perfect competition, where all firms

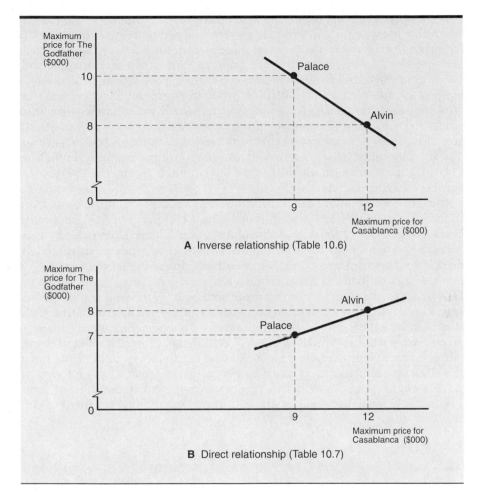

**FIGURE 10.11** *Alternative Relationships between the Maximum Amount a Theater Would Pay for* **Casablanca** *and the Maximum Amount It Would Pay for* **The Godfather** In panel A, bundling is profitable; in panel B, it is not profitable.

sell an identical product, firms under monopolistic competition sell somewhat different products. In many parts of retail trade, producers try to make their product a little different, by altering the product's physical makeup, the services they offer, and other such variables. Hathaway's shirts are not *exactly* the same as Calvin Klein's, but they are not too dissimilar either. Because of the differences among their products, producers have some control over their price, but it usually is small, because the products of other firms are very similar to their own.

Under perfect competition, the firms included in an industry are easy to determine because they all produce an identical product. But if product differentiation exists, it is no longer simple to define an industry, because each firm produces a somewhat different product. Nevertheless, it may be useful to group together firms that produce similar products and call them a *product group.* We can formulate a product group called "neckties" or "toothbrushes" or "shirts." The process by which we combine firms into product groups must be somewhat arbitrary, since there is no way to decide how close a pair of substitutes must be to belong to the same product group. But it is assumed that meaningful product groups can be established. Clearly, the broader the definition of the product group, the greater the number of firms included.

In addition to product differentiation, other conditions must be met for an industry to qualify as a case of monopolistic competition. (1) *There must be a large number of firms in the product group.* The product must be produced by perhaps 50 to 100 or more firms, with each firm's product a fairly close substitute for the products of the other firms in the product group. (2) *The number of firms in the product group must be large enough so that each firm expects its actions to go unheeded by its rivals and is unimpeded by possible retaliatory moves on their part.* Hence, when formulating their own policies with regard to price and output, they do not explicitly concern themselves with their rivals' responses. If there are a large number of firms, this condition will normally be met. (3) *Entry into the product group must be relatively easy, and there must be no collusion, such as price fixing or market sharing, among firms in the product group.* If there are a large number of firms, it generally is difficult, if not impossible, for them to collude.

# PRICE AND OUTPUT DECISIONS
# UNDER MONOPOLISTIC COMPETITION

If each firm produces a somewhat different product, it follows that the demand curve facing each firm slopes downward to the right. That is, if the firm raises its price slightly, it will lose some, but by no means all, of its customers to other firms. And if it lowers its price slightly, it will gain some, but by no means all, of its competitors' customers.

Figure 10.12 shows the short-run equilibrium of a monopolistically competitive firm. The firm in the short-run will set its price at $P_0$ and its output rate at $Q_0$, since this combination of price and output will maximize its profits. We can be sure that this combination of price and output maximizes profit because marginal cost equals marginal revenue at this output rate. Economic profits will be earned because price, $P_0$, exceeds average total costs, $C_0$, at this output rate.

One condition for long-run equilibrium is that each firm be making no

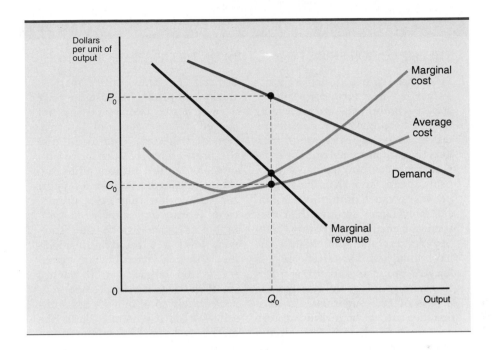

*FIGURE 10.12* **Short-Run Equilibrium, Monopolistic Competition** The firm will set price at $P_0$ and its output rate at $Q_0$, since marginal cost equals marginal revenue at this output. It will earn a profit of $C_0P_0$ per unit of output.

economic profits or losses, since entry or exit of firms will occur otherwise —and entry and exit are incompatible with long-run equilibrium. Another condition for long-run equilibrium is that each firm be maximizing its profits. At what price and output will both these conditions be fulfilled? Figure 10.13 shows that the long-run equilibrium is at a price of $P_1$ and an output of $Q_1$. The zero-economic-profit condition is met at this combination of price and output, since the firm's average cost at this output equals the price, $P_1$. And the profit-maximization condition is met, since the marginal revenue curve intersects the marginal cost curve at this output rate.[8]

# ADVERTISING EXPENDITURES: A SIMPLE RULE

Firms under monopolistic competition, as well as other market structures, spend huge amounts on advertising. How much should a profit-maximiz-

[8] The seminal work in the theory of monopolistic competition was E. Chamberlin, *The Theory of Monopolistic Competition* (Cambridge, Mass.: Harvard University Press, 1933).

## THE IMPACT OF PRICE PROMOTION ON RETAIL PERFORMANCE

Price-based promotional activities —that is, short-term price cuts to attract customers—are a leading form of competition among retailers, many of which are in markets that are monopolistically competitive. According to one survey, firms spend more than $65 billion per year on such promotions, a considerably larger amount than they spend on media advertising. Rockney Walters and Scott MacKenzie have analyzed the effects of loss leaders (products sold at low prices to attract people to the store) on the profits of two supermarkets associated with a large Midwestern supermarket chain.* They found that most of the loss-leader promotions had no effect on store profit.

(a) Some loss-leader promotions were successful in promoting the sales of the item whose price was cut, but they didn't increase the store's profits. Why? (b) According to Walters and MacKenzie, when "products are discounted heavily consumers purchase them in addition to their regular groceries, but they do not appear to purchase any complementary nonpromoted products with them." How can these supermarkets use such information? (c) In an isolated town with 3,000 inhabitants, do you think that the local supermarket behaves in accord with the theory of monopolistic competition? Why or why not? (d) To what extent do you think that the results obtained by Walters and MacKenzie can be applied validly to all supermarkets?

*Solution* (a) They didn't increase the store's profits because the price at which they were sold did not exceed average cost. (b) Information of this sort helps to indicate the profitability of such price promotions. As the authors point out, their "results provide little support for the notion that price promotions stimulate sales of unpromoted merchandise at the storewide level, yet this relationship is mentioned in virtually every retailing textbook." (c) No. In such a small market, the local supermarket is likely to be one of only a few sellers of many items. Thus, the market for these items may be an oligopoly. (d) Since these results are based on only two supermarkets, it would be hazardous to generalize from them.

* R. Walters and S. Mackenzie, "A Structural Equations Analysis of the Impact of Price Promotions on Store Performance," *Journal of Marketing Research* (February 1988).

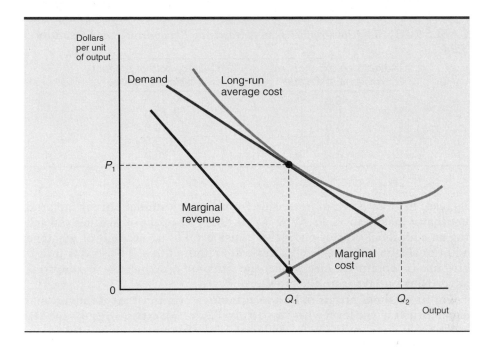

**FIGURE 10.13   Long-Run Equilibrium, Monopolistic Competition**   The long-run equilibrium is at a price of $P_1$ and an output of $Q_1$. There are zero profits, since long-run average cost equals price. Profits are being maximized, since marginal cost equals marginal revenue at this output.

ing firm spend on advertising? In this section, a simple rule is derived that helps to answer this question.[9] The quantity that a firm sells of its product is assumed to be a function of its price and the level of its advertising expenditure. There are assumed to be diminishing marginal returns to advertising expenditures, which means that beyond some point, successive increments of advertising outlays will yield smaller and smaller increases in additional sales. (Table 10.8 shows an illustrative case where successive increments of $100,000 in advertising outlays result in smaller and smaller increases in quantity sold. For example, the quantity sold increases by 2.0 million units when advertising expenditures rise from $800,000 to $900,000, but by only 1.5 million units when they rise from $900,000 to $1 million.)

Let $P$ be the price of a unit of the product and $MC$ be the marginal cost of production. If we assume that neither price nor marginal cost will be altered by small changes in advertising expenditures, the firm receives an

[9] This rule, put forth by R. Dorfman and P. Steiner, applies to monopolistic or oligopolistic firms, as well as to monopolistically competitive firms. However, since monopolistically competitive firms spend large amounts on advertising, this is a good place for this discussion.

TABLE 10.8 *Relationship between Advertising Expenditures and Quantity Sold*

| Advertising expenditures (millions of dollars) | Quantity sold of product (millions of units) |
|---|---|
| 0.8 | 15.0 |
| 0.9 | 17.0 |
| 1.0 | 18.5 |
| 1.1 | 19.5 |
| 1.2 | 20.0 |

increase in gross profit of $(P - MC)$ from each additional unit of the product that it makes and sells. Why is this the *gross* profit of making and selling an additional unit of output? Because it takes no account of whatever additional advertising expenditures were required to sell this extra unit of output. To obtain the *net* profit, the firm must deduct these additional advertising outlays from the gross profit.

For its total net profits to be a maximum, a firm must set its advertising expenditures at the level where an extra dollar of advertising results in extra gross profit equal to the extra dollar of advertising cost. Unless this is the case, the firm's total net profits can be increased by changing its advertising outlays. If an extra dollar of advertising results in more than a dollar increase in gross profit, the extra dollar should be spent on advertising (since this will raise total net profits). If an extra dollar (as well as the last dollar) of advertising results in less than a dollar increase in gross profit, advertising outlays should be cut.[10] Thus, if $\Delta Q$ is the number of extra units of output sold as a result of an extra dollar of advertising, the firm should set its advertising expenditures so that

$$\Delta Q \, (P - MC) = 1, \tag{10.9}$$

because the right-hand side of this equation equals the extra dollar of advertising cost, and the left-hand side equals the extra gross profit resulting from this advertising dollar.

If we multiply both sides of equation (10.9) by $P \div (P - MC)$, we obtain

$$P\Delta Q = \frac{P}{P - MC}. \tag{10.10}$$

Because the firm is maximizing profit, it is producing an output where marginal cost $(MC)$ equals marginal revenue $(MR)$. Thus, we can substitute $MR$ for $MC$ in equation (10.10), the result being

$$P\Delta Q = \frac{P}{P - MR}. \tag{10.11}$$

---

[10] For simplicity, we assume that the gross profit resulting from an extra dollar spent on advertising is essentially equal to the gross profit resulting from the last dollar spent. This is an innocuous assumption.

Using equation (3.16), it can be shown that the right-hand side of equation (10.11) equals $\eta$, the price elasticity of demand for the firm's product.[11] The left-hand side of equation (10.11) is the marginal revenue from an extra dollar of advertising (since it equals the price times the extra number of units sold as a result of an extra dollar of advertising). Thus, to maximize profit, the firm should set its advertising expenditure so that

Marginal revenue from an extra dollar of advertising $= \eta$.     (10.12)

This rule can be very helpful to managers.[12] Consider the Solomon Corporation, which knows that the price elasticity of demand for its product equals 1.6. To maximize profit, this firm must set the marginal revenue from an extra dollar of advertising equal to 1.6, according to this rule. Suppose Solomon's managers believe that an extra $100,000 of advertising would increase the firm's sales by $200,000, which implies that the marginal revenue from an extra dollar of advertising is about $200,000 ÷ $100,000, or 2.0 rather than 1.6. Because the marginal revenue exceeds the price elasticity, Solomon will increase its profit if it does more advertising.[13] To maximize profit, it should increase its advertising up to the point where the marginal revenue from an extra dollar of advertising falls to 1.6, the value of the price elasticity of demand.

# USING GRAPHS TO HELP DETERMINE ADVERTISING EXPENDITURE

A simple graphical technique can be used to see how much a firm, if it uses the above rule, should spend on advertising. Take the case of the Brady Chemical Company. Curve $A$ in Figure 10.14 shows the relationship between the price elasticity of demand of this firm's product and the amount it spends on advertising. With little or no advertising, this firm's product would be regarded by consumers as similar to lots of other products; hence, its price elasticity of demand would be very high.

But since appropriate advertising can induce consumers to attach impor-

---

[11] Recall from equation (3.16) that $MR = P\left(1 - 1/\eta\right)$. Thus $1 - 1/\eta = MR/P$, and $1/\eta = 1 - MR/P$, which means that

$$\eta = \frac{1}{1 - MR/P} = \frac{P}{P - MR},$$

which is the right-hand side of equation (10.11).

[12] However, this rule is based on many simplifying assumptions and is not a complete solution to this complex problem, which is considered further in Chapter 11.

[13] Had Solomon's managers believed that the marginal revenue from an extra dollar of advertising was *less* than the price elasticity of demand, a *reduction* in the firm's advertising expenditures would increase profit.

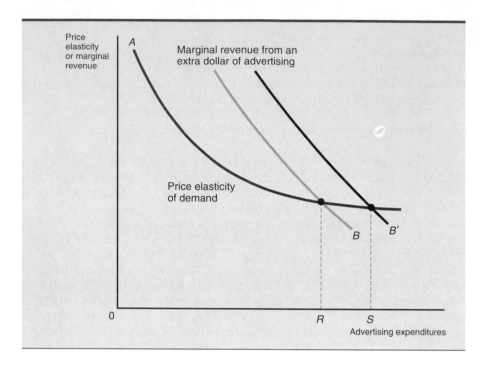

**FIGURE 10.14    *Optimal Advertising Expenditure***    The firm's optimal
advertising expenditure is *R* if the marginal revenue curve is *B* (or *S* if the
marginal revenue curve is *B′*).

tance to this product's distinguishing features, increases in advertising
expenditure reduce its price elasticity considerably (by decreasing the product's perceived substitutability with other goods).[14] At each level of advertising expenditure, the *B* curve shows the marginal revenue from an extra
dollar of advertising. Since the *A* curve intersects the *B* curve when Brady's
advertising expenditure is *R* dollars, this, based on equation (10.12), is the
level of advertising expenditures that maximizes Brady's profits.

A firm's optimal advertising expenditure depends on the position and
shape of its *B* curve and its *A* curve. For example, suppose Brady's *B* curve
shifts rightward to *B′*, as shown in Figure 10.14. Such a shift might occur if
the firm or its advertising agency found ways to increase the effectiveness
of its advertisements. An increase in the optimal level of the firm's advertising expenditures (to *S* dollars in Figure 10.14) would be the result.

---

[14] This is true for some products, but not for others. In some cases, the price elasticity of demand is
directly, not inversely, related to the amount spent on advertising.

# ADVERTISING, THE PRICE ELASTICITY OF DEMAND, AND BRAND LOYALTY: THE CASE OF THE RETAIL COFFEE MARKET

Many firms, such as retail stores, advertise changes in the prices of selected products. One effect of advertising such price changes is likely to be an increase in the price elasticity of demand for the product whose price is changed. Why? Because more consumers will be aware of the price change under these circumstances. To illustrate, consider a study carried out by Berkeley's Michael Katz and Carl Shapiro of the purchases of coffee by 935 households from 1980 to 1982.[15] For each purchase, information concerning the time of purchase, the store in which it was made, the price paid, and the use of either manufacturer or retailer coupons was obtained. (A coupon allows the buyer to obtain coffee at a lower price.) In all, about 50,000 purchase events were included in their sample. These events occurred in Pittsfield, Massachusetts.

Using regression analysis (discussed in Chapter 4), Katz and Shapiro estimated the price elasticity of demand for each of four brands of coffee— Chock Full o' Nuts, Maxwell House, Folgers, and Hills Brothers—during periods when price changes for these brands were advertised and during periods when they were not advertised. As shown in Table 10.9, the price elasticity of demand tended to be higher during the former periods than during the latter periods. For example, the price elasticity of Hills Brothers coffee was about 6.3 during periods when price changes were advertised, but only about 4.2 during periods when they were not advertised.

Katz and Shapiro also studied how frequently consumers switched from brand to brand, rather than remained loyal to a particular brand. One simple measure of brand loyalty is the percentage of customers buying a partic-

TABLE 10.9  *Price Elasticities of Demand, Periods of Advertised and Unadvertised Price Changes*

|  | Price elasticity of demand | |
| --- | --- | --- |
| Brand | Advertised price change | Unadvertised price change |
| Chock Full o' Nuts | 8.9 | 6.5 |
| Maxwell House | 6.0 | * |
| Folgers | 15.1 | 10.6 |
| Hills Brothers | 6.3 | 4.2 |

\* Not significantly different from zero.
*Source:* M. Katz and C. Shapiro, "Consumer Shopping Behavior in the Retail Coffee Market."

[15] M. Katz and C. Shapiro, "Consumer Shopping Behavior in the Retail Coffee Market," in P. Ippolito and D. Scheffman, eds., *Empirical Approaches to Consumer Protection Economics* (Washington, D.C.: Federal Trade Commission, 1986).

**TABLE 10.10**  *Percentage of Customers That Are Repeat Buyers of the Same Brand*

|  | Chock Full o' Nuts | Maxwell House | Folgers | Hills Brothers |
|---|---|---|---|---|
| All purchasers | 62 | 62 | 63 | 42 |
| Coupon users | 49 | 55 | 56 | 14 |
| Purchasers not using coupons | 63 | 70 | 65 | 44 |

*Source:* M. Katz and C. Shapiro, "Consumer Shopping Behavior in the Retail Coffee Market."

ular brand today that will buy this brand again when next they buy this sort of product. Table 10.10 shows the value of this measure for the four coffee brands studied by Katz and Shapiro. For example, about 62 percent of the buyers of Maxwell House coffee today will buy this same brand when next they buy coffee.

From the data in Table 10.10, one can conclude that brand loyalty tends to be rather high among coffees, but it varies from one brand to another. In particular, consumers tend to be less loyal to Hills Brothers than to the other three brands. Also, brand loyalty tends to be lower for consumers who purchase coffee with a coupon than for those who do not use a coupon. For example, 55 percent of consumers using a coupon to buy Maxwell House coffee were repeat buyers, whereas 70 percent of those not using coupons to buy Maxwell House coffee were repeat buyers. The fact that coupon users tend to have relatively low brand loyalty is of importance to firms. If the probability of repeat purchases by coupon users is low enough, the profitability of issuing coupons may be substantially impaired. The analysis of data of this sort concerning brand switching and brand loyalty has been very helpful to managers.

# SUMMARY

1. A perfectly competitive firm will set its output so that price equals marginal cost. If there exists an output rate where price exceeds average variable costs, it will pay the firm to produce in the short run, even though price does not cover average total costs. But if there does not exist an output rate where price exceeds average variable costs, the firm is better off to produce nothing at all. In the long run, the firm will produce at the minimum point on its long-run average total cost curve. Price tends to be at the level where the market demand curve intersects the market supply curve.
2. A constant-cost industry has a horizontal long-run supply curve; an increasing-cost industry has a positively sloped long-run supply curve. If a constant-cost industry expands, there is no increase (or decrease) in

input prices; if an increasing-cost industry expands, there is an increase in input prices.

3. Under monopoly, a firm will maximize profit if it sets its output rate at the point where marginal revenue equals marginal cost. It does not follow that a firm that holds a monopoly over the production of a particular product must make a profit. If the monopolist cannot cover its variable costs, it, like a perfectly competitive firm, will shut down, even in the short run.

4. If an industry is monopolized, it generally will set a higher price and lower output than if it is perfectly competitive. The perfectly competitive firm operates at the point at which price equals marginal cost, whereas the monopolist operates at a point at which price exceeds marginal cost.

5. A monopolist sometimes requires the consumer to pay an initial fee for the right to buy its product as well as a usage fee for each unit of the product he or she buys. This is known as a two-part tariff. Another pricing technique sometimes used by monopolists is bundling, which occurs if a firm requires customers that buy one of its products to buy another of its products as well.

6. In contrast to perfect competition, where all firms sell an identical product, firms under monopolistic competition sell somewhat different products. Producers differentiate their product from that of other producers. Thus, the demand curve facing each firm slopes downward to the right—and is not horizontal, as it would be under perfect competition. Each firm will set marginal revenue equal to marginal cost, if it maximizes profit.

7. Monopolistically competitive firms spend very large amounts on advertising. To maximize its profits, a firm should set its advertising so that the marginal revenue from an extra dollar of advertising equals the price elasticity of demand (under the conditions discussed above).

8. Advertising of price changes may increase the price elasticity of demand for the product whose price is changed. This is because the advertising makes consumers more aware of the price changes. Measures of brand loyalty are useful in guiding decisions concerning promotional activities to increase sales of particular brands.

## PROBLEMS

1. The Hamilton Company is a member of a perfectly competitive industry. Like all members of the industry, its total cost function is

$$TC = 25{,}000 + 150Q + 3Q^2,$$

where $TC$ is the firm's monthly total cost (in dollars), and $Q$ is the firm's monthly output.

(a) If the industry is in long-run equilibrium, what is the price of the Hamilton Company's product?

(b) What is the firm's monthly output?

2. In 1994, the box industry is perfectly competitive. The lowest point on the long-run average cost curve of each of the identical box producers is $4, and this minimum point occurs at an output of 1,000 boxes per month. The market demand curve for boxes is

$$Q_D = 140{,}000 - 10{,}000\,P,$$

where $P$ is the price of a box, and $Q_D$ is the quantity of boxes demanded per month. The market supply curve for boxes is

$$Q_S = 80{,}000 + 5{,}000\,P,$$

where $Q_S$ is the quantity of boxes supplied per month. ($P$ is expressed in dollars per box.)

(a) What is the equilibrium price of a box? Is this the long-run equilibrium price?

(b) How many firms are in this industry when it is in long-run equilibrium?

3. The Burr Corporation's total cost function (where $TC$ is the total cost in dollars, and $Q$ is quantity) is

$$TC = 200 + 4Q + 2Q^2.$$

(a) If the firm is perfectly competitive and if the price of its product is $24, what is its optimal output rate?

(b) At this output rate, what are its profits?

4. The supply and demand curves for pears are as follows:

$$Q_S = 10{,}000\,P$$

$$Q_D = 25{,}000 - 15{,}000\,P,$$

where $Q_S$ is the quantity (tons) supplied, $Q_D$ is the quantity (tons) demanded, and $P$ is the price per pear (in hundreds of dollars per ton).

(a) Plot the supply and demand curves.

(b) What is the equilibrium price?

(c) What is the equilibrium quantity?

5. Harry Smith is the owner of a metals-producing firm that is an unregulated monopoly. After considerable experimentation and research, he finds that its marginal cost curve can be approximated by a straight line, $MC = 60 + 2Q$, where $MC$ is marginal cost (in dollars), and $Q$ is output. The demand curve for the product is $P = 100 - Q$, where $P$ is the product price (in dollars), and $Q$ is output.

(a) If he wants to maximize profit, what output should he choose?

(b) What price should he charge?

6. The White Company is a member of the lamp industry, which is perfectly competitive. The price of a lamp is $50. The firm's total cost function is

$$TC = 1{,}000 + 20Q + 5Q^2,$$

where $TC$ is total cost (in dollars), and $Q$ is hourly output.
(a) What output maximizes profit?
(b) What is the firm's economic profit at this output?
(c) What is the firm's average cost at this output?
(d) If other firms in the lamp industry have the same cost function as this firm, is the industry in equilibrium? Why or why not?
7. The long-run supply curve for a particular type of kitchen knife is a horizontal line at a price of $3 per knife. The demand curve for such a kitchen knife is

$$Q_D = 50 - 2P,$$

where $Q_D$ is the quantity of knives demanded (in millions per year), and $P$ is the price per knife (in dollars).
(a) What is the equilibrium output of such knives?
(b) If a tax of $1.00 is imposed on each knife, what is the equilibrium output of such knives? (Assume that the tax is collected by the government from the suppliers of knives.)
(c) After the tax is imposed, you buy such a knife for $3.75. Is this the long-run equilibrium price?
8. The Wilson Company's marketing manager has determined that the price elasticity of demand for its product equals 2.2. According to studies he has carried out, the relationship between the amount spent by the firm on advertising and its sales is as follows:

| Advertising expenditure | Sales |
|---|---|
| $100,000 | $1.0 million |
| 200,000 | 1.3 million |
| 300,000 | 1.5 million |
| 400,000 | 1.6 million |

(a) If the Wilson Company is spending $200,000 on advertising, what is the marginal revenue from an extra dollar of advertising?
(b) Is $200,000 the optimal amount for the firm to spend on advertising?
(c) If $200,000 is not the optimal amount, would you recommend that the firm spend more or less on advertising?
9. The Coolidge Corporation is the only producer of a particular type of laser. The demand curve for its product is

$$Q_D = 8,300 - 2.1P,$$

and its total cost function is

$$TC = 2,200 + 480Q + 20Q^2,$$

where $P$ is price (in dollars), $TC$ is total cost (in dollars), and $Q$ is monthly output.

(a) Derive an expression for the firm's marginal revenue curve.
(b) To maximize profit, how many lasers should the firm produce and sell per month?
(c) If this number is produced and sold, what will be the firm's monthly profit?

10. The Madison Corporation, a monopolist, receives a report from a consulting firm concluding that the demand function for its product is

$$Q = 78 - 1.1P + 2.3Y + 0.9A,$$

where $Q$ is the number of units sold, $P$ is the price of its product (in dollars), $Y$ is per capita income (in thousands of dollars), and $A$ is the firm's advertising expenditure (in thousands of dollars). The firm's average variable cost function is

$$AVC = 42 - 8Q + 1.5Q^2,$$

where $AVC$ is average variable cost (in dollars).
(a) Can one determine the firm's marginal cost curve?
(b) Can one determine the firm's marginal revenue curve?
(c) If per capita income is $4,000 and advertising expenditure is $200,000, can one determine the price and output where marginal revenue equals marginal cost? If so, what are they?

*11. The Wilcox Company has two plants with the following marginal cost functions:

$$MC_1 = 20 + 2Q_1$$

$$MC_2 = 10 + 5Q_2,$$

where $MC_1$ is marginal cost in the first plant, $MC_2$ is marginal cost in the second plant, $Q_1$ is output in the first plant, and $Q_2$ is output in the second plant.
(a) If the Wilcox Company is minimizing its costs and if it is producing 5 units of output in the first plant, how many units of output is it producing in the second plant? Explain.
(b) What is the marginal cost function for the firm as a whole?
(c) Can you determine from the above data the average cost function for each plant? Why or why not?

12. If the Rhine Company ignores the possibility that other firms may enter its market, it should set a price of $10,000 for its product, which is a power tool. But if it does so, other firms will begin to enter the market. During the next 2 years, it will earn $4 million per year, but in the following 2 years, it will earn $1 million per year. On the other hand, if it sets a price of $7,000, it will earn $2.5 million in each of the next 4 years, since no entrants will appear.
(a) If the interest rate is 10 percent, should the Rhine Company set a price of $7,000 or $10,000? Why? (Consider only the next 4 years.)

---

* This question pertains to the chapter appendix.

(b) If the interest rate is 8 percent, should the Rhine Company set a price of $7,000 or $10,000? Why? (Consider only the next 4 years.)

(c) The results in parts (a) and (b) pertain only to the next 4 years. How can the firm's managers extend the planning horizon?

13. During recessions and economic hard times, many people—particularly those who have difficulty getting bank loans—turn to pawnshops to raise cash. But even during boom years, pawnshops can be very profitable. Because the collateral that customers put up (such as jewelry, guns, or electric guitars) is generally worth at least double what is lent, it generally can be sold at a profit. And because the usury laws allow higher interest ceilings for pawnshops than for other lending institutions, pawnshops often charge spectacularly high rates of interest. For example, Florida's pawnshops charge interest rates of 20 percent or more *per month.* According to Steven Kent, an analyst at Goldman, Sachs, pawnshops make 20 percent gross profit on defaulted loans and 205 percent interest on loans repaid.

(a) In late 1991, there were about 8,000 pawnshops in the United States, according to American Business Information. This was much higher than in 1986, when the number was about 5,000. Indeed, in late 1991 alone, the number jumped by about 1,000. Why did the number increase? Do you think that it will continue to increase? Why, or why not?

(b) In a particular small city, do the pawnshops constitute a perfectly competitive industry? If not, what is the market structure of the industry?

(c) Are there considerable barriers to entry in the pawnshop industry? (Note: A pawnshop can be opened for less than $125,000, but a number of states have tightened licensing requirements for pawnshops.)

# *APPENDIX: ALLOCATION OF OUTPUT AMONG PLANTS*

Many firms own and operate more than one plant. In this appendix, we show how the managers of these firms should allocate output among various plants. This is an important decision, and our results have major direct practical value. To be specific, we consider the case of the Mercer Company, a monopolist, but our results are as valid for non-monopolists as for monopolists.

The Mercer Company, a monopolist that makes a particular type of metal fixture, operates two plants with marginal cost curves shown in columns 2 and 3 of Table 10.11, output being shown in column 1. Clearly, if the firm decides to produce only 1 unit of output per hour, it should use plant I, since the marginal cost between zero and 1 unit is lower in plant I than in plant II. Hence, for the firm as a whole, the marginal cost between zero and 1 unit of output is $10 (the marginal cost between zero and 1 unit for plant I). Similarly, if the firm decides to produce 2 units of output per hour, both should be produced in plant I, and the marginal cost between the first and second unit of output for the firm as a whole is $12 (the marginal cost between the first and second unit in plant I). If the firm decides to produce 3 units of output per hour, 2 should be produced in plant I and 1 in plant II, and the marginal cost between the second and third unit of output for the firm as a whole is $14 (the marginal cost between zero and 1 unit of output for plant II). Alternatively, all 3 could be produced at plant I.

Going on in this way, we can derive the marginal cost curve for the firm as a whole, shown in column 4 of Table 10.11. To maximize profits, the firm should find that output at which marginal revenue equals the marginal cost of the firm as a whole. This is the profit-maximizing output level. In this case, it is 3 or 4 units per hour. Suppose that the firm picks 4 units. To determine what price to charge, the firm must see what price corresponds to this output on the demand curve. In this case, the answer is $23.

TABLE 10.11   Costs of the Mercer Company

| Output per hour | Marginal cost* Plant I (dollars) | Marginal cost* Plant II (dollars) | Marginal cost for firm* (dollars) | Price (dollars) | Marginal revenue* (dollars) |
|---|---|---|---|---|---|
| 1 | 10 | 14 | 10 | 40 | — |
| 2 | 12 | 18 | 12 | 30 | 20 |
| 3 | 14 | 22 | 14 | 26 | 18 |
| 4 | 20 | 26 | 14 | 23 | 14 |
| 5 | 24 | 30 | 18 | 16 | 12 |

* These figures pertain to the interval between the indicated output and 1 unit less than the indicated output.

At this point, we have solved most of the Mercer Company's problems, but not quite all. Given that it will produce 4 units of output per hour, how should it divide this production between the two plants? The answer is that it should set the marginal cost in plant I equal to the marginal cost in plant II. Table 10.11 shows that this means that plant I will produce 3 units per hour and plant II will produce 1 unit per hour. The common value of the marginal costs of the two plants is the marginal cost of the firm as a whole; this common value must be set equal to marginal revenue if the firm is maximizing profit.

Many firms have used this technique to allocate output among plants. For example, electric power companies have developed a Station-Loading Sliderule to facilitate the actual job of allocating electricity demand (or "load") among plants in accord with the above theoretical rule. This mechanical device allows a central dispatcher, who is in constant communication with the plants, to compute quickly the optimal allocation among plants. The result has been millions of dollars in savings.

As a further illustration, consider the Anderson Company which has plants at Altoona, Pennsylvania, and at High Point, North Carolina. The total cost function for the Altoona plant is

$$TC_A = 5 + 9Q_A + Q_A^2,$$

where $TC_A$ is the daily total cost (in thousands of dollars) at this plant, and $Q_A$ is its output (in units per day). The total cost curve for the High Point plant is

$$TC_H = 4 + 10Q_H + 0.5Q_H^2,$$

where $TC_H$ is the daily total cost (in thousands of dollars) at this plant, and $Q_H$ is its output (in units per day). Since the Anderson Company's demand curve is

$$P = 31 - Q,$$

its marginal revenue curve is

$$MR = \frac{dPQ}{dQ} = \frac{d(31Q - Q^2)}{dQ}$$

$$= 31 - 2Q,$$

where $Q = Q_A + Q_H$ and where $P$ is price and $MR$ is marginal revenue (both in thousands of dollars per unit).

To maximize profit, the firm must choose its price and output so that

$$MC_A = MC_H = MR, \tag{10.13}$$

where $MC_A$ is the marginal cost (in thousands of dollars) at the Altoona plant, and $MC_H$ is the marginal cost (in thousands of dollars) at the High Point plant. To obtain $MC_A$ and $MC_H$, we take the following derivatives:

$$MC_A = \frac{dTC_A}{dQ_A} = 9 + 2Q_A,$$

$$MC_H = \frac{dTC_H}{dQ_H} = 10 + Q_H.$$

According to equation (10.13), $MC_A$ must equal $MC_H$. Thus,

$$9 + 2Q_A = 10 + Q_H$$

$$Q_H = -1 + 2Q_A.$$

Also, because equation (10.13) states that $MC_A$ must equal $MR$,

$$9 + 2Q_A = 31 - 2(Q_A + Q_H)$$

$$= 31 - 2(Q_A - 1 + 2Q_A)$$

$$= 33 - 6Q_A.$$

Consequently, $Q_A = 3$. And since $Q_H = -1 + 2Q_A$, it follows that $Q_H = 5$. Moreover, $P = 23$, because $P = 31 - (Q_A + Q_H)$. Put in a nutshell, the Anderson Company should charge a price of $23,000 per unit, and produce 3 units per day at its Altoona plant and 5 units per day at its High Point plant.

# Chapter 11
# Oligopoly and Strategic Behavior

An **oligopoly** is a market structure with a small number of firms. A good example of an oligopoly is the American petroleum industry, in which eight firms have accounted in recent years for about 60 percent of the industry's refining capacity. Each of the major oil firms must take account of the reaction of the others when it formulates its price and output policy, since its policy is likely to affect theirs. Thus, when Exxon raises its price of home heating oil by 1 or 2 cents per gallon, it has to anticipate what the reaction of other firms in the industry will be. If its rivals decide against such a price increase, it is likely that the price increase will have to be rescinded; otherwise its rivals will pull away a large number of Exxon's customers.

Oligopolies abound in most countries. In the United States, the automobile industry is dominated by three domestic firms—General Motors, Ford, and Chrysler—as well as a small number of foreign producers. Many parts of the electrical equipment industry are dominated by General Electric and Westinghouse. There are many reasons for oligopoly, one being economies of scale. In some industries, because low costs cannot be achieved unless a firm is producing an output equal to a substantial percentage of the total available market, the number of firms tends to be rather small.

We devote an entire chapter to oligopoly both because of its importance and because there is no single theory of oligopoly. In contrast to perfect competition or monopoly, where there is a single unified model, many types of oligopoly models exist and are used. Each of these theories may be appropriate, depending on the circumstances.

# THE EMERGENCE OF OLIGOPOLISTIC INDUSTRIES[1]

Oligopolistic industries, like others,[2] often (but not always) pass through a number of stages—introduction, growth, maturity, and decline. As indicated in Figure 11.1, the industry's sales grow very rapidly in the introduction phase, less rapidly in the growth phase, and even less rapidly during maturity; in the stage of decline, the industry's sales fall. As an industry goes through these stages, the nature of competition often shifts.

During the early stages when industry sales are growing relatively rapidly, there frequently is a great deal of uncertainty about the industry's technology. Which product configuration will turn out to be best? Which process technology will be most efficient? Because of small production volume and the newness of the product, production costs tend to be higher than those that the industry will eventually achieve. The learning curve

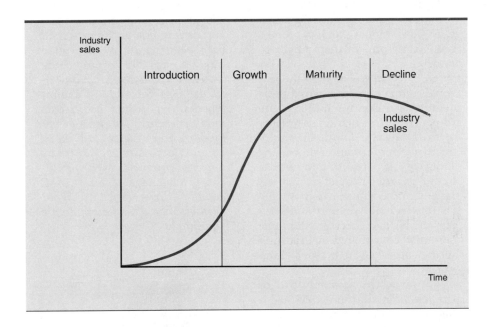

FIGURE 11.1 *Typical Stages of the Evolution of an Industry* Industry sales grow at a rapid rate in the introduction and growth stages, more modestly in the maturity stage, and not at all in the decline stage.

---

[1] The discussion in this and the following section is based largely on M. Porter, *Competitive Strategy* (New York: Free Press, 1980).

[2] Whether industries are perfectly competitive, monopolistic, monopolistically competitive, or oligopolistic, they often go through the stages discussed here. However, we focus in this chapter on the evolution of oligopolistic industries.

## IBM, THE PERSONAL COMPUTER MARKET, AND ECONOMIES OF SCALE

In 1981, the IBM Corporation introduced its personal computer, which was an enormous success. Initial estimates of sales in 1983 were about 350,000 units, but by the summer of that year the projections had risen to 600,000–800,000 units. By mid-1983, it appeared that the predicted "shakedown" of the personal computer industry was beginning to occur. In other words, a number of smaller firms in the industry, such as Vector Graphic and Interdec Data Systems, lost money, and it seemed likely that some of them might go under.

By 1984, IBM's share of the personal computer market was 60 percent. One reason for IBM's ability to penetrate this market so quickly was its already dominating presence in the information-processing industry. Its reputation, strong brand image, customer awareness, large R and D effort, heavy emphasis on customer support and service, and big and effective sales force certainly contributed significantly to the success of its personal computer.

However, this was only part of the story. In addition, IBM had a big cost advantage over its smaller competitors.

*By virtue of its enormous size the company enjoyed economies of scale, making it the low-cost producer in many cases. This allowed the firm to slash prices in any segment where it was weak. Ultimately, strength was gained by IBM through eliminating competitors who could not compete with the lower prices for a sustained period of time. With gross margins of about 40% in 1984, IBM had plenty of room for price cuts if it needed them. . . .*

*Even if companies attempted to avoid head-to-head competition with IBM by finding market niches not yet approached by the corporation, they were likely to be "blown out of the water" if the niche proved profitable. IBM was able to exploit any new opportunity because its manufacturing facilities were modern and efficient. In short, competitors survived only by offering products with significant advantages over IBM, usually a lower price or higher performance for comparable equipment.** 

* T. Wheelen and J. David Hunger, *Cases in Strategic Management and Business Policy* (Reading, Mass.: Addison-Wesley, 1987).

(recall Chapter 7) often is comparatively steep. Newly formed companies tend to be a larger percentage of the industry than in subsequent years. Many of these new firms may be started by personnel leaving other firms to start their own businesses. For example, many semiconductor firms were offshoots of Fairchild Camera and Instrument Corporation.

At these early stages of an industry's evolution, one of the major strategic questions facing managers is: Which markets for the industry's new product will tend to open up early, and which ones will open up relatively late? This question is important both because firms should allocate marketing efforts and R and D resources to relatively receptive markets and because the nature of the early markets can exert a significant influence on the way the industry evolves. To forecast which markets or market segments are likely to be most receptive to a new product, one should consider the following three factors.

First, the most receptive buyers tend to be those where the new product is most profitable. For example, if a new robot is much more profitable in the railroad industry than in the agricultural equipment industry, it is more likely to be used first by railroads, not by agricultural equipment firms. Second, buyers who face a relatively low cost of product failure are likely to be faster in adopting a new product than those where the potential costs are very high. Thus, if this new robot could cause millions of dollars of losses in the auto industry but only minor losses in the steel industry, it is more likely that steel producers will take a chance on it than that auto firms will do so. Third, buyers who would experience relatively low costs in switching from old products to the new one sold by this industry are likely to be more receptive to this industry's product than buyers who would experience high changeover costs.

# *MATURITY AND DECLINE OF OLIGOPOLISTIC INDUSTRIES*

Eventually, most industries enter the maturity phase, when industry sales grow much more modestly than before. This is often a critical phase for many members of the industry. Since firms cannot maintain the growth rates to which they are accustomed merely by protecting their market share, there is often a tendency for firms to attack the market shares of their rivals in the same industry. For example, this occurred in the dishwasher business in the late 1970s, when GE and Maytag attacked Hobart in the higher-price segments of the market, which was becoming saturated. In this phase of an industry's evolution, firms often must alter their assumptions about how their competitors are likely to behave and react. The likelihood of interfirm warfare, based on price, service, or promotion, is high in this phase.

During the maturity phase, rivalry among firms often centers on cost and service, rather than new or greatly improved products. Because of slower growth, more knowledgeable customers, and greater technological maturity, competition tends to focus on cost and service, which may prompt a significant reorientation of firms that have competed on other grounds in the past. Also, as the industry adjusts to slower growth, there generally is a reduction in the additions to productive capacity. Often, firms do not realize that they have entered this maturity phase until after they have installed more capacity than is required. Thus, for a time, the industry suffers from overcapacity.

After the maturity phase, many industries enter a stage during which sales decline. One reason for such a decline may be that this product is being supplanted by a new one (as slide rules were supplanted by electronic calculators). Another reason may be a shrinkage in the size of the customer group that buys the product, perhaps because of demographic changes. Still another reason may be a change in buyers' tastes or needs. For example, cigar sales have gone down in part because of cigars' declining social acceptability.

While firms in declining industries are often advised to curtail investment and get lots of cash out of the business as quickly as possible, this is not always the best strategy. Some industries, like some people, grow old more gracefully and profitably than others. Some firms have done well by investing heavily in a declining industry, thus making their businesses better "cash cows" later. Others have avoided losses subsequently experienced by their rivals by selling out before it was generally recognized that the industry was in decline.

## COLLUSIVE AGREEMENTS

Conditions in oligopolistic industries tend to encourage collusion, since the number of firms is small and the firms are aware of their interdependence. The advantages to the firms of collusion seem clear: increased profits, decreased uncertainty, and a better opportunity to prevent entry. But collusive arrangements are often hard to maintain, since once a collusive agreement is made, any of the firms can increase its profits by cheating on the agreement. Moreover, in the United States, collusive arrangements generally are illegal.

If a collusive arrangement is made openly and formally, it is called a **cartel**. In many other countries, cartels have been common and legally acceptable; but in the United States, most collusive agreements, whether secret or open cartels, were declared illegal by the Sherman Antitrust Act (discussed in detail in Chapter 15), which dates back to 1890. But this does not mean that such agreements do not exist. For instance, there was widespread collusion among American electrical equipment manufacturers during the

1950s. Also, trade associations and professional organizations may sometimes perform functions somewhat similar to those of a cartel. Further,
some types of cartels have had the official sanction of the United States
government. Thus, airlines flying transatlantic routes have been members
of the International Air Transport Association, which has agreed on uniform prices for transatlantic flights.

If a cartel is established to set a uniform price for a particular (homogeneous) product, what price will it charge? To answer this question, the cartel
must estimate the marginal cost curve for the cartel as a whole. If input
prices do not increase as the cartel expands, this marginal cost curve is the
horizontal sum of the marginal cost curves of the individual firms. Suppose
that the resulting marginal cost curve for the cartel is as shown in Figure
11.2. If the demand curve for the industry's product and the relevant marginal revenue curve are as shown there, the output that maximizes the total
profit of the cartel members is $Q_0$. Thus, if it maximizes cartel profits, the
cartel will choose a price of $P_0$, which is the monopoly price.

The cartel must also distribute the industry's total sales among the firms
belonging to the cartel. If the purpose of the cartel is to maximize cartel
profits, it will allocate sales to firms in such a way that the marginal cost of
all firms is equal. Otherwise the cartel could make more money by reallo-

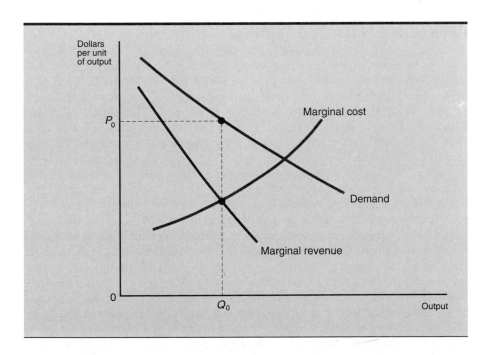

**FIGURE 11.2** *Price and Output Determination by a Cartel* The cartel
chooses a price of $P_0$ and an output of $Q_0$.

cating output among firms so as to reduce the cost of producing the cartel's total output. If the marginal cost at firm A is higher than at firm B, the cartel can increase its total profits by transferring some production from firm A to firm B.

But this allocation of output is unlikely to take place, since allocation decisions are the results of negotiation between firms with varying interests and varying capabilities. This is a political process in which firms have different amounts of influence. Those with the most influence and the shrewdest negotiators are likely to receive the largest sales quotas, even though this raises total cartel costs. Also, high-cost firms are likely to receive bigger sales quotas than cost minimization would require, since they would be unwilling to accept the small quotas required by cost minimization. In practice, sales are often distributed in accord with a firm's level of sales in the past, or the extent of its productive capacity. Also, a cartel sometimes divides a market geographically, with some firms being given particular countries or regions and other firms being given other countries or regions.

## THE BREAKDOWN OF COLLUSIVE AGREEMENTS

One of the most important things a manager should understand about collusive agreements is that they tend to break down. To understand why firms are tempted to leave the cartel, consider the case of the firm in Figure 11.3. If this firm were to leave the cartel, it would be faced with a demand curve of $DD'$ as long as the other firms in the cartel maintained a price of $P_0$. This demand curve is very elastic; the firm is able to expand its sales considerably by small reductions in price. Even if the firm were not to leave the cartel, but if it were to grant secret price concessions, the same sort of demand curve would exist.

The firm's maximum profit if it leaves the cartel or secretly lowers price will be attained if it sells an output of $Q_1$, at a price of $P_1$, since this is the output at which marginal cost equals marginal revenue. This price would result in a profit of $Q_1 \times BP_1$, which is higher than it would be if the firm conformed to the price and sales quota dictated by the cartel. A firm that breaks away from a cartel—or secretly cheats—can raise its profits as long as other firms do not do the same thing and as long as the cartel does not punish it in some way. But if all firms do this, the cartel disintegrates.

Thus, there is a constant threat to the existence of a cartel. Its members have an incentive to cheat, and once a few do so, others may follow. Price concessions made secretly by a few "chiselers" or openly by a few malcontents cut into the sales of cooperative members of the cartel who are induced to match them. Ultimately the cartel may fall apart.

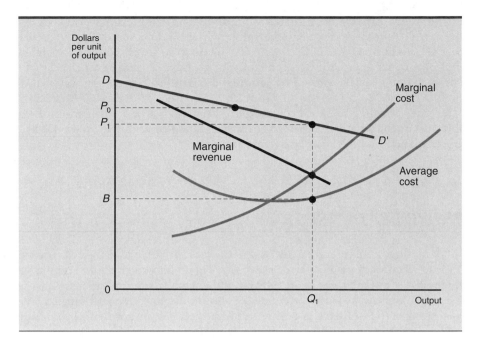

**FIGURE 11.3   Instability of Cartels**   If it leaves the cartel, the firm's profit equals $Q_1 \times BP_1$, which is higher than it would be if the firm adhered to the price and sales quota established by the cartel.

## ACRIMONY IN THE OPEC OIL CARTEL

To illustrate the difficulties in maintaining an effective cartel, consider the Organization of Petroleum Exporting Countries (OPEC), which consists of thirteen major oil-producing countries, including Saudi Arabia, Iran, Venezuela, Libya, Nigeria, and the United Arab Emirates. This cartel increased the price of crude oil dramatically during the 1970s, but by 1983, a decade after the first of its huge price increases, OPEC experienced problems in maintaining the price of oil, and from 1984 to 1986, the price fell until it was below $15 per barrel. To some extent, the downward pressure on price was due to a leftward shift in the demand for oil brought about by conservation of oil and competition from other fuels (stemming partly from the great increases in the oil price in earlier years). Also, non-OPEC oil production (in Mexico and the North Sea, for example) soared, thus putting additional pressure on OPEC.

But this is only part of the story. The price declines have also been due to the fact that there has been internal dissension and that individual members of the OPEC cartel have refused to abide by the production quotas set by the cartel. Take the case of Saudi Arabia, which said on September 27, 1991 that it would not let OPEC dictate its production level. Iran had insisted that all members be willing to cut output to push the price up to $21 per barrel. Saying that it wanted to produce 8.5 million barrels per day, Saudi Arabia refused to cut its output. Iran's oil minister, Gholamreza Aqazadeh, attacked (verbally) his Saudi counterpart, Hisham Nazer, calling him inflexible and uncooperative. Nazer in turn threatened to withdraw from OPEC. Clearly, life in a cartel can be acrimonious.

## PRICE LEADERSHIP

In many oligopolistic industries, one firm sets the price and the rest follow its lead. Examples of industries that have been characterized by such **price leadership** are steel, nonferrous alloys, and agricultural implements. In this section, we show how the price leader should set its price and output. We assume that the industry is composed of a large dominant firm—the price leader—and a number of small firms. It is also assumed that the dominant firm sets the price for the industry, but that it lets the small firms sell all they want at that price. Whatever amount the small firms do not supply at that price is provided by the dominant firm.

Under these circumstances, you can readily determine the price that the dominant firm will set if it maximizes profits. Since each small firm takes the price as given, it produces the output at which price equals marginal cost. Thus, a supply curve for all small firms combined can be drawn by summing horizontally the marginal cost curves of the small firms. This supply curve is shown in Figure 11.4. The demand curve for the dominant firm can be derived by subtracting the amount supplied by the small firms at each price from the total amount demanded at that price. Thus, the demand curve for the output of the dominant firm, d, can be determined by finding the horizontal difference at each price between the industry demand curve and the supply curve for all small firms combined.

To illustrate how $d$ is derived, suppose that the dominant firm sets a price of $P_0$. The small firms will supply $R_0$, and the total amount demanded will be $V_0$. Thus, the amount to be supplied by the dominant firm is $V_0 - R_0$, which is the quantity on the $d$ curve at price $P_0$. In other words, $d_0$ is set equal to $V_0 - R_0$. The process by which the other points on the $d$ curve are determined is exactly the same; this procedure is repeated at various levels of price.

Knowing the demand curve for the output of the dominant firm, $d$, and the dominant firm's marginal cost curve, $M$, you can readily determine the price and output that will maximize the profits of the dominant firm. The dominant firm's marginal revenue curve, $R$, can be derived from the dominant firm's demand curve, $d$, in the usual way. The optimal output for the

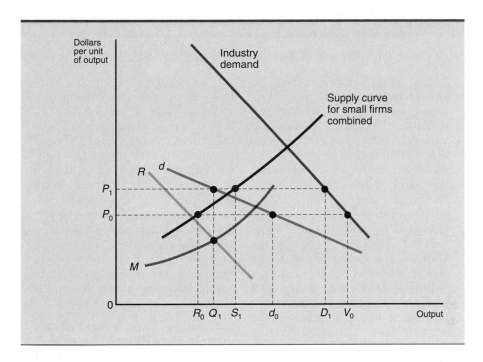

**FIGURE 11.4** *Price Leadership by a Dominant Firm* The dominant firm sets a price of $P_1$, and supplies $Q_1$ units of the product. Total industry output is $D_1$.

dominant firm is the output, $Q_1$, where its marginal cost equals its marginal revenue. This output will be achieved if the dominant firm sets a price of $P_1$. The total industry output will be $D_1$, and the small firms will supply $S_1$ $(= D_1 - Q_1)$.

## *AJAX, INC.: A NUMERICAL EXAMPLE*

To illustrate how a dominant firm can determine the price that will maximize its profits, consider Ajax, Inc., the dominant firm in a particular industry. The demand curve for this industry's product is

$$Q = 100 - 5P,$$

where $Q$ is the quantity demanded, and $P$ is the price. The supply curve for the small firms in this industry is

$$Q_S = 10 + P,$$

ANALYZING MANAGERIAL DECISIONS

## GLOBAL OLIGOPOLY IN THE DISPOSABLE SYRINGE MARKET

A disposable plastic syringe—a single-use hypodermic needle and vacuum container for the intravenous injection of drugs—is a major advance over the glass syringe. Becton Dickinson, which produced glass syringes before the advent of the plastic syringe, has been by far the biggest seller of such syringes in the world. In the early 1980s, its market share ranged from 94 percent in Mexico to 51 percent in the United States to only about 10 percent in Germany. A few producers —Becton Dickinson, Turumo (a Japanese firm), and Sherwood/Brunswick—have dominated the market, their worldwide market shares having been 31 percent, 18 percent, and 16 percent, respectively.

(a) The minimum economic scale of production for a firm in this industry has been estimated to be at least 60 percent of the combined sales of the two key national markets (the United States and Japan). Is this fact related to the oligopolistic structure of the industry? If so, how? (b) A doubling of volume has been estimated to lower the average cost of production by 20 percent. Is this fact related to the industry's structure? If so, how? (c) Becton Dickinson's strategy "was to be the world's lowest-cost producer through selling a wide line of mass-produced syringes in all the important country markets worldwide, employing large-scale plants and aggressive marketing efforts to convince doctors of the merits of disposables."* Why did it want to sell abroad as well as in the United States? (d) In each market, local competitors tended to set higher prices than Becton Dickinson and its global competitors. Why?

*Solution* (a) Yes. Given that the minimum economic scale of production is so large a proportion of total sales, one would expect that there would be only a relatively few producers. (b) Yes. Given that economies of scale are substantial, one would expect that there would be relatively few producers. (c) One important reason was to reap the benefits of economies of scale. (d) Because local competitors tended to be small, their average costs tended to be higher than those of Becton Dickinson and its global competitors.

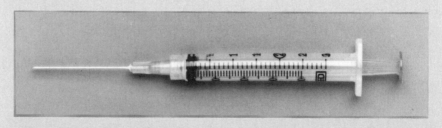

* M. Cvar, "Case Studies in Global Competition: Patterns of Success and Failure," in M. Porter, ed., *Competition in Global Industries* (Boston: Harvard Business School, 1986).

where $Q_S$ is the total amount supplied by all these small firms combined. Ajax's marginal cost curve is

$$MC = 2Q_A, \tag{11.1}$$

where $Q_A$ is Ajax's output.

To derive the demand curve for Ajax's output, we subtract $Q_S$ from $Q$, the result being

$$Q_A = Q - Q_S = (100 - 5P) - (10 + P) = 90 - 6P.$$

Thus,

$$P = 15 - \tfrac{1}{6}Q_A. \tag{11.2}$$

Remembering that Ajax's total revenue equals $P \cdot Q_A$, Ajax's total revenue equals

$$TR = (15 - \tfrac{1}{6}Q_A)Q_A$$

$$= 15Q_A - \tfrac{1}{6}Q_A^2,$$

and marginal revenue equals

$$\frac{dTR}{dQ_A} = \frac{d(15Q_A - \tfrac{1}{6}Q_A^2)}{dQ_A}$$

$$= 15 - \tfrac{1}{3}Q_A. \tag{11.3}$$

To maximize profit, Ajax must set marginal revenue, in equation (11.3), equal to marginal cost, in equation (11.1). Thus,

$$2Q_A = 15 - \tfrac{1}{3}Q_A,$$

so $Q_A$ must equal $6\tfrac{3}{7}$. Consequently, from equation (11.2), it follows that $P = 13\tfrac{39}{42}$, or \$13.93.

To sum up, if you were the chief executive officer of Ajax, and if you wanted to maximize profit, you would be well advised to charge a price of \$13.93. This is the profit-maximizing price.


# REPRESENTING OLIGOPOLY AS A GAME

Managers who must analyze and participate in oligopolistic decision making are likely to find modern **game theory** of use. Because a basic feature of oligopoly is that each firm must take account of its rivals' reactions to its own actions, oligopolistic decision making has many of the characteristics of a game. Game theory attempts to study decision making in situations where there is a mixture of conflict and cooperation, as in oligopoly. A **game** is a competitive situation where two or more persons pursue their own interests and no person can dictate the outcome. For example, poker is a game, and so is a situation in which two firms are engaged in competitive R and D programs. A game is described in terms of the players, the rules of the game, the payoffs of the game, and the information conditions that exist during the game.

Each player, and that may be a single person or an organization, is a decision-making unit with a certain amount of resources; the **rules of the game** describe how these resources can be employed. Thus, the rules of poker indicate how bets can be made and which hands are better than other hands. A **strategy** is a complete specification of what a player will do under each contingency in the playing of the game. For example, a corporation president might tell his subordinates how he wants an R and D program to start, and what should be done at subsequent times in response to various actions of competing firms. The game's outcome clearly depends on the strategies used by each player. A player's **payoff** varies from game to game: it is win, lose, or draw in checkers, and various sums of money in poker. For simplicity, this section deals only with **two-person games,** games with only two players.

The relevant features of a two-person game can be shown by constructing a **payoff matrix.** To illustrate, suppose that two firms, the Allied Company and the Barkley Corporation, are about to stage rival R and D programs and that each firm has a choice of strategies. Allied can choose strategy A or B, and Barkley can choose strategy 1 or 2. The payoff, expressed in terms of profits for each firm, is shown in Table 11.1 for each combination of strategies. For example, if Allied adopts strategy A and Barkley adopts strategy 2, Allied makes a profit of $2 million, and Barkley makes a profit of $3 million.

In this game, there is a **dominant strategy** for each player. Regardless of whether Barkley adopts strategy 1 or 2, Allied will make more profit if it chooses strategy B rather than A. Thus, strategy B is Allied's dominant strategy. Similarly, regardless of whether Allied adopts strategy A or B, Barkley will make more profit if it chooses strategy 1 rather than 2. Thus, strategy 1 is Barkley's dominant strategy. The solution to this game is quite simple. Allied chooses strategy B, and Barkley chooses strategy 1. Allied's profit equals $4 million, and Barkley's profit equals $3 million. This is the best that either firm can achieve.

*TABLE 11.1* *Payoff Matrix: R and D Programs*

| Possible strategies for Allied | Possible strategies for Barkley | |
|---|---|---|
| | 1 | 2 |
| A | Allied's profit: $3 million<br>Barkley's profit: $4 million | Allied's profit: $2 million<br>Barkley's profit: $3 million |
| B | Allied's profit: $4 million<br>Barkley's profit: $3 million | Allied's profit: $3 million<br>Barkley's profit: $2 million |

# NASH EQUILIBRIUM

Not all games have a dominant strategy for every player. For example, suppose that the payoff matrix for Allied and Barkley is that shown in Table 11.2. (This is the same as the payoff matrix in Table 11.1 except that Barkley's profit is $4 million, not $2 million, if it adopts strategy 2 and Allied adopts strategy B.) Under these circumstances, Allied still has a dominant strategy: strategy B. Regardless of which strategy Barkley adopts, strategy B is Allied's best strategy. But Barkley no longer has a dominant strategy, since its optimal strategy depends on what Allied decides to do. If Allied adopts strategy A, Barkley will make more profit if it chooses strategy 1 rather than 2. If Allied adopts strategy B, Barkley will make more profit if it chooses strategy 2 rather than 1.

**TABLE 11.2** *Payoff Matrix: No Dominant Strategy for Barkley*

| Possible strategies for Allied | Possible strategies for Barkley | |
|---|---|---|
| | 1 | 2 |
| A | Allied's profit: $3 million<br>Barkley's profit: $4 million | Allied's profit: $2 million<br>Barkley's profit: $3 million |
| B | Allied's profit: $4 million<br>Barkley's profit: $3 million | Allied's profit: $3 million<br>Barkley's profit: $4 million |

To determine what to do, Barkley must try to figure out what action Allied is likely to take. In other words, Barkley must put itself in Allied's place and see whether strategy A or strategy B is best for Allied. As pointed out in the previous paragraph, Allied's dominant strategy is strategy B. Since Barkley knows all the numbers in the payoff matrix, it can readily determine that this is the case. Thus, it will conclude that Allied will choose strategy B and that it should therefore pick strategy 2 (because strategy 2 is more profitable than strategy 1 if Allied adopts strategy B).

Thus, Allied would be expected to adopt strategy B, and Barkley would be expected to adopt strategy 2. This is the *Nash equilibrium* (named after John F. Nash, a Princeton mathematician) for this game. A Nash equilibrium occurs if each player's strategy is optimal given the strategies chosen by the other player(s). Put differently, *a Nash equilibrium is a set of strategies (in this case, strategy B for Allied and strategy 2 for Barkley) such that each player believes (accurately) that it is doing the best it can given the strategy of the other player(s).* Taking the other firm's decision as given, both Allied and Barkley are pursuing their own best interests by adopting strategy B and strategy 2, respectively. Neither regrets its own decision or has any incentive to change it.

What is the difference between a Nash equilibrium and an equilibrium where each player has a dominant strategy (as in Table 11.1)? If each player

TABLE 11.3  *Payoff Matrix: Two Nash Equilibria*

| Possible strategies for Allied | Possible strategies for Barkley | |
|---|---|---|
| | 1 | 2 |
| A | Allied's profit: $5 million<br>Barkley's profit: $5 million | Allied's profit: zero<br>Barkley's profit: zero |
| B | Allied's profit: zero<br>Barkley's profit: zero | Allied's profit: $5 million<br>Barkley's profit: $5 million |

has a dominant strategy, this strategy is its best choice *regardless of what other players do.* In a Nash equilibrium, each player adopts a strategy that is its best choice *given what the other players do.* It is also important to recognize that some games do not have a Nash equilibrium and that some games have more than one Nash equilibrium. Table 11.3 contains the payoff matrix for a game with two Nash equilibria. If Allied adopts strategy A and Barkley adopts strategy 1, each is doing the best it can given the other's choice of strategy. Also, if Allied adopts strategy B and Barkley adopts strategy 2, each is doing the best it can given the other's choice of strategy. Hence, there are two Nash equilibria in this game.

# CARPENTER COMPANY AND HANOVER CORPORATION: A NUMERICAL EXAMPLE

To illustrate further the concept of a Nash equilibrium, we consider a theory put forth by Augustin Cournot, a French economist. Although this theory is too simple to capture much of the richness of the oligopolistic situation, it has attracted considerable attention. Cournot considers the case in which there are two sellers, that is, the case of *duopoly,* but his model can easily be generalized to include the case of three or more sellers. To describe his model, it is convenient to assume that the two firms, the Carpenter Company and the Hanover Corporation, produce the same product, have the same cost functions, and are perfectly aware of the demand curve for their product, which is supposed to be linear.

Each firm assumes that, regardless of what output it produces, the other will hold its output constant at the existing level. Taking the other firm's output level as given, each firm chooses its own output level to maximize profit. Of course, the level of output that it chooses will depend on how much it thinks its rival will produce. For example, consider the situation in Figure 11.5, which shows the demand curve for Carpenter's product, based on three alternative assumptions by Carpenter concerning Hanover's output.

1. *Carpenter thinks that Hanover will produce and sell nothing.* If this is

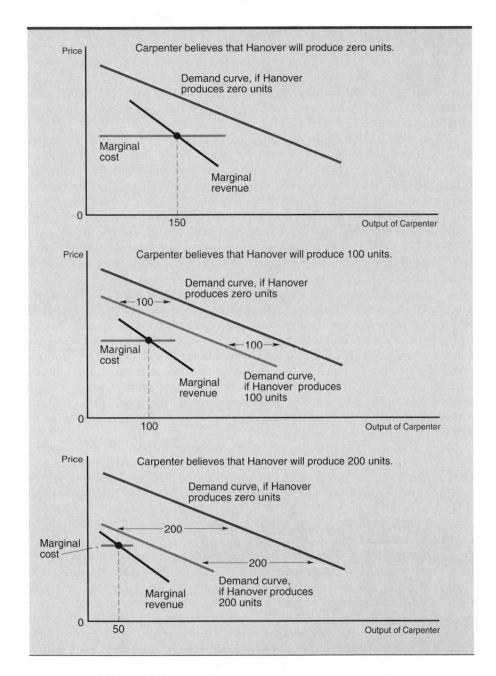

**FIGURE 11.5  Optimal Output of Carpenter Company if Hanover Corporation Produces 0, 100, or 200 Units of Output per Month**   Carpenter will produce and sell 150, 100, or 50 units, depending on whether it believes that Hanover will produce and sell 0, 100, or 200 units.

what Carpenter thinks, the demand curve for Carpenter's product is believed to be the market demand curve, since Carpenter is expected to be the sole producer. The top panel of Figure 11.5 shows the demand curve and the corresponding marginal revenue curve. To maximize profit, Carpenter will choose the output where marginal revenue equals marginal cost; this output is 150 units per month. (For simplicity, we assume that marginal cost is constant in Figure 11.5.)

2. *Carpenter thinks that Hanover will produce and sell 100 units per month.* If this is what Carpenter thinks, the demand curve for Carpenter's product is believed to be the market demand curve *shifted to the left by 100 units.* Why? Because at each possible level of price Carpenter expects to sell the total amount demanded less the 100 units that Hanover is expected to produce and sell. The middle panel of Figure 11.5 shows this demand curve and the corresponding marginal revenue curve. To maximize profit, Carpenter will choose the output where marginal revenue equals marginal cost, this output being 100 units per month in this case. (See the middle panel of Figure 11.5.)

3. *Carpenter thinks that Hanover will produce and sell 200 units per month.* If this is what Carpenter thinks, the demand curve for Carpenter's product is believed to be the market demand curve *shifted to the left by 200 units,* since at each possible level of price, Carpenter expects to sell the total amount demanded less the 200 units that Hanover is expected to produce and sell. The bottom panel of Figure 11.5 shows this demand curve and the corresponding marginal revenue curve. To maximize profit, Carpenter will choose the output where marginal revenue equals marginal cost, this output being 50 units per month in this case (as shown in the bottom panel of Figure 11.5.)

Employing these results, it is a simple matter to draw a curve showing how Carpenter's output depends on how much it thinks that Hanover will produce and sell. In the previous three paragraphs, we derived three points on this curve. These three points are plotted in Figure 11.6. Other points on this curve could be derived in the same way. This curve is called Carpenter's *reaction curve* because it shows how Carpenter will react, as a function of how much it thinks Hanover will produce and sell. Hanover also has a reaction curve which is shown in Figure 11.6. Hanover's reaction curve shows how much Hanover will produce, as a function of how much it thinks that Carpenter will produce and sell. It can be derived in precisely the same way that we derived Carpenter's reaction curve.

According to the Cournot model, an equilibrium will occur at the point where the firms' reaction curves intersect. Thus, in Figure 11.6, an equilibrium will occur if both Carpenter and Hanover are producing and selling 100 units per month. Why is this a Nash equilibrium? *Because each firm's expectation concerning the other's output is correct and because each firm is maximizing its profit (given that its rival's output is what it is).* To see that each firm's expectations concerning the other's output is correct at this intersection point, note that at this point Carpenter expects Hanover to

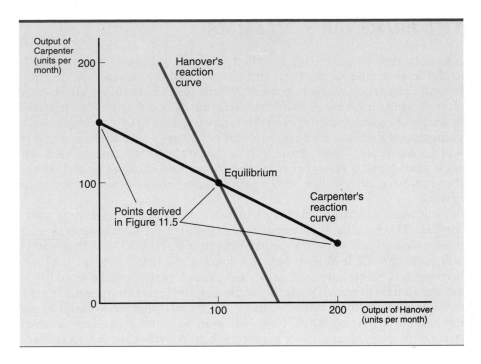

*FIGURE 11.6   Reaction Curves of Carpenter Company and Hanover Corporation*   Equilibrium occurs at the intersection of the reaction curves where each firm is producing and selling 100 units per month.

produce 100 units per month—and this in fact is what Hanover produces. Similarly, at this point Hanover expects Carpenter to produce 100 units per month—and this in fact is what Carpenter produces. Thus, there are no surprises, and equally important, there are no incentives for either firm to alter its behavior. Each firm is maximizing its profit, if (as is the case) the other produces 100 units per month.

While the Cournot model is useful in illustrating the concept of a Nash equilibrium, it has severe limitations as a representation of oligopoly behavior. For one thing, it provides no satisfactory description or explanation of the way in which firms move toward this equilibrium. Cournot's own explanation is naïve in many respects and is rejected by most economists. The lack of any explanation of the dynamic adjustment process is regarded as a serious problem by many economists. In later sections, we will take up models that pay more attention to dynamic considerations and are far richer and more interesting.

## THE PRISONER'S DILEMMA

A specific type of game—the so-called **prisoner's dilemma**—is particularly useful in analyzing oligopolistic situations. To illustrate this type of game, consider a situation where two stockbrokers, Jones and Mulloy, are arrested after making illegal use of inside information. The police lock each person in a separate room and offer each the following deal: "If you confess, while your partner does not confess, you will get a two-year jail term, while he will get ten years." Each person knows that if they both confess, each will get 8 years (not 10 years, because they cooperated with the police). If neither confesses, each will get only 4 years because the evidence against them is weak.

Both Jones and Mulloy have two possible strategies: to confess or not to confess. The four possible outcomes, depending on which strategy each person chooses, are shown in the payoff matrix in Table 11.4. What strategy will Jones choose? If Mulloy does not confess, the better strategy for Jones is to confess, since Jones will serve less time (2 years) than he would if he did not confess (4 years). If Mulloy confesses, the better strategy for Jones is to confess, since Jones will serve less time (8 years) than he would if he did not confess (10 years). Thus, Jones will confess, since regardless of which strategy Mulloy adopts, Jones is better off to confess than not to confess. Similarly, Mulloy too will confess, since regardless of which strategy Jones adopts, Mulloy is better off to confess than not to confess.

TABLE 11.4   *Payoff Matrix: Jones and Mulloy*

| Possible strategies for Jones | Possible strategies for Mulloy | |
| --- | --- | --- |
| | Confess | Do not confess |
| Confess | Both get 8-year jail terms. | Jones gets 2 years; Mulloy gets 10 years. |
| Do not confess | Jones gets 10 years; Mulloy gets 2 years. | Both get 4-year jail terms. |

Consequently, it appears that *both Jones and Mulloy will confess.* This is the dominant strategy for each person. However, it is important to recognize that each is doing worse than if neither of them confessed. If they could trust each other not to confess, each could serve 4 years rather than 8 years. But they are trapped by their incentive to pursue their own interest: interestingly, even if they could meet and agree not to confess, each one would still have an interest in cheating on the agreement.

# DOES CHEATING PAY?

To illustrate how the type of game discussed in the previous section can help to indicate the circumstances under which firms will tend to cheat (that is, secretly cut price) on a cartel agreement, suppose that the only two producers of a specialized type of scientific instrument—Acron, Inc., and the Farmer Company—form a cartel. Each firm has two possible strategies: to abide by the cartel agreement or to cheat. There are four possible outcomes, depending on which strategy each firm pursues. These are shown in Table 11.5.

Which strategy should Acron choose? If Farmer sticks by the agreement, it appears that the better strategy for Acron is to cheat, since Acron's profits will be greater than they would be if it stuck by the agreement. If Farmer cheats, the better strategy for Acron seems to be to cheat as well, since Acron's profits will be higher than they would be if it stuck by the agreement. Thus, it appears that Acron will choose the strategy of cheating, since regardless of which strategy Farmer adopts, Acron seems better off by cheating than by abiding by the agreement.

Which strategy should Farmer choose? If Acron sticks by the agreement, the better strategy for Farmer seems to be to cheat, since Farmer's profits will be greater than they would be if it stuck by the agreement. If Acron cheats, the better strategy for Farmer appears to be to cheat as well, since Farmer's profits will be higher than they would be if it stuck by the agreement. Thus, it seems that Farmer will choose the strategy of cheating, since regardless of which strategy Acron adopts, Farmer is better off by cheating than by abiding by the agreement.

Thus, it appears that both firms will cheat. Like the game in Table 11.4 involving Jones and Mulloy, this is an example of the prisoner's dilemma. Recall that because neither Jones nor Mulloy could trust the other not to confess, both wound up serving more time in jail (8 years versus 4 years) than they would have if they had trusted each other. Similarly, Acron and Farmer, because they do not trust each other to stick by their agreement, wind up with lower profits than they would if they both were to abide by the agreement ($2 million versus $5 million).

*TABLE 11.5   Payoff Matrix: Acron and Farmer*

| Possible strategies for Acron | Possible strategies for Farmer | |
|---|---|---|
| | Abide by agreement | Cheat |
| Abide by agreement | Acron's profit: $5 million<br>Farmer's profit: $5 million | Acron's profit: −$2 million<br>Farmer's profit: $8 million |
| Cheat | Acron's profit: $8 million<br>Farmer's profit: −$2 million | Acron's profit: $2 million<br>Farmer's profit: $2 million |

## A MORE SOPHISTICATED ANALYSIS

Any manager worth his salt should recognize that there is an important difference between the situation facing Acron and Farmer and that facing Jones and Mulloy. In the case of Jones and Mulloy, if this was the only crime they performed together and if they did not intend to work together again, it may have been reasonable for each of them to assume that they would play this game only once. But for Acron and Farmer, such an assumption would not be reasonable. At every point in time, each of these firms must decide whether it will cheat or not. Since they are continually dealing with customers, they must continually decide whether or not to cut price secretly.

Since Acron and Farmer play this game repeatedly, the analysis in the previous section may not be correct. To understand this, suppose that Acron refuses to cheat the first time it must make such a decision and that it continues to abide by the agreement so long as Farmer does so. But if Farmer fails even once to cooperate, Acron will revert forever to the safe policy of cheating. If Farmer adopts the same sort of policy, then each can reap profits of $5 million. If either one cheats, that firm will increase its profit to $8 million for a brief period of time, but subsequently its profit will fall permanently to $2 million. Consequently, it will not be in the interest of either firm to cheat. Moreover, Acron and Farmer can achieve this outcome even if they do not collude or make any binding agreements. If each presumes that the other will have the intelligence to maintain the monopoly price, their presumptions will tend to be correct.[3]

Under these circumstances, a good strategy for each player may be "tit for tat," which means that each player should do on this round whatever the other player did on the previous round. If Acron pursues a tit-for-tat strategy, it should abide by the agreement on the first round. If Farmer also abides by it, Acron should continue to do so, but once Farmer cheats, Acron should retaliate by cheating as well. Experimental results, based on a computer analysis of the results of various strategies, suggest that this often is a very effective approach.[4]

## MOST-FAVORED-CUSTOMER CLAUSES[5]

To illustrate how game theory can help shed light on strategic behavior, suppose that Acron and Farmer both announce to their customers that they

---

[3] We assume that each firm can readily detect whether the other firm is cheating. In reality, this may not be so easy. In some cases, trade associations have been authorized to collect detailed information concerning each firm's transactions; in this way, an attempt has been made to detect cheating quickly. Of course, the more quickly cheating is detected, the less profitable it is likely to be.

[4] R. Axelrod, *The Evolution of Cooperation* (New York: Basic Books, 1984).

[5] The discussion in this section is based on S. Salop, "Practices That (Credibly) Facilitate Oligopoly

will grant them a **most-favored-customer clause**. Such a clause stipulates that if the firm reduces its price subsequent to a purchase, the early customer will get a rebate so that he or she will pay no more than those buying after the price reduction. On the surface, this may seem to be a generous policy; indeed, one might question whether it is a profitable policy for the firms. But it is easy to show that this may be a very smart move from Acron's and Farmer's points of view.

For simplicity, suppose that both firms can sell their product at either $2,000 or $1,000. Table 11.6 shows the profits of each firm, depending on which price the firm sets. Since $2,000 is assumed to be the price that would be set if the two firms formed a cartel, and $1,000 is assumed to be the price that would be set by either of them if it cheated on such a cartel agreement, the payoff matrix in Table 11.6 is the same as that in Table 11.5. This is the payoff matrix before the announcement of the most-favored-customer clause. As indicated above, there is a temptation for both firms to cheat, although they may adopt a tit-for-tat strategy.

After the announcement by each firm of the most-favored-customer clause, the payoff matrix changes, as indicated in Table 11.7. Now each firm's profit is $4 million, not $8 million, if it sets a price of $1,000 while the other firm sets a price of $2,000. Why? Because, if $2,000 has been the price, it will have to give rebates to all of its old customers who paid $2,000.

**TABLE 11.6**  *Payoff Matrix before Most-Favored-Customer Clause*

| Possible strategies for Acron | Possible strategies for Farmer | |
|---|---|---|
| | Set price at $2,000 | Set price at $1,000 |
| Set price at $2,000 | Acron's profit: $5 million<br>Farmer's profit: $5 million | Acron's profit: −$2 million<br>Farmer's profit: $8 million |
| Set price at $1,000 | Acron's profit: $8 million<br>Farmer's profit: −$2 million | Acron's profit: $2 million<br>Farmer's profit: $2 million |

**TABLE 11.7**  *Payoff Matrix after Most-Favored-Customer Clause*

| Possible strategies for Acron | Possible strategies for Farmer | |
|---|---|---|
| | Set price at $2,000 | Set price at $1,000 |
| Set price at $2,000 | Acron's profit: $5 million<br>Farmer's profit: $5 million | Acron's profit: −$2 million<br>Farmer's profit: $4 million |
| Set price at $1,000 | Acron's profit: $4 million<br>Farmer's profit: −$2 million | Acron's profit: $2 million<br>Farmer's profit: $2 million |

Coordination," in J. Stiglitz and G. F. Mathewson, eds., *New Developments in the Analysis of Market Structures* (Cambridge, Mass.: MIT Press, 1986). For pedagogical reasons, Salop's analysis has been simplified.

Given this change in the payoff matrix, it is much more probable that both firms will adhere to the price of $2,000, since the payoff from price-cutting is less than before. Suppose Acron has the first move. Its managers are likely to think as follows: "If we establish a price of $2,000, Farmer's superior strategy is to do the same (rather than cut price to $1,000). On the other hand, if we establish a price of $1,000, Farmer's superior strategy is to follow our lead and cut price to $1,000. Thus, we are better off to establish a price of $2,000, since our profits will be greater ($5 million versus $2 million) than they would be if we charged only $1,000." Of course, Farmer's managers are likely to think the same way, with the result that the price will tend to stay at $2,000.

Thus, contrary to what one might believe at first, most-favored-customer clauses can be clever devices to discourage price-cutting. Using game theory, this fact is evident, whereas without the concepts of game theory, it is by no means obvious. General Electric and Westinghouse, among others, have adopted such clauses. The Justice Department has alleged that these clauses have facilitated tacit coordination between these two firms.

## THE THRUST AND PARRY OF OLIGOPOLISTIC RIVALRY[6]

Previous sections have demonstrated that firms in oligopolistic industries continually face a dilemma. In a broad sense, it may be in their interest to cooperate in various ways with their rivals, but nonetheless they may pursue their narrow self-interest. For members of a cartel, this tension between self-interest and cooperation is reflected in the constant temptation of cartel members to cheat. For firms that do not collude, this tension is reflected in the fact that firms, to avoid economic warfare with their rivals, may have to sacrifice some of their own potential profits.

Oligopolists, like boxers or chess players, must constantly look for ways to improve their position. Some moves that a firm can make are much less threatening to its rivals than others. Such moves have the important advantage that retaliation is much less likely if they, rather than more threatening moves, are carried out. Moves tend to be perceived as nonthreatening if rivals do not notice them or if they do not affect the level of performance of rivals (as they measure it). For example, when Timex entered the watch industry, its strategy was to produce a watch that was so cheap that it did not pay to have it repaired, and to sell it in drugstores rather than jewelry stores. The Swiss watch makers, who dominated the industry at that time, did not view this move as threatening, since it did not affect their position as the leading producers of high-quality watches.

But managers cannot always make nonthreatening moves. In deciding

---

[6] This and the following section are based on M. Porter, *Competitive Strategy*.

whether to make a threatening move, you should consider how likely it is that retaliation will occur, how soon it is likely to come, and how effective (and painful) it will be. It frequently is possible to lengthen the time lag before your rivals are aware of a threatening move, either because the move is not revealed to them or because it is on the periphery of their centers of attention. For example, years after Timex began to take significant portions of the watch market away from Swiss and American producers, its watch was still regarded by them as an inferior product not meriting retaliation.

Retaliation to some kinds of threatening moves can be very fast. If you cut your price, your rivals can do the same in a matter of days or even hours. Take the case of Bristol-Myers, which introduced a new product, Datril, and promoted it as "just as good as Tylenol, only cheaper." Literally over a weekend, Johnson & Johnson, the maker of Tylenol, decided to mobilize its sales force and match Datril's price, the result being that it successfully countered Bristol-Myers' challenge.[7]

For other types of threatening moves, it may take years to retaliate. For example Eastman Kodak had to work for over six years to develop the instant camera that it introduced in 1976 to compete with Polaroid's instant camera. In choosing which threatening moves to make, you should look carefully at your rivals' probable reaction times, and pick moves where retaliation is likely to be slow and ineffective.

One reason why your rivals may be unable to retaliate effectively is that if they do so, their action may backfire and hurt them as well. Thus, when the Swiss watch companies finally recognized that their financial and growth goals were being threatened by Timex, they found it very difficult to retaliate directly, because such retaliation would seem to legitimize the Timex concept and blur the Swiss product image.

Since, as managers, you must respond to threatening moves as well as make them, it is important to create situations where it will appear to your rivals that threatening moves against your firm will not pay off. Although economic warfare sometimes is worthwhile, it frequently is better to arrange matters so that no battle takes place. To deter a threatening move, you should do what you can to insure that competitors expect retaliation if they make such a move. Moreover, if such a move occurs, you would be well-advised to retaliate fast and effectively, since this will help to deter such moves by your competitors in the future.

# THE IMPORTANCE OF COMMITMENT

One of the central concepts in formulating and executing offensive and defensive moves is the concept of **commitment,** of which there are three

---

[7] J. Hauser, "Theory and Application of Defensive Strategy," in L. G. Thomas, ed., *The Economics of Strategic Planning* (Lexington, Mass.: D. C. Heath, 1986).

major types. First, it frequently is important that you convince your firm's rivals that your firm is committed to a strategic move that it is making. If this can be done, it increases the probability that your rivals will become resigned to the new situation and not waste their time and resources trying to prevent its occurrence. If they feel that your firm is determined at all costs to make this move, they may conclude that if they retaliate, your firm will fight back, and a mutually disadvantageous war may ensue.

Second, it frequently is important that you convince your firm's rivals that if they make particular moves, your firm is committed to retaliate swiftly and effectively. The more binding and irreversible this commitment is, the more seriously it will have to be taken by your rivals. Moreover, the greater the ability of your firm to retaliate, the more seriously this commitment will be taken. Thus, if your firm has already developed new products that it could quickly produce and market in such a way as to hurt your rivals, this fact might be leaked to them.

Third, it frequently is important that you convince your firm's rivals that your firm is committed to *not* make particular threatening moves against them. In business, as in all other walks of life, you have to build trust. This is not easy, particularly if your firm has not had an unblemished past record in this regard. The most persuasive evidence often is a demonstration that your firm can be trusted: if your firm continually lives up to its commitments, this will help.

Your firm's commitments must be credible. It is useless for your firm to commit itself to retaliate against a particular move by its rivals if it lacks the resources and know-how to do so. For example, suppose that your firm commits itself to match price reductions by its rivals, although it has no way to discover whatever secret price concessions they make. Obviously, this commitment lacks credibility.

To make a commitment credible, firms sometimes put themselves in a position where it would be difficult and costly, perhaps impossible, for them to violate their commitments. For example, a firm may make large investments in plant and equipment to produce a particular product, thus signaling to others that they have a long-run commitment to stay in the relevant market. Contracts can be signed with employees, suppliers, or customers that bind the firm to particular actions. In this way, firms enhance the credibility of their commitments. However, there are dangers in putting a firm in a position where if it reneges on a commitment, it suffers substantial losses. Sometimes a firm has to violate a commitment, despite the consequences. Hence firms sometimes put themselves in a position where it appears that they will suffer substantial losses if they violate a commitment, but like Houdini, they have a secret escape hatch. For example, it may be possible to renegotiate contracts and find alternative uses for plant and equipment.

---

CONSULTANT'S CORNER

## USING A PRICE ANNOUNCEMENT TO PREEMPT A MARKET*

Texas Instruments once announced a price for random access memories to be available two years after the announcement. A week later, Bowmar announced that it would produce this product and sell it at a lower price than Texas Instruments. A few weeks later, Motorola said it too would produce this product and sell it at a lower price than Bowmar. Finally, a couple of weeks after this, Texas Instruments announced a price that was 50 percent below Motorola's, and the other two firms said that after reconsidering their decision, they would not produce the product.

The president of a machinery firm, having heard this story at a meeting of the board of directors, decided that his company should consider the sort of strategic move that Texas Instruments used so successfully. His machinery firm was about to develop a new product, which was scheduled for commercial introduction in about two years. This product, while its production costs would not be lower than those of all competitive products that would be introduced at the same time, was expected to be cheaper to produce than some of them. The firm's president believed that his firm should announce a very low price for its forthcoming product, with an eye toward inducing other firms to drop their plans to develop their own new products. He felt that there was very little risk in doing so, since his firm really did not have to abide by the announcement. (Announcements of this sort were not regarded as binding in this industry.)

If you were a consultant to this machinery firm, would you advise the firm's president to announce a very low price for the product his firm intended to introduce in two years?

* This section is based on an actual case. For further discussion, see M. Porter, *Competitive Strategy*.

---

# WHEN IS A THREAT CREDIBLE?

Firms often transmit signals to one another to indicate their intentions, motives, and aims. Some signals are threats. Suppose, for example, that the Gelhart Company hears that the LIV Corporation, its principal rival, intends to lower its price. Gelhart may announce its intention of lowering its own price significantly, thus signaling to LIV that it is willing to engage in a price war if LIV goes ahead with its price cut. Indeed, some of Gelhart's executives may see to it that this message gets transmitted indirectly to some of LIV's managers.

However, not all threats are credible. If, for example, the payoff matrix is

TABLE 11.8    *Payoff Matrix: Gelhart and LIV*

| Possible strategies for Gelhart | Possible strategies for LIV | |
|---|---|---|
| | Low price | High price |
| Low price | Gelhart's profit: $2 million<br>LIV's profit: $3 million | Gelhart's profit: $3 million<br>LIV's profit: −$1 million |
| High price | Gelhart's profit: $7 million<br>LIV's profit: $11 million | Gelhart's profit: $11 million<br>LIV's profit: $8 million |

as shown in Table 11.8, Gelhart's threat is not very credible. To understand why, let's compare Gelhart's profits if it sets a low price with its profits if it sets a high price. (For simplicity, we assume that price can be set at only these two levels.) If LIV sets a high price, Gelhart makes $11 million if it sets a high price and $3 million if it sets a low price. If LIV sets a low price, Gelhart makes $7 million if it sets a high price and $2 million if it sets a low price. Consequently, regardless of whether LIV sets a high or low price, Gelhart will do better if it sets a high price than a low price.

Since this is the case, it certainly seems unlikely that Gelhart will carry out its threat to cut its price to the low level. After all, as we've just seen, if LIV does cut its price to the low level, Gelhart will earn higher profits by keeping its price at the high level. Consequently, if LIV can be sure that Gelhart will take the course of action that maximizes Gelhart's profit, it can dismiss Gelhart's threat as no more than an empty gesture.

But if Gelhart can convince LIV that it is not going to take the course of action that maximizes its profit, it can make its threat credible. Specifically, if it can convince LIV that, if LIV sets the low price, it will match it, *even though this lowers Gelhart's own profits*, LIV may decide not to set the low price. After all, LIV's profits are higher ($8 million versus $3 million) if it maintains a high price (and Gelhart does the same) than if LIV sets a low price (and Gelhart does the same).

How can Gelhart convince LIV that it will lower its price, even though this seems to be irrational? One way is for Gelhart's managers to develop a reputation for doing what they say, "regardless of the costs." They may have a well-publicized taste for facing down opponents and for refusing to back down, regardless of how irrational they may seem. Faced with the "crazy" Gelhart Company, the LIV Corporation may decide not to cut price. But if Gelhart cannot convince LIV of its "irrationality," LIV will rightly regard Gelhart's threat to lower price as not being credible.

## THE IMPORTANCE OF ENTRY

Up to this point, we have been concerned principally with oligopolistic behavior in the short run. In the long run, it may be possible for entry or

## POSSIBLE ENTRY-DETERRING TACTICS IN DISPOSABLE DIAPERS

Procter and Gamble has held a dominant position in the market for disposable diapers, its market share having been about 70 percent. Procter and Gamble recognized that disposable diapers could be made a mass-market product, and developed techniques to produce diapers at high speed and correspondingly low cost. Its product, Pampers, has dominated the field. According to Harvard's Michael Porter, who has made a careful study of this industry, the following are some possible ways in which Procter and Gamble might signal other firms to deter entry.*

| Tactic | Cost to Procter and Gamble | Cost to an entrant |
|---|---|---|
| 1. Signal a commitment to defend position in diapers through public statements, comments to retailers, etc. | None | Raises expected cost of entry by increasing probability and extent of retaliation |
| 2. File a patent suit | Legal fees | Legal fees plus probability that P and G wins the suit with subsequent cost to the competitor |
| 3. Announce planned capacity expansion | None | Raises expected risk of price-cutting and the probability of P and G's retaliation to entry |
| 4. Announce a new generation of diapers to be introduced in the future | None | Raises the expected cost of entry by forcing entrant to bear possible product development and changeover costs contingent on the ultimate configuration of the new generation |

(a) In considering these possible tactics, why should Procter and Gamble be concerned about the costs to itself? (b) Why should it be concerned with the costs to an entrant? (c) Procter and Gamble might also cut price to deter entry. What would be the cost of this tactic to Procter and Gamble? What would be the cost to an entrant? (d) Procter and Gamble might also increase its national advertising to deter entry. What would be the cost of this tactic to Procter and Gamble? What would be the cost to an entrant?

* M. Porter, "Strategic Interaction: Some Lessons from Industry Histories for Theory and Antitrust Policy," in S. Salop, ed., *Strategy, Predation, and Antitrust Analysis* (Washington, D.C.: Federal Trade Commission, 1981), reprinted in part in E. Mansfield, ed., *Managerial Economics and Operations Research*, 5th ed. (New York: Norton, 1987).

*Solution* (a) Obviously, Procter and Gamble must be concerned with its own costs. If it adopts a tactic that is far more costly to itself than to a potential entrant, it may cost more than it is worth. (b) The point of these tactics is to raise the cost to a potential entrant, thus discouraging entry. (c) The cost to Procter and Gamble would be an across-the-board reduction in sales revenue. The cost to an entrant would also be a reduction in potential sales revenue. (d) The cost to both Procter and Gamble and to an entrant would be the cost of the additional advertising, but for Procter and Gamble this cost increase will be spread over a larger sales volume than for the entrant. To maintain relative position, the entrant may have to match Procter and Gamble in absolute message volume.

exit of firms to take place. Whether or not the industry remains oligopolistic in the face of relatively easy entry depends on the size of the market for the product relative to the optimum size of firm. Above-average profits will attract new firms. If the market is small relative to the optimum size of firm in this industry, the number of firms will remain sufficiently small so that the industry will still be an oligopoly. If the market is large relative to the optimum size of the firm, the number of firms will grow sufficiently large so that the industry will no longer be an oligopoly.

Easy entry also tends to erode collusive agreements. We saw in Figure 11.3 that existing firms are tempted continually to "cheat" on a collusive agreement, since they can attract business from their rivals by lowering prices. The situation is similar for entrants. They too are faced by a relatively elastic demand curve as long as existing firms adhere to collusive agreements to maintain price at its existing level. As long as profits exist in the industry, firms will be tempted to enter and take business away from the collusive group by lowering the price a bit. Once entry of this sort occurs, it becomes harder and harder to keep a cartel together.

## THE DETERRENCE OF ENTRY

To understand how oligopolists try to deter entry, it is useful once again to apply game theory. Consider the Lotus Company, which faces the threat of entry by the Salem Company. Table 11.9 shows the profits of each firm, depending on whether or not Salem enters the market and on whether or not Lotus resists Salem's entry (for example, by cutting price and increasing output).

**TABLE 11.9** *Payoff Matrix before Lotus Makes Credible Its Threat to Resist*

| Possible strategies for Lotus Company | Possible strategies for Salem Company | |
|---|---|---|
| | Enter | Do not enter |
| Resist entry | Lotus' profit: $3 million<br>Salem's profit: $6 million | Lotus' profit: $13 million<br>Salem's profit: $9 million |
| Do not resist entry | Lotus' profit: $4 million<br>Salem's profit: $12 million | Lotus' profit: $13 million<br>Salem's profit: $9 million |

Salem has the first move: it must decide whether or not to enter. If it enters, Lotus must decide whether or not to resist. Based on the payoff matrix in Table 11.9, Lotus will not resist because its profits will be $1 million less (that is, $3 million rather than $4 million) if it resists than they would be if it did not resist. Knowing this, Salem will enter because its profits will be $3 million higher (that is, $12 million rather than $9 million) if it enters than they would be if it did not enter. Of course, Lotus may well threaten to resist, but given the nature of the payoff matrix in Table 11.9, this threat is not credible. Why? Because resistance would lower Lotus' profits.

To deter Salem's entry into the market, Lotus can alter the payoff matrix. For example, it can build excess production capacity, which will be employed to increase output—and slash price—if Salem enters. Since it costs money to keep excess capacity on hand, Lotus's profits are reduced by $2 million if it does not resist entry or if Salem does not enter. Consequently, the new payoff matrix is as shown in Table 11.10. Now Lotus' profits if it resists are $1 million higher than they would be if it did not resist (that is, $3 million rather than $2 million). Thus, Lotus' threat to resist becomes credible, and Salem will not enter because its profits will be $3 million lower (that is, $6 million rather than $9 million) if it enters than they would be if it did not enter.

**TABLE 11.10** *Payoff Matrix after Lotus Makes Credible Its Threat to Resist*

| Possible strategies for Lotus Company | Possible strategies for Salem Company | |
|---|---|---|
| | Enter | Do not enter |
| Resist entry | Lotus' profit: $3 million<br>Salem's profit: $6 million | Lotus' profit: $11 million<br>Salem's profit: $9 million |
| Do not resist entry | Lotus' profit: $2 million<br>Salem's profit: $12 million | Lotus' profit: $11 million<br>Salem's profit: $9 million |

## DU PONT'S ATTEMPT TO DETER ENTRY INTO THE TITANIUM DIOXIDE INDUSTRY

To illustrate how firms sometimes build up productive capacity to deter entry, consider the case of Du Pont, America's largest chemical firm, which in the early 1970s accounted for about one-third of the nation's sales of titanium dioxide, a whitener used in paints and other products. Du Pont's top executives felt at that time that the demand for titanium dioxide would grow considerably, and that new government regulations would soon be instituted that would force Du Pont's rivals to shut down their plants. (Because Du Pont's facilities used a different technology and were located in areas different from its rivals, they would not have to shut down.) Thus, many of Du Pont's rivals would have to "enter" the industry with new plants.

Du Pont's managers decided to invest over a third of a billion dollars to increase the firm's capacity to produce titanium dioxide, the strategy (according to outside observers) being to install much more capacity than was immediately necessary in order to deter Du Pont's rivals from entering the market. By making this huge investment, Du Pont, like the Lotus Company in the previous section, made credible its intention to resist if entry occurred.

In fact, however, although this strategy seemed sound, many of Du Pont's forecasts turned out to be wrong, with unfortunate consequences for the firm. The actual increase in the demand for titanium dioxide was less than was forecasted, and because the government regulations were not enforced as strongly as expected, Du Pont's rivals did not have to shut down their plants. Also, Du Pont's actions led to an antitrust case in which Du Pont was charged with attempting to monopolize the titanium dioxide market. (This case is discussed at length in Chapter 15.) Nonetheless, the fact that things did not work as Du Pont expected does not deny that the model in the previous section helps to explain Du Pont's behavior.[8]

## ADVERTISING TO RESIST ENTRY: MAXWELL HOUSE VERSUS FOLGERS

As we have seen, price cuts and the construction of excess productive capacity can be used to forestall and resist entry. But they are not the only strategies that can be used. For example, as noted in our discussion of Proctor and Gamble (page 445), advertising can be used to resist entry.

Take the case of Folgers Coffee, which began to market its product in

---

[8] See P. Ghemawat, "Capacity Expansion in the Titanium Dioxide Industry," *Journal of Industrial Economics* (December 1984).

areas of the eastern United States where it had not previously been active and where Maxwell House was the leading coffee seller. Maxwell House responded by substantially increasing its advertising, the purpose being to encourage consumers to stock up on Maxwell House Coffee and to make them less likely to pay attention to Folgers' ads asking them to try its new brand. Also, Maxwell House hoped that its additional advertising would enable it to absorb retailers' warehouse space that otherwise might be used to stock Folgers' new brand.

Specifically, Maxwell House established a target of out-advertising the entrant (Folgers) by 50 percent. Moreover, it developed advertising similar to that of Folgers to reduce the apparent novelty of Folgers' ads. If consumers were confused by this similarity, it was felt that it could help Maxwell House's sales because of greater consumer familiarity with the leading brand. The idea was to discourage potential buyers from trying Folgers Coffee and to prevent the sort of brand loyalty discussed in Chapter 10 from developing for Folgers. This is one way that an oligopolist can resist entry, and it can be effective.[9]

## PREEMPTIVE STRATEGIES: THE CASE OF WAL-MART STORES

Having studied various cases where an oligopolist wants to deter entry, let's turn to cases where an investment opportunity exists that has not been exploited by any firm, and the prize will go to the firm that exploits it first. For example, consider Wal-Mart stores, a very successful chain of discount retail stores. Sam Walton, the company's founder, established hundreds of such stores in small towns in the Southwest. Because the market in each such town was too limited to support more than one discount store, his strategy was to be the first to do so. In other words, his was a **preemptive strategy**—a strategy of setting up stores before another firm did so.

To see why such a strategy was sound, suppose that Wal-Mart and the Jones Brothers are both considering the establishment of a discount store in a small town in Oklahoma. Table 11.11 shows the relevant payoff matrix. If Wal-Mart enters the town, but Jones Brothers does not, Wal-Mart will make $5 million and Jones Brothers will make nothing. If Jones Brothers enters the town, but Wal-Mart does not, Jones Brothers will make $5 million and Wal-Mart will make nothing. If *both* Wal-Mart and Jones Brothers enter the town, both *lose* $2 million.

There are two Nash equilibria in this game—one where Wal-Mart alone enters and one where Jones Brothers alone enters. Which one occurs depends on which firm acts first. If Wal-Mart acts first, it can enter, and be

[9] J. Hilke and P. Nelson, "Noisy Advertising and the Predation Rule in Antitrust Analysis," *American Economic Review* (May 1984).

---

TABLE 11.11   *Payoff Matrix: Wal-Mart Stores versus Jones Brothers*

| Possible strategies for Wal-Mart Stores | Possible strategies for Jones Brothers | |
| --- | --- | --- |
| | Enter the town | Do not enter the town |
| Enter the town | Wal-Mart's profit: −$2 million<br>Jones Brothers' profit: −$2 million | Wal-Mart's profit: $5 million<br>Jones Brothers' profit: zero |
| Do not enter the town | Wal-Mart's profit: zero<br>Jones Brothers' profit: $5 million | Wal-Mart's profit: zero<br>Jones Brothers' profit: zero |

---

confident that Jones Brothers is very unlikely to do the same (since Jones Brothers would lose $2 million if it entered). Thus, Wal-Mart, if it is fast on its feet, can be reasonably sure to garner the prize of $5 million in profits. In fact, Wal-Mart has been very fast indeed, as evidenced by its having established more than 1,600 stores. And the late Sam Walton was very successful, as evidenced by his estimated net worth of over $6 billion.

## WHAT STRATEGIES SEEM TO PAY OFF BEST?

Having described various models of oligopolistic behavior, we conclude this chapter by considering the question that is perhaps the most important of all for managers: What business strategies seem to have been most successful? Based on the PIMS (Profit Impact of Market Strategy) data pertaining to 450 companies and 3,000 business units since 1972, Harvard's Robert Buzzell and Bradley Gale have concluded that *the most important single factor influencing a business unit's profitability is the quality of its products and services relative to those of rivals.*[10] In the short run, better quality enhances profits because the firm is able to charge premium prices. In the longer run, superior quality leads to both a gain in market share and in the expansion of the relevant market. Thus, even if there are short-term costs associated with raising quality, over a period of time these costs may be offset by economies of scale.

Of course, this does not mean that any or all attempts to improve quality will be worthwhile. Before making such attempts, it is important that a firm's managers evaluate carefully whether the prospective benefits outweigh the costs. (Chapter 14 describes in detail how such evaluations can and should be made.) Firms generally achieve quality advantages first by

---

[10] R. Buzzell and B. Gale, *The PIMS Principles Linking Strategy to Performance* (New York: Free Press, 1987). These data were cited previously on page 100. Also see National Academy of Sciences, "Competition in the Pharmaceutical Industry," and National Research Council, "Corporate Strategies in the Auto Industry," both in E. Mansfield, ed., *Managerial Economics and Operations Research*, 5th ed.

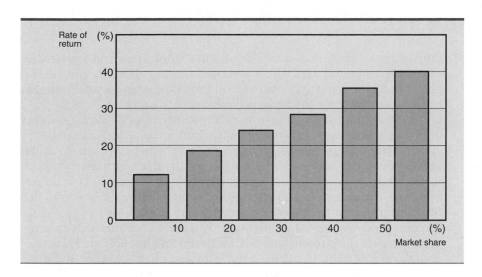

FIGURE 11.7   Relationship between Profitability and Market Share of Business Units   In general, profitability seems to be directly related to market share.

innovations in product (and service) design and subsequently by product and process improvements. In Chapter 7, we discussed many of the factors that influence the success or failure of innovative activities.

Buzzell and Gale also stress that *market share and profitability are strongly related.* As shown in Figure 11.7, a business unit's return on investment is directly related to its share of the market. As they are quick to point out, this relationship may be spurious in part, since both market share and profitability are likely to reflect other factors, such as management skill or luck. But they argue that even when a wide variety of other market and strategic factors are taken into account, market share still seems to have a positive impact on profitability. Why? Because businesses with high market shares tend to enjoy economies of scale.

While these results suggest that it often is wise to attempt to increase a firm's market share, this is not always the case. Take the case of Yamaha, which made a dramatic attack on Honda, the world leader in motorcycles, in the early 1980s. Yamaha cut prices, introduced new models, and advertised heavily in an attempt to increase its market share at Honda's expense. Honda counterattacked with ferocity, the result being that Yamaha's motorcycle sales fell by more than 50 percent, and the company incurred heavy losses. In January 1983, Yamaha's president admitted: "We cannot match Honda's product development and sales strength. . . . I would like to end the Honda-Yamaha war."

## SUMMARY

1. Oligopoly is characterized by a small number of firms and a great deal of interdependence, actual and perceived, among them. A good example of an oligopoly is the American oil industry, where a small number of firms accounts for the bulk of the industry's capacity.

2. Oligopolistic industries, like others, frequently pass through a number of phases—introduction, growth, maturity, and decline. As an industry goes through these phases, the nature of firm behavior often shifts. During the early stages, there often is considerable uncertainty regarding the industry's technology and concerning which markets will open up soonest. During the maturity phase, there frequently is a tendency for firms to attack the market shares of their rivals.

3. There is no single model of oligopoly. Instead, there are many models, depending on the circumstances. Conditions in oligopolistic industries tend to promote collusion, since the number of firms is small and firms recognize their interdependence. The advantages to be derived by the firms from collusion seem obvious: increased profits, decreased uncertainty, and a better opportunity to control the entry of new firms. However, collusive arrangements are often hard to maintain, since once a collusive agreement is made, any of the firms can increase its profits by "cheating" on the agreement. Also, firms may find it difficult to identify a course of action that is agreeable to all members of the industry.

4. Another model of oligopolistic behavior is based on the supposition that one of the firms in the industry is a price leader, because it is a dominant firm. We have shown how under these circumstances this firm should set its price to maximize its profits.

5. Game theory is often used to represent and analyze oligopolistic behavior. The relevant features of a two-person game can be shown by constructing a payoff matrix. If each firm has a dominant strategy, this strategy is its best choice regardless of what other firms do. Not all games have a dominant strategy for every firm.

6. In a Nash equilibrium, each firm adopts a strategy that is its best choice given what the other firms do. Some games do not have a Nash equilibrium; others have more than one Nash equilibrium. To illustrate the concept of a Nash equilibrium, we considered a very simple theory put forth by Augustin Cournot, a French economist.

7. The prisoners' dilemma is a type of game useful in analyzing oligopolistic situations, such as whether or not cartel members should cheat. If the game is played once, there are strong incentives to cheat, but if it is repeated, other strategies such as tit-for-tat may be better. Most-favored-customer clauses can be devices to discourage price-cutting.

8. In considering whether to make a move that threatens its rivals, an oli-

gopolist should consider how likely it is that retaliation will occur, how soon it is likely to come, and how effective (and painful) it will be. It frequently is important that you convince your firm's rivals that your firm is committed to a strategic move it is making, that if they make particular moves, your firm is committed to retaliate swiftly and effectively, and that your firm is committed not to make particular threatening moves against them.

9. Oligopolists often fight hard to deter other firms from entering their market. Game theory is useful in analyzing how they go about deterring entry. Frequently they change the payoff matrix so as to make their threat to resist entry more credible. Game theory is also useful in analyzing preemptive strategies, like that of Wal-Mart stores.

10. Statistical studies based on data pertaining to hundreds of firms suggest (a) that the single most important factor influencing a business unit's profitability is the quality of its products and services, relative to those of rivals, and (b) that market share and profitability are strongly related.

## PROBLEMS

1. The Bergen Company and the Gutenberg Company are the only two firms that produce and sell a particular kind of machinery. The demand curve for their product is

$$P = 580 - 3Q,$$

where $P$ is the price (in dollars) of the product, and $Q$ is the total amount demanded. The total cost function of the Bergen Company is

$$TC_B = 410Q_B,$$

where $TC_B$ is its total cost (in dollars), and $Q_B$ is its output. The total cost function of the Gutenberg Company is

$$TC_G = 460Q_G,$$

where $TC_G$ is its total cost (in dollars), and $Q_G$ is its total output.
   (a) If these two firms collude, and if they want to maximize their combined profits, how much will the Bergen Company produce?
   (b) How much will the Gutenberg Company produce?
   (c) Will the Gutenberg Company agree to such an arrangement? Why or why not?

2. The Ulysses Corporation and the Xenophon Company are the only producers of a very sophisticated type of camera. They each can engage in either a high or low level of advertising in trade journals. The payoff matrix is as follows:

| Possible strategies | Possible strategies for Xenophon | |
| for Ulysses | Low level | High level |
| Low level | Ulysses' profit: $12 million<br>Xenophon's profit: $13 million | Ulysses' profit: $11 million<br>Xenophon's profit: $12 million |
| High level | Ulysses' profit: $13 million<br>Xenophon's profit: $12 million | Ulysses' profit: $12 million<br>Xenophon's profit: $11 million |

(a) Will Ulysses engage in a high or low level of advertising in trade journals?

(b) Will Xenophon engage in a high or low level of advertising in trade journals?

(c) Is there a dominant strategy for each firm?

3. An oligopolistic industry selling a particular type of machine tool is composed of two firms. The two firms set the same price and share the total market equally. The demand curve confronting each firm (assuming that the other firm sets the same price as this firm) is shown below, as well as each firm's total cost function.

| Price<br>(thousands<br>of dollars) | Quantity<br>demanded<br>per day | Daily<br>output | Total cost<br>(thousands<br>of dollars) |
| --- | --- | --- | --- |
| 10 | 5 | 5 | 45 |
| 9 | 6 | 6 | 47 |
| 8 | 7 | 7 | 50 |
| 7 | 8 | 8 | 55 |
| 6 | 9 | 9 | 65 |

(a) Assuming that each firm is correct in believing that the other firm will charge the same price as it does, what is the price that each should charge?

(b) Under the assumptions in part (a), what daily output rate should each firm set?

4. The can industry is composed of two firms. Suppose that the demand curve for cans is

$$P = 100 - Q,$$

where $P$ is the price of a can (in cents), and $Q$ is the quantity demanded of cans (in millions per month). Suppose that the total cost function of each firm is

$$TC = 2 + 15q,$$

where $TC$ is total cost per month (in tens of thousands of dollars), and $q$ is the quantity produced (in millions per month) by the firm.

(a) What are the price and output if the firms set price equal to marginal cost?

(b) What are the profit-maximizing price and output if the firms collude and act like a monopolist?

(c) Do the firms make a higher combined profit if they collude than they would if they set price equal to marginal cost? If so, how much higher is their combined profit?

5. Two soap producers, the Fortnum Company and the Maison Company, can stress either newspapers or magazines in their forthcoming advertising campaigns. The payoff matrix is as follows:

| Possible strategies for Fortnum Company | Possible strategies for Maison Company | |
|---|---|---|
| | Stress newspapers | Stress magazines |
| Stress newspapers | Fortnum's profit: $8 million<br>Maison's profit: $9 million | Fortnum's profit: $7 million<br>Maison's profit: $8 million |
| Stress magazines | Fortnum's profit: $9 million<br>Maison's profit: $8 million | Fortnum's profit: $8 million<br>Maison's profit: $7 million |

(a) Is there a dominant strategy for each firm? If so, what is it?

(b) What will be the profit of each firm?

(c) Is this game an example of the prisoner's dilemma?

6. James Pizzo is president of a firm that is the price leader in the industry; that is, it sets the price and the other firms sell all they want at that price. In other words, the other firms act as perfect competitors. The demand curve for the industry's product is $P = 300 - Q$, where $P$ is the price of the product, and $Q$ is the total quantity demanded. The total amount supplied by the other firms is equal to $Q_r$, where $Q_r = 49P$. ($P$ is measured in dollars per barrel; $Q$, $Q_r$, and $Q_b$ are measured in millions of barrels per week.)

(a) If Pizzo's firm's marginal cost curve is $2.96Q_b$, where $Q_b$ is the output of his firm, at what output level should he operate to maximize profit?

(b) What price should he charge?

(c) How much will the industry as a whole produce at this price?

(d) Is Pizzo's firm the dominant firm in the industry?

7. The International Air Transport Association (IATA) has been composed of 108 American and European airlines that fly transatlantic routes. For many years, IATA acted as a cartel: it fixed and enforced uniform prices.

(a) If IATA wanted to maximize the total profit of all member airlines, what uniform price would it charge?

(b) How would the total amount of traffic be allocated among the member airlines?

(c) Would IATA set price equal to marginal cost? Why or why not?

8. Two soft drink producers, York Cola and Reno Cola, secretly collude to fix prices. Each firm must decide whether or not to abide by the agreement or to cheat on it. The payoff matrix is as follows:

| Possible strategies for Reno Cola | Possible strategies for York Cola | |
| --- | --- | --- |
| | Abide by agreement | Cheat |
| Abide by agreement | Reno's profit: $29 million<br>York's profit: $29 million | Reno's profit: $26 million<br>York's profit: $30 million |
| Cheat | Reno's profit: $30 million<br>York's profit: $26 million | Reno's profit: $28 million<br>York's profit: $28 million |

(a) What strategy will each firm choose, and what will be each firm's profit?

(b) Does it matter whether this is a one-shot agreement or whether it is meant to continue for some time?

(c) Is this game an example of the prisoner's dilemma?

9. The West Chester Corporation believes that the demand curve for its product is

$$P = 28 - 0.14Q,$$

where $P$ is price (in dollars), and $Q$ is output (in thousands of units). The firm's board of directors, after a lengthy meeting, concludes that the firm should attempt, at least for a while, to increase its total revenue, even if this means lower profit.

(a) Why might a firm adopt such a policy?

(b) What price should the firm set, if it wants to maximize its total revenue?

(c) If the firm's marginal cost equals $14, does the firm produce a larger or smaller output than it would if it maximized profit? How much larger or smaller?

10. In late 1991, two firms, Delta Airlines and the Trump Shuttle, provided air shuttle service between New York and Boston or Washington. The one-way price charged by both firms was $142 on weekdays and $92 on weekends, with lower off-peak advance-purchase fares. In September 1991, Delta increased the per-trip shuttle mileage given to members of the Delta frequent-flier program from 1,000 to 2,000 miles, even though actual mileage from New York to either Boston or Washington is about 200 miles. Moreover, Delta also offered an extra 1,000 miles to frequent fliers who made a round trip on the same day, raising a possible day's total to 5,000 miles. Almost simultaneously, Trump changed the frequent-flier mileage it gave shuttle passengers. (It participated in the One Pass frequent-flier program with Continental Airlines and some foreign carriers.) What sorts of changes do you think Trump made? Why?

11. Two firms, the Alliance Company and the Bangor Corporation, produce vision systems. The demand curve for vision systems is

$$P = 200,000 - 6(Q_1 + Q_2),$$

where $P$ is the price of a vision system (in dollars), $Q_1$ is the number of vision systems produced and sold per month by Alliance, and $Q_2$ is the number of vision systems produced and sold per month by Bangor. Alliance's total cost (in dollars) is

$$TC_1 = 8,000 \; Q_1;$$

Bangor's total cost (in dollars) is

$$TC_2 = 12,000 \; Q_2.$$

(a) If each of these two firms sets its own output level to maximize its profits, assuming that the other firm holds constant its output level, what is the equilibrium price?

(b) What will be the output of each firm?

(c) What will be the profit of each firm?

12. In Britain, price competition among book shops has been suppressed for over 90 years by the Net Book Agreement (of 1900), which was aimed at the prevention of price wars. However, in October 1991, Waterstone & Company began cutting book prices at its 85 British shops. According to Richard Barker, Waterstone's operations director, the decision to reduce the price of about 40 titles by about 25 percent was due to price cuts by Dillons, Waterstone's principal rival.

(a) According to the President of Britain's Publishers Association, the price cutting was "an enormous pity" that will "damage many booksellers who operate on very slim margins."[11] Does this mean that price cutting of this sort is contrary to the public interest?

(b) Why would Dillons want to cut price? Under what circumstances would this be a good strategy? Under what circumstances would it be a mistake?

---

[11] "British Book Shops in Price Skirmishes," *New York Times*, October 7, 1991.

# Chapter 12
# Pricing Techniques

In April 1992, Robert Crandall, chairman of American Airlines, dropped a bombshell on the travel business by drastically revising his firm's price structure. Specifically, he reduced a complex system of dozens of fares to four basic types. The result: a tidal wave of calls to all the airlines and to travel agents from customers wanting information and requesting changes in existing tickets. Although the previous two chapters covered a considerable amount of material concerning pricing, they by no means included everything a manager like Crandall needs to know about this central topic.

In this chapter, we take up four additional topics regarding pricing. First, we describe and evaluate the commonly used practice known as cost-plus pricing. Because this practice is so widespread, its advantages and disadvantages should be understood. Second, we discuss the ways in which a multiproduct firm should set prices in order to maximize its profit. This is an important extension of the material presented in previous chapters, which assumed that the firm produces only one product.

Third, we describe and analyze price discrimination, a practice whereby a firm charges different prices to different customers. Because many firms use price discrimination to enhance their profits, any manager should understand how this practice works, and the conditions under which it can be profitable. Fourth, this chapter takes up transfer pricing. If one division of a firm sells its product to another division of the same firm, the firm's top management must determine the price that the former division should charge the latter division. If this so-called transfer price is set incorrectly, the firm's profits will suffer. This chapter shows how this transfer price should be established.

## COST-PLUS PRICING

In the past half century, a great many surveys of business pricing practices have been carried out by academic researchers and others. The results, which have been surprisingly consistent from one survey to another, indicate that **cost-plus pricing** (sometimes called **full-cost pricing**) is a technique used by a large number of firms. Although there are many forms of cost-plus pricing, the typical form involves the following two steps. First, the firm estimates the cost per unit of output of the product. Since this cost will generally vary with output, the firm must base this computation on some assumed output level. Usually, firms use for this purpose some percentage, generally between two-thirds and three-quarters, of capacity. Second, the firm adds a **markup** (generally put in the form of a percentage) to the estimated average cost. This markup is meant to include certain costs that cannot be allocated to any specific product and to provide a return on the firm's investment.

In terms of basic algebra, the percentage markup can be expressed as follows:

$$\text{Markup} = \frac{\text{price} - \text{cost}}{\text{cost}}, \tag{12.1}$$

where the numerator—that is, price − cost—is the **profit margin.** Thus, if the cost of a paperback book is \$4 and its price is \$6,

$$\text{Markup} = \frac{6 - 4}{4} = 0.50,$$

or 50 percent. If we solve equation (12.1) for price, the result is

$$\text{Price} = \text{cost}(1 + \text{markup}), \tag{12.2}$$

which is the pricing formula described in the previous paragraph. In the case of the paperback book,

$$\text{Price} = 4(1 + .50)$$

$$= 6 \text{ dollars},$$

since the markup is 50 percent.

Some firms have set up a **target return** figure that they hope to earn, which determines the markup. For example, General Electric at times has established a target rate of return of 20 percent. Under target-rate-of-return pricing, price is set equal to

$$P = L + M + K + \frac{F}{Q} + \frac{\pi A}{Q}, \tag{12.3}$$

where $P$ is price, $L$ is unit labor cost, $M$ is unit material cost, $K$ is unit marketing cost, $F$ is total fixed or indirect costs, $Q$ is the number of units the firm plans to produce during the relevant planning period, $A$ is total gross operating assets, and $\pi$ is the desired profit rate on those assets. Thus, if a firm believes that its unit labor cost is $2, its unit material cost is $1, its unit marketing cost is $3, its total fixed cost is $10,000, its output will be 1,000 units, its assets are $100,000, and its target rate of return is 15 percent, its price would be set at

$$P = 2 + 1 + 3 + \frac{10,000}{1,000} + \frac{.15(100,000)}{1,000} = \$31.$$

For firms that produce more than one product, the charge for indirect cost, or overhead, is often established by allocating this cost among the firm's products on the basis of their average variable costs. Thus, if a firm's total annual indirect costs (for all products) are estimated to be $3 million and the total annual variable costs (for all products) are estimated to be $2 million, then indirect costs would be allocated to products at a rate of 150 percent of variable cost. For example, if the average variable cost of product Y is estimated to be $10, the firm would add a charge of $1.50 \times \$10$, or $15, for indirect cost. Adding this charge to the average variable cost, the firm obtains an estimated fully allocated cost of $10 + \$15$, or $25. This figure would then be marked up to allow for profit. For example, if the markup is 40 percent, the price is $1.40 \times 25$, or $35.

## COST-PLUS PRICING AT COMPUTRON, INC.: A CASE STUDY

Computron, Inc., a manufacturer of digital computers used in process control applications in chemical and other industries, adopted the following procedure to set the price for its 1000X computer. It calculated the average production cost, including indirect costs, and added on a 33⅓ percent markup, the result being as follows:

| | |
|---|---|
| Factory cost | $192,000 |
| 33⅓% markup on cost | 64,000 |
| U.S. list price | $256,000 |

The company felt that it manufactured the best all-around computer of its type, as judged by dependability, precision, and flexibility. It did not try to sell the 1000X computer on the basis of price. Although the price that the company charged was frequently higher than that of its rivals, the high quality of its products enabled it to compete successfully, both in the United States and abroad. The firm's management felt that price-cutting "not only reduced profits, but also reflected unfavorably on the company's 'quality' image." Of course, such an aversion to price-cutting, if unjustified, can cost a company dearly.[1]

# COST-PLUS PRICING AT GENERAL MOTORS: ANOTHER CASE STUDY

Cost-plus pricing has been used by the giants of American industry as well as by smaller firms like Computron. For decades, General Motors used cost-plus pricing, starting with the stated objective of earning a profit of about 15 percent (after taxes) on total invested capital. Its managers assumed that it would sell enough cars in the next year to operate at about 80 percent of its capacity; and on the basis of this assumption, they calculated what its cost per car would be. They added to this cost a markup big enough to produce the desired return on investment, the result being the so-called **standard price.** General Motors' high-level price policy committee took this standard price as a first approximation, and made small adjustments to reflect competitive conditions, long-run goals of the firm, and other factors. Since these adjustments tended to be quite small, the actual price did not differ much from the standard price.

During the 1960s, the other major American auto producers, Ford and Chrysler, also seemed to use the same sort of procedure in setting prices annually for their various models. Once announced, these prices normally stayed unchanged through an entire model year, although there were standard discounts to dealers to get rid of end-of-year inventories. The situation was described as follows:

> Each firm, figuring the prices to announce for forthcoming models, naturally looks at trends in its own production and model-change costs and at general developments in the economy. It also pays close attention to its rivals' costs and what they might be expected to charge. In this game the firm likely to prefer the lowest price has a good deal of leverage to determine the general range of prices announced for any given type of car. The firms in this industry, as in others, dislike getting caught with an overpriced model more than they fear being slightly under the market. In the 1930s Ford tended to prefer the lowest prices and hence drew close atten-

---

[1] E. R. Corey, *Industrial Marketing: Cases and Concepts*, 3d ed. (Englewood Cliffs, N.J.: Prentice-Hall, 1983).

tion from its rivals. In more recent years, General Motors has been closely watched.[2]

## DOES COST-PLUS PRICING MAXIMIZE PROFIT?

Based on the previous discussion, it seems extremely unlikely that cost-plus pricing can result in the maximization of profits. Indeed, this pricing technique seems naive, because it takes no account, explicitly at least, of the extent or elasticity of demand or of the size of marginal, rather than average, costs. Nevertheless, if applied properly, cost-plus pricing may result in firms' coming close to maximum profits. To see this, it is important to note how little has been said about the factors determining the size of the percentage markup. (Even in the case of target-rate-of-return pricing, no explanation has been given for the target rate of return that a firm chooses.) For example, why was the paperback book cited on page 459 marked up by 50 percent? Why not 25 percent, or 150 percent? If the bookseller is maximizing profit, the markup is determined by the price elasticity of demand for the book.

To understand why this is true, recall from Chapter 3 that

$$MR = P\left(1 - \frac{1}{\eta}\right), \tag{12.4}$$

where $MR$ is the product's marginal revenue, $P$ is the price, and $\eta$ is the price elasticity of demand. This, of course, is the basic relationship between price, marginal revenue, and the price elasticity of demand that we emphasized on page 90. If the firm is maximizing profit, it must be setting marginal revenue equal to marginal cost, as we have often seen (beginning in Chapter 2). Thus, if the firm is maximizing profit, we can replace $MR$ with $MC$ in equation (12.4), the result being

$$MC = P\left(1 - \frac{1}{\eta}\right), \tag{12.5}$$

where $MC$ equals the product's marginal cost. (Recall that this result was discussed in Chapter 3.)

Dividing both sides of equation (12.5) by $(1 - 1/\eta)$, we get

$$P = MC\left(\frac{1}{1 - 1/\eta}\right), \tag{12.6}$$

which means that to maximize profit, the firm should set the product's

[2] R. Caves, *American Industry: Structure, Conduct, Performance* (Englewood Cliffs, N.J.: Prentice-Hall, 1967), p. 45.

price so that it equals its marginal cost multiplied by the following term:

$$\left(\frac{1}{1 - 1/\eta}\right).$$

Glancing back at equation (12.2), you can see that according to cost-plus pricing, price is set equal to cost multiplied by (1 + Markup). Thus, if marginal (not average) cost is the cost concept that is really being used here and if the markup equals

$$\left(\frac{1}{1 - 1/\eta}\right) - 1, \tag{12.7}$$

cost-plus pricing results in the maximization of profit.

Put differently, a firm will maximize profit if it marks up marginal (not average) cost, and if the markup equals the value specified in (12.7). As (12.7) shows clearly, the markup under these circumstances depends entirely on the product's price elasticity of demand. Table 12.1 provides the profit-maximizing markup corresponding to particular values of the elasticity. If a product's price elasticity of demand equals 1.2, the optimal markup is 500 percent. If its price elasticity is 20, the optimal markup is only 5 percent. Table 12.1 should be studied carefully, since it provides interesting and useful information that can help you formulate and maintain an effective pricing policy.

Note that the optimal markup goes up as the price elasticity of demand for the product goes down. Table 12.1 shows this very clearly. In managerial economics as in other things, you ought to check whenever possible to make sure that what you're told makes sense. To see that the inverse relationship in Table 12.1 between the markup and the price elasticity is eminently reasonable, ask yourself the following question: If the quantity demanded of a product is not very sensitive to its price, should I set a relatively high or low price for this product? Obviously, you should set a high price, if you want to make as much money as possible. Since this is what Table 12.1 is telling us, it accords with common sense.

---

*TABLE 12.1* *Relationship between Optimal Markup and Price Elasticity of Demand*

| Price elasticity of demand | Optimal percentage markup of marginal cost |
|:---:|:---:|
| 1.2 | 500% |
| 1.4 | 250 |
| 1.8 | 125 |
| 2.5 | 67 |
| 5.0 | 25 |
| 10.0 | 11 |
| 20.0 | 5 |
| 50.0 | 2 |

## MARKUPS IN RETAIL GROCERY STORES

Grocery stores commonly use cost-plus pricing. Typical markups for a variety of products are as follows:

| Product | Markup (percentage) | Product | Markup (percentage) |
|---------|---------------------|---------|---------------------|
| Coffee | 5 | Cold cuts | 30 |
| Soft drinks | 5 | Fresh fruit | 45 |
| Breakfast cereal | 10 | Fresh vegetables | 45 |
| Soup | 10 | Spices | 50 |
| Ice cream | 20 | Proprietary drugs | 50 |

To the extent that the price elasticity of demand is lower for products like proprietary drugs and fresh vegetables than for products like coffee or breakfast cereal, this system of pricing may result in a grocery store's coming close to maximizing its profits, as pointed out on page 463. In general, it seems likely that stores attach high markups to products where consumers are not affected much by price—and thus where the price elasticity is low. They feel that they can safely get away with high markups. On the other hand, for products where consumers are very price-conscious, and hence where the price elasticity is high, stores realize that they must keep markups low. To do otherwise would be foolish, since consumers would go elsewhere.

This does not mean that grocery stores—or other firms, for that matter—always pursue sensible pricing policies. But it does illustrate the fact that cost-plus pricing need not be irrational.

# THE CLAWSON CORPORATION: A NUMERICAL EXAMPLE

To illustrate how cost-plus pricing can be used to maximize a firm's profits, consider the Clawson Corporation, a seller of office furniture. One of Clawson's major products is a metal desk for which the company has to pay $76 per desk, including transportation and related costs. While Clawson has a variety of overhead and marketing costs, these costs are essentially fixed, so marginal cost is approximately $76. Given that there are many firms in Clawson's geographical area that sell reasonably comparable desks, Clawson's marketing managers believe that the price elasticity of demand for its desks is quite high—about 2.5. Thus, based on Table 12.1, it should establish a markup of 67 percent, if it wants to maximize profit.

According to equation (12.2), the optimal price is

$$\text{Price} = \text{cost}(1 + \text{markup})$$

$$= 76(1 + .67)$$

$$= 127 \text{ dollars.}$$

Consequently, to maximize profit, Clawson should set a price of $127 per desk. However, this is spuriously precise. In fact, as we have seen in Chapters 8 and 4, firms very seldom can estimate their marginal costs or the price elasticity of demand with great precision. Nor is it worth what it would cost them to try to do so. Since Clawson's estimates are only approximate, so is the $127 figure. Recognizing that this is the case, Clawson's managers set a price of $127, but are prepared to push it up or down a bit in accord with their sense of what is most profitable.

# THE MULTIPLE-PRODUCT FIRM: DEMAND INTERRELATIONSHIPS

Having discussed cost-plus pricing, we turn to the pricing problems of the multiproduct firm. If a firm makes more than one product, it must recognize that a change in the price or quantity sold of one of its products may influence the demand for other products it produces. For example, if the Johnson Company produces and sells two products, $X$ and $Y$, its total revenue (i.e., sales) can be represented as

$$TR = TR_X + TR_Y, \tag{12.8}$$

where $TR_X$ is its total revenue from product $X$, and $TR_Y$ is its total revenue from product $Y$. The marginal revenue of each product is

$$MR_X = \frac{\partial TR}{\partial Q_X} = \frac{\partial TR_X}{\partial Q_X} + \frac{\partial TR_Y}{\partial Q_X} \tag{12.9a}$$

$$MR_Y = \frac{\partial TR}{\partial Q_Y} = \frac{\partial TR_Y}{\partial Q_Y} + \frac{\partial TR_X}{\partial Q_Y}. \tag{12.9b}$$

The last term in each of these equations represents the demand interrelationship between the two products. Thus, in equation (12.9a), the last term shows the effect of an increase in the quantity sold of product X on the total revenue from product Y. This effect can be either positive or negative. If products X and Y are complements, this effect will be positive, since an increase in the quantity sold of one product will increase the total revenue from the other product. On the other hand, if products X and Y are substitutes, this effect will be negative, since an increase in the quantity sold of one product will reduce the total revenue from the other product.

If you do not understand and pay proper attention to demand interrelationships of this sort among the products your firm sells, serious errors can result. For example, if product X is a fairly close substitute for product Y, and if the division of the Johnson Company producing product X launches a campaign to increase its sales, the results may be good for the division but bad for the company as a whole. Why? Because the resulting increase in product X's sales may be largely at the expense of product Y's sales.

## PRICING OF JOINT PRODUCTS: FIXED PROPORTIONS

Besides being interrelated on the demand side, a firm's products are often interrelated in production. For example, products sometimes are produced in a fixed ratio, as in the case of cattle, where beef and hide are gotten from each animal. In such a situation, there is no reason to distinguish between the products from the point of view of production or costs. Since they must be produced in fixed proportions, they are not separate products from a production point of view, but should be regarded as a **bundle**. Thus, one hide and two sides of beef might be such a bundle in the case of cattle, since they are produced from each animal. Because the products are produced jointly, there is no economically correct way to allocate the cost of producing each such bundle to the individual products.

To determine the optimal price and output of each such product, you must compare the marginal revenue of the output bundle with its marginal cost of production. If the total marginal revenue—that is, the sum of the marginal revenues gotten from each product in the package—is greater than its marginal cost, you should expand your output. Assuming that there are two joint products (A and B), Figure 12.1 shows the demand and marginal revenue curves for each,[3] as well as the marginal cost curve for the

---

[3] For simplicity, we assume that the demand curve for product A is not influenced by the price of product B, and that the demand curve for product B is not influenced by the price of product A.

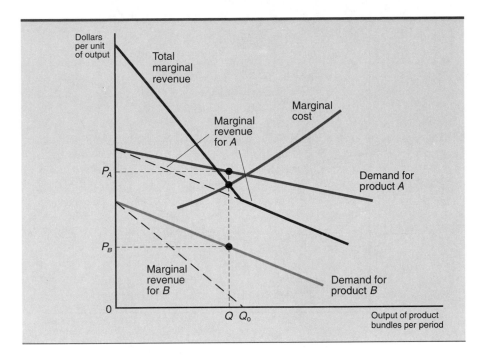

**FIGURE 12.1** *Optimal Pricing for Joint Products Produced in Fixed Proportions (Case 1)* The price of product $A$ is set at $P_A$, the price of product $B$ is set at $P_B$, and output is set at $Q$.

bundle composed of these products in the fixed proportions in which they are produced. The **total marginal revenue** curve is the **vertical** summation of the two marginal revenue curves for the individual products, since each bundle of output yields revenues from the sale of both products. Consequently, the profit-maximizing output in Figure 12.1 is $Q$, where the total marginal revenue equals marginal cost. The optimal price for product $A$ is $P_A$, and the optimal price for product $B$ is $P_B$.

It is important to note that the total marginal revenue curve coincides with the marginal revenue curve for product $A$ at all outputs beyond $Q_0$ in Figure 12.1. This is because the firm would never sell an amount of product $B$ where its marginal revenue is negative, since this would mean that greater revenues could be obtained if less were sold. Thus, if total output exceeds $Q_0$, the firm would sell only part of the product $B$ produced; specifically, it would sell the amount corresponding to an output of $Q_0$ product bundles. Consequently, if output exceeds $Q_0$, total marginal revenue equals the marginal revenue of product $A$ alone.

What if the marginal cost curve intersects the total marginal revenue curve to the right of $Q_0$ in Figure 12.1? In particular, suppose that the situa-

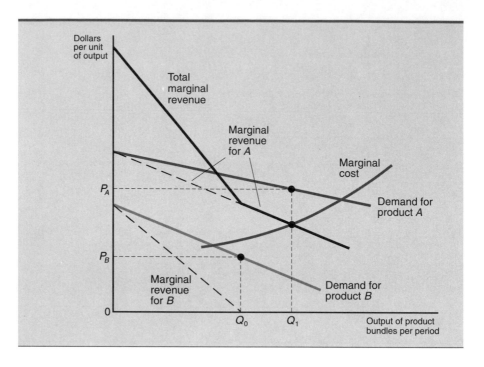

**FIGURE 12.2** *Optimal Pricing for Joint Products Produced in Fixed Proportions (Case 2)* The price of product $A$ is set at $P_A$, the price of product $B$ is set at $P_B$, and not all of product $B$ is sold.

tion is shown in Figure 12.2, where the marginal cost curve is lower than in Figure 12.1 (but the other curves are the same). The profit-maximizing output is $Q_1$, where the marginal cost and total marginal revenue curves intersect. All of product $A$ that is produced is sold, the price being $P_A$, but not all of product $B$ is sold. Instead, the amount sold is limited to the amount in output $Q_0$, so that the price of product $B$ is maintained at $P_B$. The "surplus" amount of product $B$ must be thrown away and kept off the market to avoid depressing its price.

## THE AVTECH COMPANY: A NUMERICAL EXAMPLE

To illustrate the technique discussed in the previous section, consider the Avtech Company, which manufactures two goods, $A$ and $B$, that are jointly produced in equal quantities. That is, for every unit of product $A$ that is produced, the firm also produces a unit of product $B$ (whether it wants it or not). Avtech's total cost function is

$$TC = 100 + Q + 2Q^2, \tag{12.10}$$

where $Q$ is the number of units of output. (Each unit contains 1 unit of product $A$ and 1 unit of product $B$.) The demand curves for the firm's two products are

$$P_A = 200 - Q_A \tag{12.11}$$

$$P_B = 150 - 2Q_B, \tag{12.12}$$

where $P_A$ and $Q_A$ are the price and output of product $A$, and $P_B$ and $Q_B$ are the price and output of product $B$.

How much of each product should Avtech produce and sell per period? What price should it charge for each? Avtech's total revenue equals the sum of the total revenues from its two products; thus,

$$TR = P_A Q_A + P_B Q_B. \tag{12.13}$$

Substituting the right-hand sides of equations (12.11) and (12.12) for $P_A$ and $P_B$, respectively, it follows that

$$TR = (200 - Q_A)Q_A + (150 - 2Q_B)Q_B$$

$$= 200Q_A - Q_A^2 + 150Q_B - 2Q_B^2.$$

Assuming that Avtech sells all that it produces of both products, $Q_A = Q_B = Q$, since, as stressed above, a unit of one product is produced whenever a unit of the other product is produced. Thus,

$$TR = 200Q - Q^2 + 150Q - 2Q^2$$

$$= 350Q - 3Q^2. \tag{12.14}$$

To obtain Avtech's profit, $\pi$, we must subtract its total cost in equation (12.10) from its total revenue in equation (12.14), the result being

$$\pi = (350Q - 3Q^2) - (100 + Q + 2Q^2)$$

$$= -100 + 349Q - 5Q^2.$$

Thus, the profit-maximizing output level is such that

$$\frac{d\pi}{dQ} = 349 - 10Q = 0$$

$$10Q = 349$$

$$Q = 34.9.$$

In other words, to maximize profit, Avtech should produce 34.9 units of each product per period of time.[4] To sell this amount, equation (12.11) tells

---

[4] Note that there is no reason why $Q$ must be an integer. Avtech can produce 34.9 units per period of time. How? By producing a total of 349 units during 10 periods.

us that the price of product $A$ must be

$$P_A = 200 - 34.9 = \$165.10,$$

and equation (12.12) tells us that the price of product $B$ must be

$$P_B = 150 - 2(34.9) = \$80.20.$$

At this point, it may seem that the analysis is finished—but it isn't. As indicated above, we have assumed that Avtech sells all that it produces of both products. To see whether this assumption is true, we must see whether, if $Q = 34.9$, the marginal revenues of both products are nonnegative. Only if this is the case will Avtech sell all that it produces of both products. (Recall Figure 12.2.) From equations (12.11) and (12.12), we find that $TR_A$, the total revenue from product $A$, equals

$$TR_A = P_A Q_A = (200 - Q_A)Q_A = 200Q_A - Q_A^2,$$

and that $TR_B$, the total revenue from product $B$, equals

$$TR_B = P_B Q_B = (150 - 2Q_B)Q_B = 150Q_B - 2Q_B^2.$$

Thus, the marginal revenues of products $A$ and $B$ equal

$$MR_A = \frac{dTR_A}{dQ_A} = 200 - 2Q_A = 130.2 \text{ (when } Q_A = 34.9)$$

$$MR_B = \frac{dTR_B}{dQ_B} = 150 - 4Q_B = 10.4 \text{ (when } Q_B = 34.9).$$

Since both marginal revenues $(MR_A$ and $MR_B)$ are nonnegative when $Q_A$ and $Q_B = 34.9$, the assumption underlying the above analysis is valid.[5]


# OUTPUT OF JOINT PRODUCTS: VARIABLE PROPORTIONS

Having discussed the case where two joint products are produced in fixed proportions, let's turn to the case where they are produced in variable proportions. This generally is the more realistic case, particularly if one is considering a fairly long period of time. Even in the case of cattle, the proportions of hides and beef can be altered because cattle can be bred to produce more or less beef relative to hide.

Suppose a firm produces and sells two products, $A$ and $B$, and that each **isocost curve** (labeled $TC$) in Figure 12.3 shows the amounts of these goods

---

[5] If one product's marginal revenue had been negative when $Q_A$ and $Q_B$ equal 34.9, the optimal solution would have involved producing more of this product than is sold, as indicated in Figure 12.2. The firm would sell only the amount of this product where the marginal revenue is zero. The marginal revenue for the other product would be used to determine the optimal output level, as shown in Figure 12.2.

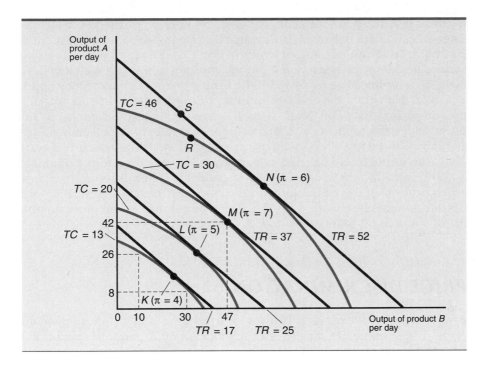

**FIGURE 12.3** *Optimal Outputs for Joint Products Produced in Variable Proportions*   The optimal point, which must be at a point where an isorevenue line is tangent to an isocost curve, is at point *M*, where profit per day is $7,000.

that can be produced at the same total cost. Thus, the isocost curve labeled $TC = 13$ shows the various combinations of outputs—for example, 26 units of product *A* and 10 units of product *B*, or 8 units of product *A* and 30 units of product *B*—that can be produced at a total cost of $13,000 per day.

Also included in Figure 12.3 are **isorevenue lines** (labeled *TR*), each of which shows the combinations of outputs of the two products that yield the same total revenue. For example, the isorevenue line labeled $TR = 52$ shows the various combinations of outputs—such as those corresponding to points *S* or *N*—that yield a total revenue of $52,000 per day. Other isorevenue lines show the output combinations that yield total revenues of $17,000, $25,000, and $37,000, respectively.

The problem facing the firm is to determine how much of products *A* and *B* to produce. The first step toward solving this problem is to observe that if an output combination is at a point where an isorevenue line is *not* tangent to an isocost curve, it *cannot* be the optimal output combination. To see this, note that if an output combination is at a point where an isorevenue line is not tangent to an isocost curve (say point *R*), it is possible to increase revenue (without changing cost) by moving to the point (on the same isocost curve) where an isorevenue line *is* tangent to the isocost curve (say point *N*). Thus, any output combination that is not at a tangency point cannot be the profit-maximizing output combination, since we have indicated how profit can be increased if the firm is at such a nontangency point.

Given that this is the case, we can find the optimal output combination by comparing the profit level at each tangency point, and choosing the point where the profit level is highest. For example, four tangency points are shown in Figure 12.3—points *K*, *L*, *M*, and *N*. As indicated in Figure 12.3, the profit levels (labeled $\pi$) corresponding to these four points are $4,000, $5,000, $7,000, and $6,000, respectively. Thus, if we must choose among the output combinations on the isocost curves in Figure 12.3, the optimal output combination for this firm is at point *M*, where the firm produces and sells 42 units of product *A* and 47 units of product *B* per day.

# PRICE DISCRIMINATION

**Price discrimination** occurs when the same product is sold at more than one price. For example, an airline may sell tickets on a particular flight at a higher price to business travelers than to college students. Even if the products are not precisely the same, price discrimination is said to occur if very similar products are sold at prices that are in different ratios to marginal costs. Thus, if a firm sells boxes of candy with a label (cost of label: 2 cents) saying "Premium Quality" in rich neighborhoods for $12 and sells the same boxes of candy without this label in poor neighborhoods for $5, this is discrimination. The mere fact that differences in price exist among similar products is not evidence of discrimination; only if these differences do not reflect cost differences is there evidence of this kind.

For a firm to be able and willing to engage in price discrimination, the buyers of the firm's product must fall into classes with considerable differences among classes in the price elasticity of demand for the product, and it must be possible to identify and segregate these classes at moderate cost. Also, buyers must be unable to transfer the product easily from one class to another, since otherwise persons could make money by buying the product from the low-price classes and selling it to the high-price classes, thus making it difficult to maintain the price differentials among classes. The differences among classes of buyers in the price elasticity of demand may be due to differences among classes in income level, tastes, or the availability of substitutes. Thus, the price elasticity of demand for the boxes of candy cited above may be lower for the rich than for the poor.

If a firm practices discrimination of this sort, it must decide two questions: How much output should it allocate to each class of buyer, and What price should it charge each class of buyer? Suppose that there are only two classes of buyers. Also, for the moment, assume that the firm has already decided on its total output, and consequently that the only real question is how it should be allocated between the two classes. The firm will maximize its profits by allocating the total output between the two classes in such a way that marginal revenue in one class is equal to marginal revenue in the other class. For example, if marginal revenue in the first class is $25 and marginal revenue in the second class is $10, the allocation is not optimal, since profits can be increased by allocating 1 less unit of output to the second class and 1 more unit of output to the first class. Only if the two marginal revenues are equal is the allocation optimal. And if the marginal revenues in the two classes are equal, the ratio of the price in the first class to the price in the second class will equal

$$\left(1 - \frac{1}{\eta_2}\right) \div \left(1 - \frac{1}{\eta_1}\right),$$

where $\eta_1$ is the price elasticity of demand in the first class, and $\eta_2$ is the price elasticity of demand in the second class.[6] Thus, it will not pay to discriminate if the two price elasticities are equal. Moreover, if discrimination does pay, the price will be higher in the class in which demand is less elastic.

Turning to the more realistic case where the firm must also decide on its total output, it is obvious that the firm must look at its costs as well as demand in the two classes. Specifically, the firm will choose the output where the marginal cost of its entire output is equal to the common value of the marginal revenue in the two classes. To see this, consider Figure 12.4, which shows $D_1$, the demand curve in class 1; $D_2$, the demand curve in class 2; $R_1$, the marginal revenue curve in class 1; $R_2$; the marginal revenue curve in class 2; and the firm's marginal cost curve. The firm begins to determine its total output by summing horizontally over the two marginal revenue curves, $R_1$ and $R_2$. The curve representing the horizontal summation of the two marginal revenue curves is $G$. This curve shows, for each level of marginal revenue, the total output that is needed if marginal revenue in each class is to be maintained at this level. The optimal output is shown by the point where the $G$ curve intersects the marginal cost curve, since marginal cost must be equal to the common value of marginal revenue in each class. If this were not the case, profits could be increased by expanding output (if marginal cost were less than marginal revenue) or by contracting output (if marginal cost were greater than marginal revenue). Thus, the firm will produce an output of $Q$ units and sell $Q_1$ units in the class 1 market and $Q_2$ units in the class 2 market. Price will be $P_1$ in the class 1 market and $P_2$ in the class 2 market. This will result in higher profits than if the firm quoted the same price in both markets.

---

[6] Recall from equation (12.4) that marginal revenue equals $P(1 - 1/\eta)$, where $P$ is price, and $\eta$ is the price elasticity of demand. Therefore, if marginal revenue is the same in the two classes, $P_1(1 - 1/\eta_1) = P_2(1 - 1/\eta_2)$. Hence $P_1/P_2 = (1 - 1/\eta_2) \div (1 - 1/\eta_1)$.

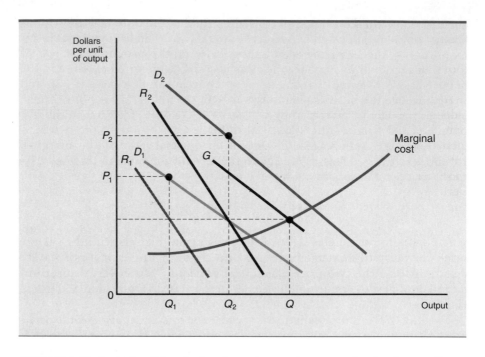

**FIGURE 12.4** *Price Discrimination* To maximize profit, the firm will produce a total output of $Q$ units, and set a price of $P_1$ in the class 1 market and a price of $P_2$ in the class 2 market.

# AIRLINE TRAVEL: A CASE STUDY

Perhaps the most frequently cited example of price discrimination is the case of airline tickets. The airlines charge a lower fare for essentially the same ticket if it is bought well in advance, if a relatively small percentage of the fare is refundable if the trip is canceled or changed, and if the trip includes a weekend stay. For example, in 1992, the price of a round-trip economy ticket from New York to San Francisco was $420 under these circumstances, but $840 if the ticket was not bought in advance, if all of the fare was refundable, and if the trip did not include a weekend stay.

One reason for these price differences is that the price elasticity of demand for business travel is much less than that for vacation travel. Business travelers must meet with clients, suppliers, and associates at particular times, often as soon as possible. Regardless of the price of an air ticket (so long as it remains within reasonable bounds), many of these trips would be well worth making. On the other hand, vacation travelers often plan their trips well in advance, are relatively flexible with regard to the timing of their trips, and are sensitive to moderate differences in ticket price. From our discussion in the previous section, it seems likely that the airlines, to maximize profit, would like to set higher prices for business travelers than for vacation travelers. And this is the effect of the price differences cited above, since business travelers are much less likely than vacation travelers to buy their tickets well in advance or to include a weekend stay.

At the same time, it is also worth noting that because the airlines can reduce their costs if demand is more predictable (as a result of better scheduling of equipment and personnel), they may enjoy savings if travelers buy their tickets well in advance. Also, if a ticket is not refundable, it clearly is not the same as a ticket that is refundable. Thus, part of the price differences cited above may be due to differences in the risk of loss by the traveler if he or she cancels or changes the trip. The price differences are not due entirely to price discrimination, pure and simple.

## PRICE DISCRIMINATION: A PHARMACEUTICAL EXAMPLE

To illustrate how price discrimination can be used, suppose a drug manufacturer sells a major drug in Europe and the United States. Because of legal restrictions, the drug cannot be bought in one country and sold in another. The demand curve for the drug in Europe is

$$P_E = 10 - Q_E, \tag{12.15}$$

where $P_E$ is the price (in dollars per pound) in Europe, and $Q_E$ is the amount (in millions of pounds) sold there. The demand curve for the drug in the United States is

$$P_U = 20 - 1.5 Q_U, \tag{12.16}$$

where $P_U$ is the price (in dollars per pound) in the United States, and $Q_U$ is the amount (in millions of pounds) sold there. The total cost (in millions of dollars) of producing the drug for sale worldwide is

$$TC = 4 + 2(Q_E + Q_U). \tag{12.17}$$

The firm's total profit from both Europe and the United States is

$$\pi = P_E Q_E + P_U Q_U - TC$$

$$= (10 - Q_E)Q_E + (20 - 1.5Q_U)Q_U - [4 + 2(Q_E + Q_U)]$$

$$= -4 + 8Q_E - Q_E^2 + 18Q_U - 1.5Q_U^2. \tag{12.18}$$

To maximize $\pi$ with respect to $Q_E$ and $Q_U$, we find first derivatives of equation (12.18) with respect to $Q_E$ and $Q_U$, and set them equal to zero.

$$\frac{\partial \pi}{\partial Q_E} = 8 - 2Q_E = 0.$$

$$\frac{\partial \pi}{\partial Q_U} = 18 - 3Q_U = 0.$$

Solving these equations for $Q_E$ and $Q_U$, we find that 4 million pounds of the drug should be sold in Europe, and 6 million pounds should be sold in the United States.

To find the optimal prices in Europe and the United States, we substitute 4 for $Q_E$ and 6 for $Q_U$ in equations (12.15) and (12.16), the result being that the price in Europe should be $6 per pound, and the price in the United States should be $11 per pound. Substituting these values of $P_E$ and $P_U$, as well as the foregoing values of $Q_E$ and $Q_U$, into equation (12.18), we find that the firm's profit equals

$$\pi = -4 + 8(4) - 4^2 + 18(6) - 1.5(6^2) = 66,$$

or $66 million.

At this point, it is important to note that if we had used the graphical technique in the previous section, we would have obtained precisely the same results. Whether the graphical technique or the calculus is used, the answer will be the same.

Having obtained the above results, it is interesting and useful to determine how much additional profit the firm makes because it engages in price discrimination. If price discrimination were not possible, $P_E$ would have to equal $P_U$. Letting this common price be $P$, it follows from equation (12.15) that $Q_E = 10 - P$, and from equation (12.16) that $Q_U = (1/1.5)(20 - P)$. Thus, the firm's total amount sold in Europe and the United States combined is

$$Q = Q_E + Q_U = 10 - P + \tfrac{1}{1.5}(20 - P) = 23\tfrac{1}{3} - \tfrac{5}{3}P,$$

which implies that

$$P = 14 - .6Q. \tag{12.19}$$

Thus, the firm's profit would be

$$\pi = PQ - TC$$

$$= (14 - .6Q)Q - (4 + 2Q)$$

$$= -4 + 12Q - .6Q^2. \tag{12.20}$$

To find the value of $Q$ that maximizes profit, we differentiate equation (12.20) with respect to $Q$ and set the derivative equal to zero.

$$\frac{d\pi}{dQ} = 12 - 1.2Q = 0.$$

Solving for $Q$, we find that the firm, if it could not engage in price discrimination, should produce a total of 10 million pounds of the drug. Substituting 10 for $Q$ in equation (12.19) and (12.20), it follows that

$$P = 14 - .6(10) = 8$$
$$\pi = -4 + 12(10) - .6(10^2) = 56.$$

Thus if the firm could not engage in price discrimination, its profit would be $56 million, rather than the $66 million it can earn by price discrimination.

# PRICE DISCRIMINATION OF OTHER TYPES

Price discrimination of the type discussed in the previous section is often called **third-degree price discrimination.** Besides third-degree price discrimination, there are also first-degree and second-degree price discrimination. In **discrimination of the first degree**, the firm is aware of the maximum amount that every consumer will pay for each amount of the commodity. Since it is assumed that the product cannot be resold, the firm can charge each consumer a different price.

For simplicity, suppose that each consumer buys only 1 unit of the commodity. The firm will establish a price for every consumer that is so high that the consumer is on the verge of refusing to buy the commodity. In the more realistic case where each consumer can buy more than 1 unit of the commodity, it is assumed that the firm knows each consumer's demand curve for the commodity and that it adjusts its offer accordingly. Thus, if the maximum amount that a particular consumer would pay for 50 units of the commodity is $100 (and if 50 units is the profit-maximizing amount for the firm to sell to this consumer), the firm will make an all-or-nothing offer of 50 units of the commodity for $100.

For first-degree price discrimination to occur, a firm must have a relatively small number of buyers, and it must be able to guess the maximum prices they are willing to accept. **Second-degree price discrimination** is much more common. Take the case of a gas company, each of whose customers has the demand curve shown in Figure 12.5. The company charges a high price, $P_0$, if the consumer purchases less than $X$ units of gas per month. For an amount beyond $X$ units per month, the company charges a medium price, $P_1$. For purchases beyond $Y$, the company charges an even lower price, $P_2$. Consequently, the company's total revenues from each consumer are equal to the shaded area in Figure 12.5, since the consumer will purchase $X$ units at a price of $P_0$, $(Y - X)$ units at a price of $P_1$, and $(Z - Y)$ units at a price of $P_2$.[7]

The gas company, by charging different prices for various amounts of the commodity, is able to increase its revenue and profits considerably. After all, if it were permitted to charge only one price and if it wanted to sell Z units, it would have to charge a price of $P_2$. Thus, the firm's total revenue would equal only the rectangle $OP_2EZ$, which is considerably less than the shaded area in Figure 12.5. By charging different prices, the firm is able to

---

[7] Of course, this assumes for simplicity that each consumer purchases Z units. Also, other simplifying assumptions (which need not concern us here) are made in this and the next paragraph.

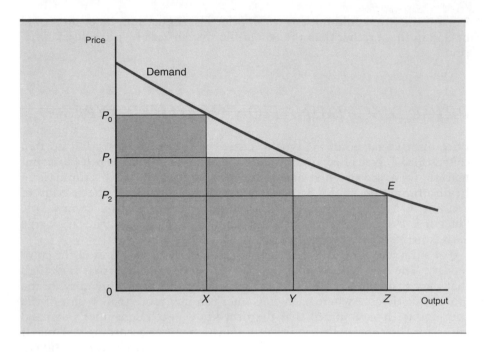

**FIGURE 12.5   *Price Discrimination, Second Degree*** The company charges a different price ($P_0$, $P_1$, or $P_2$) depending on how much the consumer purchases, thus increasing its revenue and profits.

raise its profits. According to some authorities, second-degree price discrimination plays an important role in the schedules of rates charged by many public utilities—gas, water, electricity, and others.[8]

## USING COUPONS FOR PRICE DISCRIMINATION

As pointed out in previous sections, a firm, if it is to be able to engage in price discrimination, must be able to identify and separate consumers into groups, depending on their price elasticity of demand for the firm's product. According to some observers, coupons are often used for this purpose. Producers of consumer goods like food and household products often distribute coupons through the mails or as part of a newspaper or magazine ad. These coupons enable the holder to buy the firm's product at a discount. For example, in March 1992, Maxwell House issued coupons enabling the coupon holder to save 50 cents on a can of its Lite coffee. (The coupons

[8] R. Davidson, *Price Determination in Selling Gas and Electricity* (Baltimore: John Hopkins University Press, 1955); and C. Cicchetti and J. Jurewitz, *Studies in Electric Utility Regulation* (Cambridge, Mass.: Ballinger, 1975).

## PRICING ELECTRICITY BY THE HOUR

Electric companies typically have 5 to 10 different rate schedules for their main customer groups. The average price charged large industrial users may differ substantially from that charged residences. Moreover, many consumers pay a price for electricity that is based on the time of day they use it. For example, the prices charged by Consolidated Edison, a large New York electric utility, and Pacific Gas and Electric, a major California electric utility, are as follows:

| Company and time of day of electricity use | Price (cents per kilowatt-hour) |
|---|---|
| Consolidated Edison | |
|     8 AM–10 PM (peak hours) | 27 |
|     10 PM– 8 AM (off-peak hours) | 4* |
| | |
| Pacific Gas and Electric | |
|   Summer: | |
|     Noon–6 PM (peak hours) | 28.3 |
|     6 PM–noon (off-peak hours) | 9.2 |
|   Winter: | |
|     Noon–6 PM (peak hours) | 11.3 |
|     6 PM–noon (off-peak hours) | 8.0 |

\* Approximate figure.

Electric utilities utilize their cheapest generators continuously and start up their more costly ones as demand goes up. Consequently, at 3 AM a utility might meet its requirements from a hydroelectric dam that produces electricity for 2 cents per kilowatt-hour. However, on a hot day in August when air conditioners are running full blast, demand would be so great that the utility would be forced to use its

most costly generators, perhaps an oil-fired plant where electricity costs 7 cents per kilowatt-hour.

(a) Does price discrimination occur in the market for electricity? (b) Why have some state regulatory commissions, including the Public Service Commission of New York, ordered that time-of-day rates be phased in for residential consumers? (c) In many areas, both residential and industrial consumers tend to pay a lower price per kilowatt-hour if they use more rather than less electricity. Is this price discrimination? If so, what kind of price discrimination is it? (d)

Explain why price discrimination is used by electric companies.

*Solution* (a) Yes. (b) Time-of-day rates are a way of smoothing the peaks and valleys of electricity demand. As pointed out in the paragraph before last, it is expensive to cater to peak demand. Consequently, there can be significant savings if demand is shifted from peak to off-peak times of day. (c) Yes, it is second-degree price discrimination. (d) As is evident from our discussion of Figure 12.5, price discrimination can be used to increase profit.*

* For further discussion, see W. Shepherd and C. Wilcox, *Public Policies toward Business* (Homewood, Ill.: Irwin, 1979); and *New York Times*, June 9, 1990.

were good until April 30, 1992.) This is not the first time we have encountered coupons. In Chapter 4, we saw that L'eggs issued them in its pricing experiment, and in Chapter 10, we learned that coupon users tend to have less brand loyalty than other buyers of coffee.

Available statistical evidence indicates that coupon users tend to have higher price elasticities of demand than nonusers. Thus, for cake mix, the price elasticity of demand is reported to be about 0.43 for coupon users, but only about 0.21 for nonusers. And for cat food, the price elasticity of demand is reported to be about 1.13 for coupon users, but only about 0.49 for nonusers.[9] By issuing coupons, the firms selling these and other products divide their customers into two groups: those who bother to clip and use the coupons (generally about one-fourth of all consumers) and those who don't. The more price-conscious group, the coupon users, are charged a lower price than the less price-conscious group, the nonusers.

## TYING AT IBM AND XEROX

**Tying** is a pricing technique that has been used by IBM and Xerox, among others. Tying occurs when a firm sells a product (such as a copying machine or a computer), the use of which requires the consumption of a complementary product (such as paper or paper computer cards). The consumer is

[9] C. Narasimhan, "A Price Discrimination Theory of Coupons," *Marketing Science* (Spring 1984).

required, generally by contract, to buy the complementary product from the firm selling the product itself. For example, during the 1950s, customers who leased a Xerox copying machine had to buy Xerox paper, and customers who leased an IBM computer had to buy paper computer cards made by IBM.

Why do firms engage in tying? One reason is that it is a way of practicing price discrimination. By setting the price of the complementary product well above its cost, the firm can get what is in effect a much higher price from customers who use its product intensely than from those who use it little. For example, suppose that customer A uses a Xerox copier to make 10,000 copies per month, whereas customer B makes only 1,000 copies per month. It is hard for Xerox to price its machines so as to obtain more revenue from customer A, the more intensive user, than from customer B. But if Xerox can tie the sale of copying paper to the sale of its copier, it can get more profit from customer A than from customer B because it makes more on the copying paper.

But this is not the only reason for tying. Sometimes a firm wants to insure that its product works properly and that its brand name is protected. To do so, it insists that customers use its complementary product. For example, Jerrold Electronics Corporation, which installed community antenna systems, required customers to accept 5-year maintenance contracts to avoid breakdowns resulting from improper servicing of its equipment. And McDonald's franchises have had to buy their materials and food from McDonald's so that the hamburgers are uniform, and the company's brand name is not tarnished.

## TRANSFER PRICING

In previous sections, we have assumed that the firm was selling its product to outsiders. While this generally is the case, many large firms are decentralized, and one division of a firm sells its product to another division of the same firm. For example, in the Ford Motor Company, the Engine and Foundry Division transfers its products to the Automobile Assembly Division, which in turn transfers its products to the Ford and Lincoln-Mercury Divisions. The price that the selling division charges the buying division for its product should be set so that the firm as a whole maximizes profit. In this and the following two sections, we show how this can be done.

Assume that the Orion Corporation, a chemical firm, consists of two separate divisions, a production division and a marketing division. The production division manufactures the basic chemical, which is sold internally to the marketing division. The price at which this transfer takes place is called the **transfer price**. The marketing division packages the basic chemical into the final product, and sells it to outside customers. In this section, we assume that there is no market for the basic chemical outside the firm. In the next section, we relax this assumption.

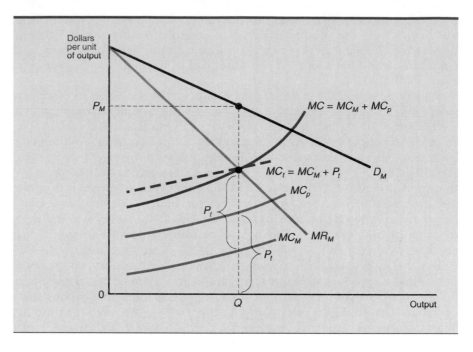

**FIGURE 12.6  Determination of Transfer Price, Given No External Market for the Transferred Good**  The optimal transfer price, $P_t$, equals the marginal production cost at the optimal output, Q.

---

With no market outside the firm for the basic chemical, the marketing division is completely dependent on the production division for its supply of the basic chemical, since it cannot buy any of this chemical outside the firm. Also, if no such market exists, the production division is not able to sell any amount of this chemical that the marketing division does not want. Thus, the quantity of the basic chemical manufactured by the production division must equal the amount sold by the marketing division.[10]

Figure 12.6 shows the optimal price and output for the firm as a whole. Looking at the two divisions combined, the marginal cost to the firm, $MC$, at any level of output is the sum of the marginal cost of production, $MC_P$, and the marginal cost of marketing, $MC_M$. Thus, as we stressed repeatedly in previous chapters, the firm will maximize profit by choosing the output, $Q$, where marginal cost $(MC)$ equals marginal revenue $(MR_M)$. To sell this output, it should establish a price of $P_M$ for its final product.

Knowing that this is the optimal output and price for the firm as a whole, at what level should the transfer price be set? In other words, how much

---

[10] For simplicity, we assume that all of the basic chemical produced during the period must be sold then. In other words, no inventories of the chemical can be carried over.

should the production division charge the marketing division for the basic chemical? If each division maximizes its own divisional profit, the transfer price, $P_t$, should equal $MC_P$, the marginal production cost at the optimal output, Q. To see this, note that once this transfer price is set, the production division will encounter a horizontal demand curve for the basic chemical that it produces, and its marginal revenue will equal $P_t$. To maximize its profit, it will choose the output level where its marginal cost, $MC_P$, equals $P_t$. As shown in Figure 12.6, this output level is Q, which was shown in the previous paragraph to be the optimal output level for the firm as a whole.

Turning to the marketing division, if the transfer price is $P_t$, this division's marginal cost curve equals $MC_t$, which is the sum of the marginal marketing cost, $MC_M$, and the transfer price, $P_t$. This division will maximize its profits by setting its output level at Q, the point where its marginal cost, $MC_t$, equals its marginal revenue, $MR_M$. To sell this amount, it charges a price of $P_M$. Thus, this division, like the production division, acts to promote the firm's overall interests. It establishes the output level, Q, and the price, $P_M$, that maximize the firm's overall profit.

# TRANSFER PRICING: A PERFECTLY COMPETITIVE MARKET FOR THE TRANSFERRED PRODUCT

In many cases, there is a market outside the firm for the product that is transferred from one division to the other. If this is true in the case of the Orion Corporation, the output levels of the production and marketing divisions no longer have to be equal. If the marketing division wants more of the basic chemical than is produced by the production division, it can buy some from external suppliers. If the production division produces more of the basic chemical than the marketing division wants, it can sell some to external customers. Assuming that the market for the basic chemical is perfectly competitive, we can readily determine the way in which the firm should set the transfer price under these circumstances.

Figure 12.7 shows the optimal price and output for the firm as a whole. Since there is a perfectly competitive market for the basic chemical, the production division is confronted with a horizontal demand curve, $D_P$, for its output, where the price is $P_t$, the price of the basic chemical in the external market. To maximize profit, the production division should produce the output, $Q_P$, where the marginal production cost $MC_P$ equals the price $P_t$. In this sense, the production division behaves like a perfectly competitive firm.

To maximize the firm's overall profit, the transfer price should equal $P_t$, the price of the basic chemical in the perfectly competitive market outside the firm. Since the production division can sell as much of the basic chemical as it wants to external customers at a price of $P_t$, it has no incentive to

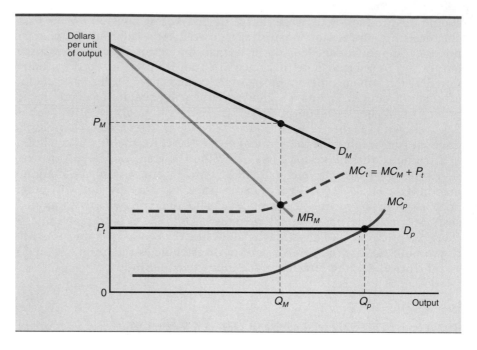

**FIGURE 12.7  Determination of Transfer Price, Given Perfectly Competitive External Market for the Transferred Product**  The optimal transfer price, $P_t$, equals the market price of the transferred product.

sell it at a price below $P_t$ to the marketing division. Similarly, since the marketing division can buy as much of the basic chemical as it wants from external suppliers at a price of $P_t$, it has no incentive to buy it from the production division at a price above $P_t$.

The marketing division, which must buy the basic chemical at a price of $P_t$ regardless of where it comes from, has a marginal cost curve, $MC_t$, which is the sum of the marketing marginal cost $MC_M$ and the price of the basic chemical, $P_t$. To maximize its own profit, the marketing division must choose that output level, $Q_M$, where its marginal cost, $MC_t$, equals its marginal revenue, $MR_M$. Since Figure 12.7 shows that the output of the marketing division, $Q_M$, is less than the output of the production division, $Q_P$, the optimal solution in this case calls for Orion's production division to sell part of its output (specifically, $Q_P - Q_M$ units) to outside customers.[11]

---

[11] Of course, it is not always true that $Q_M$ is less than $Q_p$. Whether or not this is the case depends on the shape and position of the marginal cost curves ($MC_M$ and $MC_p$) and the demand curve, as well as the price of the transferred product in the external perfectly competitive market.

## TRANSFER PRICING AT EMHART, A. O. SMITH, AND FORD

Many firms have established policies whereby one division can pay another division no more for the latter's product than what this product would cost if bought on the outside market. For example, the Emhart Corporation's policy has been that "where the total cost of material, labor, variable overhead, and transportation . . . exceeds the outside vendor's selling price, or where the delivery schedule is a factor, consideration should be given to outside vendors." Similarly, A. O. Smith, a producer of auto parts and assemblies, has stated that a division selling a particular product "will provide the buying division with a price that is at least as favorable as can be obtained from any alternate source." To the extent that the division selling the product is unwilling to sell at a less-than-market price to the buying division, these policies amount to the same thing as the optimal solution in the previous section.

Sometimes there are disputes among divisions over the proper level of transfer prices, the division selling a product wanting a higher price, the buying division wanting a lower price. At the Ford Motor Company, there has been a special intracompany pricing coordinator, a member of the corporate finance staff responsible for administering transfer-pricing policies and arbitrating disputes. At one time, six or seven employees worked almost full-time on such activities, but more recently only one person has been required, as various divisions have become more experienced and knowledgeable in this regard.

## THE ORION CORPORATION: A NUMERICAL EXAMPLE

To illustrate how a firm's managers can calculate the optimal output rates in the situation analyzed in the section before last, let's again consider the Orion Corporation, assuming that its demand and cost conditions are no longer those given in Figure 12.7. Suppose the demand curve for the finished product sold by Orion's marketing division is

$$P_M = 100 - Q_M, \tag{12.21}$$

where $P_M$ is the price (in dollars per ton) of the finished product, and $Q_M$ is the quantity sold (in millions of tons per year). Excluding the cost of the basic chemical, the marketing division's total cost function is

$$TC_M = 200 + 10\, Q_M, \tag{12.22}$$

where $TC_M$ is the division's total cost (in millions of dollars).

CONSULTANT'S CORNER

## SETTLING SOME STRIFE OVER A PRICING FORMULA*

An oil company contained two divisions, one involved in the production and sale of natural gas products and one involved in petrochemical production. The former division owned and operated about ten plants containing extraction units, which took the gas liquids out of the natural gas stream, and fractionators, which separated the gas liquid stream into particular gas liquids. The latter division, which had a variety of petrochemical plants, bought about half of the ethane it used from the former division.

The price that the gas products division charged the petrochemical division for ethane was determined by a formula that was designed to help the gas products division earn a 12 percent rate of return on its investment. This formula had evolved from negotiations between the former heads of the two divisions, but the present head of the gas products division felt that it should be abandoned because he could get much more for his ethane by selling it to buyers outside the firm. (The formula resulted in a price that was below the current market price of ethane.) On the other hand, the head of the petrochemical division pointed out that the ethane production facilities at the gas products division had been constructed to provide ethane for his division.

If you were a consultant to this firm, would you support the recommendation of the head of the gas products division, and if so, why?

* For a much more complete account of a somewhat similar situation, see M. E. Barrett and M. P. Cormack, *Management Strategy in the Oil and Gas Industries: Cases and Readings* (Houston: Gulf, 1983).

Turning to Orion's production division, its total cost function is

$$TC_P = 10 + 2Q_P + 0.5Q_P^2, \qquad (12.23)$$

where $TC_P$ is total production cost (in millions of dollars) and $Q_P$ is the total quantity produced of the basic chemical (in millions of tons per year). As indicated in the section before last, there is a perfectly competitive market for the basic chemical. Assume that its price in this market is $42 per ton.

Under these conditions, we can readily determine the optimal output rate for each division, as well as the proper transfer price for the basic chemical. The production division can sell all of the basic chemical that it wants at $42 per ton. Thus, its marginal revenue equals $42. Since its marginal cost is the first derivative of $TC_P$ [in equation (12.23)] with respect to $Q_P$, it follows that

$$MC_P = \frac{dTC_P}{dQ_P} = 2 + Q_P. \qquad (12.24)$$

## TRANSFER PRICING AND JOINT PRODUCTS AT KNOX CHEMICAL CORPORATION

Knox Chemical Corporation is one of the largest producers of isopropyl alcohol, or isopropanol, as it frequently is called. Isopropanol is used to produce acetone, an important industrial chemical; also, it is used to make various chemical intermediate products. Since Knox Chemical produces both acetone and these chemical intermediates, it uses much of the isopropanol that it makes. One of the many tasks of Knox's product manager for isopropanol was to set transfer prices for isopropanol within the company.

(a) Knox's product manager for isopropanol generally set the transfer price equal to the prevailing market price. Was this a sensible procedure? (b) When the production of phenol expanded rapidly, a great deal of acetone was produced because it was a by-prod-

uct of the process leading to phenol. What effect do you think this had on the market price of isopropanol? (c) In producing a pound of phenol, 0.6 pounds of acetone are produced. Are phenol and acetone joint products? (d) Are they produced in fixed proportions?

*Solution* (a) Yes. As stressed on page 483, to maximize the firm's overall profit, the transfer price should equal the price of the product in the external (competitive) market. (b) When the production of phenol increased, the supply of acetone increased, since acetone was a by-product. Thus, since less isopropanol was demanded to make acetone, the demand curve for isopropanol shifted to the left (as shown below), and the price of isopropanol declined (from $P_0$ to $P_1$). (c) Yes. (d) Yes.*

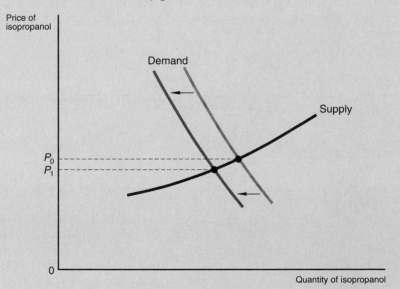

* For further discussion, see E. R. Corey, *Industrial Marketing*.

To find the output that maximizes the production division's profits, we must set its marginal revenue equal to its marginal cost:

$$42 = 2 + Q_p,$$

$$Q_P = 40.$$

Thus, the production division should produce 40 million tons per year of the basic chemical.

The transfer price for the basic chemical should be its price in the perfectly competitive market outside the firm. Since this market price is $42 per ton, the transfer price should be the same. Also, we know from the section before last that the marketing division's marginal cost, $MC_t$, is the sum of its own marginal marketing cost, $MC_M$, and the transfer price. That is,

$$MC_t = MC_M + P_t.$$

Since $P_t = \$42$, and its own marginal marketing cost equals the first derivative of $TC_M$ [in equation (12.22)] with respect to $Q_M$, it follows that

$$MC_t = \frac{dTC_M}{dQ_M} + 42 \tag{12.25}$$

$$= 10 + 42 = 52.$$

To maximize the marketing division's profit, we must set its marginal cost equal to its marginal revenue. Its total revenue is

$$TR_M = P_M Q_M = (100 - Q_M)Q_M$$

$$= 100\, Q_M - Q_M^2,$$

since its demand curve is as indicated in equation (12.21). Taking the first derivative of its total revenue with respect to $Q_M$, we obtain its marginal revenue:

$$MR_M = \frac{dTR_M}{dQ_M} = 100 - 2Q_M.$$

Setting this expression for its marginal revenue equal to its marginal cost [in equation (12.25)], we find that

$$100 - 2Q_M = 52$$

$$Q_M = 24.$$

Thus, the marketing division should sell 24 million tons per year of the basic chemical.

To sum up, the Orion Corporation's production division should produce 40 million tons per year of the basic chemical. Of this amount, 16 million tons should be sold externally at the market price of $42 per ton, and 24 million tons should be transferred to Orion's marketing division, the transfer price being the same as the market price, that is, $42 per ton.

# SUMMARY

1. Empirical studies indicate that cost-plus pricing is used by many firms. In this approach, the firm estimates the cost per unit of output of the product (based on some assumed output level) and adds a markup to include costs that cannot be allocated to any specific product and to provide a return on the firm's investment. On the surface, it is questionable whether this approach can maximize profit, but if marginal cost (not average cost) is really what is being marked up, and if the size of the markup is determined (in the appropriate way) by the product's price elasticity of demand, cost-plus pricing can result in profit maximization.

2. Firms generally produce and sell more than one product. It is important for them to recognize the demand interrelationships among the products they sell. Also, a firm's products are often interrelated in production. If two products are produced jointly in fixed proportions, the profit-maximizing output is where the total marginal revenue curve—the vertical summation of the marginal revenue curves for the individual products—intersects the marginal cost curve for the bundle of products (assuming that the marginal revenue of each product is nonnegative).

3. If two products are produced jointly in variable proportions, one can construct isocost curves, each of which shows the combinations of outputs that can be produced at the same total cost. Also, isorevenue lines can be constructed, each of which shows the combinations of outputs that yield the same total revenue. For an output combination to be optimal, it must be at a point where an isorevenue line is tangent to an isocost curve. To determine which output combination is optimal, one compares the profit levels at the tangency points. The tangency point where profit is highest is the optimal output combination.

4. Price discrimination occurs when the same product is sold at more than one price, or when similar products are sold at prices that are in different ratios to marginal cost. A firm will be able and willing to practice price discrimination if various classes of buyers with different price elasticities of demand can be identified and segregated, and if the product cannot be transferred easily from one class to another. If the total market is divided into such classes, a firm that discriminates will maximize its profits by choosing prices and outputs so that the marginal revenue in each class is equal to marginal cost.

5. Many large firms are decentralized, and one division of the firm sells its product to another division of the firm. To maximize the firm's overall profit, it is important that the price at which this transfer takes place—the so-called transfer price—be set properly. If there is no market outside the firm for the transferred product, the transfer price should equal the marginal production cost at the optimal output. If there is a perfectly competitive market for the transferred product out-

side the firm, the transfer price should equal the price of this product in that market.

## PROBLEMS

1. The Hassman Company produces two joint products, $X$ and $Y$. The iso-cost curve corresponding to a total cost of $500,000 is

$$Q_Y = 1,000 - 10Q_X - 5Q_X^2,$$

where $Q_Y$ is the quantity of product $Y$ produced by the firm, and $Q_X$ is the quantity of product $X$ produced. The price of product $X$ is 50 times that of product $Y$.
   (a) If the optimum output combination lies on this isocost curve, what is the optimal output of product $X$?
   (b) What is the optimal output of product $Y$?
   (c) Can you be sure that the optimum output combination lies on this isocost curve? Why or why not?
2. The Ridgeway Corporation produces a medical device, which it sells in Japan, Europe, and the United States. Transportation costs are a negligible proportion of the product's total costs. The price elasticity of demand for the product is 4.0 in Japan, 2.0 in the United States, and 1.33 in Europe. Because of legal limitations, this medical device, once sold to a customer in one country, cannot be resold to a buyer in another country.
   (a) The firm's vice president for marketing circulates a memo recommending that the price of the device be $1,000 in Japan, $2,000 in the United States, and $3,000 in Europe. Comment on his recommendations.
   (b) His recommendations are accepted. Sales managers send reports to corporate headquarters saying that the quantity of the devices being sold in the United States is lower than expected. Comment on their reports.
   (c) After considerable argument, the American sales manager agrees to lower the price in the United States to $1,500. Is this a wise decision? Why or why not?
   (d) Can you be sure that the firm is maximizing profit? Why or why not?
3. The McDermott Company estimates its average total cost to be $10 per unit of output when it produces 10,000 units, which it regards as 80 percent of capacity. Its goal is to earn 20 percent on its total investment, which is $250,000.
   (a) If the company uses cost-plus pricing, what price should it set?
   (b) Can it be sure of selling 10,000 units if it sets this price?
   (c) What are the arguments for and against a pricing policy of this sort?

4. The Locust Corporation is composed of a marketing division and a production division. The marginal cost of producing a unit of the firm's product is $10 per unit, and the marginal cost of marketing it is $4 per unit. The demand curve for the firm's product is

$$P = 100 - .01Q,$$

where $P$ is the price per unit (in dollars), and $Q$ is output (in units). There is no external market for the good made by the production division.
   (a) What is the firm's optimal output?
   (b) What price should the firm charge?
   (c) How much should the production division charge the marketing division for each unit of the product?

5. Ann McCutcheon is hired as a consultant to a firm producing ball bearings. This firm sells in two distinct markets, one of which is completely sealed off from the other. The demand curve for the firm's output in the one market is $P_1 = 160 - 8Q_1$, where $P_1$ is the price of the product, and $Q_1$ is the amount sold in the first market. The demand curve for the firm's output in the second market is $P_2 = 80 - 2Q_2$, where $P_2$ is the price of the product, and $Q_2$ is the amount sold in the second market. The firm's marginal cost curve is $5 + Q$, where $Q$ is the firm's entire output (destined for either market). The firm asks her to suggest what its pricing policy should be.
   (a) How many units of output should the firm sell in the second market?
   (b) How many units of output should it sell in the first market?
   (c) What price should it establish in each market?

6. The Morrison Company produces tennis rackets, the marginal cost of a racket being $20. Since there are many substitutes for the firm's rackets, the price elasticity of demand for its rackets equals about 2. In the relevant range of output, average variable cost is very close to marginal cost.
   (a) The president of the Morrison Company feels that cost-plus pricing is appropriate for his firm. He marks up average variable cost by 100 percent to get price. Comment on this procedure.
   (b) Because of heightened competition, the price elasticity of demand for the firm's rackets increases to 3. The president continues to use the same cost-plus pricing formula as before. Comment on its adequacy.

7. The Backus Corporation makes two products, $X$ and $Y$. For every unit of good $X$ that the firm produces, it produces 2 units of good $Y$. Backus' total cost function is

$$TC = 500 + 3Q + 9Q^2,$$

where $Q$ is the number of units of output (where each unit contains 1 unit of good $X$ and 2 units of good $Y$), and $TC$ is total cost (in dollars).

The demand curves for the firm's two products are

$$P_X = 400 - Q_X$$

$$P_Y = 300 - 3Q_Y,$$

where $P_X$ and $Q_X$ are the price and output of product $X$, and $P_Y$ and $Q_Y$ are the price and output of product $Y$.

(a) How much of each product should the Backus Corporation produce and sell per period of time?

(b) What price should it charge for each product?

8. The Xerxes Company is composed of a marketing division and a production division. The marketing division packages and distributes a plastic item made by the production division. The demand curve for the finished product sold by the marketing division is

$$P_0 = 200 - 3Q_0,$$

where $P_0$ is the price (in dollars per pound) of the finished product, and $Q_0$ is the quantity sold (in thousands of pounds). Excluding the production cost of the basic plastic item, the marketing division's total cost function is

$$TC_o = 100 + 15Q_0,$$

where $TC_0$ is the marketing division's total cost (in thousands of dollars). The production division's total cost function is

$$TC_1 = 5 + 3Q_1 + .4Q_1^2,$$

where $TC_1$ is total production cost (in thousands of dollars), and $Q_1$ is the total quantity produced of the basic plastic item (in thousands of pounds). There is a perfectly competitive market for the basic plastic item, the price being $20 per pound.

(a) What is the optimal output for the production division?

(b) What is the optimal output for the marketing division?

(c) What is the optimal transfer price for the basic plastic item?

(d) At what price should the marketing division sell its product?

9. The Lone Star Transportation Company hauls coal and manufactured goods. The demand curve for its services by the coal producers is

$$P_C = 495 - 5Q_C,$$

where $P_C$ is the price (in dollars) per ton-mile of coal hauled, and $Q_C$ is the number of ton-miles of coal hauled (in thousands). The demand curve for its services by the producers of manufactured goods is

$$P_M = 750 - 10Q_M,$$

where $P_M$ is the price (in dollars) per ton-mile of manufactured goods hauled, and $Q_M$ is the number of ton-miles of manufactured goods hauled (in thousands). The firm's total cost function is

$$TC = 410 + 8(Q_C + Q_M),$$

where $TC$ is total cost (in thousands of dollars).
(a) What price should the firm charge to haul coal?
(b) What price should the firm charge to haul manufactured goods?
(c) If the Interstate Commerce Commission requires the firm to charge the same price to haul both coal and manufactured goods, will this reduce the firm's profits? If so, by how much?

10. The Breen Company makes a scientific instrument used in chemical laboratories. The price of the instrument is set at 180 percent of average variable cost. The firm's marketing manager receives a telephone call from a large chemical company offering to buy 6 of the instruments at $5,000 each. To meet the terms of the offer, Breen would have to manufacture the 6 instruments in the next 3 months, which would mean that Breen would lose orders for 4 instruments because of its limited production capacity. If fulfilled, these orders would be at the regular price of $7,200 per instrument. (Because the chemical firm was ordering 6 of the instruments, it wanted a reduced price of $5,000.)
(a) Should the firm accept the offer from the chemical company? Why or why not?
(b) If not, what is the minimum price it should ask the chemical company to pay?
(c) If you were a consultant to Breen's chief executive officer, would you advise her to maintain or abandon the firm's cost-plus pricing policy? Why?

---

MANAGERIAL ECONOMICS IN CONTEXT

## A ROCKY ROAD FOR CATERPILLAR TRACTOR*

For decades, Caterpillar Tractor Company has been regarded as the leader in the world market for earth-moving equipment, a market dominated by relatively few firms. It makes products of very high quality. As one of its vice presidents once said, "Market share for us is not an objective. Building sophisticated, durable, reliable products and providing good support is." The firm also invests heavily in advanced automation to reduce its costs. Noted for its con-servative financial policies, it has been well respected by Wall Street, its customers, and its competitors.

With regard to its pricing, Caterpillar traditionally charged more than its rivals. For example, in 1981, Lee Morgan, Caterpillar's chairman, compared his firm's prices with those of Komatsu (Caterpillar's leading rival) in the following terms: "Komatsu's products are priced at least ten to fifteen percent below Caterpillar's. That says clearly what they believe our value is versus theirs." In other words, Caterpillar's managers felt that their products were sufficiently superior to that of their rivals to warrant their charging a premium price.

In the early 1980s, the dollar became very strong relative to the Japanese yen, the result being that Komatsu, a Japanese firm, could sell its products at prices that Caterpillar found difficult to meet. Moreover, the recession in the United States caused Caterpillar's American customers to emphasize its price disadvantage. As one of Caterpillar's customers stated in 1982, "Work's going cheap in our business, so we're looking particularly hard at costs." For these and other reasons, Caterpillar's sales fell by about 29 percent in 1982, and it experienced a $180 million loss. As Lee Morgan put it, "It seemed like we were in a free fall. If I had any personal despair, it was coming in every morning and wondering if we would ever hit bottom."

In 1983, Caterpillar began to change its pricing policy. In order to become more competitive, it offered price discounts. Its rival, Komatsu, priced to expand market share, and operated with very tight profit margins (about 4 to 5 percent of sales). Caterpillar felt it had to become more competitive with respect to price. To do so, the firm embarked on a major cost-reduction program, including cuts in blue-collar and white-collar employment. During 1983–84, plans were announced to close six plants. By 1985, the company was back in the black. (See Table 1.)

TABLE 1   Sales, Profits, and Employment, Caterpillar Tractor Company, 1981–90

|  | 1990 | 1989 | 1987 | 1986 | 1985 | 1984 | 1983 | 1982 | 1981 |
|---|---|---|---|---|---|---|---|---|---|
| Sales[a] | 11,436 | 11,126 | 8,180 | 7,321 | 6,725 | 6,576 | 5,424 | 6,469 | 9,154 |
| Profits[a] | 261 | 621 | 289 | 76 | 198 | −428 | −345 | −180 | 579 |
| Employees[b] | 58 | 60 | 54 | 54 | 56 | 61 | 58 | 73 | 83 |

[a] Millions of dollars.
[b] Thousands of people.

In 1987, Caterpillar's chairman stated: "We recognized that our industry was faced with substantial overcapacity, and that there would be tremendous price pressure on our products. . . . We've priced our products competitively on a value basis and offered special incentive programs to enhance the marketing effects of our dealers—perhaps at the sacrifice of some short-term profitability for longer-term improved results."

During the late 1980s, Caterpillar continued its worldwide effort to improve productivity and cut costs. In 1987, the company started a $2.1 billion program to modernize its production facilities, called "Plant With a Future." Flexible manufacturing systems (recall page 245) were installed. In 1990, Caterpillar eliminated layers of managers and organized itself into 17 profit centers. Nonetheless, because of the recession in the

United States and elsewhere, as well as a strike and lockout at the firm, Caterpillar lost money in 1991.

(a) What sort of market structure exists in the tractor industry?

(b) Does Caterpillar use cost-plus pricing? Why or why not?

(c) Did Caterpillar set its prices to deter entry?

(d) Was Caterpillar minimizing its costs in 1981 and 1982?

(e) According to Caterpillar's chairman, "New designs, new materials, new technology, and increased attention to 'manufacturability' are providing substantial cost reduction with further gains in quality and performance." Up to what point is it worthwhile to spend money on such technical improvements?

(f) As pointed out above, Caterpillar's chairman also stated that in pricing and marketing strategy, the company may have sacrificed "some short-term profitability for longer-term improved results." Is this always wise? Under what conditions is it a wise policy?

(g) In 1991, the average hourly worker represented by the United Auto Workers at Caterpillar earned $31.74 per hour. The firm asked for wage concessions to reduce its costs. On November 4, 1991, the union struck two of the firm's plants; 4 days later, the firm closed several more. In April 1992, after a five-month strike, the workers agreed to return to work on terms regarded as favorable to the firm. What effect will this have on the company's pricing?

* For further discussion, see H. Bartlett, *Cases in Strategic Management for Business* (New York: Dryden Press, 1988); Caterpillar's Annual Reports; and "Caterpillar's Trump Card," *New York Times*, April 16, 1992.

# Part Five

# Risk Analysis and Capital Budgeting

# Chapter 13
# Risk Analysis

Many business decisions involve relatively little uncertainty. For example, if the Dow Chemical Company invests $1 million in U.S. Treasury notes, it can be reasonably certain that it will receive the interest and principal in full and on time. Thus, it is not necessary that analysts and decision makers take account of uncertainty in all of their analyses; in many cases, managerial decisions, particularly those of a routine, simple sort, can be analyzed as if certainty prevailed. Moreover, even if uncertainty is substantial, models based on the assumption of certainty can provide substantial insight and help to managers.

However, for some business decisions, risk is at the very heart of the situation. For example, as we shall see below, the Tomco Oil Corporation had to decide whether or not to drill a well at Blair West, a site in Kansas. This was an important decision for Thomas Blair, president of Tomco Oil. There was a substantial risk that if Tomco drilled the well, no oil would be found. In situations of this sort, it is essential that the decision maker take proper account of risk.

In this chapter, we begin by discussing the concepts of probability and expected value. Then we see how decision trees can be used to analyze decisions involving risk and how utility functions can be constructed to describe the decision makers' attitudes toward risk. Next, we learn how certainty equivalent adjustments can be used to account for risk in the basic valuation model taken up in Chapter 1. Finally, we take up the so-called maximin rule, which is sometimes used to deal with uncertainty.

# RISK AND PROBABILITY

In ordinary parlance, risk is a hazard or a chance of loss. Thus, if you invest $10,000 in a firm carrying out research and development in biotechnology, and if there is a very substantial chance that you will lose your money because the firm will not come up with a successful new product, such an investment is risky. Moreover, in ordinary parlance, the bigger the chance of loss, the more risky a particular course of action is. Thus, an investment in a firm doing biotechnology research is riskier than an investment in Treasury notes, since there is a relatively greater chance of loss from the former investment.

To analyze risk, it is necessary to define a probability. Suppose a situation exists where one of a number of possible outcomes can occur. For example, if a gambler throws a single die, the number that comes up may be 1, 2, 3, 4, 5, or 6. A **probability** is a number that is attached to each outcome. It is the proportion of times that this outcome occurs over the long run if this situation exists repeatedly. Thus, the probability that a particular die will come up a 1 is the proportion of times this will occur if the die is thrown many, many times; and the probability that the same die will come up a 2 is the proportion of times this will occur if the die is thrown many, many times; and so on.

If a situation exists a very large number of times $R$, and if outcome $A$ occurs $r$ times, the probability of $A$ is

$$P(A) = \frac{r}{R}. \tag{13.1}$$

Thus, if a die is "true" (meaning that each of its sides is equally likely to come up when the die is rolled), the probability of its coming up a 1 is 1/6, or 0.167, because if it is rolled many, many times, this will occur 1/6 of the time.

What we have just provided is the so-called **frequency definition of probability**. In some situations, this concept of probability may be difficult to apply because these situations cannot be repeated over and over. When Porsche, the German sports car maker, introduced its new model, the 928 GTS, in March 1992, this was an "experiment" that could not be repeated over and over again under essentially the same set of circumstances. Market and other conditions vary from month to month. If Porsche's new model had not been introduced that month, the state of consumer expectations, the prices of other firms' sports cars, the advertising campaigns of other firms, and a host of other relevant factors would probably have been different.

In dealing with situations of this sort, managerial economists sometimes use a **subjective definition of probability**. According to this definition, the probability of an event is the degree of confidence or belief on the part of the decision maker that the event will occur. Thus, if the decision maker believes that outcome $X$ is more likely to occur than outcome $Y$, the probability of $X$'s occurring is higher than the probability of $Y$'s doing so. If the decision maker believes that it is equally likely that a particular outcome will or will not occur, the probability attached to the occurrence of this outcome equals 0.50. The important factor in this concept of probability is what the decision maker believes.

## PROBABILITY DISTRIBUTIONS AND EXPECTED VALUES

In a particular situation, if all possible outcomes are listed, and if the probability of occurrence is assigned to each outcome, the resulting table is called a **probability distribution**. For example, suppose that Adept Technology, a San Jose, California, manufacturer of robots, believes that the probability is .6 that it can develop a new type of robot in 1 year, and that the probability is .4 that it cannot do so in this length of time. The probability distribution is as follows:

| *Event* | *Probability of occurrence* |
|---|---|
| New robot is developed in 1 year | .6 |
| New robot is not developed in 1 year | .4 |
| | 1.0 |

Note that the probabilities sum to 1, which must be the case if all possible outcomes or events are listed.

If Adept Technology will earn a profit of $1 million if it develops the new robot in 1 year, and if it will lose $600,000 if it does not develop the new robot in 1 year, we can readily calculate the probability distribution of its profit from the new robot, which is

| *Profit* | *Probability* |
|---|---|
| $1,000,000 | .6 |
| −600,000 | .4 |

Moreover, we can also calculate the **expected value** of the profit, which is

$$(\$1,000,000) \, (.6) + (-\$600,000) \, (.4) = \$360,000.$$

The expected value is the weighted average of the profits corresponding to the various outcomes, each of these profit figures being weighted by its probability of occurrence.

In general, the expected profit can be expressed by the equation

$$\text{Expected profit} = E(\pi) = \sum_{i=1}^{N} \pi_i P_i, \tag{13.2}$$

where $\pi_i$ is the level of profit associated with the $i$th outcome, $P_i$ is the probability that the $i$th outcome will take place, and $N$ is the number of possible outcomes. Since $N = 2$, $\pi_1 = \$1,000,000$, $\pi_2 = -\$600,000$, $P_1 = .6$, and $P_2 = .4$ in the case of Adept Technology, equation (13.2) says precisely the same thing as the equation that precedes it.

## COMPARISONS OF EXPECTED PROFIT

To decide which of a number of courses of action to take, managers can compare the expected profit resulting from each one. For example, suppose that the Jones Corporation, a producer of automobile tires, is thinking of raising the price of its product by $1 per tire. Based on the firm's estimates, if it raises its price, it will experience an $800,000 profit if its current advertising campaign is successful and a $600,000 loss if the campaign is not successful. The firm believes that there is a 0.5 probability that its current advertising campaign will be successful and a 0.5 probability that it will not be successful.

Under these circumstances, the expected profit to the firm if it raises its price equals

$$(\$800,000)\,(.5) + (-\$600,000)\,(.5) = \$100,000.$$

As indicated above, the expected profit is the sum of the amount of money gained (or lost) if each outcome occurs times the probability of occurrence of the outcome. In this case, there are two possible outcomes: (1) the firm's current advertising campaign is successful, or (2) it is not successful. If we multiply the amount of money gained (or lost) if the first outcome occurs times its probability of occurrence, the result is ($800,000) (.5). If we multiply the amount of money gained (or lost) if the second outcome occurs times its probability of occurrence, the result is (−$600,000) (.5). Summing these two results, we get $100,000, which is the expected profit if the firm raises its price.

What would be the expected profit if the Jones Corporation did *not* increase its price? Suppose that the firm's executives believe that, if there were no price increase, the firm's profits would be equal to $200,000. And for simplicity, let's assume that this profit level is regarded as certain if the price is not increased. Then, if the firm wants to maximize expected profit, it should not increase its price, because its expected profit equals $200,000 if it does not do so, but only $100,000 if it raises its price. Later on in this chapter, we will discuss at length the circumstances under which it is rational to maximize expected profit—and how to proceed if it is not rational to do so.

## HOW TO CONSTRUCT A DECISION TREE

Any situation involving decision making under conditions of risk has the following characteristics. First, the decision maker must make a choice, or perhaps a series of choices, among alternative courses of action. Second, this choice leads to some consequence, but the decision maker cannot tell in advance the exact nature of this consequence because it depends on some unpredictable event, or series of events, as well as on the choice itself. For example, consider the case of the Jones Corporation, which must decide whether or not to increase the price of its automobile tires. The choice is between two alternatives: increase price or do not do so. The consequence of increasing price is uncertain, since the firm cannot be sure of whether or not its current advertising campaign will be successful.

To analyze any such problem, a decision tree is useful. A **decision tree** is a diagram that helps you visualize the relevant choices. It represents a decision problem as a series of choices, each of which is depicted by a fork (sometimes called a juncture or branching point). A **decision fork** is a juncture representing a choice where the decision maker is in control of the outcome; a **chance fork** is a juncture where "chance" controls the outcome. To differentiate between a decision fork and a chance fork, we will place a small square at the former juncture but not at the latter.

In Figure 13.1, we show the decision tree for the problem facing the Jones Corporation. Starting at the left-hand side of the diagram, the first choice is up to the firm, which can either follow the branch representing a price increase or the branch representing no such increase. Since this fork is a decision fork, it is represented by a square. If the branch representing no price increase is followed, the consequence is certain: the firm will have profits of $200,000. Thus, $200,000 is shown at the end of this branch. If the branch representing a price increase is followed, we come to a chance fork, since it is uncertain whether the firm's current advertising campaign is successful. The upper branch following this chance fork represents the consequence that it is successful, in which case the firm will have profits of $800,000, shown at the end of this branch. The lower branch following this chance fork represents the consequence that it is not successful, in which case the outcome is −$600,000 (a loss), shown at the end of this branch. The probability that "chance" will choose each of these branches is shown above the end of each branch; in both cases, this probability equals .50.

Based on such a decision tree, you can readily determine which branch the firm should choose in order to maximize expected profit. The process by which you can solve this problem, known as **backward induction**, requires that you begin at the right-hand side of the decision tree, where the profit figures are located. The first step is to calculate the expected profit when the firm is situated at the chance fork immediately to the left of these payoff figures. In other words, this is the expected profit to the firm given that "chance" will choose which subsequent branch will be followed. Because there is a .50 probability that the branch culminating in a profit of $800,000 will be followed, and a .50 probability that the branch culminating in a loss of $600,000 will be followed, the expected profit when situated at this chance fork is

$$.50(\$800,000) + .50(-\$600,000) = \$100,000.$$

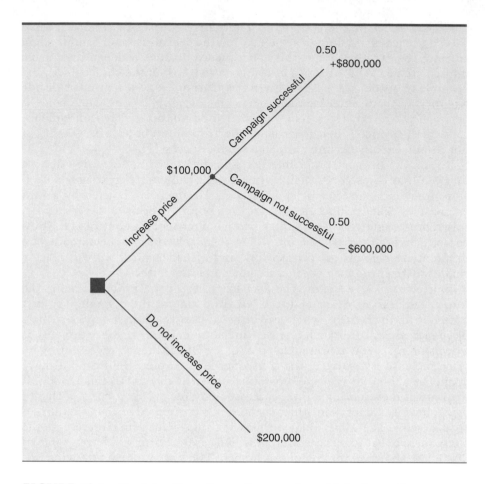

**FIGURE 13.1** *Decision Tree, Jones Corporation* If the Jones Corporation increases its price, the expected profit is $100,000. If it does not increase its price, the expected profit is $200,000.

This number is written above the chance fork in question to show that this is the expected profit when located at that fork. Moving further to the left along the decision tree, it is clear that the firm has a choice of two branches, one of which leads to an expected profit of $100,000, the other of which leads to a $200,000 expected profit. If the firm wants to maximize expected profit, it should choose the latter branch. In other words, it should not increase its price. Since the former branch (increase price) is nonoptimal, you place two vertical lines through it.

Of course, this graphic procedure for analyzing the Jones Corporation's pricing problem amounts to precisely the same thing as the calculations we made in the previous section. Recall that we compared the expected profit if the price was increased ($100,000) with the expected profit if it was not increased ($200,000) and followed the course of action that resulted in the larger of the two. Our procedure in Figure 13.1 is exactly the same.

# SHOULD TOMCO OIL CORPORATION DRILL A WELL?

One major area where the concepts presented in the previous sections have been applied is oil exploration. Very large amounts of money have been, and are being, invested in oil exploration. Oil firms use these analytical tools as an aid to decision making. To illustrate how these concepts can be applied, consider the actual case of Tomco Oil Corporation, an oil producer that had to decide whether or not to drill a well at Blair West, a site in Kansas.[1] The firm had information concerning the cost of drilling and the price of oil, as well as geologists' reports concerning the likelihood of striking oil. Suppose the geologists' reports led the firm to believe that if the well was drilled, there was a .60 probability that no oil would be found, a .15 probability that 10,000 barrels would be found, a .15 probability that 20,000 barrels would be found, and a .10 probability that 30,000 barrels would be found.

Using these probabilities alone, the firm cannot decide whether or not to drill the well. In addition, information is needed concerning the profit (or loss) that will accrue to the firm if each of these outcomes occurs. Suppose the firm believes that if it drills the well, it will incur a $90,000 loss if it finds no oil, a $100,000 profit if it finds 10,000 barrels of oil, a $300,000 profit if it finds 20,000 barrels, and a $500,000 profit if it finds 30,000 barrels. Should the firm drill the well?

Assuming that the firm wants to maximize its expected profit, it can answer this question by constructing the decision tree shown in Figure 13.2. Starting at the left-hand side of the diagram, the first choice is up to the firm, which can follow the branch representing the drilling of the well or the branch representing not drilling. If the branch representing not drilling is followed, the expected profit is zero, which is shown at the end of this branch. (Why? Because the firm neither gains nor loses if it does not drill.) If the branch representing the drilling of the well is followed, we come to a chance fork, since it is uncertain whether the firm will strike oil and if so, how much oil it will find. The highest branch following this chance fork represents the consequence that no oil is found, in which case the firm loses

---

[1] This case is described in detail in J. Hosseini, "Decision Analysis and Its Application in the Choice between Two Wildcat Oil Ventures," *Interfaces* (March–April 1986). For pedagogical reasons, we have simplified the analysis and the numbers involved. A general account of the use of decision trees in oil exploration is found in J. Pratt, H. Raiffa, and R. Schlaifer, "Introduction to Statistical Decision Theory," in E. Mansfield, ed., *Managerial Economics and Operations Research*, 5th ed. (New York: Norton, 1987).

## BIDDING FOR THE SS *KUNIANG*

Prudent application of decision tree analysis can make you a winning manager even if your bid is second best, as one utility discovered in 1981. The New England Electric System is a public utility holding company that generates and delivers electricity to over one million customers in Massachusetts, Rhode Island, and New Hampshire. Because some of its oil-fired power stations were converted to coal, it decided to obtain ships to bring coal from Virginia to New England. In 1981, the SS *Kuniang* ran aground, and the ship's owners offered to sell the salvage rights by means of a sealed bid auction. The New England Electric System was interested in making a bid, since if the *Kuniang* could be restored, it would meet the company's needs very well.

To determine how much to bid, the company carried out a detailed analysis, based on a decision tree like that in Figure 13.1 or 13.2. It calculated the expected net present value of its earnings, given each amount it might bid. For example, if it bid $5 million, it calculated that the expected net present value would be $2.85 million. On the other hand, if it bid $7 million, it calculated that the net present value would be $3.05 million.

Why was the net present value higher if it bid $7 million rather than $5 million? Because the probability was higher that its bid would win. Obviously, the company could not be sure of this probability, but according to its best estimates, this probability would increase from

about 1/6 to 1/2 if it bid $7 million rather than $5 million.

As a result of this analysis, the New England Electric System bid $6.7 million for the *Kuniang*, since this was the bid that maximized expected net present value. It came in second. The winning bid was $10 million. Of course, the fact that the company did not make the winning bid does not mean that the analysis was not useful. The point of the analysis was to determine how much it was worthwhile to bid. (If the company had made a high enough bid, it could have been reasonably sure of winning, but it would have lost money by doing so.) According to Guy W. Nichols, the company's chairman at that time, the analysis "was a useful contribution to our deliberations and to our decision regarding an appropriate bid for the ship."*

*Guy W. Nichols, Chairman of New England Electric System from 1978 to 1984*

* D. Bell, "Bidding for the S.S. *Kuniang*," *Interfaces* (March–April 1984), pp. 17–23.

$90,000, shown at the end of this branch. The second highest branch following this chance fork represents the consequence that 10,000 barrels are found, in which case the firm gains $100,000, shown at the end of this branch. Similarly, the second lowest and lowest branches following this chance fork represent respectively the consequences that 20,000 and 30,000 barrels are found; the number at the end of each of these branches is the corresponding profit to the firm.

Having constructed this decision tree, the firm's managers can compute the expected profit to the firm if it is situated at the chance fork immediately to the left of the profit (or loss) figures. If the firm is at this fork, there is a .60 probability that the branch culminating in a $90,000 loss will be followed, a .15 probability that the branch culminating in a $100,000 profit will be followed, a .15 probability that the branch culminating in a $300,000 profit will be followed, and a .10 probability that the branch culminating in a $500,000 profit will be followed. To obtain the expected profit if the firm is situated at this fork, the firm's managers should multiply each possible value of profit (or loss) by its probability, and sum the results. Thus, the expected profit if the firm is situated at this fork equals

$$.60(-\$90,000) + .15(+\$100,000) + .15(+\$300,000) \\ + .10(+\$500,000) = +\$56,000.$$

In Figure 13.2, this result is written above the chance fork in question to show that this is the expected profit if the firm is located at that fork.

Going further along the decision tree to the left, the firm has a choice of two branches, one of which leads to an expected profit of $56,000, the other of which leads to a zero expected profit. If the firm wants to maximize its expected profit, it should choose the former branch. That is, it should drill the well.

## THE EXPECTED VALUE OF PERFECT INFORMATION

Frequently, the decision maker can obtain information that will dispel (at least some of) the relevant risk. If the decision maker can get perfect information, how much is it worth? To answer this question, we define the expected value of perfect information as the increase in expected profit if the decision maker could obtain completely accurate information concerning the outcome of the relevant situation (but if he or she does not yet know what this information will be). Thus, in the case of the Jones Corporation (the firm that must decide whether or not to increase its tire price), this expected value is the increase in expected profit if the firm could obtain perfectly accurate information indicating whether or not its current advertising campaign will be successful.

To illustrate how one can compute the expected value of perfect infor-

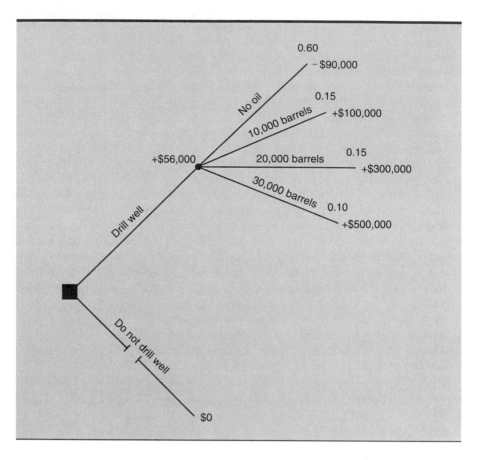

**FIGURE 13.2** **Decision Tree, Tomco Oil Corporation** If Tomco Oil drills the well, the expected profit is $56,000. If it does not, the expected profit is zero.

mation, let's return to the Jones case. To determine the expected value of perfect information, we begin by evaluating the expected monetary value to the Jones Corporation if it can obtain access to perfectly accurate information of this sort. If it can obtain perfect information, it will be able to make the correct decision, regardless of whether or not its current advertising campaign is successful. If it is successful, the firm will be aware of this fact, and will increase the price. If it is not successful, the firm will be aware of this fact also, and will not increase the price. Thus, given that the firm has access to perfect information, the expected profit is

$$.50(\$800,000) + .50(\$200,000) = \$500,000.$$

To understand why this is the expected profit if the Jones Corporation has access to perfect information, it is important to recognize that although it is assumed that the firm has access to perfect information, it *does not yet know what this information will be.* There is a .50 probability that this information will show that its advertising campaign is successful, in which case the Jones Corporation will increase its price and the profit will be $800,000. There is also a .50 probability that the information will show that it is not successful, in which case the Jones Corporation will not increase its price and its profit will be $200,000. Thus, as shown above, the expected profit if the firm has access to perfect information (that is not yet revealed to the firm) is $500,000.

At this point, we must recall that the expected profit if the firm bases its decision on existing information is $200,000 (as we saw on pages 500 to 503), not $500,000. The difference between these two figures—$500,000 minus $200,000 or $300,000—is the expected value of perfect information. It is a measure of the value of perfect information. *It shows the amount by which the expected profit increases as a consequence of the firm's having access to perfect information.*

In many circumstances, it is very important that the decision maker knows how much perfect information would be worth. Business executives are continually being offered information by testing services, research organizations, news bureaus, and a variety of other organizations. Unless you know how much particular types of information are worth, it will be difficult to decide rationally whether they should or should not be bought. The sort of analysis presented in this section is useful to guide such decisions, since it shows the maximum amount that the firm should pay to obtain perfect information.

# EVALUATING AN INVESTMENT IN A NEW CHEMICAL PLANT: A CASE STUDY

To illustrate the usefulness of the expected value of perfect information, consider an actual case where a decision tree was constructed to determine whether a major U.S. corporation should invest in a new plant. The major product of the new plant would be a brightener, but by using new processing methods, a valuable by-product could be made as well. The exact amounts of both products that would be produced were uncertain. Very small quantities of impurities in the raw materials used in the process could greatly influence the amounts of brightener and by-product produced. Also, there were uncertainties concerning the costs of raw materials and plant efficiency.

Table 13.1 shows the expected value of perfect information concerning by-product quantity, impurities, raw material costs, and plant efficiency. As you can see, the critical uncertainties were those regarding by-product quantity and the level of impurities. For example, perfect information con-

**TABLE 13.1** *Expected Value of Perfect Information Concerning Factors Influencing Whether or Not to Build New Chemical Plant*

| Factor | Expected value of perfect information (millions of dollars) |
|---|---|
| By-product quantity | 6.2 |
| Level of impurities | 3.9 |
| Raw material costs | 0.3 |
| Plant efficiency | 0.0 |

*Source:* C. Spetzler and R. Zamora, "Facilities Investment and Expansion Problem."

cerning by-product quantity would have been worth up to $6.2 million. On the other hand, information regarding raw materials and plant efficiency was of much less importance for this decision. Indeed, the expected value of perfect information concerning plant efficiency was close to zero. Based on these results, the analysts advised the company to do some research to reduce the uncertainties regarding by-product quantity and the level of impurities before committing itself to the construction of the new plant.[2]

# MEASURING ATTITUDES TOWARD RISK: THE UTILITY APPROACH

In discussing both the Jones Corporation's pricing decision and the Tomco Oil Corporation's drilling decision, we have assumed that the decision maker wants to maximize expected profit. In this and the following sections, we formulate a more realistic criterion. To understand why a decision maker may not want to maximize expected profit, consider a situation where a firm is given a choice between (1) a profit of $2,000,000 for certain and (2) a gamble in which there is a 50-50 chance of a $4,100,000 profit and a 50-50 chance of a $60,000 loss. The expected profit for the gamble is

$$0.50(\$4,100,000) + 0.50(-\$60,000) = \$2,020,000,$$

so the firm should choose the gamble over the certainty of $2,000,000 if it wants to maximize expected profit. However, it seems likely that many firms, particularly small ones, would prefer the certainty of $2,000,000, since the gamble entails a 50 percent chance that the firm will lose $60,000, a very substantial sum for a very small firm. Moreover, many people may feel that they can do almost as much with $2,000,000 as with $4,100,000, and therefore the extra profit is not worth the risk of losing $60,000.

---

[2] C. Spetzler and R. Zamora, "Decision Analysis of a Facilities Investment and Expansion Problem," in R. Howard and J. Matheson, eds., *The Principles and Applications of Decision Analysis* (Menlo Park, Calif.: Strategic Decision Group, 1984).

## CHOOSING AREAS FOR RESEARCH REGARDING POLLUTION COSTS*

The National Academy of Sciences sponsored a study to examine emission control strategies for power plants. One purpose of this study was to determine the value of reducing the uncertainty concerning the pollution costs of various strategies. Efforts to reduce harmful emissions from coal-burning power plants focus on at least four strategies: (1) treating the coal to reduce its sulfur content, (2) using premium-priced, low-sulfur coal, (3) employing a tall stack and intermittent control systems, and (4) adopting a flue-gas desulfurization process. This study was concerned with the effects of various control alternatives on the total cost of electricity. Choosing among them is not easy, partly because it has been difficult to establish, with any certainty, the pollution costs of each strategy.

Because of the limitations of existing knowledge, the study found that there was considerable uncertainty regarding which of the alternative strategies was least costly. The expected value of perfect information, shown below, depended on whether the plant was in an urban or remote area and whether low-sulfur coal was available or not.

|  | Low-sulfur coal available | Low-sulfur coal not available |
|---|---|---|
| Remote plant | $3.7 million | $2.4 million |
| Urban plant | 1.3 million | 2.8 million |

If you were a consultant to the National Academy of Sciences, what conclusions could you draw concerning the kinds of plants for which further research of this sort would be most valuable?

* This section is based on an actual case. For further discussion, see S. Watson and D. Buede, *Decision Synthesis* (Cambridge: Cambridge University Press, 1987) (which summarizes the work of D. North and M. Merkhofer).

## SHOULD MAXWELL HOUSE HAVE INCREASED ITS PRICE?

When coffee first was marketed in keyless containers, most consumers who tried it seemed to prefer the new can to the old one. Maxwell House, the nation's largest producer of coffee, developed its own keyless container (which operated on the tear-strip opening principle). One important decision that Maxwell House had to make before introducing its new can was whether or not to raise the per-

pound price of coffee in the new can by 2 cents. Coffee in the quick-strip can was expected to cost an average of 0.7 cents per pound more than in the old container.

According to Joseph Newman, who studied this case, if Maxwell House raised its price by 2 cents per pound, it might have been reasonable to expect (1) a .25 probability that its market share would decline by 1.5 percentage points, (2) a .25 probability that its market share would remain constant, (3) a .25 probability that its market share would increase by 1.0 percentage points, and (4) a .25 probability that its market share would increase by 2.5 percentage points. The change in Maxwell House's profits corresponding to each

change in its market share is given in the table below:

According to Newman, if Maxwell House did not raise its price, it might have been reasonable to expect (1) a .1 probability that its market share would decline by 0.6 percentage points, (2) a .2 probability that its market share would remain constant, (3) a .5 probability that its market share would increase by 1.0 percentage points, and (4) a .2 probability that its market share would increase by 2.8 percentage points. The change in Maxwell House's profits corresponding to each of these market-share changes is provided in the table below.

(a) Construct a decision tree representing Maxwell House's pricing

| Price per pound held constant | | Price per pound increased by 2 cents | |
|---|---|---|---|
| Change in market share (percentage points) | Change in profit (thousands of dollars) | Change in market share (percentage points) | Change in profit (thousands of dollars) |
| +2.8 | 4,104 | +2.5 | 11,939 |
| +1.0 | −591 | +1.0 | 6,489 |
| 0 | −840 | 0 | 2,856 |
| −0.6 | −1,218 | −1.5 | −1,050 |

problem. (b) If Maxwell House wanted to maximize the expected profit, should it have increased the price per pound of coffee in its new can by 2 cents?

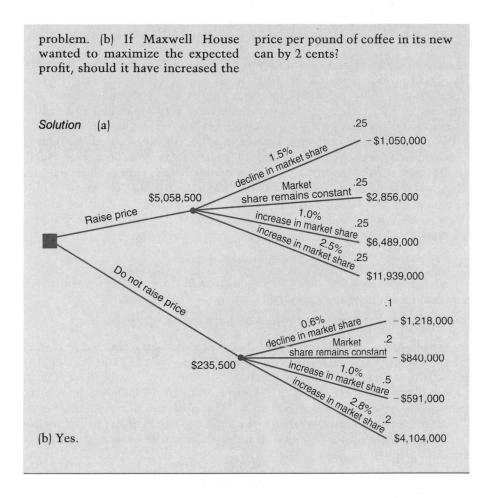

*Solution*    (a)

Raise price — $5,058,500

- 1.5% decline in market share — .25 — $1,050,000
- Market share remains constant — .25 — $2,856,000
- 1.0% increase in market share — .25 — $6,489,000
- 2.5% increase in market share — .25 — $11,939,000

Do not raise price — $235,500

- 0.6% decline in market share — .1 — $1,218,000
- Market share remains constant — .2 — $840,000
- 1.0% increase in market share — .5 — $591,000
- 2.8% increase in market share — .2 — $4,104,000

(b) Yes.

Whether or not the firm's managers will want to maximize expected profit in this situation depends on their attitude toward risk. If they are elderly people of modest means, they may be overwhelmed at the thought of taking a 50 percent chance of losing $60,000. On the other hand, if they are the heads of a big corporation, the prospect of a $60,000 loss may be not the least bit unsettling, and they may prefer the gamble to the certainty of a mere $2,000,000 gain.

Fortunately, we need not assume that the decision maker wants to maximize expected profit. Instead, we can construct a **utility function** for the decision maker that measures his or her attitudes toward risk. This concept of utility should not be confused with that discussed in the appendix to Chapter 3. As we shall see, it is a quite different sort of concept. From this utility function, we can then go on to find the alternative that is best for the decision maker, given his or her attitudes toward risk.

# CONSTRUCTING A UTILITY FUNCTION

A rational decision maker will *maximize expected utility.* In other words, the decision maker should choose the course of action with the highest expected utility. But what (in this context) is a utility? It is a number that is attached to a possible outcome of the decision. Each outcome has a utility. The decision maker's utility function shows the utility that he or she attaches to each possible outcome. This utility function, as we shall see, shows the decision maker's preferences with respect to risk. What is **expected utility**? It is the sum of the utility if each outcome occurs times the probability of occurrence of the outcome. For example, if a situation has two possible outcomes, *A* and *B*, if the utility of outcome *A* is 2 and the utility of outcome *B* is 8, and if the probability of each outcome is .50, the expected utility equals

$$.50(2) + .50(8) = 5.$$

What is the expected utility if the Tomco Oil Corporation drills the well under the circumstances described on page 503? It equals

$$.60U(-90) + .15U(100) + .15U(300) + .10U(500),$$

where $U(-90)$ is the utility that the decision maker attaches to a monetary loss of \$90,000, $U(100)$ is the utility attached to a gain of \$100,000, $U(300)$ is the utility attached to a gain of \$300,000, and so on. Since there is a .60 probability of a \$90,000 loss, a .15 probability of a \$100,000 gain, a .15 probability of a \$300,000 gain, and a .10 probability of a \$500,000 gain, this is the expected utility. What is the expected utility if the firm does not drill the well? It equals $U(0)$, since under these circumstances it is certain that the gain will be zero.

To find out the utility that the decision maker attaches to each possible outcome, we begin by setting the utility attached to two levels of profit arbitrarily. The utility of the better consequence is set higher than the utility of the worse one. In the case of the decision maker in the oil-drilling problem, we might set $U(-90)$ equal to zero and $U(500)$ equal to 50. It turns out that the ultimate results of the analysis do not depend on which two numbers we choose, as long as the utility of the better consequence is set higher than the utility of the worse one. Thus, we could set $U(-90)$ equal to 1 and $U(500)$ equal to 10. It would make no difference to the ultimate outcome of the analysis.[3]

Next, we present the decision maker with a choice between the certainty of one of the other levels of profit and a gamble where the possible outcomes are the two profit levels whose utilities we set arbitrarily. Thus, in the oil-drilling case, suppose we want to find $U(100)$. To do so, we ask the

---

[3] The utility function we construct is not unique. Because we set two utilities arbitrarily, the results will vary, depending on the values of the utilities that are chosen. If $X_1, X_2, \ldots, X_n$ are the utilities attached to $n$ possible monetary values, $(\alpha + \beta X_1), (\alpha + \beta X_2), \ldots, (\alpha + \beta X_n)$ can also be utilities attached to them (where $\alpha$ and $\beta$ are constants, and $\beta > 0$).

decision maker whether he or she would prefer the certainty of a $100,000 gain to a gamble where there is a probability of $P$ that the gain is $500,000 and a probability of $(1 - P)$ that the loss is $90,000. We then try various values of $P$ until we find the one where the decision maker is indifferent between the certainty of a $100,000 gain and this gamble. Suppose that this value of $P$ is .40.

If the decision maker is indifferent between the certain gain of $100,000 and this gamble, it must be that the expected utility of the certain gain of $100,000 equals the expected utility of the gamble. (Why? Because the decision maker maximizes expected utility.) Thus,

$$U(100) = .40U(500) + .60U(-90).$$

And since we set $U(500)$ equal to 50 and $U(-90)$ equal to zero, it follows that

$$U(100) = .40(50) + .60(0) = 20.$$

That is, the utility attached to a gain of $100,000 is 20.

Using the same procedure, we can find $U(300)$ and $U(0)$, the other utilities required to calculate the expected utility if the oil company drills the well and the expected utility if it does not drill it. For example, to obtain $U(300)$, we ask the decision maker whether he or she would prefer the certainty of a $300,000 gain to a gamble where there is a probability of $P$ that the gain is $500,000 and a probability of $(1 - P)$ that the loss is $90,000. Then we try various values of $P$ until we find the one where the decision maker is indifferent between the certainty of a $300,000 gain and this gamble. Suppose this value of $P$ is .80. Then the expected utility of a certain gain of $300,000 must equal the expected utility of this gamble, which means that

$$U(300) = .80U(500) + .20U(-90).$$

And since $U(500)$ equals 50 and $U(-90)$ equals zero, it follows that $U(300)$ equals 40.

The decision maker's utility function is the relationship between his or her utility and the amount of his or her profit (or loss). Based on our evaluation of $U(-90)$, $U(100)$, $U(300)$, and $U(500)$ in previous paragraphs, we can identify four points on the decision maker's utility function, as shown in Figure 13.3. By the repeated use of the procedure described above, we can obtain as many such points as we like. (According to Figure 13.3, $U(0) = 10$.)

## USING A UTILITY FUNCTION

Once a manager's utility function has been constructed, it can be used to indicate whether he or she should accept or reject particular gambles. Consider the actual case of Thomas Blair, president of the Tomco Oil Corpora-

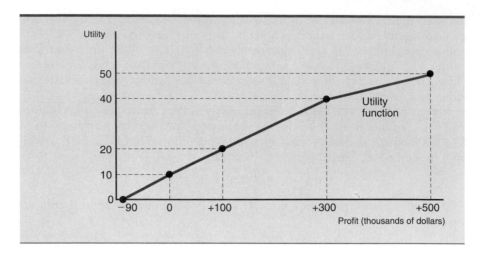

**FIGURE 13.3   *Utility Function*** The decision maker's utility function is useful in indicating whether particular gambles should be accepted.

tion. Using the above procedures, a managerial economist constructed Mr. Blair's utility function.[4] Suppose the result is as shown in Figure 13.3, and Mr. Blair must decide whether or not to drill the well described on page 503. He should drill the well if his expected utility if the well is drilled exceeds his expected utility if it is not drilled. As pointed out in the previous section, his expected utility if the well is drilled equals

$$.60U(-90) + .15U(100) + .15U(300) + .10U(500).$$

If his utility function is as shown in Figure 13.3, this expression can be evaluated. Since $U(-90)$ equals zero, $U(100)$ equals 20, $U(300)$ equals 40, and $U(500)$ equals 50, his expected utility if the well is drilled is

$$.60(0) + .15(20) + .15(40) + .10(50) = 14.$$

If the well is not drilled, Mr. Blair's expected utility equals $U(0)$, which is 10, according to Figure 13.3. Thus, he should drill the well. Why? Because if he does not drill it, his expected utility is 10, whereas if he drills it, his expected utility is 14. Since he should maximize expected utility, he should choose the action with the higher expected utility, which is to drill.

In fact, Tomco Oil Corporation did drill a well at Blair West. Subsequently, Mr. Blair stated, "Before we actually used decision-tree analysis to aid in our selection of drilling sites, we were skeptical as to the application of decision-tree analysis in oil exploration and field development decisions. Now we find it helpful, not only in choosing between two or more drilling

---

[4.] J. Hosseini, "Decision Analysis." The utility function in Figure 13.3 is hypothetical, but adequate for present purposes. As noted above, this case has been simplified in various ways for pedagogical reasons.

sites, but also in making decisions subsequent to the choice of a drilling site."[5]

## ATTITUDES TOWARD RISK: THREE TYPES

Although one can expect that utility increases with monetary gain, the shape of the utility function can vary greatly, depending on the preferences of the decision maker. Figure 13.4 shows three general types of utility functions. The one in panel A is like that in Figure 13.3 in the sense that utility increases with profit, but *at a decreasing rate.* In other words, an increase in monetary gain of $1 is associated with *smaller and smaller* increases in utility as the monetary gain increases in size. Managers with utility functions of this sort are **risk averters.** That is, when confronted with gambles with equal expected profits, they prefer a gamble with a more certain outcome to one with a less certain outcome.[6]

Panel B of Figure 13.4 shows a case where utility increases with profit, but *at an increasing rate.* In other words, an increase in monetary gain of $1 is associated with *larger and larger* increases in utility as the monetary gain increases in size. Managers with utility functions of this sort are **risk lovers.** That is, when confronted with gambles with equal expected profits, they prefer a gamble with a less certain outcome to one with a more certain outcome.[7]

Finally, panel C shows a case where utility increases with profit and *at a constant rate.* In other words, an increase of $1 in monetary gain is associated with a *constant* increase in utility as the monetary gain grows larger and larger. Stated differently, utility in this case is a linear function of profit:

$$U = a + b\pi, \tag{13.3}$$

where $U$ is utility, $\pi$ is monetary gain, and $a$ and $b$ are constants (of course, $b > 0$). People with utility functions of this sort are **risk neutral.**[8] In other words, they maximize expected profit, regardless of risk. It is easy to prove that this is true. If equation (13.3) holds,

$$E(U) = a + bE(\pi), \tag{13.4}$$

---

[5] Ibid.

[6] Consider a gamble where there is a probability of $P$ that the gain is $\pi_1$, and a probability of $(1 - P)$ that the loss is $\pi_2$. A person is a risk averter if the utility of the gamble's expected profit, $U[P\pi_1 + (1 - P)\pi_2]$, is *greater than* the expected utility of the gamble, $PU(\pi_1) + (1 - P)U(\pi_2)$.

[7] Consider the gamble described in note 6. A person is a risk lover if the utility of the gamble's expected profit, $U[P\pi_1 + (1 - P)\pi_2]$, is *less than* the expected utility of the gamble, $PU(\pi_1) + (1 - P)U(\pi_2)$.

[8] A person can be a risk averter under some circumstances, a risk lover under other circumstances, and risk neutral under still other circumstances. The utility functions in Figure 13.4 are "pure" cases where the person is always only one of these types, at least in the range covered by the graphs.

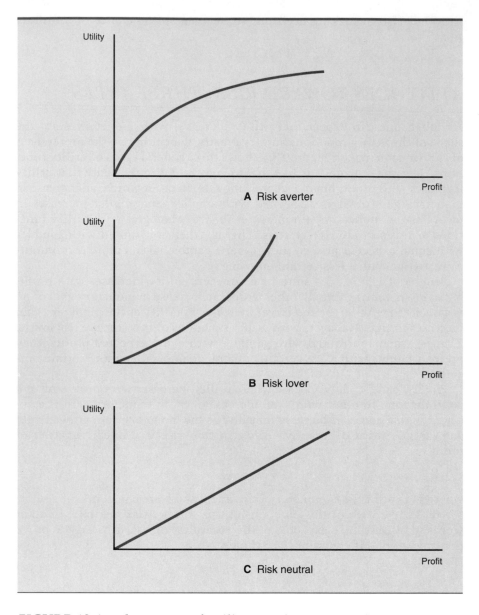

**FIGURE 13.4    Three Types of Utility Functions**    Utility functions assume a variety of shapes. In panel A, the decision maker is a risk averter; in panel B, he or she is a risk lover; and in panel C, he or she is risk neutral.

## DECIDING WHETHER TO BUY AN OPTION ON A NEW FLIGHT-SAFETY SYSTEM

Cutler-Hammer, Inc., an electronic equipment manufacturer in Milwaukee, Wisconsin, was offered the option to purchase a license to produce and sell a new flight-safety system. Because of pending legislative action, the market for the product was very uncertain. A team of Cutler-Hammer personnel and outside analysts carried out an analysis to help the company decide whether or not to purchase the option to obtain this license.

According to this team, if Cutler-Hammer purchased this option, there was a .29 probability that it would not obtain the license, in which case it would lose $125,000, and a .71 probability that it would obtain the license. If the company obtained such a license, the team estimated that there was a .85 probability that it would not obtain a defense contract, in which case it would lose $700,000, and a .15 probability that it would obtain a defense con-

tract, in which case it would gain $5.25 million.

(a) Construct the decision tree. (b) If Cutler-Hammer wanted to maximize expected profit, should it have purchased the option? (c) Cutler-Hammer also analyzed the consequences of another course of action: waiting and seeking a sublicense. The team estimated that such a course of action would result in the following probability distribution of profit:

| Probability | Profit (thousands of dollars) |
|---|---|
| 0.94 | 0 |
| 0.06 | 830 |

After considerable discussion, a unanimous decision was made by the firm's decision-making group (the president and his vice presidents for business development and operations) to adopt this course of action. Were they averse to risk?

*Solution* (a)

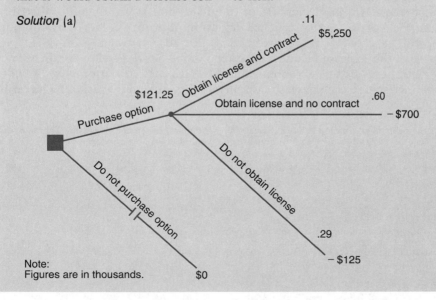

Note:
Figures are in thousands.

(b) Yes. (c) Yes. The expected profit from this course of action is $49,800, which is considerably less than it would be if the firm purchased the option [$121,250, according to part (a) above]. But there is a zero chance of loss, in contrast to a .89 probability of loss if it purchased the option.*

* For further discussion, see J. Ulvila and R. Brown, "Decision Analysis Comes of Age," *Harvard Business Review* (September–October 1982), reprinted in E. Mansfield, ed., *Managerial Economics and Operations Research*, 5th ed.

where $E(U)$ is expected utility, and $E(\pi)$ is expected profit.[9] Consequently, since expected utility is directly related to expected profit, it can only be a maximum when expected profit is a maximum.

# THE STANDARD DEVIATION AND COEFFICIENT OF VARIATION: MEASURES OF RISK

The concept of risk is not easy to measure, but it is generally agreed that the riskiness of a given decision is directly related to the extent of the dispersion of the probability distribution of profit resulting from the decision. For example, suppose the Jones Corporation must decide whether or not to invest in a new plant. If the probability distribution of profit resulting from the new plant is as shown in panel A of Figure 13.5, the decision to invest in the new plant is more risky than it would be if this probability distribution were as shown in panel B. Why? Because the profit resulting from the new plant is more uncertain and variable in panel A than in panel B.

As a measure of risk, we often use the **standard deviation,** $\sigma$, which is the most frequently used measure of the dispersion in a probability distribution.[10] To calculate the standard deviation of profit, we begin by computing the expected value of profit, $E(\pi)$. [Recall equation (13.2).] Next, we subtract this expected value from each possible profit level to obtain a set of deviations about this expected value. [The $i$th such deviation is $\pi_i - E(\pi_i)$.] Then we square each deviation, multiply the squared deviation by its prob-

[9] To illustrate that equation (13.4) is correct, suppose that $\pi$ can assume two possible values, $\pi_1$ and $\pi_2$, and that the probability that $\pi_1$ occurs is $P$ and the probability that $\pi_2$ occurs is $(1 - P)$. Then, if $U = a + b\pi$,

$$E(U) = P(a + b\pi_1) + (1 - P)(a + b\pi_2)$$
$$= a + b[P\pi_1 + (1 - P)\pi_2]$$
$$= a + b E(\pi),$$

since $E(\pi)$ equals $P\pi_1 + (1 - P)\pi_2$.

[10] While the standard deviation often is a useful measure of risk, it may not always be the best measure. Our discussion here and in subsequent sections of this chapter is necessarily simplified. The measures and techniques we describe are rough, but many analysts have found them useful.

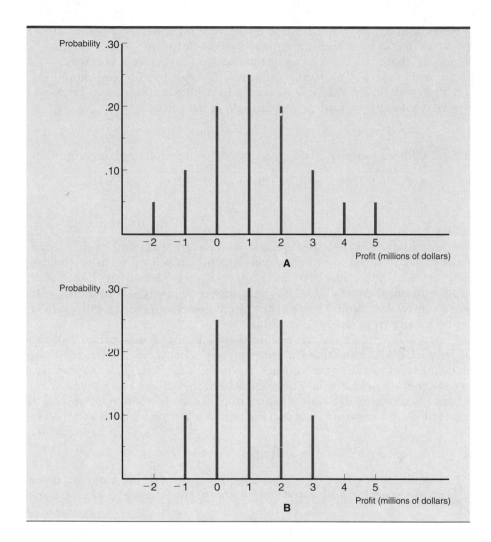

**FIGURE 13.5** *Probability Distribution of Profit from Investment in New Plant* The probability distribution in panel A shows more dispersion than that in panel B.

ability of occurrence $(P_i)$, and sum these products, the result being

$$\sigma^2 = \sum_{i=1}^{N} [\pi_i - E(\pi)]^2 P_i.$$

Taking the square root of this result, we obtain the standard deviation

$$\sigma = \sqrt{\sum_{i=1}^{N} [\pi_i - E(\pi)]^2 P_i}. \tag{13.5}$$

As an illustration, consider a company that must decide whether or not to invest in a flexible manufacturing system. According to the company's engineers, there is a .3 probability that such an investment will result in a $1 million profit, a .4 probability that it will result in a $0.2 million profit, and a .3 probability that it will result in a $0.6 million loss. Thus, the expected value of the profit from this investment is

$$E(\pi) = 1 \, (.3) + 0.2 \, (.4) + (-0.6) \, (.3) = 0.2,$$

or $0.2 million. And, based on equation (13.5), the standard deviation is

$$\sigma = \sqrt{(1 - 0.2)^2 \, (.3) + (0.2 - 0.2)^2 \, (.4) + (-0.6 - 0.2)^2 \, (.3)}$$
$$= \sqrt{0.384} = 0.62,$$

or $0.62 million.

A larger standard deviation tends to mean a larger amount of risk. Thus, if the standard deviation of the levels of profit resulting from the investment in the flexible manufacturing system were $2 million, rather than $0.62 million, there would be less certainty concerning its profitability. In other words, there would be a greater likelihood that its profitability would depart greatly from its expected value.

However, when we use the standard deviation as a measure of risk, we are implicitly assuming that the scale of the project is held constant. If one investment is twice as big as another, it would be expected that the standard deviation of its profits would be greater than that of the other investment. To take account of the scale of the project, a measure of relative risk is required. Such a measure is the **coefficient of variation**, defined as

$$V = \frac{\sigma}{E(\pi)}. \tag{13.6}$$

For example, in the case of the investment in the flexible manufacturing system, the coefficient of variation for the profit levels is $0.62 \div 0.2$, or 3.1.

## ADJUSTING THE VALUATION MODEL FOR RISK

According to the basic valuation model discussed in Chapter 1, a firm's managers must continually be concerned with the effects of their decisions on the present value of the firm's future profits, defined as

$$PV = \sum_{t=1}^{n} \frac{\pi_t}{(1 + i)^t}. \tag{13.7}$$

But the firm's managers do not know with certainty what the firm's profits in year $t$ (that is, $\pi_t$) will be. The best that they can do is use the expected profit [that is, $E(\pi_t)$] instead. How can they adjust the formula in equation (13.7) to take account of risk?

One way is to use the so-called certainty equivalent approach, which is related to the utility theory we developed in previous sections. For example, consider the manager of the firm considering the investment in the flexible manufacturing system. Suppose she is indifferent between the certainty of a $100,000 profit and the gamble involved in investing in this system. If so, the certainty equivalent ($100,000), rather than the expected profit ($200,000), should be used as $\pi_t$ in equation (13.7). If the certainty equivalent is less than the expected profit, the decision maker is a risk averter; if it is more than the expected profit, she is a risk lover; and if it equals the expected profit, she is risk neutral.

Based on the decision maker's utility function, one can construct *indifference curves* of the sort shown in Figure 13.6. Each such indifference curve shows the certainty equivalent corresponding to various uncertain outcomes. Thus, Figure 13.6 shows that the above manager is indifferent between the certainty of $100,000 and a gamble where the expected profit is $200,000 and the coefficient of variation is 3.1. Using such indifference curves, one can estimate the certainty equivalent of any uncertain situation. (In contrast to the indifference curves in the appendix to Chapter 3, these indifference curves slope upward to the right. Why? Because the manager prefers less to more risk. In the appendix to Chapter 3, the consumer preferred more of each commodity to less.)

In practice, of course, it is not easy to obtain such indifference curves,

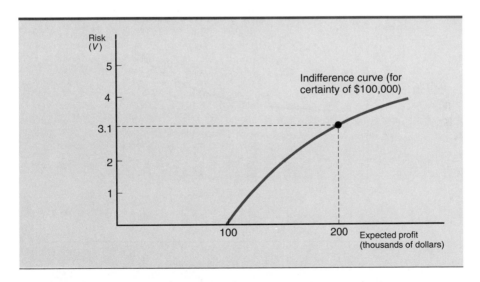

*FIGURE 13.6* **Manager's Indifference Curve between Expected Profit and Risk** The manager is indifferent between gambles with the expected profit and risk shown above. Thus, she is indifferent between the certainty of $100,000 and a gamble where the expected profit is $200,000 and the coefficient of variation is 3.1. Similar indifference curves exist for riskless amounts other than $100,000.

just as it is not easy to obtain the utility functions on which they are based. Because managers do not have unlimited time and patience, it may not be feasible to get more than a limited amount of information concerning their utility functions. Nor is it always clear which of a number of managers is the relevant one. If many managers play an important role in coming to a particular decision, and if they have very different indifference curves, they may come to quite different conclusions. But this, of course, should be expected. Indeed, it would be strange if managers with diverse attitudes toward risk did not come to divergent conclusions when faced with a choice among alternatives entailing quite different amounts of risk.

## THE USE OF RISK-ADJUSTED DISCOUNT RATES

Another way to introduce risk into the valuation model in equation (13.7) is to adjust the discount rate, *i*. This method, like that discussed in the previous section, is based on the manager's preferences with regard to risk. For example, suppose that Figure 13.7 shows a manager's indifference curve

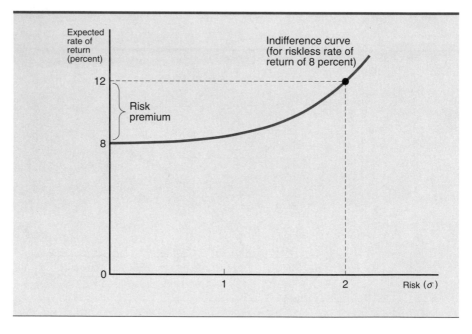

**FIGURE 13.7   *Manager's Indifference Curve between Expected Rate of Return and Risk***   The manager is indifferent between a riskless rate of return of 8 percent and gambles with the expected rate of return and risk shown above. Similar indifference curves exist for riskless rates of return other than 8 percent.

between expected rate of return and risk. As is evident from the fact that this curve slopes upward to the right, this manager is willing to accept greater risks if he obtains a higher expected rate of return. Specifically, he is indifferent between a riskless investment yielding an 8 percent return and a risky investment ($\sigma = 2$) yielding an expected rate of return of 12 percent. In other words, as risk rises, bigger expected profits are required to compensate for the higher risk.

The difference between the expected rate of return on a particular (risky) investment and that on a riskless investment is called the **risk premium** on this (risky) investment. For example, if the manager in Figure 13.7 can obtain an 8 percent rate of return from a riskless investment, he will require a risk premium of 4 percent (that is, 12 percent minus 8 percent) to compensate for the level of risk corresponding to $\sigma = 2$. This is the extra rate of return that is required to induce him to make such a risky investment. If he is offered less than this 4 percent risk premium, he will not make the investment.

Because the required rate of return depends on how risky the investment is, we can adjust the basic valuation model in equation (13.7) to take account of risk by modifying the discount rate, $i$. The adjusted version of equation (13.7) is

$$PV = \sum_{t=1}^{n} \frac{\pi_t}{(1 + r)^t},$$
(13.8)

where $r$ is the risk-adjusted discount rate. The risk-adjusted discount rate is the sum of the riskless rate of return and the risk premium required to compensate for the investment's level of risk. Thus, if the risk is such that $\sigma = 2$, the risk-adjusted discount rate would be 12 percent for the manager in Figure 13.7. This risk-adjusted rate equals 8 percent (the riskless rate) plus 4 percent (the risk premium).

## SIMULATION TECHNIQUES

Confronted with decisions involving millions of dollars where the risks are very substantial, managers frequently find simulation techniques to be useful. To illustrate the use of such techniques, suppose the officials of a chemical company must decide whether or not to build a new plant. The rate of return from the investment in this new plant depends on a number of factors—the cost of the plant, the plant's operating costs, the useful life of the plant, the size of the market for the product made by the plant, the price of this product, and this plant's share of the market. The firm's managers are uncertain concerning all of these factors, but they and their staffs can provide probability distributions for the value of each factor. These probability distributions are shown in Figure 13.8.

Based on these probability distributions, a computer program can be developed to simulate what may occur. The computer picks one value at

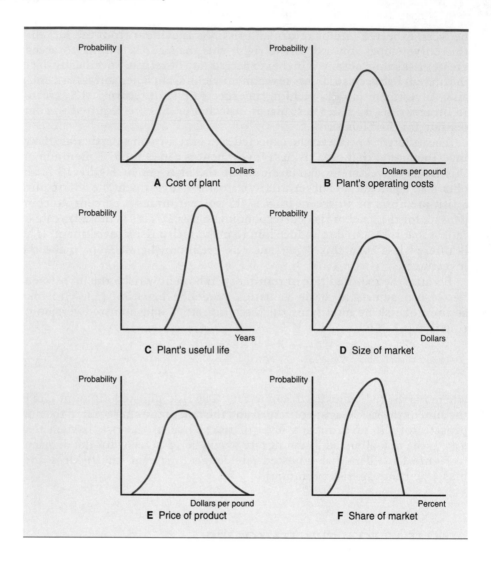

**FIGURE 13.8  Probability Distributions\* for Factors Determining the Rate of Return from Investment in New Plant**  The computer picks one value at random from each of these probability distributions, and calculates the rate of return. This is repeated over and over.

---

\* In contrast to Figure 13.5, these probability distributions are drawn as continuous curves. Depending on the circumstances, these variables can be regarded as continuous or discrete.

random from each of the probability distributions in Figure 13.8, and determines the rate of return from investing in the new plant (or the net present value), if these values prevail. For example, suppose that the computer picks a value of $2 million for the cost of the plant, $3 per pound for the plant's operating costs, 5 years for the useful life of the plant, $200 million for the market for the plant's product, $15 per pound for the price of this product, and 15 percent for this plant's share of the market. Based on these figures, the computer calculates the rate of return from the investment in this new plant.

This procedure is repeated over and over. The computer picks one set of values for the factors determining the rate of return from the investment, then a second set, then a third set, and so on. After picking each set of values, the computer calculates the rate of return from the investment. In this way, the computer builds up a frequency distribution of the rate of return. For example, the frequency distribution of the rate of return from this investment may be as shown in Figure 13.9. This frequency distribution can be of great use to managers because it summarizes concisely and effectively the extent of the risks involved in building the new plant. As pointed out in previous sections, the standard deviation (or coefficient of variation) of this frequency distribution can be used as a rough measure of risk and, together with the mean, can be used in the sorts of analyses discussed in previous sections.

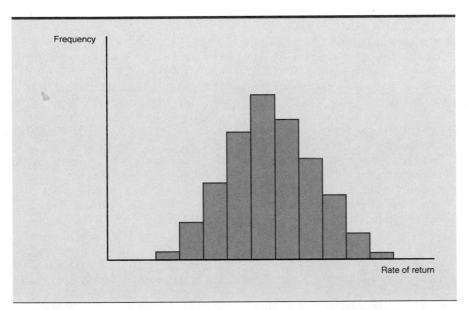

FIGURE 13.9  *Frequency Distribution of Calculated Rate of Return from Investment in New Plant*   This is the frequency distribution resulting from the procedure described in Figure 13.8 being performed repeatedly.

## USING SIMULATION TECHNIQUES IN THE COMPUTER INDUSTRY

In 1990, a major computer manufacturer was considering two investment projects. The first project involved a new technology requiring significant research. Because the technology was new and because it was hard to know whether the project would result in the desired results, there were considerable risks involved. The second project was based on existing technology. It called for incremental changes in technology and operations, and was felt to be less risky than the first project.

To compare projects of this sort, this firm has generally used analytical techniques that pay limited attention to the riskiness of the project. Using these techniques, the firm's analysts found that the two projects seemed to be about equally attractive. However, the firm's management was concerned about the large number of unknowns hidden in the sales, cost, and profit estimates for the first project.

Eventually, it was decided to use a simulation study to compare the attractiveness of the two projects. For each project, probability distributions of sales and costs were estimated. The computer then picked one value of sales at random from the probability distribution of sales and one value of costs at random from the probability distribution of costs. Then the computer calculated the discounted profit. This calculation was carried out repeatedly, first for one project and then for the other. Based on these calculations, a frequency distribution of discounted profit for each project

*Sandra L. Kurtzig, CEO of ASK Computer Systems*

was constructed; the results are shown on page 527.

On the basis of these results, it was clear that the probability of a substantial loss was much higher with the first project than with the second project, as the firm's management had thought. Indeed, this probability was so high that it was decided to reject the first project in favor of the second project. This is a good example of how the simulation techniques described on pages 523 to 527 have actually been used.

It is also a good illustration of the importance of taking proper account of risk. As Sandy Kurtzig, head of ASK Computer Systems, put it, "Charting the future in business can be like one of those game shows where you have to choose

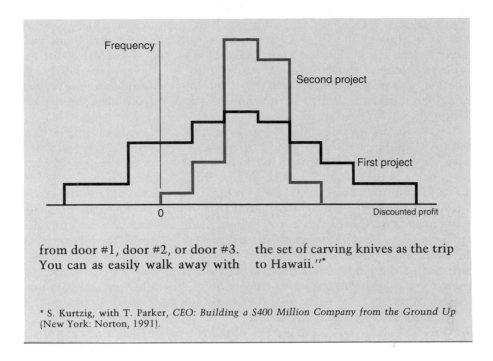

from door #1, door #2, or door #3. You can as easily walk away with the set of carving knives as the trip to Hawaii."[*]

[*] S. Kurtzig, with T. Parker, *CEO: Building a $400 Million Company from the Ground Up* (New York: Norton, 1991).

While simulation techniques of this kind are of great value, it is important to recognize that the results are no better than the original probability distributions fed into the computer. Thus, if the probability distributions in Figure 13.8 are wildly in error, it is foolish to expect the results in Figure 13.9 to be dependable. Because it frequently is expensive to obtain good estimates of the original probability distributions, this means that simulation studies of this kind, if carried out well, tend to be done to shed light only on major decisions, not minor ones.

A rougher procedure, called **sensitivity analysis,** is also worth considering. Rather than deriving the probability distributions in Figure 13.8, some analysts put together estimates of each factor (cost of plant, operating costs, and so on) that represent their best judgment of what will occur. Then they vary each of these values (within reasonable limits) to see how sensitive the rate of return is to each of them. The results indicate which factors are worth studying further, since there is little point in studying those factors that have only a minor effect on the results.

## THE WINNER'S CURSE

Firms often must bid on pieces of land or on other assets that are being auctioned off. (Recall the case on page 504 of the *SS Kuniang.*) It is important that a manager knows how to formulate an effective bid. If you bid too low, you're unlikely to get the asset in question; if you bid too high, you're likely to pay too much. To illustrate what is involved, suppose that a piece of land is to be auctioned off. This piece of land appears to have valuable oil and mineral deposits, but no one knows exactly what they are worth. (Until a variety of complex and expensive tests are performed, it is impossible to tell whether oil is present and, if so, in what amounts.) *If each bidder bids what he or she thinks the land is worth,* how much will the highest bidder be willing to pay for this land?

Unless we know more about the particular piece of land, it is impossible to provide a numerical answer to this question. Nonetheless, economists have shown that the following remarkable proposition is true. If each bidder behaves in the assumed way, *the highest bidder is likely to pay more for the land than it is worth.* To see why, suppose that each bidder makes an estimate of what the land is worth and that, *on the average, the bidders' estimates are approximately correct.* Since each bidder is assumed to submit a bid that equals his or her estimate of the land's worth, the highest bidder is likely to pay more for the land than it is worth because his or her estimate of the land's value must exceed the average estimate, which is approximately equal to the land's true value. (If his or her estimate did not exceed the average estimate, he or she would not be the highest bidder.)

To illustrate this so-called "winner's curse,"[11] suppose that 10 metals firms make bids for a particular piece of land and that each firm's estimate of its value is shown in Table 13.2. Because each firm is assumed to bid what it thinks the land is worth, the winning bid ($34,000) is made by Reynolds. But if, on the average, the firms' evaluations are approximately correct, then the true value of the piece of land is about $32,000, since this was their average estimate. Thus, Reynolds is likely to have paid too much for it.

Can the winner's curse be avoided? The answer is yes. To avoid it, sophisticated bidders make bids that are *below* their estimates of what the

---

**TABLE 13.2** *Estimates of Value of a Piece of Land, 10 Metals Firms*

| Firm | Estimate of value of land | Firm | Estimate of value of land |
|---|---|---|---|
| Alcoa | $30,000 | Reynolds | $34,000 |
| Allegheny Ludlum | 32,000 | National | 31,000 |
| Brush Wellman | 31,000 | Precision | 32,000 |
| Carpenter | 32,000 | Weirton | 33,000 |
| Intermet | 33,000 | Zemix | 32,000 |
|  |  | Average | 32,000 |

---

[11] One of the earliest discussions of the "winner's curse" was by three Atlantic Richfield engineers. See E. Capen, R. Clapp, and W. Campbell, "Competitive Bidding in High-Risk Situations," *Journal of Petroleum Technology* (June 1971). See R. Thaler, *The Winner's Curse* (New York: The Free Press, 1992).

land is really worth. Thus, the 10 metals firms, recognizing the existence of the winner's curse, may submit bids that are several thousand dollars less than their estimates of the land's true value. In this way, they try to insure that, if they are the highest bidder, they will not have paid too much for the land.[12]

## APPLICATION OF THE MAXIMIN RULE

Throughout this chapter, we have been concerned with risk, not uncertainty. Risk occurs where the outcome is not certain, but where the probability of each possible outcome is known or can be estimated. **Uncertainty** refers to a situation where these probabilities are unknown. Although managerial economists have devised a number of types of rules to help a decision maker choose among alternative courses of action under conditions of uncertainty, none of these rules is universally considered to be preferable. All of them have disadvantages and difficulties. To illustrate the sorts of rules that have been proposed, and their limitations, we take up the *maximin rule.*[13]

The decision maker, according to this rule, should determine the worst outcome that can occur if each possible course of action is chosen, and he or she should choose the course of action where this worst outcome is best. Consider a situation where the Jones Corporation, the hypothetical producer of automobile tires, must decide whether or not to move its production facilities from one location to another. The Jones Corporation is concerned that if the tax authorities in the new location were to raise taxes, such a move might cut its profits considerably. As shown in Table 13.3, the Jones Corporation believes that if it moves its facilities and a tax increase occurs, it will lose $5 million. If it moves its facilities and a tax increase does not occur, it will gain $20 million. And if it does not move its facilities, it will gain (and lose) nothing.

---

TABLE 13.3 *Jones Corporation's Gains (or Losses), with or without a Tax Increase, if a Tax Increase Does or Does Not Occur*

| | Outcome | |
| --- | --- | --- |
| Course of action | Tax increase | No tax increase |
| Firm moves facilities | −$5 million | $20 million |
| Firm does not move facilities | 0 | 0 |

---

[12] Analyses have been made to determine *how much lower* a bid should be than the bidder's estimate of what the land is really worth, but they are too advanced to be appropriate for this text.

[13] Frequently, this rule is referred to as the minimax rule; both names are in common use.

The Jones Corporation, if it applies the maximin rule, should determine the worst outcome under each course of action. There are two possible courses of action: the firm can move its facilities or not move them. Regardless of which course of action is chosen, there are two possible outcomes: a tax increase can occur or not. If these facilities are moved, the worst outcome is a $5 million loss that will result if a tax increase occurs. If these facilities are not moved, the worst (and only) outcome is a zero gain. Thus, if the Jones Corporation applies the maximin rule, it should not move its facilities. Why? Because the worst outcome if these facilities are not moved is preferable to the worst outcome if they are moved.

Whether a tax increase will occur at the new location will not be determined by a rival or competitor who is out to inflict damages on the Jones Corporation. Instead, it will be determined by a host of political, economic, social, and other factors that have little to do with this particular firm. For this and other reasons, the maximin rule has been criticized as being overly conservative. Because there is no reason why the firm should assume that the relevant political, economic, social and other factors are out to hurt it, there is no reason why it should pay attention only to the worst outcome that can occur if each course of action is taken.

Many rules other than the maximin rule have been proposed to help people make decisions under conditions of uncertainty.[14] However, each of these rules has its problems and limitations. Which, if any, is appropriate depends on the attitudes toward risk and the financial resources of the decision maker, as well as on the other aspects of the situation. There is no single rule that can be applied universally to decision making under uncertainty. The truth is that in situations where the probability of each outcome cannot be estimated (even roughly), it is very difficult to provide managers with general guidelines for decision making.

# SUMMARY

1. The probability of an event is the proportion of times that this event occurs over the long run. Expected profit is the sum of the amount of money gained (or lost) if each outcome occurs times the probability of occurrence of the outcome.
2. A decision tree is a graphical representation of a decision problem as a series of choices, each of which is depicted by a decision fork or a chance fork. A decision tree can be used to determine the course of action with the highest expected profit. A variety of examples were discussed, including Tomco Oil Corporation's decision of whether or not to drill an oil well at a site in Kansas.

---

[14] Some examples are the Bayes rule, the maximax rule, the Hurwicz rule, and L.J. Savage's minimax regret rule. See W. Baumol, *Economic Theory and Operations Analysis* (Englewood Cliffs, N.J.: Prentice-Hall, 1977); and M. Shubik, "A Note on Decision-Making under Uncertainty," in E. Mansfield, ed., *Managerial Economics and Operations Research*, 5th ed.

3. The expected value of perfect information is the increase in expected profit if the decision maker could obtain completely accurate information concerning the outcome of the relevant situation (but he or she does not yet know what this information will be). This is the maximum amount that the decision maker should pay to obtain such information. Methods have been provided to enable you to calculate the expected value of perfect information.

4. Risk is often measured by the standard deviation or coefficient of variation of the probability distribution of profit. Whether a decision maker wants to maximize expected profit depends on his or her attitudes toward risk. The decision maker's attitudes toward risk can be measured by his or her utility function.

5. To construct such a utility function, we begin by setting the utility attached to two monetary values arbitrarily. Then we present the decision maker with a choice between the certainty of one of the other monetary values and a gamble where the possible outcomes are the two monetary values whose utilities we set arbitrarily. Repeating this procedure over and over, we can construct the decision maker's utility function.

6. One way to adjust the basic valuation model for risk is to use certainty equivalents in place of the expected profit figures in equation (13.7). To do this, you construct indifference curves (based on the decision maker's utility function) showing the certainty equivalent corresponding to various uncertain outcomes.

7. Another way to introduce risk into the valuation model is to adjust the discount rate. To do this, you construct indifference curves between expected rate of return and risk, based on the decision maker's utility function. Using such indifference curves, you can estimate the risk premium (if any) that is appropriate.

8. Firms frequently must make bids on assets whose value is not known with certainty. If each firm bids what it believes the value of the auctioned item to be, the winning bid is likely to be too high. This is the "winner's curse."

9. Uncertainty refers to a situation where the relevant probabilities cannot be estimated. According to the maximin rule, the decision maker under uncertainty should choose the course of action where the worst possible outcome is least damaging. There are important problems in this rule, as well as others proposed to handle the situation of uncertainty.

# PROBLEMS

1. The president of the Martin Company is considering two alternative investments, X and Y. If each investment is carried out, there are four possible outcomes, the present value of net profit and probability of the outcome being as shown at the top of the following page.

| ─────Investment X───── | | | ─────Investment Y───── | | |
| Outcome | Net present value | Probability | Outcome | Net present value | Probability |
| --- | --- | --- | --- | --- | --- |
| 1 | $20 million | .2 | A | $12 million | .1 |
| 2 | 8 million | .3 | B | 9 million | .3 |
| 3 | 10 million | .4 | C | 16 million | .1 |
| 4 | 3 million | .1 | D | 11 million | .5 |

(a) What is the expected present value, standard deviation, and coefficient of variation of investment X?

(b) What is the expected present value, standard deviation, and coefficient of variation of investment Y?

(c) Which of these investments is riskier?

(d) The president of the Martin Company has the following utility function:

$$U = 10 + 5P - .01P^2$$

where $U$ is utility and $P$ is net present value. Which investment should she choose?

2. William J. Bryan is the general manager of an electrical equipment plant. He must decide whether or not to install a number of assembly robots in his plant. This investment would be quite risky, since both management and the work force have no real experience with the introduction or operation of such robots. His indifference curve between expected rate of return and risk is as shown below:

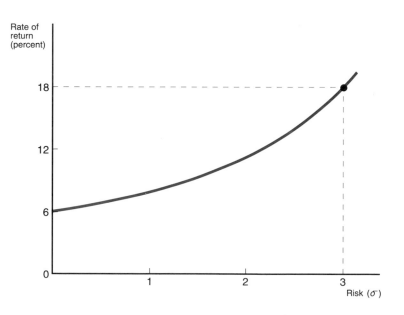

(a) If the riskiness ($\sigma$) of this investment equals 3, what risk premium does he require?

(b) What is the riskless rate of return?

(c) What is the risk-adjusted discount rate?

(d) In calculating the present value of future profits from this investment, what interest rate should be used?

3. The Zodiac Company is considering the development of a new type of plastic. Whether or not the plastic will be successful depends on the outcome of a research project being carried out at a major university. Zodiac's executives have no reasonably reliable means of estimating the university research team's probability of success. Zodiac's gains (or losses), depending on the outcome of the university research project, are as follows:

| | Outcome of university research project | |
|---|---|---|
| Action | Success | Failure |
| Zodiac develops plastic | $50 million | −$8 million |
| Zodiac does not develop plastic | 0 | 0 |

(a) If the firm's executives use the maximin rule, should they develop the new type of plastic?

(b) What are the disadvantages of the maximin rule?

(c) Based on the information given, can you calculate the expected value of perfect information? Why or why not?

4. The Electro Corporation, which manufactures television sets, has a fixed cost of $1 million per year. The gross profit from each TV set sold —that is, the price less the average variable cost—is $20. The expected value of the number of sets the company sells per year is 100,000. The standard deviation of the number of sets sold per year is 10,000.

(a) What is the expected value of the firm's annual profit?

(b) What is the standard deviation of the firm's annual profit?

(c) What is the coefficient of variation of the firm's annual profit?

5. Richard Miller, a Wall Street trader, says he is risk neutral. Suppose we let 0 be the utility he attaches to $100,000 and 1 be the utility he attaches to $200,000. If what he says is true, what is the utility he attaches to (a) $400,000; (b) $40,000; (c) −$20,000?

6. The chief executive officer of a publishing company says she is indifferent between the certainty of receiving $7,500 and a gamble where there is a .5 chance of receiving $5,000 and a .5 chance of receiving $10,000. Also, she says she is indifferent between the certainty of receiving $10,000 and a gamble where there is a .5 chance of receiving $7,500 and a .5 chance of receiving $12,500.

(a) Draw (on a piece of graph paper) four points on the utility function of this publishing executive.

(b) Does she seem to be a risk averter, a risk lover, or risk neutral? Explain.

7. The Oahu Trading Company is considering the purchase of a small firm that produces clocks. Oahu's management feels there is a 50-50 chance, if Oahu buys the firm, that it can mold the firm into an effective producer of washing machine parts. If the firm can be transformed in this way, Oahu believes that it will make $500,000 if it buys the firm; if it cannot be transformed in this way, Oahu believes that it will lose $400,000.

   (a) Construct a decision tree to represent Oahu's problem.
   (b) What are the decision forks? (Is there more than one?)
   (c) What are the chance forks? (Is there more than one?)
   (d) Use the decision tree to solve Oahu's problem. In other words, assuming that the firm wants to maximize expected extra profit, should Oahu buy the firm or not?
   (e) Before Oahu makes a decision concerning the purchase of the firm, Oahu's president learns that if the clock producer cannot be made into an effective producer of washing machine parts, there is a .2 probability that it can be resold to a Saudi Arabian syndicate at a profit of $100,000. (If the firm cannot be resold, Oahu will lose $400,000.)
      (i)   Does this information alter the decision tree?
      (ii)  Can you think of three mutually exclusive outcomes if Oahu buys the firm?
      (iii) What is the probability of each of these outcomes?
      (iv)  What is the monetary value to Oahu of each of these outcomes?
   (f) Use your results in (e) to solve Oahu's problem under this new set of conditions. In other words, on the basis of this new information, should Oahu buy the firm or not?
   (g) Oahu's executive vice president discovers an error in the estimate of how much Oahu will gain if it buys the clock manufacturer and turns it into an effective producer of washing machine parts.
      (i)   Under the circumstances in (d), how big would this error have to be to reverse the indicated decision?
      (ii)  Under the circumstances in (e), how big would the error have to be to reverse the indicated decision?

8. According to Cal Tech's Nobel Prize winning physicist the late Richard Feynman, the National Aeronautics and Space Administration (NASA) estimated the probability of a crash of the space shuttle to be 1 in 100,000, whereas the probability was in fact closer to about .01 to .02. If a decision tree had been used to determine whether or not to attempt a launch of the shuttle, what difference, if any, would this have made?

9. The *East Chester Tribune* must decide whether or not to publish a Sunday edition. The publisher thinks the probability is .6 that a Sunday edition would be a success and .4 that it would be a failure. If it is a success, she will gain $100,000. If it is a failure, she will lose $80,000.

   (a) Construct the decision tree corresponding to the problem, and use backward induction to solve the problem. (Assume that the publisher is risk neutral.)

(b) List all forks in the decision tree you constructed, and indicate whether each is a decision fork or a chance fork, and state why.

10. Roy Lamb has an option on a particular piece of land, and must decide whether to drill on the land before the expiration of the option or give up his rights. If he drills, he believes that the cost will be $200,000. If he finds oil, he expects to receive $1 million; if he does not find oil, he expects to receive nothing.

(a) Construct a decision tree to represent Lamb's decision.

(b) Can you tell whether he should drill or not on the basis of the available information? Why or why not?

Mr. Lamb believes that the probability of finding oil if he drills on this piece of land is 1/4, and that the probability of not finding oil if he drills here is 3/4.

(c) Can you tell whether he should drill or not on the basis of the available information? Why or why not?

(d) Suppose Mr. Lamb can be demonstrated to be a risk lover. Should he drill or not? Why?

(e) Suppose Mr. Lamb is risk neutral. Should he drill or not? Why?

# Chapter 14
# *Capital Budgeting*

## *INTRODUCTION*

Many of the techniques described in previous chapters are designed to help a firm do the best it can with its existing resources. While very useful, these techniques cannot help managers make decisions about expanding the firm's resource base. Manufacturing engineers propose the construction of new plant and equipment to improve efficiency. Marketing executives propose new stores and warehouses. Research administrators propose the building of new laboratories and the purchase of more advanced instrumentation. Somehow these competing claims for funds must be evaluated.

In this chapter, we turn to capital budgeting, the process of evaluating and planning capital expenditures. *A capital expenditure is a cash outlay that is expected to result in a flow of future cash benefits (extending beyond one year in the future).* Because capital expenditures affect the scale, efficiency, and nature of a firm, they are of central importance to any firm's managers (and owners). A series of capital expenditures can transform an electronics firm into a drug firm, or vice versa. Successful capital investments can turn a losing firm into a winner. Foolish capital investments can sink a firm that in other respects is well managed.

# A SIMPLE MODEL OF CAPITAL BUDGETING

Reduced to the simplest terms, capital budgeting can be viewed as an application of a basic proposition stated in Chapter 2: A firm should operate at the point where its marginal cost is just equal to its marginal revenue. In the context of capital budgeting, marginal revenue is interpreted as the rate of return on investments, and marginal cost is the firm's cost of capital. Thus, according to this rule, the firm should operate where its rate of return equals its cost of capital.

To see more clearly what this rule means, and why it makes sense, consider panel A of Figure 14.1, which represents the investment projects available to a particular firm as rectangles. Thus, rectangle G is an investment project requiring an outlay of $5 million (the width of rectangle G along the horizontal axis) and yielding a rate of return of 20 percent (the height of rectangle G along the vertical axis). In Figure 14.1, since projects are presented in the order of their rate of return, the next rectangle, rectangle H, yields the second-highest rate of return (15 percent) and requires an outlay of $2 million. The project with the third-highest rate of return is represented by rectangle K, that with the fourth-highest rate of return is represented by rectangle L, and so on.

Figure 14.1 also shows the **marginal cost of capital**, which is defined as the cost of an extra dollar acquired to make capital expenditures. For the firm in Figure 14.1, the marginal cost of capital is constant at 9 percent until the firm has raised $10 million, after which it begins to go up. To maximize profit, the firm should accept all projects where the rate of return exceeds the cost of capital. That is, projects G, H, and K should be accepted, because each generates returns that exceed the cost of capital. But projects L and M should not be accepted, since their returns do not exceed the cost of capital.

In panel A of Figure 14.1, the firm has only a few investment projects to consider. For most firms, there are many such projects to consider, and the jagged line (a series of "steps") showing investment opportunities— GHKLM in panel A—is a relatively smooth curve, like R in panel B. The optimal amount that the firm in panel B should invest is Y millions of dollars, and the marginal cost of capital (if the firm invests this optimal amount) is s percent, which is equal to the rate of return on the least profitable project accepted by the firm.

# THE INVESTMENT SELECTION PROCESS

While the simple model in the previous section is a useful introduction to capital budgeting, it ignores many important aspects of the investment selection process. This process is composed of four steps, as shown in Figure 14.2. First, the firm's managers must *generate proposals for alternative*

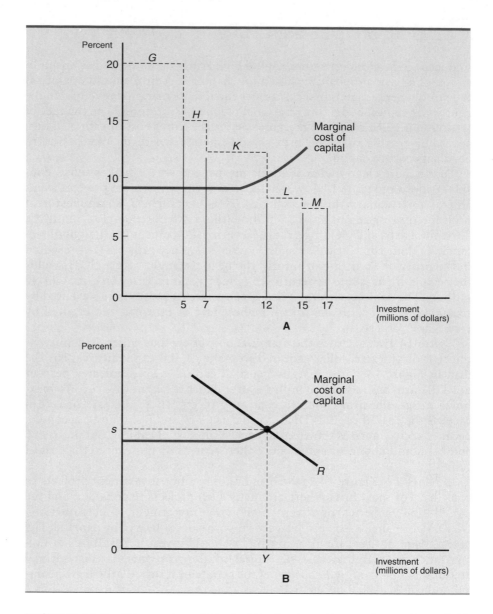

**FIGURE 14.1** *Illustration of Capital Budgeting* In panel A, projects *G*, *H*, and *K* (but not *L* and *M*) are accepted. In panel B, the optimal amount that the firm should invest is *Y* millions of dollars.

*investment projects.* Second, for each of these proposed projects, the firm's managers must *estimate cash flows for the project.* Third, the firm's managers must *evaluate each of the proposed projects, and select those to be implemented.* Fourth, the firm's managers should *review the projects after implementation.*

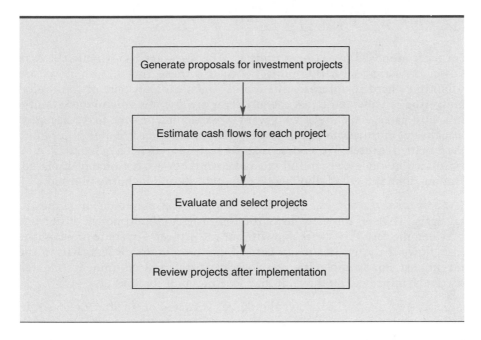

FIGURE 14.2   *The Investment Selection Process*   The process is composed of four steps, shown above.

Perhaps the most important of these steps is the first one, in which project proposals are generated. If a firm's managers and employees (as well as its advisers and consultants) cannot come up with a promising set of investment proposals, there is no way that clever selection techniques will enable the firm to make something out of nothing. It is like going to a restaurant and finding that nothing on the menu is of interest. If the choice is between poor alternatives, the result is bound to be poor. One should recognize at the outset the importance of managers doing what they can to stimulate a rich set of investment proposals.

Ideas for investment projects come from a wide variety of sources, ranging from workers in the factory to the board of directors. Suggestions frequently stem from both inside and outside the firm itself. Staff groups involved in corporate planning, research and development, marketing research, engineering, and accounting often seek out and analyze such ideas and suggestions. Because investment projects are of various types, they often are not easy to compare without detailed analysis. Some investment projects are aimed at expanding the firm's productive capacity to accommodate forecasted increases in demand. Others are meant to reduce the costs of making or distributing the firm's product. Still others are carried out to meet legal requirements or to advance the firm's technology. It is important to keep an open mind concerning their merits. Some of the most profitable projects have seemed rather weird when first suggested.

## HOW TO ESTIMATE CASH FLOWS

For each proposed investment project, it is necessary to estimate the cash flows associated with this project. Because these future cash flows are sometimes hard to forecast, this too can be a difficult part of the capital budgeting process. Note that the problems are due not only to uncertainty; in many cases, executives who want a particular project to be accepted (because of enthusiasm or self-interest) may bias the estimates to promote their being accepted. We assume that the firm's top managers insure that all estimates are reviewed carefully to make sure they are reasonably unbiased. Having done this, the following three points should be borne in mind:

*1. Incremental Analysis.* Cash flows should be estimated on an incremental basis. That is, the cash flows for the project should be the difference between the cash flows with and without the project. For some projects, the cash flows if the project is not carried out may be much less than in the recent past. For example, if a firm does not install new equipment to match its rivals' improved products, it may lose much of its market.

*2. After-Tax Basis.* Cash flows should be estimated on an after-tax basis. In making such estimates, the firm's marginal tax rate (that is, the proportion of an extra dollar of profit going for taxes) is often of central importance, as we shall see below. Noncash items like depreciation are relevant if they affect the firm's cash outflow for taxes.

*3. Indirect Effects.* In estimating the effect of a proposed investment project on the firm's cash inflows and outflows, it is essential that the analyst be sensitive to the indirect effects of the proposed project on parts of the firm's activities that may seem to be far removed from the investment. For example, although the investment in the introduction of a new product may be profitable to the division of the firm that proposes this investment, it may not be profitable to the firm as a whole because the new product may take sales away from other products produced by the firm. (Recall page 466.)

To be more specific, consider a particular investment project. For each year, it is necessary to estimate $F$, the incremental, after-tax net cash flow from the project. *This incremental, after-tax net cash flow equals* $\Delta \pi$, *the difference in net income after tax with and without the project, plus* $\Delta D$, *the difference in depreciation:*

$$F = \Delta \pi + \Delta D. \tag{14.1}$$

Since $\Delta \pi$, the difference in after-tax net income, equals $\Delta B$, the difference in before-tax income, times $(1 - t)$, where $t$ is the marginal tax rate, it follows that

$$F = \Delta B (1 - t) + \Delta D. \tag{14.2}$$

Further, since $\Delta B$, the difference in before-tax income, equals $\Delta R$, the difference in revenues, minus $\Delta C + \Delta D$, where $\Delta C$ is the difference in operating costs, it follows that

$$F = (\Delta R - \Delta C - \Delta D)(1 - t) + \Delta D. \qquad (14.3)$$

To illustrate how equation (14.3) can be applied, consider the Martin Corporation, a manufacturer of automobile parts that is considering a $500,000 investment in robots. In the current year, Martin's cash inflow would be reduced by $500,000 if it invests in the robots, but in the next 5 years (the useful life of the robots), its cash inflow would be increased because the robots would lower the firm's costs. According to Martin's engineers, its production costs would fall by about $90,000 per year. Also, because of the robots, its marketing executives feel that the quality of its product would rise, resulting in a $20,000 per year increase in revenues. The robots would be depreciated over 5 years (using straight-line depreciation) with zero salvage value at the end of the 5-year period. (Thus, the annual depreciation charge would be $100,000.) The firm's marginal tax rate is 40 percent.

Based on this information, equation (14.3) can be used to calculate the incremental, after-tax net cash flow from this project. In the current year, there is a net cash *out*flow of $500,000. During the next 5 years, there is a net cash *in*flow each year of

$$[20,000 - (-90,000) - 100,000](1 - .4) + 100,000 = \$106,000,$$

since $\Delta R = \$20,000$, $\Delta C = -\$90,000$, $\Delta D = \$100,000$, and $t = 0.4$.

Another illustration of the calculation of the cash flows from an investment project is provided in Table 14.1, which pertains to a proposed invest-

**TABLE 14.1** *Cash Flow Analysis for Investment Project (Thousands of Dollars)*

|  | 1994 | 1995 | 1996 | 1997 | 1998 | 1999 | 2000 | 2001 |
|---|---|---|---|---|---|---|---|---|
| 1. Capital expenditures* | −205.0 | −95.0 | 0 | 0 | 0 | 0 | 0 | 0 |
| Buildings | −120.0 | 0 | 0 | 0 | 0 | 0 | 0 | 0 |
| Equipment | − 85.0 | −95.0 | 0 | 0 | 0 | 0 | 0 | 0 |
| 2. Net profit (after tax) from new product† | 0 | 0 | 6.6 | 52.8 | 79.2 | 79.2 | 79.2 | 79.2 |
| Net sales | 0 | 0 | 240.0 | 450.0 | 500.0 | 500.0 | 500.0 | 500.0 |
| Cost of sales | 0 | 0 | 108.0 | 220.0 | 250.0 | 250.0 | 250.0 | 250.0 |
| Depreciation | 0 | 0 | 60.0 | 60.0 | 60.0 | 60.0 | 60.0 | 60.0 |
| Selling expense | 0 | 0 | 40.0 | 50.0 | 40.0 | 40.0 | 40.0 | 40.0 |
| Administrative expense | 0 | 0 | 22.0 | 40.0 | 30.0 | 30.0 | 30.0 | 30.0 |
| Income tax (34 percent) | 0 | 0 | 3.4 | 27.2 | 40.8 | 40.8 | 40.8 | 40.8 |
| 3. Net profit plus depreciation | 0 | 0 | 66.6 | 112.8 | 139.2 | 139.2 | 139.2 | 139.2 |
| 4. Net cash flow | −205.0 | −95.0 | 66.6 | 112.8 | 139.2 | 139.2 | 139.2 | 139.2 |

* Capital expenditures equal the sum of expenditures on buildings and expenditures on equipment. They are negative because they are a cash outflow.

† Net profit = net sales − (cost of sales + depreciation + selling expenses + administrative expense + income tax).

## ESTIMATING CASH FLOWS FOR DEVELOPING AN AIRCRAFT

Boeing, McDonnell Douglas, and other manufacturers of large airplanes must make huge investments to develop and introduce a new aircraft. The time from basic program commitment to delivery of a large transport plane is 4 to 6 years, and a total expenditure of about $4 to $6 billion must occur before a significant inflow of funds can begin. The National Research Council has published the following chart to describe the cumulative net cash flow (that is, the sum of the net cash flows from the beginning of the program) for a large transport aircraft program:*

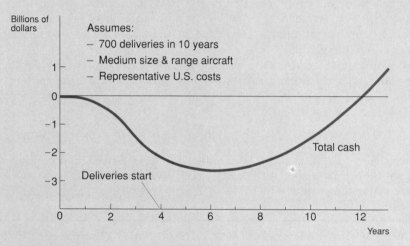

* National Research Council, *The Competitive Status of the U.S. Civil Aviation Manufacturing Industry* (Washington, D.C.: National Academy Press, 1985).

(a) In the case shown above, about how long does it take before the cumulative cash flow from the program is positive? (b) In deciding whether or not to go ahead with such a program, how would you estimate the launching cost (that is, the research and development and manufacturing and marketing start-up cost)? (c) How would you estimate the production costs? (d) This graph assumes that 700 planes of this type will be sold and delivered (over a 10-year period). In deciding whether or not to go ahead with such a program, how would you try to determine whether such an assumption is realistic?

*Solution* (a) 12 years. (b) One way to do so is to obtain data concerning the launching costs of other aircraft that the firm has developed in the recent past. These historical costs should provide a reasonable guide concerning the launching costs for a proposed program. Also, engineering managers should be able to provide rough estimates of the amount of engineering time

and other inputs required. (c) Historical data concerning the production costs of similar aircraft may be
of use. Also, engineering estimates
of the input requirements to produce such an airplane, together
with forecasts of input prices,
should be useful. (d) You might
obtain data concerning the number
of planes that the firm has sold in
the past, and potential purchasers
of aircraft of this type might be sur-
veyed to determine how many
planes of this type are likely to be
sold.

ment in buildings and equipment to produce a new product. As you can see, there is a negative cash flow in the first 2 years of the project (1994 and 1995) and a positive cash flow thereafter.

## GENERAL FOODS' "SUPER PROJECT"[1]

Before going further, it is important to recognize that the estimation of incremental cash flows can sometimes be tricky. To illustrate, consider General Foods' project to introduce a new instant dessert that would compete with its own product, Jell-O. The project, called the Super Project, would have required an investment of $400,000. Initial estimates suggested that it would be a profitable investment, but subsequent analysis raised at least two major questions:

1. The new product would make use of an agglomerator that was also used in making Jell-O. Since this machine had been completely written off against Jell-O's revenues, no cost was assigned to its use for this new product. Whether or not this procedure is correct depends on whether other new products that might be developed in the future could also make use of the machine. If it were fully used by the new instant dessert, these other products would have to bear the full cost of an extra agglomerator, which might well make them appear financially unattractive. In fact, however, these other products might be more attractive than the Super Project if the cost of the extra machine capacity were included.

2. The new product, if successful, was likely to cut into the sales of Jell-O. Thus, the General Foods analysts deducted the profit contribution that would be forgone because of Jell-O's reduced sales from the profit made by the new product. Whether or not their estimate was correct depends on whether General Foods' rivals were likely to introduce a similar new product, even if General Foods decided against it. A rival product of this sort would probably diminish Jell-O's profits, whether or not General Foods introduced the new product. The reduction in Jell-O's profits as a

---

[1] This section is based largely on R. Hayes, S. Wheelwright, and K. Clark, *Dynamic Manufacturing* (New York: Free Press, 1988), pp. 69–70.

result of its introduction of the new product would probably be much smaller if a rival product appeared than it would be if, as the analysts assumed, no rival product appeared on the scene.

The moral of this section is simple, yet profound: Estimates of incremental cash flow depend on what the alternative is, if the investment project is not carried out. Is it likely that other, more attractive products will come along—and that they will require the agglomerator's capacity? Is it likely that other firms will introduce a similar new product? These are key questions that confronted General Foods—and that its analysts had not considered fully.

## EVALUATING INVESTMENT PROJECTS: THE NET PRESENT VALUE TECHNIQUE

After cash flow estimates have been made for a particular investment project, an evaluation of the project must be carried out to determine its worth to the firm. A variety of methods are employed to rank projects and decide which ones should be accepted, but all of the correct methods are based on the concept of discounted present value.[2] In effect, we utilize the model of value discussed in Chapter 1, where we said that a firm's value equals

$$\text{Present value of expected cash flows} = \sum_{t=1}^{n} \frac{\text{net cash flow}_t}{(1+k)^t}. \qquad (14.4)$$

This equation was used in Chapter 1 to evaluate an entire firm.[3] Now we use it to evaluate a specific investment project.

Before calculating the net present value of a project, one must decide on the value of the appropriate discount rate, or cost of capital, which is represented by $k$ in equation (14.4). The ways in which the cost of capital can be estimated are discussed in detail in subsequent sections of this chapter. For now, we simply take the value of $k$ as given.

Assuming that the outlays for the investment project all occur in the current year, the net present value of a project equals

$$\text{NPV} = \sum_{t=1}^{n} \frac{F_t}{(1+k)^t} - I, \qquad (14.5)$$

---

[2] This does not mean that other techniques, such as the use of the payback period, are not in use, or that they are not reasonable approximations under some circumstances. However, in general, they cannot be counted on to provide the same answers as the techniques described here.

To simplify the exposition, we assume in this chapter that sales are for cash and that all costs (other than depreciation) are cash expenses. Throughout this chapter, an understanding of compound interest is assumed. Readers who need to review this material (or take it up for the first time) are referred to Appendix A.

[3] In Chapter 1, we sometimes assumed for simplicity that cash flow is the same as profit. No such assumption is made here. Also, $i$, rather than $k$, was used to represent the interest rate.

where $F_t$ equals incremental, after-tax net cash flow in year $t$, and $I$ equals the investment outlay for the project (assumed to occur in year 0). *If a project's NPV is greater than zero, the project should be accepted; if not, it should be rejected.* This simple rule dictates which of the investment proposals should be implemented.

## *NET PRESENT VALUE AND INTERNAL RATE OF RETURN*

Another measure of the profitability of a proposed investment project is its **internal rate of return**, which is defined as the interest rate that equates the present value of the net cash flow from the project to the project's investment outlay. To calculate the internal rate of return, we simply set the project's NPV equal to zero, which means that

$$\text{NPV} = \sum_{t=1}^{n} \frac{F_t}{(1 + k^*)^t} - I = 0. \tag{14.6}$$

Then we must solve this equation for the interest rate, $k^*$, which makes NPV equal to zero. This interest rate is the one that equates the present value of the net cash flows from the project to the project's investment outlay. It is the project's internal rate of return.

To solve equation (14.6) to find the internal rate of return, the following trial-and-error procedure generally is used. To begin with, an interest rate is chosen arbitrarily. If NPV based on this interest rate is positive, then the arbitrarily chosen interest rate must be lower than the internal rate of return, so another, *higher* rate must be tried. If NPV based on the arbitrarily chosen interest rate is negative, this interest rate must be higher than the internal rate of return, so another, *lower* rate must be tried. If this trial-and-error procedure is repeated, one eventually finds the interest rate where the NPV is approximately zero. This is the internal rate of return. (For an illustration, see pages A6 to A7 of Appendix A.) Although this procedure is laborious if done by hand, computers can perform the required calculations very quickly.

In Figure 14.1, we said that to maximize profit, a firm should accept all projects where the internal rate of return exceeds the marginal cost of capital. If a firm uses the decision rule in the previous section (that is, if it accepts all projects if and only if their NPV is greater than zero), the results are basically the same.[4] To see this, note that if the NPV of a project, using the firm's cost of capital as the interest rate, is positive, this means that the internal rate of return from the project exceeds the cost of capital. On the other hand, if the NPV is negative, this means that the internal rate of

---

[4] However, as pointed out in the next section, there sometimes can be differences. For mutually exclusive projects, the ranking can be different.

## REDESIGNING A PRODUCT LINE AT BLACK AND DECKER

Recognizing that increased foreign competition was imminent and believing that legal requirements would soon require double insulation of domestic power tools, Black and Decker, a manufacturer of power tools, invested over $17 million in a program during the 1970s to redesign its product line, simplify its products, reduce production costs, automate production, standardize components, use new materials, raise product performance, and improve quality. (Recall Chapter 1.) A graph showing the cumulative net cash flow from this project is shown below:

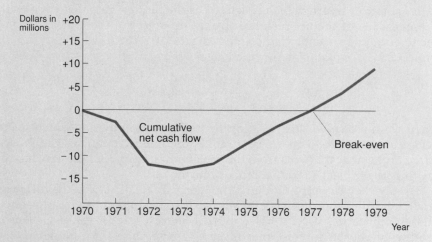

(a) Using the above data, Black and Decker calculated that the internal rate of return from this project was 30 percent. What does this mean? How can one calculate such a rate of return from the above data? (b) What is the significance of the "break-even" point shown in this graph? (c) Expenditures on development engineering and manufacturing technology constituted about $3.5 million of this investment. Is it correct to include such expenditures in an analysis of this sort, given that they arc not expenditures on plant or equipment? (d) Before this project was undertaken, what techniques could have been used to estimate the internal rate of return from this project? How accurate are these techniques?

*Solution* (a) The internal rate of return is the interest rate that sets the net present value of the project equal to zero. In other words, it is the interest rate that equates the present value of the net cash flow from the project to the project's investment outlay. The internal rate of return can be calculated from the cash flows in the graph, using equation (14.6). However, data for years after 1979 should be included. (b) This is the year when the cumulative net cash flow equals zero. In other words, the project has earned cash flows equal to the investment. (c) Yes, they are part of the total investment. (d) The firm could have estimated the cash flows, as discussed on pages 540 to 543. While such estimates frequently are not very accurate, they constitute useful, if rough, bases for decision making.*

* For further discussion, see A. Lehnerd, "Revitalizing the Manufacture and Design of Mature Global Products," in *Technology and Global Industry* (Washington, D.C.: National Academy Press, 1987).

return is less than the cost of capital. Consequently, if a firm accepts projects only if their NPV exceeds zero, this amounts to accepting only projects where the internal rate of return exceeds the cost of capital.[5]

# THE HARTMAN COMPANY: A NUMERICAL EXAMPLE

To illustrate how the net present value technique is used, consider the Hartman Company, a tool and die manufacturer, which can invest in two machines, $C$ and $D$, each costing \$25,000 and each expected to result in the increased cash inflows shown in Table 14.2. Because the cash flows from machine $C$ are riskier than those from machine $D$, Hartman's controller

TABLE 14.2    *Calculation of Net Present Value for Machines $C$ and $D$*

| | Machine C | | | | Machine D | | |
|---|---|---|---|---|---|---|---|
| | Cash flow | $\left(\dfrac{1}{1+.15}\right)^t$ | | | Cash flow | $\left(\dfrac{1}{1+.10}\right)^t$ | |
| Year(t) | (1) | (2) | (1) × (2) | Year(t) | (1) | (2) | (1) × (2) |
| 1 | 11,000 | .870 | 9,570 | 1 | 10,000 | .909 | 9,090 |
| 2 | 10,000 | .756 | 7,560 | 2 | 12,000 | .826 | 9,912 |
| 3 | 9,000 | .658 | 5,922 | 3 | 8,000 | .751 | 6,008 |
| 4 | 8,000 | .572 | 4,576 | 4 | 7,000 | .683 | 4,781 |
| Total | | | 27,628 | Total | | | 29,791 |
| | | Less cost | −25,000 | | | Less cost | −25,000 |
| | | NPV$_C$ | 2,628 | | | NPV$_D$ | 4,791 |

[5] One problem with the use of the internal rate of return is that there may be more than one value of $k^*$ that satisfies equation (14.6). In other words, there may be no unique value of the internal rate of return. However, for the typical investment project, there is an initial period when cash flows are negative, followed by a period when cash flows are positive. Under these circumstances, there is a unique internal rate of return.

indicates that machine $C$ should be evaluated with a cost of capital equal to 15 percent, whereas 10 percent should be used for machine $D$. (Recall from Chapter 13 that this is a way of adjusting for differences in risk.)

To obtain the value of NPV for machine $C$, we can use equation (14.5). Since $k = .15$, $n = 4$, $I = \$25,000$, and the values of $F_t$ are as shown in Table 14.2, it follows that

$$NPV_C = (11,000)\left(\frac{1}{1+.15}\right) + (10,000)\left(\frac{1}{1+.15}\right)^2$$

$$+ (9,000)\left(\frac{1}{1+.15}\right)^3 + (8,000)\left(\frac{1}{1+.15}\right)^4 - 25,000 = \$2,628.$$

The values of $1 \div (1 + .15)$, $[1 \div (1 + .15)]^2$, $[1 \div (1 + .15)]^3$, and $[1 \div (1 + .15)]^4$ are given in Table 14.2. (See Appendix Table 1 for the values of $[1 \div (1 + k)]^t$ corresponding to various values of $k$ and $t$. In Appendix Table 1, the symbol $i$, rather than $k$, is used, but this, of course, does not affect the numerical results.)

Equation (14.5) can also be used to calculate the NPV value for machine $D$. Since $k = .10$, $n = 4$, $I = \$25,000$, and the values of $F_t$ are as shown in Table 14.2,

$$NPV_D = (10,000)\left(\frac{1}{1+.10}\right) + (12,000)\left(\frac{1}{1+.10}\right)^2$$

$$+ (8,000)\left(\frac{1}{1+.10}\right)^3 + (7,000)\left(\frac{1}{1+.10}\right)^4 - 25,000 = \$4,791.$$

Since both machines $C$ and $D$ have positive NPVs, they should both be accepted if they are independent. Machine $C$ increases the value of the firm by $\$2,628$; machine $D$ increases it by $\$4,791$. If they are mutually exclusive investments, machine $D$ should be chosen, since it adds more to the value of the firm than does machine $C$.

Firms sometimes use the internal rate of return, rather than NPV, to select investment projects. According to this approach, projects are ranked by their internal rate of return, and those whose rate of return exceeds the risk-adjusted cost of capital are chosen. While this approach will result in the same decision to accept or reject a particular project as the NPV criterion, it can result in a different decision regarding mutually exclusive projects. This is because one project can have a higher internal rate of return but lower NPV based on the firm's cost of capital. Under the internal rate of return approach, the implied reinvestment rate for cash flows equals the internal rate of return, whereas under the NPV approach, it equals the cost of capital used in equation (14.5). Since it generally is more realistic to assume that cash flows are reinvested at an interest rate approximating the cost of capital (rather than the internal rate of return), the NPV approach usually is preferred.

## COST OF CAPITAL: DEBT

The firm's cost of capital is of central importance in capital budgeting. Although the measurement of a firm's cost of capital is a highly technical and complex topic, we can establish the basic concepts here. Firms raise funds in a variety of ways—by borrowing from banks and other financial institutions, by selling bonds, by issuing stock, by retaining part of their previous earnings, and by leasing, among others. The two principal sources of funds are **debt** and **equity,** each of which has its own cost. In this section, we consider the cost of debt.

The cost to the firm of debt capital is the rate of return that must be paid to the investors. If the price at which the debt securities are offered is $P$ and the interest payments per period are $I$, this rate of return equals $k_d$, where

$$P = \sum_{t=1}^{n} \frac{I}{(1 + k_d)^t} + \frac{U}{(1 + k_d)^n} \qquad (14.7)$$

and $U$ is the principal amount to be repaid $n$ periods after the securities are offered. To find the cost of debt capital, we must solve equation (14.7) for $k_d$. (The same procedure used on page 545 and in Appendix A to find an internal rate of return can be employed to determine the value of $k_d$.)

New long-term debt is often issued by firms at par or close to it. In other words, the price is set at $1,000 per bond, and the coupon interest rate is established at the level required by investors. If this is the case, the after-tax cost of debt capital is

$$\text{Coupon interest rate} \times (1 - t), \qquad (14.8)$$

where $t$ is the marginal tax rate. For example, suppose that the Jones Corporation sells $50 million of 9 percent bonds that are due in 2010 at par. If the corporate marginal tax rate is 40 percent, the after-tax cost of debt is $9(1 - .4)$, or 5.4 percent, since the coupon interest rate is 9 percent and the marginal tax rate is 0.4. Of course, this neglects flotation costs, but they tend to be a relatively small proportion of the total debt issued.

## COST OF INTERNAL EQUITY

As pointed out in the previous section, firms raise equity capital as well as float debt. The cost of equity capital is the equilibrium rate of return required by the investors in the firm's common stock. There are two ways to raise equity: through retained earnings and through the sale of new common stock. In this and the following section, we consider the cost of equity capital raised internally (that is, through retained earnings), after which we take up the cost of capital raised by the sale of new common stock.

One way to evaluate the cost of internal equity is through the use of the so-called **dividend-valuation model**. To the owner of common stock, the value of his or her wealth (in the firm) equals the present value of the expected future returns generated by the firm, these returns being discounted at the shareholder's required rate of return, $k_s$. Generally, these future returns are of two kinds: the receipt of dividends by the shareholder and/or the increase in the market value of the stock (commonly called a capital gain).

If the shareholder intends to hold the stock indefinitely, the shareholder's wealth (in the firm) is

$$W = \sum_{t=1}^{\infty} \frac{D_t}{(1 + k_s)^t} \tag{14.9}$$

where $D_t$ is the dividend he or she receives from the firm in period $t$. If the shareholder sells the stock after $n$ periods, his or her wealth (from the firm) is

$$W = \sum_{t=1}^{n} \frac{D_t}{(1 + k_s)^t} + \frac{M}{(1 + k_s)^n} \tag{14.10}$$

where $M$ is the value of the shareholder's stock in period $n$ when it is sold. But since $M$ is the present value of the future returns subsequent to period $n$,

$$M = \sum_{t=n+1}^{\infty} \frac{D_t}{(1 + k_s)^{t-n}}$$

which means that equations (14.9) and (14.10) are really identical.

Assuming that the dividends of the firm will grow forever at a constant compound rate of $g$ per year (see Figure 14.3), equation (14.9) implies that

$$W = \frac{D_1}{k_s - g} \tag{14.11}$$

where $D_1$ is the dividend paid next year. If $D_1$ is expressed as the dividend per share of stock, then $W$ is the market price per share of stock. Solving for $k_s$, we find that

$$k_s = \frac{D_1}{W} + g. \tag{14.12}$$

To estimate the cost of internal equity, this expression can be used.

As an illustration, consider the Miller Electronics Company. The current price of a share of its common stock is $40. Its dividend per share next year is estimated to be $2.32. In the past 15 years, its dividend per share has been growing at an annual rate of 6 percent, and this rate of increase seems likely to continue in the future. Since $D_1 = 2.32$, $W = 40$, and $g = .06$,

$$k_s = \frac{2.32}{40} + .06 = .118.$$

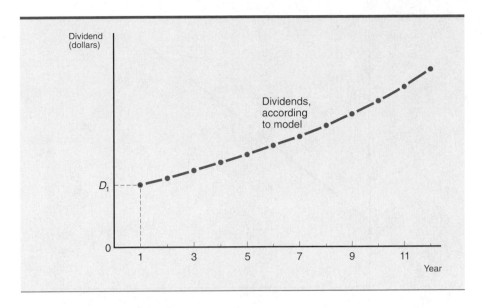

*FIGURE 14.3   Prospective Growth in the Firm's Annual Dividends, According to the Dividend-Valuation Model*   Dividends are assumed to increase at a constant rate of g per year. (Here, $g = 0.10$.)

In other words, the cost of internal equity for this firm seems to be about 11.8 percent.

## THE CAPITAL ASSET PRICING MODEL

Another way of estimating the cost of internal equity is based on the **capital asset pricing model**. This theory is concerned with the trade-off between risk and expected return for securities. It says that the rate of return required by investors is composed of a risk-free rate of return, $r_f$, plus a premium that compensates the investor for taking the risk. This risk premium, which varies from stock to stock, is greater for stocks whose returns are highly variable than for those whose returns are stable and dependable.

Figure 14.4 shows the **security market line**, the relationship between risk and expected return for all stocks in the market. Two points on this line pertain to the Jones Corporation and the Martin Company. For stock in the Jones Corporation, the risk is relatively low, so the expected return is low as well. For stock in the Martin Company, the risk is relatively high, so the expected return is relatively high too. The security market line's intercept on the vertical axis is $r_f$, the risk-free rate of return. Risk is defined as the variability of the returns. In terms of the capital asset pricing model, total

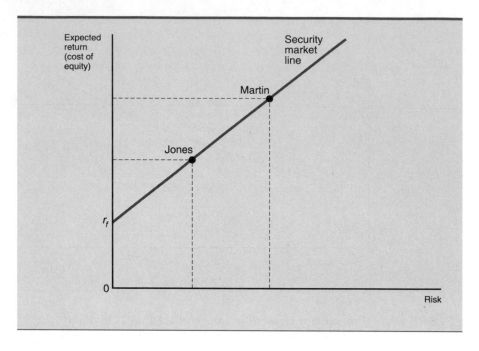

**FIGURE 14.4** *Security Market Line*   This line shows the relationship between risk and expected return for all stocks in the market.

variability of returns is not the relevant concept of risk. Total variability consists of two parts: the variability that is unique to a security and the variability that affects all securities. Only the latter concept of risk is relevant.

To see why this is the case, note that the variability of returns that is unique to a security—the **unsystematic** risk—can be minimized or eliminated if the investor diversifies his or her portfolio. This variability is caused by strikes, natural disasters, failure of major new products, and other such factors. By buying a wide variety of stocks, these factors will average out. But the variability of returns that affects all securities—the **systematic** or **nondiversifiable** risk—cannot be reduced in this way. Systematic risk is due to cyclical changes in the economy and other broad movements that affect all stocks.

The security market line can be used to estimate the cost of internal equity. To do so, one must estimate the systematic risk of individual stocks. *Beta, the slope of the regression line showing the relationship between a particular stock's returns and the returns for a market index, is a measure of the systematic risk of a stock.* The stock market as a whole has a beta of 1.0. Stocks whose prices fluctuate less than the market as a whole have betas below 1.0. For example, if a stock has a beta of 0.3, this means that a 10 percent increase in market returns tends to be associated with a 3 percent increase in this security's returns. Stocks whose prices fluctuate more than the market as a whole have betas above 1.0. For example, if a stock has a beta of 1.3, this means that a 10 percent increase in market returns tends to be associated with a 13 percent increase in this security's returns.

To use the capital asset pricing model to estimate the cost of equity capital, we calculate

$$k_e = r_f + b(k_m - r_f),\qquad(14.13)$$

where $k_m$ is the expected return on the market as a whole (or the average stock). The value $(k_m - r_f)$ is the risk premium on the average stock (which has a beta of 1.0). If we multiply this price of risk by $b$, which is a particular stock's beta (a measure of this stock's risk), we get the risk premium for this particular stock, which is $b(k_m - r_f)$. Adding this risk premium to $r_f$ (the risk-free rate of return), we get $k_e$, the stock's required return, which is used as the cost of equity capital.

To illustrate, consider the Johnson Corporation. If the beta for its stock is 0.7, if the risk-free rate of return is 7 percent, and if the rate of return on the average stock is 12 percent, it follows that $b = 0.7$, $r_f = .07$, and $k_m = .12$. If we insert these values into equation (14.13), we find that the required rate of return for its stock is

$$k_e = .07 + .7(.12 - .07) = .105,$$

or 10.5 percent. This is an estimate of its cost of equity capital. Had its beta been 1.5, an indication that its stock was above average in risk, the estimate of its cost of equity capital would have been

$$k_e = .07 + 1.5(.12 - .07) = .145,$$

or 14.5 percent.[6]

## COST OF EXTERNAL EQUITY

A firm can raise equity capital through the sale of new common stock, as well as through retained earnings. However, the costs of floating the new stock are large enough so that they must be taken into account. Also, it must be recognized that the selling price of the new stock must be less than the market price of the stock before the announcement of the issuance of the new stock. Otherwise the new stock could not be expected to sell.

Assuming that the firm's dividends will grow forever at a constant compound rate of g per year, the cost of external equity is

$$k_x = \frac{D_1}{W^1} + g,\qquad(14.14)$$

[6] In early 1992, Eugene Fama and Kenneth French of the University of Chicago published an influential paper challenging the role and influence of beta. For many years, the capital asset pricing model has been subjected to criticisms of a variety of sorts. While it is worthwhile to recognize that this is (and has been) an area of controversy, the details must be left to specialized courses on corporate finance.

where $W^1$ is the net proceeds per share to the firm from the new stock offering. Since equation (14.14) is analogous to equation (14.12), its meaning and rationale should be clear.

As an example of how equation (14.14) can be used, suppose the Miller Electronics Company can sell new stock at $38 per share (after deducting the costs of floating the stock). Recall that its dividend per share, which next year is estimated to be $2.32, is expected to grow at 6 percent per year. Thus,

$$k_x = \frac{2.32}{38} + .06 = .121,$$

or 12.1 percent.

## WEIGHTED COST OF CAPITAL

In previous sections, we described how one can estimate the cost of debt, internal equity, and external equity. At this point, two things should be stressed. First, the capital whose cost should be estimated is the marginal capital to be raised by the firm, not the cost of the capital the firm has raised in the past. Second, firms normally do not decide the extent to which equity or debt financing will be used for each particular project. The proportions of debt and equity financing are assumed to be the same for all projects— and to be equal to those in the firm's desired financial structure.

The value of the cost of capital, $k_a$, which should be used to calculate an investment's net present value, is a weighted average of the costs of debt and equity, the weights being the proportions of debt and equity financing in the firm's desired financial structure. If $P_d$ is the proportion of debt financing and $P_e$ is the proportion of equity financing in the firm's desired financial structure (and if $P_d + P_e = 1$),

$$k_a = P_d k_d + P_e k_e, \tag{14.15}$$

where $k_a$ is the weighted cost of capital, $k_d$ is the cost of debt, and $k_e$ is the cost of equity.

If a firm's after-tax cost of debt is 7 percent and its cost of equity is 14 percent, and if this firm has decided to finance all its investment projects next year through debt, it may seem obvious that this firm's weighted cost of capital is 7 percent. After all, it is using debt alone—and no equity—to finance next year's projects. But this reasoning contains a fundamental flaw. Suppose that if this firm finances these projects with debt, it exhausts some of its ability to obtain new, low-cost debt. As expansion occurs in the future, the firm at some point will have to employ additional equity financing; otherwise, its ratio of debt to total assets will be too large. Under these circumstances, 7 percent is not really the firm's opportunity cost for this kind of capital.

To see this more clearly, assume that the firm is considering a very large volume of investment projects for next year, all of which yield a return of 8 percent. If this firm's cost of capital is 7 percent, these projects should be accepted. But suppose that if these projects are accepted, the firm will use up its debt capacity, and will have to turn to equity financing, which, as indicated above, costs 14 percent. Then if there are investment projects proposed in the year after next that yield 13 percent, they will be rejected because their return would be less than the 14 percent cost of the money. Clearly, something is wrong, since projects yielding 8 percent have crowded out projects yielding 13 percent. The answer is that the firm's cost of capital should be computed as a weighted average of the costs of the various kinds of financing used. In accord with equation (14.15), the weights should be the proportion of various kinds of financing in the firm's desired financial structure.

An enormous amount of controversy has raged over whether—and if so, how—a firm's financial structure (in particular, its ratio of debt to equity capital) can affect its overall value. The traditional view was that a firm could lower its weighted cost of capital and raise its market value per share by using moderate amounts of debt. This view was challenged by Nobel laureates Franco Modigliani of MIT and Merton Miller of the University of Chicago. The issues involved are matters that are more appropriately taken up in courses on corporate finance.

It is important to recognize that the estimation of a firm's weighted cost of capital may be difficult and complex. The methods (described in earlier sections) of estimating the costs of equity and debt capital are not always easy to apply. For example, if you want to use equation (14.12) to estimate the cost of equity capital, you may have trouble finding an estimate of $g$ in which you have confidence. While capital budgeting techniques are of great practical importance, it is a mistake to think that they are simple rules that can be applied in a cut-and-dried fashion.

# THE POST-AUDIT: NATURE AND IMPORTANCE

As indicated in Figure 14.2, the last step in the process of capital budgeting is to review the projects after implementation. Such a post-completion audit, or post-audit, includes a comparison of the actual results of each investment project with the results that were forecasted in the investment proposal and an analysis of why forecasting (and other) errors occurred. Such a post-audit should not be a witch hunt. Projects often fail to meet expectations for reasons that have little to do with the competence (or lack of it) of the relevant executives. For example, few people predicted the precipitous fall in stock prices in 1987. If managers feel they will be held responsible for errors of this sort, they will tend to be overly cautious—and less aggressive and effective.

But if post-audits of this sort are carried out with the constructive objective of improving forecasting procedures and selection methods, they can

## DECIDING WHETHER TO INSTALL AN AUTOMATED MANUFACTURING SYSTEM*

A manufacturer of air-handling equipment had to decide whether or not to install a highly automated manufacturing system in its plant. This system, which would make a key component that had been manufactured with conventional equipment (with an average age of 23 years), would reduce the number of employees needed from 52 to 14, cut scrap and rework by $60,000 annually, and pare inventories from $2 million to about $1 million. Many of the firm's managers were excited about the potential benefits from the proposed new system.

But there were doubts about whether the investment in the new system would be profitable. The estimated after-tax cash flows (in thousands of dollars) from the investment were as follows:

| Year | After-tax cash flow | Year | After-tax cash flow |
|------|---------------------|------|---------------------|
| 0 | −7,380 | 6 | 714 |
| 1 | 1,370 | 7 | 714 |
| 2 | 1,675 | 8 | 714 |
| 3 | 1,632 | 9 | 714 |
| 4 | 1,632 | 10 | 714 |
| 5 | 1,632 | | |

Given that the new system would provide important intangible benefits, such as virtually unlimited flexibility to modify the mix of component models to the exact requirements of the assembly department, the firm's managers felt that they would be willing to accept only a 10 percent rate of return from the investment.

If you were a consultant to this firm, would you advise the firm's managers to invest in the new system?

* This section is based on an actual case, although some modifications have been made. For further discussion, see R. Kaplan, "Must CIM Be Justified by Faith Alone?"

be very valuable. For example, a leading pharmaceutical firm did a post-audit of its selection of research and development projects. Among other things, it found that the forecasts made by its executives of the costs of such projects tended to be biased downward, as shown in Table 14.3. This resulted in too many of these projects being accepted. After revising and improving its forecasting procedures, the firm's performance in this regard improved considerably.

TABLE 14.3   *Ratio of Actual to Forecasted Cost, 49 Projects, Major Pharmaceutical Firm*

| Ratio of actual to forecasted cost | Number of projects |
|---|---|
| Less than 1.01 | 6 |
| 1.01 and under 2.01 | 24 |
| 2.01 and under 3.01 | 16 |
| 3.01 and under 4.01 | 3 |
| Total | 49 |

*Source:* E. Mansfield, J. Rapoport, J. Schnee, S. Wagner, and M. Hamburger, *Research and Innovation in the Modern Corporation* (New York: Norton, 1971). This table also appeared on page 285.

# COMMON PITFALLS TO AVOID

In recent years, leading experts have criticized the way in which some firms use the capital budgeting techniques described in this chapter. In particular, they charge that American manufacturing firms have tended to underinvest in advanced automation (such as robots and flexible manufacturing systems) because of improper application of these techniques.[7] It is important that the following four pitfalls be noted.

1. *Firms frequently overestimate their cost of capital.* According to many experts, firms often use an estimate of the cost of capital that is too high, perhaps in the mistaken belief that it is a good idea to screen out all but the most profitable projects. This is wrong, because so long as a project's rate of return exceeds the firm's true cost of capital, its acceptance will increase the firm's value.

2. *Firms frequently assume that if they do not invest in new equipment, their profits will stay at current levels.* As stressed in previous sections, the cash flows used in capital budgeting are incremental; that is, they reflect the difference between what will occur if the project is carried out and what will happen if it is rejected. In some cases, if the project is not carried out, the firm's earnings will drop because it will not be able to compete effectively. If this is not recognized, the profitability of the project will be underestimated.

3. *Firms frequently omit the effects on cash flows of factors that cannot easily be quantified.* Advanced automation can result in a variety of benefits—better quality, greater flexibility, reduced floor space and inventory, lower throughput times, and experience with new technology—that are neglected by many firm's managers because they are hard to quantify. By

[7] For example, see R. Kaplan, "Must CIM Be Justified by Faith Alone?" *Harvard Business Review* (March–April 1986), reprinted in E. Mansfield, ed., *Managerial Economics and Operations Research,* 5th ed. (New York: Norton, 1987).

arbitrarily treating these benefits as if they were zero, these firms bias their analyses against the acceptance of various forms of advanced automation.

4. *Firms frequently create biases favoring small-scale, evolutionary projects and discouraging more ambitious ones.* In many companies, different levels of authorization must be obtained depending on the size of the project. For example, projects costing less than $100,000 may require only the approval of the plant manager, whereas those costing several million dollars may need the approval of the board of directors. One unintended result is that managers have an incentive to propose small projects where higher level approval is not needed, even though this fragmentation may not be best for the firm as a whole.

## SUMMARY

1. The investment selection process is composed of four steps. (a) The firm must generate proposals for alternative investment projects. (b) For each of these proposed projects, it must estimate cash flows for the project. (c) It must evaluate each of the proposed projects, and select those to be implemented. (d) It should review the projects after implementation.

2. For each proposed project, the difference between the cash flows with and without the project should be estimated each year on an after-tax basis. Indirect effects of the project on parts of the firm's activities seemingly far removed from the investment should be taken into account if the firm's cash flows are impacted.

3. If the outlays for an investment project all occur in the current year, the net present value of the project equals $\sum_{t=1}^{n} F_t/(1 + k)^t - I$, where $F_t$ equals the cash flow in year $t$, and $I$ equals the investment outlay. If a project's net present value is greater than zero, it should be accepted; if not, it should be rejected.

4. Another measure of the profitability of a proposed project is its internal rate of return, which is defined as the interest rate that equates the present value of the net cash flows from the project to its investment outlay. Generally, if a firm accepts projects where the internal rate of return exceeds the firm's cost of capital, the results are the same as they would be if the net present value criterion were used.[8]

5. The cost to the firm of debt capital is the rate of return that must be paid to the investors. New long-term debt is often issued by firms at (or close to) par. If so, the after-tax cost of debt capital is the coupon interest rate times $(1 - t)$, where $t$ is the firm's marginal tax rate.

6. The cost of equity capital is the equilibrium rate of return required by

[8] However, recall note 4.

the investors in the firm's common stock. Assuming that the firm's dividends per share will increase at a constant compound annual rate of g, the cost of internal equity is $(D_1/W) + g$, where $D_1$ is next year's annual dividend, and $W$ is the price per share of the firm's stock. The capital asset pricing model can also be used to estimate the cost of equity capital.

7. In calculating the net present value of a project, the firm should base the interest rate, $k$, on the weighted cost of capital, which is the weighted average of the costs of debt and equity capital.

8. The interest rate, $k$, should also be modified to reflect the riskiness of the project, as well as the attitudes of the firm's decision makers with regard to risk. The ways such modifications can be made have already been described in Chapter 13.

## PROBLEMS

1. The Secane Electronics Company is considering a $2 million investment in new manufacturing equipment. Secane's cash inflow would be reduced by $2 million this year. In the next 4 years, Secane's managers believe that its production costs will decline by $200,000 per year, its inspection costs will go down by $300,000 per year, and its revenues will rise by $150,000 per year, if the new equipment is installed. The new equipment will be depreciated over 4 years (using straight-line depreciation) with zero salvage value at the end of the 4-year period. The firm's marginal tax rate is 40 percent.

   (a) Determine the incremental after-tax cash flow each year from this investment.

   (b) If the marginal tax rate were 50 percent, not 40 percent, what would be the incremental after-tax cash flow each year?

   (c) If inspection costs were to go down by $200,000, not $300,000, per year (and if the marginal tax rate were 50 percent), what would be the incremental after-tax cash flow each year?

2. Hugh Cohen must determine whether to invest $20,000 in his own business or in another local business. Both investment projects have an expected life of five years. The incremental after-tax cash flow each year after the investment is made has the following probability distribution in each case:

| Investment in his own business | | Investment in another local business | |
|---|---|---|---|
| Probability | Annual cash flow | Probability | Annual cash flow |
| .10 | 4,900 | .20 | 4,100 |
| .40 | 5,500 | .30 | 5,800 |
| .35 | 6,500 | .25 | 7,000 |
| .15 | 7,200 | .25 | 8,000 |
| Total 1.00 | | Total 1.00 | |

Mr. Cohen decides to use a 20 percent cost of capital for the riskier project and a 15 percent cost of capital for the less risky one.

(a) What is the expected value each year of the incremental after-tax cash flow from each investment project?

(b) What discount rate is used for each project? Why does Mr. Cohen use different discount rates for the two projects?

(c) What is the risk-adjusted net present value of each project?

3. If the Hassman Company buys a particular machine in 1995, the effect will be that the firm's cash inflow will be reduced by $10,000 in 1995, and the firm's cash inflow will be increased by $2,000 annually from 1996 to 2002.

(a) If the discount rate is .10, should the firm buy this machine?

(b) If the discount rate is .20, should the firm buy this machine?

(c) What factors determine what discount rate the firm should use?

4. The Richmond Company is trying to determine whether to buy a type A or type B machine tool. The price of a type A machine tool is $80,000, while the price of a type B machine tool is $50,000. Each machine tool will last 6 years, after which its scrap value will be zero. Each machine tool produces the same quantity and quality of output, but the type A machine tool requires 2,000 hours of labor per year, whereas the type B machine tool requires 5,000 hours of labor per year.

(a) Richmond's president says that so long as the hourly wage rate exceeds $2.30 an hour, the present value of the extra labor saving with a type A machine (relative to the type B machine) exceeds the extra investment in the type A machine (relative to the type B machine). Is she correct? (The interest rate is 10 percent.)

(b) From the above data, can we be sure that the firm should buy either machine tool?

(c) Write a brief memorandum criticizing the analysis in part (a) as a means of deciding which machine tool to buy.

5. Richard Miller is trying to decide whether to install aluminum siding on his house. As matters stand, his house has wood siding, which must be painted every year at an annual cost of $500. If he installs aluminum siding now, it will cost $2,000, and the need for painting will be eliminated. If he does not install aluminum siding, he will paint the house now, a year from now, 2 years from now, 3 years from now, and 4 years from now. Then he plans to sell the house. He believes that he will be able to get no more for the house if he installs the aluminum siding than he would if he did not install it.

(a) If Mr. Miller can get 8 percent on alternative investments, should he install the aluminum siding?

(b) If Mr. Miller can get 10 percent on alternative investments, should he install the aluminum siding?

(c) How can the results of parts (a) and (b) be used by sellers of aluminum siding?

6. The Adams Company's common stock sells currently at $75 per share. Its dividend per share next year is estimated to be $4. In the past 20

years, its dividend per share has been increasing at a 5 percent annual rate, and this rate of growth is expected to continue in the future.

(a) What is the cost of internal equity capital for this firm?

(b) If the firm's common stock were to sell for $60, not $75, what would be the cost of internal equity capital?

(c) If the dividend per share were to increase at 6 percent, not 5 percent (and if the common stock price were $60), what would be the cost of internal capital?

7. The Jefferson Corporation wants to estimate its cost of internal equity capital. The beta for its stock is 0.8, the risk-free rate of return is 8 percent, and the rate of return on the average stock is 14 percent.

(a) Define what beta means.

(b) What is this firm's cost of internal equity capital?

(c) If its beta had been 1.7 rather than 0.8, what would have been its cost of internal equity capital?

(d) If its beta had been 1.0 rather than 0.8, what would have been its cost of internal equity capital?

8. A major oil company recently evaluated a proposed investment in improvements in visbreakers, a particular type of petroleum refining equipment. According to the company's analysts, such improvements would require an investment of $15 million and would result in an incremental after-tax cash inflow of $2 million per year for the following 9 years. Thus, if the investment were made in 1993, the effect on the firm's cash flow would be as follows:

| Year | Effects on cash flow (millions of dollars) | Year | Effect on cash flow (millions of dollars) |
|------|------|------|------|
| 1993 | −15 | 1998 | 2 |
| 1994 | 2 | 1999 | 2 |
| 1995 | 2 | 2000 | 2 |
| 1996 | 2 | 2001 | 2 |
| 1997 | 2 | 2002 | 2 |

(a) If the interest rate is 10 percent, what is the present value of this investment?

(b) If cost overruns result in the investment being $20 million rather than $15 million, what is the present value of the investment?

(c) In fact, the oil company decided not to carry out this investment project. Was this a wise decision? Why or why not?

9. The Madison Company's controller wants to estimate the internal rate of return from a proposed investment in a new supermarket. If the supermarket is built in 1994, it will cost $20 million. The net profit per year (after deducting depreciation) is estimated to be $4 million. This profit is estimated to continue for 5 years, beginning in 1995. Straight-line depreciation (over 5 years) will be used, the salvage value after 5 years will be zero, and the marginal tax rate is 40 percent.

(a) Determine the incremental after-tax cash flow each year from the investment in the supermarket.

(b) What are the disadvantages in the internal rate of return as a measure of the profitability of an investment project?

(c) What is the internal rate of return from the investment in the supermarket?

10. The Brown Construction and Management Company is considering two possible locations, one in Texas and one in Louisiana, where it may construct a plant and run it to produce plastic toys. The price per toy, as well as relevant cost data, for each location is given:

|  | Texas | Louisiana |
| --- | --- | --- |
| Estimated investment required to construct plant | $4,500,000 | $5,000,000 |
| Estimated price per toy | 3.00 | 3.20 |
| Production cost per toy | 0.60 | .70 |
| Marketing cost per toy | 0.40 | .40 |
| Annual sales volume (number of toys) | 500,000 | 550,000 |

In both locations, the investment in plant will occur this year, and the profits will occur for each of the next 6 years. Straight-line depreciation of the investment in plant (over 6 years) will be used, the salvage value will be zero, and the marginal tax rate is 30 percent.

(a) What is the after-tax cash flow each year from the investment at each location?

(b) If the cost of capital is 10 percent, what is the net present value of the project in Texas?

(c) If the cost of capital is 10 percent, what is the net present value of the project in Louisiana?

## HOW AMALGAMATED METALS DECIDED TO EXPAND ITS HEAT-TREATING CAPACITY*

In early 1981, the vice president of manufacturing of Amalgamated Metals directed his staff to put together a capital authorization request for the expansion of the firm's heat-treating capacity. The proposed new continuous heat-treating line had two novel elements: a continuous flow process and a computerized control system. Tom Rollins, an industrial engineer, carried out a discounted cash flow analysis of the project's financial value. As the analysis went on, it became obvious that there were considerable uncertainties concerning sales volumes and profit margins. The proposed new heat-treating line would produce materials with greater strength and greater consistency than those made with the existing process, but it was hard to tell whether customers would be willing to pay a premium for these features.

Using estimates obtained from the manufacturing, marketing, and engineering departments, Rollins calculated the project's annual cash flows. The marketing department was unwilling to provide sales forecasts for more than 4 years after the project's start-up; and since the useful life of the new equipment was believed to be about 20 years, Rollins assumed that the sales (and profit margins) in subsequent years would be the same as in the fourth year after start-up. The resulting analysis, which indicated that the internal rate of return from the project was 13 percent, was approved by the vice president for manufacturing, but the division general manager was dissatisfied, since he felt that an internal rate of return of 13 percent was too low to justify the project, given the uncertainty attached to the sales estimates.

Making new assumptions about sales and profit margins, Rollins came up with a new analysis, shown in the following table:

TABLE 1   *Financial Analysis of Continuous Heat-Treating Line (All Figures in Thousands of Dollars)*

| Year | Investment | Pretax cash flow | Operating total after-tax cash flow† |
|------|------------|------------------|--------------------------------------|
| 1 | $ 7,200 | $      0 | $ −7,200 |
| 2 | 35,200 | $      0 | −35,200 |
| 3 | 36,000 | $      0 | −36,000 |
| 4 | 1,600 | 18,080 | 9,440 |
| 5 | 0 | 20,480 | 12,240 |
| 6 | 0 | 24,160 | 14,080 |
| 7 | 0 | 25,840 | 14,920 |
| . | . | . | . |
| . | . | . | . |
| . | . | . | . |
| 23 | 0 | 25,840 | 14,920 |
| Present value at 10% | | | $ 26,869 |
| Internal rate of return | | | 15% |

† After-tax cash flow = (pretax cash flow − depreciation) (1 − tax rate) −investment + depreciation.

This analysis was submitted to Amalgamated's Office of Financial Analysis, which was skeptical of both the sales estimates and the investment data. With regard to the investment data, the Office of Financial Analysis pointed out that changes would probably have to be made in the coating line once the new heat-treating line went into operation. If the investment required to make these changes was included in the analysis, the internal rate of return fell considerably, and the project was no longer very attractive. The vice president for manufacturing argued successfully that altering the coating line was a decision that should be considered separately, and the proposal was sent to the executive committee and then to the board of directors, which approved it.

(a) Several potential advantages of the new heat-treating line, such as the value of the new products and information that could be obtained from a computer-based process, were ignored by Mr. Rollins because they were hard to quantify. Is this the best procedure? Why or why not?

(b) Was the Office of Financial Analysis correct in arguing that the follow-on costs required to change the coating line should be included in the analysis? Why or why not?

(c) If Amalgamated did not introduce the new heat-treating process and its competitors did, would its sales revenues be affected? The above analysis assumes that the answer is no. Is this a problem? Why?

(d) How would you determine whether 10 percent is a reasonable estimate of Amalgamated's cost of capital?

(e) Given the indicated uncertainties attached to the sales estimates, should a risk premium be included in the discount rate? How big should it be?

---

* This case is based on material in R. Hayes, S. Wheelwright, and K. Clark, *Dynamic Manufacturing* (New York: Free Press, 1988).

# Part Six

# Government-Business Relations and the Global Economy

# Chapter 15
# Government and Business

According to *Business Week*, Bill Gates, chairman of Microsoft, the computer software firm, was a billionaire seven times over in 1992. Yet he and other top executives of Microsoft had to be concerned with the reported investigation by the Federal Trade Commission of the firm's competitive practices. The moral: If you plan to move to the top of the executive ranks, you had better be prepared to deal not only with your colleagues and your competitors, but with government agencies as well. In this chapter, we discuss the nature and effects of public regulation, antitrust policy, and the patent system. Managers must not only understand the nature of public policy in these areas; they must also understand what public policy is designed to achieve. Too frequently business executives lack the breadth of viewpoint and knowledge required to act effectively to promote their firm's interests (let alone society's) in the public arena.

## COMPETITION VERSUS MONOPOLY

The Supreme Court has stated that "competition is our fundamental national policy." Many economists agree that competition is preferable to monopoly (or other serious departures from perfect competition), because it is likely to result in a better allocation of resources. As we saw in Chapter

10, a monopolist tends to restrict output, thus driving up price. These economists argue that, from the point of view of social welfare, it would be better if the monopolist raised its output to the competitive level. (Also, in their view, monopolists are likely to be less efficient than competitive firms.) While economists are by no means unanimous on this score, the majority seems to prefer competition over monopoly.

One way society deals with these problems is to establish government commissions like the Federal Communications Commission or the Interstate Commerce Commission to regulate the behavior of monopolists. In this way, as we will see in subsequent sections of this chapter, the government tries to reduce the harmful effects of monopoly. In addition, Congress has enacted antitrust laws that are meant to promote competition and control monopoly. These laws too are discussed at length in this chapter. Any manager must be aware of the nature of these laws, since violating them may mean fines and jail sentences.

Although the United States has gone further in promoting competition than other major industrialized countries, this does not mean that our dedication to competition is complete. National policies are too ambiguous and rich in contradictions to be characterized so simply. The truth is that we as a nation have adopted many measures to promote monopoly and to limit competition. For example, this is the effect of the patent system, which is designed to promote invention and innovation. In later sections of this chapter, we will see why it is felt that the patent system is beneficial, despite the fact that it creates temporary monopolies.

## REGULATION OF MONOPOLY

In some areas of the economy, such as the distribution of gas and electricity, it is not economical for more than one firm to exist, because there are important economies of scale. This firm, a so-called **natural monopolist**, is in a position to charge a higher-than-competitive price for its product. Since such a price may lead to an inefficient allocation of society's resources, as well as to monopolistic profits regarded by the public as excessive and unjustifiable, government regulatory commissions often are established to set limits on the prices that a monopolist of this sort can charge.

Consider the Acme Electric Company, whose demand curve, marginal revenue curve, average cost curve, and marginal cost curve are shown in Figure 15.1. Without regulation, the firm would charge a price of $P_0$, and it would produce $Q_0$ units of the product. By setting a maximum price of $P_1$, the commission can make the monopolist increase output, thus pushing price and output closer to what they would be if the industry were organized competitively. If the commission imposes a maximum price of $P_1$, the firm's demand curve becomes $P_1AD'$, its marginal revenue curve becomes $P_1ABR'$, its optimum output becomes $Q_1$, and it will charge the maximum price of $P_1$. By setting the maximum price, the commission aids consumers

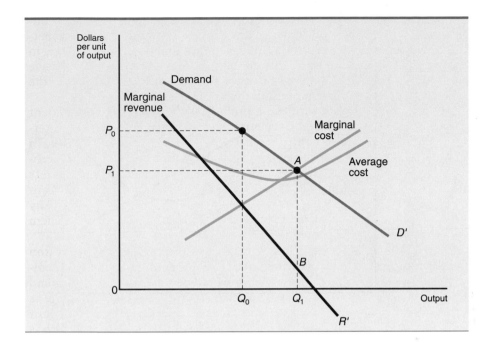

**FIGURE 15.1** *Regulation of Acme Electric Company: Maximum Price*
By setting a maximum price of $P_1$, a regulatory commission can make
Acme increase output to $Q_1$.

who pay a lower price for more of the product. By the same token, the commission takes away some of the Acme Electric Company's monopoly power.

Regulatory commissions often establish the price—or the maximum price—at the level at which it equals average total cost, including a "fair" rate of return on the company's investment. In Figure 15.2, the price would be set by the commission at $P_2$, where the demand curve intersects the average total cost curve. The latter curve includes what the commission regards as a fair profit per unit of output. There has been considerable controversy over what constitutes a fair rate of return, as well as over what should be included in the company's investment on which the fair rate of return is to be earned.

To illustrate the workings of the regulatory process, consider the telephone industry in Michigan. The two organizations that have played a key role in the regulation of the telephone industry there are one firm, Michigan Bell Telephone System (a subsidiary of Ameritech),[1] and one commis-

[1] Ameritech (American Information Technologies Corporation) is one of seven regional holding companies resulting from the breakup of the American Telephone and Telegraph Company (AT&T), which is discussed on page 579.

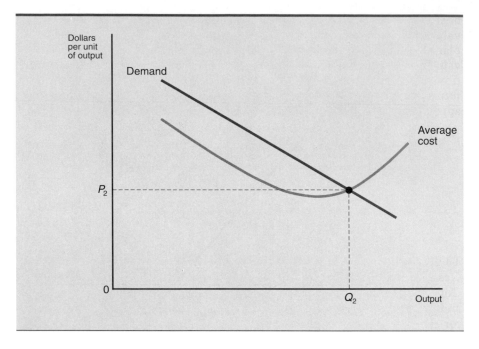

**FIGURE 15.2** *Regulation of Acme Electric Company: Fair Rate of Return* The regulated price is $P_2$, where the demand curve intersects the average total cost curve, which includes what the commission regards as a fair profit per unit of output.

sion, the Public Service Commission in Michigan. Although Michigan Bell is not the sole telephone company in the state, it is the dominant firm, and there is no direct competition between firms in the industry. The commission, composed of three people appointed by the governor, has had authority over the telephone industry for about half a century.

General-rate cases play an important role in the regulatory process. Such cases are initiated by the firms and are based on company claims that earnings are too small and a higher price level is needed. Demand is generally assumed to be price inelastic; consequently, higher prices are assumed to result in greater revenues. The industry usually receives less than it requests (and commission decisions lag behind the industry's revenue requests). However, the fact that the commission does not approve all Bell requests does not imply that the company is constrained much by the commission, since the company may have asked for more than it thought it would receive.

The commission tries to regulate the industry so that earnings equal a "reasonable return on the value of a firm's existing plant." Yet there is a host of questions concerning what is a "reasonable return" and what is "the value of a firm's existing plant." The original cost or historical cost of the plant is the measure on which most commissions base their estimates of the value of the plant; but some permit firms to use replacement-cost valuations instead. In the early 1980s, regulated firms often asked for a rate of return of about 10 to 15 percent; commissions in recent years have approved rates of return of about 6 to 10 percent.[2]

# THE TRENTON GAS COMPANY: A NUMERICAL EXAMPLE

To illustrate the workings of public utility regulation, consider the Trenton Gas Company, which has assets of $300 million. The State Public Utility Commission, after considering the extent of the risks assumed by the firm and the conditions in the financial markets, decides that a fair rate of return for the firm would be 10 percent. Thus, Trenton Gas is allowed to earn profits of 0.10($300 million) = $30 million per year. These profits are not economic profits; they are accounting profits. As stressed above, commissions try to allow firms to earn only a normal or fair rate of return, which tends to rule out economic profits. (Recall Chapter 1.)

What price will the firm set, and what will its output be? To answer these questions, it is important to note that the demand curve for gas provided by the firm is

$$P = 30 - 0.1Q, \tag{15.1}$$

where $P$ is the price per customer (in dollars), and $Q$ is the number of customers served (in millions). The firm's total cost equals

$$TC = 10 + 5Q + 0.9Q^2, \tag{15.2}$$

where $TC$ is total cost (in millions of dollars). Note that this concept of total cost does not include the opportunity cost of the capital invested in the firm by its owners. Thus, the firm's accounting profit equals

$$\pi = (30 - 0.1Q)Q - (10 + 5Q + 0.9Q^2)$$

$$= -Q^2 + 25Q - 10,$$

where $\pi$ is the firm's profit (in millions of dollars).

Since the commission has decided that the firm's accounting profit

[2] See R. Noll and B. Owen, eds., *The Political Economy of Regulation* (Washington, D.C.: American Enterprise Institute, 1983); W. Shepherd and C. Wilcox, *Public Policies toward Business*, 6th ed. (Homewood, Ill.: Irwin, 1979); and W. Shepherd, ed., *Public Policies toward Business: Readings and Cases* (Homewood, Ill.: Irwin, 1979).

should equal $30 million, we set $\pi$ equal to 30, which implies that

$$30 = -Q^2 + 25Q - 10$$
$$-Q^2 + 25Q - 40 = 0, \qquad (15.4)$$

which is an equation of the form $aQ^2 + bQ + c = 0$. We can use the following equation to solve for the roots of this equation:

$$Q = \frac{-b \pm \sqrt{b^2 - 4ac}}{2a}$$

$$= \frac{-25 \pm \sqrt{25^2 - 4(-1)(-40)}}{2(-1)}$$

$$= \frac{-25 \pm \sqrt{465}}{-2}$$

$$= 1.7 \text{ or } 23.3.$$

Because commissions generally want public utilities to serve as many customers as possible, the larger figure, $Q = 23.3$, is the relevant one. Thus, price will be set as follows:

$$P = 30 - 0.1(23.3)$$

$$= 27.67.$$

To sum up, the Trenton Gas Company's price will be $27.67, and it will serve 23.3 million customers.

## THE LONE STAR GAS COMPANY: A CASE STUDY

As a further illustration of how regulatory commissions work, let's look at an actual case. In 1978, the Lone Star Gas Company, which provides gas to 1.1 million residential and commercial customers in the Dallas–Fort Worth area, requested an increase in its price. The Texas Railroad Commission is the state regulatory body with authority over the rates that gas companies can charge. To decide whether an increase should be granted, the commission began by determining the appropriate rate base. The company's assets that were "used and useful" were identified, and valued at historical cost. After allowing for accumulated depreciation, the original cost of invested capital was calculated to be $185 million.

To establish the rate of return that Lone Star Gas should earn on this invested capital, the cost of both debt and equity capital and the percent of each to total capitalization were estimated. The cost of capital was estimated to be 13.87 percent for common equity, 9.75 percent for preferred equity, 8.59 percent for long-term debt, and 9.98 percent for short-term debt. After weighting each of these costs of capital by the percent of total capitalization it represented, the result was 11.1 percent. Thus, the commission concluded that Lone Star Gas should earn an 11.1 percent return on its invested capital of $185 million.

To earn this return, the firm should make an annual profit of .111 ($185 million), or $20.5 million. Since the firm's actual profit was only about $9.8 million, the commission decided to allow the firm to raise its price to the extent necessary to bring its profit up to the "reasonable" level of $20.5 million.[3]

# EFFECTS OF REGULATION ON EFFICIENCY

Regulators try to prevent a monopoly from earning excessive profits. As we have seen in previous sections, the firm is permitted only a "fair" rate of return on its investment. One difficulty with this arrangement is that the firm is guaranteed this rate of return, regardless of how well it performs. If the regulators decide that the Acme Electric Company should get a 9 percent rate of return on its investment, this is the rate of return it will get regardless of whether the Acme Electric Company is managed well or poorly. Why is this a problem? Because unlike a competitive firm, there is no incentive for the firm to increase its efficiency.

The regulatory process is characterized by long delays, which, ironically, may go part way toward encouraging efficiency in regulated firms. In many regulated industries, a proposed rate increase or decrease may be under review for months before a decision is made by the commission. In cases where such a price change is hotly contested, it may take years for the required hearings to take place before the commission and for appeals to be made subsequently to the courts. Such a delay between a proposed price change and its ultimate disposition is called a **regulatory lag.** Long regulatory lags are often criticized by people who would like the regulatory process to adapt more quickly to changing conditions and to yield more timely decisions. But one advantage of regulatory lags is that they result in some penalties for inefficiency and rewards for efficiency.

To illustrate, consider a regulated company whose price is established so that the firm can earn a rate of return of 9 percent (which is what the commission regards as a "fair" rate of return). The firm develops and introduces some improved manufacturing processes that cut the firm's costs, thus allowing it to earn 11 percent. If it takes 15 months for the commission to review the prices it approved before and to modify them to take account of the new (lower) cost levels, the firm earns a higher rate of return (11 percent rather than 9 percent) during these 15 months than it would if it had not developed and introduced the improved manufacturing processes.

---

[3] For further discussion, see M. E. Barrett and M. P. Cormack, *Management Strategy in the Oil and Gas Industries: Cases and Readings* (Houston: Gulf, 1983). The present treatment is simplified for pedagogical reasons.

---

### CONSULTANT'S CORNER

## A DISPUTE OVER A REQUESTED GAS RATE INCREASE*

The Boston Gas Company's request for a $17 million rate increase was examined at hearings conducted by the Massachusetts Department of Public Utilities. One consumers' group, which opposed the rate increase, argued that the gas company should be allowed a 10.5 percent rate of return, while the company asked for a 12.46 percent rate of return. The company also argued that because of regulatory lag, it was receiving considerably less than the 12 percent return it was allowed by the commission. Since previous rate increases had not become effective until almost a year after they were requested, the company earned about 9 percent, not 12 percent.

At the hearing, an economist testifying for the consumers' group argued that the company's cost of equity capital was about 12 percent, whereas an economist hired by the company testified that it was about 16 percent. This was an important issue in the case. Both economists used equation (14.12) to estimate the company's cost of equity capital, but the economist hired by the consumers' group assumed that the annual rate of dividend growth, g, would equal 0.01, whereas the company's economist assumed that it would equal 0.05.

If asked to advise this firm, what suggestions would you make concerning ways to reduce the adverse effects of regulatory lag on the company's earnings? What sorts of analyses would you carry out to determine which of the two estimates of the cost of equity capital is closer to the truth?

* For further discussion, see M. E. Barrett and M. P. Cormack, *Management Strategy in the Oil and Gas Industries: Cases and Readings.*

---

While the regulatory lag does restore some of the incentives for efficiency (and some of the penalties for inefficiency), it does not result in as strong a set of incentives as do competitive markets. One of the fundamental problems with regulation is that if a regulatory commission prevents a firm from earning higher-than-average profits, there may be little incentive for the firm to increase its efficiency and to introduce innovations.

## THE DEREGULATION MOVEMENT

Much controversy has centered on the regulatory process; many observers feel that the commissions are lax and that they tend to be captured by the industries they are supposed to regulate. Also, in some cases, regulation, although effective, seems to have had unfortunate effects, the result being that major steps toward deregulation occurred during the 1970s and 1980s in airlines, trucking, railroads, banking, and communications, among others.

Take, for example, the case of the Civil Aeronautics Board (CAB), which regulated the prices charged by the interstate scheduled airlines as well as entry into the industry. The airlines, not being permitted to compete through lower prices, attempted to lure travelers away from their rivals through more flights, more planes, and more frills like in-flight gourmet meals. This resulted in an upward spiral of fare increases because the increased profits from each fare raise were soon dissipated through more scheduling and service competition. Critics argued that if price competition were permitted, fares would tend to fall as travelers opted for lower prices rather than more service.

Hearings were held by a subcommittee of the U.S. Senate Judiciary Committee in 1975, the aim being to make the case for flexible pricing and easier entry. During the late 1970s, the CAB carried out extensive policy reforms. Airlines were allowed to institute discount fares. For example, American Airlines began to offer the Super-Saver fare (which was 30 percent below economy fare) in the New York–San Francisco and New York–Los Angeles markets. Also, entry restrictions were loosened. In 1977 and 1978, the first years in which the deep discount fares were allowed, average air fares increased by considerably less than the consumer price index. Indeed, average air fares actually decreased from 1977 to 1978, even though all consumer prices went up by 8 percent.

The airlines as well as consumers seemed to be benefiting from regulatory reform. Because the price elasticity of demand for air travel is about 1.3 (according to the CAB's Bureau of Economics), lower prices meant a substantial increase in passengers. The general economic upturn also boosted the number of air passengers and the amount of air freight, the result being that the airlines' profits were much higher in 1978 than in 1977. With fares going down and profits going up, the Congress was enthusiastic about the steps toward deregulation, and in 1978, it passed legislation that ended various powers of the CAB. The power to regulate routes was phased out at the end of 1981, and the power to regulate rates was phased out at the end of 1982. The airlines were given much more freedom with regard to pricing and entry.

In recent years, deregulation has become more controversial. The airlines have experienced losses, as a result of higher fuel prices, recession, and price wars, particularly on the long hauls. There have been complaints that deregulation has resulted in poorer service, particularly to medium- and small-size towns. The airline industry has become much more concentrated, as a number of firms have merged. Nonetheless, there is no indication that the airlines will be regulated once more and that the CAB will be revived.

# THE CONCENTRATION OF ECONOMIC POWER

Government regulatory commissions are not the only device used by society to deal with the problem of monopoly; another device is the application of the nation's antitrust laws. The antitrust laws reflect a feeling that there is excessive power in the hands of relatively few firms. According to the latest available figures, the 100 largest manufacturing firms control about half of all manufacturing assets in the United States, and this percentage seems to have increased considerably since the end of World War II. Although bigness is not the same as monopoly power, there is a widespread feeling that economic power is concentrated in relatively few hands.

The antitrust laws are aimed at promoting competition and limiting monopoly. As stressed above, many economists believe that competition is preferable to monopoly because competition tends to result in a more effective allocation of resources. To measure how close a particular industry is to being perfectly competitive (or monopolized), economists have devised the *market concentration ratio,* which shows the percentage of total sales or production accounted for by the industry's four largest firms. The higher the percentage, the more concentrated the industry.

Table 15.1 shows the market concentration ratios for selected industries. These ratios vary widely from industry to industry. In the automobile industry, the concentration ratio is very high—90 percent. In the commercial printing industry, it is very low—7 percent. The concentration ratio is only a rough measure of an industry's market structure, which must be supplemented with data on the extent and type of product differentiation in the industry, as well as on barriers to entry. Even with these supplements, it

**TABLE 15.1**   *Concentration Ratios in Selected Manufacturing Product Markets*

| Industry | Market share of 4 largest firms (percent) |
|---|---|
| Automobiles | 90 |
| Photographic equipment | 77 |
| Tires | 69 |
| Aircraft | 72 |
| Blast furnaces and steel plants | 44 |
| Electronic computers | 43 |
| Petroleum refining | 32 |
| Bread and cake | 34 |
| Pharmaceuticals | 22 |
| Radio and TV equipment | 37 |
| Newspapers | 25 |
| Commercial printing (lithographic) | 7 |

*Source: U.S. Department of Commerce.*

is still a crude measure because, for one thing, it takes no account of competition from foreign suppliers. Nonetheless, the concentration ratio has proved to be a valuable tool, although its limitations must be recognized.

Another measure of concentration is the **Herfindahl-Hirschman index**, which equals the sum of the squared market shares of the firms in the market. For example, if two firms exist in a market, and each has 50 percent of the market, this index equals $50^2 + 50^2 = 5,000$. The Herfindahl-Hirschman index was used by the Justice Department in its 1982 merger guidelines. According to the department, if this index (after the merger) was less than 1,000, the merger was unlikely to be challenged. If it was between 1,000 and 1,800, a merger that changed the index by less than 100 points probably would not be challenged. If it was greater than 1,800, a merger that changed the index by less than 50 points probably would not be challenged.

# THE SHERMAN ACT

The first federal antitrust law, the Sherman Act, was passed by Congress in 1890. While the common law had long outlawed monopolistic practices, it seemed to many Americans in the latter part of the nineteenth century that legislation was needed to discourage monopoly and to preserve and encourage competition. The formation of "trusts"—monopolistic combines that colluded to raise prices and restrict output—brought the matter to a head. The essence of the Sherman Act lies in the following two sections:

> Sec. 1. Every contract, combination in the form of trust or otherwise, or conspiracy, in restraint of trade or commerce among the several states or with foreign nations, is hereby declared to be illegal. Every person who shall make any such contract or engage in any such combination or conspiracy, shall be deemed guilty of a misdemeanor. . . .
> Sec. 2. Every person who shall monopolize, or attempt to monopolize or combine or conspire with any other person or persons, to monopolize any part of the trade or commerce among the several States, or with foreign nations shall be deemed guilty of a misdemeanor.

In 1974, the Sherman Act was amended, making violations felonies rather than misdemeanors. Corporations can now be fined up to $1 million, and individuals can be fined up to $100,000 and can receive prison terms of up to three years. Besides criminal fines and jail sentences, firms and individuals can be sued for triple damages in civil suits brought by those hurt by an antitrust violation.

It is important to recognize that if executives of two or more firms in a particular industry talk about prices and agree to fix them, this is a violation of Section 1 of the Sherman Act. To illustrate this point, consider Robert Crandall, chief executive officer of American Airlines, who was discussed previously on page 458. He called Howard Putnam, chief executive officer of Braniff Airways, on February 21, 1982, and proposed that they raise prices. The telephone call, which (unknown to Crandall) was taped, went as follows:

Putnam: Do you have a suggestion for me?

Crandall: Yes, I have a suggestion for you. Raise your goddamn fares 20 percent. I'll raise mine the next morning.

Putnam: Robert, we . . .

Crandall: You'll make more money and I will, too.

Putnam: We can't talk about pricing!

Crandall: Oh [expletive deleted], Howard. We can talk about any goddamn thing we want to talk about.[4]

After finding out about the call, the Justice Department filed a suit accusing Robert Crandall of breaking the antitrust laws by proposing to fix prices. But because there had been no agreement to fix prices, Section 1 had not been violated. Nonetheless, the court decided that a proposal of this sort could be an attempt to monopolize part of the airline industry, which is forbidden by Section 2 of the Sherman Act. American Airlines said that it would not do such a thing again.

## THE CLAYTON ACT, THE ROBINSON-PATMAN ACT, AND THE FEDERAL TRADE COMMISSION ACT

During its first 20 years, the Sherman Act was not regarded by its supporters as being very effective. The ineffectiveness of the Sherman Act led in 1914 to passage by Congress of two other laws—the Clayton Act and the Federal Trade Commission Act. The Clayton Act attempted to be more specific than the Sherman Act in identifying certain practices that were illegal because they would "substantially lessen competition or tend to create a monopoly."

The Clayton Act outlawed unjustified price discrimination, which (as you will recall from Chapter 12) is a practice whereby one buyer is charged more than another buyer for the same product. However, discrimination resulting from differences in the quality or quantity of the product sold, or resulting from differences in cost or competitive pressures, were allowed. In 1936, the Robinson-Patman Act amended the Clayton Act. It prohibited charging different prices to different purchasers of "goods of like grade and quality" where the effect "may be substantially to lessen competition or tend to create a monopoly in any line of commerce, or to injure, destroy, or prevent competition with any person who either grants or knowingly receives the benefit of such discrimination, or with customers of either of

---

[4] *New York Times*, February 24, 1983.

them." The Robinson-Patman Act was aimed at preventing price discrimination in favor of chain stores that buy goods in large quantities. The small independent retailers felt threatened by the chain stores, and pushed hard for this law.

The Clayton Act also outlawed the use of tying contracts that reduce competition. As Chapter 12 indicated, tying contracts make buyers purchase other items to get the product they want. For a long time, IBM rented, but would not sell, its machines and insisted that customers buy IBM punch cards and use IBM maintenance services. The Supreme Court required IBM to end its tying contracts. However, not all tying contracts have been prohibited. If a firm needs to maintain control over complementary goods and services to make sure that its product works properly, this can be an adequate justification for a tying contract. Also, if the tying arrangements are voluntary and informal, there is no violation of the law. Thus, if a customer continually buys IBM punch cards because he or she feels that they work best on IBM equipment, this is no violation of the law, so long as this customer does not have to buy IBM punch cards.

Further, the Clayton Act outlawed mergers that substantially lessen competition; but since it did not prohibit one firm's purchase of a competitor's plant and equipment, it really could not stop mergers. In 1950, this loophole was closed by the Celler-Kefauver Antimerger Act. However, this does not mean that mergers have become less prevalent. On the contrary, there was an epidemic of mergers in the 1980s, as we shall see below.

The Federal Trade Commission Act was aimed at preventing undesirable and unfair competitive practices. It established the Federal Trade Commission to investigate unfair and predatory practices and to issue cease-and-desist orders. The act stated that "unfair methods of competition in commerce are hereby declared unlawful." The commission—composed of five commissioners, each appointed by the president for a term of 7 years—was given the formidable task of defining exactly what was "unfair." Eventually, the courts took away much of the commission's power; but in 1938, the commission acquired the function of outlawing untrue and deceptive advertising. Also, the commission has authority to investigate various aspects of the structure of the American economy.

# THE INTERPRETATION OF THE ANTITRUST LAWS

The real impact of the antitrust laws depends on how the courts interpret them, and the judicial interpretation of these laws has varied substantially from one period of time to another. Typically, charges are brought against a firm or group of firms by the Antitrust Division of the Department of Justice, a trial is held, and a decision is reached by the judge. In major cases, appeals are made that eventually reach the Supreme Court.

In 1911, as a consequence of the first major set of antitrust cases, the Standard Oil Company and the American Tobacco Company were forced to give up a large share of their holdings of other firms. The Supreme Court, in deciding these cases, put forth and used the famous **rule of reason**—that only unreasonable combinations in restraint of trade, not all trusts, required conviction under the Sherman Act. In 1920, the rule of reason was employed by the Supreme Court in its finding that U.S. Steel had not violated the antitrust laws even though it had tried to monopolize the industry —since the court said the company had not succeeded. U.S. Steel's large size and its potential monopoly power were ruled beside the point, since "the law does not make mere size an offense. It . . . requires overt acts."

In the 1920s and 1930s, the courts, including the conservative Supreme Court, interpreted the antitrust laws in such a way that they had little impact. While Eastman Kodak and International Harvester controlled very substantial shares of their markets, the court, using the rule of reason, found them innocent on the grounds that they had not built up their near-monopoly position through overt coercion or predatory practices.

During the late 1930s, this situation changed dramatically, with the prosecution of the Aluminum Company of America (Alcoa). This case, decided in 1945 (but begun in 1937), reversed the decisions in the *U.S. Steel* and *International Harvester* cases. Alcoa had achieved its 90 percent of the market by means that would have been regarded as "reasonable" in the earlier cases—keeping its price low enough to discourage entry, adding capacity to take care of increases in the market, and so forth. Nonetheless, the court decided that Alcoa, because it controlled practically all the industry's output, violated the antitrust laws.

Frustrating as it sometimes may be to managers, the antitrust laws are rather vague and ambiguous, the result being that it is not easy to tell whether certain actions are permissible. Take the case of two breweries, Pabst and Blatz, which wanted to merge in 1958. The government objected to this merger even though the two firms together accounted for less than 5 percent of the nation's beer sales. What troubled the government was that they accounted for about 24 percent of beer sales in Wisconsin. The district court judge, agreeing with Pabst and Blatz that Wisconsin should be viewed as only part of the relevant market, dismissed the complaint, but the Supreme Court ruled against the firms. This case shows how difficult it can be to establish even the boundaries of the relevant market.

## ANTITRUST POLICY DURING THE 1960s AND 1970s

The 1960s and 1970s generally were vigorous decades from the viewpoint of antitrust. In 1961, the major electrical equipment manufacturers were convicted of collusive price agreements. Executives of General Electric, Westinghouse, and other firms in the industry admitted that they met secretly and communicated in order to maintain prices, share the market, and eliminate competition. Some of the executives were sentenced to jail on criminal charges, and the firms had to pay large amounts to customers to make up for the overcharges. There were 1,800 triple-damage suits against the firms, which resulted in payments estimated at about $0.5 billion.

During the 1960s, horizontal mergers—mergers of firms making essentially the same good—became increasingly likely to run afoul of the antitrust laws. In the *Von's Grocery* case in 1965, the court disallowed a merger between two supermarkets that together had less than 8 percent of the Los Angeles market. Also, vertical mergers—mergers of firms that supply or sell to one another—were viewed with suspicion by the courts. For example, in the *Brown Shoe* case, the Supreme Court said that the merger of Brown with R.G. Kinney would mean that other shoe manufacturers would be frozen out of a substantial part of the retail shoe market. Another leading problem confronting the Justice Department was conglomerate mergers —mergers of firms in unrelated industries. However, this problem diminished in importance in the late 1960s, when the conglomerates began to show relatively disappointing earnings.

In 1969, the Antitrust Division sued IBM Corporation under Section 2 of the Sherman Act, thus beginning one of the biggest and most expensive antitrust cases in history. The government alleged that IBM held a monopoly and that the firm's 360 line of computers was introduced in 1965 in a way that eliminated competition. IBM's defense was that its market position resulted from its innovative performance and economies of scale, that its pricing was competitive, and that its profit rate really had not been high. After the trial began in 1975, it took the government almost three years to present its case. In early 1982, the Reagan administration dropped the IBM case, on the grounds that it was "without merit and should be dismissed."

In 1974, the government brought an antitrust suit against the American Telephone and Telegraph Company (AT&T), which was settled on the same day in 1982 as the IBM case. According to the settlement, AT&T divested itself of 22 companies that provide most of the nation's local telephone service, and kept its Long Lines Division, Western Electric, and the Bell Laboratories. The Federal Communications Commission estimated that long-distance rates dropped 38 percent after the divestiture. (For example, the cost of a 10-minute call from New York to Boston fell from $4.09 in December 1983 to $2.34 in December 1988.) But the cost of local telephone service rose substantially, according to some estimates, and divestiture seemed to cause a great deal of confusion among customers and costly adjustments within AT&T. Nonetheless, many observers believe that AT&T is a leaner and more dynamic firm, and that new technologies and services will be introduced more rapidly than in the past.

## ANTITRUST POLICY DURING THE 1980s AND 1990s

The 1980s were not a period of intense antitrust activity. Antitrust officials felt they should attack conspiracies to fix prices, but they were less concerned than their predecessors about many kinds of mergers. While critics argued that antitrust enforcement was too lax, the Reagan administration maintained that it was enforcing the laws in ways that advanced, rather than hindered, competition.

There was an epidemic of mergers during the 1980s. For example, Chevron took over Gulf Oil, and General Electric took over RCA. In many cases, the acquiring firm bypassed the target corporation's management and tried to purchase a controlling interest directly from the target's stockholders. For example, Saul Steinberg, a prominent investor, tried to acquire Walt Disney Productions (page 78) in this way. A continuing debate has gone on concerning the social costs and benefits of this wave of takeovers. Without question, mergers can have substantial benefits; for example, they can result in economies of scale, the more accurate valuation of particular resources, or the substitution of a more efficient management for a less efficient one. However, these benefits are not assured. A firm may be less efficient, not more so, after a merger than before.

Some prominent analysts argue that stock market prices provide a good barometer of the consequence of a takeover. According to this view, if the aggregate net change in the value of the acquirers' and targets' shares is positive as a result of a takeover, then the merger is socially beneficial. Other analysts believe that accounting data are more useful for this purpose than stock market prices. Some well-known economists have concluded from accounting data that there is no evidence that the acquiring companies managed their acquired assets either worse or better than the average. However, critics argue that accounting studies do not take into account the real market values of acquired assets, since they are based on accounting valuations, which may understate (or overstate) their value.

The Bush administration was more actively involved in antitrust than its predecessor. The Justice Department filed suit against the American Institute of Architects on the grounds that it unreasonably restrained price competition among architects. Also, the Federal Trade Commission complained that Capital Cities–ABC Inc. and the College Football Association had illegally conspired to limit the number of football games shown on television. Nonetheless, many observers feel that, for better or worse, antitrust activity during the early 1990s was not relatively aggressive.

However, in late 1991, the Federal Trade Commission was reported to be investigating Intel's practices in the microprocessor business and Microsoft's practices in the computer software business. (Recall page 565.) And Advanced Micro Devices filed a lawsuit accusing Intel of attempting to monopolize the market for microprocessors. (Previously, Intel had sued Advanced Micro Devices for copyright infringement.) And Cyrix Corporation filed suit alleging that Intel was trying to monopolize the market for math processing chips (after Intel sued Cyrix for patent infringement). Thus, there continued to be some noteworthy antitrust activity.

## TWO APPROACHES TO ANTITRUST POLICY

In judging antitrust cases, some lawyers and economists look primarily and directly at **market performance**—the industry's rate of technological change, efficiency, and profits, the conduct of individual firms, and so on. Those favoring this approach argue that in deciding antitrust cases, one should review in detail the performance of the firms in question to see how well they have served the economy. If they have served well, they should not be held in violation of the antitrust laws merely because they have a large share of the market. This test, as it is usually advocated, relies heavily on an evaluation of the technological "progressiveness" and "dynamism" of the firms in question. One problem with this approach is that it is very difficult to tell whether a particular industry's performance is "good" or "bad." Economists do not have the sorts of measurement techniques required to obtain reasonably accurate measures of an industry's performance.

Another approach to antitrust policy emphasizes the importance of an industry's **market structure**—the number and size distribution of buyers and sellers in the market, the ease with which new firms can enter, and the extent of product differentiation. Advocates of this approach say that one should look to market structure for evidence of undesirable monopolistic characteristics. The basic idea behind this approach, as Chicago's Nobel laureate George Stigler put it, is that "an industry which does not have a competitive structure will not have competitive behavior."

For example, it has been suggested that if for 5 years or more, one firm has accounted for 50 percent or more of annual sales in a market, or if 4 or fewer firms have accounted for 80 percent of such sales, it should be presumed that "market power" exists. Unless such "market power" can be defended by economies of scale or some other justification, it has been suggested that such "market power" be declared illegal. One problem with this approach is that the relationship between market structure and market performance may be so weak that it may be a mistake to choose, more or less arbitrarily, some level of concentration and to say that if concentration exceeds this level, market performance is likely to be socially unacceptable.

## DU PONT'S TITANIUM DIOXIDE PIGMENTS: A CASE STUDY

To understand the nature of antitrust law, it is useful to look closely at particular cases. Consider the case involving the chemical giant Du Pont, which produces titanium dioxide, a white chemical pigment used to make paint. In 1970, because of its development of the ilmenite chloride process for manufacturing titanium oxide, Du Pont held a substantial cost advantage (16 cents per pound versus 21 cents per pound) over its rivals. From 1972 to 1977, Du Pont increased its capacity and raised its market share from about 30 percent to 42 percent. (Recall our discussion of Du Pont's huge investment program in Chapter 11.) In 1978, the government charged that Du Pont had used unfair methods of competition and unfair acts and practices by using its dominant position in an attempt to monopolize the production of titanium dioxide (TiO2) pigments. The Federal Trade Commission described the situation as follows:

> Du Pont's growth strategy consists of three interrelated elements: a) expansion of capacity by construction of a large-scale plant; b) exploitation of its cost advantage by pricing its products high enough to finance its own expanded capacity, yet low enough to discourage rivals from expanding; and c) refusal to license its cost-saving ilmenite chloride technology with which rivals could learn to take advantage of the economies of scale inherent in the low-grade ore technology. In addition, the allegedly strategic behavior of Du Pont consisted of premature expansion of its TiO2 capacity and exaggerated announcements of its expansion intentions, all for the primary purpose of preempting competitors' expansion plans.
>
> Complaint counsel contend that this conduct amounted to exclusionary and anticompetitive behavior insulating Du Pont's cost advantage from competitive erosion since the ilmenite chloride technology actually changes as the scale of operation increases and, without large-scale operations, no competitor will be able to reduce or eliminate Du Pont's cost advantage through "learning-by-doing" ilmenite chloride technology. The inevitable result of this strategy, according to complaint counsel, will be to give Du Pont the power to raise prices at will, restrict output and prevent competition. Indeed, complaint counsel argue that Du Pont's expansion plan "made no sense unless it results in a monopoly."
>
> Du Pont admits that it sought to capitalize on its cost advantage in order to capture or serve the major portion of the growth in demand for TiO2 well into the 1980's. Even so, it denies that the cost advantage was "fortuitous," claiming instead that it was due to its costly innovations in low-grade ilmenite chloride technology in earlier years. It further denies that its capacity expansion had any purpose other than to satisfy the expected increase in demand for TiO2. Du Pont also denies that it engaged in an unlawful strategic pricing strategy, contending that its pricing during the period was attributable to market forces beyond its control. Indeed, Du Pont asserts that complaint counsel failed to prove that its prices were not profit-maximizing under the prevailing economic conditions.
>
> Furthermore, Du Pont claims that it was under no duty to license its ilmenite chloride technology to any competitor, and contends that its competitors, all large corporations engaged in TiO2 manufacture, are not

prevented from developing their own low-grade ore technology or constructing large-scale plants if they choose to make such investments. Finally, Du Pont points to its failure to achieve the anticipated growth in its market share and denies that it could attain monopoly power in the TiO2 market.[5]

What was the outcome of this case? In 1980, the complaint was dismissed on the following grounds: "Du Pont engaged in conduct consistent with its own technological capacity and market opportunities. It did not attempt to build excess capacity or to expand temporarily as a means of deterring entry. Nor did respondent engage in other conduct that might tip the scales in the direction of liability, such as pricing below cost, making false announcements about future expansion plans, or attempting to lock up customers in requirements contracts to assure the success of its growth plans. In short, we find Du Pont's conduct to be reasonable."[6]

One point that should be recognized is that Du Pont's strategy did not work very well, since demand did not grow as rapidly as the company had forecasted, with the result that there was considerable excess capacity in the industry. But whether or not Du Pont's strategy worked, it won the antitrust case, which is our primary interest here.

## STATE ANTITRUST LAWS

It is also worth noting that states, as well as the federal government, have antitrust laws. Indeed, state antitrust legislation sometimes is broader than federal law, and in 1989, the Supreme Court affirmed that states may pass laws permitting consumers to bring antitrust suits that would not be allowed under federal laws. Specifically, many states, including California, Illinois, and Michigan, have laws permitting "indirect" purchasers—retail customers who did not deal directly with manufacturers—to bring damage suits against manufacturers that conspire to fix prices. In contrast, federal law generally bars most antitrust damage suits by "indirect" purchasers.

These state laws played an important role in an antitrust case that four states (Alabama, Arizona, California, and Minnesota) and many other plaintiffs brought against a group of cement makers. The cases were settled with the creation of a $32 million settlement fund. When the fund was about to be distributed, the "direct" purchasers claimed that the "indirect" purchasers had no right to share in the settlement, since they were barred from doing so by federal law. The "indirect" purchasers argued that this did not mean that state laws permitting them to share in the settlement were invalid or irrelevant—and the Supreme Court agreed with them.

---

[5] Federal Trade Commission, *In the Matter of E.I. DuPont de Nemours and Company,* docket no. 9108, October 20, 1980.

[6] Ibid., p. 51.

## UNITED AIRLINES' PURCHASE OF PAN AM'S PACIFIC DIVISION

In 1985, United Airlines purchased Pan Am's Pacific Division for $750 million. As part of the transition to a deregulated environment (recall pages 572 to 573), the U.S. Department of Transportation had the responsibility of approving such acquisitions. A hearing was held by the Department of Transportation. The Department of Justice, as well as American, Eastern, and Northwest Airlines, opposed the purchase. The percentage of total passengers carried across the Pacific by each airline in 1984 was as follows:

| Firm | Percentage |
| --- | --- |
| Northwest | 27.5 |
| JAL | 21.9 |
| Pan American | 18.5 |
| Korean Air | 9.3 |
| United | 7.3 |
| China Airlines | 6.8 |
| Singapore Airlines | 2.9 |
| Thai International Airways | 2.2 |
| CAAC | 1.6 |
| Philippine Airlines | 1.3 |
| Other | 0.7 |
| Total | 100.0 |

(a) What was the concentration ratio before the purchase? Was it relatively high? (b) What was the concentration ratio after the purchase? (c) Entry into the U.S.–Japan air transport market is governed by the U.S.–Japan Civil Aviation Agreement, and Japan has been reluctant to permit entry. Is this an important consideration in judging whether the purchase should have been approved? If so, why? (d) The Department of Transportation approved the purchase, although some experts, like MIT's Frank Fisher, believe that "with Pan American's Tokyo and other Pacific service added to its large domestic route system (and with its Apollo computer reservation system), United could expect to

*Stephen M. Wolf, Chairman, President and CEO, UAL Corporation and United Airlines*

attract a large share of the traffic without competing on price."* *Why is this relevant?*

*Solution* (a) It equaled $27.5 + 21.9 + 18.5 + 9.3 = 77.2$ percent. Yes. (b) It was $27.5 + 21.9 + (18.5 + 7.3) + 9.3 = 84.5$ percent, if we simply combine United's and Pan Am's shares to approximate United's post-purchase share. (c) If there are substantial barriers to entry, existing airlines in this market do not have to be concerned about price competition from entrants. Thus, they have greater power over price. (d) A free enterprise system is built on the presumption that there will be price competition in markets. If this purchase weakens the incentive for firms in this market to compete in this way, this effect is of obvious relevance to the department's decision.†

* F. Fisher, "Pan American to United: The Pacific Division Transfer Case," *RAND Journal of Economics* (Winter 1987).
† For further discussion of this case, see ibid.

## THE PATENT SYSTEM

While the antitrust laws are designed to limit monopoly, not all public policies have this effect. The patent system is a good example. The United States patent laws grant the inventor exclusive control over the use of an invention for seventeen years in exchange for his or her making the invention public knowledge. Not all new knowledge is patentable. In separate cases, courts have ruled that a patentable invention "is not a revelation of something which existed and was unknown, but the creation of something which did not exist before,"[7] and that there "can be no patent upon an abstract philosophical principle".[8] A patentable invention must have as its subject matter a physical result or a physical means of attaining some result, not a purely human means of attaining it. Moreover, it must contain a certain minimum degree of novelty. " 'Improvement' and 'invention' are not convertible terms. . . . Where the most favorable construction that can be given . . . is that the article constitutes an improvement over prior inventions, but it embodies no new principle or mode of operation not utilized before by other inventors, there is no invention."[9]

Three principal arguments are used to justify the existence of the patent laws. First, these laws are regarded as an important incentive to induce the inventor to put in the work required to produce an invention. Particularly

[7] *Pyrene Mfg. Co. v. Boyce,* C.C.A.N.J., 292 F.480.
[8] *Boyd v. Cherry,* 50 F.279, 282.
[9] *William Schwarzwaelder and Co. v. City of Detroit,* 77 F.886, 891.

in the case of the individual inventor, it is claimed that patent protection is a strong incentive. Second, patents are regarded as a necessary incentive to induce firms to carry out the further work and make the necessary investment in pilot plants and other items that are required to bring the invention to commercial use. If an invention became public property when made, why should a firm incur the costs and risks involved in experimenting with a new process or product? Another firm could watch, take no risks, and duplicate the process or product if it were successful. Third, it is argued that because of the patent laws, inventions are disclosed earlier than otherwise, the consequence being that other inventions are facilitated by the earlier dissemination of the information.

Unlike most other goods, new technological knowledge cannot be used up. A person or firm can use an idea repeatedly without wearing it out; and the same idea can serve many users at the same time. No one need be getting less of the idea because others are using it too. This fact creates an important difficulty for any firm that would like to make a business of producing knowledge. For an investment in research and development to be profitable, a firm must be able to sell its results, directly or indirectly, for a price. But potential customers would be unwilling to pay for a commodity that, once produced, becomes available to all in unlimited quantity. There is a tendency to let someone else pay for it, since then it would become available for nothing.

The patent laws, which are a way of addressing this problem, make it possible for firms to produce new knowledge and to sell or use it profitably. But the patent system has the disadvantage that new knowledge is not used as widely as it should be, because the patent holder, who attempts to make a profit, will set a price sufficiently high so that some people who could make productive use of the patented item will be discouraged from doing so. From society's point of view, everyone who can use the idea should be allowed to do so at a very low cost, since the marginal cost of their doing so is often practically zero. However, this would be a rather short-sighted policy because it would provide little incentive for invention.

Without question, the patent system enables innovators to appropriate a larger portion of the social benefits from their innovations than would be the case without it, but this does not mean that patents are very effective in this regard. Contrary to popular opinion, patent protection does not make entry impossible, or even unlikely. Within four years of their introduction, 60 percent of the patented successful innovations included in one study were imitated.[10] Nonetheless, patent protection generally increases imitation costs. In the above study, the median estimated increase in imitation cost (the cost of developing and commercially introducing an imitative product) was 11 percent. In the ethical drug industry, patents had a bigger impact on imitation costs than in the other industries, which helps to

---

[10] E. Mansfield, M. Schwartz, and S. Wagner, "Imitation Costs and Patents: An Empirical Study," *Economic Journal* (December 1981).

account for the fact that patents are regarded as more important in ethical drugs than elsewhere. The median increase in imitation cost was about 30 percent in ethical drugs, in contrast to about 10 percent in chemicals and about 7 percent in electronics and machinery.

# PATENTS AND THE RATE OF INNOVATION

One of the most important and controversial questions concerning the patent system is: What proportion of innovations would be delayed or not introduced at all if they could not be patented? To shed light on this question, carefully designed surveys have been carried out to determine the proportion of their patented innovations that firms report they would have introduced (with no appreciable delay) if patent protection had not been available. According to the firms in one such study, about one-half of the patented innovations would not have been introduced without patent protection. The bulk of these innovations occurred in the drug industry. Excluding drug innovations, the lack of patent protection would have affected less than one-fourth of the patented innovations in the sample.

Patents frequently are not regarded as crucial because they often have only a limited effect on the rate at which imitators enter the market. For about half of the innovations in the above study, the firms believed that patents had delayed the entry of imitators by less than a few months. Although patents generally increased the imitation costs, they did not increase the costs enough in these cases to have an appreciable effect on the rate of entry. But although patent protection seems to have only a limited effect on entry in about half of the cases it seems to have a very important effect in a minority of them. For about 15 percent of the innovations, patent protection was estimated to have delayed the time when the first imitator entered the market by four years or more.

In another study based on a random sample of 100 firms from 12 industries (excluding very small firms) in the United States,[11] the results indicate that patent protection was judged by the firms to have been essential for the development or introduction of 30 percent or more of the inventions commercialized in two industries—pharmaceuticals and chemicals. In another three industries (petroleum, machinery, and fabricated metal products), patent protection was estimated to be essential for the development and introduction of about 10 to 20 percent of their inventions. In the remaining seven industries (electrical equipment, office equipment, motor vehicles, instruments, primary metals, rubber, and textiles), patent protection was estimated to be of much more limited importance in this regard. Indeed, in office equipment, motor vehicles, rubber, and textiles, the firms were unanimous in reporting that patent protection was not essential for the develop-

---

[11] E. Mansfield, "Patents and Innovation: An Empirical Study," *Management Science* (February 1986).

ment or introduction of any of their inventions during the years 1981 to 1983.

This does not mean, however, that firms make little use of the patent system. On the contrary, even in those industries in which practically all inventions would be introduced without patent protection, the bulk of the patentable inventions seem to be patented. And in such industries as pharmaceuticals and chemicals, in which patents are important, over 80 percent of the patentable inventions are reported to have been patented. Clearly, firms generally prefer not to rely on trade secret protection when patent protection is possible. Even in industries like motor vehicles, in which patents are frequently said to be relatively unimportant, about 60 percent of the patentable inventions seem to be patented.

## THE PROTECTION OF INTELLECTUAL PROPERTY RIGHTS

In many high-technology industries, there is a widespread feeling among top managers that inadequate protection is being given to intellectual property rights, such as patents and copyrights. There are important and well-known differences between the industrialized countries and the developing countries in their attitudes toward such rights. The latter countries tend to feel that intellectual property rights give inventors and innovators an undesirable monopoly on advanced technology that can be used to extract unjustifiably high prices, as well as unwarranted restrictions on the application of the technology. In their view, the enforcement of intellectual property rights would do little to aid their own development; indeed, it would tend to hinder their development and to prolong the period during which their per capita income falls considerably short of that in the industrialized countries.

A view sometimes expressed in developing countries is that knowledge should be made available at minimal cost to everyone, since it is a common property of all. Also, it is argued that because the development of the relatively impoverished countries of the world is a goal that benefits everyone, the technology needed by these countries should be given to them at a low cost. For these and other reasons, many developing countries have relatively weak laws to protect intellectual property and less than diligent enforcement of the laws that exist. Also, they have adopted policies with regard to direct foreign investment and licensing designed to improve the terms on which they can obtain advanced technology.

Obviously, the industrialized countries tend to disagree with the foregoing arguments. In their view, intellectual property rights must be respected to provide a fair return to the private investors who take the substantial risks involved in developing and commercializing a new technology.

TABLE 15.2   *Percentage of Major U.S. Chemical (and Drug) Firms Reporting That Intellectual Property Rights Protection in Each of 16 Countries Is Too Weak to Permit Them to Transfer Their Newest and/or Most Effective Technology to Wholly Owned Subsidiaries There, 1991*

| Country | Percent of firms | Country | Percent of firms |
|---------|------------------|---------|------------------|
| Argentina | 44 | Nigeria | 67 |
| Brazil | 50 | Philippines | 47 |
| Chile | 47 | Singapore | 12 |
| Hong Kong | 21 | South Korea | 31 |
| India | 81 | Spain | 0 |
| Indonesia | 40 | Taiwan | 19 |
| Japan | 0 | Thailand | 60 |
| Mexico | 31 | Venezuela | 50 |

*Source:* E. Mansfield, "Unauthorized Use of Intellectual Property: Effects on Investment, Technology Transfer, and Innovation," Conference on Global Dimensions of Intellectual Property Rights in Science and Technology, Washington, D.C., National Research Council, 1992.

Unless such returns are forthcoming, the incentives for inventive and innovative activity will be impaired, to the detriment of all nations, rich or poor. Moreover, the industrialized countries sometimes argue that the establishment of stronger intellectual property rights would help to promote indigenous technological and innovative activities in the developing countries, although it is recognized that this is only one of many factors involved. As shown in Table 15.2, many U.S. firms, particularly in the chemical industry, feel that intellectual property rights protection in many developing countries is too weak to permit them to transfer their newest and/or most effective technology to wholly owned subsidiaries there.

Superimposed on these differences of philosophy between industrialized and developing countries is a bewildering array of exceedingly complex issues that have arisen as a result of the development and diffusion of new information and communications technologies. There are basic questions concerning data ownership and control, and concerning ways to monitor computer activity. Governments find it hard to control the information crossing their borders, and firms have difficulties in protecting their data bases. A variety of new technologies have come into being that fit awkwardly, if at all, into traditional concepts of intellectual property.

Consider, for example, the case of computer software. In the United States, West Germany, and the United Kingdom, there has been a tendency to use copyright law to protect software, but others, such as Japan's Ministry of International Trade and Industry, have opposed copyright protection, and the issues are by no means decided. Proponents of copyright protection say that software is like writing, except that it is in a new form resulting from technological advance. Opponents argue, among other things, that object code is not like writing because it is addressed to

CONCEPTS IN CONTEXT

## HOW TO PROTECT INTELLECTUAL PROPERTY RIGHTS

In the late 1980s, American high-tech firms put much more emphasis than in previous years on protecting intellectual property rights. Take the case of Texas Instruments, which decided it was not receiving enough money from Japanese and Korean chip manufacturers that were using its patents. After a long legal struggle, it got nine of the firms to pay higher royalties, which amounted in 1987 to $191 million. Or consider the IBM Corporation, which in 1988 approached rivals using its RISC (reduced instruction set computing) technology, and informed them that they might be violating IBM's patents.

*Court of Appeals for the Federal Circuit*

Part of the reason for this increased emphasis on intellectual property rights is the change in the legal treatment of such rights. In 1982, Congress established the Court of Appeals for the Federal Circuit, to which all patent cases are sent on appeal. This has resulted in rulings that often favor patent holders, and stiff penalties for infringers. It is important to recognize that patent suits can involve very large amounts of money. Eastman Kodak was forced out of the instant photography business when it lost a patent suit to the Polaroid Corporation, which sought damages of $5.7 billion.

Another reason for emphasizing intellectual property rights is that many firms are losing large sums of money as a result of what they regard as piracy. In a dozen developing countries in 1984, Pfizer sold about $47 million worth of a dozen pharmaceuticals on which it had patents. According to Pfizer, pirates sold about $42 million of these same drugs in those countries that year. In the early 1980s, Pfizer introduced Feldene—an anti-arthritic drug—in Argentina. Within 18 months, 14 firms were marketing what Pfizer said was the same drug. In 1984, whereas Pfizer sold $1.6 million of Feldene, pirates sold over $17 million of it.

machines, not people. Even if all nations agreed that copyright protection should be granted, it is not clear whether imitators could not still duplicate the essential features of a program, if they changed it in minor ways.[12]

---

[12] For a recent discussion, see P. Menell, "Tailoring Legal Protection for Computer Software," *Stanford Law Review* (July 1987).

A myriad of problems have also arisen with regard to the protection of semiconductor chips. Patents are regarded by many observers as inappropriate because the fundamental technology for making chips is well known. Congress has rejected the argument that copyright protection should be granted in this area. Instead, the Semiconductor Chip Protection Act of 1984 gives creators of mask works exclusive rights concerning the sale, distribution, import, and reproduction of a mask work for ten years if it is original (but not novel or nonobvious) and registered within 2 years of its creation.[13]

Coupled with these vexing problems associated with new technologies are very significant losses by American manufacturers and others resulting from outright piracy and counterfeiting. The International Trade Commission has estimated that in 1982, American business lost about $6.8 billion in worldwide sales on this account. The Department of Commerce has claimed that the loss could be as high as $20 billion. Among the industrial sectors where counterfeiting is particularly serious are wearing apparel and footwear, transportation equipment parts and accessories, computer hardware, chemicals, records and tapes, sporting goods, toys, video games, and machinery and electrical products.[14]

Given losses of this magnitude, it is not hard to understand why American firms have been, and are, concerned about these issues. But it is hard to change foreign practices, and it seems fair to say that from an American point of view, progress has been limited.[15]

# REGULATION OF ENVIRONMENTAL POLLUTION

Having looked briefly at antitrust policy and the patent system, let's return to the topic of government regulation. Government agencies regulate many aspects of economic life, not just the prices charged by electric, telephone, or transportation companies. Managers of firms in a wide variety of industries, ranging from steel or chemicals to paper or petroleum, must understand and cope with a huge number of government regulations to protect the environment. To illustrate the situation, consider the Reserve Mining Company, which produces iron pellets from taconite rock. For every ton of

---

[13] Ibid.

[14] U.S. Department of Commerce, Statement by Malcolm Baldrige on Proposed "Intellectual Property Rights Improvement Act of 1986," April 7, 1986; and International Trade Commission, *The Effects of Foreign Product Counterfeiting on U.S. Industry*, USITC Publication 1479, January 1984.

[15] For further discussion, see E. Mansfield, "Intellectual Property Rights, Technological Change, and Economic Growth," in M. Bloomfield and C. Walker, eds., *Intellectual Property Rights and Capital Formation in the Next Decade* (Landham, Md.: University Press of America, 1988).

iron pellets it manufactures, Reserve also produces 2 tons of waste taconite tailings, which for over a decade were dumped into Lake Superior. In 1969, Reserve found itself in a court battle, one of the most hotly debated matters being the discovery of asbestoslike fibers in the water supply of Duluth, Minnesota. When the legal battle was resolved in 1977, Reserve was granted the necessary permits to begin construction of a new dumping facility, which cost about $400 million. The price was high, but asbestos levels in Lake Superior seem to have dropped substantially.

In the following sections, we explain why our economy, in the absence of government action, is likely to generate too much pollution. Then we discuss the optimal level of pollution control and describe the various forms of government regulation. In view of the importance of the environment both to managers and to the public at large, this discussion should be of considerable interest.

## EXTERNAL ECONOMIES AND DISECONOMIES

To understand why our economy is likely to generate too much pollution, you must know what is meant by an external economy or an external diseconomy. An *external economy* occurs when an action taken by a firm or individual results in uncompensated benefits to others. Thus, a firm may train workers that eventually go to work for other firms that do not have to pay the training costs. Or a firm may carry out research that benefits other firms that do not have to pay for the research. In general, there is a tendency for activities resulting in external economies to be underperformed from society's point of view. If a firm or individual takes an action that contributes to society's welfare but receives no payment for it, the firm or the individual is likely to take this action less frequently than would be socially desirable.

An *external diseconomy* occurs when an action taken by a firm or individual results in uncompensated costs or harm to others. Thus, a firm may generate smoke that harms neighboring families and businesses, or a person may fail to keep up his or her property, thus reducing the value of neighboring houses. In general, there is a tendency for activities resulting in external diseconomies to be overperformed from society's point of view. If a firm or individual takes an action that results in costs borne by others, the firm or the individual is likely to take this action more frequently than is socially desirable.

## THE GENESIS OF THE POLLUTION PROBLEM

The key to understanding why our economy generates too much pollution (from society's point of view) is the concept of an external diseconomy.

When firms and individuals pollute our waterways and atmosphere, they are engaged in activities resulting in external diseconomies. For example, a firm may pollute a river by pumping out waste materials, or it may pollute the air with smoke or materials. These activities generate external diseconomies, and as pointed out above, they are likely to be overperformed from a social viewpoint.

In a competitive economy, resources tend to be used in their socially most valuable way because they are allocated to the people and firms that find it worthwhile to bid most for them, assuming that prices reflect true social costs. Suppose, however, that because of the presence of external diseconomies, people and firms do not pay the true social costs for certain resources. In particular, suppose that some firms or people can use water or air for nothing, but that other firms or people incur costs as a consequence of this prior use. In this case, *the price paid by the user of water or air is less than the true cost to society.* In a case like this, users of water and air are guided in their decisions by the prices they pay. Since they pay less than the true social costs, water and air are artificially cheap to them, so that they will use too much of these resources, from society's point of view.

## THE OPTIMAL LEVEL OF POLLUTION CONTROL

Managers, like other members of society, should be able to look at matters from a social, as well as private, standpoint. They should be sensitive to the effects of their actions on society as a whole, as well as on their firm's interests. An industry generally can vary, at each level of output, the amount of pollution it generates. For instance, it may install pollution control devices like scrubbers to lower the amount of pollution it generates at each level of output. In this section, we determine the socially optimal level of pollution control.

The total social cost of each level of discharge of an industry's wastes, holding constant the industry's output, is shown in Figure 15.3. The more untreated waste the industry discharges into the environment, the greater the total costs. Figure 15.4 shows the costs of pollution control at each level of discharge of the industry's wastes. The more the industry reduces the amount of wastes it discharges, the higher are its costs of pollution control. Figure 15.5 shows the sum of these two costs—the cost of pollution and the cost of pollution control—at each level of discharge of the industry's wastes.

From society's point of view, the industry should lower its discharge of pollution to the point where the sum of these two costs—the cost of pollution and the cost of pollution control—is a minimum. Specifically, the optimal level of pollution in the industry is B in Figure 15.5. To see why this is the optimal level, note that if the industry discharges *less* than this amount of pollution, a 1-unit increase in pollution will lower the cost of pollution control by more than it will increase the cost of pollution, whereas if the

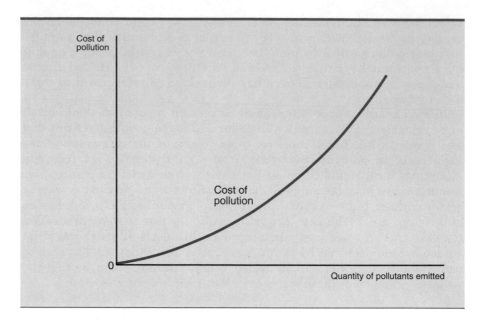

**FIGURE 15.3   Pollution Cost**   The cost of pollution increases as larger quantities of pollutants are emitted.

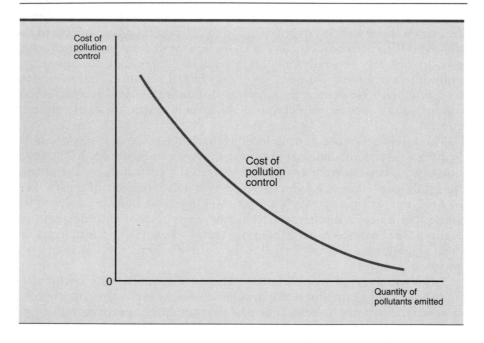

**FIGURE 15.4   Pollution Control Cost**   The cost of pollution control decreases as larger quantities of pollutants are emitted.

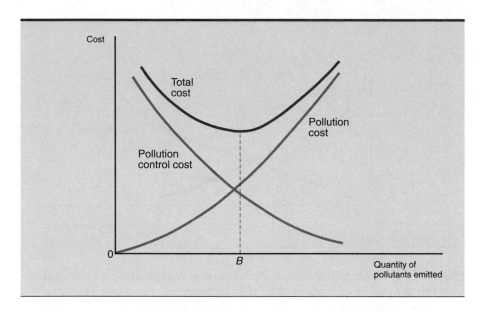

*FIGURE 15.5    Sum of Pollution Cost and Pollution Control Cost*   From the point of view of society as a whole, the optimal level of pollution in this industry is *B*.

industry discharges *more* than this amount of pollution, a 1-unit reduction in pollution will lower the cost of pollution by more than it will increase the cost of pollution control.

Figure 15.6 shows the marginal cost of an extra unit of discharge of waste, at each level of discharge of the industry's wastes; this is designated by *UU'*. Figure 15.6 also shows the marginal cost of reducing the industry's discharge of waste by one unit; this is designated by *VV'*. The socially optimal level of pollution for the industry is at the point where the two curves intersect. At this point, the cost of an extra unit of pollution is just equal to the cost of reducing pollution by an extra unit. Regardless of whether we look at Figure 15.5 or 15.6, the answer is the same: *B* is the socially optimal level of pollution.

## FORMS OF GOVERNMENT REGULATION

Because it does not pay all of the social costs of its pollution, the industry in Figure 15.6 will not find it profitable to reduce its pollution level to *B*. One way that the government can establish incentives for firms to reduce their pollution is by direct regulation. For example, the government may decree

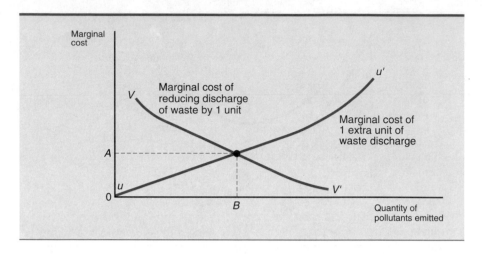

**FIGURE 15.6** *Marginal Cost of Pollution and Marginal Cost of Pollution Control* At the socially optimal level of pollution, *B*, the cost of an extra unit of pollution is equal to the cost of reducing pollution by an extra unit.

that this industry is to limit its pollution to *B* units. Direct regulation of this sort is relied on in many sectors of the American economy.

Another way to induce firms to reduce pollution is to establish effluent fees. An **effluent fee** is a fee that a polluter must pay to the government for discharging waste. For instance, in Figure 15.6, an effluent fee of *A* per unit of pollution discharge might be charged. If so, the marginal cost of an additional unit of pollution discharge to the industry is *A*, with the result that it will cut back its pollution to the socially optimal level, *B* units. To maximize their profits, the firms in the industry will reduce pollution to *B* units because it will be profitable to cut back pollution so long as the marginal cost of reducing pollution by a unit is less than *A*—and, as you can see from Figure 15.6, this is the case when the pollution discharge exceeds *B*.

To illustrate the usefulness of effluent fees, take the case of Germany's Ruhr Valley, a highly industrialized area with limited water supplies. Effluent fees have been used in the Ruhr to help maintain the quality of the local rivers, and the results have been highly successful. But this does not mean, of course, that direct regulation is not useful too. Some ways of disposing of certain types of waste are so dangerous that the only sensible thing to do is to ban them. Also, it sometimes is not feasible to impose effluent fees—for example, in cases where it is very difficult to meter the amount of pollutants emitted by various firms and households.

Yet another way that the government can reduce the amount of pollution is to issue **transferable emissions permits,** which are permits to generate a particular amount of pollution. These permits, which are limited in total

## BUYING AND SELLING POLLUTION PERMITS AT THE CHICAGO BOARD OF TRADE

On July 16, 1991, the Chicago Board of Trade voted to create a private market for rights to emit sulfur dioxide. This was made possible by the Clean Air Act of 1990, which gave polluters the right to meet sulfur dioxide standards by buying and selling pollution emissions permits that the Environmental Protection Agency will issue to electric utilities. Moreover, individuals can speculate on a rise or fall in the price of such pollution permits, in essentially the same way that they speculate now on bonds or stocks.

The Clean Air Act establishes a particular limit on total emissions of sulfur dioxide from 110 power plants beginning in 1995. In the year 2000, this limit will be reduced substantially (to less than half the 1991 level). One object of this program is to reduce acid rain. Firms finding it relatively expensive to cut down on their sulfur dioxide emissions are likely to buy pollution permits because such permits cost less than cutting down on their emissions. On the other hand,

firms finding it relatively cheap to cut down on their sulfur dioxide emissions are likely to sell pollution permits because their costs of reducing the emissions are less than what they can sell the permits for. Thus, the reduction in the total emission of sulfur dioxide will occur at relatively low cost.

For such a scheme to work, the electric utilities must be able to buy and sell permits. The Chicago Board of Trade will begin to allow such trading to occur in 1993, even though the permits will not be issued until 1995. (Firms will be able to make agreements to deliver permits after they are issued.) According to Richard Sandor, an executive managing director at Kidder, Peabody, and Company, the price of a right to emit a ton of sulfur dioxide is likely to be about $400. This price will be set by the supply and demand curves for permits. However, it cannot exceed $2,000 per ton since utilities can exceed their legal limits and pay fines of $2,000 per ton.*

* For further discussion, see *New York Times*, July 17, 1991.

number so that the aggregate amount of pollution equals the level the government decides on, are allocated among firms. They can be bought and sold. Firms that find it very expensive to curb pollution are likely to buy these permits; firms that find it cheap to do so are likely to sell them. The Clean Air Act of 1990 called for the use of such permits to reduce the emission of sulfur dioxide, and the Chicago Board of Trade has voted to create a market for these permits. (See page 597.)

## EFFECTS OF REGULATION-INDUCED COST INCREASE ON PRICE AND OUTPUT

Regardless of how the government induces firms to reduce pollution, the result is an increase in firms' costs, as in the case of the Reserve Mining Company discussed above. (Du Pont is reported to have spent about ‘$500 million on environmental equipment in 1991 alone.[16]) It is important to recognize this fact, and to see how you can determine the extent to which this cost increase will be passed on to consumers in the form of a price increase—and the extent that it will be borne by the firms. In this section, we learn how this can be done.

Suppose a new regulation is enacted that says that paper mills must use new methods to reduce water pollution. Assuming that the paper industry is perfectly competitive, we can compare the situation in the industry after the regulation's enactment with that prior to its enactment. Before the regulation, the marginal cost function of each paper producer is assumed to be

$$MC = 20 + 40Q, \tag{15.5}$$

where $Q$ equals the number (in thousands) of tons of paper produced per week. Thus, if the price is $P$, the firm, to maximize profit, will set price equal to marginal cost, which means that

$$P = 20 + 40Q,$$

or

$$Q = -0.5 + 0.025P.$$

If there are 1,000 paper producers, all with the same cost function, the industry's supply curve is

$$Q_S = 1,000(-0.5 + 0.025P)$$
$$= -500 + 25P. \tag{15.6}$$

---

[16] "How Clean-Air Bill Will Force Du Pont into Costly Moves," *Wall Street Journal*, May 25, 1990.

Assuming that the market demand curve for paper is

$$Q_D = 3,500 - 15P, \tag{15.7}$$

we can find the equilibrium price and output of paper by setting the quantity demanded, in equation (15.7), equal to the quantity supplied, in equation (15.6):

$$3,500 - 15P = -500 + 25P$$

$$40P = 4,000$$

$$P = 100.$$

Thus, the quantity demanded equals

$$Q_D = 3,500 - 15P = 3,500 - 15(100) = 2,000.$$

And the quantity supplied equals the same amount:

$$Q_S = -500 + 25P = -500 + 25(100) = 2,000.$$

In other words, before the new regulation, the price of paper is $100 per ton, and 2,000 thousands of tons are produced per week.

What is the effect of the new regulation on the price and output of paper? Suppose the regulation raises the marginal cost of producing paper by 25 percent. Thus, after the regulation, the marginal cost function of each paper producer is

$$MC = 1.25 \, (20 + 40Q)$$

$$= 25 + 50Q.$$

To maximize profit, each firm sets marginal cost equal to price, which means that

$$25 + 50Q = P,$$

or

$$Q = -0.5 + 0.02P.$$

Thus, the industry's postregulation supply curve is

$$Q'_S = 1,000(-0.5 + 0.02P)$$

$$= -500 + 20P, \tag{15.8}$$

if all 1,000 of the paper producers stay in the industry. (Some may drop out if they cannot avoid losses. Recall Chapter 10.) To find the equilibrium price after the enactment of the new regulation, we set the quantity demanded in equation (15.7), equal to the quantity supplied, in equation (15.8):

$$3,500 - 15P = -500 + 20P$$

$$35P = 4,000$$

$$P = 114.3.$$

Thus, the postregulation quantity demanded equals

$$Q_D = 3,500 - 15P = 3,500 - 15(114.3) = 1,786.$$

And the quantity supplied equals the same amount:

$$Q_S' = -500 + 20P = -500 + 20(114.3) = 1,786.$$

In other words, after the new regulation, the price of paper is $114.30 per ton, and 1,786 thousands of tons of paper are produced per week.

Clearly, the new regulation results in an increase in price (from $100 to $114.30 per ton) and a reduction in output (from 2,000 to 1,786 thousands of tons per week). This will typically be the effect of such regulations, but the extent of the price increase (and the output reduction) will depend on the price elasticity of demand for the product. If the price elasticity is very low, the price increase will be greater (and the output reduction will be smaller) than it would be if the price elasticity were very high.

## PUBLIC GOODS

Besides regulating the environment and the behavior of monopolists, the government performs a wide variety of economic functions, including the provision of goods and services. For example, the government is responsible for the provision of national defense, a critically important product in any society. Why does the government provide some goods and not others? One important reason is that some goods—so-called *public goods*—are unlikely to be produced in sufficient amounts by the private (non-governmental) sector of the economy. Thus, the government is given the task of providing these goods. Before concluding this chapter, we must describe briefly what a public good is and why the private sector is unlikely to provide a public good in sufficient amounts.

A major hallmark of a public good is that *it can be consumed by one person without diminishing the amount that other people consume of it.* Public goods tend to be relatively indivisible; they often come in such large units that they cannot be broken into pieces that can be bought or sold in ordinary markets. Also, *once such goods are produced, there is no way to bar citizens from consuming them.* Whether or not citizens contribute toward their cost, they benefit from them. Obviously, this means that it would be very difficult for any firm to market them effectively.

As pointed out above, national defense is a public good. The benefits of expenditure on national defense apply to the entire nation. Extension of the benefits of national defense to an additional citizen does not mean that any other citizen gets less of these benefits. Also, there is no way of preventing citizens from benefiting from them, whether they contribute to their cost or not. Thus, there is no way to use ordinary markets (such as exist for wheat, steel, or computers) to provide for national defense. Since it is a public good, national defense, if it is to reach an adequate level, must be provided by the government. Similarly with flood control, environmental protection, and other such services.

However, it is important to recognize that, although these services are provided by the government, this does not mean that they must be produced entirely by the government. The U.S. Air Force does not produce the B-2 Stealth Bomber; Northrop Corporation does. The U.S. Navy does not produce the F-14 fighter; Grumman does. Firms play a central role in developing and producing the weapons systems on which our military establishment relies, although national defense is a public good.

Government agencies have a major influence over a wide variety of industries, not just defense contractors like Northrop or Grumman. This chapter has described in detail many of the activities of government agencies that are of most importance to managers. Much more will be said on this score in the following chapter, which deals with managerial economics in a global context.

# SUMMARY

1. Commissions regulating public utilities often set price at the level at which it equals average total cost, including a "fair rate of return" on the firm's investment. One difficulty with this arrangement is that since the firm is guaranteed this rate of return (regardless of how well or poorly it performs), there is no incentive for the firm to increase its efficiency. Although regulatory lag results in some incentives of this sort, they often are relatively weak.

2. There has been a great deal of controversy over the practices of the regulatory commissions. Many economists have viewed them as lax or ill-conceived. In many areas, like transportation, there has been a movement toward deregulation. In the airline industry, this movement has been particularly dramatic.

3. The Sherman Act outlaws any contract, combination, or conspiracy in restraint of trade and makes it illegal to monopolize or attempt to monopolize. The Clayton Act outlaws unjustified price discrimination and tying contracts that reduce competition, among other things. The Robinson-Patman Act was aimed at preventing price discrimination in favor of chain stores that buy goods in large quantities. The Federal Trade Commission Act was designed to prevent undesirable and unfair competitive practices.

4. The real impact of the antitrust laws depends on the interpretation placed on these laws by the courts. In its early cases, the Supreme Court put forth and used the famous rule of reason—that only unreasonable combinations in restraint of trade, not all trusts, required conviction under the Sherman Act. The situation changed greatly in the 1940s when the court decided that Alcoa, because it controlled practically all of the nation's aluminum output, was in violation of the antitrust laws. In the early 1980s, two major antitrust cases—against American Telephone and Telegraph and the IBM Corporation—were decided.

5. The patent laws grant the inventor exclusive control over the use of an invention in exchange for his or her making the invention public knowledge. The patent system enables innovators to appropriate a larger portion of the social benefits from their innovations than would be the case without it, but it frequently has only a limited effect on the rate at which imitators appear. Nonetheless, firms continue to make extensive use of the patent system.

6. In many high-technology industries, there is a widespread feeling among top managers that inadequate protection is being given to intellectual property rights, such as patents and copyrights. The developing countries have particularly weak laws to protect intellectual property rights and less than diligent enforcement of the laws that exist.

7. An external economy occurs when an action taken by a firm or individual results in uncompensated benefits to others. An external diseconomy occurs when an action taken by a firm or individual results in uncompensated costs or harm to others. When firms and individuals pollute our waterways and atmosphere they are engaged in activities resulting in external diseconomies.

8. The socially optimal level of pollution (holding output constant) is at the point where the marginal cost of pollution equals the marginal cost of pollution control. In general, this will be at a point where a nonzero amount of pollution occurs. To formulate incentives that will lead to a more nearly optimal level of pollution, the government can establish effluent fees, issue transferable emissions permits, and enact direct regulations, among other things.

9. Regulations (and other measures) designed to reduce pollution tend to increase the costs of the regulated firms. The price of their product generally goes up, and industry output tends to go down. If the price elasticity of demand is relatively low, more of the cost increase can be passed along to consumers in the form of a price increase than would be the case if the price elasticity of demand were relatively high.

10. A public good can be consumed by one person without diminishing the amount of it that other people consume. Also, once a public good is produced, there is no way to bar citizens from consuming it. Public goods, such as national defense, are unlikely to be produced in sufficient quantities by the private (nongovernmental) sector of the econ-

omy. Thus, the government often is given the task of providing these goods.

# PROBLEMS

1. The Harrison Electric Company is engaged in a rate case with the local regulatory commission. The demand curve for the firm's product is

$$P = 1000 - 2Q,$$

where $P$ is price per unit of output (in dollars), and $Q$ is output (in thousands of units per year). Its total cost (excluding the opportunity cost of the capital invested in the firm by its owners) is

$$TC = 50 + .25Q,$$

where $TC$ is expressed in millions of dollars.

(a) The Harrison Electric Company has requested an annual rate (that is, price) of $480. If the firm has assets of $100 million, what will be its rate of return on its assets if this request is granted?

(b) How much greater would the firm's accounting profits be if it were deregulated?

2. The cost of pollution (in billions of dollars) originating in the paper industry is

$$C_p = 2P + P^2,$$

where $P$ is the quantity of pollutants emitted (in thousands of tons). The cost of pollution control (in billions of dollars) for this industry is

$$C_c = 5 - 3P.$$

(a) What is the optimal level of pollution?

(b) At this level of pollution, what is the marginal cost of pollution?

(c) At this level of pollution, what is the marginal cost of pollution control?

3. There are seven firms that produce kitchen tables. Suppose their sales in 1994 are as follows:

| Firm | Sales (millions of dollars) |
|------|------|
| A | 100 |
| B | 50 |
| C | 40 |
| D | 30 |
| E | 20 |
| F | 5 |
| G | 5 |

(a) What is the concentration ratio in this industry?

(b) Would you regard this industry as oligopolistic? Why or why not?

(c) Suppose that firm A merges with firm G. What now will be the concentration ratio in this industry?

(d) Suppose that after they merge, firms A and G go out of business. What now will be the concentration ratio in this industry?

4. The cost of pollution emanating from the chemical industry (in billions of dollars) is

$$C_p = 3P + 3P^2,$$

where $P$ is the quantity of pollutants emitted (in thousands of tons). The cost of pollution control (in billions of dollars) is

$$C_c = 7 - 5P.$$

(a) What is the optimal effluent fee?

(b) If the cost of pollution control falls by $1 billion at each level of pollution, does this alter your answer to part (a)?

5. In the cardboard box industry, the minimum value of average cost is reached when a firm produces 1,000 units of output per month. At this output rate, average cost is $1 per unit of output. The demand curve for this product is as follows:

| Price (dollars per unit of output) | Quantity (units demanded per month) |
|---|---|
| 3.00 | 1,000 |
| 2.00 | 8,000 |
| 1.00 | 12,000 |
| 0.50 | 20,000 |

(a) Is this industry a natural monopoly? Why or why not?

(b) If the price is $2, how many firms, each of which is producing an output such that average cost is a minimum, can the market support?

6. The Kravis Company, which sells engines, has a uniform price of $500, which it charges all its customers. But after its competitors begin to cut their prices in the California market to $400, Kravis reduces its price to $400.

(a) Does this tend to violate the Clayton Act?

(b) If the Kravis Company had cut its price to $300, might this tend to violate the Clayton Act?

(c) Suppose the Kravis Company decides to purchase enough of the stock of competing firms so that it can exercise control over them and see to it that the price-cutting in the California market stops. Is this legal? If not, what law does it violate?

7. Bethlehem and Youngstown, two major steel producers, accounted for about 21 percent of the national steel market in the late 1950s, when they proposed to merge.

(a) Should the two steel companies have been allowed to merge? Why or why not?

(b) According to the companies, Bethlehem sold most of its output in the East, whereas Youngstown sold most of its output in the Midwest. Was this fact of relevance? Why or why not?

(c) In fact, the district court did not allow Bethlehem and Youngstown to merge. Yet in 1985 (as we saw on page 584), the Department of Transportation allowed United Airlines (with about 7 percent of the service between Japan and the U.S. mainland) to acquire Pan Am's Pacific Division (with about 19 percent). How can you explain this?

8. One of the most celebrated antitrust cases of recent years involved Eastman Kodak and Berkey Photo. Eastman Kodak has long been a dominant producer of cameras and film. Berkey Photo competed with Kodak as photofinisher, and less successfully (until 1978) as a camera manufacturer. Berkey bought much of its film and photo finishing equipment and supplies from Kodak. In 1973, Berkey filed suit, saying that Kodak had violated the antitrust laws when in 1972 it introduced its new 110 "Pocket Instamatic" camera. Because the camera was introduced with no advance notice to Kodak's competitors, Berkey could not introduce its own version of the new camera until late 1973, and did not reach a substantial sales volume until 1974. Berkey claimed that Kodak's failure to disclose the innovation to its competitors before introducing it violated Section 2 of the Sherman Act.

The jury was instructed that if it found monopoly power in the relevant markets (cameras or film), it could then consider "whether in the light of other conduct [it] determine[d] to be anticompetitive, Kodak's failure to predisclose was on balance an exclusionary course of conduct," and thus in violation of Section 2. The jury found that Berkey should be awarded damages, after trebling, of $45,750,000 for lost profits on the 110 camera and $167,100 for lost profits on photo finishing services. The court also instructed Kodak to disclose (before introduction) to competitors all camera and film innovations that it provides its own photo finishing division.

(a) Does withholding from others advance knowledge of a firm's new products ordinarily constitute valid and legal competitive conduct?

(b) What effect would the court's decision have on the incentives to innovate?

(c) Kodak appealed the decision, and the circuit court reversed the damage awards. Give several reasons why such a reversal was reasonable.

9. *Telex Corporation v. International Business Machines Corporation*, decided in 1975, was one of the most important cases in the antitrust field in recent decades. The following passages are taken from the opinion of the court of appeals, which is commenting on the decision of a lower court.

We recognize that market definition is generally treated as a matter of fact and that findings on this subject are not to be overturned unless clearly erroneous. Our question is, therefore, whether it was clearly erroneous for the court to exclude peripheral products of systems other than IBM such as Honeywell, Univac, Burroughs, Control Data Corp. and others, together with peripheral products plug compatible with the systems and, indeed, whether the systems themselves manufactured by the companies are to be taken into account. It is significant, of course, that peripheral products constitute a large percentage of the entire data processing system, somewhere between 50 and 75 percent.

Inasmuch as IBM's share of the data processing industry as a whole is insufficient to justify any inference or conclusion of market power in IBM, the exclusion from the defined market of those products which are not plug compatible with IBM central processing units has a significant impact on the court's decision that IBM possessed monopoly power.

We then must inquire whether this market definition was correct in light of the following factors:

Should peripheral products not plug compatible with IBM systems be considered part of the relevant market in view of the existence of easy and practicable interchange of these products by use of interfaces designed for this purpose?

Should not the peripheral products plug compatible with systems other than IBM be considered part of the relevant market because of the admitted competition existing as between system manufacturers on a system by system basis in which the peripherals are a significant part of the system?

In dealing with the issue whether peripheral products non-compatible with IBM systems ought to be considered, the court said in Finding 47 that as a *practical* matter there is no direct competition between IBM peripherals and the peripherals of other systems manufacturers. However, this finding is out of harmony with other findings which the court made. . . .

It seems clear that reasonable interchangeability is proven in the case at bar and hence the market should include not only peripheral products plug compatible with IBM CPUs, but all peripheral products, those compatible not only with IBM CPUs but those compatible with non-IBM systems. This is wholly justifiable because the record shows that these products, although not fungible, are fully interchangeable and may be interchanged with minimal financial outlay, and so cross-elasticity exists within meaning of the *Du Pont* decision.

The court's very restrictive definition of the product market in the face of evidence which established the interchangeable quality of the products in question, together with the existence of cross-elasticity of demand, must be regarded as plain error.[17]

---

[17] U.S. Court of Appeals, "Telex Corporation v. International Business Machines Corporation," in E. Mansfield, ed., *Managerial Economics and Operations Research*, 5th ed. (New York: Norton, 1987).

(a) Why does this opinion put so much emphasis on the definition of the relevant market?

(b) Why does the court dwell so much on the question of interchangeability of products?

(c) Why is the concept of cross elasticity of demand, discussed in Chapter 3, relevant here?

10. During the 1990s, there has been an enormous amount of attention devoted to global warming. According to many scientific theories, increases in carbon dioxide and other so-called greenhouse gases may produce significant climatic changes over the next century. To cope with this potential problem, it has been suggested that firms reduce energy consumption and switch to nonfossil fuels. William Nordhaus, a leading expert on this topic, has estimated that the worldwide costs (in 1989 U.S. dollars) of various percentage reductions in the quantity of greenhouse gases emitted into the atmosphere would be as follows:

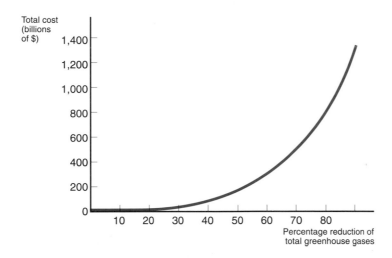

*Source:* R. Dornbusch and J. Poterba, eds., *Global Warming: Economic Policy Responses* (Cambridge, Mass.: MIT Press, 1991), p. 50.

(a) Does this graph show the cost of pollution or the cost of pollution control?

(b) Can this graph alone indicate the socially optimal amount of greenhouse gases that should be emitted into the atmosphere? Why, or why not?

(c) If world output is about $20 trillion, by what percentage would world output be reduced if the nations of the world agreed to cut greenhouse gas emission by 50 percent?

(d) The single most common policy that is proposed to decrease greenhouse gas emission is a so-called carbon tax, a tax on fossil fuels in proportion to the amount of carbon they emit when burned. Why would such a tax have the desired effect?

11. On August 28, 1991, the New York State Electric and Gas Corporation filed a request for a 10.7 percent increase in electric revenues. The reasons given to justify the increase were that the value of the firm's plant and equipment had increased by $140 million, that operating costs had increased, and that investors required a higher rate of return.

   (a) Why should an increase in the value of the firm's plant and equipment result in an increase in the amount of revenue allowed by the Public Service Commission?

   (b) Why should an increase in operating costs have the same effect?

   (c) Why should the attitude of investors regarding what they require as a rate of return be relevant here?

# Chapter 16
# Managerial Economics: Taking a Global View

Competition in many industries is global. In automobiles, electronics, machine tools, computers, and a host of other industries, Japanese, European, and American firms—sometimes with considerable help from their governments—are battling hard for supremacy, or at least survival. If you want to be an effective manager in such industries, you must understand relevant aspects of international economics. In this chapter, we take up the factors influencing whether a country will export or import a particular product, the determinants of exchange rates, and the nature and effects of tariffs, quotas, and strategic trade policy. Also, we discuss the factors that should be considered by managers in deciding whether to build a plant abroad, where to build it, and how quickly, and in choosing whether—and, if so, how—to transfer technology overseas. These topics are of central importance in today's world, where advances in transportation and communication have brought Tokyo and London much closer to New York or Los Angeles than the map indicates.

## FOREIGN TRADE

To begin with, it is important to recognize that foreign trade is of great importance to the United States. As shown in Table 16.1, we exported

TABLE 16.1    *U.S. Merchandise Exports and Imports, 1990*

| Exports | | Imports | |
|---|---|---|---|
| Product | Amount *(billions of dollars)* | Product | Amount *(billions of dollars)* |
| Food, feed, and beverages | 35 | Food, feed, and beverages | 27 |
| Industrial supplies | 106 | Petroleum and oil products | 62 |
| Machinery | 120 | Other industrial supplies | 82 |
| Autos and parts | 37 | Capital goods | 117 |
| Aircraft | 32 | Auto vehicles and parts | 86 |
| Other | 59 | Consumer goods (except autos) | 106 |
| | | Other | 18 |
| Total | 389 | | |
| | | Total | 498 |

*Source: Survey of Current Business.*

about $390 billion in merchandise in 1990, much of it being machinery and industrial supplies, and we imported about $500 billion, much of it being capital goods and autos and other consumer goods. As shown in Table 16.2, about half our exports went to Western Europe and Canada in 1990, and over 45 percent of our imports were from Western Europe and Japan.

Why does trade occur among nations? As economists have pointed out for over a century, *trade permits specialization, and specialization increases output.* Because the United States can trade with other countries, it can specialize in the goods and services it produces well and cheaply. Then it can trade them for goods that other nations are particularly good at producing. The result: both we and our trading partners can benefit.

International differences in resource endowments, and in the relative quantity of various types of human and nonhuman resources, are important bases for specialization. Consider nations with lots of fertile soil, little

TABLE 16.2    *Geographical Distribution of U.S. Exports and Imports, 1990*

| Area | Percentage Distribution | |
|---|---|---|
| | Exports | Imports |
| Japan | 13 | 16 |
| Western Europe | 32 | 30 |
| Latin America | 16 | 15 |
| Canada | 17 | 15 |
| Eastern Europe | 1 | * |
| Other | 21 | 24 |
| Total | 100 | 100 |

* Less than $\frac{1}{2}$ of 1 percent.
*Source:* See Table 16.1.

capital, and much unskilled labor. They are likely to find it advantageous to produce agricultural goods, while nations with poor soil, much capital, and highly skilled labor will probably do better to produce capital-intensive, high-technology goods. However, the bases for specialization do not remain fixed over time. Instead, as technology and the resource endowments of various nations change, the pattern of international specialization changes as well. For example, the United States specialized more in raw materials and foodstuffs a century ago than it does now.

## COMPARATIVE ADVANTAGE

Even if one country is able to produce everything more cheaply than another country, it still is likely that they both can benefit from specialization and trade. This proposition, known as the *law of comparative advantage,* must be understood. Suppose that the United States is twice as efficient as China in producing computers and 50 percent more efficient than China in producing textiles. In particular, suppose that the United States can produce 2 computers or 6,000 pounds of textiles with 1 unit of resources, and China can produce 1 computer or 4,000 pounds of textiles with 1 unit of resources. In this case, the United States is a more efficient producer of both computers and textiles, but it has a comparative advantage in computers, not textiles. In other words, its efficiency advantage over China is greater in computers than in textiles, so its comparative advantage lies in computers. (Why is its efficiency advantage greater in computers than in textiles? Because it can produce double as many computers, but only 50 percent more textiles, from a unit of resources than China can.)

If countries specialize in producing goods and services where they have a comparative advantage and trade with one another, each country can improve its standard of living. Figure 16.1 shows the *production possibilities curve* in the United States—the curve that shows the maximum number of computers that can be produced, given various outputs of textiles. The United States must give up 1 computer for every additional 3,000 pounds of textiles it produces; thus, the slope of the American production possibilities curve is $-1/3,000$. Also, Figure 16.1 shows China's production possibilities curve. Since China must give up 1 computer for every additional 4,000 pounds of textiles it produces, the slope of its production possibilities curve is $-1/4,000$.

Suppose that the United States has 1,000 units of resources and uses all of them to produce computers, while China has 800 units of resources and uses all of them to produce textiles.[1] In other words, the United States oper-

---

[1] By resources we mean here a combination of labor, capital and other types of inputs, not just labor alone, so it is realistic to suppose that the United States has more resources than China. Note too that it generally is more realistic to assume that production possibilities curves are curvilinear, rather than linear (as in Figure 16.1). Usually, the slope of a production possibilities curve becomes steeper as one moves to the right along the horizontal axis. However, for present purposes, we assume that these curves are linear to keep the analysis as simple as possible.

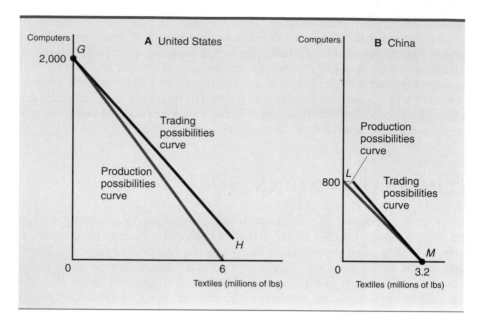

*FIGURE 16.1* *Production and Trading Possibilities Curves, United States and China* Each country's trading possibilities curve lies above its production possibilities curve. This means that both countries can have more of both commodities by specializing and trading than by trying to be self-sufficient.

ates at point *G* on its production possibilities curve and China operates at point *M* on its production possibilities curve. Then suppose that the United States trades its computers for China's textiles. The line *GH* in panel A of Figure 16.1 shows the various amounts of computers and textiles the United States can end up with if it specializes in computers and trades them for Chinese textiles. The line *GH* is called the *trading possibilities curve* of the United States. The slope of *GH* is

$$- \frac{\text{price of textiles (per pound)}}{\text{price of a computer}},$$

which (in absolute value) equals the number of computers the United States must give up to get a pound of Chinese textiles. Similarly, the line *LM* in panel B of Figure 16.1 shows China's trading possibilities curve. That is, *LM* represents the various amounts of computers and textiles China can wind up with if it specializes in textiles and trades them for U.S. computers.

The big point to note about both panels of Figure 16.1 is that *each country's trading possibilities curve—GH in panel A and LM in panel B—lies above its production possibilities curve*. This means that both countries can have more of both commodities by specializing and trading than by trying to be self-sufficient—even though the United States is more efficient than China at producing both commodities. Moreover, firms in the United States can make money by producing computers and selling them in both countries, and firms in China can make money by producing textiles and selling them in both countries.

# CHANGES IN COMPARATIVE ADVANTAGE

Any good manager must recognize that, if a country has a comparative advantage in the production of a particular commodity, it cannot count on this situation lasting indefinitely. To illustrate, consider the case of watches. In 1945, Switzerland produced about 90 percent of the world's watches and watch movements. The production of watches was labor intensive; about 60 percent of the production cost of a watch went for labor. The Swiss firms concentrated on making high-quality, expensive watches (so-called jewel-levered watches). Their watches were sold largely in jewelry stores (and some department stores), where profit margins were typically about 50 percent. During the 1950s and 1960s, Switzerland's share of world watch output declined, in part because Timex, a U.S. firm, successfully produced and marketed inexpensive watches that were popular and the Japanese became a bigger factor in the watch market. (Recall page 441 of Chapter 11.) Nonetheless, the Swiss still produced about half the world's watches in 1970.

During the 1970s, the technology of watchmaking was revolutionized, resulting in the quartz watch. This new technology permitted the design of watches that were very accurate; also, it allowed miniaturization and the digital display of time. For analog quartz watches (those with the traditional face and hands), average variable production costs fell by about 83 percent between 1974 and 1979. By 1979, direct labor accounted for less than 20 percent of the production cost of an analog quartz watch. In the case of digital quartz watches, many semiconductor firms, often in the United States or Hong Kong, constructed fully automated production processes to make them.

By 1980, Switzerland no longer had a comparative advantage in watch manufacture. It produced only about 15 percent of the world's watches, less than Hong Kong or Japan. The leading producer was Hong Kong, where most watches were made by semiconductor firms, not the traditional watch manufacturers. What happened to the Swiss watch industry? It shrank. In 1980, it contained about half as many firms—and employed about half as many employees—as in 1970.

Clearly, the managers of any firm selling largely to foreign markets (or competing against foreign rivals in domestic markets) must constantly be on their guard against the loss of comparative advantage. In some cases, if such a loss occurs, the answer is to locate the firm's factories in some other part of the world where costs are lower. For example, Timex produced overseas many of the watches it sold in the United States. In other cases, the firm may be best off to get out of the business and invest its resources elsewhere. Thus, as pointed out in Chapter 2, John Welch, chairman of General Electric, decided in 1987 to sell its consumer electronics business to Thomson-Brandt, France's government-owned consumer electronics manufacturer.[2]

## USING DEMAND AND SUPPLY CURVES TO DETERMINE WHICH COUNTRY WILL EXPORT A PRODUCT

How can a manager tell whether his or her country has a comparative advantage in the production of a particular product? One important indicator is whether this country's firms can make money by producing and exporting the product. Consider the Wilton Company, maker of a new product produced and sold only in Germany and the United States, the only two countries where this product has a significant market. In the United States, the demand curve for this product is such that[3]

$$Q_d^u = 100 - 2P_u, \tag{16.1}$$

and the supply curve is such that[4]

$$Q_s^u = 5 + 2.6P_u, \tag{16.2}$$

where $P_u$ is the price of the product (in dollars) in the United States, $Q_d^u$ is the quantity demanded (in millions of units) per month in the United States, and $Q_s^u$ is the quantity supplied (in millions of units) per month in the United States. In Germany, the demand curve for this product is such that

$$Q_d^g = 120 - 4P_g, \tag{16.3}$$

and the supply curve is such that

$$Q_s^g = 2 + 2P_g, \tag{16.4}$$

where $P_g$ is the price of the product (in German marks) in Germany, $Q_d^g$ is

---

[2] For further discussion, see D. Yoffie, *International Trade and Competition* (New York: McGraw-Hill, 1990).

[3] As pointed out in Chapter 3, the demand curve for a product is an equation where price is on the left-hand side of the equation, and quantity demanded is on the right-hand side. To derive equation (16.1) [and equation (16.3)], we move price to the right-hand side and quantity demanded to the left-hand side.

[4] As pointed out in Chapter 10, the supply curve for a product is an equation where price is on the left-hand side of the equation, and quantity supplied is on the right-hand side. To derive equation (16.2) [and equation (16.4)], we move price to the right-hand side and quantity supplied to the left-hand side.

the quantity demanded (in millions of units) per month in Germany, and $Q_s^g$ is the quantity supplied (in millions of units) per month in Germany.

Since this new product is now being introduced for the first time in Germany and the United States, managers and analysts in both countries would like to predict whether, after markets in both countries settle down, this product will be exported, and if so, by which of these two countries. To answer this question, we must begin by noting that, if the cost of transporting this product from the United States to Germany (or back) is negligible, the price of this product must be the same in both countries. Why? Because if it were different, a firm could make money by purchasing it in the country where its price is lower and selling it in the country where its price is higher. As this continued, the price would rise in the former country and fall in the latter country, until eventually the price in both countries would be equal.

But what do we mean by the price in both countries being equal? Prices in the United States are quoted in dollars; prices in Germany are quoted in marks. What we mean is that, based on prevailing exchange rates, the prices in the two countries are the same. If the U.S. dollar exchanges (at banks and elsewhere) for 1.6 German marks, a price of $10 in the United States is equivalent to a price of 16 marks in Germany. Consequently, if this is the exchange rate, what we mean when we say that the prices in the two countries are the same is that

$$P_g = 1.6P_u. \tag{16.5}$$

If there is no government intervention in the market for this product and if this market is competitive, the price of this product will tend to be at the level where the total world demand for the product equals the total world supply. In other words, in equilibrium,

$$Q_d^u + Q_d^g = Q_s^u + Q_s^g. \tag{16.6}$$

Using equations (16.1) to (16.4), we can express each of the $Q$'s in equation (16.6) as a function of $P_u$ or $P_g$. Substituting each of these functions for each of the $Q$'s in equation (16.6), we obtain

$$(100 - 2P_u) + (120 - 4P_g) = (5 + 2.6P_u) + (2 + 2P_g).$$

And substituting $1.6P_u$ for $P_g$, we find that

$$(100 - 2P_u) + (120 - 4 \times 1.6P_u) = (5 + 2.6P_u) + (2 + 2 \times 1.6P_u),$$

or

$$220 - 8.4P_u = 7 + 5.8P_u$$
$$213 = 14.2P_u$$
$$P_u = \$15.$$

And since $P_g = 1.6P_u$, $P_g = 1.6(15) = 24$ marks. In other words, the price of the product will be $15 in the United States and 24 marks in Germany.

Given these prices, we can determine whether Germany or the United

States will be an exporter of the product. Based on equation (16.1), the monthly demand in the United States will be $100 - 2P_u = 100 - 2(15) = 70$ millions of units. Based on equation (16.2), the amount supplied per month in the United States will be $5 + 2.6P_u = 5 + 2.6(15) = 44$ millions of units. Thus, the United States will import $70 - 44 = 26$ millions of units per month. Based on equation (16.3), the monthly demand in Germany will be $120 - 4P_g = 120 - 4(24) = 24$ millions of units. Based on equation (16.4), the amount supplied per month in Germany will be $2 + 2P_g = 2 + 2(24) = 50$ millions of units per month. Thus, Germany will export 26 millions of units per month.

In sum, the answer is that Germany will be the exporter of this new product—and that its exports will be 26 million units per month.

## EXCHANGE RATES

Practically any manager of a large firm (and many managers of small firms) must be concerned with exchange rates. For example, suppose that an American firm wants to buy a machine tool from a Japanese firm. To buy the machine tool, it must somehow get Japanese yen to pay the machine-tool maker, since this is the currency in which the machine-tool maker deals. Or, if the machine-tool maker agrees, the American firm might pay in dollars; but the Japanese firm would then have to exchange the dollars for yen, since its bills must be paid in yen. Whatever happens, either the American firm or the Japanese firm must somehow exchange dollars for yen, since international business transactions, unlike transactions within a country, involve two different currencies.

As pointed out in the previous section, *the exchange rate is the number of units of one currency that exchanges for a unit of another currency.* In 1992, an American dollar exchanged for about 125 yen; thus, this was the exchange rate between these two currencies. Exchange rates can vary considerably over time; for example, in 1970, a dollar exchanged for about 360, not 125, yen. (See Figure 16.2.) To a large extent, exchange rates, like any price in a competitive market, are determined by supply and demand.[5] In the case of the Japanese yen, the demand and supply curves may look like those shown in Figure 16.3. The demand curve shows the amount of Japanese yen that people with dollars will demand at various prices of a yen.

---

[5] Prior to 1973, exchange rates generally were fixed by government agreements. The International Monetary Fund was established to maintain a stable system of fixed exchange rates and to insure that when exchange rates had to be changed because of significant trade imbalances, disruption was minimized. This system, set up at the end of World War II, broke down and was replaced by flexible exchange rates in 1973.

However, governments still intervene to some extent in the currency markets. That is, they step in to buy and sell their currency. Thus the United States has agreed that "when necessary and desirable," it would support the value of the dollar. Also, some European countries have decided to maintain fixed exchange rates among their own currencies, but to float jointly against other currencies.

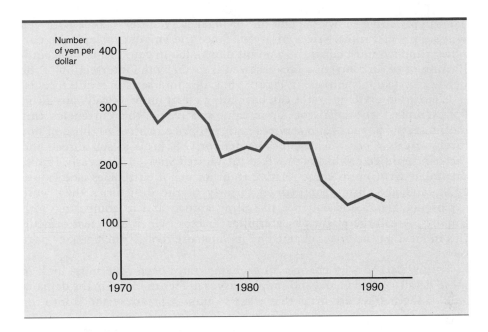

FIGURE 16.2 *Number of Japanese Yen That Could Be Bought for a U.S. Dollar, 1970–90* The exchange rate between the dollar and the yen has varied greatly.

*Source:* Economic Report of the President.

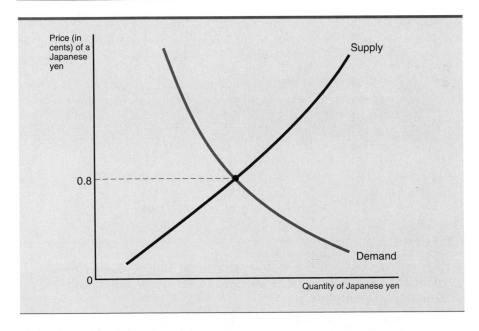

FIGURE 16.3 *Demand and Supply Curves for Japanese Yen* The equilibrium price of a yen is 0.8 cents.

The supply curve shows the amount of Japanese yen that people with yen will supply at various prices of a yen. Since the amount of Japanese currency supplied must equal the amount demanded in equilibrium, the equilibrium price (in cents) of a Japanese yen is given by the intersection of the demand and supply curves. In Figure 16.3, this intersection is at 0.8 cents.

Changes in exchange rates can have a big effect on practically any firm. For example, if the dollar goes up in value relative to other currencies, this means that U.S. goods and services go up in price relative to those of our foreign rivals. Consequently, it is harder for U.S. firms to sell abroad and easier for foreign producers to sell in the United States. In the early 1980s, the dollar went up in value relative to other major currencies (see Figure 16.4), and U.S. firms complained bitterly of the difficulties they were experiencing as a consequence in selling abroad and in competing with imports. Recall the plight of Caterpillar Tractor, which had great difficulties in meeting the prices charged by its Japanese rival, Komatsu. (See page 494.)

To understand why changes in exchange rates occur, we must look in more detail at the demand and supply curves in Figure 16.3. On the demand side of the market are firms that want to import Japanese goods into the

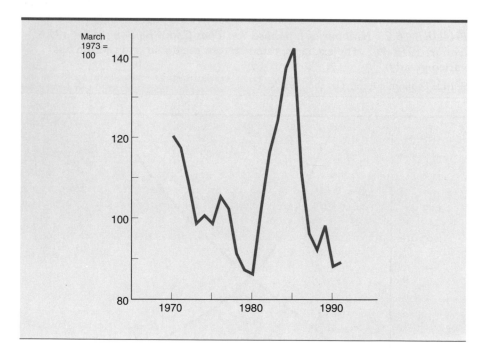

FIGURE 16.4   *Value of U.S. Dollar in Terms of Major Foreign Currencies,*
*1970–91*   The value of the dollar rose greatly (relative to other major
currencies) in the early 1980s.

*Source:* Economic Report of the President, 1991

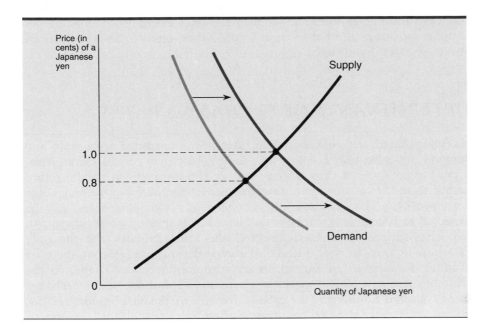

FIGURE 16.5   *Effect of Rightward Shift of the Demand Curve for Japanese Yen*   Because of the rightward shift of the demand curve, the equilibrium price of a yen increases from 0.8 to 1.0 cents.

United States, people who want to travel in Japan (where they'll need Japanese money), firms that want to invest in facilities in Japan, and other with dollars who want Japanese currency. The people on the supply side of the market are those who want to import U.S. goods into Japan, Japanese who want to travel in the United States (where they'll need U.S. money), firms with yen that want to invest in facilities in the United States, and others with yen who want U.S. currency.

When U.S. firms and individuals demand more Japanese goods and services, thus causing the demand curve in Figure 16.3 to shift upward and to the right, the price (in cents) of the Japanese yen will tend to increase. For example, if the demand curve for yen shifts as shown in Figure 16.5, the result will be an increase in the equilibrium price of the yen from 0.8 cents to 1.0 cents. On the other hand, when the Japanese demand more U.S. goods and services, thus causing the supply curve in Figure 16.3 to shift downward and to the right, the price (in cents) of the Japanese yen will tend to decrease.

Why does an increase in Japanese demand for U.S. goods and services cause the supply curve in Figure 16.3 to shift downward and to the right? Because this supply curve shows the amount of yen that will be supplied at each price of a yen. Since an increase in Japanese demand for U.S. goods and services would be expected to result in a greater amount of yen being put forth at a given price of the yen, it would be expected to shift this supply curve downward and to the right.

# DETERMINANTS OF EXCHANGE RATES

Having pointed out that exchange rates are determined by supply and demand, we must now go on to cite some of the major factors that determine the position of these supply and demand curves. In the long run, according to the so-called *purchasing power parity theory of exchange rate determination*, the exchange rate between any two currencies may be expected to reflect differences in the price levels in the two countries. To see why, suppose that Germany and the United States are the only exporters or importers of automobiles and that automobiles are the only product they export or import. If an automobile costs $10,000 in the United States and 20,000 marks in Germany, what must be the exchange rate between the dollar and the mark? Clearly, a mark must be worth $0.50, because otherwise the two countries' automobiles would not be competitive in the world market. If a mark were set equal to $0.60, this would mean that a German automobile would cost $12,000 (that is 20,000 times $0.60), which is more than what a U.S. automobile would cost. Thus, foreign buyers would obtain their automobiles in the United States.

Based on this theory, one would expect that, *if the rate of inflation in Country A is higher than in Country B, Country A's currency is likely to fall in value relative to Country B's.* Suppose that costs double in the United States, but increase by only 50 percent in Germany. After this burst of inflation, an automobile costs $20,000 (that is, 2 times $10,000) in the United States and 30,000 marks (that is, 1.50 times 20,000 marks) in Germany. Thus, based on the purchasing power parity theory, the new value of the mark must be $0.67, rather than the old value of $0.50. (Why $0.67? Because this is the exchange rate that makes the new cost of an automobile in the United States, $20,000, equivalent to the new cost of an automobile in Germany, 30,000 marks.) Because the rate of inflation is higher in the United States than in Germany, the dollar falls in value relative to the mark.

While relative price levels may play an important role in the long run, other factors tend to exert more influence on exchange rates in the short run. In particular, *if one country's rate of economic growth is higher than the rest of the world, its currency is likely to depreciate* (that is, fall in value relative to other nations' currencies). If a country's economy is booming, this tends to increase its imports. If there is a boom in the United States, Americans will tend to make more money and buy more of all goods, including foreign-made goods. If a country's imports tend to grow faster than its exports, its demand for foreign currency will tend to grow more rapidly than the amount of foreign currency that is supplied to it. Consequently, its currency is likely to depreciate.

Furthermore, if the rate of interest in Germany is higher than in the United States, banks, multinational corporations, and other investors in the United States will sell dollars and buy marks in order to invest in the high-yielding Germany securities. Also, German investors (and others) will be less likely to find U.S. securities attractive. Thus, the mark will tend to appreciate (that is, rise in value) relative to the dollar, since the demand curve for marks will shift to the right and the supply curve for marks will shift to the left. In general, *an increase in a country's interest rates leads to an appreciation of its currency, and a decrease in its interest rates leads to a depreciation of its currency.* In the short run, interest rate differentials can have a major impact on exchange rates, since huge amounts of money are moved from country to country in response to differentials in interest rates.

## TARIFFS AND QUOTAS

When an industry is threatened by foreign competition, it sometimes presses for a *tariff*, a tax that the government imposes on imports. The object of a tariff is to reduce imports in order to protect domestic industry and workers from foreign competition. Obviously, if foreign firms are faced with a tariff, they will cut down on the amount they export to this country. Indeed, if the tariff is high enough (a so-called prohibitive tariff), foreign firms will find it unprofitable to export to this country at all.

For example, during the early 1950s, watches imported from Switzerland rose from 38 to 58 percent of the American market. In 1954, U.S. watch manufacturers petitioned the federal government to increase tariffs on Swiss watches. They argued that the Swiss had a cost advantage because of lower wage rates and that watch manufacturing technology was important to national defense. The government agreed to increase tariffs by 50 percent on watches with 1 to 17 jewels.

Besides tariffs, other barriers to free trade are *quotas*, which are limits that many countries impose on the quantities of certain commodities that can be imported annually. In many cases, a quota insulates local industry from foreign competition even more effectively than a tariff does. Foreigners, if their costs are low enough, can surmount a tariff barrier; but if a quota exists, there is no way they can exceed the quota. The United States has imposed quotas on the imports of sugar and steel, among other commodities. In the case of sugar, imports in 1990 were limited to 1.6 million tons. In the case of steel, quotas were instituted in 1984, after American steel firms experienced substantial losses in the early 1980s and turned to the government for help. By 1989, steel imports were limited to about 20 percent of the U.S. market. In early 1992, the Bush administration, citing the improved position of American steel firms, allowed the steel import quotas to expire.

While economists traditionally have argued for free trade, there are circumstances where, from society's point of view, tariffs and quotas make sense. If a particular industry is essential for national defense, it may be reasonable to protect it in this way. Also, if an industry is young (a so-called *infant industry*), it may be sensible for the government to shelter it temporarily from the rigors of international competition, thus enabling it to develop to the point where it becomes strong and viable. However, even if there is a legitimate case on such grounds for protecting a domestic industry, government subsidies may be a more straightforward means to do so than tariffs or quotas.

# THE EFFECTS OF A QUOTA: THE CASE OF THE WILTON COMPANY'S PRODUCT

To illustrate the effects of a quota, let's return to the Wilton Company, producer of the new product produced and sold only in Germany and the United States. According to the analysis presented earlier in this chapter, Germany would be expected to export 26 million units of this product to the United States per month. Suppose that the Wilton Company and other American producers of the product succeed in getting the federal government to establish a quota of 3 million units per month on imports of this product from Germany. What will be the effect on the price of this product in the United States?

Since $Q_d^u$ is the quantity demanded in the United States and $Q_s^u$ is the quantity supplied in the United States, our imports of this product from Germany equal

$$Q_d^u - Q_s^u = (100 - 2P_u) - (5 + 2.6P_u) \qquad (16.7)$$
$$= 95 - 4.6P_u.$$

And since the quota says that these imports must not exceed 3 million units, it follows that

$$95 - 4.6P_u = 3,$$

which means that

$$P_u = 20.$$

Thus, the price of this product will be $20 in the United States, not $15 as it was before the quota. Clearly, this increase in price is a welcome development for the Wilton Company and other U.S. producers of the product, but not for U.S. consumers.

## WHY BRIDGESTONE PAID $2.6 BILLION FOR FIRESTONE'S TIRE PLANTS

The Bridgestone Tire Company is the biggest tire producer in Japan and the third largest tire producer in the world. During the 1970s and 1980s, its sales grew rapidly, both in Japan and in the rest of the world. Because its tires are part of the original equipment on exported Japanese cars, many of its tires enter foreign markets with little or no effort on its part. But direct exports of its tires are also important, and Bridgestone's management has wanted to expand its export sales.

In 1988, Bridgestone surprised many observers by buying the tire operations of Firestone Rubber, a major U.S. producer. Bridgestone paid Firestone $2.6 billion, for which it received five tire plants in North America (which provided at that time about 40 percent of the tires for North American cars built by Ford and 20 percent of those built by General Motors), and other plants in Europe and South America.

To understand this key decision, you must look carefully at two topics emphasized in this chapter —the imposition by governments of tariffs and quotas, and the movements of exchange rates. With regard to tariffs and quotas, Bridgestone's decision was influenced by actual and potential limitations by the United States government on U.S. imports of Japanese automobiles. These limitations led four major Japanese auto producers to start making cars in the United States, and all of them put U.S.–made tires on their U.S.–made cars.

Clearly, the purchase of Firestone's plants enabled Bridgestone to elude many of the effects of these limitations.

Turning to the movement of exchange rates, Bridgestone's decision was also influenced by its need to keep its costs competitive with those in the United States. During the early 1980s, Bridgestone's costs were no higher than its U.S. competitors (despite its much higher transportation costs) because of the low value of the yen relative to the U.S. dollar. (Recall Figure 16.2.) But in the late 1980s the value of the yen increased, so that the price of tires in the United States, when expressed in yen, fell below Bridgestone's unit costs. By buying

*Yoichiro Kaizaki, Chairman and CEO of Bridgestone/Firestone, Inc.*

Firestone's plants, Bridgestone could prevent increases in the value of the yen from increasing the cost of its tires to its U.S. customers.

Further, its purchase of these plants reduced very significantly Bridgestone's transportation costs in serving the U.S. market. Because the cost of shipping a tire to the United States is relatively high ($3 to $12 per tire for Bridgestone), there are obvious problems in trying to sell tires in the United States except as part of original vehicle equipment. By buying Firestone's plants, Bridgestone cut its transportation costs greatly.

Returning to the central point here, you can't understand why Bridgestone made this huge investment in Firestone's plants unless you understand the nature and effects of import restrictions like tariffs and quotas and unless you understand the implications for firms of changes in exchange rates.*

*For further discussion, see J. Daniels and L. Radebaugh, *International Business: Environments and Operations,* 5th ed. (Reading, Mass.: Addison-Wesley, 1989).

## THE RECENT UPSURGE OF PROTECTIONISM

During most of the period since World War II, the United States pushed hard for reductions in tariffs, quotas, and other barriers to trade. In 1947, the United States and 22 other nations signed the General Agreement on Tariffs and Trade (GATT), which calls for all participating countries to meet periodically to negotiate bilaterally on tariff cuts. Any tariff cut negotiated in this way will be extended to all participating countries. During the 1960s, the "Kennedy Round" negotiations took place among about 40 countries in an effort to reduce tariffs; and during the 1970s, over 100 countries met in Tokyo as part of a further round of trade negotiations. The result was a substantial reduction of tariffs and other trade barriers.

However, as Western Europe and Japan have become tougher competitors, many U.S. industries have begun to lobby for quotas and higher tariffs. In the 1980s, hundreds of petitions were filed by industry and labor, requesting the federal government to protect them from imports. Worried auto workers found a strong advocate in Representative John Dingell, one of the leaders of an emerging protectionist movement in Congress. Dingell threatened that, if the Japanese did not agree to voluntary restrictions on their auto exports to the United States, Congress would impose mandatory ones. In 1981, the Japanese agreed to export no more than 1.68 million cars per year to the United States. In 1985, the United States stopped asking for such restraints, but the Japanese decided to maintain them anyway.

One reason why U.S. firms found it so difficult to compete with foreign rivals during the early 1980s was the big increase then in the value of the dollar relative to other currencies. As shown in Figure 16.4, the value of the dollar (relative to other major currencies) rose by over 50 percent between 1980 and 1985. Besides making American goods and services much more expensive to foreigners, which hurt our exports, this made foreign goods and services cheaper in the United States, and this helped foreign firms invade our domestic markets.

During the late 1980s and 1990s, the value of the dollar was much lower than in the early 1980s. (See Figure 16.4.) Nonetheless, the presssure for protectionism has continued, and many economists have pointed out that the U.S. consumer is the one who takes a beating. For example, after the restrictions on auto imports from Japan were imposed, higher prices could be charged for Toyotas and Datsuns—and General Motors, Ford, and Chrysler could raise their prices too. The result: billions of extra dollars paid by U.S. consumers for autos. According to some estimates, each auto worker's job protected in this way cost consumers about $160,000 per year!

# STRATEGIC TRADE POLICY

Traditionally, economists have tended to argue that free trade is the best policy to promote the interests of society as a whole. Thus, they generally applauded the lowering of tariffs in the 1960s and early 1970s, and they generally looked with disfavor on the growth of protectionism during the 1980s. But some economists have begun to dispute these traditional beliefs. In their view, the U.S. government should control the access of foreign firms to our domestic markets, as well as promote the activities of our firms in foreign markets. For example, if particular high-technology industries result in large technological benefits to other domestic industries, the government may be justified in using subsidies or tariffs to protect and promote these industries. And if economies of scale mean that only two highly profitable producers can exist in the world market for a particular product, the government may be justified in using subsidies or tariffs to increase the chances that a U.S. firm will be one of the lucky pair.

According to these economists, there are strategic industries that, from the point of view of a particular country, are worth protecting in this way. However, it is very difficult to identify which industries fall into this category and to estimate how much the country would gain from such policies. Consequently, critics of such strategic trade policies worry that special-interest groups will use such policies to advance their own interests, not those of the nation as a whole. Given the vagueness of the criteria for identifying which industries should be protected, many industries could use these ideas to justify protection for themselves and their allies, regardless of whether it was merited.[6]

[6] P. Krugman, *Journal of Economic Perspectives* (Fall 1987).

# AIRBUS VERSUS BOEING: STRATEGIC TRADE POLICY IN ACTION

To illustrate the workings of strategic trade policy, suppose that only two firms, Airbus and Boeing, are capable of producing a new 150-seat passenger aircraft. Each firm must decide whether or not to produce and market such a plane. Because Boeing has a headstart, it will be able to make this decision first. Table 16.3 shows the payoff matrix for the two firms.[7] If either firm is the sole producer of the plane, it will make $120 million, but if both firms decide to produce and market such a plane, both will lose $8 million. Clearly, Boeing, which has the first move in this game, will decide to produce the plane; and Airbus, once it realizes that Boeing is committed to this course of action, will decide not to produce it.

TABLE 16.3 *Payoff Matrix: Airbus and Boeing*

| Possible strategies for Airbus | Possible strategies for Boeing | |
| --- | --- | --- |
| | Produce the new plane | Do not produce the new plane |
| Produce the new plane | Airbus's profit: −$8 million<br>Boeing's profit: −$8 million | Airbus's profit: $120 million<br>Boeing's profit: zero |
| Do not produce the new plane | Airbus's profit: zero<br>Boeing's profit: $120 million | Airbus's profit: zero<br>Boeing's profit: zero |

But Boeing is a U.S. firm, while Airbus is a joint venture of French, British, German, and Spanish aerospace firms (with their governments' blessings and participation). If European governments decide to pay Airbus a subsidy of $10 million if it will produce the plane, the game has quite a different outcome. Since the payoff matrix is now as shown in Table 16.4, it is clear that Airbus will produce the plane, regardless of whether or not Boe-

TABLE 16.4 *Payoff Matrix after Subsidy to Airbus*

| Possible strategies for Airbus | Possible strategies for Boeing | |
| --- | --- | --- |
| | Produce the new plane | Do not produce the new plane |
| Produce the new plane | Airbus's profit: $2 million<br>Boeing's profit: −$8 million | Airbus's profit: $130 million<br>Boeing's profit: zero |
| Do not produce the new plane | Airbus's profit: zero<br>Boeing's profit: $120 million | Airbus's profit: zero<br>Boeing's profit: zero |

[7] The concept of a payoff matrix is discussed in detail on pages 429 to 430.

ing commits itself to produce it. Thus, Boeing, recognizing that this will be Airbus's decision, will not find it profitable to produce it. Instead, Boeing will decide against production of the plane.

In effect, the European governments have taken the profit of $120 million away from Boeing and bestowed it on Airbus. Admittedly, they have to pay a subsidy of $10 million, but this is relatively small. Without question, this example seems to indicate that government intervention of this sort can pay off. But things are not so simple. For one thing, such government actions are likely to provoke retaliation. Thus, the U.S. government may retaliate by granting a $10 million subsidy to Boeing to produce the plane, with the result that both firms may produce it, although this is not economically desirable.

## INTERNATIONAL TRADE DISPUTES

Many American industries are influenced in an important way by international trade disputes. For example, the semiconductor industry has been involved in a series of disputes with the Japanese. Among other things, the semiconductor firms have charged that the Japenese have *dumped* chips (that is, sold them at a lower price than in Japan, and perhaps below cost) in the United States and that the Japanese have not allowed American firms to gain access to Japanese markets.

In 1974, Congress passed major legislation relating to international trade, often referred to as the 1974 Trade Act. Section 301 of this act gave the President of the United States the authority to take action to remove foreign trade barriers. In 1988, the Omnibus Trade and Competitiveness Act gave the United States Trade Representative the authority to determine whether a foreign trade practice was unfair. The Trade Representative, subject to presidential direction, could then choose what action to take.

These pieces of legislation have given the President considerable leeway in deciding what sorts of retaliatory action to take against other countries. The President can suspend or withdraw any trade concessions, can impose tariffs or other restrictions on imports from the countries involved and can retaliate against goods or services other than those cited in the complaints. Section 301 can be invoked if American firms file a complaint with the Trade Representative or if the Trade Representative on his or her own decides to do so.

In 1985, the semiconductor firms filed a petition with the federal government asking for the use of Section 301 against the Japanese. The Trade Representative expressed support for the semiconductor firms' position. The Japanese then agreed to increase their purchase of foreign-made chips and to have their government monitor export prices on semiconductor products to prevent their going below fair market value in the United States and elsewhere. The United States in turn agreed to drop the 301 case. But

## IS AIRBUS PLAYING BY THE RULES?

In March 1986, European and American officials met in Geneva, Switzerland to discuss allegations by both sides of unfair competitive practices, including an allegation by the United States about Airbus subsidies. There were rumors that the Reagan administration was considering a Section 301 case against Airbus, and the governments of France, Germany, and the United Kingdom (the biggest governments involved in the Airbus program) asked for the meeting.

The United States government charged that "direct program subsidies by [France, Germany, and the United Kingdom] . . . are leading to trade distortions in large transport aircraft. The United States believes that continued support of this type will result in increased trade tensions in the area of civil aircraft—a sector that has generally been one of cooperation in trade."* According to the president of Boeing's commercial aircraft unit, these governments had put about $10 billion into Airbus without regard to profit.

By 1990, the conflict had intensified, as Airbus's share of the world aircraft market rose to about 30 percent, as shown below:

|  | Percent of passenger jet market (based on orders) | |
|---|---|---|
|  | *1988* | *1990* |
| Airbus | 15 | 34 |
| Boeing | 59 | 45 |
| McDonnell Douglas | 22 | 15 |
| Other | 4 | 6 |
|  | 100 | 100 |

(a) Why does the U.S. government say that it is unfair for the European governments to subsidize Airbus in this way? (b) The European governments retort that American firms like Boeing also receive large government subsidies, since the work they do for the Department of Defense under government contracts yields great benefits to their civilian business. Is this true? (c) If the U.S. aircraft manufacturers feel that Airbus constitutes unfair competition, why hasn't a Section 301 case been brought against Airbus?

*Jean Pierson, President of Airbus Industrie*

> *Solution* (a) In the U.S. view, Airbus is selling its airplanes at well under their true cost, which the European governments refuse to divulge. (b) Yes. However, the U.S. points out that there was not direct U.S. government support for commercial aircraft programs, and it argues that there was "only negligible" indirect benefits to U.S. civil aircraft manufacturers from their defense work. (The latter argument is often challenged.) (c) Neither Boeing nor McDonnell Douglas filed a petition because they feared that sanctions could disrupt the market. Many of the components of their aircraft are produced abroad, and many of their customers are in Europe. They feared that, if the U.S. tried to get tough, the Europeans might retaliate.[†]
>
> [*]U.S. press release, March 21, 1986, quoted by D.Yoffie, *International Trade and Competition*, p. 352.
> [†]For further information, see J. Pierce and R. Robinson, *Cases in Strategic Management*, 2d ed. (Homewood, Ill.: Irwin, 1991); D. Yoffie, *International Trade and Competition*; and *New York Times*, June 23, 1991.

problems continued. The semiconductor firms have complained repeatedly that the Japanese have violated this and other agreements.[8]

International trade disputes of this sort are very hard to resolve. Despite its obvious economic, political, and military strength, the United States cannot dictate to the rest of the world. Indeed, despite its superpower status, the United States sometimes has remarkably little influence over other countries' economic policies. Moreover, as in all disputes, there are two sides of the story, and it would be naïve to believe that the United States has a monopoly on righteousness.

## MAKING DIRECT INVESTMENTS ABROAD

To survive and prosper, many firms must produce and sell in a number of countries. One of the most important questions faced by a variety of industrial managers is whether—and if so, where—to establish sales outlets, manufacturing facilities, and R and D laboratories abroad. In other words, what sorts of direct investments should be made in other countries?

Many firms are multinational—that is, they already have facilities in other countries. (Recall the case of Bridgestone, described on page 623.) In some industries like aluminum and oil, firms have established overseas facilities to control foreign sources of raw materials. Frequently, firms have invested overseas in an attempt to defend their competitive position. In many cases, firms have set up foreign branches to exploit a technological lead. That is, after exporting a new product to a foreign market, a firm may

---

[8] See D. Yoffie, *International Trade and Competition*.

decide to establish a plant overseas to supply that market. Once a foreign market is large enough to accommodate a plant of minimum efficient size, this decision does not conflict with economies of scale. Moreover, transport costs often can be reduced in this way; and in some cases, the only way a firm can introduce its innovation into a foreign market is by establishing a production facility there.

What factors are important in deciding where to locate a new plant? Firms seem to be particularly interested in the size of the local market, both because a large local market tends to reduce freight and delivery costs and because it means lower tariffs (since much of the plant's output will be sold within the nation where the plant is located). Another important factor is the country's investment and political climate—whether the country allows foreign ownership, whether its government is reasonably stable, and whether profits can be taken out of the country. Still another major factor is the availability of skilled labor and relevant technology or know-how in the country.

Table 16.5 shows the total amount that had been invested abroad by U.S. firms in 1990. As you can see, the total investment was over $400 billion, over half being in the oil and manufacturing industries. Close to half was invested in Europe; Latin America and Canada together account for about one-third of the total.

---

**TABLE 16.5   *U.S. Direct Investment Abroad, Selected Regions, by Industry, 1990 (billions of dollars)***

| Region | All industries | Oil | Manu-facturing | Wholesale trade | Banking | Financial | Services | Other |
|---|---|---|---|---|---|---|---|---|
| All countries | 421 | 60 | 168 | 41 | 21 | 99 | 11 | 21 |
| Canada | 68 | 11 | 33 | 4 | 1 | 12 | 2 | 6 |
| Europe | 204 | 24 | 84 | 24 | 9 | 52 | 7 | 4 |
| Japan | 21 | 3 | 11 | 4 | * | 2 | * | * |
| Latin America | 72 | 5 | 24 | 3 | 8 | 27 | 2 | 4 |

*Under $1 billion.
Source: U.S. Department of Commerce.

---

## ESTABLISHING A PLANT ABROAD: TIME-COST TRADE-OFFS

If a firm decides to establish a plant overseas, there often is a time-cost trade-off that is somewhat similar to that which pertains to industrial innovation. (Recall Chapter 7.) That is, if the firm decides to design and construct this plant in a relatively short period of time, the costs often will be higher than if more time is taken to do the work. As additional engineers are brought on to the project to speed the design work, diminishing returns

ANALYZING MANAGERIAL DECISIONS

## WHY SO MANY U.S. PLANTS ARE LOCATED SOUTH OF THE BORDER

Mexico began the Border Industrialization Program—or Maquiladora Program—in 1965. According to this program, a U.S. company establishes two plants under a single management, one on each side of the Mexican border. The U.S. plant supplies components duty-free to its sister plant in Mexico for assembly, processing, or repair; these components are then returned to the United States for further processing or as final goods. The United States imposes tariffs on only the non-U.S. components used and the value added by Mexican labor. By the mid 1980s, almost 800 plants were participating in the Maquiladora Program, and they employed over 250,000 persons.

Whether or not they have taken part in the Maquiladora Program, many well-known American companies, such as Alcoa, Johnson and Johnson, Rohm and Haas, and Westinghouse, have established plants in Mexico. In 1991, Alcoa's eight Mexican plants (in Acuna, Monterey, and elsewhere) employed about 5,000 workers, and Johnson and Johnson's two Mexican plants (in Juarez and Tijuana) employed about 2,900. Small firms, as well as big ones, have located manufacturing facilities south of the border. For example, Stabilus, a Pennsylvania firm, opened its first Mexican assembly plant in 1991. Parts are transported from the firm's main factory in suburban Philadelphia to Nuevo Laredo, where a crew of 30 workers

assembles gas springs for office chairs. Thomas Blomquist, president of Stabilus, has said that "This is something we had to do."

(a) According to many estimates, U.S. companies, by establishing their own plants in Mexico, often can save a great deal. Why? (b) Other countries besides Mexico have relatively low wage rates. What are the advantages of locating a plant in Mexico rather than in these other countries? (c) What are the disadvantages of locating a plant in Mexico?

*Solution* (a) Wage rates are much lower in Mexico than in the United States. Mexican workers in manu-

*Paul H. O'Neill, Chairman of Alcoa*

facturing earn, on the average, about $1.85 per hour in wages and benefits, as compared with about $15 in the United States. In 1987, the minimum wage in Mexico was about $3 per day, even lower than in Hong Kong where it was about $14 per day. (b) For U.S. firms, there are many advantages stemming from Mexico's geographical proximity. Communications and transportation costs can be reduced. For example, a firm can cut shipping time from weeks to days by locating a plant in Mexico rather than Asia. (c) Transportation, communications, and electrical service are not very well developed. In addition, the turnover rate in the work force is sometimes found to be relatively high. Also, in the past, Mexico has sometimes confiscated foreign assets.*

* For further discussion, see T. Wheelen and J. D. Hunger, *Cases in Strategic Management and Business Policy*, and the references cited there, as well as *Philadelphia Inquirer*, November 3, 1991.

can generally be expected. Attempts to reduce project time by speeding equipment procurement can also be expected to increase project costs. The available evidence indicates that the relationship between $C$, the present value of the costs of establishing the plant, and $t$, the number of months it takes to establish the plant, is generally like that shown in Figure 16.6.[9]

To determine how quickly to do the design and construction work, the firm must estimate, for each value of $t$, the present value of gross profit if the duration of the project is $t$ months. If the results are as shown in Figure 16.6, the optimal duration of the project is $Y$ months, since this is the value of $t$ where the present value of net profit is highest. To see that this is true, note that the present value of *net profit* at each value of $t$ is the vertical distance between the present value of *gross profit* (given by the "Gross profit" curve in Figure 16.6) and the present value of the *costs* (given by the "Cost" curve in Figure 16.6). Clearly, this vertical distance is greatest when the duration of the project is $Y$ months.

## CHANNELS OF INTERNATIONAL TECHNOLOGY TRANSFER

In today's global economy, international technology transfer is of vital importance in many industries. Firms want both to make profitable use of their technology in other countries and to obtain technology at minimum cost from foreign firms, universities, and other sources. Thus, international technology transfer is a two-way street. To understand the nature of inter-

[9] E. Mansfield, A. Romeo, M. Schwartz, D. Teece, S. Wagner, and P. Brach, *Technology Transfer, Productivity, and Economic Policy* (New York: Norton, 1982).

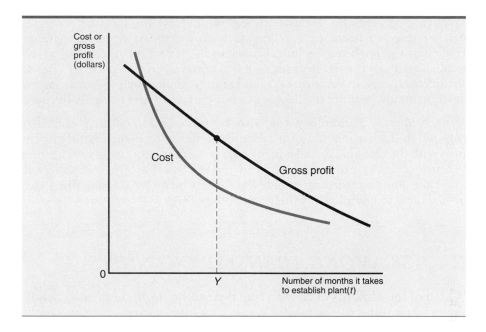

**FIGURE 16.6    Time-Cost Trade-Off in Design and Construction of Overseas Plant**    The optimal duration of the project is Y months, since this is the value of *t* where the present value of net profit is highest.

national technology transfer, it is necessary to describe the principal ways in which technology can be transferred across national borders.

*Export of goods.* The mere existence or availability of a good in a foreign country may result in the transfer of technology since the good may provide information to the importers of the good. Thus, the export of advanced computers to a particular country may result in technology transfer. In addition, the importing country may gain technology because the exporters of the good, to promote their sales, may help the importing country's personnel to use the good efficiently—and this training is a form of technology transfer. Also, if the country that imports the good is able to reverse-engineer it (that is, take it apart to discover how it is constructed), there is the opportunity for further technology transfer.

*Direct investment in wholly owned subsidiaries.* Another way of transferring technology is through direct investment in overseas subsidiaries. For example, firms like IBM and Hewlett-Packard have established a global network of facilities. They train foreign operatives and managers, communicate information and capabilities to foreign engineers and technicians, help the foreign users of their products to use them more effectively, and help foreign suppliers to upgrade their technology.

*Licensing agreements.* Firms with significant new products or processes often engage in licensing agreements with foreigners covering patents, trademarks, franchises, technical assistance, and so on. Licensing agreements often call for the licensee to pay a certain percentage of its sales to the licensor, plus, in some cases, a flat fee for technical help. Some licensing agreements also require the licensee to buy certain inputs from the licensor.

*Joint ventures.* Technology can also be transferred to other countries through the formation of a joint venture, an operation owned jointly by the firm with the technology and a firm or agency of the host country. The joint venture generally produces a good or service based on the technology in question. Joint venture agreements are often made by smaller firms that need capital to complement their technology.[10]

## CHOICE AMONG TRANSFER CHANNELS

Which of these means of transferring their technology, do firms generally prefer? According to the available evidence, direct investment in wholly owned subsidiaries is generally preferred if firms can obtain the necessary resources and if they believe that licensing will give away valuable know-how to foreign producers who are likely to become competitors in the future. Of course, the longer the estimated life of the innovation, the less inclined a firm is to enter into a licensing agreement. Also, firms prefer direct investment over licensing when the technology is sophisticated and foreigners lack the know-how to assimilate it or when a firm is concerned about protecting quality standards. For example, if a firm licenses technology to a less-than-capable foreign firm, and the foreign firm produces defective merchandise, it may reflect adversely on the firm whose technology was used (or abused).

On the other hand, licensing is often preferred when the foreign market is too small to warrant direct investment, when the firm with the technology lacks the resources required for direct investment, or when advantages accrue through cross licensing. Also, in some countries, direct investment has been discouraged by the government. (Particularly in the less-developed countries, there has sometimes been considerable hostility toward multinational firms. Some governments feel that their sovereignty is threatened by the great power of the multinational firm over their national economies.) Turning to joint ventures, they have advantages with regard to forging good relations with host countries, but they have disadvantages and problems in operation, personnel matters, and division of profits.

To the host country's government, the choice among these alternative

---

[10] There are other ways that technology is transferred. For example, scientists and engineers exchange information at international meetings, and one country's scientists and engineers read the publications of other countries' scientists and engineers. Also, emigration can sometimes be an important channel of international technology transfer.

## REORGANIZING A FIRM'S GLOBAL R AND D NETWORK*

Boehringer Ingelheim was the first German pharmaceutical firm to establish subsidiaries in the United States and Japan. The American subsidiary (in Ridgefield, Connecticut) began to carry out research and development in about 1975; the Japanese subsidiary began to do so in the early 1980s. Decision making regarding R and D was completely decentralized. The head of research and development of each subsidiary could develop products for his or her own geographical markets. Thus, the American subsidiary could develop a new product for the American market, and the Japanese subsidiary could develop a new product for the Japanese market. This seemed to be the best way for Boehringer Ingelheim to expand its market share in the American and Japanese markets.

In the late 1980s, however, the firm's top managers became convinced that this was not the optimal way to manage its global network of R and D laboratories. Too much money was being spent on developing products that could not be transferred from one market to another. Given the very high costs of developing a new drug, there were obvious advantages in being able to spread these costs over a number of markets, not just one.

If you were a consultant to Boehringer Ingelheim, what changes would you recommend in the organization and administration of its global R and D activities?

* This case is based on material in P. Roussel, K. Saad, and T. Erickson, *Third Generation R and D* (Boston: Harvard Business School Press, 1991).

means of obtaining technology looks quite different than it does to the firm with the technology. To the host government, direct investment creates many problems because the wholly owned subsidiary of a foreign firm is partly outside the government's control. The direct investor is only partly responsive to the host nation's economic policies. The investor can draw on funds and resources outside the host country. Moreover, the investor has a global strategy, which may be at odds with the optimal operation of the subsidiary from the viewpoint of the host government. Joint ventures may overcome some of these disadvantages of direct investment, but they have the disadvantage that the host country must invest more capital. Licensing arrangements eliminate many of the problems of control, but they have the disadvantage that the firm with the technology has little commitment or incentive to help the licensee with managerial and technical problems.

The choice of the channel of technology transfer may in fact depend on the age of the technology being transferred. Consider the case of petrochemicals. When various important petrochemicals were relatively new, direct investment was the dominant form of technology transfer, but as they became mature, licensing became dominant. One reason for this sort of pattern lies in the changes over time in the relative bargaining positions of the innovating firm and the country wanting the technology. When the technology is quite new, it is closely held, and countries wanting the technology are under pressure to accept the firm's conditions, which often are a wholly owned subsidiary. But as time goes on, the technology becomes more widely known, and the host country can take advantage of competition among technologically capable firms to obtain joint ventures or sometimes licenses. Eventually, the technology may become available in plants that can be acquired by the host country on a turnkey basis from independent engineering firms.

## STRATEGIC ALLIANCES

In recent years, more and more firms have been forming strategic alliances with firms in other countries (as well as those in their own countries). In the auto industry, major companies have begun to cooperate in joint development and supply of complete vehicles, engines, and transmissions. For example, during the 1980s, Renault, a French firm, jointly produced transmissions with Volkswagen (Germany), gasoline engines with Volvo (Sweden) and Peugeot (France), and diesel engines with Fiat (Italy). Practically all the major firms in the auto industry are involved in this global cooperative network. Figure 16.7 shows the various links between the leading firms. As you can see, American firms like General Motors have ties with a variety of Japanese and European auto producers.[11]

Many strategic alliances involve the sharing of technological information. In the semiconductor industry, U.S. firms often trade design information regarding their products for information concerning Japanese firms' production techniques. (Recall from Chapter 7 that Japanese firms tend to devote a larger proportion of their industrial R and D to processes than do U.S. firms.) For example, in the alliance between VLSI Technology (United States) and Hitachi (Japan), VLSI Technology traded design technology for Hitachi's process technology in integrated circuits.[12]

Strategic alliances of this sort can be of considerable value, since they enable firms to gain access to technology that is complementary to their own technology and help them to enter new markets or defend existing market positions. But they also can be hazardous. If a firm provides valuable technology to others and gets little in return, such an alliance can be very costly. Unfortunately, some firms have had this happen. It is important that a firm's managers be clear as to exactly what benefits an alliance of this sort will bring—and how they can be reasonably sure that these benefits will be forthcoming.

[11] K. Clark and T. Fujimoto, *Product Development Performance* (Boston: Harvard Business School Press, 1991).

[12] D. Methé, *Technological Competition in Global Industries* (New York: Quorum Books, 1991).

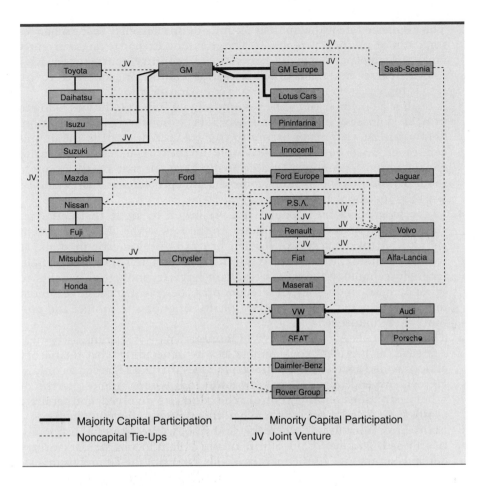

*FIGURE 16.7    Global Network of Auto Producers, 1980s*    Practically all the major firms in the auto industry are involved in a global cooperative network.

*Source:* K. Clark and T. Fujimoto, *Product Development Performance,* p. 326.

# SUMMARY

1. If countries specialize in producing goods and services where they have a comparative advantage, and trade with one another, each country can improve its standard of living. Whether or not a particular country has a comparative advantage in the production or a given product depends on the country's resource endowments and technological expertise. Managers must constantly be on their guard against the loss of comparative advantage.

2. The exchange rate is the number of units of one currency that exchanges for a unit of another currency. To a large extent, exchange rates currently are set by supply and demand. The value of a country's currency (relative to other currencies) tends to fall if its inflation rate or economic growth rate is high or if its interest rates are comparatively low.

3. A tariff is a tax imposed by the government on imports, the aim being to protect domestic industry and workers from foreign competition. Quotas are another major barrier to free trade. While tariffs and quotas can sometimes be justified (for example, on the basis of national security considerations), economists traditionally have felt that a tariff or quota tends to cost the general public more than the protected industry (and its workers and suppliers) gains.

4. In recent years, some economists have begun to argue that countries should adopt strategic trade policies. In their view, the U.S. government should control the access of foreign firms to our domestic markets, as well as promote the activities of our firms in foreign markets. If particular high-technology industries result in large technological benefits to other domestic industries, these economists believe that the government may be justified in using subsidies, tariffs, or quotas to protect and promote these industries.

5. The 1974 Trade Act and the 1988 Omnibus Trade and Competitiveness Act gave the President considerable leeway in deciding what retaliatory action to take against foreign trade practices that are regarded as unfair. He can suspend or withdraw any trade concessions, impose tariffs or other restrictions on imports from the countries involved, and retaliate against goods and services other than those cited in the complaints.

6. Many firms must decide whether—and if so, where—to establish facilities abroad. Whether or not a firm locates a plant in a particular country depends on the size of the market in that country, the country's investment climate, and the availability of skilled labor there. If a firm decides to build a plant overseas, there often is a time-cost trade-off.

7. International technology transfer is of vital importance to many firms. There are four principal ways by which technology can be transferred across national borders: export of goods, direct investment in wholly owned foreign subsidiaries, licensing agreements, and joint ventures. Direct investment is often preferred by firms if they can obtain the necessary resources and if they believe that other methods of transfer will give away valuable know-how to foreign producers who are likely to become competitors in the future.

8. In recent years, more and more firms have been forming strategic alliances with firms in other countries (as well as those in their own countries). Many strategic alliances involve the sharing of technological information. It is important that a firm's managers be clear as to exactly what benefits an alliance of this sort will bring—and how they can be confident that these benefits will be obtained.

# PROBLEMS

1. Donald R. Keough, president of the Coca-Cola Company, said in 1991, "Our single and relentless focus has been internationalizing this business."[13] In 1991, Coke had pushed the international contribution to its profits to 80 percent from 50 percent in 1985. By the year 2000, the United States may account for no more than 10 percent of the firm's profits.

   (a) In the United States, per capita consumption of soft drinks made by Coca-Cola equals 292 eight-ounce servings per year, whereas it equals 48 in France and 112 in Japan. Does this help to account for the fact that Coke's unit sales are growing at an annual rate of 8 to 10 percent overseas, as compared with 3.5 percent in the United States? If so, how?

   (b) Mr. Keough has said that, "When I think of Indonesia—a country on the Equator with 180 million people, a median age of 18, and a Moslem ban on alcohol, I feel I know what heaven looks like." Why is he so enthusiastic about Indonesia? (Note: Indonesia's per capita consumption of soft drinks made by Coca-Cola equals 4 eight-ounce servings per year.)

   (c) In some countries, like Britain and Taiwan, Coke has used joint ventures with bottlers to enter foreign markets; in others like France, it has established wholly owned bottling operations. What factors influence Coke's decision in this regard?

   (d) Coke's principal rival, Pepsi Cola, obtains less than 20 percent of its profits from outside the United States. Whereas Coke has 41 percent of the domestic soft drink market, as compared with Pepsi's 33 percent, it outsells Pepsi 4 to 1 outside the United States. According to some analysts, this helps to explain why Coke makes 3 or 4 times as much profit per gallon sold in many overseas markets as in the United States. Why do they think that this is the explanation?

2. In 1991, local cement makers in Florida filed a complaint against Venezuelan firms charging that they were dumping cement in Florida. According to U.S. law, dumping occurs when foreigners set their price below "fair market value," which is defined as either the price they establish at home or their cost of production. More than half of Florida's cement is supplied by local firms, such as a subsidiary of Texas-based Southdown Inc. The rest comes from overseas. The price of cement is roughly $60 in both Florida and Venezuela.[14]

   (a) Why is it profitable for Venezuelan firms to enter the Florida cement market? (Hint: Ocean transportation is cheap relative to railroads or trucks.)

---

[13] "For Coke, World Is Its Oyster," *New York Times*, November 21, 1991.
[14] "Cement Shoes for Venezuela," *New York Times*, September 25, 1991.

(b) If transportation and storage add about $10 to $15 per ton to the cost of sending Venezuelan cement to Florida, does it appear that the Venezuelan firms are selling cement at a lower price in Florida than in their home markets?

(c) According to Kenneth Clarkson of the University of Miami and Stephen Morrell of Barry University, both consultants for the Venezuelan firms, Florida consumers would pay over $600 million more for cement in the period 1991 to 1996 if foreign firms were no longer permitted to ship into the Florida market. If this is true, should foreign firms be allowed to continue selling cement at $60 per ton in Florida?

3. Suppose that Japan and the United States are the only producers and consumers of a particular sort of flashbulb. The demand and supply curves for this flashbulb in the United States are as follows:

| Price (dollars) | Quantity demanded (millions) | Quantity supplied (millions) |
|---|---|---|
| 5 | 10 | 4 |
| 10 | 8 | 6 |
| 15 | 6 | 8 |
| 20 | 4 | 10 |

The demand and supply curves for this flashbulb in Japan are:

| Price (expressed in dollar equivalent of Japanese price) | Quantity demanded (millions) | Quantity supplied (millions) |
|---|---|---|
| 5 | 5 | 2 |
| 10 | 4 | 6 |
| 15 | 3 | 10 |
| 20 | 2 | 14 |

(a) Suppose that there is free trade in these flashbulbs. What will be the equilibrium price?

(b) Which country will export flashbulbs to the other country?

(c) How large will be the exports?

(d) Suppose that the United States imposes a tariff of $10 per flashbulb. What will happen to exports and imports?

4. According to a (hypothetical) government report, the United States can produce 3 computers or 3,000 cases of wine with 1 unit of resources, while Germany can produce 1 computer or 5,000 cases of wine with 1 unit of resources.

(a) If this report is accurate, will specialization increase world output of computers and wine?

(b) If the maximum number of computers that can be produced per year in the United States is 1,000, draw the U.S. production possibilities curve on the graph below.

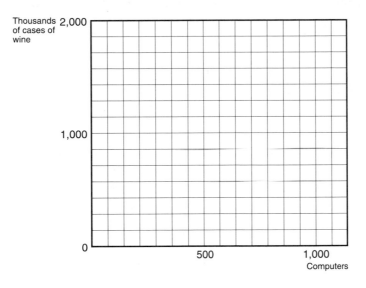

(c) In the diagram above draw the trading possibilities curve if the United States produces only computers and trades them for German wine (at a price for each computer that is equivalent to 2,000 cases of German wine). Does this curve lie above the production possibilities curve?

(d) If the maximum number of cases of wine that can be produced per year in Germany is 2 million, draw the German production possibilities curve below.

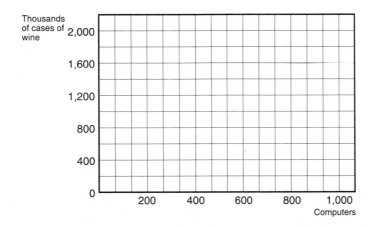

(e) In the diagram above draw the trading possibilities curve if Germany produces only wine and trades it for U.S. computers (at a price for each computer that is equivalent to 2,000 cases of German wine). Does this curve lie above the production possibilities curve?

5. If labor is the only input, a study indicates that two countries, Honduras and Panama, can produce the following amounts of two commodities, bananas and coffee, with a day of labor.

|  | Bananas (lbs.) | Coffee (lbs.) |
| --- | --- | --- |
| Honduras | 20 | 6 |
| Panama | 10 | 8 |

(a) In order for both countries to gain from trade with one another, between what limits must the ratio of the prices lie?

(b) Suppose that there is free trade and the price of bananas increases relative to the price of coffee. Is this change in relative prices to the advantage of Honduras or Panama?

6. The supply curve for Japanese cameras to the U.S. market is shown below for two periods of time.

(a) One curve is before a depreciation of the dollar relative to the yen; one curve is after it. Which curve is which? Why?

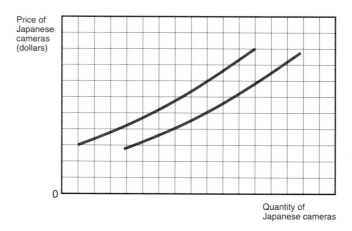

Price of Japanese cameras (dollars)

0

Quantity of Japanese cameras

(b) What will be the effect of the depreciation on the dollar price of Japanese cameras?

(c) What will be the effect on U.S. expenditures (in dollars) for Japanese cameras if the demand for them in the United States is price elastic?

(d) What will be the effect on U.S. expenditures (in dollars) for Japanese cameras if the demand for them in the United States is price inelastic?

7. The demand curve in Italy for U.S. computers is as shown below.

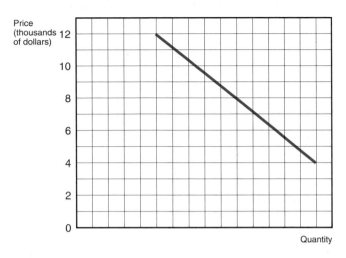

(a) If the Italian lira depreciates relative to the U.S. dollar, will the quantity of computers sold in Italy at a dollar price of $8,000 rise or fall?

(b) Under these circumstances, will the demand curve rise or fall?

8. The demand and supply curves for the Swiss franc are as follows:

| Price of franc (dollars) | Millions of francs demanded | Millions of francs supplied |
|---|---|---|
| .80 | 600 | 800 |
| .70 | 640 | 740 |
| .60 | 680 | 680 |
| .50 | 720 | 620 |
| .40 | 760 | 560 |

(a) What is the equilibrium rate of exchange for the dollar?

(b) What is the equilibrium rate of exchange for the Swiss franc?

(c) How many dollars will be bought in the market?

(d) How many Swiss francs will be bought in the market?

9. The demand curve for British pounds is as follows:

| Price of British pound (dollars) | Millions of pounds demanded |
|---|---|
| 2.00 | 400 |
| 2.10 | 380 |
| 2.20 | 360 |
| 2.30 | 340 |
| 2.40 | 320 |
| 2.50 | 300 |

(a) Suppose that the British government sets the exchange rate at $2.40 and that the quantity of pounds supplied at this exchange rate is 360 million pounds. Will the British government have to buy or sell pounds? If so, how many?

(b) If the British government has to buy pounds with dollars, where will it get the dollars?

10. The Liverous Company is the maker of a new product made and bought only in Japan and the United States. In the United States, the demand curve for this product is such that

$$Q_d^u = 20 - 2P_u,$$

and the supply curve is such that

$$Q_s^u = 5 + 3P_u,$$

where $P_u$ is the price of the product (in dollars) in the United States, $Q_d^u$ is the quantity demanded (in thousands of units) per week in the United States, and $Q_s^u$ is the quantity supplied (in thousands of units) per week in the United States. In Japan, the demand curve for this product is such that

$$Q_d^j = 45.5 - 3P_j,$$

and the supply curve is such that

$$Q_s^j = -5 + 2P_j,$$

where $P_j$ is the price of the product (in yen) in Japan, $Q_d^j$ is the quantity demanded (in thousands of units) per week in Japan, and $Q_s^j$ is the quantity supplied (in thousands of units) per week in Japan. Assume that a U.S. dollar exchanges for 130 Japanese yen.

(a) What will be the price of this product in Japan? In the United States?

(b) How much of this product will each country supply?

(c) Will the United States be an importer or exporter of this product?

11. During the 1980s, Black and Decker (B & D), the manufacturer of power tools, encountered a number of problems. The recession of the early 1980s hurt B & D's sales, as did the subsequent strength of the U.S. dollar. Its rival, Japan's Mikita Electric Works, reduced its costs and was able to nearly equal B & D's 20 percent share of the world market. In part, B & D's problems were of its own making, according to some observers, for reasons given below.

By 1982, B & D operated twenty-five manufacturing plants in thirteen countries on six continents. It had three operating groups, as well as the headquarters in Maryland. Each group had its own staff. In addition, B & D companies, such as B & D of West Germany, operated autonomously in each of the more than fifty countries where B & D sells and services products. The company's philosophy had been to let each country adapt products and product lines to fit the unique characteristics of each market. The Italian firm produced power tools for Italians, the British subsidiary made power tools for Britons, and so on.

As a result, countries did not communicate well with each other. Successful products in one country often took years to introduce in others. In order to meet the tailor-made specifications of different markets, design centers were not being used efficiently. At one point, eight design centers around the world had produced 260 different motors, even though it was determined that the firm needed fewer than ten different models.[15]

If you were asked by B & D's top managers to recommend changes to improve this situation, what advice would you give?

---

### MANAGERIAL ECONOMICS IN CONTEXT

## A FREE TRADE AGREEMENT FOR NORTH AMERICA?*

For decades, there has been talk about a free trade agreement for North America. All tariffs and quotas would be eliminated on trade among Canada, Mexico, and the United States. The result would be the world's largest free market, with about 400 million consumers and a total output of $6 trillion (about 25 percent larger than the European Community). In recent years, this talk has become much more serious. Indeed, in 1988, the Canada–U.S. Free Trade Agreement was signed by Prime Minister Brian Mulroney and President Ronald Reagan.

According to some estimates, this agreement was supposed to create an additional 750,000 jobs in the United States and 150,000 in Canada. On both sides of the U.S.– Canadian border, there were misgivings about the agreement. On the Canadian side, people were concerned that they would lose their cultural identity and be overwhelmed by the economic and political juggernaut to their south. On the U.S. side, some people were worried that they would lose production and jobs to Canada. Nonetheless, on January 1, 1989, the historic agreement went into operation. All bilateral tariffs were to be removed in 10 equal, annual steps, which began on that date (except for those cases where the relevant industries agreed to a faster phaseout of the tariffs).

In late November 1990, Presidents George Bush and Carlos Salinas de Gortari met to launch trade talks between Mexico and the United States. Mexico wanted to weaken U.S. quotas on textiles and steel and to open U.S. markets to its fruits and vegetables. The United States wanted Mexico to allow foreign investment in its oil industry. (Such investment currently is prohibited by the Mexican

---

* The material in this case came from J. Daniels and L. Radebaugh, *International Business;* and *Business Week,* November 12, 1990, May 27, 1991, and March 16, 1992.

---

[15] Daniels and L. Radebaugh, *International Business*, 5th ed. (Reading, Mass.: Addison-Wesley, 1989), pp. 449–50.

*Brian Mulroney, Prime Minister of Canada*

*Carlos Salinas de Gortari, President of Mexico*

constitution.) As these talks continued, alarm bells went off among U.S. labor leaders, who feared the export of jobs to Mexico. Also, environmentalists warned that Mexico could degrade clean-air and toxic-waste standards across the continent. Industries that might be hurt by free trade with Mexico also were concerned. For example, Bill Becker, chairman of the Florida Citrus Commission warned that the removal of the U.S. tariff on orange juice would "wipe out the Florida industry. We can't compete with our environmental constraints, labor constraints, and the other regulations."[†]

Actually, many of the barriers to trade between Mexico and the United States have already been torn down. Take the important case of automobiles. In 1991, Mexico produced over 1 million vehicles. If a North American Free Trade Agreement is signed, many auto executives think that Mexican output could hit 3 million by the year 2000. Even if it is not signed, they think that Mexican auto output could hit 2 million. Thus, by the end of the 1990s, one in six cars and light trucks made in North America could come from Mexico.

Many of these cars are made by Ford, Chrysler, and General Motors. For example, at Ramos Arizpe, General Motors makes the Buick Century and the Chevrolet Cavalier for export and for local sale. At Hermosillo, Ford makes Tracers and Escorts for export to California and elsewhere. At Toluca, Chrysler's plant exports Shadows and Spirits. But Mexico is not the home of only U.S. auto producers; France's Renault, Japan's Nissan, and Germany's Volkswa-

[†] *Business Week*, May 27, 1991, p. 33

gen, among others, have plants there.

Why are auto producers moving into Mexico? One reason, as we stressed earlier in this chapter, is low wages. An experienced welder at Chrysler's Toluca plant makes about $1.75 an hour, much less than the $16 an hour earned by experienced welders at Chrysler's Michigan plant. However, this is only part of the story. Surprising as it has been to many observers, the quality of the cars produced is high. Within 2 years after its start-up in 1987, Ford's Hermosillo plant was winning quality awards. Ramos Arizpe, only 5 years old, is General Motors' top plant of its kind, out-scoring other plants in Oklahoma City and Quebec.

According to auto executives, Mexico's young workers learn new industrial methods more quickly than their older counterparts in the United States. For example, the labor force at Ramos Arizpe quickly learned Japanese-style manufacturing techniques. Highly trained workers in small teams can substitute for one another and effectively monitor quality. In contrast, many U.S. plants still have rigid work rules. At Hermosillo, Ford provides trainees with a 7-week program where they study statistics and economics.

While U.S. auto companies are enthusiastic about their experiences in Mexico, the United Auto Workers (UAW) is protesting loudly. In particular, the UAW has tried to torpedo the proposed North American Free Trade Agreement. According to Owen Bieber, president of the UAW, if the agreement passes, "you can kiss the jobs and livelihoods of thousands of Americans goodbye."[‡] If the Agreement is passed, the UAW wants it to contain a clause protecting U.S. jobs.

(a) On August 13, 1992, the United States, Canada, and Mexico announced a free trade agreement. However, the agreement still needed to be ratified by lawmakers in the three countries. Among other things, tariffs on all farm products would be phased out, but many would fall slowly. What are the arguments in support of U.S. tariffs on orange juice? What are the arguments against them?

(b) Does it appear that the United States has lost its comparative advantage in the production of automobiles? Is the evidence clear-cut?

(c) On February 12, 1992, the U.S. Customs Service ruled that Honda Motor Company had to pay tariffs of about $180 per car on the Civics it shipped from its plant in Alliston, Ontario to the United States because, in its view, too little of these cars was produced in North America to allow them to enter the United States duty-free. Some leading Canadians said Canada should abrogate its free trade agreements with the United States. Why were they so concerned?

(d) Have Ford, General Motors, and Chrysler transferred technology to Mexico? If so, through what channels have they done so? Why have they chosen these channels?

‡ *Business Week*, March 16, 1992, p. 100.

(e) According to *Business Week,* "If the Administration hopes to make a convincing case for North American free trade, it should not overlook the needs of job-losers at home. . . . U.S. workers who do lose their jobs should be granted generous assistance for retraining so they may qualify for new jobs."[§] Do you agree? Why or why not?

(f) Environmentalists cite the sludge in the Rio Grande river and the smog over Mexico City. (The lower Rio Grande is the most polluted river in the United States.) How can one tell whether existing levels of pollution in these cases are excessive? If they are excessive, what can the governments of Mexico and the United States do to reduce pollution?

[§] *Ibid.,* p. 138.

# Appendix A
# *Discounting and Present Values*

When a manager chooses between two courses of action, A and B, he or she is choosing between the cash flows resulting if A is chosen and the cash flows when B is chosen. These cash flows generally occur over a number of periods. For example, if A is chosen, the firm may experience an outflow of $1 million this year and an inflow of $300,000 during each of the next 5 years. On the other hand, if B is chosen, the firm may experience an outflow of $1 million this year, and an inflow of $250,000 for each of the next 6 years. How can a manager compare these two alternatives?

To answer this question, it is convenient to begin by pointing out one of the basic propositions in managerial economics: *A dollar received today is worth more than a dollar received a year from today.* Why? Because one can always invest money that is available now and obtain interest on it. If the interest rate is 6 percent, a dollar received now is equivalent to $1.06 received a year hence. Why? Because if you invest the dollar now, you'll get $1.06 in a year. Similarly, *a dollar received now is equivalent to* $(1.06)^2$ *dollars 2 years hence.* Why? Because if you invest the dollar now, you'll get 1.06 dollars in a year, and if you reinvest this amount for another year at 6 percent, you'll get $(1.06)^2$ dollars.

More generally, suppose that you can invest at a compound rate of $i$ percent per year. What is the *present value*—that is, the value *today*—of a dollar received $n$ years hence? Based on the foregoing argument, its present value is

$$\frac{1}{(1 + i)^n}. \tag{A.1}$$

Thus, if the interest rate is .10 and if $n = 4$ (which means that the dollar is received in 4 years), the present value of a dollar equals

$$\frac{1}{(1 + .10)^4} = \frac{1}{1.4641} = \$.683.$$

In other words, the present value of the dollar is 68.3 cents.

To see that this answer is correct, let's see what would happen if you invested 68.3 cents today. As shown in Table A.1, this investment would be worth 75.1 cents after 1 year, 82.6 cents after 2 years, 90.9 cents after 3 years, and $1 after 4 years. Thus, 68.3 cents is the present value of a dollar received 4 years hence, because if you invest 68.3 cents today, you will have exactly $1 in 4 years.

TABLE A.1   Value of 68.3 Cents Invested at 10 Percent Interest

| Number of years hence | Return received | Value of investment |
|---|---|---|
| 1 | 68.3(.10)   = 6.830¢ | 68.3 + 6.830 =   75.13¢ |
| 2 | 75.13(.10)  = 7.513¢ | 75.13 + 7.513 =   82.64¢ |
| 3 | 82.643(.10) = 8.264¢ | 82.643 + 8.264 =   90.91¢ |
| 4 | 90.907(.10) = 9.091¢ | 90.907 + 9.091 = 100.00¢ |

Appendix Table 1 shows the value of $1 \div (1 + i)^n$, for various values of $i$ and $n$. For example, according to this table, the present value of a dollar received 10 years hence is 46.3 cents if the interest rate is .08. To see this, note that the figure in Appendix Table 1 corresponding to $n = 10$ and $i = .08$ is .46319.

Using this table, you can readily determine the present value of any amount received $n$ years hence, not just $1. If you receive $R_n$ dollars $n$ years hence, the present value of this amount is

$$\frac{R_n}{(1 + i)^n}. \tag{A.2}$$

Thus, to determine the present value of $R_n$, all that you have to do is multiply $R_n$ by $1 \div (1 + i)^n$. Since Appendix Table 1 provides us with the value of $1 \div (1 + i)^n$, this is a simple calculation.

To illustrate, suppose you will receive $10,000 ten years hence and the interest rate is .12. According to equation (A.2), the present value of this amount equals $10,000 \times [1 \div (1 + i)^n]$. Since Appendix Table 1 shows that $1 \div (1 + i)^n = .32197$ when $n = 10$ and $i = .12$, the present value of this amount is $10,000 (.32197) = $3,219.70.

## Present Value of a Series of Payments

As pointed out at the beginning of this appendix, managers generally must consider situations where cash flows occur at more than a single time. For example, investment in a new machine tool is likely to result in a cash outflow now and a series of cash inflows in the future. To determine the present value of such an investment, it is convenient to begin by considering the simple case where you receive $1 per year for $n$ years, the interest rate being $i$. More specifically, the $n$ receipts of $1 occur 1 year from now, 2 years from now, ..., and $n$ years from now. The present value of this stream of $1 receipts is

$$\frac{1}{1 + i} + \frac{1}{(1 + i)^2} + \cdots + \frac{1}{(1 + i)^n} = \sum_{t = 1}^{n} \frac{1}{(1 + i)^t}. \tag{A.3}$$

For example, the present value of $1 to be received at the end of each of the next 5 years, if the interest rate is .10, is

$$\sum_{t = 1}^{5} \frac{1}{(1 + .10)^t} = \frac{1}{(1 + .10)} + \frac{1}{(1 + .10)^2} + \frac{1}{(1 + .10)^3} + \frac{1}{(1 + .10)^4}$$

$$+ \frac{1}{(1 + .10)^5} = .90909 + .82645 + .75131 + .68301 + .62092$$

$$= \$3.79. \tag{A.4}$$

To obtain each of the terms on the right in equation (A.4), we use Appendix Table 1. For example, the final term on the right is .62092, which is the present value of a dollar received 5 years hence (if the interest rate is .10), according to Appendix Table 1.

Table A.2 shows that $3.79 is indeed the present value of $1 to be received at the end of each of the next 5 years, if the interest rate is .10. As you can see, if you invest $3.79 at 10 percent interest, you will be able to withdraw $1 at the end of each year, with nothing left over or lacking. Since analysts frequently must calculate the present value of a dollar received at the end of each of the next $n$ years, the expression in equation (A.3)—that

---

TABLE A.2  *Demonstration That $3.79 (Invested at 10 Percent Interest) Provides Exactly $1 at the End of Each of the Next 5 Years*

| Number of years hence | Return received | Amount withdrawn | Net value of investment |
|---|---|---|---|
| 1 | $3.79(.10)  = .379 | $1.00 | $3.79 + .379 − 1.00  = 3.169 |
| 2 | $3.169(.10) = .3169 | $1.00 | $3.169 + .3169 − 1.00 = 2.486 |
| 3 | $2.486(.10) = .2486 | $1.00 | $2.486 + .2486 − 1.00 = 1.735 |
| 4 | $1.735(.10) = .1735 | $1.00 | $1.735 + .1735 − 1.00 = 0.909 |
| 5 | $0.909(.10) = .0909 | $1.00 | $0.909 + .0909 − 1.00 = 0 |

is, $\sum_{t=1}^{n} 1 \div (1 + i)^t$—has been tabled, the results being shown in Appendix Table 2. For example, if you receive $1 at the end of each of the next 10 years, and if the interest rate is .06, the present value is $7.36. To see this, note that the figure in Appendix Table 2 corresponding to $n = 10$ and $i = .06$ is 7.3601.

More generally, if you receive $R$ dollars at the end of each of the next $n$ years, and if the interest rate is $i$, the present value is

$$\sum_{t=1}^{n} \frac{R}{(1 + i)^t} = R \sum_{t=1}^{n} \frac{1}{(1 + i)^t}. \tag{A.5}$$

Thus, the present value of $5,000 to be received at the end of each of the next 5 years, if the interest rate is .08, is $5,000(3.9927) = $19,964, since Appendix Table 2 shows that the value of $\sum_{t=1}^{n} 1 \div (1 + i)^t = 3.9927$, when $n = 5$ and $i = .08$.

Finally, we must consider the case where there is a series of unequal, not equal, payments. Suppose that a payment is received at the end of each of the next $n$ years, that the amount received at the end of the $t^{th}$ year is $R_t$, and that the interest rate is $i$. The present value of this series of unequal payments is

$$\sum_{t=1}^{n} \frac{R_t}{(1 + i)^t}. \tag{A.6}$$

Appendix Table 1 can be used to help carry out this computation. For example, suppose that $i = .10$, that $n = 3$, and that the amount received at the end of the first year is $3,000, the amount received at the end of the second year is $2,000, and the amount received at the end of the third year is $1,000. Table A.3 shows how to calculate the present value of this series of unequal payments, which in this case equals $5,131.48.

TABLE A.3   *Present Value of Stream of Unequal Payments, Where* i = .10 *and* n = 3

| Number of years hence | (1) Amount received $R_t$ | (2) $\frac{1}{(1 + .10)^t}$ | (1) × (2) Present value of amount received |
|---|---|---|---|
| 1 | $3,000 | .90909 | $2,727.27 |
| 2 | 2,000 | .82645 | 1,652.90 |
| 3 | 1,000 | .75131 | 751.31 |
| | | Total | $5,131.48 |

## The Use of Periods Other Than a Year

Thus far, we have assumed that the interest or return from an invested amount is paid annually. In other words, we have assumed that a dollar invested at the beginning of a year earns interest of $i$ percent at the end of that year. In many situations, this is not correct. Instead, interest, dividends, or other returns from an investment may be received semiannually, quarterly, or even monthly. Because you earn a return in the next period on the return received in this period, the results differ from those given in previous sections of this appendix.

If interest is received *semiannually*, the present value of a dollar received $n$ years hence is

$$\frac{1}{(1 + i/2)^{2n}} \tag{A.7}$$

where $i$ is the annual interest rate. To understand this expression, note that the interest rate for each semiannual period is $i/2$, and that there are $2n$ semiannual periods in $n$ years. Bearing this in mind, this expression can be derived in the same way as expression (A.1).

If interest is received *quarterly*, the present value of a dollar received $n$ years hence is

$$\frac{1}{(1 + i/4)^{4n}} \tag{A.8}$$

where $i$ once again is the annual interest rate. To see why this is true, note that the interest rate for each quarterly period is $i/4$, and that there are $4n$ quarterly periods in $n$ years. Bearing this in mind, this expression can be derived in the same way as expression (A.1).

More generally, suppose that interest is received $c$ times per year. Under these circumstances, the present value of a dollar received $n$ years hence is

$$\frac{1}{(1 + i/c)^{cn}}. \tag{A.9}$$

Appendix Table 1 can be used to determine present values under these circumstances. To evaluate the expression in (A.9), let the interest rate be $i/c$, and let the number of years be $cn$; using these values, Appendix Table 1 will give the correct answer. Thus, the present value of $1 to be received 3 years hence, where the interest rate is 8 percent paid quarterly, can be obtained by finding in the table the present value of $1 to be received 12 years hence where the interest rate is 2 percent. Specifically, the answer is 78.849 cents.

## Determining the Internal Rate of Return

Previous sections of this appendix have been concerned entirely with determining the present value of a stream of cash flows. While this is of great importance in managerial economics, it also is important to calculate the internal rate of return—the interest rate that equates the present value of the cash inflows with the present value of the cash outflows. Put differently, the internal rate of return is the interest rate that makes the present value of a stream of cash flows equal zero. In other words, we want to find $i$ where

$$R_0 + \frac{R_1}{1 + i} + \frac{R_2}{(1 + i)^2} + \cdots + \frac{R_n}{(1 + i)^n} = 0,$$

or

$$\sum_{t = 0}^{n} \frac{R_t}{(1 + i)^t} = 0. \tag{A.10}$$

To solve equation (A.10) for $i$, it often is necessary to use trial and error (if you do not have access to a computer or calculator). The first step is to make a rough estimate of the value of $i$ that will satisfy equation (A.10). The second step is to adjust this estimate. If the present value based on the original estimated rate of interest is *positive, increase* the value of $i$. If the present value based on the original estimated rate of return is *negative, reduce* the value of $i$. The third step is to continue to adjust this estimate until you find the value of $i$ that will satisfy equation (A.10).

As an illustration, consider the following stream of cash flows: $R_0 = -\$5,980, R_1 = \$3,000, R_2 = \$2,000, R_3 = \$2,000$. As a first step, we estimate (roughly) that the internal rate of return is in the neighborhood of 8 percent. As shown in Table A.4, the present value of this stream of cash flows, given that the interest rate is 8 percent, is $101, which is positive. Thus, a higher value of $i$ must be tried. We choose 9 percent. As shown in Table A.4, the present value of this stream of cash flows, given that the interest rate is 9 percent, is zero. Thus, the internal rate of return is 9 percent.

TABLE A.4 **Determination of the Internal Rate of Return**

| Year $t$ | Cash flow $R_t$ | $i = 8$ percent | | $i = 9$ percent | |
|---|---|---|---|---|---|
| | | $\frac{1}{(1 + i)^t}$ | Present value | $\frac{1}{(1 + i)^t}$ | Present value |
| 0 | −$5,980 | 1.00000 | −5,980 | 1.0000 | −5,980 |
| 1 | 3,000 | .92593 | 2,778 | .91743 | 2,752 |
| 2 | 2,000 | .85734 | 1,715 | .84168 | 1,683 |
| 3 | 2,000 | .79383 | 1,588 | .77228 | 1,545 |
| Total | | | 101 | | 0 |

If the cash flows (in years other than year 0) are all equal, there is a simpler way to determine the internal rate of return. Under these circumstances, equation (A.10) can be written as follows:

$$R_0 + \sum_{t=1}^{n} \frac{R}{(1 + i)^t} = 0,$$

where $R$ is the cash flow in years 1 to $n$. Thus,

$$\sum_{t=1}^{n} \frac{1}{(1 + i)^t} = \frac{-R_0}{R}. \qquad (A.11)$$

Since we are given the value of $-R_0/R$, we can find the value of $i$ in Appendix Table 2 where the entry in the $n$th row equals $-R_0/R$. This value of $i$ is the internal rate of return.

To illustrate, suppose that a machine tool costs \$10,000, and that it will result in a cash inflow of \$2,500 for each of the next 6 years. Since $R_0 = -\$10,000$ and $R = \$2,500$, the value of $-R_0/R$ is 4. Looking in the row of Appendix Table 2 where $n = 6$, we look for the interest rate where the entry in the table is 4. Since the entry is 3.9976 when $i = 13$ percent, the internal rate of return is about 13 percent.

Finally, it is worth pointing out that if an investment yields an infinite series of equal cash flows, the present value of this series is

$$\sum_{t=1}^{\infty} \frac{R}{(1 + i)^t} = R \sum_{t=1}^{\infty} \frac{1}{(1 + i)^t} = \frac{R}{i}. \qquad (A.12)$$

For example, if an investment yields a perpetual annual return of \$4,000 per year, and if the interest rate is 8 percent, the present value of this perpetual stream of returns equals \$4,000 ÷ .08 = \$50,000.

# Appendix B
## The Normal, t, and F Distributions

The formula for the probability distribution of a variable with a normal distribution is

$$f(x) = \frac{1}{\sqrt{2\pi}\,\sigma}\, e^{-\frac{1}{2}[(x-\mu)/\sigma]^2} \tag{B.1}$$

where $\mu$ is the variable's mean, $\sigma$ is its standard deviation, $e$ is approximately 2.718 and is the base of the natural logarithms, and $\pi$ is approximately 3.1416. This is often called the **normal curve**.

Although normal curves vary in shape because of differences in mean and standard deviation, all normal curves have the following characteristics in common:

1. *All normal curves are symmetrical about the mean.* In other words, the height of the normal curve at a value that is a certain amount *below* the mean is equal to the height of the normal curve at a value that is the same amount *above* the mean. Besides being symmetrical, the normal curve is *bell-shaped,* as in Figure B.1. (Note that a normal variable can assume values ranging from $-\infty$ to $+\infty$.)

2. Regardless of its mean or standard deviation, the probability that the value of a normal variable will lie within *one* standard deviation of its mean is 68.3 percent, the probability that it will lie within *two* standard deviations of its mean is 95.4 percent, and the probability that it will lie within *three* standard deviations of its mean is 99.7 percent. Panel B of Figure B.1

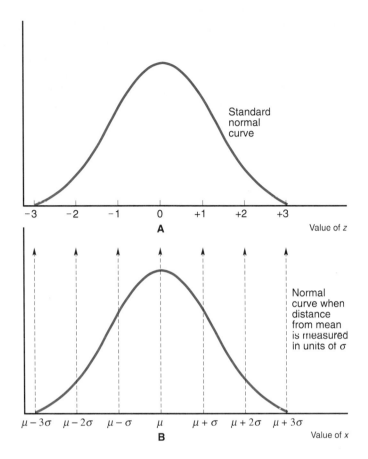

*FIGURE B.1   Comparison between Any Normal Curve (when Distance from Mean Is Measured in Units of σ) and the Standard Normal Curve*

shows the distance from the mean, $\mu$, in units of the standard deviation, $\sigma$. Clearly, almost all the area under a normal curve lies within three standard deviations of the mean.

3.  The location of a normal curve along the horizontal axis is determined *entirely* by its mean, $\mu$. For example, if the mean of a normal curve equals 4, it is centered at 4; if its mean equals 400, it is centered at 400. The amount of spread in a normal curve is determined *entirely* by its standard deviation, $\sigma$. If $\sigma$ increases, the curve's spread widens; if $\sigma$ decreases, the curve's spread narrows.

If one expresses any normal variable as a deviation from its mean, and measures these deviations in units of its standard deviation, the resulting variable, called a **standard normal variable,** has the probability distribution shown in panel A of Figure B.1. This probability distribution is called the **standard normal curve.**

If any normal variable is expressed in standard units (that is, if it is expressed as a deviation from its mean, and measured in units of its standard deviation), its probability distribution is given by the standard normal curve. Thus, if a firm's sales are normally distributed and if we express them in standard units, their probability distribution is given by the standard normal curve. Put more formally, if $X$ is a normally distributed variable, then

$$Z = \frac{X - \mu}{\sigma} \qquad \text{(B.2)}$$

has the standard normal distribution regardless of the values of $\mu$ and $\sigma$.

Appendix Table 3 shows the area under the standard normal curve from zero to the positive number $(z)$ given in the left-hand column (and top) of the table. In other words, this table provides the probability that a standard normal variable lies between zero and $z$. Thus, the probability that a standard normal variable lies between zero and 1.10 equals .3643. Because of the symmetry of the normal curve, this is also the probability that it lies between zero and $-z$. Thus, the probability that a standard normal variable lies between zero and $-1.10$ equals .3643.

*The t Distribution*     The $t$ distribution is really a family of distributions, each of which corresponds to a particular number of degrees of freedom. From a mathematical point of view, the number of degrees of freedom is simply a parameter in the formula for the $t$ distribution. The shape of the $t$ distribution is rather like that of the standard normal distribution. Figure B.2 compares the $t$ distribution (with 2 degrees of freedom) with the stan-

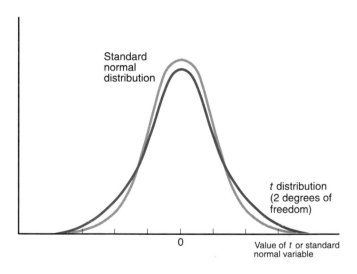

FIGURE B.2    *Comparison between Normal and* t *Distributions*

dard normal distribution. As you can see, both are symmetrical, bell-shaped, and have a mean of zero. The $t$ distribution is somewhat flatter at the mean and somewhat higher in the tails than the standard normal distribution. As the number of degrees of freedom becomes larger and larger, the $t$ distribution tends to become exactly the same as the standard normal distribution. The $t$ distribution is often called Student's $t$ distribution because the statistician W. S. Gosset, who first derived this distribution, published his findings under the pseudonym Student.

To find the probability that the value of $t$ exceeds a certain number, we can use Appendix Table 4. As you can see, each row of this table corresponds to a particular number of degrees of freedom. The numbers in each row are the numbers that are exceeded with the indicated probability by a $t$ variable. For example, the first row indicates that if a $t$ variable has 1 degree of freedom, there is a .40 probability that its value will exceed .325, a .25 probability that its value will exceed 1.000, a .05 probability that its value will exceed 6.314, a .01 probability that its value will exceed 31.821, and so on. Since the $t$ distribution is symmetrical, it follows that if a $t$ variable has 1 degree of freedom, there is a .40 probability that its value will lie below −.325, a .25 probability that its value will lie below −1.000, and so on.

*The* F *Distribution*     The $F$ distribution, like the $t$ distribution, is in reality a family of probability distributions, each corresponding to certain numbers of degrees of freedom. But unlike the $t$ distribution, the $F$ distribution has two numbers of degrees of freedom, not one. Figure B.3 shows the $F$ distribution with 2 and 9 degrees of freedom. As you can see, the $F$ distribution is skewed to the right. However, as both numbers of degrees of freedom become very large, the $F$ distribution tends toward normality. Once again, it should be emphasized that any $F$ random variable has *two* numbers of degrees of freedom. Be careful to keep these numbers of degrees of freedom in *the correct order*, because an $F$ distribution with $v_1$ and $v_2$ degrees

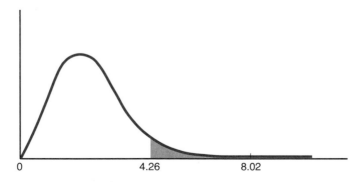

*FIGURE B.3   The* F *Probability Distribution, with 2 and 9 Degrees of Freedom*

of freedom is *not* the same as an $F$ distribution with $v_2$ and $v_1$ degrees of freedom.

Tables are available that show the values of $F$ that are exceeded with certain probabilities, such as .05 and .01. Appendix Table 5 shows, for various numbers of degrees of freedom, the value of $F$ that is exceeded with probability equal to .05. For example, if the numbers of degrees of freedom are 2 and 9, the value of $F$ that is exceeded with probability equal to .05 is 4.26. Similarly, Appendix Table 6 shows, for various numbers of degrees of freedom, the value of $F$ that is exceeded with probability equal to .01. For example, if the numbers of degrees of freedom are 2 and 9, the value of $F$ exceeded with probability equal to .01 is 8.02. (In Appendix Tables 5 and 6, the first number of degrees of freedom is labeled "degrees of freedom for numerator," and the second number is labeled "degrees of freedom for denominator.")

# Brief Answers to Odd-Numbered End-of-Chapter Questions and Problems

## Chapter 1

1. They tend to exacerbate it, since the executive's pay is not so directly related to his or her effectiveness in raising the firm's profits.

3. Managerial economics draws on microeconomics and the decision sciences; it applies and extends them to solve management problems. It provides analytical tools and serves an integrating role. Whereas microeconomics is largely descriptive, managerial economics is largely prescriptive.

5.

| Number of years in the future | Profit (millions of dollars) | $\dfrac{1}{(1+i)^t}$ | Present value |
|---|---|---|---|
| 1 | 8 | .90909 | 7.27272 |
| 2 | 10 | .82645 | 8.26450 |
| 3 | 12 | .75131 | 9.01572 |
| 4 | 14 | .68301 | 9.56214 |
| 5 | 15 | .62092 | 9.31380 |
| 6 | 16 | .56447 | 9.03152 |
| 7 | 17 | .51316 | 8.72372 |
| 8 | 15 | .46651 | 6.99765 |
| 9 | 13 | .42410 | 5.51330 |
| 10 | 10 | .38554 | 3.85540 |
| | | Total | 77.55047 |

Thus, the answer is $77.55047 million.

7. These differences are described on pages 11–12.
9. The differences between "satisficing," on the one hand, and the traditional theory are described on pages 13–15.
11. If the cash flow is very risky, investors generally will want a higher interest rate (or rate of return) to compensate for the risk than they would if the cash flow were not very risky. This point is discussed in detail in Chapter 13.
13. (a) He will receive 80(50)($5) = $20,000, from which he must pay $3,000 for the umbrellas and 3($3,000) = $9,000 for rent. Thus, his accounting profit equals $20,000 − $3,000 − $9,000, or $8,000.
    (b) Since he could earn $4,000 doing construction work, his economic profit is $8,000 − $4,000 = $4,000. (For simplicity, we ignore the fact that he could have earned interest on the money he invested in this business during the summer.)
15. (a) The supply curve for coffee shifted to the left, as shown below.

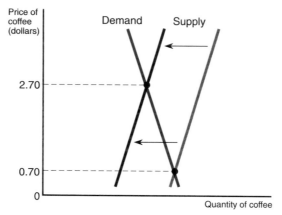

    (b) No. With more normal weather conditions, the supply curve for coffee would be expected to shift back toward the right—and price would be expected to recede to more normal levels.

## Chapter 2

1. (a) $5,000; −$3,000.
   (b) 7 units per day.
   (c) No, because profit is higher at 9 units per day than at 7 units per day.
3. (a) Since marginal cost equals 4 + 16Q, it is 164 if Q = 10.
   (b) 4 + 16(12) = 196.
   (c) 4 + 16(20) = 324.
5. (a) 6.

(b) $24X$.

(c) $48X^2$.

(d) $8/X^3$.

7. (a) 2.

(b) $12X^2$.

(c) $1.6Z^{.2} X^{-.2}$.

(d) $-3Z \div (4 + X)^2$.

9. (a) $\partial C/\partial X_1 = -3 + 4X_1 + X_2 = 0$

$$\partial C/\partial X_2 = -4 + 6X_2 + X_1 = 0.$$

Solving these two equations simultaneously,

$X_1 = 14/23$

$X_2 = 13/23$.

(b) The answer will not change.

11. (a) If the overhead, depreciation, and insurance are not increased by the introduction of the new product, the incremental cost is the out-of-pocket cost of $4 million, which is less than the incremental revenue of $5 million. Thus, under these circumstances, Trumbull's chairman is not right, since the product's introduction would increase the firm's profits.

(b) The development costs incurred in the past are *sunk* costs. Because they have been substantial is no good reason to introduce the product. The vice president of research is wrong.

## Chapter 3

1. (a) If $Q = 20$, $P = 2,000 - 50(20) = 1,000$. Thus, price would have to equal $1,000.

(b) Since $500 = 2,000 - 50Q$, $Q = 1,500 \div 50 = 30$. Thus, it will sell 30 per month.

(c) Because $Q = (2,000 - P) \div 50 = 40 - .02P$,

$$\frac{dQ}{dP} = -.02.$$

Thus,

$$\frac{-dQ}{dP} \cdot \frac{P}{Q} = .02\left(\frac{500}{30}\right) = .33.$$

(d) If $.02\left(\dfrac{P}{(2,000 - P) \div 50}\right) = 1,$

$$.02\left(\frac{50P}{2,000 - P}\right) = 1,$$

or

$P = 2,000 - P$

$P = 2,000/2 = 1,000$.

Thus, if price equals $1,000, the demand is of unitary elasticity.

3. (a) $\dfrac{-\partial Q}{\partial P} \cdot \dfrac{P}{Q} = \dfrac{3(10)}{500 - 3(10) + 2(20) + .1(6,000)}$

$= \dfrac{30}{500 - 30 + 40 + 600} = \dfrac{30}{1,110}.$

(b) $\dfrac{\partial Q}{\partial I} \cdot \dfrac{I}{Q} = \dfrac{.1(6,000)}{1,110} = \dfrac{600}{1,110}.$

(c) $\dfrac{\partial Q}{\partial P_r} \cdot \dfrac{P_r}{Q} = \dfrac{2(20)}{1,110} = \dfrac{40}{1,110}.$

(d) Population is assumed to be essentially constant (or to have no significant effect on Q, other than via whatever effect it has on per capita disposable income).

5. (a) Yes.
   (b) Yes.

7. (a) Because there are lots of very close substitutes for a particular brand, but not for cigarettes as a whole. It appears that the elasticity exceeded 2.
   (b) No. More will be said on this score on pages 151–52.

9. (a) 3.1.
   (b) Decreases.
   (c) 2.3.
   (d) 0.1.
   (e) The quantity demanded will increase by 10 percent. (Note that Q in this problem is defined as quantity demanded *per capita*.)

11. (a) Price should be set equal to $MC\left(\dfrac{1}{1 - 1/\eta}\right) = 18\left(\dfrac{1}{1 - 1/3}\right) = 27$ dollars.
    (b) $18.

## Chapter 4

1. (a) The evidence appears to be very strong that increases in the firm's advertising expenditure do have a positive effect on the quantity demanded of the firm's product.
   (b) $Q = -104 + 3.2(5,000) + 1.5(20) + 1.6(1,000) - 2.1P$
   $= 17,526 - 2.1P.$
   Thus,
   $$P = \dfrac{17,526 - Q}{2.1} = 8,346 - .476Q.$$
   (c) From the answer to part (b),
   $Q = 17,526 - 2.1P.$
   Thus, if $P = 500$,
   $Q = 17,526 - 2.1(500) = 16,476.$
   (d) Since $R^2$ equals .89, the regression equation seems to fit the data

quite well. However, we have no way of knowing (from the information given here) whether the error terms are serially correlated or whether a nonlinear equation fits significantly better.

3. (a) Let profit equal $Y$ and sales equal $X$. Plotting $Y$ against $X$, we get the following:

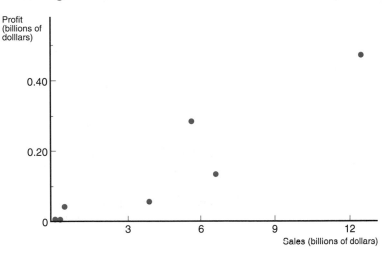

$\Sigma X = 30.0$; $\Sigma Y = 0.94$; $\Sigma X^2 = 248.72$; $\Sigma XY = 8.307$; $n = 7$; $\Sigma Y^2 = .3030$.

$$b = \frac{7(8.307) - (30)(0.94)}{7(248.72) - 30^2} = \frac{58.149 - 28.200}{1,741.04 - 900} = \frac{29.949}{841.04}$$
$$= .0356.$$

$a = .134 - (.0356)(4.286) = .134 - .153 = -.019.$

The regression line is $\hat{Y} = -0.019 + .0356X$.

(b) $-0.019 + .0356(2) = -.019 + .071 = .052$. Thus, the answer is about .05 billions of dollars.

(c) No. Prices and costs will be different in 1998 than in 1980.

5. (a) 40.833.

(b) $-1.025$.

(c) 0.006667.

(d) 0.916.

(e) 1.361.

(f) Less than .001.

(g) Less than .001.

(h) 0.244.

(i) The average relationship is $C1 = 40.8 - 1.02\ C2 + 0.00667\ C3$. This relationship seems to fit the data quite well, $R^2$ being .916. There is a very small probability that the estimated effect of $C2$ (price) is due to chance, but a much higher probability (.244) that the effect of $C3$ (disposable income) could be due to chance.

7. (a) Let General Electric's profits be $Y$ and gross national product be $X$. If we plot $Y$ against $X$, we get the following graph:

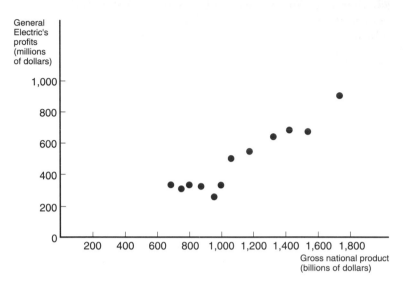

To calculate $a$ and $b$, we can compute the following:

| | X | Y | X² | Y² | XY |
|---|---|---|---|---|---|
| | 688 | 355 | 473,344 | 126,025 | 244,240 |
| | 753 | 339 | 567,009 | 114,921 | 255,267 |
| | 796 | 361 | 633,616 | 130,321 | 287,356 |
| | 868 | 357 | 753,424 | 127,449 | 309,876 |
| | 936 | 278 | 876,096 | 77,284 | 260,208 |
| | 982 | 363 | 964,324 | 131,769 | 356,466 |
| | 1,063 | 510 | 1,129,969 | 260,100 | 542,130 |
| | 1,171 | 573 | 1,371,241 | 328,329 | 670,983 |
| | 1,306 | 661 | 1,705,636 | 436,921 | 863,266 |
| | 1,407 | 705 | 1,979,649 | 497,025 | 991,935 |
| | 1,529 | 688 | 2,337,841 | 473,344 | 1,051,952 |
| | 1,706 | 931 | 2,910,436 | 866,761 | 1,588,286 |
| Sum | 13,205 | 6,121 | 15,702,585 | 3,570,249 | 7,421,965 |
| Mean | 1,100.42 | 510.08 | | | |

The results are

$$b = \frac{12(7,421,965) - (13,205)(6,121)}{12(15,702,585) - 13,205^2}$$

$$= \frac{89,063,580 - 80,827,805}{188,431,020 - 174,372,025}$$

$$= \frac{8,235,775}{14,058,995} = .586.$$

$$a = 510.08 - (.586)(1,100.42) = 510.08 - 644.85 = -134.77.$$

Thus, the slope equals .586, and the intercept equals −134.77 millions of dollars.

(b) On the average a $1 increase in the GNP seems to be associated with a $.000586 increase in General Electric's profits (recalling that GNP is measured in billions of dollars, while General Electric's profits are measured in millions of dollars).

(c) The forecast equals − 134.77+ .586(2,000) = −134.77 + 1,172 = 1,037.23. That is, it equals 1,037.23 millions of dollars.

(d) $r^2 = .90$.

(e) No. No. A nonlinear relationship might be as good or better.

(f) If nothing else is available, this model may be serviceable, but it is so crude that it is difficult to believe that the analyst could not improve upon it by taking other independent variables into account.

9. (a) Taking antilogs,

$$Q = 102P^{-.148}Z^{.258}$$

$$\frac{\partial Q}{\partial P} = -.148(102P^{-1.148}Z^{.258})$$

$$= -.148 \, Q/P.$$

Since the price elasticity of demand equals $-\partial Q/\partial P \cdot P/Q$, it follows that the price elasticity of demand equals .148.

(b) $\frac{\partial Q}{\partial Z} = .258(102P^{-.148}Z^{-.742})$

$$= .258Q/Z.$$

Since the cross elasticity of demand equals $\partial Q/\partial Z \cdot Z/Q$, it follows that the cross elasticity of demand equals .258.

(c) The regression seems to provide a good fit. The fact that $\overline{R}^2$ equals .98 means that 98 percent of the variation in log Q can be explained by the regression. (See the chapter appendix.) Also, see Figure 4.6.

11. (a) No.

(b) The market supply curve for wine.

## Chapter 5

1. (a) Yes. Room occupancy in August tends to be about 57 percent greater than in January.

(b) There are more tourists during the summer than the winter. Because of the recession, there may have been fewer tourists, and hence the seasonal variation may have been less pronounced during the recession than before it.

(c) It might be of use in scheduling labor inputs and in ordering supplies. Certainly, the manager would want to take proper account of this seasonal variation in his or her hiring and purchasing decisions.

3. (a) Because the seasonal index shows by what percent sales for a particular month tend to be above or below normal.
   (b) Deseasonalized sales are as follows:
   | | | | |
   |---|---|---|---|
   | January | 2.5 ÷ | .97 = | $2.58 million |
   | February | 2.4 ÷ | .96 = | 2.50 million |
   | March | 2.7 ÷ | .97 = | 2.78 million |
   | April | 2.9 ÷ | .98 = | 2.96 million |
   | May | 3.0 ÷ | .99 = | 3.03 million |
   | June | 3.1 ÷ | 1.00 = | 3.10 million |
   | July | 3.2 ÷ | 1.01 = | 3.17 million |
   | August | 3.1 ÷ | 1.03 = | 3.01 million |
   | September | 3.2 ÷ | 1.03 = | 3.11 million |
   | October | 3.1 ÷ | 1.03 = | 3.01 million |
   | November | 3.0 ÷ | 1.02 = | 2.94 million |
   | December | 2.9 ÷ | 1.01 = | 2.87 million |

   (c) Because they want to see how sales are changing, when the seasonal factor is deleted.
5. (a) Yes. Yes.
   (b) Yes. No.
7. (a) $\Delta Y = 7.36 + .20\Delta C_{-1} - .26\Delta Y_{-1} + 2.00\Delta G.$
   (b) Inserting the changes in $C$ and $Y$ between this period and the last period into the equation in the answer to part (a)—and inserting a forecast of the change in $G$ between this and the next period into this equation—we can forecast the change between this and the next period in $Y$ (that is, GNP).
9. (a) Let $t' = 0$ when $t = 1963$. Let $y$ be General Electric's sales.

| $t'$ | $y$ | $t'^2$ | $y^2$ | $t'y$ |
|---|---|---|---|---|
| −13 | 2.2 | 169 | 4.84 | −28.6 |
| −12 | 2.6 | 144 | 6.76 | −31.2 |
| −11 | 3.0 | 121 | 9.00 | −33.0 |
| −10 | 3.5 | 100 | 12.25 | −35.0 |
| −9 | 3.3 | 81 | 10.89 | −29.7 |
| −8 | 3.5 | 64 | 12.25 | −28.0 |
| −7 | 4.1 | 49 | 16.81 | −28.7 |
| −6 | 4.3 | 36 | 18.49 | −25.8 |
| −5 | 4.2 | 25 | 17.64 | −21.0 |
| −4 | 4.5 | 16 | 20.25 | −18.0 |
| −3 | 4.2 | 9 | 17.64 | −12.6 |
| −2 | 4.5 | 4 | 20.25 | −9.0 |
| −1 | 4.8 | 1 | 23.04 | −4.8 |
| 0 | 4.9 | 0 | 24.01 | 0.0 |
| 1 | 4.9 | 1 | 24.01 | 4.9 |
| 2 | 6.2 | 4 | 38.44 | 12.4 |
| 3 | 7.2 | 9 | 51.84 | 21.6 |
| 4 | 7.7 | 16 | 59.29 | 30.8 |

*(table continues)*

| $t'$ | $y$ | $t'^2$ | $y^2$ | $t'y$ |
|------|------|--------|---------|--------|
| 5 | 8.4 | 25 | 70.56 | 42.0 |
| 6 | 8.4 | 36 | 70.56 | 50.4 |
| 7 | 8.8 | 49 | 77.44 | 61.6 |
| 8 | 9.6 | 64 | 92.16 | 76.8 |
| 9 | 10.5 | 81 | 110.25 | 94.5 |
| 10 | 11.9 | 100 | 141.61 | 119.0 |
| 11 | 13.9 | 121 | 193.21 | 152.9 |
| 12 | 14.1 | 144 | 198.81 | 169.2 |
| 13 | 15.7 | 169 | 246.49 | 204.1 |
| Sum 0 | 180.9 | 1,638 | 1,588.79 | 734.8 |
| Mean 0 | 6.7 | | | |

$$b = \frac{734.8 - (180.9)(0)}{1,638 - (0)(0)} = \frac{734.8}{1,638} = .449.$$

$$a = 6.7 - (.449)(0) = 6.7.$$

Thus, the trend is $6.7 + .449t'$.

(b) The graph is as follows:

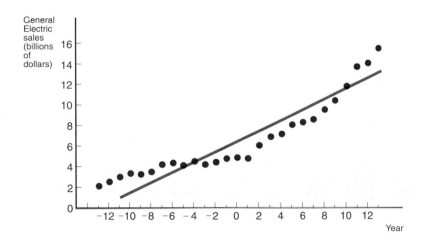

(c) It appears from the graph that the trend may be curvilinear, and that an exponential or quadratic trend might do better.

(d) The forecast would be $6.7 + .449(28) = 19.3$ billions of dollars, which was not much higher than actual sales in 1976. In fact, GE's sales were about $60 billion in 1991, which indicates how poor linear extrapolations of this sort can be, particularly when one is using them to forecast many years (15 years in this case) into the future.

## Appendix

1. (a) Let $S_0$ be the smoothed value for 1983, $S_1$ be the smoothed value for 1984, and so on.

$S_0 = 2.$
$S_1 = (1/4)(4) + (3/4)(2) = 2.50.$
$S_2 = (1/4)(8) + (3/4)(2.50) = 3.88.$
$S_3 = (1/4)(12) + (3/4)(3.88) = 5.91.$
$S_4 = (1/4)(20) + (3/4)(5.91) = 9.43.$
$S_5 = (1/4)(28) + (3/4)(9.43) = 14.07.$
$S_6 = (1/4)(38) + (3/4)(14.07) = 9.50 + 10.55 = 20.05.$
$S_7 = (1/4)(50) + (3/4)(20.05) = 12.50 + 15.04 = 27.54.$
$S_8 = (1/4)(70) + (3/4)(27.54) = 17.50 + 20.66 = 38.16.$
$S_9 = (1/4)(90) + (3/4)(38.16) = 22.50 + 28.62 = 51.12.$

(b) $S_0 = 2.$
$S_1 = (1/2)(4) + (1/2)(2) = 3.00.$
$S_2 = (1/2)(8) + (1/2)(3.00) = 5.50.$
$S_3 = (1/2)(12) + (1/2)(5.50) = 8.75.$
$S_4 = (1/2)(20) + (1/2)(8.75) = 14.38.$
$S_5 = (1/2)(28) + (1/2)(14.38) = 21.19.$
$S_6 = (1/2)(38) + (1/2)(21.19) = 29.60.$
$S_7 = (1/2)(50) + (1/2)(29.60) = 39.80.$
$S_8 = (1/2)(70) + (1/2)(39.80) = 54.90.$
$S_9 = (1/2)(90) + (1/2)(54.90) = 72.45.$

(c) $S_0 = 2.$
$S_1 = (3/4)(4) + (1/4)(2) = 3.50.$
$S_2 = (3/4)(8) + (1/4)(3.50) = 6.88.$
$S_3 = (3/4)(12) + (1/4)(6.88) = 10.72.$
$S_4 = (3/4)(20) + (1/4)(10.72) = 17.68.$
$S_5 = (3/4)(28) + (1/4)(17.68) = 25.42.$
$S_6 = (3/4)(38) + (1/4)(25.42) = 28.50 + 6.36 = 34.86.$
$S_7 = (3/4)(50) + (1/4)(34.86) = 37.50 + 8.72 = 46.22.$
$S_8 = (3/4)(70) + (1/4)(46.22) = 52.50 + 11.56 = 64.06.$
$S_9 = (3/4)(90) + (1/4)(64.06) = 67.50 + 16.02 = 83.52.$

## Chapter 6

1. (a) To see whether 400 hours of skilled labor and 100 hours of unskilled labor are the optimal input combination, recall from equation (6.11) that to minimize cost, the Elwyn Company should pick an input combination where

$$\frac{MP_s}{P_s} = \frac{MP_u}{P_u},$$

where $MP_s$ is the marginal product of skilled labor, $MP_u$ is the marginal product of unskilled labor, $P_s$ is the price of skilled labor, and $P_u$ is the price of unskilled labor. Since $P_s = 10$, $P_u = 5$, and

$$MP_s = \frac{\partial Q}{\partial S} = 300 - 0.4S$$

$$MP_u = \frac{\partial Q}{\partial U} = 200 - 0.6U,$$

it follows that the Elwyn Company should pick an input combination where

$$\frac{300 - 0.4S}{10} = \frac{200 - 0.6U}{5},$$

or

$$1,500 - 2S = 2,000 - 6U$$
$$S = -250 + 3U.$$

Thus, 400 hours of skilled labor and 100 hours of unskilled labor are not the optimal input combination, because, if $S = 400$ and $U = 100$, this equation does not hold.

(b) If a total of $5,000 is spent on skilled and unskilled labor,
$$10S + 5U = 5,000,$$
since $P_s = 10$ and $P_u = 5$. From the answer to part (a), we know that
$$S = -250 + 3U.$$
Solving these two equations simultaneously, $S = 392.9$ and $U = 214.3$. Thus, to maximize output, Elwyn should hire about 393 hours of skilled labor and about 214 hours of unskilled labor.

(c) From equation (6.4), we know that $MP_u \cdot P$ must equal $P_u$, where $P$ is the price of the product. (Under present circumstances, the marginal revenue product of unskilled labor equals $MP_u \cdot P$, and the marginal expenditure on unskilled labor equals $P_u$.) Thus, since $P = 10$, $P_u = 5$, and $MP_u = 200 - 0.6U$,
$$10(200 - 0.6U) = 5$$
$$U = 332.5.$$
To maximize profit, Elwyn should hire 332.5 hours of unskilled labor. [Note that we no longer assume that a total of $5,000 is spent on labor. Thus, the answer is different from that in part (b).]

3. (a) No.
  (b) 50 pounds, since half of these amounts (that is, 50 pounds of hay and 125.1 pounds of grain) results in a 25-pound gain.
  (c) $-(125.1 - 130.9) \div (50 - 40) = 0.58$.
  (d) No, because it is impossible to tell (from the information given in the question) how much hay and grain can be used to produce a 25-pound gain after the advance in technology.

5. (a) No.
  (b) General farms.
  (c) No.

7. (a) and (b). The average and marginal products of grain when each amount is used are calculated as follows on page A-24.

| Amount of grain | Average product | Marginal product |
|---|---|---|
| 1,200 | $5{,}917 \div 1{,}200 = 4.93$ | $\dfrac{7{,}250 - 5{,}917}{1{,}800 - 1{,}200} = 2.22$ |
| 1,800 | $7{,}250 \div 1{,}800 = 4.03$ | $\dfrac{8{,}379 - 7{,}250}{2{,}400 - 1{,}800} = 1.88$ |
| 2,400 | $8{,}379 \div 2{,}400 = 3.49$ | $\dfrac{9{,}371 - 8{,}379}{3{,}000 - 2{,}400} = 1.65$ |
| 3,000 | $9{,}371 \div 3{,}000 = 3.12$ | |

(c) Yes. The marginal product of grain decreases as more of it is used.

9. (a) To minimize cost, the firm should choose an input combination where $MP_L/P_L = MP_K/P_K$, where $MP_L$ is the marginal product of labor, $MP_K$ is the marginal product of capital, $P_L$ is the price of labor, and $P_K$ is the price of capital. Since

$$MP_L = \frac{\partial Q}{\partial L} = 5K$$

$$MP_K = \frac{\partial Q}{\partial K} = 5L,$$

it follows that

$$\frac{5K}{1} = \frac{5L}{2},$$

or $K = L/2$. Since $Q = 20$, $K = 4/L$. Thus,

$$\frac{L}{2} = \frac{4}{L},$$

or

$$L^2 = 8,$$

which means that the firm should use $2\sqrt{2}$ units of labor and $\sqrt{2}$ units of capital.

(b) If the price of labor is $2 per unit, the optimal value of $K$ is 2, and the optimal value of $L$ is 2. Thus, output per unit of labor is $20 \div 2$, or 10, whereas it formerly was $20 \div 2\sqrt{2}$, or $10 \div \sqrt{2}$. Thus, output per unit of labor will rise.

(c) No, because a 1 percent increase in both $K$ and $L$ results in more than a 1 percent increase in $Q$.

11. (a) Total annual costs equal $C = 40\ L/2 + (8{,}000)(1{,}000)/L$. Thus, $dC/dL = 20 - 8{,}000{,}000/L^2$, and the optimal lot size is

$$\sqrt{(8{,}000)(1{,}000)/20} = \sqrt{400{,}000} = 632.5.$$

(b) The optimal lot size is

$$\sqrt{(8{,}000)(10{,}000)/20} = \sqrt{4{,}000{,}000} = 2{,}000.$$

(c) The optimal lot size is

$$\sqrt{(8{,}000)(100{,}000)/20} = \sqrt{40{,}000{,}000} = 6{,}324.6.$$

## Chapter 7

1. (a) $\dfrac{200,000}{10(20,000) + .02(50,000) + 5(10,000)} = \dfrac{200,000}{251,000} = .797.$

   (b) $\dfrac{300,000}{10(30,000) + .02(100,000) + 5(14,000)} = \dfrac{300,000}{372,000} = .806.$

   (c) The base year is 1994.

3. (a) $\log C = 5.1 - .25 \log 100$

   $\qquad = 5.1 - .25(2)$

   $\qquad = 4.6.$

   Thus, $C = 39,811.$

   (b) $\log C = 5.1 - .25 \log 200$

   $\qquad = 5.1 - .25\,(2.30)$

   $\qquad = 4.525.$

   Thus, $C = 33,497.$

   (c) $1 - 33,497/39,811 = 16$ percent.

5. Let $E$ equal the output of electric power, $X$ equal the output of coal, and $C$ equal the output of chemicals, all expressed in millions of dollars. To meet the consumption targets, $C = 818$, $E = 159$, $X = 144$. (To see this, use the technique on pages 273–75.) The amount of labor used is $.2E + .6X + .1C$. Thus if, $C = 818$, $E = 159$, and $X = 144$, it follows that $200 million of labor must be used.

7. (a) 0.5 ($1 million) + 0.5 ($2 million) = $1.5 million.

   (b) 0.75 ($1 million) + 0.25 ($2 million) + $150,000 = $1.4 million. This assumes that whether each approach costs $1 million or $2 million is independent of what the other approach costs. Also, the total cost figure for each approach, if adopted, includes the $150,000. Thus, only the $150,000 spent on the aborted approach is lost. The $150,000 spent on the approach that is adopted is part of the total cost figure given in the problem.

   (c) Comparing the answers to parts (a) and (b), parallel approaches result in lower expected cost.

9. (a) 0.6 ($5 million) + 0.4 ($3 million) = $4.2 million.

   (b) 0.7 ($3 million) + 0.3 ($5 million) = $3.6 million.

   (c) .18 ($5 million) + .82 ($3 million) + $500,000 = $3.86 million.

## Chapter 8

1. (a) It is the cheapest of these three ways of making steel. Using this method, cost per ton is $310.34, as compared with $368.86 and $401.73 with the other methods.

   (b) If the price of scrap rises, the cost of producing steel based on the electric-furnace continuous-casting route will increase, because this route uses scrap. Thus, the cost advantage of this route will be reduced if the price of scrap goes up.

(c) It implies that American steel producers will have a hard time competing with Korean and other steel producers.

(d) If each figure is the minimum value of long-run average cost for a particular technique, it also equals the long-run marginal cost for the technique, since marginal cost equals average cost when the latter is a minimum. (Recall page 294.)

3. (a) If $Q$ is the sales volume,
$$Q \, (\$200) - \$5,000 = \$10,000,$$
so $Q$ must equal 75.

(b) Since $Q \, (\$250) - \$5,000 = \$10,000$, $Q$ must equal 60.

(c) Since $Q \, (\$265) - \$5,000 = \$10,000$, $Q$ must equal 56.6.

5. The table is as follows:

| Total fixed cost | Total variable cost | Average fixed cost | Average variable cost |
|---|---|---|---|
| 50 | 0 | — | — |
| 50 | 25 | 50 | 25 |
| 50 | 50 | 25 | 25 |
| 50 | 70 | 16⅔ | 23⅓ |
| 50 | 85 | 12½ | 21¼ |
| 50 | 100 | 10 | 20 |
| 50 | 140 | 8⅓ | 23⅓ |
| 50 | 210 | 7⅐ | 30 |

7. (a) Yes. Since $\partial TC/\partial Q \cdot Q/TC = \alpha_1$, this is true.

(b) Yes. If $\alpha_1 < 1$, a 1 percent increase in output results in a less than 1 percent increase in total cost, so average cost falls with increases in output; in other words, there are economies of scale. If $\alpha_1 > 1$, a 1 percent increase in output results in a more than 1 percent increase in total cost, so average cost increases with increases in output; in other words, there are diseconomies of scale.

(c) If we assume that a 1 percent increase in both $P_L$ and $P_K$ will result in a 1 percent increase in $TC$, $\alpha_2 + \alpha_3 = 1$. Thus,
$$\frac{TC}{P_k} = \alpha_0 \, Q^{\alpha_1} \left(\frac{P_L}{P_K}\right)^{\alpha_2},$$
and
$$\log\left(\frac{TC}{P_k}\right) = \log \alpha_0 + \alpha_1 \log Q + \alpha_2 \log\left(\frac{P_L}{P_K}\right).$$
If this is treated as a regression equation, one can estimate the $\alpha$'s, using the regression technique discussed in Chapter 4, subject to the caveats concerning various kinds of possible errors cited there.

9. (a) Since marginal cost equals $dTVC/dQ$, it equals
$$MC = 50 - 20Q + 3Q^2.$$
It is a minimum when
$$\frac{dMC}{dQ} = -20 + 6Q = 0,$$

or

$Q = 20/6$.

(b) Average variable cost equals

$$AVC = \frac{TVC}{Q} = 50 - 10Q + Q^2.$$

It is a minimum when

$$\frac{dAVC}{dQ} = -10 + 2Q = 0,$$

or

$Q = 5$.

(c) If $Q = 5$, average variable cost equals $50 - 10(5) + 5^2 = 25$. Marginal cost equals $50 - 20(5) + 3(5^2) = 25$. Thus, marginal cost equals average variable cost at this output level.

11. (a) Using equation (8.7), $S = (23,000 + 11,000 - 30,000) \div 30,000 = .13$.

(b) Production facilities used to make one product sometimes can be used to make another product, and by-products resulting from the production of one product may be useful in making other products.

## Chapter 9

1. (a) Maximize $50L + 25M + 12.5S$, where $L$ is the number of large cabinets produced, $M$ is the number of medium cabinets produced, and $S$ is the number of small cabinets produced per day.

(b) The constraints are

$$25L + 15M + 10S \leq 3,500$$
$$40L + 15M + 5S \leq 2,500$$
$$L \geq 0, M \geq 0, S \geq 0.$$

(c) To maximize profit, the firm should produce 100 medium cabinets and 200 small cabinets; that is, $M = 100$ and $S = 200$. Thus, Mr. Casey should allocate 1,500 hours of labor to the production of medium cabinets and 2,000 hours of labor to the production of small cabinets; and he should allocate 1,500 hours of machine time to the production of medium cabinets and 1,000 hours of machine time to the production of small cabinets.

To derive this solution, we construct rays for the production of large, medium, and small cabinets, as shown on page A-28. These rays ($R_L$ for large cabinets, $R_M$ for medium cabinets, and $R_S$ for small cabinets) show the amount of labor time and machine time required to produce various numbers of cabinets. The black lines are isoprofit curves corresponding to profit levels of $2,500 and $5,000 per day. To satisfy the constraints, the firm must choose a point within the rectangle *OABC*. Clearly, the highest isoprofit curve that can be reached is the one corresponding to a daily profit

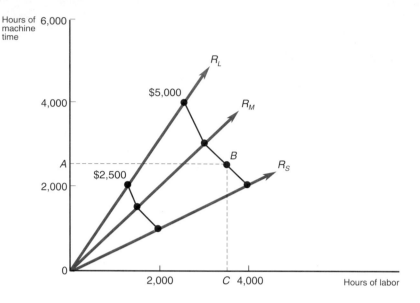

of \$5,000, the optimal point being *B*, where only medium and small cabinets are produced. Since all of the available labor and machine time is used at point *B*,

$$15M + 10S = 3,500$$
$$15M + 5S = 2,500.$$

Solving these two equations simultaneously, $M = 100$ and $S = 200$. Thus, to maximize profit, 100 medium cabinets and 200 small cabinets should be produced per day.

3. Both the rays and the isoquant are shown below.

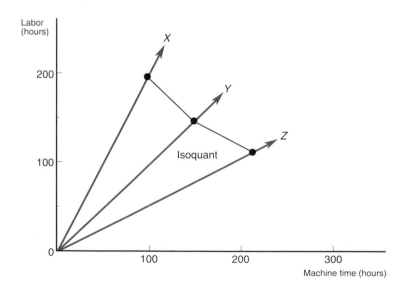

5. (a) Minimize $3{,}500U + 2{,}500V$, subject to

$$25U + 40V \geq 50$$
$$15U + 15V \geq 25$$
$$10U + 5V \geq 12.5$$
$$U \geq 0, V \geq 0.$$

(b) $U = .83$ and $V = .83$. To see that this is the solution to the problem in part (a), note that if $(3{,}500U + 2{,}500V)$ equals $k$,

$$U = \frac{k}{3{,}500} - \frac{2{,}500}{3{,}500}V = \frac{k}{3{,}500} - .714V.$$

Thus, to minimize $k$, we must find a point on the lowest of the black parallel lines in the diagram below. To meet the constraints, this point must not be inside $OWXYZ$, since the three colored lines represent the three constraints

$$U \geq \frac{50}{25} - \frac{40}{25}V = 2 - 1.6V$$

$$U \geq \frac{25}{15} - \frac{15}{15}V = 1\tfrac{2}{3} - 1.0V$$

$$U \geq \frac{12.5}{10} - \frac{5}{10}V = 1.25 - 0.5V.$$

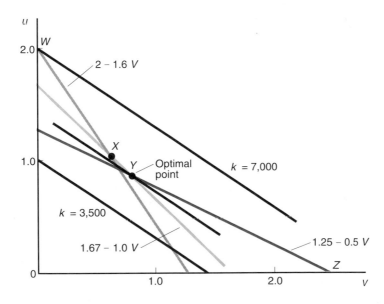

Clearly, the point on the lowest black line that does not lie below any of the colored lines is point $Y$, where

$$U = 1.25 - 0.5V$$

$$U = 1\tfrac{2}{3} - 1.0V.$$

Solving these equations simultaneously, $U = .83$ and $V = .83$.

(c) An extra hour of labor is worth 83 cents an hour. An extra hour of machine time is also worth 83 cents an hour.

7. (a) 60.
   (b) 40.
   (c) Zero.
9. (a) No.
   (b) Yes.

## Chapter 10

1. (a) Since average cost (AC) must be a minimum, and since
$$AC = \frac{25,000}{Q} + 150 + 3Q,$$
$$\frac{dAC}{dQ} = \frac{-25,000}{Q^2} + 3 = 0.$$
   Thus, $Q = \sqrt{25,000/3} = 91.3$, and
$$AC = 25,000/91.3 + 150 + 3(91.3) = 697.7,$$
   so the price must be $697.7, since in long-run equilibrium, price equals the minimum value of average cost.
   (b) 91.3 units.
3. (a) Marginal cost equals the following:
$$MC = \frac{dTC}{dQ} = 4 + 4Q.$$
   Setting marginal cost equal to price, we have
   $4 + 4Q = 24$
   $4Q = 20$
   $Q = 5.$
   Thus, the optimal output rate is 5.
   (b) Profit equals total revenue minus total cost. Since total revenue equals 24Q, profit equals
   $\pi = 24Q - 200 - 4Q - 2Q^2 = -200 + 20Q - 2Q^2.$
   Because $Q = 5$,
   $\pi = -200 + (20)(5) - (2)(5)^2 = -200 + 100 - 50 = -150.$
   Thus, the firm loses $150 (which is less than if it shuts down).
5. (a) Marginal revenue $= 100 - 2Q$; marginal cost $= 60 + 2Q$. Thus, if marginal revenue equals marginal cost, $100 - 2Q = 60 + 2Q$, which means that $Q = 10$.
   (b) Since $P = 100 - Q$, $P$ must equal 90 if $Q = 10$. Thus, he should charge a price of $90.
7. (a) Since the equation for the supply curve is $P = 3$, the long-run equilibrium output can be determined by finding the value of $Q_D$ if $P = 3$. (This is the value where the supply and demand curves intersect.) Thus, since $Q_D = 50 - 2P$, the equilibrium output is $50 - (2)(3)$, or 44 million knives per year.

(b) A tax of $1 will raise the supply curve by $1, which means that its equation will be $P = 4$. (To see why, note that producers, to have the same amount left over after the tax, must charge $1 more.) Thus, the long-run equilibrium output can be determined by finding the value of $Q_D$ if $P = 4$. (This is the value where the demand curve intersects the new supply curve.) Thus, since $Q_D = 50 - 2P$, the equilibrium output is $50 - (2)(4)$, or 42 million knives per year.

(c) No.

9. (a) Since $P = (8,300 - Q) \div 2.1 = 3,952 - .476Q$,
$$MR = 3,952 - .952Q.$$

(b) $MC = 480 + 40Q$. If $MC = MR$,
$$480 + 40Q = 3,952 - .952Q$$
$$40.952Q = 3,472$$
$$Q = 84.8.$$
Thus, the firm would produce 84.8 lasers per month. If $Q = 84.8$, $P = 3,952 - .476(84.8) = 3,912$. Thus, the price should be $3,912.

(c) The firm's monthly profit equals
$$(84.8)(3,912) - [2,200 + 480(84.8) + 20(84.8)^2] = \$145,012.80.$$

11. (a) If the firm is producing 5 units in the first plant, the marginal cost in the first plant equals $20 + 2(5)$, or 30. Thus, if the firm is minimizing costs, marginal cost in the second plant must also equal 30, which means that
$$10 + 5Q_2 = 30$$
$$Q_2 = 4.$$
Thus, the second plant must be producing 4 units of output.

(b) Since $MC_1 = MC_2 = MC$ and the firm's output, Q, equals $Q_1 + Q_2$,
$$Q_1 = MC_1/2 - 10$$
$$Q_2 = MC_2/5 - 2$$
$$Q = Q_1 + Q_2 = 0.7MC - 12$$
$$MC = (1/0.7)(Q + 12).$$

(c) No, because we do not have information concerning the fixed costs of each plant.

13. (a) It probably tended to increase because high profits induced entry. Also, the 1990–91 recession may have resulted in more demand for the services of pawnshops. So long as pawnshops are earning substantial economic profits, further increases seem likely.

(b) No. It is likely to be an oligopoly, since there generally are not a very large number of pawnshops in a small city.

(c) Apparently not, but licensing requirements may exist.

## Chapter 11

1. (a) They would want to set marginal revenue equal to the marginal cost of each firm, but this is impossible since Bergen's marginal cost is $410 and Gutenberg's marginal cost is $460. Because Bergen's marginal cost is always less than Gutenberg's, it will produce all of the output. Equating its marginal cost to marginal revenue (MR),

$$MR = 580 - 6Q = 410,$$

so $Q = 170/6$. This is Bergen's output.

(b) Nothing.

(c) Not unless Gutenberg receives an attractive share of the profit from Bergen's output even though it produces nothing.

3. (a) $9,000.

(b) 6.

5. (a) Yes. Fortnum should stress magazines, and Maison should stress newspapers.

(b) Fortnum's profit will be $9 million, and Maison's profit will be $8 million.

(c) No.

7. (a) To find the profit-maximizing price, the IATA should construct the marginal cost curve for the cartel as a whole. Then, as shown in Figure 11.2, it should determine the amount of traffic (which is the output of this industry) where marginal revenue equals marginal cost. The price that will elicit this amount of traffic is the profit-maximizing price.

(b) If IATA wants to maximize profit, it will allocate this traffic among the airlines in such a way that the marginal cost of all airlines is equal. (However, for reasons discussed on page 424, it may not want to maximize profit.)

(c) No. This would not maximize profit.

9. (a) The size of a firm is often measured by its total revenue. Perhaps a firm might feel that a higher total revenue would make the firm more visible to investors and customers. Also, its managers may be more interested in the growth of the firm than in profits. (However, they are likely to feel that profits should not fall below some minimum level.)

(b) To maximize its total revenue, it should set

$$\frac{d(PQ)}{dQ} = \frac{d(28Q - .14Q^2)}{dQ} = 28 - .28Q = 0.$$

Thus, $Q$ should equal 100, and $P$ should equal $14.

(c) If it maximizes profit, it sets

$$28 - .28Q = 14,$$

so $Q = 50$. Consequently, the firm produces 50,000 units more than it would if it maximized profit.

11. (a) Letting Alliance's profit be $\pi_1$,

$$\pi_1 = Q_1 [200,000 - 6(Q_1 + Q_2)] - 8,000 Q_1.$$

Letting Bangor's profit be $\pi_2$,

$\pi_2 = Q_2 [200,000 - 6(Q_1 + Q_2)] - 12,000\, Q_2.$

If Alliance maximizes its profit, assuming that Bangor will hold its output constant,

$$\frac{\partial \pi_1}{\partial Q_1} = 192,000 - 6Q_2 - 12Q_1 = 0.$$

If Bangor maximizes its profit, assuming that Alliance will hold its output constant,

$$\frac{\partial \pi_2}{\partial Q_2} = 188,000 - 6Q_1 - 12Q_2 = 0.$$

Solving these equations simultaneously, $Q_1 = 196,000/18 = 10,889$, and

$$Q_2 = (188,000 - 196,000/3) \div 12 = 122,667/12 = 10,222,$$

so

$P = 200,000 - 6(10,889 + 10,222) = 73,334$ dollars.

(b) Alliance's output is 10,889, and Bangor's output is 10,222.

(c) Alliance's profit is

10,889 (73,334 − 8,000), or approximately $711 million.

Bangor's profit is

10,222 (73,334 − 12,000), or approximately $627 million.

## Chapter 12

1. (a) The slope of the isocost curve is $dQ_Y/dQ_X = -10 - 10Q_X$. If total revenue equals a constant $(K)$,

$P_X Q_X + P_Y Q_Y = K,$

which means that

$$Q_Y = \frac{K}{P_Y} - \frac{P_X Q_X}{P_Y}.$$

Thus, the slope of the isorevenue curve is $-P_X/P_Y$, or $-50$. If the isorevenue curve is tangent to the isocost curve,

$-10 - 10Q_X = -50,$

or $Q_X = 4$.

(b) $Q_Y = 1,000 - 10(4) - 5(4^2) = 880$.

(c) No. There is no evidence that this is true.

3. (a) To earn 20 percent on its total investment of $250,000, its profit must equal $50,000 per year. Thus, if it operates at 80 percent of capacity (and sells 10,000 units), it must set a price of $15 per unit. (Since average cost equals $10, profit per unit will be $5, so total profit per year will be $50,000.)

(b) From the information given, there is no assurance that it can sell 10,000 units per year if it charges a price of $15 per unit.

(c) Unless the markup bears the proper relationship to the price elasticity of demand, the firm probably is sacrificing profit.

5. (a) $MR_1 = 160 - 16Q_1$
$MR_2 = 80 - 4Q_2$
$MC = 5 + (Q_1 + Q_2)$.
Therefore
$$160 - 16Q_1 = 5 + Q_1 + Q_2$$
$$80 - 4Q_2 = 5 + Q_1 + Q_2.$$
Or
$$155 - 17Q_1 = Q_2$$
$$75 - 5Q_2 = Q_1.$$
Thus,
$$155 - 17(75 - 5Q_2) = Q_2$$
$$155 - 1275 + 85Q_2 = Q_2$$
$$84Q_2 = 1,120$$
$$Q_2 = 1,120/84 = 13\tfrac{1}{3}.$$
It should sell $13\tfrac{1}{3}$ units in the second market.

(b) $Q_1 = 75 - 5Q_2$
$= 75 - 5(1120/84)$
$= 75 - 5,600/84$
$= 75 - 66\tfrac{2}{3}$
$= 8\tfrac{1}{3}$.
It should sell $8\tfrac{1}{3}$ units in the first market.

(c) $P_1 = 160 - 8(8\tfrac{1}{3}) = 93\tfrac{1}{3}$.
$P_2 = 80 - 2(13\tfrac{1}{3}) = 53\tfrac{1}{3}$.

7. (a) Backus' total revenues equal
$$TR = P_X Q_X + P_Y Q_Y = (400 - Q_X)Q_X + (300 - 3Q_Y)Q_Y,$$
and since $Q_Y = 2Q_X$,
$$TR = (400 - Q_X)Q_X + (300 - 6Q_X)(2Q_X)$$
$$= 400\,Q_X - Q_X^2 + 600\,Q_X - 12Q_X^2 = 1,000Q_X - 13Q_X^2.$$
Thus, the firm's profit equals
$$\pi = 1,000Q_X - 13Q_X^2 - 500 - 3Q_X - 9Q_X^2$$
$$= -500 + 997Q_X - 22Q_X^2.$$
Setting $d\pi/dQ_X = 997 - 44Q_X = 0$, we find that the profit-maximizing value of $Q_X = 997/44 = 22.66$. Thus, Backus should produce and sell 22.66 units of product $X$ and 45.32 units of product $Y$ per period of time.

(b) The price of product $X$ must be $400 - 22.66 = \$377.34$, and the price of product $Y$ must be $300 - 3(45.32) = \$164.04$.

We have assumed that Backus sells all that it produces of both products. The marginal revenue of product $X$ equals $400 - 2(22.66) = 354.68$, and the marginal revenue of product $Y$ equals $300 - 6(45.32) = 28.08$. Since both are non-negative, this assumption is true, if Backus maximizes profit.

9. (a) The firm's profit equals $P_C Q_C + P_M Q_M - TC$, or
$$\pi = (495 - 5Q_C)Q_C + (750 - 10Q_M)Q_M - 410$$
$$- 8(Q_C + Q_M).$$
Thus,
$$\frac{\partial \pi}{\partial Q_C} = 495 - 10Q_C - 8 = 0$$
$$\frac{\partial \pi}{\partial Q_M} = 750 - 20Q_M - 8 = 0.$$
Consequently, $Q_C = 48.7$ and $Q_M = 37.1$, so
$P_C = 495 - 5(48.7) = 251.5$.
(b) $P_M = 750 - 10(37.1) = 379$.
(c) Yes. Under these circumstances,
$$Q_C = \frac{495 - P}{5} \text{ and } Q_M = \frac{750 - P}{10},$$
so
$$Q = Q_C + Q_M = 174 - .3P;$$
and
$$P = (174 - Q) \div .3 = 580 - \frac{10}{3}Q.$$
Thus,
$$\pi = \left(580 - \frac{10}{3}Q\right)Q - 410 - 8Q$$
$$= -410 + 572Q - \frac{10}{3}Q^2.$$
If $\pi$ is a maximum,
$$\frac{d\pi}{dQ} = 572 - \frac{20}{3}Q = 0,$$
so $Q = 572 (3/20) = 85.8$. Consequently,
$$\pi = -410 + 572(85.8) - \frac{10}{3}(85.8^2)$$
$$= 24,129,$$
which compares with
$$\pi = [495 - 5(48.7)]48.7 + [750 - 10(37.1)]37.1 - 410$$
$$- 8(48.7 + 37.1)$$
$$= (251.5)48.7 + (379)37.1 - 1,096.4$$
$$= 12,248.05 + 14,060.9 - 1,096.4 = 25,213,$$
the value of profits when price discrimination is allowed.

## Chapter 13

1. (a) The expected present value is $10.7 million, the standard deviation
is $5.06 million, and the coefficient of variation is 47 percent.
(b) The expected present value is $11.0 million, the standard deviation
is $1.95 million, and the coefficient of variation is 18 percent.

(c) Investment *X*.

(d) Investment *Y*, since she is a risk averter (as indicated by the fact that *U* increases at a decreasing rate as *P* rises). Investment *Y* has both a higher expected present value and a lower standard deviation than investment *X*.

3. (a) No.

(b) It is very conservative, as discussed on page 530.

(c) No, because no probability distribution of the outcome can be given.

5. (a) 3.

(b) −0.6.

(c) −1.2.

7. (a) See diagram below.

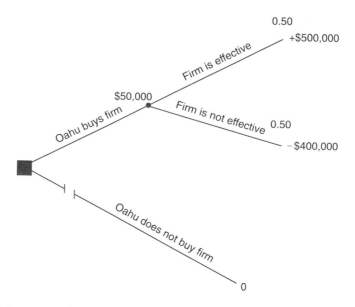

(b) There is only one: whether or not to buy the firm.

(c) There is only one: whether the firm becomes an effective producer of washing machine parts or not.

(d) Yes, it should buy the firm.

(e) (i)  Yes.

(ii)  Three mutually exclusive outcomes are: (1) The firm becomes an effective producer of washing machine parts. (2) The firm does not become an effective producer of washing parts and is sold to the Saudis. (3) The firm does not become an effective producer of washing machine parts and cannot be sold to the Saudis.

(iii)  The probability of the first outcome (in part ii) is .5, the probability of the second outcome is (.5)(.2), or .1, and the probability of the third outcome is (.5)(.8), or .4.

(iv) The extra profit to Oahu from the first outcome is $500,000; the extra profit from the second outcome is $100,000; the extra profit from the third outcome is − $400,000.

(f) Oahu should buy the firm. The expected extra profit if it does so is (.5)($500,000) + (.1)($100,000) + (.4)(−$400,000) = $100,000.

(g) (i) If the extra profit if the firm is made into an effective producer of washing machine parts is $400,000 or less, the decision will be reversed. Put differently, if the *error* was an *overstatement* of this extra profit by $100,000 or more, the decision will be reversed.

(ii) If the extra profit if the firm is made into an effective producer of washing machine parts is $300,000 or less, the decision will be reversed. Put differently, if the *error* was an *overstatement* of this extra profit by $200,000 or more, the decision will be reversed.

9. (a)

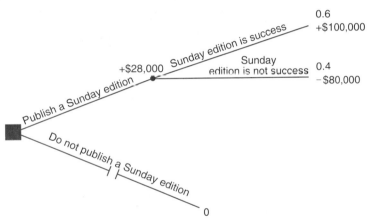

If the publisher is risk neutral, she wants to maximize expected profit. Thus, she should publish the Sunday edition.

(b) Whether or not to publish the Sunday edition is a decision fork. Whether or not it is a success, if published, is a chance fork.

## Chapter 14

1. (a)

| Year* | Incremental after-tax cash flow |
|-------|---------------------------------|
| 0 | −$2 million |
| 1 | $150,000(1 − .4) + $500,000 = $590,000 |
| 2 | $150,000(1 − .4) + $500,000 = $590,000 |
| 3 | $150,000(1 − .4) + $500,000 = $590,000 |
| 4 | $150,000(1 − .4) + $500,000 = $590,000 |

(b)

| Year* | Incremental after-tax cash flow |
|---|---|
| 0 | −$2 million |
| 1 | $150,000(1 − .5) + $500,000 = $575,000 |
| 2 | $150,000(1 − .5) + $500,000 = $575,000 |
| 3 | $150,000(1 − .5) + $500,000 = $575,000 |
| 4 | $150,000(1 − .5) + $500,000 = $575,000 |

(c)

| Year* | Incremental after-tax cash flow |
|---|---|
| 0 | −$2 million |
| 1 | $50,000(1 − .5) + $500,000 = $525,000 |
| 2 | $50,000(1 − .5) + $500,000 = $525,000 |
| 3 | $50,000(1 − .5) + $500,000 = $525,000 |
| 4 | $50,000(1 − .5) + $500,000 = $525,000 |

*The present year is year 0.

3. (a) The net present value equals

$$-\$10,000 + \$2,000 \left[\frac{1}{1.10} + \frac{1}{(1.10)^2} + \cdots + \frac{1}{(1.10)^7}\right]$$

$$= -\$10,000 + \$2,000(4.8684) = -\$263.20.$$

The firm should not buy this machine.

(b) The net present value equals

$$-\$10,000 + \$2,000 \left(\frac{1}{1.20} + \frac{1}{(1.20)^2} + \cdots + \frac{1}{(1.20)^7}\right)$$

$$= -\$10,000 + \$2,000(3.6046) = -\$2,790.80.$$

The firm should not buy this machine.

(c) The riskiness of the investment and the cost of capital.

5. (a) The present value of painting costs is

$$\$500 \left[1 + \frac{1}{1.08} + \frac{1}{(1.08)^2} + \frac{1}{(1.08)^3} + \frac{1}{(1.08)^4}\right]$$

$$= \$500(1 + 0.926 + 0.857 + 0.794 + 0.735)$$

$$= \$500(4.312) = \$2,156.$$

This must be compared with $2,000, the cost of installing aluminum siding now. Since the latter is less than the former, it is cheaper to install the aluminum siding.

(b) Since the present value of the painting costs is $500 (4.170) = $2,085, it is cheaper to install the aluminum siding.

(c) They can use as a selling point the fact that for consumers like Mr. Miller, aluminum siding is cheaper than continuing to paint.

7. (a) Beta is the slope of the regression line showing the relationship between a particular stock's returns and the returns for a market index.

(b) $k_e = .08 + 0.8(.14 − .08) = .128$. Thus, the cost of equity capital is 12.8 percent.

(c) $k_e = .08 + 1.7(.14 − .08) = .182$. Thus, the cost of equity capital is 18.2 percent.

(d) $k_e = .08 + 1.0(.14 − .08) = .14$. Thus, the cost of equity capital is 14 percent.

9. (a)

| Year | Incremental after-tax cash flow (millions) |
|---|---|
| 1994 | $-20$ |
| 1995 | $4(1 - 0.4) + 4 = 6.4$ |
| 1996 | $4(1 - 0.4) + 4 = 6.4$ |
| 1997 | $4(1 - 0.4) + 4 = 6.4$ |
| 1998 | $4(1 - 0.4) + 4 = 6.4$ |
| 1999 | $4(1 - 0.4) + 4 = 6.4$ |

(b) There may be more than one internal rate of return. In other words, the answer may not be unique.

(c) About 18 percent.

## Chapter 15

1. (a) If $P = 480$, $Q = 260$, according to the demand curve. Thus, the firm's total revenue equals $260(480)$ thousands of dollars, or $124,800,000. The firm's total cost equals $50 + .25(260) = 115$ millions of dollars. Thus, the firm's accounting profit is $9,800,000, which means that its rate of return would be 9.8 percent.

(b) If it were deregulated, it would maximize

$$\pi = [1/1,000][Q(1,000 - 2Q)] - 50 - .25Q = -50 + .75Q.$$
$$- .002Q^2.$$

Setting $d\pi/dQ = .75 - .004Q = 0, Q = 187.5$. Thus, under deregulation,

$$\pi = -50 + .75(187.5) - .002(187.5^2) = \$20.3125 \text{ million}.$$

3. (a) $220/250 = 88$ percent.

(b) Yes, because it is dominated by a few firms.

(c) $225/250 = 90$ percent.

(d) $140/145 = 97$ percent.

5. (a) No. If price is $1, 12 firms of optimal size can exist in the market.

(b) Eight.

7. (a) The district court ruled against the merger.

(b) The court held that transportation costs were small enough so that competition on a national basis was practical.

(c) Obviously, the views of courts and government agencies change over time. The prevailing climate of opinion was quite different in the 1980s than in the 1950s.

9. (a) Whether or not a firm has substantial monopoly power depends on how big the market is.

(b) If products are interchangeable, they should be included in the same market.

(c) Because the cross elasticity of demand is a measure of how closely one good substitutes for another, and thus of how legitimate it is to consider them as part of a single market.

11. (a) Because the commission tries to provide the firm with a "fair" rate of return on its investment.
    (b) Because this increase reduced the firm's profit.
    (c) See page 572.

## Chapter 16

1. (a) Yes. Since consumption levels are much less in other countries, there appears to be far more room for growth than in the United States.
   (b) Because the conditions in Indonesia seem to be very favorable to the consumption of soft drinks, and at present, Coca-Cola is selling relatively little there, it appears that great sales growth there is quite possible.
   (c) Trade barriers and regulatory considerations are important. So are costs and local custom.
   (d) Because Coke does not have to compete so aggressively against Pepsi, it can spend much less on marketing than domestically and thus increase its profits abroad.
3. (a) $10.
   (b) Japan.
   (c) 2 million flashbulbs.
   (d) They will cease.
5. (a) The price of a pound of bananas must be between 3/10 and 8/10 of the price of a pound of coffee.
   (b) Honduras.
7. (a) It will fall.
   (b) It will fall.
9. (a) Buy, 40 million pounds.
   (b) From its reserves.
11. Basically, much more effort should be devoted to coordinating the work and planning of B&D's farflung (and largely uncoordinated) subsidiaries.

# Brief Answers to "Consultant's Corner"

## Planning to Meet Peak Engineering Requirements (Chapter 2)

The firm wanted an estimate of when the number of engineers required to carry out this project would reach a maximum. Since $a = 18$ and $b = 1$,

$$Y = 18t - t^2$$

and

$$\frac{dY}{dt} = 18 - 2t.$$

Setting $dY/dt$ equal to zero,

$$18 - 2t = 0$$
$$t = 9.$$

Thus, $Y$ reaches a maximum when $t = 9$. (Because $d^2Y/dt^2 = -2$, we can be sure that this is a maximum, not a minimum.)

The firm also wanted an estimate of the maximum number of engineers that would be required to carry out this project. To obtain such an estimate, we find the value of $Y$ when $t = 9$.

$$Y = 18(9) - (9)^2$$
$$= 81.$$

Thus, when engineering requirements for this project reach their peak, 81 engineers will be needed.

To sum up, the engineering requirements for this project will reach their peak 9 months after the project begins, when 81 engineers will be needed.

## Estimating the Quantity Demanded of Fresh Premium Salmon (Chapter 3)

Because the income elasticity of demand is about 4 in countries other than Japan, a 10 percent increase in income would result in about a 40 percent increase in quantity demanded between 1986 and 1990. In Japan, since the income elasticity is estimated to be about 2, there would be about a 20 percent increase in quantity demanded. Thus, the estimate for 1990 (in thousands of tons) would be as follows:

| Country | Estimate |
|---|---|
| United States | 90(1.4) = 126 |
| Canada | 14(1.4) = 20 |
| Japan | 110(1.2) = 132 |
| France | 35(1.4) = 49 |
| United Kingdom | 16(1.4) = 22 |
| Germany | 8(1.4) = 11 |
| Other European countries | 22(1.4) = 31 |
| Total | 391 |

In other words, about 391 thousand tons of fresh premium salmon would be demanded in 1990, under the assumed circumstances. Obviously, this was a rough estimate.

## Price and Market Share for a New Electrical Drive (Chapter 4)

If the total market is 10,000 units, the relationship between price and quantity demanded is as follows:

| Price | Quantity demanded |
|---|---|
| $ 800 | 10,000 (.110) = 1,100 |
| 900 | 10,000 (.102) = 1,020 |
| 1,000 | 10,000 (.092) = 920 |
| 1,100 | 10,000 (.084) = 840 |
| 1,200 | 10,000 (.075) = 750 |
| 1,300 | 10,000 (.066) = 660 |
| 1,400 | 10,000 (.056) = 560 |

To obtain a simple equation expressing quantity demanded as a function of price, regression analysis can be used, the independent variable being price and the dependent variable being quantity demanded. The resulting regression equation is

$$Y = 1822 - 0.8964X,$$

where $Y$ is the quantity demanded, and $X$ is price (in dollars). The equation seems to be reliable in the sense that it fits the above data very well, as indicated by the fact that $r^2 = 0.999$. However, the above data may or may not be very reliable, depending on how thoroughly the market research department did its job. It is risky to extrapolate a regression equation beyond the range to which the data apply. Thus, the firm cannot safely assume that this equation can predict quantity demanded if price is $1,500 or $1,600.

Without data on the costs of producing and marketing the electrical drive, one cannot say what the price should be.

## Deciding Whether to Finance the Purchase of an Oil Field (Chapter 5)

In deciding whether or not to approve this loan application, the bank's forecasts of the price of oil are very important. Yet the simple extrapolation technique that is used is very crude. It is clear from the figures that this forecast was the result of a simple trend extrapolation that assumed a steady increase, beginning at $25 in 1986 and reaching $49 in 1998. Econometric models based on a more sophisticated analysis of the demand and supply of oil might be more effective. In fact, the bank's forecasts were very poor. For example, the price was about $13, not $25, in 1986, and about $20, not $31, in 1989.

## Choosing the Size of an Oil Tanker (Chapter 6)

If the company needs to transport enough oil to warrant building a larger tanker, the cost of carrying a barrel of oil will decrease if a larger tanker is built. Because there are economies of scale in tanker construction and operation, costs fell as the average size of a tanker rose during 1958–76. According to one major oil company, the average cost per barrel of a typical 11,000-mile voyage fell from about 2.25 cents in 1954 to about 1.00 cents in 1974.

## Evaluating a Large-Scale Program of Product and Process Improvement (Chapter 7)

The available data show that the average cost of a dishwasher fell by 12 percent, in part a result of a 42 percent increase in labor productivity. Also, the number of service calls was reduced by 45 percent, and the reject rate was cut by 7.5 percentage points. Thus, these data certainly indicate that cost has been reduced and that product quality has been raised. But they tell us nothing about how General Electric's sales volume was influenced by product and process changes. (In fact, there was a substantial increase in its market share in the first year after the new product's introduction.) Even more important, these data tell us nothing about the rate of return that the firm obtained from its $40 million investment.

## An Intrafirm Dispute over a Break-Even Chart (Chapter 8)

All of the president's points are relevant. The fact that the product mix changes with increases in output may be quite important. It may be misleading to lump all three products together as the accountant did. Also, contrary to the assumption that the total cost curve is linear, the marginal cost of the first type of chair would increase with increases in output. Further, the price used for the second type of chair is not the relevant one.

## Evaluating the Organization of a Shipping Program (Chapter 9)

It is very unlikely that the firm is minimizing its total freight costs. Each regional sales manager cannot see all of the interrelated aspects of the problem, and each is concerned with minimizing only his or her own freight costs. Moreover, the choice of which orders are fulfilled by the distant plant is being made on the basis of when the orders are received (by the other plants), not with an eye toward minimizing total freight costs. To see how much those costs could be reduced, the firm might use the sort of linear programming model described in the Essex Corporation example (and used by H. J. Heinz). This model should be used to determine how much each plant should ship to each warehouse to minimize total freight costs.

## Forecasting the Price of Salmon (Chapter 10)

If the quantity supplied in 1990 is in accord with the firm's estimate, regardless of whatever price changes occur, the quantity demanded must increase by about 15 percent to close the gap between the quantity supplied and the quantity demanded. Since the price elasticity of demand is about 1.5, a 10 percent decrease in price would increase the quantity demanded by about 15 percent. Thus, a very rough estimate would be that the price would fall by about 10 percent.

## Using a Price Announcement to Preempt a Market (Chapter 11)

It seems doubtful that such a price announcement would have the desired effect. Since this firm will not be the lowest-cost producer of the next generation of products, it will not be able to announce a price that is low enough to make it unprofitable for all its rivals to enter the market. Unless it announces a price that is so low that it, as well as its rivals, would lose money, it is unlikely to induce its rivals to drop their plans to develop their own new products of the relevant kind. Moreover, even if it did announce a price at which it would lose money, it seems likely that its rivals would not take it too seriously, because announcements of this sort are not regarded as binding. Thus, such an announcement might well be regarded as a bluff. To be effective, an announcement must be credible. The firm's rivals would have to be convinced that the firm really would sell the product at a price that would impose unacceptable losses on them.

## Settling Some Strife over a Pricing Formula (Chapter 12)

From our discussion of transfer pricing, we know that if there is a competitive market for ethane, the transfer price should equal the price in this market. However, it must be recognized that there can be heated disputes between divisions over transfer pricing. In this case, the petrochemical division may resist the increase in the transfer price of ethane because it will make the petrochemical division look less profitable—and make the division's managers appear less successful.

## Choosing Areas for Research Regarding Pollution Costs (Chapter 13)

The expected value of perfect information seems to be greatest for a remote plant with low-sulfur coal available and least for an urban plant with low-sulfur coal available. However, this tells us nothing about the costs involved in obtaining perfect information. Unless you have some idea of these costs, it is very difficult to say much about the relative desirability of various areas of research.

## Deciding Whether to Install an Automated Manufacturing System (Chapter 14)

If 10 percent is the appropriate discount rate, the net present value of this investment is $283, as shown below.

| Year | Cash flow | $(1/1.10)^t \times$ Cash flow |
|------|-----------|-------------------------------|
| 0 | −7,380 | $1.00000(−7,380) = −7,380$ |
| 1 | 1,370 | $.90909(1,370) = 1,245$ |
| 2 | 1,675 | $.82645(1,675) = 1,384$ |
| 3 | 1,632 | $.75131(1,632) = 1,226$ |
| 4 | 1,632 | $.68301(1,632) = 1,115$ |
| 5 | 1,632 | $.62092(1,632) = 1,013$ |
| 6 | 714 | $.56447(714) = 403$ |
| 7 | 714 | $.51316(714) = 366$ |
| 8 | 714 | $.46651(714) = 333$ |
| 9 | 714 | $.42410(714) = 303$ |
| 10 | 714 | $.38554(714) = 275$ |
| | Total | 283 |

Thus, this investment should be carried out, according to the simple rule in the text. But there could be a question concerning the appropriate discount rate. Although the firm's managers state that they would be willing to accept only a 10 percent rate of return, more analysis might be carried out to see whether the discount rate should be higher or lower.

## A Dispute over a Requested Gas Rate Increase (Chapter 15)

To reduce the adverse effects of regulatory lag, you might suggest that the firm file for an interim rate increase (besides the permanent rate increase). The firm might promise to refund any difference between the interim rate and the permanent rate if the former turned out to be higher than the latter. (In fact, this is what the company proposed.) To see which of the two estimates of the cost of equity capital is closer to the truth, you might study the historical rate of growth of the firm's dividends, the object being to estimate g. Also, you might try to forecast the growth of the firm's dividends, based on various estimates published by brokerage firms as well as on statistical analysis. Other techniques in Chapter 14 might be used as well. (Recall from Chapter 14 that the cost of equity capital is not the same as the firm's weighted cost of capital.)

## Reorganizing a Firm's Global R and D Network (Chapter 16)

There are advantages in coordinating decisions regarding which products to develop with an eye toward the total world market, not just regional markets. In fact, Boehringer Ingelheim has altered its organization in this way. Decisions regarding which products to develop are now made centrally, but all of the subsidiaries have a voice in these centralized decisions, which are made by an International Steering Committee, composed of executives from all the major subsidiaries as well as from Germany.

# Brief Answers to "Managerial Economics in Context"

## Part Two: How to Forecast the Sales of Paper, According to McKinsey

(a) Yes. One can calculate a regression where the quantity demanded of plain-paper copy paper is the dependent variable, while cents per copy and gross national product are the independent variables. However, in a time-series analysis of this sort, one must be careful to recognize that serial correlation may be present.

(b) The multiple coefficient of determination.

(c) Based on the graph on page 198, one cannot calculate the elasticity of demand for plain-paper copy paper with respect to cost per copy, because there are no numbers along the horizontal axis. But if these numbers were supplied, such a calculation could be made. This elasticity might be of use because it would indicate how sensitive the quantity demanded is to changes in cost per copy.

(d) Not necessarily. The annual rate of growth of the quantity demanded may have varied from one year to another. If an exponential curve fits well, the annual rate of growth is relatively constant from year to year.

(e) No. The procedures described on pages 174–76 might be used to calculate such a seasonal index. To make monthly or quarterly forecasts, a seasonal index would be useful.

(f) If the multiple regression described in the answer to question (a) were calculated, one would need forecasts of gross national product and of cents per copy to forecast quantity demanded. The Wharton model and other such models might be used to forecast gross national product.

## Part Three: Apple's Lisa-Macintosh Development Project

(a) 50,000 computers per year.
(b) Perhaps the most important question is whether or not it would have been worth $2 million to have had the Macintosh computers available for sale a year earlier. As pointed above, the Mac's introduction was postponed almost a year. Such delays are frustrating to potential customers and users, as well as to marketing and other personnel. Also, rivals can use the time to develop and implement counterstrategies. You would have to estimate whether the firm's revenues would have increased by $2 million or more, if the Macintosh had been available a year earlier.
(c) Apparently, it was inefficient, since about $7 million of its equipment was removed because of lack of effectiveness.
(d) As pointed out on page 260, it is very important for close links to be created and maintained between marketing and R and D. Otherwise products may be developed that do not fit the needs and tastes of potential users and consumers.
(e) No. As indicated in equation (6.11), a firm should increase the amount of capital used only to the point where $MP_K/P_K = MP_L/P_L$, where $MP_K$ is the marginal product of capital, $MP_L$ is the marginal product of labor, $P_K$ is the price of capital, and $P_L$ is the price of labor. Beyond that point, increases in capital raise, not lower, a firm's costs.
(f) Yes. As pointed out in Chapter 9, linear programming can help to solve many relevant problems, such as: Which production processes should be used? How much of a factory's output should be shipped to particular warehouses?

## Part Four: A Rocky Road for Caterpillar Tractor

(a) Oligopoly.
(b) Caterpillar clearly has not maintained a constant percentage markup of price over average cost. During the 1980s, its profit margins often were less than in earlier years. As shown on page 494, its profits were negative in 1982 to 1984.
(c) No. It charged a price that was higher than that of its rivals in 1981.
(d) Faced with large losses, Caterpillar cut back on many expense items that would probably have not been cut so much otherwise. As pointed out on

page 494, the firm engaged in a major cost-reduction program in 1983 and 1984.

(e) It is worthwhile to spend money on them up to the point where the extra expenditure equals the extra savings. There are some technical improvements of this sort that require little expenditure relative to the savings they produce. Others require greater expenditure and yield smaller savings. Eventually one reaches a point where it is worthwhile to spend no more on such improvements, since the extra savings are less than the extra expenditures.

(f) No. It is wise only if the longer-term improved results are worth more than the short-term profits that are sacrificed. If a firm sacrifices $2 million in profits this year to obtain $1 million in profits 5 years from now, this is not a wise policy. Caterpillar estimated that the longer-term improved results were well worth the sacrifice.

(g) It will tend to reduce costs, thus allowing the firm more latitude in keeping its prices down.

## Part Five: How Amalgamated Metals Decided to Expand Its Heat-Treating Capacity

(a) No. By ignoring these potential advantages, their value is assumed to be zero. It is better to make rough estimates of their value than to ignore them entirely.

(b) Yes. If it is true that these changes would have to be made, their costs should be included in the analysis. Otherwise the complete costs of introducing the new heat-treating process are understated.

(c) Its sales revenues might be affected if customers preferred its rivals' products, which were stronger and more consistent because they introduced the new process. The fact that the analysis ignores this possibility could be a problem. Whether it is serious depends on how likely its rivals are to introduce the new process and the extent to which customers prefer products made by this process.

(d) You should use the techniques described on pages 549–55 to estimate the firm's cost of capital.

(e) There probably should be a risk premium included in the discount rate, the size of which depends on the risk preferences of the decision maker. To determine how large it should be, the procedures described on pages 522–23 might be employed.

## Part Six: A Free Trade Agreement for North America?

(a) Such tariffs help the U.S. orange juice producers and their workers and suppliers, but they tend to hurt U.S. consumers, who are likely to pay more for orange juice.

(b) Based on the fact that U.S. auto plants have found it difficult to compete with the Japanese and others, some observers have argued that the United States has lost its comparative advantage, but it is a complex question, and more time is required to settle it.

(c) Canadians felt that this ruling put their exporters at a disadvantage and that it would discourage investment in their country.

(d) Yes. Direct investment in subsidiaries located in Mexico has been very important, for reasons cited in Chapter 16.

(e) Many people believe that society as a whole, which tends to benefit from free trade, should help the minority that is hurt by it. The United States has established "adjustment assistance" for firms and workers who have suffered idleness or unemployment due to an increase in imports. However, such programs were reduced substantially in the early 1980s.

(f) In theory, one should carry out the sort of analysis shown in Figure 15.5, but in practice it is very difficult to do this with any precision. They can use transferable emissions permits, effluent fees, and/or direct regulation.

# Appendix Tables

APPENDIX TABLE 1 *Value of* $\dfrac{1}{(1+i)^n}$

*Value of* i

| n | 1% | 2% | 3% | 4% | 5% | 6% | 7% | 8% | 9% | 10% |
|---|------|------|------|------|------|------|------|------|------|------|
| 1 | .99010 | .98039 | .97007 | .96154 | .95233 | .94340 | .93458 | .92593 | .91743 | .90909 |
| 2 | .98030 | .96117 | .94260 | .92456 | .90703 | .89000 | .87344 | .85734 | .84168 | .82645 |
| 3 | .97059 | .94232 | .91514 | .88900 | .86384 | .83962 | .81639 | .79383 | .77228 | .75131 |
| 4 | .96098 | .92385 | .88849 | .85480 | .82270 | .79209 | .76290 | .73503 | .70883 | .68301 |
| 5 | .95147 | .90573 | .86261 | .82193 | .78353 | .74726 | .71299 | .68058 | .64993 | .62092 |
| 6 | .94204 | .88797 | .83748 | .79031 | .74622 | .70496 | .66634 | .63017 | .59627 | .56447 |
| 7 | .93272 | .87056 | .81309 | .75992 | .71063 | .66506 | .62275 | .58349 | .54705 | .51316 |
| 8 | .92348 | .85349 | .78941 | .73069 | .67684 | .62741 | .58201 | .54027 | .50189 | .46651 |
| 9 | .91434 | .83675 | .76642 | .70259 | .64461 | .59190 | .54393 | .50025 | .46043 | .42410 |
| 10 | .90529 | .82035 | .74409 | .67556 | .61391 | .55839 | .50835 | .46319 | .42241 | .38554 |
| 11 | .89632 | .80426 | .72242 | .64958 | .58468 | .52679 | .47509 | .42888 | .38753 | .35049 |
| 12 | .88745 | .78849 | .70138 | .62460 | .55684 | .49697 | .44401 | .39711 | .35553 | .31683 |
| 13 | .87866 | .77303 | .68095 | .60057 | .53032 | .46884 | .41496 | .36770 | .32618 | .28966 |
| 14 | .86996 | .75787 | .66112 | .57747 | .50507 | .44230 | .38782 | .34046 | .29925 | .26333 |
| 15 | .86135 | .74301 | .64186 | .55526 | .48102 | .41726 | .36245 | .31524 | .27454 | .23939 |
| 16 | .85282 | .72845 | .62317 | .53391 | .45811 | .39365 | .33873 | .29189 | .25187 | .21763 |
| 17 | .84436 | .71416 | .60502 | .51337 | .43630 | .37136 | .31657 | .27027 | .23107 | .19784 |
| 18 | .83602 | .70016 | .58739 | .49363 | .41552 | .35034 | .29586 | .25025 | .21199 | .17986 |
| 19 | .82774 | .68643 | .57029 | .47464 | .39573 | .33051 | .27651 | .23171 | .19449 | .16354 |
| 20 | .81954 | .67297 | .55367 | .45639 | .37689 | .31180 | .25842 | .21455 | .17843 | .14864 |
| 21 | .81143 | .65978 | .53755 | .44883 | .35894 | .29415 | .24151 | .19866 | .16370 | .13513 |
| 22 | .80340 | .64684 | .52189 | .42195 | .34185 | .27750 | .22571 | .18394 | .15018 | .12285 |
| 23 | .79544 | .63414 | .50669 | .40573 | .32557 | .26180 | .21095 | .17031 | .13778 | .11168 |
| 24 | .78757 | .62172 | .49193 | .39012 | .31007 | .24698 | .19715 | .15770 | .12640 | .10153 |
| 25 | .77977 | .60953 | .47760 | .37512 | .29530 | .23300 | .18425 | .14602 | .11597 | .09230 |

## APPENDIX TABLE 1 (Cont'd)

Value of i

| n | 11% | 12% | 13% | 14% | 15% | 16% | 17% | 18% | 19% | 20% | 24% |
|---|-----|-----|-----|-----|-----|-----|-----|-----|-----|-----|-----|
| 1 | .90090 | .89286 | .88496 | .87719 | .86957 | .86207 | .85470 | .84746 | .84043 | .83333 | .8065 |
| 2 | .81162 | .79719 | .78315 | .76947 | .75614 | .74316 | .73051 | .71818 | .70616 | .69444 | .6504 |
| 3 | .73119 | .71178 | .69305 | .67497 | .65752 | .64066 | .62437 | .60863 | .59342 | .57870 | .5245 |
| 4 | .65873 | .63552 | .61332 | .59208 | .57175 | .55229 | .53365 | .51579 | .49867 | .48225 | .4230 |
| 5 | .59345 | .56743 | .54276 | .51937 | .49718 | .47611 | .45611 | .43711 | .41905 | .40188 | .3411 |
| 6 | .53464 | .50663 | .48032 | .45559 | .43233 | .41044 | .38984 | .37043 | .35214 | .33490 | .2751 |
| 7 | .48166 | .45235 | .42506 | .39964 | .37594 | .35383 | .33320 | .31392 | .29592 | .27908 | .2218 |
| 8 | .43393 | .40388 | .37616 | .35056 | .32690 | .30503 | .28478 | .26604 | .24867 | .23257 | .1789 |
| 9 | .39092 | .36061 | .33288 | .30751 | .28426 | .26295 | .24340 | .22546 | .20897 | .19381 | .1443 |
| 10 | .35218 | .32197 | .29459 | .26974 | .24718 | .22668 | .20804 | .19106 | .17560 | .16151 | .1164 |
| 11 | .31728 | .28748 | .26070 | .23662 | .21494 | .19542 | .17781 | .16192 | .14756 | .13459 | .0938 |
| 12 | .28584 | .25667 | .23071 | .20756 | .18691 | .16846 | .15197 | .13722 | .12400 | .11216 | .0757 |
| 13 | .25751 | .22917 | .20416 | .18207 | .16253 | .14523 | .12989 | .11629 | .10420 | .09346 | .0610 |
| 14 | .23199 | .20462 | .18068 | .15971 | .14133 | .12520 | .11102 | .09855 | .08757 | .07789 | .0492 |
| 15 | .20900 | .18270 | .15989 | .14010 | .12289 | .10793 | .09489 | .08352 | .07359 | .06491 | .0397 |
| 16 | .18829 | .16312 | .14150 | .12289 | .10686 | .09304 | .08110 | .07073 | .06184 | .05409 | .0320 |
| 17 | .16963 | .14564 | .12522 | .10780 | .09293 | .08021 | .06932 | .05998 | .05196 | .04507 | .0258 |
| 18 | .15282 | .13004 | .11081 | .09456 | .08080 | .06914 | .05925 | .05083 | .04367 | .03756 | .0208 |
| 19 | .13768 | .11611 | .09806 | .08295 | .07026 | .05961 | .05064 | .04308 | .03669 | .03130 | .0168 |
| 20 | .12403 | .10367 | .08678 | .07276 | .06110 | .05139 | .04328 | .03651 | .03084 | .02608 | .0135 |
| 21 | .11174 | .09256 | .07680 | .06383 | .05313 | .04430 | .03699 | .03094 | .02591 | .02174 | .0109 |
| 22 | .10067 | .08264 | .06796 | .05599 | .04620 | .03819 | .03162 | .02622 | .02178 | .01811 | .0088 |
| 23 | .09069 | .07379 | .06014 | .04911 | .04017 | .03292 | .02702 | .02222 | .01830 | .01509 | .0071 |
| 24 | .08170 | .06588 | .05322 | .04308 | .03493 | .02838 | .02310 | .01883 | .01538 | .01258 | .0057 |
| 25 | .07361 | .05882 | .04710 | .03779 | .03038 | .02447 | .01974 | .01596 | .01292 | .01048 | .0046 |

## APPENDIX TABLE 2 Value of $\sum\limits_{t=1}^{n} \dfrac{1}{(1+i)^t}$

Value of i

| n | 1% | 2% | 3% | 4% | 5% | 6% | 7% | 8% | 9% | 10% |
|---|---|---|---|---|---|---|---|---|---|---|
| 1 | .9901 | .9804 | .9709 | .9615 | .9524 | .9434 | .9346 | .9259 | .9174 | .9091 |
| 2 | 1.9704 | 1.9416 | 1.9135 | 1.8861 | 1.8594 | 1.8334 | 1.8080 | 1.7833 | 1.7591 | 1.7355 |
| 3 | 2.9410 | 2.8839 | 2.8286 | 2.7751 | 2.7233 | 2.6730 | 2.6243 | 2.5771 | 2.5313 | 2.4868 |
| 4 | 3.9020 | 3.8077 | 3.7171 | 3.6299 | 3.5459 | 3.4651 | 3.3872 | 3.3121 | 3.2397 | 3.1699 |
| 5 | 4.8535 | 4.7134 | 4.5797 | 4.4518 | 4.3295 | 4.2123 | 4.1002 | 3.9927 | 3.8896 | 3.7908 |
| 6 | 5.7955 | 5.6014 | 5.4172 | 5.2421 | 5.0757 | 4.9173 | 4.7665 | 4.6229 | 4.4859 | 4.3553 |
| 7 | 6.7282 | 6.4720 | 6.2302 | 6.0020 | 5.7863 | 5.5824 | 5.3893 | 5.2064 | 5.0329 | 4.8684 |
| 8 | 7.6517 | 7.3254 | 7.0196 | 6.7327 | 6.4632 | 6.2093 | 5.9713 | 5.7466 | 5.5348 | 5.3349 |
| 9 | 8.5661 | 8.1622 | 7.7861 | 7.4353 | 7.1078 | 6.8017 | 6.5152 | 6.2469 | 5.9852 | 5.7590 |
| 10 | 9.4714 | 8.9825 | 8.7302 | 8.1109 | 7.7217 | 7.3601 | 7.0236 | 6.7101 | 6.4176 | 6.1446 |
| 11 | 10.3677 | 9.7868 | 9.2526 | 8.7604 | 8.3064 | 7.8868 | 7.4987 | 7.1389 | 6.8052 | 6.4951 |
| 12 | 11.2552 | 10.5753 | 9.9589 | 9.3850 | 8.8632 | 8.3838 | 7.9427 | 7.5361 | 7.1601 | 6.8137 |
| 13 | 12.1338 | 11.3483 | 10.6349 | 9.9856 | 9.3935 | 8.8527 | 8.3576 | 7.9038 | 7.4869 | 7.1034 |
| 14 | 13.0088 | 12.1062 | 11.2960 | 10.5631 | 9.8986 | 9.2950 | 8.7454 | 8.2442 | 7.7860 | 7.3667 |
| 15 | 13.8651 | 12.8492 | 11.9379 | 11.1183 | 10.3796 | 9.7122 | 9.1079 | 8.5595 | 8.0607 | 7.6061 |
| 16 | 14.7180 | 13.5777 | 12.5610 | 11.6522 | 10.8377 | 10.1059 | 9.4466 | 8.8514 | 8.3126 | 7.8237 |
| 17 | 15.5624 | 14.2918 | 13.1660 | 12.1656 | 11.2740 | 10.4772 | 9.7632 | 9.1216 | 8.5435 | 8.0215 |
| 18 | 16.3984 | 14.9920 | 13.7534 | 12.6592 | 11.6895 | 10.8276 | 10.0591 | 9.3719 | 8.7556 | 8.2014 |
| 19 | 17.2201 | 15.2684 | 14.3237 | 13.1339 | 12.0853 | 11.1581 | 10.3356 | 9.6036 | 8.9501 | 8.3649 |
| 20 | 18.0457 | 16.3514 | 14.8774 | 13.5903 | 12.4622 | 11.4699 | 10.5940 | 9.8181 | 9.1285 | 8.5136 |
| 21 | 18.8571 | 17.0111 | 15.4149 | 14.0291 | 12.8211 | 11.7640 | 10.8355 | 10.0168 | 9.2922 | 8.6487 |
| 22 | 19.6605 | 17.6581 | 15.9368 | 14.4511 | 13.1630 | 12.0416 | 11.0612 | 10.2007 | 9.4424 | 8.7715 |
| 23 | 20.4559 | 18.2921 | 16.4435 | 14.8568 | 13.4885 | 12.3033 | 11.2722 | 10.3710 | 9.5802 | 8.8832 |
| 24 | 21.2435 | 18.9139 | 16.9355 | 15.2469 | 13.7986 | 12.5503 | 11.4693 | 10.5287 | 9.7066 | 8.9847 |
| 25 | 22.0233 | 19.5234 | 17.4181 | 15.6220 | 14.9039 | 12.7833 | 11.6536 | 10.6748 | 9.8226 | 9.0770 |

## APPENDIX TABLE 2 *(Cont'd)*

### Value of i

| n | 11% | 12% | 13% | 14% | 15% | 16% | 17% | 18% | 19% | 20% | 24% |
|---|-----|-----|-----|-----|-----|-----|-----|-----|-----|-----|-----|
| 1 | .9009 | .8929 | .8850 | .8772 | .8696 | .8621 | .8547 | .8475 | .8403 | .8333 | .8065 |
| 2 | 1.7125 | 1.6901 | 1.6681 | 1.6467 | 1.6257 | 1.6052 | 1.5852 | 1.5656 | 1.5465 | 1.5278 | 1.4568 |
| 3 | 2.4437 | 2.4018 | 2.3612 | 2.3126 | 2.2832 | 2.2459 | 2.2096 | 2.1743 | 2.1399 | 2.1065 | 1.9813 |
| 4 | 3.1024 | 3.0373 | 2.9745 | 2.9137 | 2.8550 | 2.7982 | 2.7432 | 2.6901 | 2.6386 | 2.5887 | 2.4043 |
| 5 | 3.6959 | 3.6048 | 3.5172 | 3.4331 | 3.3522 | 3.2743 | 3.1993 | 3.1272 | 3.0576 | 2.9906 | 2.7454 |
| 6 | 4.2305 | 4.1114 | 3.9976 | 3.8887 | 3.7845 | 3.6847 | 3.5892 | 3.4976 | 3.4098 | 3.3255 | 3.0205 |
| 7 | 4.7122 | 4.5638 | 4.4226 | 4.2883 | 4.1604 | 4.0386 | 3.9224 | 3.8115 | 3.7057 | 3.6046 | 3.2423 |
| 8 | 5.1461 | 4.9676 | 4.7988 | 4.6389 | 4.4873 | 4.3436 | 4.2072 | 4.0776 | 3.9544 | 3.8372 | 3.4212 |
| 9 | 5.5370 | 5.3282 | 5.1317 | 4.9464 | 4.7716 | 4.6065 | 4.4506 | 4.3030 | 4.1633 | 4.0310 | 3.5655 |
| 10 | 5.8892 | 5.6502 | 5.4262 | 5.2161 | 5.0188 | 4.8332 | 4.6586 | 4.4941 | 4.3389 | 4.1925 | 3.6819 |
| 11 | 6.2065 | 5.9377 | 5.6869 | 5.4527 | 5.2337 | 5.0286 | 4.8364 | 4.6560 | 4.4865 | 4.3271 | 3.7757 |
| 12 | 6.4924 | 6.1944 | 5.9176 | 5.6603 | 5.4206 | 5.1971 | 4.9884 | 4.7932 | 4.6105 | 4.4392 | 3.8514 |
| 13 | 6.7499 | 6.4235 | 6.1218 | 5.8424 | 5.5831 | 5.3423 | 5.1183 | 4.9095 | 4.7147 | 4.5327 | 3.9124 |
| 14 | 6.9819 | 6.6282 | 6.3025 | 6.0021 | 5.7245 | 5.4675 | 5.2293 | 5.0081 | 4.8023 | 4.6106 | 3.9616 |
| 15 | 7.1909 | 6.8109 | 6.4624 | 6.1422 | 5.8474 | 5.5755 | 5.3242 | 5.0916 | 4.8759 | 4.6755 | 4.0013 |
| 16 | 7.3792 | 6.9740 | 6.6039 | 6.2651 | 5.9542 | 5.6685 | 5.4053 | 5.1624 | 4.9377 | 4.7296 | 4.0333 |
| 17 | 7.5488 | 7.1196 | 6.7291 | 6.3729 | 6.0472 | 5.7487 | 5.4746 | 5.2223 | 4.9897 | 4.7746 | 4.0591 |
| 18 | 7.7016 | 7.2497 | 6.8389 | 6.4674 | 6.1280 | 5.8178 | 5.5339 | 5.2732 | 5.0333 | 4.8122 | 4.0799 |
| 19 | 7.8393 | 7.3650 | 6.9380 | 6.5504 | 6.1982 | 5.8775 | 5.5845 | 5.3176 | 5.0700 | 4.8435 | 4.0967 |
| 20 | 7.9633 | 7.4694 | 7.0248 | 6.6231 | 6.2593 | 5.9288 | 5.6278 | 5.3527 | 5.1009 | 4.8696 | 4.1103 |
| 21 | 8.0751 | 7.5620 | 7.1016 | 6.6870 | 6.3125 | 5.9731 | 5.6648 | 5.3837 | 5.1268 | 4.8913 | 4.1212 |
| 22 | 8.1757 | 7.6446 | 7.1695 | 6.7429 | 6.3587 | 6.0113 | 5.6964 | 5.4099 | 5.1486 | 4.9094 | 4.1300 |
| 23 | 8.2664 | 7.7184 | 7.2297 | 6.7921 | 6.3988 | 6.0442 | 5.7234 | 5.4321 | 5.1668 | 4.9245 | 4.1371 |
| 24 | 8.3481 | 7.7843 | 7.2829 | 6.8351 | 6.4338 | 6.0726 | 5.7465 | 5.4509 | 5.1822 | 4.9371 | 4.1428 |
| 25 | 8.4217 | 7.8431 | 7.3300 | 6.8729 | 6.4641 | 6.0971 | 5.7662 | 5.4669 | 5.1951 | 4.9476 | 4.1474 |

## APPENDIX TABLE 3 *Areas under the Standard Normal Curve*

This table shows the area between zero (the mean of a standard normal variable) and z. For example, if $z = 1.50$, this is the shaded area shown below, which equals .4332.

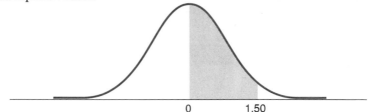

| z | .00 | .01 | .02 | .03 | .04 | .05 | .06 | .07 | .08 | .09 |
|---|---|---|---|---|---|---|---|---|---|---|
| 0.0 | .0000 | .0040 | .0080 | .0120 | .0160 | .0199 | .0239 | .0279 | .0319 | .0359 |
| 0.1 | .0398 | .0438 | .0478 | .0517 | .0557 | .0596 | .0636 | .0675 | .0714 | .0753 |
| 0.2 | .0793 | .0832 | .0871 | .0910 | .0948 | .0987 | .1026 | .1064 | .1103 | .1141 |
| 0.3 | .1179 | .1217 | .1255 | .1293 | .1331 | .1368 | .1406 | .1443 | .1480 | .1517 |
| 0.4 | .1554 | .1591 | .1628 | .1664 | .1700 | .1736 | .1772 | .1808 | .1844 | .1879 |
| 0.5 | .1915 | .1950 | .1985 | .2019 | .2054 | .2088 | .2123 | .2157 | .2190 | .2224 |
| 0.6 | .2257 | .2291 | .2324 | .2357 | .2389 | .2422 | .2454 | .2486 | .2517 | .2549 |
| 0.7 | .2580 | .2611 | .2642 | .2673 | .2704 | .2734 | .2764 | .2794 | .2823 | .2852 |
| 0.8 | .2881 | .2910 | .2939 | .2967 | .2995 | .3023 | .3051 | .3078 | .3106 | .3133 |
| 0.9 | .3159 | .3186 | .3212 | .3238 | .3264 | .3289 | .3315 | .3340 | .3365 | .3389 |
| 1.0 | .3413 | .3438 | .3461 | .3485 | .3508 | .3531 | .3554 | .3577 | .3599 | .3621 |
| 1.1 | .3643 | .3665 | .3686 | .3708 | .3729 | .3749 | .3770 | .3790 | .3810 | .3830 |
| 1.2 | .3849 | .3869 | .3888 | .3907 | .3925 | .3944 | .3962 | .3980 | .3997 | .4015 |
| 1.3 | .4032 | .4049 | .4066 | .4082 | .4099 | .4115 | .4131 | .4147 | .4162 | .4177 |
| 1.4 | .4192 | .4207 | .4222 | .4236 | .4251 | .4265 | .4279 | .4292 | .4306 | .4319 |
| 1.5 | .4332 | .4345 | .4357 | .4370 | .4382 | .4394 | .4406 | .4418 | .4429 | .4441 |
| 1.6 | .4452 | .4463 | .4474 | .4484 | .4495 | .4505 | .4515 | .4525 | .4535 | .4545 |
| 1.7 | .4554 | .4564 | .4573 | .4582 | .4591 | .4599 | .4608 | .4616 | .4625 | .4633 |
| 1.8 | .4641 | .4649 | .4656 | .4664 | .4671 | .4678 | .4686 | .4693 | .4699 | .4706 |
| 1.9 | .4713 | .4719 | .4726 | .4732 | .4738 | .4744 | .4750 | .4756 | .4761 | .4767 |
| 2.0 | .4772 | .4778 | .4783 | .4788 | .4793 | .4798 | .4803 | .4808 | .4812 | .4817 |
| 2.1 | .4821 | .4826 | .4830 | .4834 | .4838 | .4842 | .4846 | .4850 | .4854 | .4857 |
| 2.2 | .4861 | .4864 | .4868 | .4871 | .4875 | .4878 | .4881 | .4884 | .4887 | .4890 |
| 2.3 | .4893 | .4896 | .4898 | .4901 | .4904 | .4906 | .4909 | .4911 | .4913 | .4916 |
| 2.4 | .4918 | .4920 | .4922 | .4925 | .4927 | .4929 | .4931 | .4932 | .4934 | .4936 |
| 2.5 | .4938 | .4940 | .4941 | .4943 | .4945 | .4946 | .4948 | .4949 | .4951 | .4952 |
| 2.6 | .4953 | .4955 | .4956 | .4957 | .4959 | .4960 | .4961 | .4962 | .4963 | .4964 |
| 2.7 | .4965 | .4966 | .4967 | .4968 | .4969 | .4970 | .4971 | .4972 | .4973 | .4974 |
| 2.8 | .4974 | .4975 | .4976 | .4977 | .4977 | .4978 | .4979 | .4979 | .4980 | .4981 |
| 2.9 | .4981 | .4982 | .4982 | .4983 | .4984 | .4984 | .4985 | .4985 | .4986 | .4986 |
| 3.0 | .4987 | .4987 | .4987 | .4988 | .4988 | .4989 | .4989 | .4989 | .4990 | .4990 |

*Source:* This table is adapted from National Bureau of Standards, *Tables of Normal Probability Functions,* Applied Mathematics Series 23, U.S. Department of Commerce, 1953.

## APPENDIX TABLE 4 *Values of* t *That Will Be Exceeded with Specified Probabilities*

This table shows the value of $t$ where the area under the $t$ distribution exceeding this value of $t$ equals the specified amount. For example, the probability that a $t$ variable with 14 degrees of freedom will exceed 1.345 equals .10.

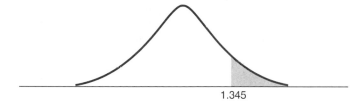

1.345

| Degrees of freedom | .40 | .25 | .10 | Probability .05 | .025 | .01 | .005 |
|---|---|---|---|---|---|---|---|
| 1 | 0.325 | 1.000 | 3.078 | 6.314 | 12.706 | 31.821 | 63.657 |
| 2 | .289 | 0.816 | 1.886 | 2.920 | 4.303 | 6.965 | 9.925 |
| 3 | .277 | .765 | 1.638 | 2.353 | 3.182 | 4.541 | 5.841 |
| 4 | .271 | .741 | 1.533 | 2.132 | 2.776 | 3.747 | 4.604 |
| 5 | 0.267 | 0.727 | 1.476 | 2.015 | 2.571 | 3.365 | 4.032 |
| 6 | .265 | .718 | 1.440 | 1.943 | 2.447 | 3.143 | 3.707 |
| 7 | .263 | .711 | 1.415 | 1.895 | 2.365 | 2.998 | 3.499 |
| 8 | .262 | .706 | 1.397 | 1.860 | 2.306 | 2.896 | 3.355 |
| 9 | .261 | .703 | 1.383 | 1.833 | 2.262 | 2.821 | 3.250 |
| 10 | 0.260 | 0.700 | 1.372 | 1.812 | 2.228 | 2.764 | 3.169 |
| 11 | .260 | .697 | 1.363 | 1.796 | 2.201 | 2.718 | 3.106 |
| 12 | .259 | .695 | 1.356 | 1.782 | 2.179 | 2.681 | 3.055 |
| 13 | .259 | .694 | 1.350 | 1.771 | 2.160 | 2.650 | 3.012 |
| 14 | .258 | .692 | 1.345 | 1.761 | 2.145 | 2.624 | 2.977 |
| 15 | 0.258 | 0.691 | 1.341 | 1.753 | 2.131 | 2.602 | 2.947 |
| 16 | .258 | .690 | 1.337 | 1.746 | 2.120 | 2.583 | 2.921 |
| 17 | .257 | .689 | 1.333 | 1.740 | 2.110 | 2.567 | 2.898 |
| 18 | .257 | .688 | 1.330 | 1.734 | 2.101 | 2.552 | 2.878 |
| 19 | .257 | .688 | 1.328 | 1.729 | 2.093 | 2.539 | 2.861 |
| 20 | 0.257 | 0.687 | 1.325 | 1.725 | 2.086 | 2.528 | 2.845 |
| 21 | .257 | .686 | 1.323 | 1.721 | 2.080 | 2.518 | 2.831 |
| 22 | .256 | .686 | 1.321 | 1.717 | 2.074 | 2.508 | 2.819 |
| 23 | .256 | .685 | 1.319 | 1.714 | 2.069 | 2.500 | 2.807 |
| 24 | .256 | .685 | 1.318 | 1.711 | 2.064 | 2.492 | 2.797 |

## APPENDIX TABLE 4 (Cont'd)

| Degrees of freedom | | | | Probability | | | |
|---|---|---|---|---|---|---|---|
| | .40 | .25 | .10 | .05 | .025 | .01 | .005 |
| 25 | 0.256 | 0.684 | 1.316 | 1.708 | 2.060 | 2.485 | 2.787 |
| 26 | .256 | .684 | 1.315 | 1.706 | 2.056 | 2.479 | 2.779 |
| 27 | .256 | .684 | 1.314 | 1.703 | 2.052 | 2.473 | 2.771 |
| 28 | .256 | .683 | 1.313 | 1.701 | 2.048 | 2.467 | 2.763 |
| 29 | .256 | .683 | 1.311 | 1.699 | 2.045 | 2.462 | 2.756 |
| 30 | 0.256 | 0.683 | 1.310 | 1.697 | 2.042 | 2.457 | 2.750 |
| 40 | .255 | .681 | 1.303 | 1.684 | 2.021 | 2.423 | 2.704 |
| 60 | .254 | .679 | 1.296 | 1.671 | 2.000 | 2.390 | 2.660 |
| 120 | .254 | .677 | 1.289 | 1.658 | 1.980 | 2.358 | 2.617 |
| ∞ | .253 | .674 | 1.282 | 1.645 | 1.960 | 2.326 | 2.576 |

*Source: Biometrika Tables for Statisticians* (Cambridge, Eng.: Cambridge University, 1954).

## APPENDIX TABLE 5 Value of an F Variable That Is Exceeded with Probability Equal to .05

| | | | | Degrees of freedom for numerator | | | | | |
|---|---|---|---|---|---|---|---|---|---|
| | 1 | 2 | 3 | 4 | 5 | 6 | 7 | 8 | 9 |
| 1 | 161.4 | 199.5 | 215.7 | 224.6 | 230.2 | 234.0 | 236.8 | 238.9 | 240.5 |
| 2 | 18.51 | 19.00 | 19.16 | 19.25 | 19.30 | 19.33 | 19.35 | 19.37 | 19.38 |
| 3 | 10.13 | 9.55 | 9.28 | 9.12 | 9.01 | 8.94 | 8.89 | 8.85 | 8.81 |
| 4 | 7.71 | 6.94 | 6.59 | 6.39 | 6.26 | 6.16 | 6.09 | 6.04 | 6.00 |
| 5 | 6.61 | 5.79 | 5.41 | 5.19 | 5.05 | 4.95 | 4.88 | 4.82 | 4.77 |
| 6 | 5.99 | 5.14 | 4.76 | 4.53 | 4.39 | 4.28 | 4.21 | 4.15 | 4.10 |
| 7 | 5.59 | 4.74 | 4.35 | 4.12 | 3.97 | 3.87 | 3.79 | 3.73 | 3.68 |
| 8 | 5.32 | 4.46 | 4.07 | 3.84 | 3.69 | 3.58 | 3.50 | 3.44 | 3.39 |
| 9 | 5.12 | 4.26 | 3.86 | 3.63 | 3.48 | 3.37 | 3.29 | 3.23 | 3.18 |
| 10 | 4.96 | 4.10 | 3.71 | 3.48 | 3.33 | 3.22 | 3.14 | 3.07 | 3.02 |
| 11 | 4.84 | 3.98 | 3.59 | 3.36 | 3.20 | 3.09 | 3.01 | 2.95 | 2.90 |
| 12 | 4.75 | 3.89 | 3.49 | 3.26 | 3.11 | 3.00 | 2.91 | 2.85 | 2.80 |
| 13 | 4.67 | 3.81 | 3.41 | 3.18 | 3.03 | 2.92 | 2.83 | 2.77 | 2.71 |
| 14 | 4.60 | 3.74 | 3.34 | 3.11 | 2.96 | 2.85 | 2.76 | 2.70 | 2.65 |
| 15 | 4.54 | 3.68 | 3.29 | 3.06 | 2.90 | 2.79 | 2.71 | 2.64 | 2.59 |
| 16 | 4.49 | 3.63 | 3.24 | 3.01 | 2.85 | 2.74 | 2.66 | 2.59 | 2.54 |
| 17 | 4.45 | 3.59 | 3.20 | 2.96 | 2.81 | 2.70 | 2.61 | 2.55 | 2.49 |
| 18 | 4.41 | 3.55 | 3.16 | 2.93 | 2.77 | 2.66 | 2.58 | 2.51 | 2.46 |
| 19 | 4.38 | 3.52 | 3.13 | 2.90 | 2.74 | 2.63 | 2.54 | 2.48 | 2.42 |
| 20 | 4.35 | 3.49 | 3.10 | 2.87 | 2.71 | 2.60 | 2.51 | 2.45 | 2.39 |
| 21 | 4.32 | 3.47 | 3.07 | 2.84 | 2.68 | 2.57 | 2.49 | 2.42 | 2.37 |
| 22 | 4.30 | 3.44 | 3.05 | 2.82 | 2.66 | 2.55 | 2.46 | 2.40 | 2.34 |
| 23 | 4.28 | 3.42 | 3.03 | 2.80 | 2.64 | 2.53 | 2.44 | 2.37 | 2.32 |
| 24 | 4.26 | 3.40 | 3.01 | 2.78 | 2.62 | 2.51 | 2.42 | 2.36 | 2.30 |
| 25 | 4.24 | 3.39 | 2.99 | 2.76 | 2.60 | 2.49 | 2.40 | 2.34 | 2.28 |
| 26 | 4.23 | 3.37 | 2.98 | 2.74 | 2.59 | 2.47 | 2.39 | 2.32 | 2.27 |
| 27 | 4.21 | 3.35 | 2.96 | 2.73 | 2.57 | 2.46 | 2.37 | 2.31 | 2.25 |
| 28 | 4.20 | 3.34 | 2.95 | 2.71 | 2.56 | 2.45 | 2.36 | 2.29 | 2.24 |
| 29 | 4.18 | 3.33 | 2.93 | 2.70 | 2.55 | 2.43 | 2.35 | 2.28 | 2.22 |
| 30 | 4.17 | 3.32 | 2.92 | 2.69 | 2.53 | 2.42 | 2.33 | 2.27 | 2.21 |
| 40 | 4.08 | 3.23 | 2.84 | 2.61 | 2.45 | 2.34 | 2.25 | 2.18 | 2.12 |
| 60 | 4.00 | 3.15 | 2.76 | 2.53 | 2.37 | 2.25 | 2.17 | 2.10 | 2.04 |
| 120 | 3.92 | 3.07 | 2.68 | 2.45 | 2.29 | 2.17 | 2.09 | 2.02 | 1.96 |
| $\infty$ | 3.84 | 3.00 | 2.60 | 2.37 | 2.21 | 2.10 | 2.01 | 1.94 | 1.88 |

Degrees of freedom for denominator

## APPENDIX TABLE 5 (Cont'd)

| | | | | | Degrees of freedom for numerator | | | | | |
|---|---|---|---|---|---|---|---|---|---|---|
| | 10 | 12 | 15 | 20 | 24 | 30 | 40 | 60 | 120 | ∞ |
| 1 | 241.9 | 243.9 | 245.9 | 248.0 | 249.1 | 250.1 | 251.1 | 252.2 | 253.3 | 254.3 |
| 2 | 19.40 | 19.41 | 19.43 | 19.45 | 19.45 | 19.46 | 19.47 | 19.48 | 19.49 | 19.50 |
| 3 | 8.79 | 8.74 | 8.70 | 8.66 | 8.64 | 8.62 | 8.59 | 8.57 | 8.55 | 8.53 |
| 4 | 5.96 | 5.91 | 5.86 | 5.80 | 5.77 | 5.75 | 5.72 | 5.69 | 5.66 | 5.63 |
| 5 | 4.74 | 4.68 | 4.62 | 4.56 | 4.53 | 4.50 | 4.46 | 4.43 | 4.40 | 4.36 |
| 6 | 4.06 | 4.00 | 3.94 | 3.87 | 3.84 | 3.81 | 3.77 | 3.74 | 3.70 | 3.67 |
| 7 | 3.64 | 3.57 | 3.51 | 3.44 | 3.41 | 3.38 | 3.34 | 3.30 | 3.27 | 3.23 |
| 8 | 3.35 | 3.28 | 3.22 | 3.15 | 3.12 | 3.08 | 3.04 | 3.01 | 2.97 | 2.93 |
| 9 | 3.14 | 3.07 | 3.01 | 2.94 | 2.90 | 2.86 | 2.83 | 2.79 | 2.75 | 2.71 |
| 10 | 2.98 | 2.91 | 2.85 | 2.77 | 2.74 | 2.70 | 2.66 | 2.62 | 2.58 | 2.54 |
| 11 | 2.85 | 2.79 | 2.72 | 2.65 | 2.61 | 2.57 | 2.53 | 2.49 | 2.45 | 2.40 |
| 12 | 2.75 | 2.69 | 2.62 | 2.54 | 2.51 | 2.47 | 2.43 | 2.38 | 2.34 | 2.30 |
| 13 | 2.67 | 2.60 | 2.53 | 2.46 | 2.42 | 2.38 | 2.34 | 2.30 | 2.25 | 2.21 |
| 14 | 2.60 | 2.53 | 2.46 | 2.39 | 2.35 | 2.31 | 2.27 | 2.22 | 2.18 | 2.13 |
| 15 | 2.54 | 2.48 | 2.40 | 2.33 | 2.29 | 2.25 | 2.20 | 2.16 | 2.11 | 2.07 |
| 16 | 2.49 | 2.42 | 2.35 | 2.28 | 2.24 | 2.19 | 2.15 | 2.11 | 2.06 | 2.01 |
| 17 | 2.45 | 2.38 | 2.31 | 2.23 | 2.19 | 2.15 | 2.10 | 2.06 | 2.01 | 1.96 |
| 18 | 2.41 | 2.34 | 2.27 | 2.19 | 2.15 | 2.11 | 2.06 | 2.02 | 1.97 | 1.92 |
| 19 | 2.38 | 2.31 | 2.23 | 2.16 | 2.11 | 2.07 | 2.03 | 1.98 | 1.93 | 1.88 |
| 20 | 2.35 | 2.28 | 2.20 | 2.12 | 2.08 | 2.04 | 1.99 | 1.95 | 1.90 | 1.84 |
| 21 | 2.32 | 2.25 | 2.18 | 2.10 | 2.05 | 2.01 | 1.96 | 1.92 | 1.87 | 1.81 |
| 22 | 2.30 | 2.23 | 2.15 | 2.07 | 2.03 | 1.98 | 1.94 | 1.89 | 1.84 | 1.78 |
| 23 | 2.27 | 2.20 | 2.13 | 2.05 | 2.01 | 1.96 | 1.91 | 1.86 | 1.81 | 1.76 |
| 24 | 2.25 | 2.18 | 2.11 | 2.03 | 1.98 | 1.94 | 1.89 | 1.84 | 1.79 | 1.73 |
| 25 | 2.24 | 2.16 | 2.09 | 2.01 | 1.96 | 1.92 | 1.87 | 1.82 | 1.77 | 1.71 |
| 26 | 2.22 | 2.15 | 2.07 | 1.99 | 1.95 | 1.90 | 1.85 | 1.80 | 1.75 | 1.69 |
| 27 | 2.20 | 2.13 | 2.06 | 1.97 | 1.93 | 1.88 | 1.84 | 1.79 | 1.73 | 1.67 |
| 28 | 2.19 | 2.12 | 2.04 | 1.96 | 1.91 | 1.87 | 1.82 | 1.77 | 1.71 | 1.65 |
| 29 | 2.18 | 2.10 | 2.03 | 1.94 | 1.90 | 1.85 | 1.81 | 1.75 | 1.70 | 1.64 |
| 30 | 2.16 | 2.09 | 2.01 | 1.93 | 1.89 | 1.84 | 1.79 | 1.74 | 1.68 | 1.62 |
| 40 | 2.08 | 2.00 | 1.92 | 1.84 | 1.79 | 1.74 | 1.69 | 1.64 | 1.58 | 1.51 |
| 60 | 1.99 | 1.92 | 1.84 | 1.75 | 1.70 | 1.65 | 1.59 | 1.53 | 1.47 | 1.39 |
| 120 | 1.91 | 1.83 | 1.75 | 1.66 | 1.61 | 1.55 | 1.50 | 1.43 | 1.35 | 1.25 |
| ∞ | 1.83 | 1.75 | 1.67 | 1.57 | 1.52 | 1.46 | 1.39 | 1.32 | 1.22 | 1.00 |

*Degrees of freedom for denominator* (row labels)

Source: Biometrika Tables for Statisticians.

## APPENDIX TABLE 6 Value of an **F** Variable Exceeded with Probability Equal to .01

| | | | | Degrees of freedom for numerator | | | | | |
|---|---|---|---|---|---|---|---|---|---|
| | 1 | 2 | 3 | 4 | 5 | 6 | 7 | 8 | 9 |
| 1 | 4052 | 4999.5 | 5403 | 5625 | 5764 | 5859 | 5928 | 5982 | 6022 |
| 2 | 98.50 | 99.00 | 99.17 | 99.25 | 99.30 | 99.33 | 99.36 | 99.37 | 99.39 |
| 3 | 34.12 | 30.82 | 29.46 | 28.71 | 28.24 | 27.91 | 27.67 | 27.49 | 27.35 |
| 4 | 21.20 | 18.00 | 16.69 | 15.98 | 15.52 | 15.21 | 14.98 | 14.80 | 14.66 |
| 5 | 16.26 | 13.27 | 12.06 | 11.39 | 10.97 | 10.67 | 10.46 | 10.29 | 10.16 |
| 6 | 13.75 | 10.92 | 9.78 | 9.15 | 8.75 | 8.47 | 8.26 | 8.10 | 7.98 |
| 7 | 12.25 | 9.55 | 8.45 | 7.85 | 7.46 | 7.19 | 6.99 | 6.84 | 6.72 |
| 8 | 11.26 | 8.65 | 7.59 | 7.01 | 6.63 | 6.37 | 6.18 | 6.03 | 5.91 |
| 9 | 10.56 | 8.02 | 6.99 | 6.42 | 6.06 | 5.80 | 5.61 | 5.47 | 5.35 |
| 10 | 10.04 | 7.56 | 6.55 | 5.99 | 5.64 | 5.39 | 5.20 | 5.06 | 4.94 |
| 11 | 9.65 | 7.21 | 6.22 | 5.67 | 5.32 | 5.07 | 4.89 | 4.74 | 4.63 |
| 12 | 9.33 | 6.93 | 5.95 | 5.41 | 5.06 | 4.82 | 4.64 | 4.50 | 4.39 |
| 13 | 9.07 | 6.70 | 5.74 | 5.21 | 4.86 | 4.62 | 4.44 | 4.30 | 4.19 |
| 14 | 8.86 | 6.51 | 5.56 | 5.04 | 4.69 | 4.46 | 4.28 | 4.14 | 4.03 |
| 15 | 8.68 | 6.36 | 5.42 | 4.89 | 4.56 | 4.32 | 4.14 | 4.00 | 3.89 |
| 16 | 8.53 | 6.23 | 5.29 | 4.77 | 4.44 | 4.20 | 4.03 | 3.89 | 3.78 |
| 17 | 8.40 | 6.11 | 5.18 | 4.67 | 4.34 | 4.10 | 3.93 | 3.79 | 3.68 |
| 18 | 8.29 | 6.01 | 5.09 | 4.58 | 4.25 | 4.01 | 3.84 | 3.71 | 3.60 |
| 19 | 8.18 | 5.93 | 5.01 | 4.50 | 4.17 | 3.94 | 3.77 | 3.63 | 3.52 |
| 20 | 8.10 | 5.85 | 4.94 | 4.43 | 4.10 | 3.87 | 3.70 | 3.56 | 3.46 |
| 21 | 8.02 | 5.78 | 4.87 | 4.37 | 4.04 | 3.81 | 3.64 | 3.51 | 3.40 |
| 22 | 7.95 | 5.72 | 4.82 | 4.31 | 3.99 | 3.76 | 3.59 | 3.45 | 3.35 |
| 23 | 7.88 | 5.66 | 4.76 | 4.26 | 3.94 | 3.71 | 3.54 | 3.41 | 3.30 |
| 24 | 7.82 | 5.61 | 4.72 | 4.22 | 3.90 | 3.67 | 3.50 | 3.36 | 3.26 |
| 25 | 7.77 | 5.57 | 4.68 | 4.18 | 3.85 | 3.63 | 3.46 | 3.32 | 3.22 |
| 26 | 7.72 | 5.53 | 4.64 | 4.14 | 3.82 | 3.59 | 3.42 | 3.29 | 3.18 |
| 27 | 7.68 | 5.49 | 4.60 | 4.11 | 3.78 | 3.56 | 3.39 | 3.26 | 3.15 |
| 28 | 7.64 | 5.45 | 4.57 | 4.07 | 3.75 | 3.53 | 3.36 | 3.23 | 3.12 |
| 29 | 7.60 | 5.42 | 4.54 | 4.04 | 3.73 | 3.50 | 3.33 | 3.20 | 3.09 |
| 30 | 7.56 | 5.39 | 4.51 | 4.02 | 3.70 | 3.47 | 3.30 | 3.17 | 3.07 |
| 40 | 7.31 | 5.18 | 4.31 | 3.83 | 3.51 | 3.29 | 3.12 | 2.99 | 2.89 |
| 60 | 7.08 | 4.98 | 4.13 | 3.65 | 3.34 | 3.12 | 2.95 | 2.82 | 2.72 |
| 120 | 6.85 | 4.79 | 3.95 | 3.48 | 3.17 | 2.96 | 2.79 | 2.66 | 2.56 |
| ∞ | 6.63 | 4.61 | 3.78 | 3.32 | 3.02 | 2.80 | 2.64 | 2.51 | 2.41 |

*Degrees of freedom for denominator*

## APPENDIX TABLE 6 (Cont'd)

|  | Degrees of freedom for numerator | | | | | | | | | |
|---|---|---|---|---|---|---|---|---|---|---|
|  | 10 | 12 | 15 | 20 | 24 | 30 | 40 | 60 | 120 | ∞ |
| 1 | 6056 | 6106 | 6157 | 6209 | 6235 | 6261 | 6287 | 6313 | 6339 | 6366 |
| 2 | 99.40 | 99.42 | 99.43 | 99.45 | 99.46 | 99.47 | 99.47 | 99.48 | 99.49 | 99.50 |
| 3 | 27.23 | 27.05 | 26.87 | 26.69 | 26.60 | 26.50 | 26.41 | 26.32 | 26.22 | 26.13 |
| 4 | 14.55 | 14.37 | 14.20 | 14.02 | 13.93 | 13.84 | 13.75 | 13.65 | 13.56 | 13.46 |
| 5 | 10.05 | 9.89 | 9.72 | 9.55 | 9.47 | 9.38 | 9.29 | 9.20 | 9.11 | 9.02 |
| 6 | 7.87 | 7.72 | 7.56 | 7.40 | 7.31 | 7.23 | 7.14 | 7.06 | 6.97 | 6.88 |
| 7 | 6.62 | 6.47 | 6.31 | 6.16 | 6.07 | 5.99 | 5.91 | 5.82 | 5.74 | 5.65 |
| 8 | 5.81 | 5.67 | 5.52 | 5.36 | 5.28 | 5.20 | 5.12 | 5.03 | 4.95 | 4.86 |
| 9 | 5.26 | 5.11 | 4.96 | 4.81 | 4.73 | 4.65 | 4.57 | 4.48 | 4.40 | 4.31 |
| 10 | 4.85 | 4.71 | 4.56 | 4.41 | 4.33 | 4.25 | 4.17 | 4.08 | 4.00 | 3.91 |
| 11 | 4.54 | 4.40 | 4.25 | 4.10 | 4.02 | 3.94 | 3.86 | 3.78 | 3.69 | 3.60 |
| 12 | 4.30 | 4.16 | 4.01 | 3.86 | 3.78 | 3.70 | 3.62 | 3.54 | 3.45 | 3.36 |
| 13 | 4.10 | 3.96 | 3.82 | 3.66 | 3.59 | 3.51 | 3.43 | 3.34 | 3.25 | 3.17 |
| 14 | 3.94 | 3.80 | 3.66 | 3.51 | 3.43 | 3.35 | 3.27 | 3.18 | 3.09 | 3.00 |
| 15 | 3.80 | 3.67 | 3.52 | 3.37 | 3.29 | 3.21 | 3.13 | 3.05 | 2.96 | 2.87 |
| 16 | 3.69 | 3.55 | 3.41 | 3.26 | 3.18 | 3.10 | 3.02 | 2.93 | 2.84 | 2.75 |
| 17 | 3.59 | 3.46 | 3.31 | 3.16 | 3.08 | 3.00 | 2.92 | 2.83 | 2.75 | 2.65 |
| 18 | 3.51 | 3.37 | 3.23 | 3.08 | 3.00 | 2.92 | 2.84 | 2.75 | 2.66 | 2.57 |
| 19 | 3.43 | 3.30 | 3.15 | 3.00 | 2.92 | 2.84 | 2.76 | 2.67 | 2.58 | 2.49 |
| 20 | 3.37 | 3.23 | 3.09 | 2.94 | 2.86 | 2.78 | 2.69 | 2.61 | 2.52 | 2.42 |
| 21 | 3.31 | 3.17 | 3.03 | 2.88 | 2.80 | 2.72 | 2.64 | 2.55 | 2.46 | 2.36 |
| 22 | 3.26 | 3.12 | 2.98 | 2.83 | 2.75 | 2.67 | 2.58 | 2.50 | 2.40 | 2.31 |
| 23 | 3.21 | 3.07 | 2.93 | 2.78 | 2.70 | 2.62 | 2.54 | 2.45 | 2.35 | 2.26 |
| 24 | 3.17 | 3.03 | 2.89 | 2.74 | 2.66 | 2.58 | 2.49 | 2.40 | 2.31 | 2.21 |
| 25 | 3.13 | 2.99 | 2.85 | 2.70 | 2.62 | 2.54 | 2.45 | 2.36 | 2.27 | 2.17 |
| 26 | 3.09 | 2.96 | 2.81 | 2.66 | 2.58 | 2.50 | 2.42 | 2.33 | 2.23 | 2.13 |
| 27 | 3.06 | 2.93 | 2.78 | 2.63 | 2.55 | 2.47 | 2.38 | 2.29 | 2.20 | 2.10 |
| 28 | 3.03 | 2.90 | 2.75 | 2.60 | 2.52 | 2.44 | 2.35 | 2.26 | 2.17 | 2.06 |
| 29 | 3.00 | 2.87 | 2.73 | 2.57 | 2.49 | 2.41 | 2.33 | 2.23 | 2.14 | 2.03 |
| 30 | 2.98 | 2.84 | 2.70 | 2.55 | 2.47 | 2.39 | 2.30 | 2.21 | 2.11 | 2.01 |
| 40 | 2.80 | 2.66 | 2.52 | 2.37 | 2.29 | 2.20 | 2.11 | 2.02 | 1.92 | 1.80 |
| 60 | 2.63 | 2.50 | 2.35 | 2.20 | 2.12 | 2.03 | 1.94 | 1.84 | 1.73 | 1.60 |
| 120 | 2.47 | 2.34 | 2.19 | 2.03 | 1.95 | 1.86 | 1.76 | 1.66 | 1.53 | 1.38 |
| ∞ | 2.32 | 2.18 | 2.04 | 1.88 | 1.79 | 1.70 | 1.59 | 1.47 | 1.32 | 1.00 |

Degrees of freedom for denominator

Source: Biometrika Tables for Statisticians.

## APPENDIX TABLE 7 Values of $d_L$ and $d_U$ for the Durbin-Watson Test

A. Significance level = .05

| | k = 1 | | k = 2 | | k = 3 | | k = 4 | | k = 5 | |
|---|---|---|---|---|---|---|---|---|---|---|
| n | $d_L$ | $d_U$ | $d_L$ | $d_U$ | $d_L$ | $d_U$ | $d_L$ | $d_U$ | $d_L$ | $d_U$ |
| 15 | 1.08 | 1.36 | 0.95 | 1.54 | 0.82 | 1.75 | 0.69 | 1.97 | 0.56 | 2.21 |
| 16 | 1.10 | 1.37 | 0.98 | 1.54 | 0.86 | 1.73 | 0.74 | 1.93 | 0.62 | 2.15 |
| 17 | 1.13 | 1.38 | 1.02 | 1.54 | 0.90 | 1.71 | 0.78 | 1.90 | 0.67 | 2.10 |
| 18 | 1.16 | 1.39 | 1.05 | 1.53 | 0.93 | 1.69 | 0.82 | 1.87 | 0.71 | 2.06 |
| 19 | 1.18 | 1.40 | 1.08 | 1.53 | 0.97 | 1.68 | 0.86 | 1.85 | 0.75 | 2.02 |
| 20 | 1.20 | 1.41 | 1.10 | 1.54 | 1.00 | 1.68 | 0.90 | 1.83 | 0.79 | 1.99 |
| 21 | 1.22 | 1.42 | 1.13 | 1.54 | 1.03 | 1.67 | 0.93 | 1.81 | 0.83 | 1.96 |
| 22 | 1.24 | 1.43 | 1.15 | 1.54 | 1.05 | 1.66 | 0.96 | 1.80 | 0.86 | 1.94 |
| 23 | 1.26 | 1.44 | 1.17 | 1.54 | 1.08 | 1.66 | 0.99 | 1.79 | 0.90 | 1.92 |
| 24 | 1.27 | 1.45 | 1.19 | 1.55 | 1.10 | 1.66 | 1.01 | 1.78 | 0.93 | 1.90 |
| 25 | 1.29 | 1.45 | 1.21 | 1.55 | 1.12 | 1.66 | 1.04 | 1.77 | 0.95 | 1.89 |
| 26 | 1.30 | 1.46 | 1.22 | 1.55 | 1.14 | 1.65 | 1.06 | 1.76 | 0.98 | 1.88 |
| 27 | 1.32 | 1.47 | 1.24 | 1.56 | 1.16 | 1.65 | 1.08 | 1.76 | 1.01 | 1.86 |
| 28 | 1.33 | 1.48 | 1.26 | 1.56 | 1.18 | 1.65 | 1.10 | 1.75 | 1.03 | 1.85 |
| 29 | 1.34 | 1.48 | 1.27 | 1.56 | 1.20 | 1.65 | 1.12 | 1.74 | 1.05 | 1.84 |
| 30 | 1.35 | 1.49 | 1.28 | 1.57 | 1.21 | 1.65 | 1.14 | 1.74 | 1.07 | 1.83 |
| 31 | 1.36 | 1.50 | 1.30 | 1.57 | 1.23 | 1.65 | 1.16 | 1.74 | 1.09 | 1.83 |
| 32 | 1.37 | 1.50 | 1.31 | 1.57 | 1.24 | 1.65 | 1.18 | 1.73 | 1.11 | 1.82 |
| 33 | 1.38 | 1.51 | 1.32 | 1.58 | 1.26 | 1.65 | 1.19 | 1.73 | 1.13 | 1.81 |
| 34 | 1.39 | 1.51 | 1.33 | 1.58 | 1.27 | 1.65 | 1.21 | 1.73 | 1.15 | 1.81 |
| 35 | 1.40 | 1.52 | 1.34 | 1.58 | 1.28 | 1.65 | 1.22 | 1.73 | 1.16 | 1.80 |
| 36 | 1.41 | 1.52 | 1.35 | 1.59 | 1.29 | 1.65 | 1.24 | 1.73 | 1.18 | 1.80 |
| 37 | 1.42 | 1.53 | 1.36 | 1.59 | 1.31 | 1.66 | 1.25 | 1.72 | 1.19 | 1.80 |
| 38 | 1.43 | 1.54 | 1.37 | 1.59 | 1.32 | 1.66 | 1.26 | 1.72 | 1.21 | 1.79 |
| 39 | 1.43 | 1.54 | 1.38 | 1.60 | 1.33 | 1.66 | 1.27 | 1.72 | 1.22 | 1.79 |
| 40 | 1.44 | 1.54 | 1.39 | 1.60 | 1.34 | 1.66 | 1.29 | 1.72 | 1.23 | 1.79 |
| 45 | 1.48 | 1.57 | 1.43 | 1.62 | 1.38 | 1.67 | 1.34 | 1.72 | 1.29 | 1.78 |
| 50 | 1.50 | 1.59 | 1.46 | 1.63 | 1.42 | 1.67 | 1.38 | 1.72 | 1.34 | 1.77 |
| 55 | 1.53 | 1.60 | 1.49 | 1.64 | 1.45 | 1.68 | 1.41 | 1.72 | 1.38 | 1.77 |
| 60 | 1.55 | 1.62 | 1.51 | 1.65 | 1.48 | 1.69 | 1.44 | 1.73 | 1.41 | 1.77 |
| 65 | 1.57 | 1.63 | 1.54 | 1.66 | 1.50 | 1.70 | 1.47 | 1.73 | 1.44 | 1.77 |
| 70 | 1.58 | 1.64 | 1.55 | 1.67 | 1.52 | 1.70 | 1.49 | 1.74 | 1.46 | 1.77 |
| 75 | 1.60 | 1.65 | 1.57 | 1.68 | 1.54 | 1.71 | 1.51 | 1.74 | 1.49 | 1.77 |
| 80 | 1.61 | 1.66 | 1.59 | 1.69 | 1.56 | 1.72 | 1.53 | 1.74 | 1.51 | 1.77 |
| 85 | 1.62 | 1.67 | 1.60 | 1.70 | 1.57 | 1.72 | 1.55 | 1.75 | 1.52 | 1.77 |
| 90 | 1.63 | 1.68 | 1.61 | 1.70 | 1.59 | 1.73 | 1.57 | 1.75 | 1.54 | 1.78 |
| 95 | 1.64 | 1.69 | 1.62 | 1.71 | 1.60 | 1.73 | 1.58 | 1.75 | 1.56 | 1.78 |
| 100 | 1.65 | 1.69 | 1.63 | 1.72 | 1.61 | 1.74 | 1.59 | 1.76 | 1.57 | 1.78 |

## APPENDIX TABLE 7 (Cont'd)

B. Significance level = .025

| n | k = 1 | | k = 2 | | k = 3 | | k = 4 | | k = 5 | |
|---|---|---|---|---|---|---|---|---|---|---|
| | $d_L$ | $d_U$ | $d_L$ | $d_U$ | $d_L$ | $d_U$ | $d_L$ | $d_U$ | $d_L$ | $d_U$ |
| 15 | 0.95 | 1.23 | 0.83 | 1.40 | 0.71 | 1.61 | 0.59 | 1.84 | 0.48 | 2.09 |
| 16 | 0.98 | 1.24 | 0.86 | 1.40 | 0.75 | 1.59 | 0.64 | 1.80 | 0.53 | 2.03 |
| 17 | 1.01 | 1.25 | 0.90 | 1.40 | 0.79 | 1.58 | 0.68 | 1.77 | 0.57 | 1.98 |
| 18 | 1.03 | 1.26 | 0.93 | 1.40 | 0.82 | 1.56 | 0.72 | 1.74 | 0.62 | 1.93 |
| 19 | 1.06 | 1.28 | 0.96 | 1.41 | 0.86 | 1.55 | 0.76 | 1.72 | 0.66 | 1.90 |
| 20 | 1.08 | 1.28 | 0.99 | 1.41 | 0.89 | 1.55 | 0.79 | 1.70 | 0.70 | 1.87 |
| 21 | 1.10 | 1.30 | 1.01 | 1.41 | 0.92 | 1.54 | 0.83 | 1.69 | 0.73 | 1.84 |
| 22 | 1.12 | 1.31 | 1.04 | 1.42 | 0.95 | 1.54 | 0.86 | 1.68 | 0.77 | 1.82 |
| 23 | 1.14 | 1.32 | 1.06 | 1.42 | 0.97 | 1.54 | 0.89 | 1.67 | 0.80 | 1.80 |
| 24 | 1.16 | 1.33 | 1.08 | 1.43 | 1.00 | 1.54 | 0.91 | 1.66 | 0.83 | 1.79 |
| 25 | 1.18 | 1.34 | 1.10 | 1.43 | 1.02 | 1.54 | 0.94 | 1.65 | 0.86 | 1.77 |
| 26 | 1.19 | 1.35 | 1.12 | 1.44 | 1.04 | 1.54 | 0.96 | 1.65 | 0.88 | 1.76 |
| 27 | 1.21 | 1.36 | 1.13 | 1.44 | 1.06 | 1.54 | 0.99 | 1.64 | 0.91 | 1.75 |
| 28 | 1.22 | 1.37 | 1.15 | 1.45 | 1.08 | 1.54 | 1.01 | 1.64 | 0.93 | 1.74 |
| 29 | 1.24 | 1.38 | 1.17 | 1.45 | 1.10 | 1.54 | 1.03 | 1.63 | 0.96 | 1.73 |
| 30 | 1.25 | 1.38 | 1.18 | 1.46 | 1.12 | 1.54 | 1.05 | 1.63 | 0.98 | 1.73 |
| 31 | 1.26 | 1.39 | 1.20 | 1.47 | 1.13 | 1.55 | 1.07 | 1.63 | 1.00 | 1.72 |
| 32 | 1.27 | 1.40 | 1.21 | 1.47 | 1.15 | 1.55 | 1.08 | 1.63 | 1.02 | 1.71 |
| 33 | 1.28 | 1.41 | 1.22 | 1.48 | 1.16 | 1.55 | 1.10 | 1.63 | 1.04 | 1.71 |
| 34 | 1.29 | 1.41 | 1.24 | 1.48 | 1.17 | 1.55 | 1.12 | 1.63 | 1.06 | 1.70 |
| 35 | 1.30 | 1.42 | 1.25 | 1.48 | 1.19 | 1.55 | 1.13 | 1.63 | 1.07 | 1.70 |
| 36 | 1.31 | 1.43 | 1.26 | 1.49 | 1.20 | 1.56 | 1.15 | 1.63 | 1.09 | 1.70 |
| 37 | 1.32 | 1.43 | 1.27 | 1.49 | 1.21 | 1.56 | 1.16 | 1.62 | 1.10 | 1.70 |
| 38 | 1.33 | 1.44 | 1.28 | 1.50 | 1.23 | 1.56 | 1.17 | 1.62 | 1.12 | 1.70 |
| 39 | 1.34 | 1.44 | 1.29 | 1.50 | 1.24 | 1.56 | 1.19 | 1.63 | 1.13 | 1.69 |
| 40 | 1.35 | 1.45 | 1.30 | 1.51 | 1.25 | 1.57 | 1.20 | 1.63 | 1.15 | 1.69 |
| 45 | 1.39 | 1.48 | 1.34 | 1.53 | 1.30 | 1.58 | 1.25 | 1.63 | 1.21 | 1.69 |
| 50 | 1.42 | 1.50 | 1.38 | 1.54 | 1.34 | 1.59 | 1.30 | 1.64 | 1.26 | 1.69 |
| 55 | 1.45 | 1.52 | 1.41 | 1.56 | 1.37 | 1.60 | 1.33 | 1.64 | 1.30 | 1.69 |
| 60 | 1.47 | 1.54 | 1.44 | 1.57 | 1.40 | 1.61 | 1.37 | 1.65 | 1.33 | 1.69 |
| 65 | 1.49 | 1.55 | 1.46 | 1.59 | 1.43 | 1.62 | 1.40 | 1.66 | 1.36 | 1.69 |
| 70 | 1.51 | 1.57 | 1.48 | 1.60 | 1.45 | 1.63 | 1.42 | 1.66 | 1.39 | 1.70 |
| 75 | 1.53 | 1.58 | 1.50 | 1.61 | 1.47 | 1.64 | 1.45 | 1.67 | 1.42 | 1.70 |
| 80 | 1.54 | 1.59 | 1.52 | 1.62 | 1.49 | 1.65 | 1.47 | 1.67 | 1.44 | 1.70 |
| 85 | 1.56 | 1.60 | 1.53 | 1.63 | 1.51 | 1.65 | 1.49 | 1.68 | 1.46 | 1.71 |
| 90 | 1.57 | 1.61 | 1.55 | 1.64 | 1.53 | 1.66 | 1.50 | 1.69 | 1.48 | 1.71 |
| 95 | 1.58 | 1.62 | 1.56 | 1.65 | 1.54 | 1.67 | 1.52 | 1.69 | 1.50 | 1.71 |
| 100 | 1.59 | 1.63 | 1.57 | 1.65 | 1.55 | 1.67 | 1.53 | 1.70 | 1.51 | 1.72 |

## APPENDIX TABLE 7 *(Cont'd)*

C. Significance level = .01

| | k = 1 | | k = 2 | | k = 3 | | k = 4 | | k = 5 | |
|---|---|---|---|---|---|---|---|---|---|---|
| n | $d_L$ | $d_U$ | $d_L$ | $d_U$ | $d_L$ | $d_U$ | $d_L$ | $d_U$ | $d_L$ | $d_U$ |
| 15 | 0.81 | 1.07 | 0.70 | 1.25 | 0.59 | 1.46 | 0.49 | 1.70 | 0.39 | 1.96 |
| 16 | 0.84 | 1.09 | 0.74 | 1.25 | 0.63 | 1.44 | 0.53 | 1.66 | 0.44 | 1.90 |
| 17 | 0.87 | 1.10 | 0.77 | 1.25 | 0.67 | 1.43 | 0.57 | 1.63 | 0.48 | 1.85 |
| 18 | 0.90 | 1.12 | 0.80 | 1.26 | 0.71 | 1.42 | 0.61 | 1.60 | 0.52 | 1.80 |
| 19 | 0.93 | 1.13 | 0.83 | 1.26 | 0.74 | 1.41 | 0.65 | 1.58 | 0.56 | 1.77 |
| 20 | 0.95 | 1.15 | 0.86 | 1.27 | 0.77 | 1.41 | 0.68 | 1.57 | 0.60 | 1.74 |
| 21 | 0.97 | 1.16 | 0.89 | 1.27 | 0.80 | 1.41 | 0.72 | 1.55 | 0.63 | 1.71 |
| 22 | 1.00 | 1.17 | 0.91 | 1.28 | 0.83 | 1.40 | 0.75 | 1.54 | 0.66 | 1.69 |
| 23 | 1.02 | 1.19 | 0.94 | 1.29 | 0.86 | 1.40 | 0.77 | 1.53 | 0.70 | 1.67 |
| 24 | 1.04 | 1.20 | 0.96 | 1.30 | 0.88 | 1.41 | 0.80 | 1.53 | 0.72 | 1.66 |
| 25 | 1.05 | 1.21 | 0.98 | 1.30 | 0.90 | 1.41 | 0.83 | 1.52 | 0.75 | 1.65 |
| 26 | 1.07 | 1.22 | 1.00 | 1.31 | 0.93 | 1.41 | 0.85 | 1.52 | 0.78 | 1.64 |
| 27 | 1.09 | 1.23 | 1.02 | 1.32 | 0.95 | 1.41 | 0.88 | 1.51 | 0.81 | 1.63 |
| 28 | 1.10 | 1.24 | 1.04 | 1.32 | 0.97 | 1.41 | 0.90 | 1.51 | 0.83 | 1.62 |
| 29 | 1.12 | 1.25 | 1.05 | 1.33 | 0.99 | 1.42 | 0.92 | 1.51 | 0.85 | 1.61 |
| 30 | 1.13 | 1.26 | 1.07 | 1.34 | 1.01 | 1.42 | 0.94 | 1.51 | 0.88 | 1.61 |
| 31 | 1.15 | 1.27 | 1.08 | 1.34 | 1.02 | 1.42 | 0.96 | 1.51 | 0.90 | 1.60 |
| 32 | 1.16 | 1.28 | 1.10 | 1.35 | 1.04 | 1.43 | 0.98 | 1.51 | 0.92 | 1.60 |
| 33 | 1.17 | 1.29 | 1.11 | 1.36 | 1.05 | 1.43 | 1.00 | 1.51 | 0.94 | 1.59 |
| 34 | 1.18 | 1.30 | 1.13 | 1.36 | 1.07 | 1.43 | 1.01 | 1.51 | 0.95 | 1.59 |
| 35 | 1.19 | 1.31 | 1.14 | 1.37 | 1.08 | 1.44 | 1.03 | 1.51 | 0.97 | 1.59 |
| 36 | 1.21 | 1.32 | 1.15 | 1.38 | 1.10 | 1.44 | 1.04 | 1.51 | 0.99 | 1.59 |
| 37 | 1.22 | 1.32 | 1.16 | 1.38 | 1.11 | 1.45 | 1.06 | 1.51 | 1.00 | 1.59 |
| 38 | 1.23 | 1.33 | 1.18 | 1.39 | 1.12 | 1.45 | 1.07 | 1.52 | 1.02 | 1.58 |
| 39 | 1.24 | 1.34 | 1.19 | 1.39 | 1.14 | 1.45 | 1.09 | 1.52 | 1.03 | 1.58 |
| 40 | 1.25 | 1.34 | 1.20 | 1.40 | 1.15 | 1.46 | 1.10 | 1.52 | 1.05 | 1.58 |
| 45 | 1.29 | 1.38 | 1.24 | 1.42 | 1.20 | 1.48 | 1.16 | 1.53 | 1.11 | 1.58 |
| 50 | 1.32 | 1.40 | 1.28 | 1.45 | 1.24 | 1.49 | 1.20 | 1.54 | 1.16 | 1.59 |
| 55 | 1.36 | 1.43 | 1.32 | 1.47 | 1.28 | 1.51 | 1.25 | 1.55 | 1.21 | 1.59 |
| 60 | 1.38 | 1.45 | 1.35 | 1.48 | 1.32 | 1.52 | 1.28 | 1.56 | 1.25 | 1.60 |
| 65 | 1.41 | 1.47 | 1.38 | 1.50 | 1.35 | 1.53 | 1.31 | 1.57 | 1.28 | 1.61 |
| 70 | 1.43 | 1.49 | 1.40 | 1.52 | 1.37 | 1.55 | 1.34 | 1.58 | 1.31 | 1.61 |
| 75 | 1.45 | 1.50 | 1.42 | 1.53 | 1.39 | 1.56 | 1.37 | 1.59 | 1.34 | 1.62 |
| 80 | 1.47 | 1.52 | 1.44 | 1.54 | 1.42 | 1.57 | 1.39 | 1.60 | 1.36 | 1.62 |
| 85 | 1.48 | 1.53 | 1.46 | 1.55 | 1.43 | 1.58 | 1.41 | 1.60 | 1.39 | 1.63 |
| 90 | 1.50 | 1.54 | 1.47 | 1.56 | 1.45 | 1.59 | 1.43 | 1.61 | 1.41 | 1.64 |
| 95 | 1.51 | 1.55 | 1.49 | 1.57 | 1.47 | 1.60 | 1.45 | 1.62 | 1.42 | 1.64 |
| 100 | 1.52 | 1.56 | 1.50 | 1.58 | 1.48 | 1.60 | 1.46 | 1.63 | 1.44 | 1.65 |

*Source:* J. Durbin and G. S. Watson, "Testing for Serial Correlation in Least Squares Regression," *Biometrika* 38 (June 1951).

# *Photo Credits*

P. 14: courtesy of Bantam Doubleday Dell Publishing Group, Inc.; p. 17: courtesy of the Banc One Corporation; p. 27: courtesy of the Federal Communications Commission; p. 48: courtesy of General Foods Corporation; p. 57: courtesy of the United States Air Force; p. 78: courtesy of the Bettmann Archives; p. 87: courtesy of Abitibi-Price, Inc.; pp. 97, 404, 464, 479, 510: courtesy of Jay Bruff; p. 147: courtesy of General Motors; p. 175: courtesy of University of North Carolina Hospitals; pp. 182, 210, 232: courtesy of the American Petroleum Institute; p. 185: courtesy of Kim Newton/Woodfin Camp and Associates; p. 189: courtesy of Cummins Engine Company, Inc.; p. 213: courtesy of the Nucor Corporation; pp. 258, 420: courtesy of International Business Machines Corporation; p. 265: courtesy of Boeing Commercial Airplane Group; p. 278: courtesy of the Rowland Company; p. 280: courtesy of the Warder Collection; p. 288: courtesy of Harley-Davidson, Inc.; p. 319: courtesy of Ogilvy and Mather Worldwide; p. 343: courtesy of Delta Airlines; p. 348: courtesy of the Du Pont Corporation; p. 367: courtesy of Apple Computer, Inc.; p. 428: courtesy of Becton-Dickinson and Company; p. 504: courtesy of New England Electric System; p. 526: courtesy of ASK Computer Systems; p. 584: courtesy of the UAL Corporation and United Airlines; p. 590: courtesy of the United States Court of Appeals for the Federal Circuit; p. 597: courtesy of the Chicago Board of Trade; p. 623: courtesy of Bridgestone/Firestone, Inc.; p. 628: courtesy of Airbus Industrie; p. 631: courtesy of Alcoa; p. 646: courtesy of Wide World Photos, Inc.

# Index

# Among the case studies and examples in this book:

1. The Comeback of the Xerox Corporation
2. Harley-Davidson versus the Japanese Goliaths
3. How Should Heinz Distribute Its Ketchup?
4. Bantam's Big Bet on Schwarzkopf's Book
5. How Banc One Deals with the Principal-Agent Problem
6. The 1991 Collapse of Wool Prices
7. Why the Drop in the Price of Radio Stations?
8. The Allocation of the Tang Brand Advertising Budget
9. The Optimal Size of a Hospital
10. An Alleged Blunder in the Stealth Bomber's Design
11. The Effects of Advertising on the Sales of Tang
12. Planning to Meet Peak Engineering Requirements
13. Walt Disney Productions and Attendance at Theme Parks
14. The Demand for Newsprint
15. Estimating the Quantity Demanded of Fresh Premium Salmon
16. Using PIMS Data to Estimate Elasticities of Demand
17. L'eggs: A Market Experiment
18. How the Japanese Motorcycle Makers Used the Coefficient of Determination
19. Price and Market Share for a New Electrical Drive
20. Color Balance and Shelf-Life Performance of Polaroid Film
21. How Good Are *Ward's* Projections of Auto Output?
22. How Fed Economists Forecast Auto Output
23. The Demand Function for Cigarettes
24. Forecasting the Demand for Blood Tests at North Carolina Memorial Hospital
25. The Wharton Econometric Model
26. Deciding Whether to Finance the Purchase of an Oil Field
27. Forecasting Shipments of Cement by CEMCO
28. How the Cummins Engine Company Forecasts Sales
29. How to Forecast the Sales of Paper, According to McKinsey
30. How to Determine the Optimal Horsepower for an Oil Pipeline
31. How Nucor Stays on the Production Function
32. What Toyota Taught the World
33. Advantages of Just-in-Time Production
34. Choosing the Size of an Oil Tanker
35. Benchmarking at Xerox
36. The Telephone Industry in Canada
37. Poultry Production in the United States
38. Using Total Factor Productivity to Track Factory Performance
39. Evaluating a Large-Scale Program of Product and Process Improvement
40. Parallel Development Efforts at IBM
41. The Time-Cost Trade-Off Function for Airlines
42. Henry Ford's Model T and Douglas Aircraft's DC-9
43. The Development and Introduction of Canon's Personal Copier
44. Forecasting the Rate of Diffusion of Numerically Controlled Machine Tools
45. The Spread of Industrial Robots in Japan and the United States
46. How Harley-Davidson Has Reduced Costs
47. The Effects of Output on the Cost of Producing Aircraft
48. Economies of Scale in Producing Methanol from Coal
49. Should We Continue to Make Autos from Steel?
50. A Hosiery Mill's Short-Run Cost Functions
51. A Transportation Firm's Short-Run Cost Functions
52. The Long-Run Average Cost Function for Electric Power
53. Economies of Scope in Advertising Agencies